THE
ENGLISH NOVEL,
1700–1740

THE
ENGLISH NOVEL,
1700–1740

∞

An Annotated Bibliography

Robert Ignatius Letellier

Bibliographies and Indexes in World Literature,
Number 56

GREENWOOD PRESS
Westport, Connecticut • London

Library of Congress Cataloging-in-Publication Data

Le Tellier, Robert Ignatius.
    The English novel, 1700–1740 : an annotated bibliography / Robert Ignatius Letellier.
        p. cm—(Bibliographies and indexes in world literature, ISSN 0742-6801 ; no. 56)
    Includes index.
    ISBN 0-313-31746-1 (alk. paper)
    1. English fiction—18th century—Bibliography. 2. English fiction—18th
    century—History and criticism—Bibliography. I. Title. II. Series.
Z2014.F4L47 2002
[PR851]
016.823'508—dc21   2002069648

British Library Cataloguing in Publication Data is available.

Library of Congress Catalog Card Number: 2002069648
ISBN: 0-313-31746-1
ISSN: 0742-6801

First published in 2002

Greenwood Press, 88 Post Road West, Westport, CT 06881
An imprint of Greenwood Publishing Group, Inc.
www.greenwood.com

Printed in the United States of America

The paper used in this book complies with the
Permanent Paper Standard issued by the National
Information Standards Organization (Z39.48–1984).

10 9 8 7 6 5 4 3 2 1

Contents

Contents vii

Sources and Abbreviations

1650-1850: ideas, aesthetics and inquiries

AAA = Arbeiten aus Anglistik und Amerikanistik
AHR = American Historical Review
American Political Science Review
ANQ = American Notes and Queries
Ang = Anglia: Zeitschrift für englische Philologie
Annales de l'Université de Paris

BB = Bulletin of Bibliography
BIHS = Bulletin of Humanistic Science
BNYPL = Bulletin of New York Public Library
BC = The Book Collector
BSEAA = XVIIe-XVIIe: Bulletin de la Société d'Études anglo-américaines des XVIIe et XVIIIe siècles
Bulletin of Hispanic Studies

Caliban
CCV = Cahiers Charles V
CEACrit = CEA Critic: an Official Journal of the College English Association
CentR = Centennial Review
ConLit = Contemporary Literature
CI = Critical Inquiry
CL = Comparative Literature
CLAJ = College Association Journal
Clio: a Journal of Literature, History, and the Philosophy of History
CLS = Comparative Literature Studies
Comparitive Literature
CRCL = Canadian Review of Comparative Literature
Criticism: a Quarterly for Literature and the Arts
Current Writing
Cycnos

DA/DAI = Dissertation Abstracts International
Diacritics: a Review of Contemporary Criticism
DSS = Dix-Septième Siècle
DUJ = Durham University Journal
DVLG   =   Deutsche   Vieteljahrschrift   für   Literaturwissenschaft   und
     Geistesgeschichte

E & S = Essays and Studies
EA = Études anglaises
EC = Essays in Criticism: a Quarterly Journal of Literary Criticism
ECF = Eighteenth-Century Fiction
ECL = Eighteenth-Century Life
ECS = Eighteenth-Century Studies
ECSTC = The Eighteenth-Century Short Title Catalogue
EigoS = Eigo Seinen [The Rising Generation]
ELH: a journal of English literary history
ELit = Essays in Literature
ELN = English Language Notes
EngA = English in Africa
English Studies in Africa
EngS = English Studies: a Journal of English Language and Literature
ERR = European Romantic Review
ES = English Studies
ESCan = English Studies in Canada
Essays by Divers Hands
Études littéraires

French Review
French Studies

GBB = George Borrow Bulletin
Genre
Gramma

Harvard Studies and Notes in Philology and Literature
Harvard University Summaries of Theses
Hispanic Review
HLB = Harvard Library Bulletin
HLQ = Huntingdon Library Bulletin: a Journal for the History and Interpretation
     of English and American Civilization
HR = Hudson Review
HSNPL = Harvard Studies and Notes in Philology and Literature

Illinois Studies in Language and Literature

Imaginaire
*IT = Index to Theses for Higher degrees by the Universities of Great Britain
        and Ireland*

JEPG = Journal of English German Philology
JGE = Journal of General Education
JH = Journal of Humanities
JHI =Journal of the History of Ideas
JLS = Journal of Literary Studies
JNT = Journal of Narrative Technique
Journal: College of Arts and Essays
JEurS = Journal of European Studies
JSBC = Journal for the Study of British Culture

KR = Kenyon Review
Kunapipi

La Licorne
Language and Literature
Library
Literature & History
LHR = Lock Haven Review
*LLComp = Literary and Linguistic Computing: journal for the Association for
            Literary and Linguistic Computing*
London Mercury

Malahat Review
MedLit
Million
MLN (Baltimore, MD)
MLQ = Modern Language Quarterly
MLR = Modern Language Review
MLS = Modern Language Studies
Moreana

Neophil = Neophilologus
NLB = Newberry Library Bulletin
Die neueren Sprachen
NLH = New Literary History: a Journal of Theory and Interpretation
Novel: a Forum on Fiction
NQ = Notes and Queries
NRam = New Rambler: the Journal of the Johnson Society

OL Orbis Litterarum: International Review of Literary Studies

PAAS = Proceedings of the American Antiquarian Society
Pacific Historical Record
PBSA = Papers of the Bibliographic Society of America
PLL = Papers on Language and Literature
PMLA = Publications of the Modern Language Association of America
Poetica: Zeitschrift für Srach- und Literaturwissenschaft
Political Science Quarterly
POMPA = Publications of the Mississippi Philological Association
PP = Philologica Pragensia: journal of modern philology
PQ = Philological Quarterly
PS = Prose Studies: History, Theory, Criticism

Q/W/E/R/T/Y: ars, littératures & civilsations du monde anglophone

RANAM = Recherches anglaises et américaines: a quarterly review
RECTR = Restoration and Eighteenth-Century Theatre Research
ReLit = Religion and Literature
Ren = Renascence
Representations
RES = Review of English Studies: a Quarterly Journal of English Literature and
        the English Language
Rev = Review
Revue des Cours et Conférences
Revue d'Histoire littéraire de France
RF = Romanische Forschungen
Rhetorica
RLC = Revue de Littérature Comparée
RLV = Revue des Langues vivantes
RMRLL = Rocky Mountain Review of Language and Literature: the journal of the
        Rocky Mountain Language Association
Romanic Review
RomN = Romance Notes
Room of One's Own

SAQ = South Atlantic Quarterly
SB = Studies in Philology: Papers of the Bibliographical Society of the Univ. of
        Virginia
SBHT = Studies in Burke and His Times
Scriblerian and Kit-Cats: a Newsjournal Devoted to Pope, Swift, and Their
        Circle, the Kit-Cats and Dryden
SECC = Studies in Seventeenth-Century Culture
SEL = Studies in English Literature/Eibunga ke Kenkyu
SELit = Studies in English Literature 1500-1900
SHogg = Studies in Hogg and His World

SLI = Studies in the Literary Imagination
SM = Studia Mystica
SoRA = Southern Review: Literary and Interdisciplinary Essays
SP = Studies in Philology
SSF = Studies in Short Fiction
StudECC = Studies in Eighteenth-Century Culture
Studies in Scottish Literature
Studies in Short Fiction
StudN = Studies in the Novel
SVEC = Studies on Voltaire and Eighteenth Century

TamKR = TamKang Review: a journal primarily devoted to comparative studies between Chinese and foreign literatures
TCEL = Thought Currents in English Literature
Temps modernes
Texas Studies in Literature and Language
TLS = Times Literary Supplement
TSL = Tennessee Studies in Literature
TSLL = Texas Studies in Literature and Language: a Journal of the Humanities
TSWL = Tulsa Studies in Women's Literature

University of California Publications in Modern Philology
USt = Utopian Studies
UTQ = University of Toronto Quarterly: a Canadian Journal of the Humanities

YFS = Yale French Studies

Virginia Magazine of History and Bibliography

Women and Literature
Women's Studies
Work & Days

YWES = Year's Work in English Studies

ZAA = Zeitschrift fur Anglistik und Amerikanistik

Introduction

1. Origins and models

This bibliography has been compiled as a contribution to the work of the Salzburg Centre for Research on the Early English Novel, in its project of re-publishing fiction from the sixteenth, seventeenth and early eighteenth centuries, and providing a data base for scholarly materials in this field. It was made possible by the commitment of Holger Klein, its director, and professor at the Institut für Anglistik und Amerikanistik at the University of Salzburg; he was intrumental in obtaining the research funding from the Fonds zur Förderung der Wissenschaftlichen Forschung in Vienna. Without the assistance of the Fonds, this project would not have been possible: I owe them a fundamental debt of gratitude.

The model for this task has been the work of Prof. James HARNER, whose *English Renaissance prose fiction, 1500-1660: An annotated bibliography* (1978, with subsequent supplements in 1985 and 1992) is a quarry of materials on the earliest phase of the novel.

The present study represents the third part of a trilogy begun in 1992 with a ground-clearing exercise, *A bibliography of the English novel from the Restoration to the French Revolution: A checklist of sources and critical materials, with particular reference to the period 1660 to 1740* (1995). This was followed by the more specialized *The English Novel, 1660-1700: An annotated bibliography* (1997) which sought to throw more light on the fiction written in these years, and its broad socio-historical context. This work seeks to extend this process a step further, and illuminate the next 40 years, from 1700 to 1740, the late dawn immediately preceding the sunburst of the classic English novel with Samuel Richardson's *Pamela*. This innovative work, which ushers in the new, expanded novel of the 1740s, is the point of departure, and does not come under the aegis of this study.

2. Historical contexts

The period 1660-1700 had been dominated by the dramatic events of the Restoration and the Glorious Revolution, events of immense political and sociological import for the emergence of modern Britain. The first forty years of the eighteenth century were to see other changes that would radically affect the future, but on the whole was marked by a greater sense of stability and consolidation, and an exhilarating expansion on both national and international fronts.

Queen Anne (1702-14) succeeded those paragons of the Protestant succession, William and Mary. Her reign was important for the development of party politics (the Whig influence dominant under the Duchess of Marlborough until 1710; the Tories thereafter under Robert Harley and Lord Bolingbroke). Marlborough's successes in the War of the Spanish Succession gave Britain a new consciousness of its military prowess, and prepared it for ever more daring imperial ventures. The Union with Scotland (1707) and the resultant United Kingdom fuelled a new perception of national power, with the Protestant cause vindicated by the accession of the Elector of Hanover as George I (1714-27). This was underlined in the defeat of the Catholic Stuart cause in 1715 and, decisively, at Culloden in 1745. The absence of the German George I from meetings of the Cabinet left government in the hands of Whig ministers (Stanhope, Townshend, Walpole), with constitutional control over the Crown thus increasing. This process continued in the reign of George II (1727-60) whose son Frederick, Prince of Wales, became the centre of opposition, and forced the resignation of the mighty Walpole.

The period was marked by a growing awareness of the power of the printed word, and its relation to true freedom. Even during the Restoration the control and licensing of the press had continued. This forbade the printing of any book or pamphlet contrary to the doctrine and discipline of the Church of England. It was revived in 1685 until 1694 when Parliament refused to renew it. It must be remembered that the abandonment of the Act was not due to any change of opinion in Parliament or government in favor of liberty of expression, and that the detection of authors and publishers of libels was entrusted to salaried 'messengers of the press'; Parliament, further, was active in drawing the attention of government to obnoxious publications. Daniel Defoe was arrested and pilloried in 1703 for his pamphlets on ecclesiastical matters; John Matthews was hanged in 1719 in consequence of his pamphlet asserting that James III was the rightful king of England.

After the extraordinary freedom of the Restoration stage, a sense of greater sobriety in the theatre followed on the royal order of 1698 prohibiting the acting of anything contrary to religion and good manners. In the early part rof the eighteenth-century control of the stage appears to have been exercised largely by the Lord Chamberlain himself. But the gradual chastening of the drama, which led to such plays as those by Rowe, Addison and Steele, may be attributed more to a change in public sentiment than to the action of the censor. This change is also much in evidence in the development of prose fiction in which women playwrights like Manley and Rowe were to play a major role.

Addison and Steele, indeed, are figures of great representative importance for these years. Joseph Addison demonstrated profiency in many literary fields. But it was as an essayists and moralist that he made his mark. With his old school friend, Richard Steele, he founded the *Spectator* (1711), the tone of which is often light and funny, but is always concerned with promoting the virtues of reasonableness, common sense and benevolent moderation. Their essays, so often in the mode of short stories, and in the clear and unpretentious prose which makes it possible to communicate their ideas to people of ordinary intelligence, had immense influence on the form, content and medium of fiction. This went hand in hand with the new forces of enlightenment that were beginning to dominate European thought, the questioning of traditions and prejudices, especially in religion, with emphasis on the primacy of reason and strict scientific method. In England this built on the work of Newton and Locke. Interestingly, one of the best prose writers of the time, Jonathan Swift, used prose only as a vehicle for philosophical satire: *Gulliver's Travels* is not a novel.

These first 40 years of the eighteenth century marked a vital stage in the process by which the novel came to birth. The fantastical trappings of the romances were being discarded; prose style had become appropriately simple enough for the reproduction of everyday experience. A huge new reading public was emerging, gradually freed of the old Puritan suspicions that fiction was an incitement to sin, and a huge waste of time, and hence was increasingly able to identify with the characters and events devised by authors. Hand in hand with this was the expansion of the book trade to the point where substantial numbers of books could be distributed to larger numbers of people for reasonable prices.

All was leading to the phenomenal moment which saw the publication of Samuel Richardson's *Pamela* in 1740, to be followed two years later by *Joseph Andrews* (1742), Fielding's send-up of the former. Richardson brought his achievement to a peak with *Clarissa Harlowe* (1747-48) in which his complex insights into character and exploration of the darker aspects of human nature are carried even further. Fielding again responded in his own very different way with *Tom Jones* (1749); here the whole of English society is surveyed with understanding, humour and compassion. The decade of the 1740s function as a turning point - and not only in the history of the novel. "The decade [...] might well be nominated the most innovative in English literature, with striking departures not only in fiction and poetry, but in history, philosophy, and other sorts of intellectual prose" (Lawrence Lipking, "Inventing the Eighteenth Centuries" in Leopold Damrosch, *The Progress of Eighteenth-Century Literature* [1988], p. 10).

3. The wider background

The prose fiction of these 40 years must be understood in the context of the times. In this bibliography the general and specific perception of the period results in a corresponding division of materials into two sections. The first half part of this work (Chapters 1-3) is devoted to providing the necessary resources and backgrounds. The principal concerns of fiction are carefully surveyed in the bibliographies of the English novel in the early eighteenth century. Then follow the anthologies of shorter novels, short stories, essays, tales, documentary collections, biographies, and other historical or social extracts pertaining to this period, all invariably with introductions or other critical apparatus (Chapter 2). Next come the surveys and general studies of the era, covering the broad context historically, socially, and culturally, and listing works pertinent to literary theory, themes and topics (Chapter 3). This selection, which cannot hope to achieve completeness or total inclusiveness, aims at providing a nonetheless comprehensive, complementary and topical context of sources, critical materials, backgrounds, matters surrounding the fiction of these years that throw some light on the wider literary and social issues.

Apart from my own checklist mentioned above, attention must be drawn to the following authorities who have in different ways covered the background of the first 40 years, each having his own angle and emphasis:

- LUND, R. D. *Restoration and early eighteenth-century English literature: A selected bibliography of resource materials* (1980), who provides an annotated guide to information on the period, albeit missing more current data, and not specifically aimed at prose fiction;

- HAHN, H. George and BEHM, Carl III. *The eighteenth-century British novel and its background: An annotated bibliography and guide to topics* (1985), who provide surveys of criticism, studies of eighteenth-century life and background to the novel, and lists of criticism pertaining to major and minor novelists, each item characterized by a descriptive word or phrase;

- SPECTOR, Robert D. *Backgrounds to Restoration and eighteenth-century English literature: An annotated bibliographical guide to modern scholarship* (1991), who gives a detailed survey of the period from the daily lives of the people to the philosophical foundations of society, with a sociological rather than a literary interest;

- MAZZENO, Lawrence W. *The British novel, 1680-1832: An annotated bibliography* (1997), who provides an overview of the essential tools of eighteenth-century bibliographical investigation and selected works of criticism on individual authors.

My own selection concentrates on the first 40 years of the century specifically and keeps the literary emphasis of my subject (early English prose fiction) in focus. It presents a single list arranged alphabetically by contributor's name, which seeks to be up-to-date and comprehensive. A key to its potential usefulness is provided by indices of scholars and themes.

4. Annotation

Each item is listed in bibliographical detail, according to the practice of the *Annual Bibliography of English Language and Literature* (ABELL) and the *MLA Annual Bibliography*. A brief commentary is provided, a concise guide to contents and any particular features which could be of use to scholars, especially the presence of specific bibliographies, special tables, appendices or illustrations. In rare instances, a text or its abstract have not been available for inspection, but an entry is retained all the same for the sake of completeness. On occasion, the entry is succinct where the contents are uncomplicated (as in books devoted to life and works). Where the work concerned is very complex, or has particular relevance to the prose fiction of the period, or the development of the novel generally, the commentary is sometimes given more extensive space, even if it covers only an article or dissertation.

5. Chronology

The second part of this bibliography (Part II, Chapters 4 and 5) is devoted to the individual novelists and anonymous titles that appeared between 1700 and 1740. The novelists of this period still remain largely unknown. Thus in the interests of usefulness and convenience, the section ends with chronological survey of a cross-section of works printed during these 40 years and featured in this study (Chapter 5). Such a shortlist makes no pretence at completeness, but tabulates the more prominent works. The guidelines have been provided by George WATSON's *New Cambridge bibliography of English literature II: 1600-1800* (1974) [=NCBEL], H. McBURNEY'S *A checklist of English prose fiction 1700-39* (1960), and F. J. G. ROBINSON'S *Eighteenth-century British books: An author catalogue extracted from the British Museum Catalogue of Printed Books* (1981). Supplementary listings can be found in:
- MORGAN, C. *The rise of the novel of manners* (1911) and
- DAY, R. A. *Told in letters* (1966).

6. Authors and individual works

The main part of Part II is devoted to an alphabetical listing of the authors of fiction active between 1700 and 1740 who feature in the chronology (Chapter 5). Each entry provides title, date, pagination, source, and descriptive tag. The entries vary from simple records of obscure anonymous works to substantial accounts of the *oeuvre* of famous writers.
1) The authors are arranged in alphabetical order by name rather than title. Those known only by initials are placed first under the letter of the surname.
2) Anonymous works are gathered together and listed first, the place of each item determined by the first word after the article.
3) Each author's work is listed chronologically.
4) Where a translation is listed, the translator and original title and dates are provided.
5) All contemporary or immediately subsequent contemporary editions are listed after the original date of appearance. Any modern (twentieth-century) editions are given under the subheading EDITIONS (collections coming before individual titles).
6) Each work is briefly categorized according to the descriptive tag used by the NCBEL.
7) In listing the works themselves, the original orthography has been retained.
8) All critical works are listed under STUDIES and are arranged in the usual alphabetical order within each entry. Where bibliographies already exist, the

listings are supplementary (as with Daniel Defoe).

7. Prominent people: Daniel Defoe

Any single entry provides immediate perceptions of the relative obscurity or prominence of any particular author. Three in particular emerged as the dominant figures of prose fiction in these years: Defoe, Manley and Haywood. Defoe has been the subject of such intensive study that materials on him outweigh many times over even his nearest contenders. Specific bibliographies have appeared already, especially:
- PAYNE, W. "An annotated bibliography of works about Daniel Defoe, 1719-1974," *Bulletin of Bibliography* 32 (1975);
- STOLER, J. A. *Daniel Defoe: An annotated bibliography of modern criticism, 1900-1980* (1984); with the same scholar's updates "Daniel Defoe: A partly annotated bibliography of criticism, 1981-1994 (Parts 1 and 2)," *Bulletin of Bibliography* 53:1+2 (1996).
In the present bibliography attention is focussed, therefore, on those studies appearing between 1994 and 1999.

Defoe is also a figure whose life and work covers such a wide spectrum of interrelated bibliographical and literary themes, with a great deal of work devoted to exploring and sifting the content of the 'Defoe canon'. Obviously some selection of what is included is necessary, but it is important to be as representative as possible of Defoe's many facets. Materials discussing his canon, therefore, are listed but not always annotated, and readers are directed to the definitive studies by P. N. FURBANK and W. R. OWENS, *The canonisation of Daniel Defoe* (1988) and *A critical bibliography of Daniel Defoe* (1998).

In this study attention is focused on Defoe's fiction, and especially on the immense fame of his two illustrious novels, *Robinson Crusoe* (1719) and *Moll Flanders* (1722). The archetypal force of the former has given it a legendary status, with editions translations and criticism generating its own volume and momentum. See, for example:
- DÉTIS, E. "*The Life and Strange Adventures of Robinson Crusoe, of York, Mariner*: A selective critical bibliography." *BSEAA* 33 (Nov. 1991); and
- LOVETT, R. W. '*Robinson Crusoe*': *A bibliographical checklist of English language editions* (1991).
The literature on this novel since 1994 alone give an extraordinary entrée into the life and work of Defoe, let alone the manifold implications of the work itself which continues to fascinate every generation anew, its themes as fresh and challenging to the contemporary post-modernist, post-structuralist, post-feminist, post-colonial literary scene as ever before.

8. The women novelists

The cases of Mary Delarivière Manley and Eliza Haywood are special. The lists provided indicate any author's contemporary popularity, and revival in scholarly interest. Indeed the growth of women's studies in recent times not only reflects the mid- to late- twentieth-century topicality of feminism, but focuses attention on the dynamic role played by women in the rise of the novel. Following on figures like Margaret Cavendish and Aphra Behn in the late seventeenth century, Penelope Aubin, Jane Barker, Mary Davys and Elizabeth Rowe are significant exponents of the novel form in the early eighteenth. After Defoe, no figures are more prominent than Manley or more productive than Haywood.

Information on the nature of women's contribution to fiction in this period can be supplemented by reference to other bibliographical studies, each with their own particular specializations, like:

- BACKSCHEIDER, P. (et al) *An annotated bibliography of twentieth-century studies of women and literature* (1977);
- SCHWARZ, N. L. *Articles on women writers 1960-1975: A bibliography* (1977), both of which are very general.

Of major importance is D. A. SAAR and M. A. SCHOFIELD's *Eighteenth-century Anglo-American women novelists: A critical reference guide* (1996), which provides well-annotated bibliographies on 35 women writers, covering criticism from most of the twentieth century (1900-92).

In this present bibliography, all the women authors mentioned above (Aubin, Barker, Davys, Haywood, Manley, Rowe) have a section dedicated to selected pre-1992 studies which the compiler has found particularly helpful, followed by a section on criticism that has appeared since 1992 that complements the materials collated in Saar and Schofield.

The women novelists are indeed central to the development of the early novel, and crucial in affecting the transition between the mental world of the late seventeenth century and the new ideas of the early eighteenth century, not least in the movement from romance to the realistic novel. The ancient heritage of the romance tradition had already begun acquiring a sharper sense of human observation in Mme de Scudéry's work, a process that gained in psychological perception in the fiction of Mme de Lafayette. The role of Cavendish, Behn, and Manley in the development of the epistolary novel, with its new depth of first-person self-revelation in letters, is fundamental. This, coupled with the proliferation of the lives of criminals and rogues (the extraordinary case of Mary Carleton between 1663 and 1673 being a case in point), and a change from the ethos the Restoration period, with Queen Mary II setting the scene for a far more restrained and responsible moral tone, was to have distinct influence on the novel. Behn's libertine heroines are continued in the work of Haywood with much 'immoral' description, but there is a turn to the moral, didactic novel in the writings of Aubin, Davys and Rowe. Conversely, Behn, while using sometimes stereotypically romance characters, has more ordinary settings that have little to do with romance. Haywood used more developed characters, but the structure and some recurrent elements (like the journey) are strongly reminiscent of romance, as in Aubin. Davys on the other hand used rather more developed characters and rejected the romance tradition, fostering domesticated settings even more than Behn. All of them have something to say about the treatment of women - and depict the movement or process from woman as subject to woman as object.

It is interesting to observe that these trends - the literature of shabby adventurers and delinquents, the growing depth and exploration of self-revelation (especially in letters, journals and other autobiographical material), the shift to 'moral' teaching, the ambiguity of women in society, and the interplay between woman as subject and object - reaches its supreme expression in the enduringly fascinating (and intangibly ambiguous) masterpiece of the early novel, Defoe's *Moll Flanders*. Here, as later in Richardson, Prévost, and Marivaux, the dynamic female protagonist is the creation of the male mind. Only Haywood, whose *Love in excess* (1719) proved one of the few best-sellers of the age, after Defoe and Swift, came close to producing a novel with anything like the same popular appeal.

9. Different kinds of novels

The productions of the women writers focus attention on the generic variety of fiction in the early eighteenth century. If romance was giving way to a new sense of human vibrancy in both the low-mimetic vitality of the picaresque and the psychological subtlety of the epistolary novel, a combination of first-person central adventure and first-person peripheral satirical observation of society, as well as interest in exotic places and scenery, gave rise to a different type of travel adventure, the imaginary voyage into remote or fictional regions, often ideal worlds, in the manner of Sir Thomas More's *Utopia*. Whether with satirical social observation, or the promotion of an optimum state or mode of human behaviour, the topos of the journey and the remote or ideal land, receiving new impetus from Margaret Cavendish's *Blazing World* (1666) and Henry Neville's *Island of Pines* (1668), was to attain new popularity in the early eighteenth century, and lead straight to Robinson Crusoe's confrontation with isolation, true meaning and the 'vocation' of life on his desert isle (1719), or the ideal world of Cristoforo Armeno's Serindip (1722).

The vogue for the East, stimulated by Jean de Préchac's *The chaste seraglian: or Yolanda of Sicily* (trans. 1686), Antoine Galland's version of *The Arabian Nights* (1706), and the 'strange adventures' of Mrs Aubin's *Count de Vinevil and his family* (1721) with its Turkish setting, and *Lucinda, an English lady* (1722) who is captured by Algerian pirates, the challenge of confronting an alien, Islamic culture, was to combine a satirical and idealistic consideration of world views with picaresque captivities and escapes from Barbary, to form the Oriental tale which was to retain its popularity throughout the eighteenth century, as both medium of exotic adventure and vector of social critique.

Here there are again critical-bibliographic studies, both old and new, which are indispensible points of reference, like:
- CONANT, M. P. *The Oriental tale in the eighteenth century* (1908);

- GOVE, P. B. *The imaginary voyage in prose fiction, 1700-1800* (1941);
- PERRY, Ruth. *Women, letters, and the novel* (1980);
- KLEIN, H.-G. *Der Briefroman in der englischen Literatur vom 16. bis zum 18. Jahrhundert* (1986).

10. The translations

Montesquieu's *Persian Letters* appeared in English in 1722, was reprinted again in 1730, and reached 6 editions by 1773. The work was of great importance, not only being epistolary in form, but also combining picaresque adventures with an imaginary voyage to an exotic, indeed Oriental place, half-historical half-fictional in its sociological concerns and Utopian aspirations. The observations of life and institutions in a faraway land served as the vehicle for a radical discussion of France of the *ancien régime*, and in its pioneering psychological and sociological concerns, this new and yet composite 'foreign observer' genre proved very influential and much imitated.

Montesquieu's fiction serves to focus attention on the great popularity of French literature in translation in the first 40 years of the eighteenth century. The imaginary voyage, with its mixture of Utopian idealism and actual historical observation, found important expression in François Misson's *A new voyage to the East-Indies by Francis Leguat and his companions* (1708), while the picaresque found one of its late, great manifestations in Le Sage's *Histoire de Gil Blas* (trans. 1716, with 5 editions by 1744), while the epistolary novel reached a new highpoint of subtlety and psychological density in Pierre Carlet de Chamberlain Marivaux's *The life of Marianne: or the adventures of the Countess of *** (1736-42), the first part of which antedates Richardson's magisterial achievements in *Pamela* by four years. The Abbé Prévost's *The Life of Mr Cleveland, natural son of Oliver Cromwell* (from *Le Philosophe anglais*, 1731, 1734-35, 1736, with numerous editions through the century) is another instance of immensely popular translation from the French which exercised a profound influence on the English novel. The fusion of emotional sensibility with a fervent philosophical Deism is unfolded in a series of colorful and bizarre adventures that range across the globe. The emotional world, the loose structure and vibrant sense of setting and adventure, was to have enormous impact.

Constructing a bibliographic study of such famous figures as Montesquieu, Marivaux and Prévost is a difficult challenge, since these are major figures of French literature, while the recurrence and popularity of their work as translation has not endured the testing of the past 300 years. To compile thorough bibliographies would be a huge task, each an end, if not a book, in itself; to have only those studies in English, or that relate solely to the English translations of these works, is a very limiting exercise. A degree of selection has been necessary here, to keep this exercise within acceptable limits, and yet to provide some stimulus to research or further enquiry, on the principle that something is better than nothing.

11. Conclusion and thanks

While this bibliography of sources and critical materials is broad in scope, there are inevitable omissions (apart from the conscious selection that has on occasion been necessary). It is nonetheless hoped that it will serve as a sourcebook, helpful to the scholar and the general reader alike, and make some contribution to the further exploration of the early English novel.

My special thanks go to Nicholas Southey of the University of South Africa who located several Defoe studies from South African journals for me, to the staff of the Reading Room, West Room, Manuscripts Room, Periodicals Desk, and, most especially, Interlibrary Loans of the University Library, Cambridge. I would like to mention Neil Hudson and Alison Zammer for their special kindness. Holger Klein and Linda Reschen have been painstaking readers and critics of my text, Patrick Welche has been an irreplaceable help in matters of computing, and Terry Letellier has been my constant support and encouragement during my long labours.

Robert Ignatius Letellier
Cambridge
16 February 2002

Part I

THE GENERAL PERIOD
1700-1740:
MISCELLANEOUS WORKS

1

Bibliographies

1 *ANNUAL BIBLIOGRAPHY OF LANGUAGE AND LITERATURE*. London: Modern Humanities Research Association, 1920-.

Standard annual bibliography listing (without annotation) Festschriften, bibliography, scholarly method, computer technology, newspapers, English language, traditional culture, English literature (general, Old English, Middle English, then by century). Index of authors and subjects. Index of scholars.

2 BACKSCHEIDER, Paula R., NUSSBAUM, Felicity and ANDERSON, Philip B. *An annotated bibliography of twentieth-century studies of women and literature, 1660-1800*. New York: Garland, 1977; pp. x, 287.

Includes critical and scholarly books and articles published between 1900 and 1975, with women, not just literary women, the subject. Aimed at scholars of the Restoration and the 18c, of social history and of women's studies. Annotations are descriptive rather than critical. Divided into I. General Studies and II. Genre Studies (biographies, letters and memoirs, conduct books, drama, fiction, women's studies, major authors (Cleland, Defoe, Fielding, Richardson, Smollett, Sterne), periodicals and poetry. III. provides bibliographies on individuals (Mary Astell, Penelope Aubin, Joanne Baillie, Anna Laetitia Barbauld, Jane Barker, Elizabeth Barry, Aphra Behn, Georgina Anne Bellamy, Anna Bracegirdle, Charlotte Brooke, Fanny Burney, Elizabeth Carter, Margaret Cavendish, Susannah Centlivre, Mary Chandler, Hester Chapone, Charlotte Clarke, Sarah Churchill, Catherine Clive, Catherine Trotter Cockburn, Hannah Cowley, Mary Davys, Catherine Hyde Douglas, Maria Edgeworth,

Elizabeth Elstob, Sarah Fielding, Anne Firth, Nell Gwynn, Laetitia Hawkins, Mary Hays, Eliza Haywood, Queen Henrietta Maria, Lucy Hutchinson, Elizabeth Inchbald, Esther Johnson, Dorothy Jordan, Ellis Cornelia Knight, Charlotte Lennox, Sarah Lennox, Mary Delarivière Manley, Elizabeth Montague, Lady Mary Wortley Montague, Hannah More, Amalia Opie, Dorothy Osborne, Kathleen Phillips, Laetitia Pillington, Hester Piozzi, Ann Radcliffe, Mary Robinson, Elizabeth Singer Rowe, Sarah Scott, Anna Stewart, Frances Sheridan, Sarah Keble Siddons, Charlotte Smith, Johanna Southcote, Frances Thynne, Mary Toft, Susanna Wesley, Jane West, Peggy Woffington, Mary Wollstonecraft, Ann Yearsley, Individual Women. Index of Restoration and 18c Women (257-61), Author Index (263-87).

3 BAKER, Ernest Albert. *A guide to the best fiction in English and American: Including translations from foreign languages* (1913). Rev. J. PACKMAN. London: Routledge & Kegan Paul, 1932; pp. vii, 634.

An attempt to survey the whole field of English and American fiction, characterizing every individual item of any perceived importance. Also embraces fiction in foreign languages, alphabetical listing of selected major works: author, full title, date, descriptive précis, translation details, and later/modern editions. Index (521-634).

4 BATESON, F. W. (ed.). *Cambridge bibliography of English literature.* 5 vols. Cambridge: Cambridge UP, 1940-57. See also WATSON.

Section on prose fiction with chronological listing of general studies, anthologies, original work and translations.

5 BATTESIN, Martin C. (ed.). *British novelists, 1660-1800. Part 1: A-L.* (*Dictionary of Literary Biography*, 39:1.) *Part 2: M-Z.* (*Dictionary of Literary Biography*, 39:2.) Detroit, New York and London: A Bruccoli Clark Layman Book, 1985; pp. xvii, 325; ix, 329-700.

Presents a series of detailed articles on a whole range of late 17c and 18c novelists, books for further reading, and a cumulative index to the whole series. Each entry begins with a list of works, continues with an extended literary-critical biography, and concludes with a series of references (letters, bibliographies, critical works on the subject). Each entry is generously illustrated with portraits and facsimiles.
Part 1: Amory, Aubin, Bage, Barker, Beckford, Behn, Blackamore, Frances Brooke, Henry Brooke, Bunyan, Burney, Cleland, Collier, Congreve, Coventry, Davys, Day, Defoe, Fielding, Godwin, Goldsmith, Graves, Griffiths, Haywood, John Hill, Holcroft, Inchbald, Samuel

Johnson, Charles Johnson, Harriet and Sophie Lee, Lennox, Lewis.
Part 2: Mackenzie, Manley, Paltock, Pratt, Radcliffe, Reeve, Richardson, Rowe, Sarah Scott, Shebbeare, Frances Sheridan, Charlotte Smith, Smollett, Sterne, Swift, Walpole, Mary Wollstonecraft.
Appendix: *Novelists on the Novel* (557-658) collects a series of prefaces by Bunyan, Congreve, Manley, Huet, Defoe, Aubin, Haywood, Davys, Richardson, Fielding, Smollett, Sarah Fielding, Samuel Johnson, Francis Coventry, Horace Walpole, Elizabeth Griffith, Sarah Reeve, Fanny Burney, Thomas Holcroft, Mackenzie, Godwin. Books for further reading (659-64).

6 BEASLEY, Jerry C. (ed.). *English fiction 1660-1800: a guide to information sources.* (American Literature, English Literature, and World Literatures in English. Information Guide Series, 14.) Detroit, MI: Gale Research Company, 1978; pp. xvi, 313.

Provides a comprehensive annotated listing of most critical materials available on the English novel (1600-1800). Divided into 2 parts. Part I is a General Bibliography giving background sources, general reference works on the English novel, the novel as genre, English fiction (history and criticism), checklists and other biographical resources, serials and reprint series. Part II provides a bibliography of individual authors.

7 BELL, Inglis F. and BAIRD Donald. *The English novel 1578-1956: a checklist of twentieth-century criticisms.* London: Clive Bingley/ Hamden, CT: Linnet Books 1959. Rpt. Hamden: The Shoe String Press, 1974; pp. xix, 168.
Introd. discusses historical and critical issues (ix-xiv). Systematic checklist of criticism available to 1956, tabulated alphabetically by author. The 18c is represented by the usual famous five novelists. Adds a further list of sources in which novel criticism is found. Straightforward listing without description or comment.

8 BELL, Maureen; PARFITT, George and SHEPHERD, Simon. *A biographical dictionary of English women writers, 1580-1720.* Brighton: Harvester Wheatsheaf, 1990; pp. xxiv, 298.

Collates crucial information about women writing in this period. Introduction and Appendices. Concentrates on the writing women produced. Includes all women known to have written.

9 BERNBAUM, Ernest. "Recent works on prose fiction before 1800." *MLN* 42 (1927): 281-93; 43 (1928): 416-25; 46 (1931): 95-107; 47 (1932): 104-13; 48 (1933): 370-78; 49 (1934): 524-34; 51 (1936): 244-55; 52 (1937):

580-93; 55 (1940): 54-65.

Examines various books covering subjects of prose fiction from antiquity to the 18c. The sections on the 17c to 18c deal with translations of Boccaccio, Bunyan, French and English literary ideas, translations of English novels, the role of personal memoirs, and various individual novelists. The organization is roughly based on J. A. K. Thomson's distinctions: 1) myth (or religion); 2) legend (or history); *Märchen* (or ordinary life).

10 BIBLIOTHEQUE NATIONALE. *Catalogue général des livres imprimés.* Paris: Impr. Nationale, 1900-80.

11 BLACK, Frank Gees. *The epistolary novel in the late eighteenth-century: a descriptive and bibliographic study.* Eugene, ON: Univ. of Oregon, 1940; pp. iv,184.

While devoted principally to the epistolary novel between 1781 and 1800, this is an invaluable resource for the general study of the novel in the 18c, particularly because of the five appendices:
A. Alphabetical List of Epistolary Fiction, 1740-1840 (112-53);
B. Chronological List of Epistolary Fiction, 1740-1840 (154-68);
C. Epistolary Fiction in Verse, 1766-1835 (169-70);
D. Illustrative List of Epistolary Fiction in Periodicals (171-72);
E Charts (173-4); author index (175-7); title index (178-84).

12 BLAIN, Virginia; CLEMENTS, Patricia and GRUNDY, Isobel. *The feminist companion to literature in English. Women writers from the Middle Ages to the Present.* London: B. T. Batsford Ltd., 1990. pp. xiv, 1231.

Introduction, with succinct life and works, and limited critical accounts of hundreds of women authors (about 280 entries for the 18c). List of works frequently cited. Index of topics (1205-08). Index of Names (chronological) (1210-18). Index of Cross References (1219-31).

13 BLAKEY, D. *The Minerva Press 1790-1820.* London: Bibliographical Society, 1939.

Chronological list of popular fiction 1773-1820.

14 BLOCK, Andrew. *The English novel 1740-1850: a catalogue including prose romances, short stories and translations of foreign fiction with introductions by J. Crow and E. A. Baker.* London, 1939. Rev. London: Dawson, 1961; pp. 349.

Alphabetical listing by author, with transcription of title pages from the earliest known editions (author - title - place - publisher - date). Translations are given under the original author. Record of frontispieces and other illustrations. No pagination indicated. Items are unnumbered. Index of titles (259-349).

15 BONHEIM, Helmut W. *The English novel before Richardson: a checklist of texts and criticisms to 1970*. Metuchen, NJ: The Scarecrow Press, Inc., 1971; pp. vi, 145.

Checklist indicating where the chief novels 'before the novel' are found, and listing the relevant works of criticism. 1. Alphabetically arranged lists of authors, their narrative prose and relevant criticism; 2. anthologies and libraries; 3. secondary literature according to topics which have received particular attention from the critics. Lists 26 individual authors: Behn, Breton, Congreve, Davys, Defoe, Dekker, Deloney, Forde, Gascoigne, Gosson, Grange, Greene, Hall, Harvey, Haywood, Lodge, Lyly, Manley, Thomas More, Munday, Nashe, Painter, Pettie, Riche, Shakespeare, Sidney. Provides bibliographies on 16 topics: autobiography, background (general and literary), characters, conduct and courtesy books, imagery, influences (Classical, French, German, Italian, Spanish), jest books, novels, pamphlets, roguery, romance and legend, satire, translations, travel literature, Utopian fiction, women and literature. Index.

16 BOWERS, Fredson. *Principles of bibliographic description* [1946]. Rpt. New York: Russell & Russell, 1962; pp. xvii, 505.

Of pertinence is ch.3 "Bibliographical Descriptions of Sixteenth-, Seventeenth- and Eighteenth-Century Books: a Preview" (124-34). Index (501-5).

17 BRAKE, Laurel and CAMBELL, Gordon (eds). *The year's work in English studies*, 69 (1988); 70 (1989). Oxford: Basil Blackwell for the English Association; Cambridge, MA: Humanities Press, Atlantic Headlands, NJ: 1991, 1992.

Annual report providing full critical discussions of new publications covering literary history and criticism, English language, and the various periods from Old English literature to the 20c (with a special section on American literature).

18 THE BRITISH LIBRARY. *GENERAL CATALOGUE OF BOOKS PRINTED TO 1975*. 272 vols. London: Clive Bingley, 1979-.

19 CLARIDGE, Henry. "American literature to 1900: general, early and eighteenth-century literature." *YWES* 72 (1991): 422-32.

Survey of bibliographical listings with important reviews updating the field. See esp. Section 2: Early and Eighteenth-Century Literature (429-32). List of books reviewed (451-53).

20 *COMPREHENSIVE DISSERTATION INDEX, 1861-1972.* Ann Arbor: Xerox University Microfilms, 1973.

21 CONGER, Sydney Macmillan and CONROY, Peter V, Jr."Sensibility: a Select Bibliography of Secondary Sources." In (pp. 208-29) CONGER, Syndy McMillen (ed.). *Sensibility in transformation: creative resistance to sentiment from the Augustans to the Romantics. Essays in honor of Jean H. Hagstrum.* Rutherford: Fairleigh Dickinson UP, 1990; pp. 235.

See below, **332**.

22 COPLEY, Stephen and BOWER, Alan. "The eighteenth century." *YWES* 66 (1985): 318-42; 67 (1986): 320-52; 68 (1987): 337-80; 69 (1988): 366-80; 70 (1989): 351-400; 71 (1990): 358-95; 72 (1991): 249-68; 73 (1992) 274-335; 74 (1993): 279-304; 75 (1994): 334-81 ; COPLEY, Stephen with MAJOR, Emma; O'BRIEN, Karen and JUSTICE, George. 76 (1995): 328-79; LYNN, Steven; JUSTICE, George; O'BRIEN, Karen; BACKSCHEIDER, Paula R.; ENNIS, Daniel J.; MUSE, Amy and NAUGLE, Nancy. 77 (1996): 382-449.

The annual critical review and bibliography is arranged as follows: 1. General; 2. Poetry; 3. Drama; 4. Prose; 5. The Novel.

23 CORDASCO, Francesco. *Eighteenth century bibliographies. Handlists of critical studies relating to Smollett, Richardson, Sterne, Fielding, Dibdin, eighteenth century medicine, the eighteenth century novel, Godwin, Gibbon, Young, and Burke. To which is added John P. Anderson's bibliography of Smollett.* Metuchen, NJ: The Scarecrow Press, Inc., 1970; pp. iii, 230.

Of particular pertinence is ch. viii "The Eighteenth Century Novel. Handlist of General Histories and Articles of the Last Twenty-five Years with a Notice of Bibliographical Guides" (153-65). Contains a preface and introductory note by Prof. James R. FOSTER. I. General Bibliographic Guides (153-54); II. General Histories and Articles of the Last Twenty-five Years (155-63); III. Important French Literary Histories (164-65). Subject index (165). Lists some 110 items with occasional brief commentary.

24 CRADDOCK, Patricia B. "Recent studies in Restoration and eighteenth-century literature." *SELit* 32:3 (1992): 571-601.

Accounts of books of interest to scholars of Restoration and 18c literature published between March 1991 and March 1992. Identifies trends such as "the interest in particular authors and the rise of the novel, and changing ones, such as the greater interest in genres other than the novel, and the study of literary theory within the Restoration and 18c in the light of modern enquiries..." (601).

25 CRANE, Ronald Salmon. "Review of *A list of English tales and prose romances printed before 1740* by Arundell Esdaile." *MLN* 29 (Feb. 1914): 45-49.

Provides additions and corrections to ESDAILE. See below, **36**.

26 DE VOOGT, Peter J. "A critical bibliography: the eighteenth century." *Dutch Quarterly Review* 17 (1987): 129-41.

Critical review of book-length works published in 1984 and 1985 on Restoration and 18c British and American literature, history and sociology and philosophy.

27 *DISSERTATION ABSTRACTS INTERNATIONAL.* 1969 - Feb. 1985. Also *DISSERTATION ABSTRACTS,* 1952-1969. See also *COMPREHENSIVE DISSERTATION INDEX.*

28 DRAPER, John William. *Eighteenth-Century English Aesthetics: a bibliography.* (Englische Forschungen, 71.) Heidelberg: Carl Winter, 1931; pp. 140.
Lists 1) 110 general books on aesthetics; 2) 103 treatises on architecture and 65 on gardening; 3) pictorial and plastic arts; 4) 244 literary discourses (literature and drama); 5) music (including opera); 6) some recent comment on 18c aesthetics, all for the period 1750-1800.

29 DURANT, Jack D. "Books about the early English novel: a survey and a list." In J. M. ARMISTEAD (pp. 269-84) *The first English novelists.* Knoxville, Tennessee, 1985. See Ch. 3 under ARMISTEAD, **173**.

Brief and selectively chosen bibliography with sharply pointed annotation.

30   DYSON, A. E. (ed.). *The English novel: select bibliographical guides.* London: Oxford UP, 1974; pp. ix, 372.

Provides introductory texts, critical studies and commentaries, biographies and a background reading list.

31   *THE EIGHTEENTH CENTURY: A CURRENT BIBLIOGRAPHY.* Philadelphia, 1978; New York: AMS Press, Inc., 2001-.

Bibliography listing significant books, articles and reviews relating to:
1. printing and bibliographical studies;
2. historical, social and economic studies;
3. philosophy, science and religion;
4. the fine arts.
Index.

32   *EIGHTEENTH-CENTURY FICTION.* Hamilton, Ont.: McMaster Univ., 1978-.

33   *EIGHTEENTH-CENTURY LIFE: PUBLISHED TRI-ANNUALLY FOR THE COLLEGE OF WILLIAM AND MARY BY THE JOHNS HOPKINS UNIVERSITY PRESS.* Pittsburgh, then Baltimore 1974-.

34   *EIGHTEENTH-CENTURY STUDIES: A JOURNAL OF LITERATURE AND THE ARTS.* Davis, CA: American Society for Eighteenth-Century Studies, 1967-.

35   *ENGLISH LITERATURE, 1600-1800: A BIBLIOGRAPHY OF MODERN STUDIES, 1926-72.* Founded by Ronald S. CRANE. Compiled for the *Philological Quarterly.* By C. B. WOODS, G. S. ALLEMAN, G. S. KOLB, C. A. ZIMONSKY and H. K. MILLER. 6 vols. Princeton: Princeton UP, 1950-74. Rpt. from *Philological Quarterly.*

Collation of all the articles published in the *Philological Quarterly* (1925-70) under the headings: I. Bibliographical Aids, II. General Studies, III. Studies of Authors, sometimes with annotations (often very substantial in the case of reviews). Index of Names.

36   ESDAILE, Arundell. *A list of English tales and prose romances printed before 1740.* London: The Bibliographic Society, 1912; pp. xxxv, 329.

Alphabetical listing by author of editions, including some locations. Divided into two parts: 1475-1642 and 1643-1739.

37 EVANS, James E. and WALL, John N., Jr. *A guide to prose fiction in the 'Tatler' and the 'Spectator'.* (Garland Reference Library of the Humanities, 71.) New York; London: Garland, 1977; pp. 396.

Full accounts are provided of the prose fiction found in the *Tatler* and the *Spectator* by date. Each is followed by an index to the catalogue of the two papers. The fifth section is devoted to an annotated bibliography of the critical studies of the prose fiction.

38 FREY, Linda; FREY, Marsha and SCHNEIDER, Joanne. *Women in western European history: a select chronological, geographical and topical bibliography from Antiquity to the French Revolution.* Westport, CT: Greenwood, 1982; pp. liv, 1024.

Vast bibliography (unannotated) devoted to all aspects of women in life, history, culture and literature: historical surveys of Antiquity, the Middle Ages, Renaissance, Reformation, Seventeenth Century and Eighteenth Century. Subject, Name and Author Indices.

39 GARBER, Linda and COOPPAN, Vilashini. "An annotated bibliography of lesbian literary critical theory, 1970-1989". In (pp. 340-54) WOLFE, Susan J. and PENELOPE, Julia (eds). *Sexual practice/textual theory: Lesbian cultural criticism.* Oxford and Cambridge, MA: Blackwell, 1993; pp. xii, 388. See below, **1061**.

40 GASKELL, Philip. *A new introduction to bibliography.* New York; Oxford: Oxford UP, 1972; pp. x, 438.

Important for the chapter "Book Production: the Hand Press Period 1500-1800" (including printing type, composition, paper, imposition, presswork, warehouses, binding, decoration and illustration, patterns of production, the English booktrade to 1800).

41 GAVERLEY, A.; FLOWERS, F. J. C.; ROBINSON, E. A.; THOMPSON, R. V. and WALLIS, P. J., assisted by HEAL, J. G. B. and JONES, B. *Eighteenth-century British books: A subject catalogue extracted from the British Museum General Catalogue of Printed Books.* (Project for Historical Bibliography.) 4 vols. University of Newcastle upon Tyne, Dawson and Co. Ltd., 1979. See below **91**.

42 GECKER, S.; SCHMULBACH, F. and DUNCOMBE, R. *English fiction to 1820 in the University of Pennsylvania Library.* Philadelphia: Univ. of Philadelphia Library, 1954; pp. 132.

Short-title listing of works arranged alphabetically by author.

43 GLOCK, Waldo Summer. *Eighteenth-century English literary studies: a bibliography.* Metuchen, NJ; London: Scarecrow Press, 1984; pp. xviii, 847.

Purpose is "to provide the undergraduate and graduate student and the scholar [...] a comprehensive but not exhaustive survey of the critical literature on the most important writers of the eighteenth century" (xi). 3701 entries. Divided into Collected Studies (without annotation), General Studies (with annotation) with chapters on Joseph Addison, Mark Arkenside, James Boswell, Fanny Burney, Robert Burns, Charles Churchill, William Collins, William Cowper, George Crabbe, Daniel Defoe, Henry Fielding, John Gay, Oliver Goldsmith, Thomas Gray, Samuel Johnson, Alexander Pope, Matthew Prior, Samuel Richardson, Christopher Smart, Tobias Smollett, Richard Steele, Laurence Sterne, Jonathan Swift, Arthur Young, Edward Young. The entries vary between 6 and 16 lines and are succinct and helpful. Author index (829-47).

44 GOVE, Philip Babcock. *The imaginary voyage in prose fiction, 1700-1800: A history of its criticism and a guide for its study, with an annotated checklist of 215 Imaginary Voyages from 1700 to 1800.* New York: Columbia UP, 1941; pp. 445. See below, **472**.

45 GRIEDER, Josephine. "English translations of French non-sentimental prose fiction, 1760-1800." *BB* 32:4 (1975): 168-71.

Translations of French prose fiction formed the staple of the British public's literary diet between 1760 and 1800. Attempts to document the minor non-sentimental French fiction: 1) French works translated into English (38 titles); 2) checklist of French authors translated (22 names).

46 GREENOUGH, Chester Noyes. *A bibliography of Theophrastan Character in England with several portrait characters* (1947). Westport, CT: Greenwood Press, 1970; pp. xii, 347.
Bibliography of the Character, listing thousands of items between 1495 and 1941. The years 1700 to 1740 (147-201) list author, title, details of size, location, list of contents, sometimes some commentary. Indices (281-347).

47 GROLIER CLUB, THE. *Catalogue of original and early editions of some English writers from Wither to Prior.* 3 vols. New York, 1905.

Descriptive catalogue of 1088 items taken mainly from libraries of

Grolier Club members, arranged chronologically by author with extensive title page facsimiles and indices of printers, booksellers and engravers.

48 HAHN, H. George and BEHM, Carl, III. *The eighteenth-century British novel and its background: an annotated bibliography and guide to topics.* Metuchen, NJ; London: The Scarecrow Press, Inc., 1985; pp. ix, 392.

Contains 3188 items, each provided with a descriptive word or phrase. Divided into 7 parts: 1. A guide to topics, an index of subjects, themes and critical issues (1-48); 2. Bibliographies and surveys of criticism (49-56); 3. Studies of 18c life: backgrounds of the novel (57-111); 4. General criticism of the 18c British novel and related studies (115-52); 5. Major novelists (153-68): Defoe, Fielding, Richardson, Smollett, Sterne; 6. Minor novelists (269-330): Aubin, Bage, Barker, Beckford, Blackamore, Frances More Brooke, Hervey Brooke, Fanny Burney, Cleland, Coventry, Cumberland, Davys, Day, Sarah Fielding, Godwin, Goldsmith, Graves, Hawkeworth, Hays, Hayworth, Holcroft, Inchebald, Ch. Johnstone, Lee, Lennox, Lewis, Mackenzie, Manley, Moore, Radcliffe, Reeve, Robinson, Row, Scott, Sheridan, Smith, Walker, Walpole, Wollstonecraft; 7. 'Near'-novelists (Johnson, Swift) (331-72). Index of critics and scholars (373-92).

49 HALKETT, Samuel and LAING, John. *Dictionary of anonymous and pseudonymous English literature.* Ed. J. KENNEDY; W. A. SMITH and A. F. JOHNSON. 8 vols. and 2 vols. supplement. London: Oliver & Boyd, 1926-62.

Each entry provides the highlighted first word of the anonymous title, the full title and subtitle, description of the author as given, the author's actual name in parentheses (if known), size of the book, pages, sources of origin, place and date of publication. Sometimes a small descriptive note is appended.

50 HARDY, J. C. *A catalogue of English prose fiction, mainly of the eighteenth century, from a private library.* Foss, Perthshire: Duval, 1982; pp. 171.

List of 826 titles of mainly 18c works with a small overspill at the end of each century, nearly all first, or first collected, editions. Sufficient information of the imprint is given to identify the edition.

51 HOE, Robert. *Catalogue of the library of Robert Hoe of New York: illuminated manuscripts, incunabula, historical bindings, early English literature, rare Americana, French illustrated books, eighteenth-century*

English authors, autographs, manuscripts etc. To be sold by auction on Monday, April 24, 1911. 8 vols. New York: The Anderson Auction Company, 1911.

Divided into four parts: 1 (3538 items); 2 (3621 items); 3 (3412 items); 4 (4017). Each entry provides name, full title, details of imprint, binding and publishing, sometimes annotated with descriptive details and illus.

52 HOWARD, Patsy C. *Theses in English literature, 1894-1970.* Ann Arbor: The Perian Press, 1973; pp. 387.

Bibliography of unpublished baccalaureate and master's theses from American universities. Entries are arranged alphabetically under the names of the writers across the spectrum of English literature. Provides a foreword (vii-viii), a list of institutions.

53 HOWARD-HILL, T. H. *Index to British literary bibliography.* 7 vols. Oxford: Clarendon Press, 1969-80. Second ed., rev. and enlarged, 1987.

Lists all major bibliographies and catalogues for the period. Also has entries under individual authors.

54 HUBIN, Allen J. *Crime fiction II: a comprehensive bibliography, 1749-1990. A completely revised and updated edition.* (Garland Reference Library for the Humanities, 1353.) 2 vols. New York and London: Garland Publishing, Inc., 1994. I, xxix, 1-887; II, 891-1568.

Crime fiction is defined very broadly as fiction intended for adult readers, or featuring adult protagonists and containing crime or the threat of crime as a major plot element. Included are mystery, detective, suspense thriller, gothic (romance suspense), police and spy fiction. The intent is to cover all such fiction in the English language published in book form through the end of 1990. Magazine and dime novel fiction, juvenile and children's material are not included. Divided into Author Index, Title Index, Settings Index, Series Index, Series Character, Chronology, Film Index, Screenwriters Index, Directors Index.

55 HUNTER, J. Paul. "Studies in eighteenth-century fiction". *PQ* 55 (1976): 507-32.
Review of bibliographies of 18c novel (1975): major novelists (Defoe, Richardson, Fielding, Smollett, Sterne), lesser known writers of fiction, general studies (history, tradition, theory). Review of the year's work in 1975 showed the increasing sophistication about 18c fiction. Readings of novels still predominated, and reliable information about how the novel

relates to historical processes, and to cultural artifacts, and modes of thinking seemed wanting. Discerns a need for studies that would precisely establish the 18c novel in relation to other writers, artists and thinkers of the period, as well as to other times and places.

56-----"Studies in eighteenth-century fiction, 1976". *PQ* 56 (1977): 498-539.

Review article surveying critical works on 18c for 1976.

57 JONES, Claude E. "Prose fiction and related matters to 1832." *BB* 21 (1956): 234-36.
Chronological listing of authors and short titles "intended to organize the major types and writings which feed the novel proper" for the period 1300 B.C. to 1832 A.D. Continued in *BB* 22 (1957).

58------"Modern books dealing with the novel in English." *BB* 22 (1957).

Continuation of above.

59 KAY, Donald. *Short fiction in 'The Spectator'*. (Studies in the Humanities, 8, Literature.) Alabama: Alabama UP, 1975; pp. 145.

Provides a succinct introduction to the shorter forms of prose fiction in the late 17c and early 18c. Useful discussion of individual genres: the Character, the fable, the dream vision-cum-allegory, the Oriental tale, the mock-sentimental tale, the fabliau and rogue literature, the satirical adventure story, the domestic apologue. Select Bibliography (136-42).

60 LETELLIER, Robert Ignatius. *A bibliography of the English novel from the Restoration to the French Revolution: a checklist of sources and critical materials, with particular reference to the period 1660-1740*. (Salzburg English and American Studies, 17.) Salzburg: Institut für Anglistik und Amerikanistik; Lewiston, NY; Queenston, Ont.; Lampeter: Edwin Mellen Press, 1995; pp. xxxvii, 428.

Introduction (xxix-xxxvii). Part A - "The General Period (1660-1800): Miscellaneous Works" is divided into seven subsections:
1. Bibliographies; 2. Anthologies; 3. General Studies (historical, intellectual and cultural backgrounds, literary theory, criticism and motifs); 4. American Fiction; 5. Women's Studies; 6. Types of Fiction (epistolary novel, Oriental tale, picaresque novel, Gothic Novel); Part B - "Individual Authors and Specific Work of Fiction (1660-1740)" is divided into four subsections: 1. A Chronological Shortlist of Principal Works of Fiction; 2. Bunyan (bibliography 1970-90); 3. Defoe

(bibliography 1980-90); 4. Alphabetical List of Individual Authors, Titles, and Translations; Index of Scholars (315-42). Thematic Index (343-428).

61-----*The English Novel, 1660-1700: an annotated bibliography.* (Bibliographies and Indices in World Literature, 53.) Westport, CT and London: Greenwood Press, 1997; pp. xxxiv, 448.

Divided into: Part I: The General Period 1660-1700: Miscellaneous Works; 1. Bibliographies; 2. Anthologies; 3. General Studies; Part II: Individual Authors and Specific Works of Fiction 1660-1700; 4. Alphabetical List of Individual Authors, Titles, and Translations; 5. A Selected Chronological Shortlist of Prose Fictions in English between 1660 and 1700. Index of Scholars (419-432). Subject and Thematic Index (433-48). The 1360 items are extensively annotated.

62 LEVERNIER, James and WILMES, Douglas R. (eds). *American writers before 1800: a bibliographical and critical reference.* 3 vols. Westport, CT: Greenwod Press, 1984; pp. xxiii, 1764.

Covers hundreds of American writers, listing the works of each, giving a short biography, a critical appraisal and a selected bibliography (or "suggested reading"). Appendices provide years of birth, places of birth, principal places of residence, and a chronology. Index (1725-64).

63 LINK, Viktor. "Bank note, corkscrew, flea and sedan: additions to a checklist of eighteenth-century fiction." *LC* 42 (1978): 159-67.

See below under MEEKER, **76**.

64 LOWNDES, William T. *The bibliographer's manual of English literature.* Rev. Henry G. BOHN. 6 vols. London: Bell, 1890; pp. 3414.

Lists authors, titles, and subjects. Annotations include collations, notes on contents and locations of copies.

65 LUND, Roger D. *Restoration and early eighteenth-century English literature, 1660-1740: a selected bibliography of resource materials.* New York: MLA, 1980; pp. 42.

A concise (unannotated) guide to current periodicals, bibliographies, concordances, and other resource materials readily available for the study of Restoration and early 18c literature: 1. current journals and newspapers; 2. annual bibliographies; 3. general bibliographies; 4. poetry; 5.drama; 6. fiction; 7. literary criticism and language studies; 8. translations; 9. publishing and bookselling; 10. newspapers and periodicals; 11 .art and music; 12. history, biography and autobiography; 13. religious literature; 14. miscellaneous bibliographies; 15. individual authors.

66-----"The modern reader and the 'truly feminine novel', 1660-1815: a critical reading list." In SCHOFIELD, Mary Anne and MACHESKI, Cecile (eds). *Fetter'd or free? British women novelists, 1670-1815*. Athens, GA: Ohio UP, 1986; pp. xvii, 441.

Provides a discussion of works devoted to novels by women, covering both general studies and anthologies of articles, also articles on individual authors from the late 17c to the early 19c, from Aphra Behn to Jane Austen.

67 McBURNEY, W. H. *A checklist of English prose fiction 1700-39*. Cambridge, MA: Harvard UP, 1960; pp. x, 154.

"Although many studies have been devoted to the social, philosophical and literary sources from which the major novelists of the eighteenth century received their specific inspirations, there is a persistent [...] tendency [...] to ignore or dismiss the numerous minor writers of prose fiction who were the contemporaries of Defoe and Richardson. These works [...] were the only immediate prose fictional background that the acknowledged masters of the novel had, and as such, they are worthy of attention". Provides a chronological checklist by year of 337 titles, listing first anonymous works, works of English fiction, then translations. Provides full title, imprint information, details of edition, pagination, size, library where held, sometimes a brief descriptive sentence. Appended are 54 "Dubious or Unauthenticated Titles, 1700-1739" (111-22). Bibliography (125-28). Index (129-54).

68-----and TAYLOR, C. *English prose fiction 1700-1800 in the University of Illinois Library*. Urbana, 1965.

Lists 966 items.

69 McKERROW, Ronald. *An introduction to bibliography for literary students*. Oxford: Clarendon Press, 1927; pp. 359.

General introduction to the history of printing and details of bibliographical practice.

70   McNAMEE, Lawrence F. *Dissertations in English and American literature.* 3 vols. New York: Bowker, 1965-74.

      Vol. I covers 1865 to 1964; vol. II 1965 to 1969; vol. III 1970 to 1973.

71   MAGILL, Frank N. (ed.). *Magill's bibliography of literary criticism: 1300 critical evaluations of selected novels and plays: offprints of all the new material from the 12-volume revised editions of 'Masterplots'.* 4 vols. Englewood Cliffs, NJ: Salem, 1976; Epping: Bowker Publishing Co., 1976, 1978.

      Devoted to critical commentaries and evaluations of 1300 novels and plays which appeared in *Masterplots* as digests. Author and title index (IV, i-xvi).

72   MAHL, Mary and KOON, Hélène (eds). *The Female Spectator: English women writers before 1800.* Bloomington, IN: Indiana UP/ Old Westbury: Feminist Press, 1977; pp. 310.

      Introduction (1-11). Series of essays on individual women writers from the Middle Ages to 1800. Each essay contains a short introductory survey of the life, works and critical importance, and a bibliography of texts, editions and related readings.

73   *MAN AND NATURE: PROCEEDINGS OF THE CANADIAN SOCIETY FOR EIGHTEENTH-CENTURY STUDIES.* Edmonton: Academic Printing & Publishing, 1981 etc.

74   MAYO, Robert. *The English novel in the magazines, 1740-1815. With a catalogue of 1375 magazine novels and novelettes.* Evanston: Northwestern UP, 1962; pp. x, 695.

      Covers the magazine tradition in prose fiction, the single-essay periodical, historical miscellanies and associated periodicals, miscellanies and miscellaneous fiction: reprinted pieces, original fiction in the miscellanies. Appendices (religious magazines, prose fiction, foreign fiction in translation). Notes, glossary, catalogue of magazine novels and novelettes (431-620). Index of catalogue references (621-47), chronological index (648-52), register of periodicals containing long prose fiction (653-77). Index (678-95). Illus.

75   MAZZENO, Lawrence W. *The British novel, 1680-1832: an annotated bibliography.* (Magill Bibliographies.) Lanham, MD/ London: Scarecrow Press, 1997; pp. 247.

Provides a series of (unnumbered) critical texts, covering the novel from Aphra Behn to Sir Walter Scott. An introduction (1-26) provides background on bibliographical matters, and an overview of the essential tools of eighteenth-century bibliographical investigation. General Studies lists a series of studies fundamental to the criticism, history and theory of the novel in this period. The 20 chapters which follow are dedicated to selected works of criticism on individual authors, each divided into general studies and individual works on essential studies of the principal works of fiction: Jane Austen, William Beckford, Aphra Behn, Fanny Burney and Mme D'Arblay, Daniel Defoe, Maria Edgeworth, Henry Fielding, William Godwin, Oliver Goldsmith, Samuel Johnson, Matthew Lewis, Henry Mackenzie, Charles Robert Maturin, Ann Radcliffe, Samuel Richardson, Sir Walter Scott, Mary Shelley, Tobias Smollett, Laurence Sterne, Horace Walpole. Author index (233-38). Subject index (239-46). Entries are succinct (8-10 lines), but most informative.

76 MEEKER, R. K. "Bank note, corkscrew, flea and sedan: a checklist of eighteenth-century fiction." *The Library Chronicle* 35 (1969): 52-57.

Detailed survey of 18c works of fiction written from a non-human point of view: 61 titles of works which employ non-human narration. See also LINK, Viktor. "Bank note, corkscrew, flea and sedan: additions to a checklist of eighteenth-century fiction." *LC* 42:3 (1978): 159-67: 94 titles added to the original list.

77 MODERN HUMANITIES RESEARCH ASSOCIATION. *Annual Bibliography of English Language and Literature*. 1920-99. See above, **1**.

78 *MLA INTERNATIONAL BIBLIOGRAPHY OF BOOKS AND ARTICLES ON THE MODERN LANGUAGES AND LITERATURES.* E. Terence FORD (director). New York: The Modern Language Association of America, 1922-92.
Standard annual publication listing current publications. Provides both a *Subject Index* and *Classified Listings* (groupings under languages, with subsections general, fiction, theater, drama, novel, periodicals, poetry, prose). Brief annotations. Both are now available on line and on CD rom.

79 MOULTON, Charles W. *The library of literary criticism of English and American authors*. 2 vols. Buffalo: Moulton, 1901. Abridged, revised, and with additions by Martin TUCKER. Vol. II *Neo-Classicism to the Romantic Period*. New York: Frederick Unger Publishing Co., 1966; pp. viii, 602.

Selection of extracts from authors of the early 18c: George Farquhar, Antony Ashley Cooper, William Wycherley, Joseph Addison, Sir John Vanbrugh, Cotto Mather, William Congreve, Sir Richard Steele, Daniel Defoe, John Gay, George Lillo, Alexander Pope, Jonathan Swift, James Thomson (1-184). Each entry contains a biographical chronology, a very select bibliography, a section of 'Personal' attestations, excerpts from major works, and a small 'General' section of later critical perspectives. The section on Daniel Defoe (82-98) is of particular relevance.

80 *NATIONAL UNION CATALOG, THE. PRE-1956 IMPRINTS.* 738 vols. London: Mansell, 1975.

"A cumulative author list representing Library of Congress printed cards and titles reported by other American libraries. Compiled and edited with the cooperation of the Library of Congress and National Union Catalog Subcommittee of the Resources Committee of the Resources and Technical Services Division, American Library Associations."

81 NEUBURG, Victor E. *Chapbooks: a bibliography of reference to English and American chapbook literature of the eighteenth and nineteenth centuries.* London: The Vine Press, 1964; pp. 88.

Introd. (1-6) provides definition of chapbooks ("the paper-covered books offered for sale by peddlers, hawkers, and other itinerant merchants known as 'chapmen'"). They were circulated in their thousands during the 18c, the successors of the jest book and ballad of the Elizabethan Age, and the only reading matter in the 18c available to the poor. Looks at sources, classification, printers (London, provincial, Scottish, American), the development of chapbook bibliography, collectors and collections. Notes (50-54). The bibliography itself is divided into chronological items, undated items, MSS, sales catalogues, addenda, with an index of authors and printers (79-80), authors of works recorded in the bibliography and subjects (81-88). Full details of 161 items with annotations. 10 illus.

82 ORR, Leonard. *A catalogue checklist of English prose fiction 1750-1800.* Troy, NY: Whitston, 1979; pp. xi, 204.

Preface (v). Introduction (1-26). Essay "The Audience for the Novel, 1750-1800" (27-40). Chronological checklist (43-136). Author index (137-46). Title index (147-204). Introd. describes the literary scene, discussing the major works of the dominant authors. Lists 1190 titles by year, giving author, title and date, but no publisher or pagination. Locates sources for all the titles.

83 PALMER, Helen H. and DYSON, Anne J. *English novel explications.* Hamden: The Shoe String Press, 1973. 5 supplements, 1976, 1981, 1986, 1990, 1994.

The checklist of BELL and BAIRD (1959) covers the 20c criticism through 1957. This lists criticism for 1958-91 with supplements to Bell and Baird. Articles concerned with the novel as a whole, or important aspects of it, are included.

84 PITCHER, Edward. "Some emendations to Melvin R. Watson's checklist of eighteenth-century magazine serials." *NQ* 23 (1976): 506-9.

85-----"Fiction in *The Philadelphia Minerva* (1795-1798): A contribution toward the establishment of the American canon." *RALS* 9 (1979): 3-23.

Provides a catalogue of 227 items from *The Philadelphia Minerva*, with information for answering the questions: 1) What proportion of fiction was reprinted from non-American sources?; 2) Which stories clearly belong to the American tradition?; 3) What were some of the frequently used sources for the fiction of the magazine articles?; 4) To what extent could one establish authorship for the 227 mostly anonymous tales? Author index (20-21). Pseudonyms and initials (21). Non-periodical sources (21-22). Periodicals (22-23).

86-----"The fiction in *The American Museum* (1787-1792): a checklist with notes on sources." *AEB* 5 (1981): 100-06.

Provides a checklist of fiction in *The American Museum*, attempting to identify sources (or prior appearances) of stories, to isolate fiction, probably by Americans, and to show how editions of this and other American magazines published the originals with reprinted material in a manner that has inhibited identification. Lists 58 items. Index (105-6).

87-----"Robert Mayo's *The English Novel in the Magazines 1740-1815*: further emendations." *Library* 9:2 (1987): 162-64.

88 PRICE, Mary Bell and PRICE, Lawrence Marsden. *The publication of English literature in Germany in the eighteenth century. University of California Publications in Modern Philology*, 17 (1934): 1-288.

Preface (i-viii). Introd. (1-22). Works of reference (23-27). Bibliography of translations (29-258). Appendices (259-68). Index of translators, adaptors, and editors (269-88). "It seems safe to assert that no really important English novel of these years [1700 to 1740] escaped the attention of the translators, and no important English novelist. Perhaps the best selection was not always made [...]. It would appear that some of the more interesting novels of Mrs Manly and of Eliza Haywood were neglected for certain others of less value [...]." Translations rose from 5 in 1710, to 12 in 1730, 52 in 1770, to 159 in 1780.

89   Q., R. S. "Jest and song books." *NQ* 18 (20 Oct. 1856): 272-73.

List of jest books.

90   RILEY, David W. "English books of the seventeenth to nineteenth centuries in the John Rylands Library of Manchester, with particular reference to history and literature." *BJRL* 71:2 (Summer 1989): 87-102.

Description of the holdings of the John Rylands Library. The collection of the 18c English works numbers some 50,000 items, and details are internationally available by accessing the ECSTC = the Eighteenth-Century Short Title Catalogue, a computer data-base with administration offices in London and the United States.

91   ROBINSON, F. J. G.; AVERLEY, G.; ESSLEMONT, D. R. and WALLIS, P. G. *Eighteenth-century British books: an author union catalogue extracted from the British Museum Catalogue of Printed Books, the Catalogue of the Bodleian Library, and of the University Library Cambridge.* 5 vols. Folkstone: Dawson & Sons Ltd., 1981. xxi, 754, 716, 627, 715, 707.

Provides the most complete listing of books printed in the 18c, wholly or partly in England, or printed in Britain, America, or the British Colonies, including all books translated into or from English. Most editions prior to 1701 of works which have an 18c imprint are also included. Introduction, classification tables. Each entry provides name, number, short title, date, publishing and location details.

92   ROUSE, H. B. "A selective and critical bibliography of studies in prose fiction." *JEGP* 48-51 (1949-52).

Presents bibliographies which offer a selection of more important studies in prose fiction of English and European scholarship and criticism, published in 1948 (192 titles), 1949 (198 titles), 1950 (223 titles), 1951 (193 titles).

93   SAAR, Doreen Alvarez and SCHOFIELD, Mary Anne (eds). *Eighteenth-century Anglo-American women novelists: a critical reference guide.*

(Critical Reference Guides.) New York: G. K. Hall; London: Prentice Hall, 1996; pp. xxii, 664.

Major bibliographic contribution. Provides annotated entries on some 35 women writers with critical works, beginning from the first decade of the 20c (1900-92). Introd. (xii-xxii) discusses aspects of the changing styles, emphases and concerns of critical fashion. Entries are limited to one or two line observations, sometimes longer paragraphs. Items are divided into years, and numbered within each year. "Feminist criticism has changed not only the literary but the cultural map of issues [...]. While literary critics at the beginning of the twentieth century evinced only sporadic interest in women writers, by the end of the seventies critical approaches to women writers of the eighteenth century were dramatically different. Women writers who were once neglected became the object of regular scholarly activity" (xxi). Authors covered: Penelope Aubin, Jane Barker, Frances Moore Brooke, Charlotte Charke, Mary Collyer, Maria Edgeworth, Sarah Fielding, Hannah Webster Foster, Susannah Minifie Gunning, Mary Hays, Eliza Haywood, Elizabeth Inchbald, Harriet and Sophia Lee, Charlotte Lennox, Delarivière Manley, Margaret Minifil, Amelia Alderson Opie, Ann Radcliffe, Clara Reeve, Perdita Robinson, Susanna Haswell Rowson, Frances Chamberlaine Sheridan, Charlotte Turner Smith, Tabitha Tenney, Sukey Vickery, Jane West, Helen Marie Williamson, Mary Wollstonecraft, Sally Bareth Keating Wood, Anne Cromartie Yearsley. Index (651-64).

94 SARGENT, Lyman Tower. *British and American Utopian literature, 1576-1985.* (Garland Reference Library of the Humanities, 831.) New York; London: Garland, 1988; pp. xix, 559.

Chronological list of Utopias published in English, or in a few cases, Latin, with brief annotations. Author index, title index.

95 SAWYER, Charles James and HARVEY DARTON, F.J. *English books 1475-1900: a signpost for collectors.* 2 vols. Westminster: Chas. J Sawyer; New York: E.P. Dutton & Co., 1927; pp. 384, 431.

Looks at several works of prose fiction, considering matters of special interest for collectors.

96 SERAFIN, Steven (ed.). *Eighteenth-Century British literary biographers.* (*Dictionary of Literary Biography*, 142.) Detroit, New York and London: A Bruccoli Clark Layman Book, 1994; pp. xi, 370.

Presents a series of detailed articles on a whole range of 18c biographers.

Each entry begins with a list of works, continues with an extended literary-critical biography, and concludes with a series of references (letters, bibliographies, biographies, critical works on the subject). Generously illustrated with portraits and facsimiles. Lists books for further reading and cumulative index to the whole series. Covers Anderson, Barbauld, Bisset, Boswell, Brydges, Currie, Davies, Godwin, Goldsmith, Hawkesworth, Sir John Hawkins, William Hayley, Hays, Hoon, Johnson, Malone, Mason, Murphy, Piozzi, Roberts, Southey.

97 SHERBO, Arthur. "Eighteenth-century English fiction in print: an uncritical census." *College Eng* 21 (Nov. 1959): 105-11.

Looks at the available editions of the 18c novel in 1959. There is virtually no modern form which does not stem from some 18c prototype. Lists various editions, tabulating author, title, edition, introduction, notes, bibliography and price, including Swift, Fielding, Smollett, Richardson, Burney, Sterne, Johnson, Goldsmith, Defoe, Mackenzie, Lewis.

98 SIEBERT, Donald T. (ed.). *British prose writers, 1660-1800. First series.* (Dictionary of Literary Bibliography, 101.) *Second series.* (Dictionary of Literary Biography, 104.) Detroit, New York and London: A Bruccoli Clark Layman Book, 1991; pp. xv, 440; xiii, 434.

Presents a series of detailed articles on a range of late 17c and 18c literary figures (novelists, essayists, journalists, history, political writers). Each entry begins with a list of works, continues with an extended literary-critical biography, and concludes with a series of references (letters, bibliographies, biographies, critical works on the subject). Generously illustrated with portraits and facsimiles. Books for further reading and a cumulative index to the whole series.
First series: Addison, Arbuthnot, Berkeley, Bolingbroke, Burnet, Butler, Hyde, Defoe, Dennis, Dryden, Fielding, Hervey, Locke, Mandeville, Lady Mary Wortley Montague, Pepys, Pope, Rymer, Shaftesbury, Steele, Swift, Temple.
Second series: Boswell, Burke, Chesterfield, Cowper, Gibbon, Godwin, Goldmith, Hawkins, Hume, Johnson, Henry Home Lord Kames, Catherine Macaulay, Pery, Hester Piozzi, Reynolds, Smith, Smollett, Walpole, Warburton, Joseph Warton, Thomas Warton, John Wesley, Mary Wollstonecraft.

99 SMITH, Alpheus Ward. "Collections and notes of prose fiction in England, 1660-1714." Unpub. doct. diss., Harvard Univ., 1932.

Provides a critical bibliography.

100 SOUVAGE, Jacques. *An introduction to the study of the novel: with special reference to the English novel.* Ghent: Storia-Scientia, 1967; pp. ix, 254.

Divided into two parts: I. The Theory of the Novel (3-100), which seeks to define the novel, looking at theories of structure and form, narrative technique, old and dramatized novels, telling and showing, point of view, characterization, character. II. A Systematic Bibliography of the Novel (103-234): A. Bibliographies, checklists, catalogues, reference works, miscellaneous works (103-9);B. Periodicals devoted to the novel (110); C. Philosophy and sociology of the novel (110-17); D. Novel as literary genre. Trends in the novel (social, utopian, political, symbolical, psychological) (118-28); E. Theory of the novel; F. History of the novel; G. The modern novel (1850 onwards); H. Comparative study of the novel; I. Studies of topics; J. Form and Structure in the novel; K. Technique (narrative, character and characterization); M. Style in the novel; N. Studies in individual novelists.

101 SPECTOR, Robert D. (comp.). *Backgrounds to Restoration and eighteenth-century English literature: an annotated bibliographical guide to modern scholarship.* (Bibliographies & Indices in World Literature 17.) Westport, CT: Greenwood, 1989; pp. xxiv, 553.

Gives a broad and detailed view of the period, ranging from the daily lives of the people, through the institutions which governed their existence, to the cultural, social, scientific, philosophical foundations of their society. The annotation for every entry is intended to provide a guide to what can be found at each source, a summary of contents, and often an evaluative comment on the source itself:
1. bibliographies; 2. publishing, printing and journalism; 3. history and politics: 4. religion;5. philosophy; 6. science, medicine and technology; 7. economics; 8.crime and law; 9. society, manners, customs and attitudes; (A. general sociology B. family; C. women; D. sex; E. race, nationalities, religion); 10. education and rhetoric; 11. language and rhetoric; 12. literature and the arts; (A. literature, dramatic history and criticism; B. satire; C. music; D. painting, engraving, sculpture; E. architecture, gardening, decorative arts; F. the sister arts).

102 STREETER, Harold W. *Eighteenth-century English novels in French translation: a bibliographic study.* New York: Institute of French Studies, 1936; pp. viii, 256.

The preface sketches the vogue and influence of the 18c English novel in

France. Analyzes the periodical intermediaries and the dominant theories of translation in the period. The second section is devoted to the main channels of the diffusion of the English novel through French translations, with the chief names Manley, Swift, Defoe, Fielding, Richardson, and Sterne. The last section deals with the extent and diversity of the French translation of English novels, examining the different novels translated as 'satirical', 'politico-philosophical', 'moral or didactic', and 'sentimental'. Lists 520 titles, arranged by these various genres or groups, and a selective list of spurious translations. Mistakes corrected by Donald F. BOND (*MP* 35 [1937-38]: 457-61) who comments on and supplements various entries, and adds to the general bibliography. The introduction provides a useful outline of the movement. It does not exaggerate the effect of the English novel upon the French, and rightly regards Prévost as a greater influence than Richardson.

103 *STUDIES IN EIGHTEENTH-CENTURY CULTURE: PROCEEDINGS OF THE AMERICAN SOCIETY FOR EIGHTEENTH-CENTURY STUDIES.* Vol. 1. Cleveland; London: The Press of Case Western Reserve U, 1971; Vol. 6. Madison: Wisconsin UP for the American Society for Eighteenth-Century Studies, 1977; Vol. 28. Baltimore and London: The Johns Hopkins UP, 1998, etc.

104 *STUDIES IN ENGLISH LITERATURE, 1500-1900* (Summer issue: "Studies in the Restoration and Eighteenth Century"). Rice Univ., Houston, TX, 1961-.

105 *STUDIES IN SHORT FICTION*, annual bibliography. Newberry, SC: Newberry College, 1963-.

106 TODD, Janet (ed.). *A dictionary of British and American women writers, 1660-1800.* London: Methuen, 1984; pp. xxiv, 344.

Provides biographical and bibliographical details of hundreds of British and American women writers. Their lives are recounted in some detail, with critical reference to works, and brief summaries of the principal ones. Lists of selected works and references.

107 TRILL, Suzanne. "Early modern women's writing: texts and contexts." *CritS* 4:2 (1992): 724- 32.

Survey of modern texts of early women's writing: British poetry, works about Mary Astell and other early feminists, women dramatists of the Restoration period, witchcraft, Mrs Manley, relationships between women, challenging the canon, bibliographies.

108 UMI. *Early English Books (1661-1799): a cumulative index to units 1-60 of the Microfilm Collection.* 9 vols. Ann Arbor, MI: University Microfilms, 1990; pp. 7386.

Vols I-II: *Author Index* (1685); Vols III-V: *Title Index* (4258); Vols VI-VIII: *Subject Index* (7088); Vol. IX: *Wing Nos and Reel Position Indices* (7386).

109 UPHAM, Alfred Horatio. "Notes on English prose fiction." *MLN* 30 (1915): 246-47.

Provides additions to ESDAILE from an unpublished list by Augustus H. Shearer.

110 WATSON, George (ed.). *The New Cambridge Bibliography of English Literature, II: 1660-1800.* Cambridge: Cambridge UP, 1974. 2476 col.

Revision of BATESON. See columns 975-84.

111 WILES, R. M. *Serial publication in England before 1750.* Cambridge: Cambridge UP, 1957; pp. xv, 391.

Much on minor fiction, including chronological lists of titles.

112 *YEAR'S WORK IN ENGLISH STUDIES, THE.* See above under COPLEY, **22**.

113 ZALL, P.M. "English prose jestbooks in the Huntingdon Library: a chronological checklist (1535?-1799)." *SRO* 4 (1969): 78-91.

Provides a chronological short-title list, indicating number and nature of jests.

2

Anthologies

114 ANON. (ed.). *Women critics 1660-1820: an anthology.* Bloomington and Indianapolis: Indiana UP, 1995; pp. xxv, 410.

Presents a range of critical writings by 41 of the nearly 100 women who produced criticism between 1660 and 1820. The breadth and depth of these women's thought demonstrates their participation in diverse critical traditions and the distinctive insights they brought to critical theory and practice. While drawn principally from England, there is a sampling from France, Germany, and the United States. Includes Mme de Scudéry, Aphra Behn, Jane Barker, Anne Dacier, Anne Finch, Catherine Trotter Cockburn, Elizabeth Elstob, Eliza Haywood, Elizabeth Cooper, Sarah Fielding, Elizabeth Robinson Montague, Louise d'Epinay, Elizabeth Griffith, Charlotte Lennox, Clara Reeve, Sophie Guntermann von La Roche, Isabelle von Tyll de Zuylen de Charrière, Mary Alcock, Anna Seward, Anna Laetitia Barbauld, Hannah Cowley, Hannah More, Comtesse de Genlis, Charlotte Smith, Judith Murray, Frances Burney, Phyllis Wheatley, Elizabeth Inchbald, Mary Robinson, Elizabeth Hamilton, Hannah Foster, Mary Wollstonecraft, Mary Hays, Joanna Baillie, Anne Kidd, Dorothea Schlegel, Mme de Staël, Maria Edgeworth, Jane Austen, Rachel Lazarus. Biographical and bibliographical sources (391-401).

115 ALDINGTON, R. (ed.). *A book of 'Characters': compiled and translated with introduction and notes.* London: George Routledge, 1924; pp. xvi, 559.

"Characters" from Theophrastus, Joseph Hall, Sir Thomas Overbury, Nicholas Breton, John Earle, Thomas Fuller, Samuel Butler and others including Richard Flecknoe, John Denham, John Oldham, *The Tatler*, *The Spectator*, Jean de la Bruyère, Luc de Chapiers, Abel Boyer, Cyrano de Bergerac, Pierre de Gouz, Pierre Jacques Britten, Abbé Goussault, Comtesse de Genlis. Introduction (1-26).

116   ALLOTT, Miriam. *Novelists on the novel*. New York: Columbia UP and London: Routledge & Kegan Paul, 1959; pp. xv, 336.

Gathers together discussions about the nature and crafts of fiction by novelists, "believing that these are the most likely people to clear up the confusions of novel criticism" (xv): Part I "The Nature of Prose Fiction" (the novel and the marvellous, the novel as a portrait of life, the ethics of the novel); Part II "The Genesis of the Novel" (the novelist's approach and equipment, germination at work, effort and inspiration); Part III "The Craft of Fiction" (structural problems - unity and coherence, plot and story, time factors, narrative technique, characterization dialogue, background style).

117   ANDREWS, William L.; BUSH, Sergeant, Jr.; KOLODNY, Annette; LANG, Amy Schlaeger and Daniel B. SHEA, Daniel B. (eds.). *Journey in New Worlds: early American women narratives*. Madison: U of Wisconsin P, 1990; pp. 232.

Republishes critical editions of texts of Mary Rowlandson, the journal of Madame Knight, the life of Elizabeth Ashbridge, and the travel diary of Elizabeth House Trust covering the period from the late 17c to the late 18c.

118   ASHTON, John. *Chapbooks of the eighteenth century, with facsimiles, notes and introduction*. London: Chatto & Windus, 1882. Rpt. London: Skoob Books Publishing, n.d; pp. xvi, 486.

Introd. (iii-xii) discusses the genre, format, repertoire, market and readership in the 18c. Chapbooks were virtually the only reading matter for the poorer classes and provide for the modern reader a fascinating way into the heroes and legends, folklore and superstitions that prevailed in the popular literature of the age. Provides over 100 chapbooks and facsimiles of the original covers and woodcut illustrations.

119   BACKSCHEIDER, Paula R. and RICHETTI, John J. (eds.). *Popular fiction by women, 1660-1730: an anthology*. Oxford: Clarendon Press; New York: Oxford UP, 1996; pp. xxvi, 336.

The introduction (ix-xxiv) provides a critical context for the selected stories, and reassesses the understanding of the rise of the English novel over the past 50 years. M. D. McKillop and I. Watt provided seminal studies, but "the unspoken masculine assumptions of both [...] are now embarrassingly apparent" (ix). Over the past 25 years literary historians have begun "reading beyond and around the work of the male masters" on whom these two critics concentrated. The text raises important questions on the virtual disappearance from literary history of this body of fiction by women, about the history of the English novel, the formation of the canon, and about aesthetics. Discusses and provides the texts of: 1. Aphra Behn, *The History of the Nun* (1689) (1-44); 2. Delarivière Manley, *The Secret History of Queen Zara and the Zarazians* (1705) (45-80); 3. Jane Barker, *Love Intrigues* (1713) (81-112); 4. Penelope Aubin, *The Strange Adventures of the Count de Vinevil and His Family* (1721) (113-152); 5. Eliza Haywood, *The British Recluse* (1722) (153-226); 6. Eliza Haywood, *Fantomima* (1725) (227-50); 7. Mary Davys, *The Reformed Coquet* (1724) (251-322); 8. Elizabeth Singer Rowe, *Friendship in Death* (selections) (1728) (323-34). Chronology (xxv-vi). Facs. reprints of the first pages. Bibliography (335-6).

120 BATTESIN, Martin C. (ed.). *British novelists, 1660-1800. Part 1: A-L.* (*Dictionary of Literary Biography*, 39:1.) *Part 2: M-Z.* (*Dictionary of Literary Biography*, 39:2.) etc.

Appendix: *Novelists on the Novel* (557-658) collects a series of prefaces by Bunyan, Congreve, Manley, Huet, Defoe, Aubin, Haywood, Davys, Richardson, Fielding, Smollett, Sarah Fielding, Samuel Johnson, Francis Coventry, Horace Walpole, Elizabeth Griffith, Sarah Reeve, Fanny Burney, Thomas Holcroft, Mackenzie, Godwin. Books for further reading (659-64).

121 BOYCE, Benjamin (ed.). *Prefaces to fiction: with an introduction by Benjamin Boyce.* (Augustan Reprint Society, 32.) Los Angeles: William Andrews Clark Memorial Library, Univ. of California, 1952.

Facs. reprints. Introduction (i-xii). George de Scudéry, Preface to *Ibrahim* (1674); Manley, Preface to *The secret history of Queen Zarah* (1709). Other 18c prefaces by D'Argens, Warburton, Derrick.

122 CAREY, John (ed.). *The Faber book of Utopias.* London: Faber & Faber, 1999; pp. xxxvi, 531.

Collection of excerpts from 104 pieces of utopian writing, from c. 1940 BC to 1998. Each extract has its own introduction. The general introd. (xi-xxvi) discusses the genre and reasons for selection: " [...] we all want our loved ones to live free of suffering, injustice and heartbreak. Those who construct utopias build on that universal human longing. What they build, however, carries within it its own potential for crushing or limiting human life' (xi). [...] I have extended the definition of utopia beyond the strictly formal [...]. [U]topianism permeates literature and life far beyond the narrow boundaries of bibliographical classification" (xxxvi). For the period 1660-1740, the selection covers:

1. Margaret Cavendish: *The Blazing World* (1666);
2. Henry Neville: *The Isle of Pines* (1668);
3. Denis Vairasse: *The History of the Severambians* (1667-69);
4. Gabriel de Foigny: *A New Discovery* (1693);
5. Anon.: *The Sophick Constitution* (1700);
6. Ambrose Evans: *Adventures of James Dubourdieu* (1719);
7. Daniel Defoe: *Robinson Crusoe* (1719);
8. Ambrose Philps: *The Fortunate Shipwreck* (1720);
9. Jonathan Swift: *Gulliver's Travels* (1726);
10. Ludwig Holberg: *Niels Klim's Journey* (1741).

123 CLAEYS, Gregory (ed.). *Utopias of the British Enlightenment.* (Cambridge Texts in the History of Political Thought.) Cambridge and New York: Cambridge UP, 1994; pp. xli, 305.

While once thought hardly to exist, there were many 18c Enlightenment satires upon the notions of primitive innocence and of terrestrial moral perfectibility in this era, as well as widespread use of the utopian format to lampoon existing social imperfections, rather than to recommend a superior regime. 18c Britain was given to imagining a variety of fictional ideal societies and model commonwealths. Provides an extended introduction (vii-xxviii), a chronology of main 18c Utopias and anti-utopian texts (xxix-xxxii), a bibliographical note (xxxiii), biographical notes (xxxvi-xxxviii). Provides 7 texts: 1. Anon. *The Island of Content* (1709); 2. Anon. *A Description of New Athens in Terra Autralis Incognita* (1720); 3. David Hume: *Idea of a Perfect Commonwealth* (1752); 4. James Burgh: *An Account of [...] Cessares, A People of South America* (1764); 5. James North More: *Memoirs of Planetes* (1795); 6. Wieland Hodgeson: *The Common Wealth of Reason* (1795); 7. Anon. *Bruce's Voyage to Naples* (1802).

124 CRAIK, Henry (ed.). *English Prose: selections with critical introductions by various writers and general introductions to each Period. Vol. IV: Eighteenth Century.* London and New York: Macmillan & Co., 1894; pp. xii, 639.

Introduction (1-11). Extracts from Conyers Middleton, Bishop Berkeley, William Law, Samuel Richardson, Bishop Butler, Lord Chesterfield,

William Warburton, John Wesley, Henry Fielding, Samuel Johnson, David Hume, Laurence Sterne, Thomas Gray, Horace Walpole, Gilbert White, Tobias Smollett, William Robertson, Richard Price, Sir Joshua Reynolds, Adam Smith, Thomas Warton, Oliver Goldsmith, Edmund Burke, William Cowper, Joseph Priestley, Samuel Horsley, Edward Gibbon, James Boswell, William Paley, Henry Mackenzie, Hannah More, Jeremy Bentham, Madame D'Arblay, Dugald Stewart, William Beckford, William Corbett, James Macintosh, Isaac Disraeli, Maria Edgeworth. Notes (635-36).

125 FRENCH, Laura. "Measuring others by themselves: Images of Native Americans in American literature, 1607-1887." Unpub. doct. diss., Indiana Univ. of Pennsylvania, 1994. [*DA* 55 (1994): 963A.]

Annotated anthology that provides piercing examples and critical analysis of images of native Americans as reflected in American prose literature from 1607-1887. The purpose is to show how changing political and economic agendas of Anglo-Americans in the New World led to changing images of the natives in the prose literature of the periods. The anthology is in chronological order, introduced by brief background, date of publication, reception and current canonical status. Texts by non-native writers demonstrate the high level of awareness of natives throughout the 17c, 18c and 19c, and help to deflect criticism of multiculturism as a new trend that disrupts historic patterns of American culture.

126 GREENFIELD, John R. (ed.); BRAILOW, David and BRUCCOLI, Arlyn (assoc. ed.). *Dictionary of British literary characters: 18th- and 19th-century novels.* New York: Facts on File, 1993; pp. 655.

Part I of a two-volume compendium comprising over a thousand novels and more than ten thousand characters. The selection of novels has been as inclusive as space permits, and, apart from established novelists, there is extensive coverage of lesser-known authors, including many women writers. Seeks to cover all major characters and all other characters who contribute to the themes and plots in any significant way. Each character is listed alphabetically by first name, or by some salient identifying characteristic. Description, author, and title are provided, and there is an index, alphabetical by author, of all titles, followed by an alphabetical list of all the characters in that work, as listed in the *Dictionary*. Provides useful information about the characters' occupations, family relations, relations with other characters, class and gender roles, as well as contributions to the theme and plot of the novel concerned.

127 HARRIS, Sharon M. (ed.). *American women writers to 1800*. New York and
Oxford: Oxford UP, 1996; pp. 452.

Relatively little research has been published about early American
women writers. This anthology seeks to advance the process of filling the
documentary and intellectual gap in American culture and history, and
to encourage further explorations in this field. A majority of the texts
included have not been reprinted since their original publication, and, in
the case of letters and diaries, have never been published. Provides
samples of the available writings by women in this period, with a general
introduction, and biographical introductions from the perspective of a
feminist scholar and theorist. Categorizes the extracts as youthful
reflections, women's education, domestic records, business women's
writing, deathbed declarations, feminist visions, first women, spiritual
narratives, captivity narratives, travel journals, epistolary exchanges,
petitions, political essays and organizational tracts, revolutionary war
writings, poetry, histories, drama, novels. Each extract is preceded by a
brief biographical-critical note. List of Notable Early American Women
(413-20). Select Bibliography (421-31). Index (432-52).

128 HENDERSON, Philip (ed.). *Shorter novels*. 3 vols. Vol. III: *Eighteenth
century*. (Everyman's Library.) London and Toronto: J. M. Dent & Sons
Ltd., 1930; pp. xii, 306.

A general preface to the 3 vols is provided by George SAINTSBURY,
with particular introductions and notes to each vol. by Philip
HENDERSON. Vol. 3 contains an Introduction (vii-xii), and the texts of
Johnson's *Rasselas*, Walpole's *The Castle of Otranto*, Beckford's *Vathek*.
Biographical notices at the beginning of each novel. Notes (278-306).

129 HOPKINS, Annette Brown and HUGHES, Helen Sard (eds). *The English
novel before the nineteenth century: excerpts from representative types*.
Boston: Ginn, 1915; pp. xxi, 794.

Asserts that the excerpts in this anthology have been chosen to illustrate
"definite technical and historical features in the development of the
novel".

130 JONES, C. E. (ed.). *Prefaces to three eighteenth-century novels (1708 -
1751 - 1797)*. (Augustan Reprint Society, 64.) Los Angeles: William
Andrews Clark Memorial Library, Univ. of California, 1952; Augustan
Reprint Society, 1957; pp. iv, [58].

Fasc. reprints. Introduction (i-iv). Important for Alemán, preface to *The*

Life of Guzman d'Alfarache. Also prefaces by Coventry and Tyler.

131   JONES, J. C. (ed.). *Women in the eighteenth century: constructions of femininity.* London and New York: Routledge, 1990; pp. vi, 257.

Anthology gathering together various texts by and about women, ranging from 'conduct' manuals to pamphlets on prostitution, from medical ethics to critical definitions of women's writing, from anti-female satire to appeals for female equality. Aims to completement the upsurge in feminist writing on 18c literary history, and offer students the opportunity to make their own re-readings of literary texts and their ideological contexts. Contributors include Mary Astell, Elizabeth Carter, Susanna Centlivre, Hester Chapone, Charlotte Clarke, Lady Mary Chudleigh, Mary Collier, Daniel Defoe, Joseph Dorman, John Duncombe, Anne Dulton, François de Salignac de la Mothe-Fénelon, Jane Fordyce, Robert Gould, Catherine Manley Graham, John Gregory, Letitia Hawkins, Mary Hays, Eliza Haywood, Vicesimus Knox, Bernard Mandeville, Delarivière Manley, Martha Mears, Hannah More, Teresia Constantia Phillips, Richard Polwhele, Clara Reeve, Samuel Richardson, Mary Robinson, Eliza Singer Rowe, George Savile Marquis of Halifax, Mary Scott, Priscilla Wakefield, Wetenhall Wilkes, Mary Wollstonecraft. Select bibliography (historical and literary) (249-50). Index (253-57).

132   KIMPEL, Dieter and WIEDEMANN, Conrad (eds). *Theorie und Technik des Romans im 17. und 18. Jahrhundert.* (Deutsche Texte, 16, 17.) 2 vols. Tübingen: Niemeyer, 1970; pp. 159.

Collection of original writings on prose fiction (prefaces, dedications, treatises, advertisements, commentaries) covering the period from the Baroque to early Romanticism. Early 18c fiction is discussed in the anonymous "Raisonnement über die Romane" (1708) (61-68), by Wilhelm Richter ("Avertissement zum sächsischen Robinson", 1723) (68), and in the anonymous "Einige Gedanken und Regeln von den deutschen Romanen" (1744) (69-76).

133   McBURNEY, William H. (ed.). *Four before Richardson: Selected English novels, 1720-7.* Lincoln, NA and London: U of Nebraska P, 1963; pp. xxxv, 373.
Modern reprints of: 1. Arthur Blackamore, *Luck at Last; or, The Happy Unfortunate* (1723) (1-81); 2. W. P., *The Jamaica Lady; or, The Life of Bavia* (1720) (83-152); 3. Eliza Haywood, *Philidor and Placentia; or L'Amour trop Delicat* (1727) (153-271); 4. Mary Davys, *The Accomplished Rake; or, Modern Fine Gentlemen* (1727) (233-373).
"The four works presented here are arranged in a progression of technical

skill and general interest although my introduction suggests interrelations. All texts are taken from the first editions, and are reproduced without omissions [...]. Punctuation, capitalization, and paragraphing have been modernized; and spelling has been adapted to accepted American usage" (viii). Title pages are reprinted with detailed annotations. Extended introduction (xi-xxxv) places the novels in the historical and critical context of the fiction of the early 18c, and provides detailed discussion of the four authors: Blackamore (xvi-xix), W.P. (xix-xxii), Haywood (xxii-xxix), Davys (xxix-xxxv).

134   McCORMICK, Ian (ed.). *Secret sexualities: A sourcebook of 17th- and 18th-century writing.* London and New York: Routledge, 1997; pp. x, 262.
Presents a series of primary texts concerning sex, sexuality, and gender. The texts range from trial records and newspaper items to medical pamphlets and anatomical treatises. There is a general introduction (1-11) providing a theorectical framework for the collection, "to provide a range of texts that supply a sense of the diversity of thinking about sexuality in the seventeenth and eighteenth centuries" (10). Groups the documents as: 1) Anatomies; 2) Crimes and Punishments; 3) Representatives; 4) Sapphic Texts. Glossary (237-40). Notes (241-48). Bibliography (249-54). Index (255-62).

135 McGOWAN, Ian (ed.). *The Restoration and eighteenth century.* Basingstoke, Macmillan, 1989; pp. xxviii, 584.

Collection of pieces from the Restoration and the 18c. The introduction provides a historical and cultural overview: religion and ideas, Augustanism, writers and readers, drama, fiction and poetry (xv-xxvii). Extracts by Samuel Butler, John Aubrey, John Bunyan, John Dryden, Samuel Pepys, Thomas Sprat, John Wilmot, William Dampier.

136   MACK, Robert L. (ed.). *Oriental tales.* (World's Classics.) Oxford: Oxford UP, 1992; pp. lix, 277.

Editions of John Hawkworth, *Almoran and Hamet,* Frances Sheridan, *The History of Nourjahad,* Clara Reeve, *The History of Charaba, Queen of Egypt,* Maria Edgeworth, *Murad the Unlucky.*

137   MAHL, Mary R. and KOON, Helen (eds). *The female spectator: English women writers before 1800.* Bloomington, IN: Indiana UP; Old Westbury: Feminist Press, 1977; pp. 310.

Anthology of writings covering many centuries: Julian of Norwich,

Margery Kempe, Catherine Parr, Queen Elizabeth I, Elizabeth Grymeston, Mary Sidney Herbert, Amelia Lanier, Elizabeth Clinton, Elizabeth Cary, Bathsua Makin, Margaret Cavendish, Katherine Philips, Aphra Behn, Mary Delarivière Manley, Susannah Centlivre, Eliza Haywood, Frances Grenville Boscawen, Anna Laetitia Barbauld, Hannah More, Anna Seward.

138 MOULTON, Charles Wells. *The library of literary criticism of English and American literature.* Esp. Vol. II: 1639-1729. Buffalo: Moulton, 1901. Abridged, rev. and with additions by Martin TUCKER. New York: Frederick Unger Publishing Co., 1967; pp. 602.

Critical anthology comprising contributions from the 18c, 19c and 20c, with biographical notes, lists of works and additions.

139 PEROSA, Sergio. *Teorie inglesi del romanzo 1700-1900 da Fielding a Dickens, da Stevenson a Conrad, una grande tradizione narrativa nell'interpretazione dei suoi protagonisti.* Milan: Bompiani, 1983; pp. 360.

In Italian. Source book of extracts from theoretical writing on prose fiction by a selection of novelists over two centuries. The introduction (9-52) places the anthology of 100 extracts in a critical perspective looking at the themes: 1) dalla Francia; 2) il primo settecento; 3) la metà del secolo; 4) la ripresa del 'romance'; 5) il romanzo storico; 6. classificazione, detrattori, difesi; 7) dibatti sul realismo; 8) l'arte del romanzo; 9) naturalismo e nuovo romanzo; 10) il romanzo d'arte. The texts concerning the early 18c are: 1. Congreve's preface to *Incognita* (1671); 2. Peter Motteux's preface to his translation of *The History of Don Quixote* (1700); 3. Manley's preface to *The Secret History of Queen Zarah* (1705); 4. Sir Richard Blackmore's "An Essay on Epick Poetry" (1716); 5. Defoe's preface to *Robinson Crusoe* (1719); 6. Defoe's preface to *Roxana* (1724); 7. Ephraim Chambers, from his *Cyclopaedia* (1728); 8. Nathan Bailey, from the *Dictionarium Britannicum* (1730); 9. Thomas Dyche and William Pardon, from *A New General English Dictionary* (3rd ed.,1740);10. Philip Dormer Stanhope, Earl of Chesterfield, Letter (1740);11. Henry Fielding, preface to *Joseph Andrews* (1742);12. Samuel Richardson, preface to vol.1 of *Clarissa* (1747); 13. Tobias Smollett, preface to *Roderick Random* (1748); 14. Henry Fielding, opening chapters of *Tom Jones* (1749); 15. Samuel Johnson, *The Rambler* (31 March 1750).

The Italian medium means limited accessibility to this very useful book. Apart from the inclusive and imaginative choice of material, the study is particularly rich as a sourcebook, and further provides a descriptive Register of Names (345-48), Essential Bibliography (349-60): 1) primary sources (72 items); 2) secondary sources (95 items); 3) general subjects (27 items); 4) individual authors (60 items). Index of sources quoted (361-65).

140 PRESTON, James and POUPARD, Dennis (eds). *Literature criticism from 1400 to 1800: excerpts from the works of fifteenth, sixteenth, seventeenth and eighteenth century novelists, poets, playwrights, philosophers and other creative writers, from the first published critical appraisals to current evaluations.* Vol. IV. Detroit: Gale Research Co., 1986.

The selection of criticism is designed to provide an historical overview of cultural responses to the author's work through the ages. Gives biocritical information, background, bibliographies (primary and secondary), cumulative indices.

141 PRINGLE, David. *Imaginary people: a who's who of fictional characters from the eighteenth century to the present day.* Aldershot and Brookfield, VT: Scolar Press, 1987; 2nd ed. 1996; pp. v, 296.

Short entries provide information on more than 1300 modern fictional characters, ranging from Defoe's Robinson Crusoe, concentrating on the period of the modern novel (1719-1989), but including plays, short stories, opera, ballet, comic strips, musicals, films, radio and TV. Many illus.

142 RAWLINGS, Philip (ed.). *Drunks, whores and idle apprentices: criminal biographies of the eighteenth century.* London and New York: Routledge, 1992; pp. xi, 224.

Small selection of 18c accounts of the lives of contemporary criminals, providing the flavor of a body of literature which was very popular in its time. The General Introduction (1-35) discusses some of the problems surrounding its use, looking at the literature of crime and its popularity, the readers, the writers (with problems of authenticity and accuracy), the criminal biography as literature, as history, issues and tensions in criminal biography, changes in the literature. Further reading (27-28). Bibliographical notes (28-35). The 5 texts all have their own extended introductions with bibliographical notes:
1. *The History of [...] John Sheppard* (1724) (39-46, 47-78);
2. *The Life and Actions of James Dalton* (1730) (79-84, 85-112);
3. *The Ordinary Newgate's 'Account': Mary Young* (1741) (113-21);
4. *The Discoveries of John Poulter* (1753-54) (139, 147);
5. *The Life, Travels, Exploits, Frauds and Robberies of Charles Speckman* (1763) (181, 185). Index (217-24).

143 SAINTSBURY, George (ed.). *Specimens of English prose style from Malory to Macaulay: selected and annotated with an introduction by George Saintsbury*. London: Kegan Paul, Trench & Co., 1885; pp. xlvi, 367.

Provides extracts for the period 1700-40 from John Locke, Robert South, Gilbert Burnet, Charles Leslie, Daniel Defoe, Richard Bentley, Jonathan Swift, Sir Richard Steele, Joseph Addison, Henry St John Viscount Bolingbroke, Conyers Middleton, George Berkeley, Alexander Pope, Samuel Richardson, Lady Mary Wortley Montague, Joseph Butler, Philip Dormer Stanhope Earl of Chesterfield, Robert Paltock, Henry Fielding, Samuel Johnson, David Hume, Laurence Sterne, Thomas Gray, Horace Walpole, Gilbert White, Tobias Smollett, Adam Smith, Sir Joshua Reynolds. Introduction and brief annotations.

144 SHARROCK, Roger (ed.). *The Pelican Book of English prose*. Vol.I: *From the beginnings to 1790*. Harmondsworth: Penguin Books, 1970; pp. 708.

Introduction (21-51) gives an historical-critical survey, with attention to the 18c (47-49).The section "Augustan" (387-694) includes 'Life and Action', 'Imagination', 'Argument', with selections by the Earl of Shaftesbury, the Earl of Clarendon, Dorothy Osborne, George Fox, Thomas Fuller, Henry Power, Robert Hook, John Bunyan, Samuel Pepys, John Evelyn, Izaak Walton, the Marquis of Halifax, Celia Fiennes, Ned Ward, Gilbert Burnet, Roger North, Thomas Brown, Joseph Addison, Lawrence Eckart, Daniel Defoe, William Law, Joseph Spence, Thomas Gray, Horace Walpole, Oliver Goldsmith, Richard Graves, William Robertson, Samuel Johnson, James Cook, Fanny Burney, Edward Gibbon, William Cowper, James Boswell, Gilbert White. Biographical notes (695-708).

145 UPHAUS, Robert and FORSTER, Gretchen M. (eds). *The other eighteenth century: English women of letters, 1660-1800*. East Lansing, MI: Colleagues Press, 1991; pp. 465, 13 illus.

Attempts to restore women's writing in England "to its rightful place in the present day canon of 18c literature". Extensive introd. (1-16). Anthologizes a wide range of works of many genres by 22 writers: Margaret Fell, Judith Drake, Mary Astell, Aphra Behn, Sarah Fyge Egerton, Lady Mary Chudleigh, Katherine Philips, Anne Finch Countess of Winchelsea, Lady Rachel Russell, Eilzabeth Tollet, Elizabeth Singer Rowe, Elizabeth Carter, Catherine Talbot, Jane Collier, Lady Mary Wortley Montague, Lady Sarah Dennington, Hannah Cowley, Joanne Baillie, Mary Wollstonecraft, Hannah More, Maria Edgeworth, Anna Laetitia Barbauld. Themes exemplified: women writers' sense of belonging to a tradition and a community, opposition to subordination and the silencing of women, determination to use talents and create a space for themselves. Each set of readings is prefaced by a short historical-critical introd. Appendix (13 plates).

146   WARDROPER, John (ed.). *Jest upon jest: a selection from the jestbooks and collections of merry tales published from the reign of Richard III to George III*. London: Routledge & Kegan Paul, 1970; pp. vii, 216.

Chronological survey of jest collections, discussing matter and themes. Introd. (1-25), 244 texts (28-150), sources (151-5), notes (156-99), bibliography (200-5), index (207-16).

147   WILLIAMS, Ioan M. *The novel and romance 1700-1800: a documentary record*. London: Routledge & Kegan Paul, 1970; pp. xi, 484.

Documentary record tracing the development of novel criticism from 1700 to 1800. Material includes prefaces to collections, translations, and original novels; essays written for journals modelled on the *Spectator*; passages from miscellanies and from books written primarily for some purpose connected with the novel; reviews from the monthly reviews; introductions to the works of certain authors. 18c criticism of prose fiction in England falls into two sections, dividing at the year 1740. The century began with the rejection of the previously popular heroic romance. The first 40 years was a period of great activity and experiment, but was marked by a lack of confidence on the part of the novelists, and a generally hostile attitude on the part of the critics who were offended by the frivolity and immorality of much of the contemporary fiction. The period ended suddenly with the publication of Richardson's *Pamela* (1740) and Fielding's *Joseph Andrews* (1742) which was partly stimulated by his rival's success. These two writers consolidated their achievements with *Clarissa* (1748) and *Tom Jones* (1749). Together they demonstrated that fiction could be popular, and yet have artistic and intellectual appeal. There followed such an enormous increase in the production of fiction that many observers felt that the novel was a threat to cultural and moral standards. Between 1740 and the end of the century, a great deal of discussion went on and very positive advances were made towards the serious consideration of prose fiction as a branch of literature on equal terms with poetry and drama. There are 101 critical extracts: nos. 1-25 cover the period 1691 to 1741. The introduction (1-24) is very important: the decline of the heroic romance; between romance and novel: 1700-40; the importance of Richardson; after Richardson: the conservative reaction to the novel; the development of theory. Detailed notes (449-74). Index of titles (475-79). Index of names

(480-84).

148 WILLIAMSON, Marilyn L. *Raising their voices: British women, 1650-1750.* Detroit: Wayne State UP, 1990; pp. 339.

Survey with Introduction (14-36) of the women writers of 17c and 18c.

149 WÜRZBACH, Natascha (ed.). *The novel in letters: Epistolary fiction in the early English novel, 1678-1740.* Introd. trans. rev., Jean BONHEIM and John F. DAVIS. London: Routledge & Kegan Paul, 1969; pp. xxiii, 288.

Important introduction (ix-xxiii) discussing the letter as a literary convention, models and manuals, the autobiography, diaries and journals, development of dialogue, the role of the reader, characterizations, the narrative traditions. The novel at the end of the 17c and beginning of the 18c had not emerged from the shadow cast by the "dubious respectability" cast by its predecessors, the romance and the scandalous chronicle. The epistolary novel has much in common with other narrative fiction, and feeds directly into the achievements of the 18c novel - psychological analysis and point- of-view technique, as well as the attainment of a high dramatic immediacy. Each reprint is prefaced with its own introduction. 1. Aphra Behn, *Five Love-Letters from a Nun to a Cavalier* (1678) (1-22); 2. Abel Boyer, From *Letters of wit, politics and morality* (1701) (23-36); 3. Delarivière Manley, From *A Lady's pacquet of letters* (1707) (37-52); 4. Anon., *A Letter from Mrs Jane Jones* (1737) (53-64);5. Mary Hearne, *The Lover's Week* (1718) (65-90); 6. Anon., *The Double Captive* (1718) (91-101); 7. John Costeker, From *The Constant Lovers* (1731) (105-48);8. John Campbell, *The Polite Correspondence* (1730) (149-96); 9. Aphra Behn, *Love letters between a nobleman and his sister* (1684)(197-282).Select bibliography (283-85).

150 ZIPES, Jack (trans.). *Beauties, beasts and enchantment: Classic French fairy tales. Translated with an Introduction by Jack Zipres.* Harmondsworth: Penguin Books Ltd. and New York: A Meridian Book, 1991; pp. viii, 589.

Anthology of the most important fariy tales to appear in France between 1690 and 1789. Includes works by Charles Perrault (10), Marie-Jeanne L'Héritier (1), Catherine Bernard (1), Charlotte-Rose Caumont de la Force (1), Jean de Mailly (1), Henriette Julie de Murat (1), Jean-Paul Bignon (1), Gabrielle-Suzanne de Villeneuve (1), Jeanne-Marie Leprince de Beaumont (2), Philippe de Caylus (1), Mlle. de Lubert (1), Marie-Catherine d'Aulnoy (15). The introduction, "The Rise of the French Fairy Tale and the Decline of France" (1-12), provides a survey of the genre in the context of the politico-social circumstances of the late 17c, and discussion of the various subtypes: the salon fairy tale, the Oriental fairy tale, the comic and conventional fairy tale. Also see below, **1080**.

3

General Studies

HISTORICAL, INTELLECTUAL AND CULTURAL BACKGROUNDS, LITERARY THEORY, CRITICISM, AND MOTIFS

151 ANON. "Defoe, Ward, Brown and Tutchin, 1700-1703." *NQ* 162 (1932): 416-23.

Collections of newspaper references. After a long period of repression and persecution, the English Press, with a history reaching back to the early newsletters, gained its freedom in 1694 when the Licensing Act was finally abrogated.

152 ANON. "English humour 1500-1800." *TLS* (21 May 1938): 360.

Describes jest books displayed at the Bodleian exhibition illustrating English humor from the Renaissance to the beginning of the 19c.

153 ANON. "Le passé présent: études sur la culture britannique pré-industrielle. Mélanges en l'honneur d'André Parreaux." *CCV* 9 (1988); pp. 159.

Collection of essays exploring the nature of pre-industrial British society. The emphasis is predominantly on 18c literature, but other contributions highlight aspects of life in the late 17c and 18c.

154 ANON. "Making and rethinking the canon: the eighteenth century." *MLS* 18:1 (Winter 1988).

Explores the notion of canon, and the formation of a body of enduringly popular works of literature.

155 ADAMS, Percy G. *Travelers and travel-liars, 1660-1800.* Berkeley: U of California P, 1962; rpt. New York: Dover; London: Constable, 1980; pp.

x, 292; illus. (8 pp. of plates).

Surveys the objects, methods and effects of travel books and writers, and analyzes the conscious purpose of deceiving.

156-----"The anti-hero in eighteenth-century fiction." *SLI* 9:1 (1976): 29-51.

Many 18c novels contain elements of the picaresque and of the *Bildungsroman*. First-person narrative techniques, the rise of the lower servant classes to middle-class, even upper-class status, pseudo-autobiography and biography, all contributed to popularize the story of a young man or woman who survives years of troubled experience to arrive at some kind of earthly reward. Few of these heroes are in the Hector tradition; most are like Jason or Odysseus, willing to employ subterfuge to fight a cruel world on its own terms. So many anti-heroes in 18c fiction indicate the variety of fiction.

157-----*Travel literature and the evolution of the novel.* Lexington: U of Kentucky P, 1983; pp. xi, 368.

Persistent but changing traditions of travel literature form a major contribution to our understanding of the evolution of the novel. Points to relationships in structure, language and philosophy between the two analogous and continuously developing forms.

158 ADAMS, Robert M. *The land and literature of England: a historical account.* New York and London: W. W. Norton & Co., 1983; pp. 555.

Ch. 11 "The Early Eighteenth Century: The Rising Novel (1714-1748)" (286-313) discusses the growing maturity of the novel in a detailed historical context. Investigates various themes (Whigs and the paths of prudence, progress and poverty, the rise of Robert Walpole, the reign of 'sly King Log', the rising flood of imperial ambition). The section 'The Opening Up of Fiction: Defoe and Richardson' (300-3) is a very curtailed survey that gives virtually no idea of the vibrancy of lesser writers of fiction. Aubin and Haywood are ignored, Manley briefly mentioned, the important French translations overlooked. Many illus. Appendices. Suggestions for Further Reading (520-34). Index (535-55).

159 ADAMSON, David McLaren. "Eighteenth-century rhetorics and rhetafictions." Unpub. doct. diss., Univ. of California, Los Angeles, 1991. [*DAI* 52:6 (1991): 2146A.]
Examines the history of 18c British rhetoric. It urges reconsideration of its history from a broader definition than has hitherto been applied.

Argument uses generic, historical and historiographical methods. The historiographic argument suggests that 18c rhetoric has been studied only from the philosophical point of view. Because this view is narrow, scholars have dismissed rhetoric as irrelevant to their special fields. In the early 18c rhetoric became oriented towards an English-speaking readership. Examines 18c techniques that try to restore rhetoric's performative dimension (Pope, Fielding, George Campbell).

160   ADBURGHAM, Allison. *Women in print: writing women and women's magazines from the Restoration to the accession of Victoria.* London: Allen & Unwin, 1972; pp. 302, illus.

The aim is to salvage pre-Victorian periodicals from the limbo of forgotten publications, and investigate self-supporting women of the middle-classes in the late 17c and 18c. Ch. 1 "From the Restoration to Queen Anne" (19-36) considers women dramatists: Aphra Behn, Catherine Cockburn, Susannah Centlivre, as well as John Dunton, the *Athenian Mercury*, the *Gentlemen's Journal*, and sexual mores -- seduction and marriage, aristocratic adultery, purity through innocence. Ch. 2 "Fashionable Education and Lonely Scholars" (37-52) looks at boarding schools for young ladies, the fashion for all things French, scholarly eccentrics, manuals of direction. Ch. 3 "Essay Papers and Newpaper Women" (53-67) looks at Richard Steele's championship of women, his writing for them in the *Tatler* and the *Spectator*, and Mrs Manley in her *New Atlantis*. Chronology of periodicals mentioned (273-81) and bibliography (282-90).

161   ALDISS, Brian W. and WINGROVE, David. *Trillion year spree: the history of science fiction.* New York: Atheneum, 1986; pp. 528.

Traces the history of science fiction, seeing it as originating in the Gothic with Mary Shelley, continuing with Edgar Allan Poe and H. G. Wells, and reaching its peak in the 20c (1950s-1970s). Surely utopian ideas and the imaginary voyage must also have made their contribution to this genre?

162   ALLEN, Don Cameron. "Early eighteenth-century literary relations between England and Germany." *MLN* 49 (1934): 99-101.

In an oration *De Charlataneria Eruditorum* (Amsterdam, 1716) delivered by J. B. Menken to the students, faculty and townspeople of Marburg on 9 February 1713, he provided interesting evidence of the literary relationship between England and Germany at that time, referring to Dryden, Thomas Fuller, Boyle and Bentley, and satirists, indicating that the fame of the Partridge pamphlets had already reached Germany.

163   ALLEN, Walter. *The English novel: a short critical history.* London: Phoenix House Ltd., 1954; pp. xv, 336.

Ch. 1 "The Beginnings" (19-32) covers the late 17c before centering on Defoe, who is as much entitled to be considered the founder of English journalism as the father of the novel. Concentrates mainly on *Robinson Crusoe*: "It was Coleridge's contention that Crusoe was the universal representative, the person for whom every reader could substitute himself" (36). The sense of partnership between God and man is with Crusoe all the time. In *Moll Flanders* the emphasis is on the effect of the environment on character. Here Defoe is revealed as the first wholly unambiguous instance in English literature of that interest in character in itself, that obsession to impart character, which Virginia Woolf found the distinguishing mark of the novelist. In this respect, Defoe is the archetypal novelist (39).

164   ALLISTON, April. *Virtue's faults: Correspondences in eighteenth-century British and French women's fiction.* Stanford, CA: Stanford UP, 1996; pp. xiv, 318.

Despite the advances made in English and French studies of women's literature, the amount of comparative work in this field remains negligible. The fiction of women's correspondence includes elements of both domestic fiction and romance, and investigates a strain in fiction that works out the relations between the public and private spheres. Offers serious and sympathetic readings of some neglected women's novels of the later 18c, and recontextualizes them in relation to rereading better-known women's novels across the whole 18c. Notes (245-90). Bibliography (291-310). Index (311-18).

165   ALTER, Robert. *Rogue's progress: studies in the picaresque novel.* Cambridge, MA: Harvard UP, 1963; pp. 148.

Inquires into the inner structure of the picaresque. Traces a genuine tradition of picaresque narrative, extending in time and place far beyond the borders of Spain. There is a variety of picaresque experience, not simply *the* picaresque experience. Looks at Lazarillo and the picaresque hero, a bourgeois picaroon, the picaroon as fortune's plaything, the picaresque domesticated, heirs of the tradition. Works cited (136-37), notes (139-46), index (147-48).

166   ALTMAN, Janet Gurkin. *Epistolarity: approaches to a form.* Columbus:

Ohio State UP, 1982; pp. viii, 235.

Provides a critical survey of the history of the epistolary novel,
concentrating by and large on the 18c efflorescence, but invaluable for its
general study of the topic. Epistolary fiction tends to flourish at those
moments when novelists most openly reflect upon the relation between
storytelling and intersubjective communication, and begin to question the
way in which writing reflects, betrays or constitutes the relations between
self, other and experience.

167   AMELINCKX, Frans C. and MEGAY, Joyce N. *Travel, quest, and
      pilgrimage as a literary theme: studies in honor of Reino Virtanen.* n.p.:
      Society of Spanish and Spanish-American Studies, 1978; pp. vii, 292.

Autobiography, epistolary novels and travel literature have been much
neglected, yet are venerable, varied, rich and entertaining. Considers
travel literature from antiquity to modern times in a series of 27 essays.
The most significant travel literature of the years 1500-1700 remains the
utopian kind, the "extraordinary voyage". Fénelon, Voltaire, Swift,
Diderot developed into a field of philosophical and political writing,
resuming links with Plato and Sir Thomas More. A. M. VAZQUEZ-BIGI
("Lunarians and Lunatics from Aphra Behn to Goldoni-Haydn: the Don
Quixotes and Harlequins of extraterrestrial travel" [138-52]) provides an
overview of the copious literature of such voyages and a corresponding
new public taste.

168   AMOS, Flora Ross. *Early theories of translation.* (Columbia Univ. Studies
      in English and Comparative Literature.) New York: Columbia UP, 1920;
      pp. xiv, 184.
      Survey of the theory and practice of English translators from Medieval
      times. Ch.4 "From Cowley to Pope" (138-78) sees the period of Dryden
      and Pope as the golden age of English translators. Index (181-84).

169   ANDERSON, Howard. "The idea of the novel in the mid-eighteenth century:
      Richardson, Fielding and Sterne." In (pp. 311-27) AHRENS, Rüdiger
      and   WOLFF,   Erwin   (eds).   *Englische   und   amerikanische
      Literaturtheorie: Studien zur ihrer historischen Entwicklung; Band I:
      Renaissance, Klassizismus und Romantik.* (Anglistische Forschungen,
      126.) Heidelberg: Winter, 1978. I, 438; II, 618.

There is a remarkable sense of dislocation as the reader moves from
Clarissa to *Tom Jones* to *Tristram Shandy*. The sense of each as a
different world, is a valid response to 3 distinct ways of describing and
patterning experience, 3 unique narrative approaches to the reader.

Extraordinary expansion and deepening consciousness was the work that all these founders of the English novel passed on to the next century. Their perception that, in an increasingly disintegrated society, fiction could provide impressive experience with inescapable value for the reader's reaction to himself and his world, has indeed been a vital base of the novel's power through the 19c and into our own time. Select bibliography (325-37).

170   ANDREW, Donna T. *Philanthropy and police: London charity in the eighteenth century*. Princeton: Princeton UP, 1989; pp. x, 229.

Survey of the sociology of 'welfare' in the 18c, looking at religion, commerce and charity from 1680-1740 (11-43), charity and the charitable community at mid-century, charitable foundations from 1750-70, poverty and the attack on dependency, charities of self-help. Bibliographical notes. Appendix of donors. Index (223-9).

171   ANNANDALE, E. T. and LEBRUN, Richard A. (eds). *L'Homme et la nature/Man and nature*. Proceedings of the Canadian Society of Eighteenth-Century Studies. (Man & Nature 5.) Edmonton: Academic Printing & Publishing, 1986; pp. x, 213.

Provides articles on the 18c French novel (Alexandre AMPRIMOZ, "Le roman du XVIIIe siècle: Signification de l'encadrement, pp. 1-14), Beaumarchais, Defoe, the Grenville programme, Diderot, Goethe, Burney, rebellion in SW Germany after the Seven Years' War, the Lovejovian universe, Dante in the 18c, the German England, 18c Russian music and translations of the English novel, the development of the French and Italian spectacle, the Canadian outback, Lillo and More.

172   ARAVMUDAN, Srinivas. "Tropical figures: colonial representation in England and France, 1688-1789." Unpub. doct. diss., Cornell Univ., 1991. [*DA* 52 (1992): 3271A.]

Investigates the metropolitan colonial ideal from the historical compromise of the Glorious Revolution to the rupture marked by the French Revolution: the textured backgrounds of tropical narrative, the historiography of slavery and imperialism, and the construction of literary genres. Argues that literary representations of colonial peoples - like Caribbean slaves - had a profound impact on the formation of Enlightenment-inspired Western political subjects because discourses of individualism, economic freedom, secularism, and national liberation were linked with colonial modes of domination and repression. Looks at Behn's *Oroonoko* and the complementary oppression of metropolitan women in Thomas Southerne's successful dramatic adaptation.

173 ARMISTEAD, J. M. (ed.). *The first English novelists: essays in understanding. Honoring the retirement of Percy G. Adams.* (Tennessee Studies in Literature, 29.) Knoxville: Tennessee UP, 1985; pp. 295.

Provides a comprehensive account of studies on the novel from the beginning of the 18c to its conclusion, and has an annotated list of major works on the rise of fiction by J.D. DURANT (275-84).

174 ARMSTRONG, Nancy. "The rise of femine authority in the novel". *Novel* 15 (1982): 127-45.

Domestic fiction provided a way of telling about conflict and contradictions within the socio-economic sphere, while remaining remote from the world. To this special connotative power of the primitive voice and subject matter, we can probably attribute the development of a distinctively feminine mode of literature. The novel early on assumed the distinctive features of a specialized language for women. It might have an explicitly female source, concentrate on women's experience, address an audience of young middle-class ladies, and find itself censored by female reviewers.

175-----*Desire and domestic fiction: A political history of the novel.* New York: Oxford UP, 1987; pp. x, 300.

Domestic fiction has tried to disentangle the language of sexual relations from the language of politics, and so introduced a new form of political power which emerged with the rise of the domestic woman, and established its hold over British culture through her dominance over all objects and practices we associate with private life: authority over the household, leisure time, courtship procedure, kinship relations. Under her jurisdiction, the most basic qualities of human identity were supposed to develop. Looks at the rise of female authorship in the novel, the rise of the domestic woman, the rise of the novel, the rhetoric of violence and disorder, the politics of domestic fiction. Notes (261-90).

176-----and TENNENHOUSE, Leonard (eds). *The ideology of conduct: essays on literature and the history of sexuality.* (Essays on Literature and Society.) New York; London: Methuen, 1987, pp. 243.

These essays demonstrate that conduct books for women in particular strove to reproduce, if not always to revise, the culturally approved forms of desire. Such instructional literature had the sole purpose of telling women how to make themselves desirable. Looks at Medieval courtly literature, early conduct books, Defoe's ideas of conduct, the rise of the domestic woman. Bibliographic notes.

177-----and TENNENHOUSE, Leonard. *The imaginary Puritan: literature, intellectual labor, and the origins of personal life.* Berkeley; Oxford: U of California P, 1992; pp. 275.

Studies the appearance of "the author" during the late 17c and early 18c, and what happens to traditional historical narratives once the importance of this event is understood. The appearance of the author coincides with the onset of modernity itself. Looks at the mind of Milton, the English Revolution, family history, the influence of literature, the vanishing intellectual, signs of personal life, the reproductive hypothesis, why categories thrive.

178 ASHLEY, Leonard R.N. "Short fiction: beginnings to 1800." In (pp. 133-52) MAGILL, Frank (ed.). *Critical survey of short fiction.* Vol. I. Englewood Cliffs: Salem Press, 1981.

Provides a broad survey of short fiction in verse and prose.

179 ATKINSON, Geoffroy. *The extraordinary voyage in French literature.* Vol. 2: *From 1700 to 1720.* Paris: Champion, 1922. Vols. 1 & 2 rpt New York: Burt Franklin, 1969; pp. 147.

Deals with works published in the years immediately preceding the appearance of Defoe's *Robinson Crusoe.* Until 1720, the novel of extraordinary voyage developed in France without any indebtedness to English or Spanish writers. The realistic settings of these accounts were based almost entirely upon French accounts of travel. After 1720, there was much conscious French imitation of *Robinson Crusoe.* Provides 1) an extended definition of the extraordinary voyage; 2) looks at the type as a document for ideas; 3) real and imaginary realms (accounts of real voyages, imaginary realms); 4) a precursor of the extraordinary voyage (Vincent Le Blanc, *Voyages du sieur Vincent Le Blanc*); 5) Foigny's *La Terre australe connue* (voyage and adventure, ideal lands, sources and influences); 6) Denis Vairasse's *Histoire des Sévarambes* (voyage, ideal land, sources); 7) Fénelon's *Les Aventures de Télémaque* (voyage setting, relation to earlier voyages, *Le Bétique, Salente*). Provides close analysis of:
1. Claude Gilbert, *Histoire de Calejava*;
2. Lahotan and 'the Good Savage';
3. Maximilien Misson, *Voyage de François Leguat*;

4. Simon Tyssot, *Voyages de Jacques Massé*;
5. Simon Tyssot, *Voyage de Groenland.*
Appendices (111-35). Index (137-47).

180-----*Les relations de voyage du XVIIe siècle et l'évolution des idées.* Paris: Librairie Ancienne Édouard Champion, 1924. Rpt New York: Burt Franklin, 1971; pp. 220.

Draws out the influence of voyages of discovery on the growth of ideas in the late 17c and early 18c. Looks at philosophers and ideas (Montaigne's "Les Cannibales", rationalists and *libertins*, philosophers, Vauban), theories and political activity (liberty, equality, fraternity), overseas republics (savage republics, missionary republics, republican colonies), the concepts of the Noble Savage and the Wise Chinese, economic and political theories, deist ideas, anti-Christian ideas (direct and indirect criticisms), other ideas (progress, Ancients and Moderns, relativism, the exotic spirit, sensibility, rationalism, the experimental method). Conclusions. Appendix (197-200). Bibliography (201-14). Index (215-20).

181-----*Le Sentiment de la nature et le retour à la vie simple, 1690-1740.* (Société de Publications Romanes et Françaises, 64.) Geneva: Librairie E. Droz; Paris: Librairie Minard, 1960; pp. 89.

The first half of the 18c in France not only saw the decadence of classicism, but also the rising of the philosophic spirit. The authors of this period prepared the ground for the sentimental flowering in the second half of the 18c. Admiration for the beauties of natural scenery and the yearning for a simple and virtuous life far from crowded and sordid cities were increasingly expressed after 1690. Looks at *Le plein air, La nature (la nature indifférente, la nature admirable), le mensonge passioné, la retour à la vie simple.* Bibliography (85-89).

182-----*The sentimental revolution: French writers of 1690-1740.* Ed. A. C. KELLER. Seattle/London: U of Washington P, 1965; pp. 188.

An enlightenment began to appear in France as early as the time of Amyot, Bodin, and Montaigne in the 1500s. It went into eclipse among the best authors for 50 or 60 years in the century following, but rose rapidly again in more open questioning of traditional institutions and beliefs between the late 17c and the publication of the *Encyclopédie* in 1750, a rationalist protest against traditions in France from 1600 until the mid-18c. Considers periodicals, second-rate novels, plays, poems, accounts of travel in Europe, letters, diaries, memoirs and sermons, some books on nature, science, all published in this transitional period of 50 years. Looks at famine, plague and bankruptcy, witnesses of war and wretchedness; growth of self-esteem among commoners; growth of compassion; praise of lay benevolence; moral reprobation; recrimination of Protestants. Bibliography (175-81). Index (182-88).

183-----and KELLER, Abraham C. *Prelude to the Enlightenment: French literature, 1690-1740.* London: George Allen & Unwin, Ltd., 1971; pp. 221.

Third volume of a study of French history and literature from 1690 to 1740. Numerous passages are quoted from documents written by members of the middle class, as well as members of the petty nobility, who had been reduced to poverty and disappointed by the changing times. There was a significant growth in the reading public, a wider, more varied public, with a greater variety of tastes. There was evidence of a growing diversity, part of the social development where middle-class authors were writing for the enjoyment of their fellow commoners, often with open or tacit disregard of the approved values of traditional aristocratic society. The history of 18c France was very much taken up with efforts of the middle class to break down the barriers and restrictions which the monarchy and nobility had erected against them. Looks at emotional revolutions (personal emotions, literary attitudes and stances), the broadening world of 1700 (expression of the real world, intellectual horizons. Bibliography (209-14). Index (215-21).

184 AUTY, Susan Garis. "Anti-splenetic mirth in the novels of the mid-eighteenth-century." Unpub. doct. diss., Univ. of Toronto, 1971. [*DA* 34:8 (1972): 5131A.]

Approaching 18c novels solely from satire and sentiment constricts their spirit, and ignores the vitality and interest in expansive, comic narrative flowing from the recognition of good nature stimulated by Addison and Steele. Examines the anti-splenetic process, the ways in which writers of the mid-18c promoted laughter to stave off the melancholy that arises from an unduly serious contemplation of human absurdity. Conscious lightheartedness fulfills the primary objective of all comedy, that of making all human contradictions seem bearable, even wonderful, in spite of the philosophical objections to the grotesquerie, pain and uncertainty of life. Looks at social and literary movements, Fielding and his influence, his delight in the unpredictability of life's adventures, Sterne and Smollett. Life is worth the trouble it takes to live, and laughter counterbalances spleen-provoking trouble.

185-----*The comic spirit of eighteenth-century novels.* (Kennikat Press International Univ. Pbns: Literary Criticism Series.) Port Washington, NY: Kennikat Press, 1975; pp. 198.

Investigates the shift from satire to 'amiable' humour, the influence of liberal attitudes on literary forms visible in changing subjects and styles. The suitability of the new novel forms to the new temperament is a factor in its rise at the time. Devoted mainly to Fielding, Smollett and Sterne. Bibliography (190-95).

186 BABB, Moira Campbell Ferguson. "Declarations of independence: The rebel heroine, 1684-1800". Unpub. doct. diss., Univ. of Washington 1973. [*DA* 34 (1974): 5088A.]

Examines the development of the rebel heroine in the British novel from Bunyan's Christiana, Defoe's Moll Flanders, Richardson's Pamela and Clarissa, through heroines of minor novelists in the late 18c, to the quasi-autobiographical heroines of Mary Wollstonecraft. Investigates those women who reflect in one way or another the growth of political, social and religious individualism after the Bloodless Revolution of 1689. Heroines who defied the strict social code of obedience placed themselves outside the pole of society and became rebels in conflict with the accepted order.

187 BABCOCK, R. W. "The idea of taste in the eighteenth century." *PMLA* 50 (1935): 922-26.

Presents some periodical items which discuss taste in formal theoretical style from 1712-98. The accent is on taste and morality, natural and acquired taste, taste and elegance, taste and sentiment, taste and novelty, taste and the soul, taste and delicacy.

188 BACCOLINI, Raffaella; FORTUNATI, Vita and MINERVA, Nadia (eds). *Viaggi in utopia.* (Forme dell'utopia: sezioni studi, 6.) Ravenna: Longa, 1996; pp. 450.

Collection of essays in Italian, English and French, focusing on 'decentralized' notions of utopia, based on the central topoi of the journey and the traveller. "La sfida di questo volume consiste nel prospettare un'utopia decentrata, che faccia proprio un punto di vista nomadico, capace di accogliere il decentramento prospettico, di transitare tra culture e pensieri diversi, di valicare il limite."
Looks at:
1. La tipologia del viaggio;

2. Viaggitori utopici tra cinquecento e settecento;
3. Il viaggio utopico come avventura filosofica e initiazione;
4. Viaggatori moderni in utopia;
5. Utopia viaggio e estraneità femminile;
6. Itinerari e miti utopici.
Index of names (425-38).

189 BACKSCHEIDER, Paula R. (ed.). *Probability, time and space in eighteenth-century literature.* New York: AMS Press, 1979; pp. xv, 307.

Series of 14 essays investigating concepts of probability, time and space in late 17c and 18c science, culture and especially literature. The secularization of the idea of history and of change, the mathematization of thinking about natural phenomena, and the growth of empirical science revolutionized thought. There was a revolution in the calculation of time, and thinking about space was equally revolutionary. Space, like time, became a concept in which objects exist and move. The literature of the period also demonstrates the incorporation of and preoccupation with science. Each essay has extensive bibliographical notes. Index (301-7).

190-----"Women's influence". *StudN* 11 (1979): 2-22.

Sets out to delineate the means and limits of feminine influence in novels by women in the 18c where the heroine had to find the means to exert influence in a male-dominated world, where violence was by no means unusual, and where a female character saw herself as a representative of her sex, a victim of the 'wrongs of women'. Examines some of the conventions. Immediacy of danger elicits extreme behavior from the heroines. By the mid-century, domestic intrigue and social limitations replace rapes, poisonings, sorceries and convents in escape literature. The recognition of external and internal limits circumscribing women's lives, and the demands for more realistic fiction, reduced the kinds of influence women writers assigned to their heroines. The scandalous memoirs of the 18c provided an important release for liberating fantasies for women in a time of great social limitation. Success for the heroine should be measured in terms of self-mastery and renunciation. Modern criticism has underestimated the impact of social restrictions and of women's frustrations and emotional outrage. Detailed notes.

191-----"'I died for love': esteem in eighteenth-century novels by women". In (pp. 152-68) SCHOFIELD, Mary Anne and MACHESKI, Celia (eds). *Fetter's or free? British women novelists, 1670-1815.* Athens, OH; London: Ohio UP, 1986; pp. 441.

For hundreds of years marriage was the most important event in a woman's life. The 18c novel by and for women has the ideal of happy marriage as its central subject. For all the heroine's assertions of indifference, future happiness and the resolution of the book depends upon the hero's final judgement. This essay is divided into the discussion of courtship and marriage. It was entirely accepted that satisfaction in marriage is impossible without esteem. Early 18c novels reflect the pressure on women to marry even marginally acceptable men, and also the desire to have the unmarried life accepted as a respectable alternative. A large number of 18c novels portray marriage, and find their subject matter in the vicissitudes and aspirations of this state of life. Childbirth is anticipated with uniform dread, regardless of the heroine's status or hopes for respect. Investigates two of the most remarkable treatments of childbirth in the 18c -- by Defoe in *Roxana* and Richardson in *Pamela*. The women novelists of the 18c increasingly resisted the temptation of novels to give an unrealistic idea of the world. The first half of the century developed the novel of heightened emotions and hysterical posturing, but after the mid-century, novels began exploring the grinding problems of middle-class women. Bibliographic notes (67-68).

192 BAER, Cynthia Marie. "Wise and worthier women: Lady Mary Wroth's *Urania* and the development of women's narrative." Unpub. doct. diss., Univ.of Washington, 1993. [*DA* 55 (1994): 282A.]

Reads Lady Mary Wroth's *The Countess of Montgomerie's Urania* (1621) in the context of Renaissance Court culture and the development of negotiation characterizing Wroth's text, structures that reveal a pattern of female authority in women's emerging voice within patriarchy. Read alongside the novels of 18c women writers, the pattern of female authority in Wroth's narrative links her text to the development of a female narrative tradition. Eliza Haywood's *The History of Miss Betsy Thoughtless* (1751) and Fanny Burney's *Cecilia* (1782) and *Camilla* (1796) all reveal similar patterns of female authority negotiating the traditional definitions of femininity that locate women within patriarchy. The pattern of protest/containment underlying these early women's narratives begins to define a female tradition of narrative and a pattern of reading women within patriarchy that is still evidenced today in studies like Janice Radway's *Reading the Romance*.

193 BAGULEY, David. "Parody and the realist novel." *UTQ* 55 (1985): 94-108.

In theory, the presence of parody in realist discourse is incongruent since the devices of parody and realism are seemingly incongruent. Parody does not imitate actions and phenomena, but provides another text and literary practice. It does not imitate but distort. Explores the degree of realism that parody can enjoy in texts whose primary motivation would seem to preclude it.

194   BAINES, Paul Timothy. "Authenticity and forgery in eighteenth-century Britain." Unpub. doct. diss., University of Bristol, 1988. [*DAI* 50:10 (1990): 3232A.]

Documents the use of the vocabulary of criminality in dealing with certain literary acts of the 18c. By drawing comparisons with contemporary writing on forgery as a crime, it is hoped to derive the common cultural factors which made 'the house of forgery' a common theme in the period. At a time when the laws against forgery were being strengthened, Pope made detailed attacks on forgers. An economy of document-collecting and evidence-gathering, and a palaeography which concentrates on writing as money or property and intensified notions of literary authenticity.

195-----"'Able mechanick': The Life and Adventures of *Peter Wilkins* and the eighteenth-century fantastic voyage." In (pp. 1.-25) SEED, David (ed.). *Anticipations: essays on early science fiction and precursors.* (Liverpool Science Fictions Texts and Studies, 2.). Syracuse, NY; Liverpool: Liverpool UP, 1995; pp. xvi, 225.

Investigates the extraterrestrial theme and the image of technology in sublunar travel fictions. Many of the moon voyages of the 17c and 18c engender a recognition like that encountered in Hogarth's engraving 'Some of the Principal Inhabitants of the Moon: Royalty, Episcopacy and Law' (1724). The moon is a reflection of the earth. Examines particularly the anonymous tale *Peter Wilkins* (1750) where an entire economic system is reflected and a Gulliverian fantasy is grafted on to Crusoe's colonial ambition. Bibliographical notes.

196   BAKER, Ernest Albert. *The history of the English novel.* Vol. III: *The later romances and the establishment of realism.* London: H. F. & G. Witherby, 1930; pp. 278.

Provides a critical history of the unfolding of fiction in the late 17c and early 18c. Ch. 5 "The Followers of Mrs Behn" (107-29) looks individually at Manley (108-14), Haywood (114-21), Rowe (122-24), Barker (124), Aubin (124-26), Davys (126-28), Boyd (128-29). Provides detailed summaries of plots with cogent critical observation (e.g., "Mrs Haywood could make some show of the workings of motive, especially under the influence of febrile sentiment; she lacked the power of giving individuality to the figures swayed by these gusty emotions", 116-17). Sums up the whole period in succinct clarity: "Between Mrs Behn and Mrs Boyd fiction had on the whole, however, begun to settle down to its own proper sphere [...]. Romance was getting old-fashioned and ridiculous [...]. The object of both romance and *nouvelle* was to tell a touching and exciting story. The novel [...] has a further duty to perform, to establish life actually going on. This the professional writers were beginning dimly to understand. They acknowledged the need for verisimilitude" (129). Ch. 6 "The Establishment of Realism - Defoe and *Robinson Crusoe*" (130-74) and ch. 7 "The Later Fiction of Defoe" (175-229) provide detailed historico-critical introduction to Defoe's fiction, looking at his life, early work, political satire, use of circumstantial realism, his creative fecundity, detailed examination of *Robinson Crusoe*, its realism, sources, indebtedness to travel literature, multiple influences on its composition, extended analysis of Hendrik Smeek, utopian romance, Defoe's use of materials, the autobiographical elements, the second part (*Farther Adventures*), as an allegory, Defoe on storytelling. Ch. 7 (175-229) looks at *The King of Pirates, The History of Duncan Campbell, Memoirs of a Cavalier* (180-83) ("a realistic version of history"), *Captain Singleton* (183-90), *Moll Flanders* (190-98), *A Journal of the Plague Year* (199-202). Looks at character drawing, Defoe's prose, the origins of his style, *Colonel Jacques* (206-9), *Roxana* (209-17), *A Voyage around the Whole Island of Great Britain*, criminal biographies, *Captain Carleton* (221-23), Defoe's part in the foundation of the modern novel, his stories as a portrayal of life, differences between old fiction and new, Defoe's renewal of popular literature, his strengths and weaknesses. "Defoe gave us human histories, not stories of human characters" (229).

See also Vol. IV: *Intellectual realism from Richardson to Sterne* (1930); Vol. V: *The novel of sentiment and the Gothic romance* (1934).

197 BAKER, Lesley Ann. "Rape and resistance: Sexual violence and the production of culture in eighteenth-century culture." Unpub. doct. diss., Tulane Univ., 1994. [*DA* 56 (1995): 2244A.]

In the early modern period, Western culture increasingly divided itself into the public sphere and the intimate domestic sphere. Sexual discourse also proliferated during this period, and this is used to explore esp. sexual violence in the production of this new dichotomized society. Women are placed in a larger cultural context. Examines Richardson's use of rape to analyze its cultural role to control women's behavior, Fielding's to maintain classical homo-social order. Burney condemned this new social order. Use of the topos by Eliza Haywood, Elizabeth Inchbald, Tobias Smollett and Sir Walter Scott prove that the discourse of sexual violence was widespread, and needs more exploration.

198 BAKER, S. "The idea of romance in the eighteenth-century novel." *SELit* 40 (1963): 49-61.

Discusses the influence of earlier romances (esp. 17c French ones) on the 18c novel.

199 BALLASTER, Ros. *Seductive forms: women's amatory fiction from 1648-1740*. Oxford: Clarendon Press; New York: Oxford UP, 1992; pp. 232.

Study of women's novelistic writing in England prior to the rise of the sentimental myth inaugurated by Richardson's *Pamela*, seeking to understand the importance of ideologies of gender in the construction of genre. Examines 20c theories of the early modern novel (formalist and historicist) and late 17c traditions in feminocentric prose fiction so as to situate the works of Behn, Manley and Haywood more precisely in relation to predecessors and successors in love fiction. The depiction of the woman reader in contemporary periodical and prose fiction is used as a formal device introducing new concepts concerning the male and his relation to the state. Investigates the prevailing conventions in amatory fiction in the last decade of the 17c developed from French models (romance, *nouvelle*, scandal chronicle, epistolary fiction). Then looks at the fiction of Behn, Manley and Haywood and their transformation of these feminocentric forms in the context of the late 17c and early 18c party politics and gender ideology. Finally looks at the critical fate of Behn, Manley and Haywood in the 18c when the novel was purged of disreputable associations with female sexuality. Bibliography (212-25).

200 BARBAULD, Anna Letitia. "On the origin and progress of novel writing." In (pp.1-59) of *The British novelists. With an essay and prefaces biographical and critical. Vol. I*. London G. Woodall, 1810; 1820.

Survey of the history of novel writing, returning to look for "the origins of fictions, tales and adventures" of every age and country. Looks at the ancient world (Greek, Latin, Arabic, and Gothic romances), the Medieval romance, Cervantes, the French heroic romance, and the picaresque novel, before considering the 18c (Marivaux, Rousseau, Genlis, Prévost, Goethe, Schiller, Musäus). Then focuses on England, looking at the 17c, turning to the 18c (Defoe, Richardson, Fielding, Sterne) and a discussion at length of the sentimental novel and the reading habits of the late 18c and early 19c.

201 BARKER, Gerard A. *Grandison's heirs: the paragon's progress in the late* *eighteenth-century novel.* Newark, NJ: Delaware UP; London: Assoc. UPs, 1985; pp. 187.

Examines the nature and influence of Richardson's *Sir Charles Grandison*, positively and negatively, and the evolutions of the Grandisonian hero in the 18c. Looks at Sheridan, Burney, Inchbald, Holcraft, Godwin, Austen. Selected bibliography (173-82).

202 BARKER, Hannah and CHALUS, Elaine. *Gender in eighteenth-century England: roles, representations and responsibilities.* London and New York: Longman, 1997; pp. xi, 266.

Seeks to redress the history of gender in 18c England. Examines the relationship between men and women through a wide assortment of subjects and sources in order to introduce new research through contemporaries' understanding of themselves (esp. with regard to roles, representations and responsibilities) revealing the complexity and multiplicity of gender roles in a society where boundaries between public and private, social and political were blurred and permeable. Looks at social reputations; work and poverty; periodicals and printed page; patriarchy; spinsterhood, marriage, divorce and widowhood, property and the law; separate spheres; gender history/women's history; a gendered history of men, sexuality, reputation and the body; work-poverty, consumption, crime; politics and social élites; print culture and the arts; education; religion; demography; the family; parents and children. Provides a very useful bibliography (250-60). Index (261-66).

203 BARKER-BENFIELD, G. J. *The culture of sensibility.* Chicago and London: U of Chicago P, 1992; pp. 520.

Sensibility was synonymous with consciousness, with feeling, and eventually with sexual characteristics. Its meaning rested on materialist assumptions, but it came to be invested with spiritual and moral values. There was a continuous struggle over its meaning and values. Britain became a mass consumer society in the preindustrial period (1650-1750). The Industrial Revolution vastly extended needs and appetites. Prospects for creating and furthering commerce led men to change themselves as males, changes nourished by the character of a public, popular male culture dating back to the Reformation. Cultural change was generated privately as well as in the public institutions monoplized by men. 18c consumerism also had a meaning for women and their cultivation of sensibility. There was a transformation of women's lives in the household. The culture of sensibility became a culture of reform expressed in humanitarianism. The gendering of sensibility sexualized it: desire was associated with the rake/victim dyad. Men tried to express themselves in commerce, not war; the more mannerly men became, the more women pressed on with their own wishes, entered public space for pleasure, became more emergent and self-conscious. Bibliographic notes (397-504). Index (505-20).

204 BARKHAUSEN, Jochen. *Die Vernunft des Sentimentalismus: Untersuchungen zur Entstehung der Empfindsamkeit und empfindsamen Tragödie in England.* (Mannheimer Beiträge zur Sprach- und Literaturwissenschaft, 3.) Tübingen: Narr, 1983; pp. 288.

In German. Investigates the origins of literary sentimentalism in the late 17c and its effects on literature, esp. the drama. Distinguishes between sentimentality and sentimentalism, looking at the negative connotations associated with sentimentalism, the development of this attitude in the 17c. Focuses particularly on Locke, Shaftesbury and Steele. Important bibliography on the subject and wider period (277-88).

205 BARNOUW, Jeffrey. "Feeling in Enlightenment aesthetics." *SECC* 18 (1988): 323-42.

What the 18c meant by the term 'aesthetics' was different from the present understanding. Appreciating works of art or the beauty of nature was only a secondary application. It really was concerned with the analysis, nurture and refinement of feeling as a principal element of knowledge, and of motivation or character. Aesthetic judgment was seen as a 'sense' akin to sight or hearing.

206 BARRELL, John. *English literature in history 1730-80: an equal, wide survey.* London: Hutchinson, 1983; pp. 228.

Examines shifting meanings of literature and its presumed relations with 'history'. History has a significant range of reference, and as an account of actions grouped by period and place and a narrative, is a form of 'literature'. The Introduction ("Artificers and Gentlemen" [17-50]) outlines the problem in detail, and presents the essays which provide a wide range of social knowledge and experience, and exhibit society as a various and complex organization in which a 'gentleman' "is adequate to the task of comprehending that organization", and thereby justify his claim to be a member of the ruling class. Note and references (211-24). Index (225-28).

207 BARRON, Sarah Susan. "'Female difficulties': Women's role and women's fate in eighteenth-century women's fiction". Unpub. doct. diss., Ohio

State Univ., 1982. [*DA* 43 (1983): 2675A.]

Study of 16 novels written by Eliza Haywood, Sarah Fielding, Charlotte Lennox, Frances Sheridan and Fanny Burney. Undertaken to determine their beliefs about specific issues of concern to women in 18c England: the economic problems of women, the question of proper education for women, the double sexual standards, the emotional and physical repression of women experienced as a result of following the accepted code of behavior for their sex. Explores what each novelist believed about these issues and how they expressed these beliefs in their novels.

208 BARTOLOMEO, Joseph Francis. "A poetics of fiction: Eighteenth-century foundations." Unpub. doct. diss., Harvard Univ., 1984. [*DA* 47 (1986): 2165A.]

Attempts to retrieve the earliest theoretical commentary on the English novel by its first avowed authors and critics. Considers the interpretive difficulties posed by the preface form, the principal form of criticism before Richardson, the 'moral' and 'aesthetic' strands. Analyzes Richardson, Fielding and Johnson, trying to liberate them from stereotypes by examining the tensions underlying their commentary. Finally looks at the more comparative and comprehensive criticism offered by the anonymous reviewers of the *Monthly Review* and the *Critical Review*.

209-----*A new species of criticism: Eighteenth-century discourse on the novel.* Newark: U of Delaware; London and Toronto: Assoc. UPs, 1994; pp. 209.

Examines the construction of a valorized notion of the novel by focusing on the explicit commentary on the genre offered by the earliest novelists and critics. 18c writers initiated a discussion of many central concerns, such as a) the ethos of writing and reading; b) historicity and the boundary of fact and fiction; c) narrative as a gendered phenomenon; d) formal conventions and transgressions; e) the limits of probability; f) conflicts between popular and mythical culture; g) the role of the reader as both consumer and concoctor of literary technique. Concentrates attention primarily on comments by novelists about their novels as genre and on reviews from the two leading organs of institutionalized criticism, the *Monthly Review* and the *Critical Review* where formal conventions and rhetorical strategies were analyzed: where, how and whence novels (Congreve, Defoe), respect and readers (later novelists), periodical reviewers. Notes (162-87). Bibliography (188-98). Index (199-209).

210   BATTEN, Charles L. *Pleasurable instruction: form and convention in eighteenth-century travel literature.* London and Los Angeles: U of California Press (Berkeley), 1978; pp. xii, 170.

Generic description of one of the popular literary forms of the 18c, the nonfictional travel account. Looks at the importance and popularity of 18c travel literature together with definitions of form and convention, the basic conventions used by travellers to narrative experiences and description of geographic regions, and how these changed towards the end of the century. Finally recounts ways in which they should and should not be interpreted by readers since many in the past have tried to see the century's travellers as precursors of a new romantic sensibility. Notes (121-54). Index (155-70). Illus. (4 plates).

211   BATTESTIN, Martin C. *The providence of wit: aspects of form in Augustan literature and arts.* New York: Oxford UP, 1974; pp. xv, 331.

Accounts for a special quality in certain works of Augustan literature and art -- their deliberate artificiality, our sense of the craftman's pleasure in careful shapes and bold contrivances. Tries to make this aspect of early 18c aesthetics more understandable as a historical phenomenon by showing its relation to ontological assumptions that were losing currency by the end of the 18c. The poetry of Pope and Gay, the fiction of Fielding and Goldsmith, the music and buildings and gardens of the period, all in various ways attest to the faith of "the age in order", the conviction that art is the attribute of reality. Balance, proportion design, whether conceived geometrically, or as a movement through time towards some pre-determined ending - are best understood in terms of ontological assumptions of the Christian-humanist tradition, that great coherent tradition of Western thought which Newton seemed to have confirmed, but which soon disintegrated under pressure of a new subjectivism influenced by Locke's epistemology. Illus. (17 plates). Bib. notes (272-315). Index (317-31).

212   BAUGH, Albert C. (ed.). *A literary history of England.* London: Routledge & Kegan Paul Ltd., 1950; pp. xii, 1673.

Of pertinence is Book III, "The Restoration and Eighteenth Century (1660-1789)", and particularly ch. 8 'Types of Prose Fiction' (793-805) which looks at fiction for various classes, French romances, English romances, philosophical romances, epistolary narratives, crime and adventure, John Bunyan, the short story or 'novel', Aphra Behn. The early 18c is investigated in 'Defoe and Journalism' (847-56) which locates Defoe in the context of politics, journalism, and news pamphlets, before discussing his life and works, esp. the novels (853-56). Mention is made of his facility in writing, his vividness, characterizations, lack of structure, handling of truth and the picaresque tradition, and his persona of preacher and commentator. Ch. 10 "The Mid-Century Novel" (950-64) concentrates on Richardson, Fielding, and Smollett, with passing reference to Manley, Haywood, and the French translations of Marivaux and Prévost (951). Index (1607-73).

213 BAUM, Rosalie Murphy. "Early American literature: reassessing the Black contribution." *ECS* 27:4 (1994): 533-49.

When the black voice has any role in the general anthologies of American literature, it lies in the black's outcry as outsider and sufferer, as in the slave narrative, not in the black voice as independent, innovative and intelligent contribution to the American heritage. Even though many white authors now included in general anthologies of early American literature wrote about the black experience of the 1700s and 1800s, these works are seldom anthologized. Including more black writers and writings by whites about blacks in anthologies will profoundly affect understanding and discussion of the early days of the country. Detailed bibliographical notes.

214 BAYNE-POWELL, Rosamund. *English country life in the eighteenth century*. London: John Murray, 1935; pp. 319.

Series of essays covering agriculture (conditions of agriculture at the beginning of the 18c); the village and its government; the country folk (Coke of Norfolk); the village doctor (Claver Morris of Wells); the farmer (Robert Blakeley of Dishley); the village tradesman (Thomas Turner of East Hoathley, Sussex); the village schoolmaster and education (Walter Gale); the laborer; village amusements; sport; folklore; travel; gardens and nature. Bibliography (313-14). Index (315-19). Illus. (10 plates).

215-----*The English child in the eighteenth century*. London: John Murray, 1935; pp. 322.

Of esp. interest are the chapters "Children's Books" and "Some Children in Eighteenth-Century Fiction". Finds Maria Edgeworth's tales incomparably the best in their day. A parade of fictitious children is reviewed: 'Colonel' Jack, little Tom Jones, Humphrey Clinker, and Roderick Random, David Simple, Moses Primrose. Bibliography (306-8). Index (311-22).

216-----*Eighteenth-century London life*. London: John Murray, 1937; pp. 385.

Provides an historical survey, looking at: London's aspects and characteristics; means of communications; the life of the upper classes, the middle classes, the poor; the government of London; trade; politics; inns, taverns, and coffee houses; pleasure gardens, spas, parks and fairs; amusements; dress and fashion; lotteries, gambling, bubbles; crimes and the police; superstitions and churching; education; religion, ancient customs; servants; food, drink and the household; literature, art and music; newspapers and magazines; some national events. Index (381-85). Illus. (14 plates).

217-----*Housekeeping in the eighteenth century.* London: John Murray, 1956; pp. 208.

Survey by individual essay on houses; interior decorating; furniture; pictures, statuary, china, clocks; table appointments; linen; the kitchen premises; food; drink; entertaining, meals; water, washing, sanitation; heating and lighting; servants; illness and remedies; death and mourning; handicrafts and needlework; money and taxation; household superstitions and customs. Bibliography (200-2). Index (203-8).

218 BEACHCROFT, Thomas Owen. *The English short story.* (Writers and their Work, 168.) London: Longmans, 1964; pp. 42.

Considers the development of the short story, with attention to types of fiction and stylistic trends. Ch. 4 "The Eighteenth Century - the Moral Story enclosed in the Essay" (30-37) points out that "[...] it was the essayist who took the decisive steps towards modern fiction" (30). Examines the contribution of Addison and Steele's stories to deal with affairs of belief or lasting interest, with strong ethical purpose, and the virtues of civilized living. Other magazines followed, the *Spectator*, like the *Rambler* and the *Adventurer.* Another graceful invention of the urge to moralize in story form was the Oriental tale. The author who really could practise fiction in its short form for its own sake was Defoe. His greatest contribution was the gift of building complete verisimilitude with quiet authentic touches. One does not know whether he is writing fiction or reporting fact (33-34). Discusses "The Apparition of Mrs Veal". Defoe's contribution to the short story was not followed up in the succeeding years until Charles Lamb at the end of the 18c. Select Reading List (41-42).

219-----*The modest art: a survey of the short story in English.* London: Oxford UP, 1968; pp. 394.

Discusses types of works, narrative techniques and subject matter. Looks particularly at innovations in form and the handling of place in the short story. Of particular interest is ch. 7 "The Character Books, and the Story Emerging from the Essay" (176-88), which traces the history of the short story from the end of the Restoration to the early 18c. It considers the contribution of Congreve, the study of the Theophrastan Character, the essays in the *Spectator* and the *Tatler*, and esp. Defoe ("The Apparition of Mrs Veal"). "Defoe's contribution to the short story was not followed up in succeeding years. When the fictional element in the letter writers broke away from the essay, it developed into the novel rather than the short story" (85-86). Attention then moves to Charles Lamb and Leigh Hunt. Select bibliography (264-69), Index (271-86).

220   BEASLEY, Jerry C. "English fiction in the 1740s: some glances at the major and minor novels." *StudN* 5 (1973): 155-75.

The vast area of pre-Richardsonian fiction has already been explored and mapped. The decade which ushered in *Pamela*, however, witnessed the publication of more than 300 works of prose fiction, or perhaps two-thirds as many as appeared in England during all the years between 1700 and 1739. Apart from the six major works of Richardson, Fielding and Smollett, this total includes numerous foreign works of fiction in translation, and a great many forgotten native pieces of remarkable diversity. Sketches some of this background and suggests ways in which the work of the major novelists relates to it. They "developed a potential mode which enabled the English novel to become a serious story of familiar life and credible characters, widely accessible, yet shaped by artistic vision and control, into a formal interpretive statement on the universal human condition" (173).

221-----*Novels of the 1740s*. Athens, GA: Georgia UP, 1982; pp. 238.

"During the years between 1740 and 1749 the English novel as we know it today was born and nurtured through its infancy. This was the important decade when Samuel Richardson, Henry Fielding and Tobias Smollett made their sudden appearance as novelists of the first rank. So great and concentrated a burst of artistic energy as it occurred at this time is rare indeed in literature and therefore very interesting" (xi). Studying the lesser works can tell us a lot about how the major novels came to be what they were - the themes, conventions, and methods explored by the great novelists. Looks at Romance, Fiction as Contemporary History, as Contemporary Biography, as Records of Spiritual Life, Novelistic Fiction in the 1740s, Fiction as Artifice. Notes (211-31). Index

222-----"Politics and character in the eighteenth century." *StudECC* 13 (1984): 3-

17.

English literature and the arts during the years 1700-1800 were deeply affected by changing and often volatile political circumstances. Sketches out and exemplifies different kinds of 'political characters' in the 18c, and offers a few speculations concerning the important reciprocal relations between the practices of political writers and some of the age's prevailing arts of characterization. Contains a full account of Manley's *The Secret History of Queen Zarah* (1705). Sarah Churchill's alliance with the Whigs gave Mrs Manley ammunition for malicious barrages on behalf of the Tories.

223------"Politics and moral idealism: The achievement of some early women novelists". In (pp. 216-36) SCHOFIELD and MACHESKI, *'Fetter'd or free'* etc., **860**.

Women wrote stories by the dozen, particularly during the early years of the 18c, not merely for the diversion or titillation of their readers, but using their works to give urgent and meaningful expression to female consciousness. Even the most trite and conventional novels often dramatize a subversive affirmation of the dominant value of the female as the active embodiment of emotional sensitivity and moral integrity, and a chief force for domestic stability.

224 BECK, Hamilton. "The novel between 1740 and 1780: parody and historiography." *JHI* 46 (1985): 405-16.

Investigates parody and the imitation of historical writing in the novel, esp. with reference to Richardson, Fielding, Sterne, Diderot, Theodor Gottlieb von Hippel. The 18c novel was in part an imitation of historical writing, an imitation which was then parodied, leading finally to a return to historical techniques, this time on a new level in a to-and-fro motion.

225 BELL, Ian A. *Literature and crime in Augustan England*. London and New York. Routledge, 1991; pp. 250.

Study of information about deviance, misinformation and disinformation. Concentrates on the diverse representation of crime and legality in early 18c England, on ways in which the various constituent performers in these cultural practices were portrayed, and on the significance of such representation for their producers and consumers. Aims at serving wider cultural history where close reading of works of literature are informative, not just about the internal ordering of texts, but also about the creation and dissemination of ideology and the diversity of cultural practice. Looks at literature/crime/society, representing the criminal, the harlot's progress, satires, royal music, Fielding and the discipline of fiction. Bibliographic notes (231-45). Index (246-50).

226 BEHRENS, Laurence. "Plotting the eighteenth-century novel: Narrative constructs from Defoe to Goldsmith." Unpub. doct. diss., Univ. of California, Los Angeles, 1972. [*DA* 35 (1975): 1613A.]

Demonstrates that the exact manner in which a plot is configured has far-reaching effects on the responses of readers. By comparing the plot structures of five of the most popular novels of the 18c, with alternative plot structures devised by abridgers and adapters, shows that even the slightest tampering with the original plot will inevitably alter the emotional and intellectual response which the author intended (*Robinson Crusoe, Pamela , Clarissa, Tom Jones, The Vicar of Wakefield*).

227 BENDER, John. *Imagining the penitentiary: fiction and architecture of mind in eighteenth-century England*. Chicago; London: Chicago UP, 1987; pp. xvii, 337.

Attitudes formulated between 1719 and 1779 in narrative literature and art, especially in prose fiction, enabled the conception and construction of actual prisons later in the 18c. These penitentiaries "assumed the novelistic ideas of character and re-presented the sensible world [...] in order to alter motivation and, ultimately, to reconstruct the fictions of personal identity that underlie consciousness" (1-2). Looks at the prison in the novel as cultural system, the novel and the rise of the penitentiary (*Moll Flanders* and *Robinson Crusoe*), the city and the rise of the penitentiary (*A Journal of the Plague Year*), generic conflict and reformist discourse (Gay and Hogarth), narration and cultural power (Fielding), Fielding and the juridical novel, the aesthetic of isolation as social system, the public execution. Notes (253-316).

228 BENEDICT, Barbara M. "Literary miscellanies: the cultural mediation of fragmented feelings." *ELH* 57 (Summer 1990): 407-30.

From the 1780s to the 1820s, collections of tales and poems appeared which were designed to exploit the current rage for sentiment while offering high literature at affordable prices. The demand for a consumable literary culture was stimulated by rising literacy. One characteristic was the fictional language of sentimental fiction. This feature of sentimental literature was replicated in the cheaper literary miscellanies in the more accessible form of a plenitude of visual signals which combined 'high' and popular culture. Literary sentimentalism found a new home in the literary miscellany.

229-----"The 'curious attitude' in eighteenth-century Britain: observing and owning." *ECLife* 14:3 (Nov. 1990): 59-98.

Curiosity in the 18c is perceived not only as the sanction for exploration, but also as a threat to the established hierarchies of society. As an aesthetic category, it violates neo-classical formalities; as a scientific term, it overleaps the boundaries established by religion. By dislocating traditional meanings and sources to vaunt the power of empirical judgement, "curiosity fractures culture into a cabinet of curiosities" (98).

230 BENITO-VESSELS, Carmen and ZAPPALA, Michael (eds). *The Picaro: a symposium on the rogue's tale*. Newark: U of Delaware P; London and Toronto: Assoc. UPs, 1994; pp. 191.

Social despair and its immediate consequences - moral abjection - contributed to the forging of the rogue as a literary character. Organizations of rogues existed all over Spain and were quite sophisticated. Picaresque literature was immersed in a cultural ambience in clear contrast to the artificiality of the chivalric romance. 10 essays explore the various aspects and facets of the genre: discursive parameters; classicity in the Spanish Golden Age; *Lo Lozana andaluza* as a precursor to the Spanish picaresque; the picaresque and autobiography; Richard Head and the origins of the picaresque in England; translations and cultural *translatio*; from duplicitous delinquents to superlative simpleton (*Simplicissimus* and the German Baroque); Latin American Enlightenment versus the picaresque; Don Picaro: Lord Byron and the reclassification of the picaro; the Brazilian picaro; Each essay has bibliographic notes. Selected bibliography (179-84). Index (185-91).

231 BENSADON, Michel Emile. "Transformations of the self in the European picaresque novel: *Guzman de Alfarache, Moll Flanders, Gil Blas de Santillane*." Unpub. doct. diss., New York Univ., 1987. [*DAI* 48:11 (1988) 2865A.]

Extricates the picaresque persona from the traditional literary classification to which it has been relegated as a prototype of the rogue, and interprets the "hero's" actions as the outer manifestations of a self tormented not only by social determinants, but also by inner conflicts. Such types present a false self to the world, an idealized self-image behind which feelings of bitterness and disillusionment are expressed in criminal actions, and in a generally hostile attitude preceded are followed by an appeal to the reader for understanding and support.

232 BENTLEY, G. E., Jr. (ed.). *Editing eighteenth-century novels.* Toronto: Hakkert, for the Committee for the Conference on Editorial Problems, 1975; pp. 134.

Editing of 18c works has been scandalously neglected. Growing criticism of the four greatest 18c novelists has been based on unsatisfactory or corrupt texts, but the correction of this lamentable situation is now well under way. Describes the editorial process and trustworthy foundations for responsible criticism of the future. Points out the role played by unique features like the use of capitals, eccentric punctuations, typographical variations which may signal an allusion, the use of different type faces, the self-conscious 18c exploration of the novel as physical and visual object. Looks forward to enhanced appreciation that will ensue when the critical editions are in print.

233 BERMINGHAM, Ann. "The popularisation of the picturesque taste." *SVEC* 265 (1989): 1212-13.

The popularization of picturesque taste in England climaxed in the last decade of the 18c. As a practice, or way of viewing nature, it inspired hundreds of tourists to tour the Cumberland lakes, Devonshire coast and other canonized spots in search of picturesque beauty. The popular success of the picturesque can be attributed to the ways in which its theory and practice accommodated late 18c forces of individualism while appearing aesthetically to reject or even transcend them.

234-----and BREWER, John (eds). *The consumption of culture, 1600-1800: language, object, text.* London and New York: Routledge, 1995; pp. 548.

Consumption, even conspicuous consumption, has a long and complex history. Data comes not only from paintings, but from the consumer objects themselves in museums, antique shops and others. Dutch still-life paintings are not only a reflection of wealth, but reflect on wealth by a society transformed through the rising tide of capitalism. They reminded their owners of the transitory nature of earthly pleasures and the vanity of newly acquired riches. Presents 26 diverse histories of consumption which compel one to see the culture of the early modern period in a new way since they reveal a culture already formed by consumption, and one struggling to come to terms with the fact. It was not merely a celebration of the *status quo*, but a progressive look for social change in which the modern conditions of class, gender, and racial inequalities are exposed and understood. New theories of material culture promote social justice by understanding modern history and its political instrumentality. Looks at 1) the formation of a public for art and literature; 2) engendering the literary canon; 3) consumption and the modern state; 4) the social order:

culture high and low; 5) what women want. Bibliographical notes. Index
(535-48). Illus. profusely.

235   BIBER, Douglas and FINEGAN, Edward. "Drift in three English genres
from the 18th to the 20th centuries: a multidimensional approach." In
(pp. 83-102) KYTO, Merja (et al eds). *Corpus linguistics, hard and soft.*
(Language & Computers: Studies in Practical Linguistics 2.) Amsterdam:
Rodopi, 1988; pp. iii, 293.

Uses factor analysis to identify underlying textual dimensions, identifying
sets of linguistic features that co-occur frequently in texts. Chosen texts
represent a wide range of spoken and written texts, and illustrate basic
functional dimensions of variation in English. Focuses on genres
representing three types of communication: narrative and description
(mostly fiction), essays (expository, argumentative, and biographical) and
personal. Major authors of 84 historical texts from 18c and 19c and the
modern period. Part A looks at 18c British essays (18 texts) (Addison,
Boswell, Burke, Defoe, Dryden, Johnson, Steele, Swift); narrative and
description (5 texts) (Johnson, Swift). Multidimensional analysis can be
used to trace the historical evidence of genres in England. Sketches how
narratives, essays, and letters have evolved with respect to underlying
dimensions of variation. Both synchronic and diachronic studies vary in
different ways with respect to each dimension.

236   BIRKHEAD, Edith. "Sentiment and sensibility in the eighteenth-century
novel." *E & S* 2 (1925): 91-116.

The history of the word 'sensibility' is closely associated with that of
'sentimental'. The Oxford English Dictionary notes it as rare before the
middle of the 18c. Before that period it was usually applied to physical
sensations, although Addison uses it in reference both to emotional and
bodily susceptibility. During the later half of the 18c it came to be
regarded as essential to emotional respectability. In 17c and early 18c
formal literature made little provision for the emotional as opposed to the
intellectual reader. Translations from the French were widely read in the
first half of the 18c. Towards the middle of the 18c the romances of
Marivaux and Crébillon *fils* began to be fashionable. Sentimentalism,
which had shown itself in the drama of the 18c, now found a new
channel in the novel.

237   BIRNBAUM, J. *Die 'Memoirs' um 1700: eine Studie zur Entwicklung der
realistischen Romankunst vor Richardson.* Halle: Max Niemeyer Verlag,
1934; pp. 117.

Deeply believing citizens were led to the reading of memoirs by a wish to learn from the experiences of others, and a desire for the presentation of worldly trials and weaknesses. Bibliography of memoirs written between 1671-1740 (138 titles), and those works of fiction which qualify as a type of memoir (28-29). Looks at prefaces and particular types: Court-, Noble- and Bourgeois-Memoirs, Robinsonades and Adventure Stories, role of true stories in literature and their meaning for the novel.

238 BJORNSON, Richard. *The picaresque hero in European fiction*. Madison: U of Wisconsin P, 1977; pp. x, 308.

Ch.7 ("Translations and Transitions", 139-65) provides a survey of English translations of Spanish picaresque fiction.

239-----"The picaresque novel in France, England and Germany." *CL* 29 (1977): 124-47.

Considers the spread and transformation of Spanish picaresque fiction in England, esp. through translations.

240 BLACK, F. G. "The technique of letter fiction in English from 1740 to 1800." *HSNPL* 15 (1933): 290-312.

Of the 3000 novels written between 1740 and 1799, 506 were epistolary. From 4 in 1740 to 81 in 1771, a high peak of production was reached in 1788 (108), and after 1788 there was a decline with the form becoming numerically unimportant. The rise in popularity can be accounted for by the successes of Richardson and Rousseau (*Eloisa*, Eng. trans. 1761), the decline by the emergence of the new fictional forms which could not well fit into the epistolary mode, esp. the Gothic and historical novels, and perhaps by the exhaustion of its literary possibilities. The number of its variations was limited, and half a century saw it worked out. But the form was of service to the novel generally. It called attention to point of view and left suggestions for bringing story and reader into closer association. It stressed familiar conversation and circumstantial realism. It encouraged a generous inclusiveness and leisureliness of style. It found a place for discussion and commentary along with the recital narrative.

241 BLACK, Jeremy. "Tourism and cultural challenge: the changing scene of the eighteenth century." In (pp. 185-202) McVEAGH, John (ed.). *1660-1780: All the world before them*. London: Ashfield, 1990; pp. 305.

Describes how travel for pleasure increased in the 18c, esp. after the Seven Years' War in 1763, a phenomenon not restricted to Britain. The

18c began living at a higher social level, as an increasingly consumer society affected by fashion. The increase in travel literature can be understood only in the context of a savage public attack on tourism. Much of this criticism in the first half of the century was made by commentators such as newspaper writers. In the opening decades of the century English travel literature was characterized by a political fervor directed against arbitrary power; in the second half of the century a shift occurred towards a more conciliatory stance. Bibliographical notes (200-2).

242-----and GREGORY, Jeremy (eds). *Culture, politics and society in Britain, 1660-1800*. Manchester and New York: Manchester UP, 1991; pp. viii, 216.

Comprises seven essays concerned with the interlocking world of culture, politics, and society, presenting some of the most recent research on these themes. There is still a need for 18c historians to pay attention to the political import of literature, and for literary criticism to take historical issues more into account. They go some way to unpicking the popular image of the 18c as an age of political stability by showing the strength of the forces of opposition to the Georgian establishment, from the world of popular politics and culture, and from Jacobitism. They also show by what means the political and cultural establishment was able to construct its own cultural identity. A concern for such an interdisciplinary study tries to establish various kinds of contexts in which cultural and political activity can be mutually analyzed. Helps understanding of the nature and preoccupations of 18c society: thinkers and writers from a wide range of the political spectrum shared a common assumption that political and cultural activity went hand in hand. Topics include royal representations, the press, Anglicanism and the arts, Jacobite Latinity, patronage and power (the portrait), civilization and disease (medical ideology), xenophobia and world of print. Introd. (1-12). Bibliographic notes.

243   BLACK, Sidney J. "Eighteenth-century 'histories' as a fictional mode." *Boston Univ Stud in Eng* 1 (1955): 38-44.

The beginning of the 18c conveniently illustrates the general growth of the realistic narrative into an aesthetic that has become a permanent aspect of the modern novel. It was then axiomatic to critics that the narrative of a life, a voyage, or a journey offered the maximum looseness of structure, permitted digression and reflection, and offered opportunities for circumstantial details, that helped to avert the moral disapproval connected with fiction. It made possible the widest variety of subject matter: survey of social levels, of geographic space and political time, as well as copious digressions of a moral and psychological nature. The literal interpretations which Defoe had insisted upon presenting when he called his fictions true to fact ceased to be necessary in the time of Fielding and Smollett. Fielding heralded a new dispensation which allowed fiction to be true, provided it reflected the general experience of mankind.

244 BLACKBURN, Alexander L. "The picaresque novel: A literary idea, 1554-1954." Unpub. doct. diss., Univ. of Cambridge, 1963; pp. 374.

Presents the picaresque novel as a literary idea, with critical distinctions defining the type over 400 years, so addressing critical confusion about the nature of the English variety, and focusing on the American strain. Considers the classical picaresque novel (in the 17c), and the dialectical picaresque novel (in the 18c). Selected bibliography (355-74).

245-----*The myth of the picaro: continuity and transformation of the picaresque novel, 1554-1954.* Chapel Hill: U of North Carolina P, 1979; pp. x, 267.

Comparative critical study of the picaresque novel through history, as well as a study of its influence on the nature and origins of modern fiction. The genre includes a variety of novels that depict either a personal or symbolic picaro. Looks at 1) the classic form of the Spanish novels, 29 the "dialectical" form of the mixed picaresque and non-picaresque novels of France and England in the 18c and early 19c; 3) the symbolic form of certain 19c and early 20c novels written in Russia and Germany, but particularly the USA where the picaresque seems to have been spontaneously reborn. Notes (217-38). Bibliography (239-62). Index (263-67). Studies of Lazarillo, Buscón, Le Sage, Defoe (*Colonel Jack*), Fielding (*Jonathan Wild*), Smollett (*Count Fathom*), Dickens (*Oliver Twist*), Thackeray (*Barry Lyndon*), Melville (*The Confidence Man*).

246 BLAMIRES, Harry. *A short history of English literature.* London: Methuen & Co. Ltd., 1974; pp. 536.

Ch. 11 "Origins of the novel" (182-92) provides a succinct overview of the history of English prose fiction from Elizabethan times to Defoe. This is one of the most helpful accounts of this neglected area available in any of the various histories of English fiction, combining chronological facts with precise critical insights. Beginning with Lyly, Lodge, Greene and Deloney, he moves to the late 17c with a helpful description of Congreve and Behn's contributions, before focusing on Defoe's achievement most pertinently (188-92). Chronological table of writers (by birth) (474-79).

Bibliography (480-93). Index (495-536).

247 BLAND, D. S. "Endangering the reader's neck: background description in the novel." *Criticism* 3 (1961).

Examines the use of landscape by the novelists of the 18c.

248 BLONDEL, Madeleine. *Images de la femme dans le roman anglais de 1740 à 1771*. Paris: Librairie Honoré Champion; Lille: Atelier Reproduction de Thèses, 1976; pp. 1196.

Socio-literary survey of the role of women in the English novel, looking at 1) the social milieu; 2) the young girl; 3) marriage, its moral manners, widowhood; 4) the women outside the confines of marriage; 5) whether the novel really mirrors the social and historical realities. Bibliography: 1) catalogues; 2) 18c novels in England; 3) French and German novels of the 18c; 4) journals; 5) essays; 6) periodicals; 7) poetry; 8) life and society; 9) the novel in the 18c; 10) women; 11) writers and their public (1046-1118). Illustrations (1181-90). Index.

249 BLOOR, Robert Henry Underwood. *The English novel from Chaucer to Galsworthy*. (University Extension Library.) London: I. Nicholson & Watson, 1935; pp. 248.

General survey of the novel by chapters, from the Medieval romance.

250 BOND, R. P. (ed.). *Studies in the early English periodical*. Chapel Hill, NC: U of North Carolina P, 1957; pp. 206, index.

Introduction to the early periodical press in England, especially in the years 1700-60, illustrating its growth and summarizing the contemporary forces responsible for this enlargement. During the period 1620-1700, no fewer than 700 newspapers and periodicals were offered to the public, but the vast majority collapsed from literary exhaustion or starvation. Looks particularly at Steele and Bickerstaff.

251 BONHEIM, Helmut. *The narrative mode: Techniques of the short story*. Cambridge: D. S. Brewer, 1982; pp. 197.

Systematic "scientific" approach to the narrative techniques of story-telling, chosen from a study of 600 short stories and 300 novels, covering 1) theories of narrative modes; 2) mode chopping; 3) the mode in concert; 4) the submodes of speech; 5) inquiry; 6) short story beginnings; 7) how stories end (the static mode); 8) how stories end (the dynamic mode); 9) conclusion: novel and short story. Notes (170-71). Bibliography (A. short story collections and anthologies; B. literature on speech and fiction, esp. narrative monologue; C. works consulted). Index (193-97). Full of sharp and useful information about the literary techniques of writing: "Before the advent of the gothic novel and romanticism, scene played practically no role in the novel; this is true even of the 'realistic' work of Defoe and Fielding. People are described, places only rarely" (9).

252-----*Literary semantics*. Cambridge: D. S. Brewer, 1990; pp. ix, 381.

Discusses the application of cladistics to the categorization of literary genres, using the development of the short story and the novel (141-62).

253 BOOTH, Wayne C. "The self-conscious narrator in comic fiction before *Tristram Shandy*." *PMLA* 67 (1952): 163-85.

Sterne's novel is not as chaotic as it seems. He takes the novel beyond the limits carefully avoided by earlier novelists, beyond various kinds of unities and cohesive forces at work in older "facetious" and "chaotic" traditions. What he learnt was how to employ a kind of narrator to impose unity of however "loose" or unconventional a kind. His true achievement is in taking forces which had become more and more disruptive in comic fiction and synthesizing them with the help of older models provided by Cervantes, Furetière, Dunton, Congreve, Marivaux, Fielding. Attention is focused on the self-conscious narrator who intrudes into his novel to comment on himself as a writer, and on his book, not simply as a series of events with moral implications, but as a created literary product.

254-----*The rhetoric of fiction* (1961). Second rev. ed. Chicago: Chicago UP, 1983; pp. xix, 552.

Magisterial analysis of the constituent parts of prose fiction, divided into 1) General; 2) Techniques as Rhetoric; 3) The Author's Objectivity and the 'Second Self'; 4) Artistic Purity and the Rhetoric of Fiction (telling and showing, realism, objectivism, true art and audience, belief and reader objectivity, types of narration); 5) Narrative Irony and Unreliable Narration (the author's voice in fiction, reliable commentary, telling and showing, control and distance, impersonal narration, authorial silence, confusion and distance, impersonal narration). Afterword to the second edition (401-58). The supplementary bibliography (covering 1961 to 1982) by James PHELAN is an indispensable guide to fictional aesthetics up to the given dates, and is divided into substantial subsections reflecting the major parts of the study (364-510).

255 BORINSKI, Ludwig. *Der englische Roman des 18. Jahrhunderts*. Frankfurt and Bonn: Athenäum Verlag, 1968; pp. 333.

In German. Devotes chapters to Defoe, Richardson, Fielding, Smollett, Sterne, the English novel (1760-90), Jane Austen. Of particular importance are the first two chapters: Ch. 1 "Defoe und seine Vorgänger" (9-66) places Defoe in the picaresque tradition, going back to Elizabethan times, also looking at the Puritan autobiography, a national version of history, Defoe and the American tradition; Ch.2 "Die Voraussetzungen des klassischen englischen Romans" (67-97) looks at social elements, moralizing weeklies, Anglican theology, social reform, the psychology of piety, pietistic reactions to the Enlightenment, the heroic-gallant novel, the works of French Classicism after 1660, the English novella after 1680 (Aphra Behn), the novel of manners, the novel of letters, the notion of sentiment, types of narrative forms, stereotypes, motives. Very restricted critical apparatus, few footnotes. Index.

256 BORSAY, Peter. *The English urban renaissance: culture and society in the provincial town, 1660-1770*. Oxford: Oxford UP, 1989; pp. xxii, 416.

Throughout the middle and upper reaches of the urban system there was a new wave of prosperity after 1660, the most striking sign of which was the cultural refinement and prestige it brought to the towns it affected. The introduction looks at the urban scenes, landscape (house, street, prospect, square), leisure society (economic foundations, pursuit of status, civility and cultural differentiation), town and nation.

257 BOSTRIDGE, Ian. "Debates about witchcraft in England, 1650-1736." Unpub. doct. diss., Univ. of Oxford, 1990. [*DA* 53:7 (1993) 3337A.]

Shows the evolution of an educated belief in witchcraft in England from 1650 (at the end of the last decade of large-scale persecution) to 1736 (when Jacobean witchcraft was repealed). Witchcraft theory had ideological import in the years 1650 to 1670; the theory continued into the 18c, and its demise had specific political and ideological reasons.

258------*Witchcraft and its transformations, c.1650-c.1750*. Oxford: Clarendon Press, 1997; pp. 274.

The last execution for witchcraft took place in 1685. Suggests that witchcraft theory had a serious constituency well beyond 1700, and that the reasons for its loss of credibility were partially political. Between

1650 and 1750 this theory, centered upon the notion that men and women could make covenants with the Devil to do harm to their communities, thus setting themselves up against the divine and social order, lost its mainstream ideological roots, and was eliminated from the world view of the polite classes in England. Seeks to discover when witchcraft theory ceased to be credible, when it became ridiculous, when it was so marginalized that it was no longer controversial and rejected from the public domain. The laws against witchcraft were repealed in 1736. Bibliography (245-64). Index (265-74). Illus. (9 plates).

259 BOUCÉ, Paul-Gabriel. *Sexuality in eighteenth-century Britain*. Manchester: Manchester UP; Totowa, NJ: Barnes & Noble, 1982; pp. xii, 262.

Presents an interdisciplinary approach to the complex and inescapable phenomenon of sexuality. Half the book deals with the socio-cultural context of sexuality, with emphases on the medical and para-medical background, the sexual mores of Scotland, and pornography. More specifically literary topics cover Mary Astell's feminism, sexual patterns in the novels of Defoe, Fielding, Richardson, Smollett and Sterne, the mythology and iconography of love in Pope, Fielding, Cleland and Sterne. See esp. John Vladimir PRICE, "Patterns of sexual behavior in some eighteenth-century novels" (159-75).

260-----and HALIMI, Suzy (eds). *Le corps et l'âme en Grande-Bretagne au XVIIIe siècle*. Colloques 1983-5 du Center d'Études anglaises du XVIIIe siècle. Paris: Publications de la Sorbonne, 1986; pp. 180.

In French. Series of 14 essays exploring the dialectical interplay between between body and soul in 18c Britain. This is put into perspective by the unprecedented growth of the pre-capitalist economy, by an extraordinary literary and artistic development and progress in science and technology. Covers: 1) *maux de corps et de l'âme* (illness and pharmacology); 2) *corps social et âme de la cité* (prison and policing); 3) *corps et âme ludiques* (comedy, actors, caricature); 4) *corps et âme: la quête du bonheur* (lost women, love, pleasure, the search for happiness, happiness and sorrow). Bibliographical notes. There is a particularly apposite essay by Françoise DU SORBIER: "À la recherche de la femme perdue: *Moll Flanders* and *Roxana*" (121-30).

261-----(ed.). *Constraintes et libertés dans la Grand-Bretagne du XVIIIe siècle*. Centre d'Etudes anglaises du XVIIIe siècle de Paris III-Sorbonne Nouvelle; Colloques 6-7 déc. 1985 et avril 1986. (Sér. Langues & Langages 18.) Paris: Publications de la Sorbonne, 1988; pp. 194.

Series of 11 essays exploring the 18c approach to constraint/ restraint and liberty, various notions of liberty in the context of the politics and culture of the age. Preface by BOUCÉ (7-20) is divided into 3 sections: critique/criticism (the fiction artist and the critic, Adam Smith); essays and novels (Fielding, Sterne, Walpole, Burney); theater, satire and music (comedy, satire, profane and religious music). Each essay has bibliographical notes.

262   BOWERS, Toni O'Shaughnessey. "Maternal ideology and matriarchal authority: British literature and the making of middle-class motherhood, 1680-1750." Unpub. doct. diss., Stanford Univ., 1991. [*DA* 52 (1992): 3289A.]

Argues that representation of mothers in British discourse of the 17c and early 18c helped to make powerful the notion that motherhood is defined against, rather than within, creative participation in the public world - a notion which continues today to limit and bifurcate female experience. Looks at novels by Defoe and Richardson, as well as popular works of many genres, broadside news reports, engravings, portraits, sermons, autobiographies, memoirs. pamphlet tales, drinking songs and coinage.

263----- "Lies, sex and invisibility: amatory fiction from the Restoration to the mid-eighteenth century." In (pp. 50-72) RICHETTI, John (et al eds). *The Columbia history of the British novel.* See below, **806.**

Sensational tales of sexual intrigue published for English women in the late 17c and early 18c were among the most widely read texts of the day. They demonstrate the historical fabrication of authority systems which have come to seem eternal and inevitable. They offer a chance to imagine alternatives to the rigid roles of victim and oppressor, and to understand both social and literary history as narrative of reciprocal pleasures and shared anxieties. Extensive bibliography.

264-----"Rites of passage: inventions of self and community in eighteenth-century British travel literature." Unpub. doct. diss., Univ. of Chicago, 1994. [*DA* 55 (1995): 2399-400A.]

The 18c witnessed an explosion in the production of travel literature, whose output was second only to theology. Considers the cultural needs fulfilled by travel writing. It structured the way people understood themselves, and their habitat took on heightened importance as England changed its own borders (being 'Great Britain'), and as an international presence. It functioned as a medium for the construction of new national, social and civic identities. Part 1 analyzes the travel narratives of Defoe,

Fielding and Smollett; Part 2 the works of female travellers (Lady Mary Wortley Montague and Mary Wollstonecraft). These narratives constitute radical acts of self-assertion that invent novel concepts of personhood, citizenship and country.

265-----*The politics of motherhood: British writing and culture, 1680-1760.* Cambridge, New York and Melbourne: Cambridge UP, 1996; pp. xvi, 262.

Seeks to make two arguments. Firstly, the struggle to define material virtue, authority, and responsibility was crucial to the construction of models for legitimate power and allegiance in Augustan England, a society where relations of authority on all levels were undergoing revision. Secondly, the increasingly narrow definition of material virtue which emerged during the first half of the 18c was vital to the containment of matriarchal authority at a time when patriarchal authority was undergoing radical reconception, and was therefore particularly vulnerable. Much discourse was preoccupied with motherhood. In novels, visual art, conduct literature, and printed ephemera of all kinds, questions about maternal agency, and the scope of maternal authority, emerge as central. Again and again the maternal becomes a crucial site on which battles over agency and authority were fought. Part I investigates royal motherhood: Queen Anne and the politics of maternal representation. Part II looks at monstrous motherhood: violence, difference, and the subversion of maternal ideals (Defoe and Haywood) (98-123; 124-46). Part III explores domestic motherhood, constraint, complexity and the failure of maternal authority (Richardson). Illus. (13 plates). Bibliography (235-56). Index (257-62).

266 BOYCE, Benjamin. "News from hell: satiric communications with the nether world in English writing of the seventeenth and eighteenth centuries." *PMLA* 58 (1943): 402-37.

In addition to the extraordinary voyage and journey to the moon, there is another kind of imaginary voyage, the satirical descent to Hell (which goes back to Lucian). Traces the history of this topos from Antiquity to its appearance in the English literature of the late 17c and early 18c where the nether world is depicted for purposes of entertainment and satire. Bibliography of works from 1590-1939 (201 in all).

267-----"English short fiction in the eighteenth century: a preliminary view." *SSF* 5 (1968): 95-112.

Outside the periodicals, the realm of short fiction is quite unmapped.

Where does one find a bibliography of such short stories? The article investigates a "fragmentary part" of the "vast and uncharted territory". Part I looks at the "The Main Kinds of Short Fiction" (98-106). One popular sort of fiction in the 18c developed out of the character sketch, the conflicts between young love and all the motives of social advantage, parental preference, and financial benefit, as well as of lust, egoism, and waning affection, produced countless pieces of fiction, esp. in the periodicals. Part II investigates the instructive power of these stories (the personal letter, psychological realism, the art of dialogue). There was a neglect of physical setting, but wittily effective formal language is characteristic. In the absence of stream of consciousness and the point of view of an unjudging spectator author, a controlled, formal, even elegant style of omniscient writing gives distinction in general to this form of fiction.

268   BRACK, Gae Annette. "Samuel Johnson and four literary women." Unpub. doct. diss., Arizona State univ., 1979. [*DAI* 40 (1979): 231A.]

This study in literary history analyzes the careers of four 18c English literary women who enjoyed the patronage of Dr Johnson: Elizabeth Carter, Charlotte Lennox, Fanny Burney, and Hannah More. The professional careers of these women, because so diverse, provide information about the kind of literary work available to women and the methods of publication current at the time (patronage, subscription, periodicals and booksellers).

269   BRADBROOK, Frank W. *Jane Austen and her predecessors*. Cambridge: Cambridge UP, 1966; pp. viii, 179.

Investigates the influences working on Jane Austen. Useful for its survey of "The General Literary Tradition" (periodicals, moralists in prose, the picturesque, drama and poetry) and "The Tradition in the Novel" (beginnings, the feminist tradition, other influences). Ch.6 "The Feminist Tradition" (90-119) is of particular interest in linking the first half of the century with later trends in female writing. Bibliography (175-9).

270   BRANT, Clare V. "Eighteenth-century letters: Aspects of the genre with reference to the epistolary novel and the familiar letter of personal correspondence." Unpub. doct. diss., Univ. of Oxford, 1987. [*IT* 37 (1988): 1341.]

Letters participate in almost all types of 18c century prose forms. Investigates the epistolary novel and the familiar letters of personal correspondence, and argues that each reflects interestingly on the other.

Clarifies the conventions of each form, where they overlap, how they differ and why. Discusses the limitations of the epistolary novel, and investigates the transmission of texts: why certain letters have been published, how different editorial policies affected their reading.

271-----and PURKISS, Diane (eds). *Women, texts and histories, 1575-1760.* London: Routledge, 1992; pp. xi, 299.

Explorations of historical and critical intersections concerning women of the early modern period. Extensive bibliography (271-87).

272 BRAUDY, Leo. "The form of the sentimental novel." *Novel* 7 (1973): 5-13.

Structure in the sentimental novel strives to imitate feeling rather than intellect, and to embody direct experience rather than artistic premeditation. The basic imperative of the novel from Defoe on is made only a little more apparent in the work of Sterne, Mackenzie and others. Sterne extends a literary form whose first appearance showed fidelity to real life and moral correctness.

273 BRAVERMAN, Richard. *Plots and counterplots: sexual politics and the body politic in English literature, 1660-1730.* (Cambridge Studies in Eighteenth-Century Literature and Thought, 18.) Cambridge; New York: Cambridge UP, 1993; pp. xviii, 333.

Studies the way in which literary forms mediate the dynastic politics of later 17c and early 18c England. The rupture between Crown and Parliament led to a quest "for the discursive means to bridge it" (xii). Focuses on the period from the Restoration to the rise of the oligarchy in the 1720s, exploring works of satire, tragedy, comedy, romance, georgic and the novel. What connects them all is sexual politics, with the body politic refigured as a feminized body. Bibliography (317-25).

274 BREDVOLD, L. I. *The natural history of sensibility.* Detroit: Wayne State UP, 1962; pp. vii, 104.

Investigates the unfolding of the taste of sensibility: the ethics of feeling; Diderot: the frustration of a scientific moralist; the exaltation of unhappiness; the culmination of horror.

275 BREE, L. J. "'Cits and traders': commerce and industry in the British novel 1700-1832." Unpub. doct. diss., Univ. of London, Queen Mary and Westfield College, 1991. [*IT* 43:2 (1994): 447.]

Studies the treatment of commerce and industry in the novel in the context of social and literary conditions in the 18c and early 19c. This reveals a growing perception of the vast political and social changes, and casts new light on the theory of the novel as a 'middle class' form. Novelists after Defoe were reluctant to consider commerce in detail or sympathetically. They restricted themselves largely to characters and subjects of interests to the gentry, writing within literary traditions which emphasized traditional hierarchical distinctions.

276 BREWER, John. *The sinews of power: war, money and the English state 1688-1783*. London: Unwin Hyman, 1989; pp. xxii, 289.

Intensive sociological survey of the period.The English state in the medieval and modern era is discussed before focusing on the particular period, the contours of the fiscal-military state, the political crisis which led to the emergence of this state, the effects of war on the economy, the state and civil society (the clash over information and interest).

277 BRISSENDEN, Robert Francis. *Virtue in distress: studies of the novel of sentiment from Richardson to Sade*. London: Macmillan; New York: Barnes & Noble, 1974; pp. 306.

Endeavors to explain the meaning of 'sentimentalism' and 'novel of sentiment' by investigating the terms, and then explaining some individual novels - all from the late 18c. Provides essential background for 18c fiction, and looks at the emergence of important topoi - the sentimental traveller (3-10) and the theme of virtue in distress (65-95).

278 BRITTON, W. E. "Fiction and disillusionment." *Papers of the Michigan Academy of Science, Arts & Letters* 38 (1952): 459-66.

Literature is the handmaid of virtue in Richardson's simplified view of reward and punishment. Realists like Fielding and Smollett wanted their fiction to perform worthwhile service without a distorted picture of life. No enduring prose can be divorced from a recognition of the grim realities of the world.

279 BROOKS, Douglas. *Number and pattern in the eighteenth-century novel: Defoe, Fielding, Smollett and Sterne*. Boston, MS: Routledge & Kegan Paul, 1973; pp. 198.

Exploration of repetitive patterns in 18c fiction. Ch.1 provides a brief account of the origins and continuity of the numerological tradition in Western European thought as it affected literary structures. The rest of the book is devoted to analysis of the major novels of Defoe, Fielding, Smollett and Sterne.

280 BROPHY, Elizabeth Bergen. *Women's lives and the eighteenth-century English novel.* Tampa: U of South Florida P, 1991; pp. 291.

Presents 18c women in their various roles and examines the novels of the period to assess both the accuracy of their portrayal of women, and the influence they might have had on women readers. Looks at daughters, courtship, wives, spinsters and widows, 'reinforcement or rebellion?' Notes (269-72). Bibliography (273-84): Primary Sources, Non-Fiction, Secondary Sources. Index.

281 BROWN, Homer Obed. "Of the title to things real: conflicting stories." *ELH* 55:4 (Winter 1988): 917-54.

Treatment of the emergence of the novel in Ian WATT, Michael McKEON and Nancy ARMSTRONG. The novel did not achieve the cultural, let alone the terminological, stability McKeon claims by the 1740's. Instead 'the novel' is given an 18c coherence *après coup* through those acts of editing and literary history (by Letitia Barbauld and Sir Walter Scott) in the early decades of the 19c.

282-----*Institutions of the English novel from Defoe to Scott.* Philadelphia: Pennsylvania UP, 1997; pp. xxiii, 228.

Insistence that the novel fully realized its generic identity, or was institutionalized by 1750, is based on a misconception of institution. This presupposes that the identity of the novel is defined by its contextualization at this particular moment, and discounts the massive change in meaning undergone not only by the term 'novel', but also by the particular texts of Defoe, Richardson, and Fielding in the next two centuries, and especially the crucial next 70 years. It ignores the later historical contexts that actually change the meaning of texts as they are historicized at later vantage points. Bibliographic notes (203-24). Index (225-28).

283 BROWN, Jane. *The art and architecture of English gardens: designs for the garden from the collection of the Royal Institute of British Architects 1609 to the present day.* London: Weidenfeld & Nicolson, 1989; pp. 320, illus.

Exploration of the relationship between architects and gardens, examining the Drawings Collections of the Royal Institute of British

Architects.

284 BROWN, Laura S. "English drama 1660 to 1760: the development of its form and its relation to the emergence of the novel." Unpub. doct. diss., Univ. of California, Berkeley, 1977. [*DA* 39 (1978): 891A-2A.]

From the Restoration to the mid-18c the drama undergoes a major transformation which ends in the decline of this genre. This is the consequence of the formal history of the drama over the century and is logically related to the contrasting success of the emergent novel. The drama of the early Restoration is a social form, its comprehensibility and the standards of its fictional world depending on aristocratic assessment of social status. Novelistic moral actions, however, achieve their formal success through the very means - psychological complexity and extended moral scope - which were denied to the drama by its particular history. In this respect the rise of the novel depicts the formal causes of the decline of the drama.

285-----"Drama and the novel in eighteenth-century England." *Genre* 13 (1980): 287-304.

In the 18c the drama gave way to the novel as the major literary genre in England, a central index to a much larger historical transformation. The Renaissance was the age of the drama, the 19-20cc the age of the novel, so that the meeting of the drama and the novel in the century between represents the special generic location of one of the major turning points in literary history. The drama of the 18c was a direct and self-conscious successor to the Restoration theater. All the dramatists (like Lillo and Rowe) are struggling with the confined context and flat characterization bequeathed to them by the social drama of the Restoration. Prose narrative before 1740 has a discontinuous history. French *nouvelles* and esp. romances, 18c secret histories, erotic and pious novellas, and pathetic tales, present a relatively weak and diffuse tradition. Even the autobiographical Puritan tradition (Defoe) is so distinct as to isolate and emphasize Richardson's original achievement. Richardson and Fielding are free to use the methods and materials of prior narrative and contemporary dramatists, but remain relatively unconstrained by them. It is psychological complexity and social scope which constitute the crucial point of distinction between a genre with strong ties to past conventions and a genre equipped to respond to the requirements of the new bourgeois vision.

286-----*Ends of empire: Woman and ideology in early eighteenth-century English literature*. Ithaca and London: Cornell UP, 1993; pp. 203.

Examines the way in which the literature of the 18c served the purposes of empire, and also ways in which a radical critique might recruit that literature to uncover the operations of imperialism in the 18c and help to put a stop to empire in the 20c. There has been a neglect of the historical materials that indicate the 18c cultural crisis - intercultural collision, institutionalized racism, class tension, changes in women's roles in the family and in the economy. Also seeks to redress conceptual resistance to political criticism and to 'theory', whether of structuralism, Marxism, Foucauldianism, feminism, or the interrelated topics of race, ethnicity, minority discourse, and post-colonialism. This leads to the categories of empire, slavery and colonialism in which the novel has provided a fertile field for new approaches. Looks at the feminization of ideology, the trade in slaves (*Oroonoko*), staging sexuality (the domestic 'she-tragedy'), capitalizing on war (dress and aesthetics in Pope), Amazons and Americans (Defoe), imperial disclosures (Swift). Bibliographic footnotes. Index (201-3).

287 BROWN, Richard D. *Knowledge is power: the diffusion of information in early America, 1700-1865.* Oxford and New York: Oxford UP, 1991; pp. xii, 372.

Explores the history of the United States during the period 1700 to 1865, seeking to delineate some of the ways in which information moved through society in an attempt to discern who commanded what sort of knowledge with what kind of social consequences. Also seeks to grasp the social significance of the possession of various types of information. Analyzes what kinds of information various sorts of people have craved, traces the way in which they acquired the knowledge and fitted it into their lives. In this way clarifies several dimensions of the information and communication revolution as it was sweeping through the Anglo-American world. Looks at information and authority, the challenge of rusticity, rural clergymen and communication, lawyers, public office and communication patterns, communicators and commerce, information and usability, domestic roles in the mastery of effective information, the idea of universal information. Notes (303-62). Index (363-72).

288 BROWN, Stephen William. "Changing concepts of character and plot from Dryden to Sterne." Unpub. doct. diss., Queen's Univ. at Kingston, Canada 1989. [*DAI* 49:11 (1989): 3366A.]

Examines the development of the novel from 1660 to 1760 to demonstrate that the novelistic form which came together in the 1740's is an expression of a radical shift in sensibility which can be located in Dryden and Pope. It is important to study the novel in wider contexts than the traditional emphasis on Richardson and Fielding.

289   BROWNE, Alice. *The eighteenth-century feminist mind.* Brighton: The
Harvester Press, 1987; pp. viii, 237.

Examines the place and work of women writers in the 18c, esp. the call
for women's education to be equal to men; the legal and economic
weaknesses in a woman's position, esp. if married; and the attack on the
double standards in sexuality whereby men demanded chastity of women,
but not of themselves. Looks at: 1) 18c notions of women (advice to
women, novels and heroines - Clarissa and Julie); 2) feminist responses
(beginnings of 18c feminism, women's education, women in society, the
double sexual standards, the protests of the 1790s). Notes (179-213).
Bibliography (214-32). Index (233-37).

290 BRUSS, Elizabeth Patton Wissman. "Autobiography: the changing structure
of a literary act." Unpub. doct. diss., Univ. of Michigan, 1972. [*DA* 33
(1973): 6302A.]

Attempts to categorize a genre like autobiography are often rigid and
prescriptive: how is a text evaluated under given conventions as a kind
of communicative act? The major evidence for autobiography is
linguistic, since linguistic variables such as deixis, tense, person and
modulation, reflect its functional context.

291   BUCK, Gerhard. *Die Vorgeschichte des historischen Romans in der
modernen enlischen Literatur.* (Britannica, 2.) Hamburg: Friedrichsen,
de Gruyter & Co., 1931; pp. 114.

In German. Literature on the historical novel before Sir Walter Scott is
limited. Only Defoe's *Journal of the Plague Year* (1722) and Leland's
Longworth (1762) are authentic examples. Regards Roger Boyles's
English Adventures (1676) as the first actual historical novel. Provides
a survey of the Restoration works which recount historical subjects,
before moving on to other such works in the early 18c, prior to the
emergence of Defoe. Bibliography lists texts (chronologically from 1762
to 1811) and studies (98-101).

292   BURNHAM, Michelle. *Captivity and sentiment: cultural exchange in
American literature, 1682-1861.* Hanover, PA and London (Dartmouth
College); UP of New England, 1997; pp. x, 211.

Explores critically the strategic element of captivity literature and
complicates it by examining a further dynamic observed by the paradigm

of sympathy it traditionally elicits in the reader. There is a hidden dynamic and fascination, an almost subversive pleasure, with which audiences have responded to captivity scenarios. A number of texts from Mary Rowlandson's months among the Indians to *Uncle Tom's Cabin* were once popular literature, even bestsellers. Why and how does captivity literature function as escape literature? What does the sentimentality of these texts tell us of the terms of such escape? What is the source of pleasure that underwrites such sympathetic response? Examines texts published in North America from the 17c through the 19c that depend on the central, sympathetic figure of a captive woman. The colonial captivity narrative, the Anglo-American sentimental novel, and the American slave narrative, are linked by the texts across various borders. They traverse the very cultural, national, and racial boundaries they seem to inscribe. Captivity literature, like its heroines, negotiates zones of contact such as the frontier, the Atlantic Ocean, the master/slave division and the color line. Notes (177-92). Bibliography (193-206). Index (207-11). Illus. (11 plates).

293 BURWICK, Frederick. *Illusion and the drama: critical theory of the Enlightenment and Romantic era.* University Park, PA: Penn State Univ., 1991; pp. vii, 326.

Seeks to appraise the functions of 'illusion' in 18c aesthetics and dramatic criticism. Considers perfect illusion and the skeptics (Rousseau, Johnson, Stendhal), illusion in the players (Diderot, Tieck, Lamb), illusion and the audience (Lessing, Mendelssohn, Schiller), illusion and the play (W.A. Schlegel), illusion and the romantic imagination (Coleridge), illusion and the stage (Goethe, Hugo), illusion and melodrama (Coleridge, Tieck). Bibliography (305-18). Index (319-26).

294 BUTLER, Sydney James. "Masks of reality: the rhetoric of narration in the eighteenth-century novel." Unpub. doct. diss., Univ. of British Columbia, 1974. [*DA* 35 (1975): 7249A-50A.]

Investigates how the development of the English novel during the 18c is illustrated by the author's "mask of reality", or rhetorical stance adopted for telling his story. Creates a fictional world or *kosmos*, and the success of his work depends on his power to invest this illusory world with an air of reality. Through his medium of the printed word, he tries to convince the reader of the truth of his vision. Defoe excludes the author from the life of the novel. In Richardson the authorial presence becomes visible in the critical prefaces and postscripts. In Fielding and Sterne the role of the narrator becomes still more explicit, so that the reader's attention is diverted from contemplation of an imaginary world to consideration of the world as a piece of fiction.

295   BUTT, John. *The mid-eighteenth century*. Ed. and completed by Geoffrey
CARNELL. (Oxford History of Literature, 8.) Oxford: Clarendon Press,
1979; pp. vii, 671.

Looks at the period 1740-90, considering Samuel Johnson, poetry (1740-
60, 1760-89), Scottish poetry, drama, history, travel literature, memoirs
and biography, essays, letters, dialogues and speeches, four major
novelists (Richardson, Fielding, Smollett, Sterne), other prose fiction.
The conclusion explores the 18c 'quest for energy'. Very useful
Chronological Table (515-31). Bibliography (532-60). Index (661-71).

296 BUXTON, John. *The Grecian taste: literature in the age of Neo-Classicism*.
London; New York: Macmillan, 1978; pp. 188.

Examines the prevalence of neo-classical (actually 'Grecian') taste and
ideas in the 18c, influenced by Winckelmann's vision of Ancient Greece.
Looks at the contribution of Mark Akenside, William Collins, Oliver
Goldsmith, William Blake, Walter Savage Landor, Thomas Love
Peacock and Percy Bysshe Shelley. References (170-83). Index (184-8).

297   BYRD, Max. *Visits to Bedlam: madness and literature in the eighteenth
century*. Columbia, SC: U of South Carolina P, 1974; pp. 200.

Examines the universal ambiguity of the response to madness in the
historical setting of 18c England. For approximately 100 years from the
late 17c to the late 18c, English society addressed the idea of the
extraordinary madman, the person of madman himself, with astonishing
energy and vehemence. The period saw the intensified practice of the
incarceration of the insane. Describes the Augustan response to madness,
to distinguish it from the traditional view, and to suggest how this
attitude, which was a denial, evolved into the Romantic response, which
was an embracing one. Draws on the imaginative literature of the 18c for
examples of the response at its most intense and complex, but also
medical and social history for support. Bibliographic notes (177-94).
Index (195-200). Illus. (8 plates).

298-----*London transformed: images of the city in the eighteenth century*. New
Haven, CT and London: Yale UP, 1978; pp. x, 202.

Study of London, examining its great vitality, social confidence, civility,
and arts of living. The extraordinary growth of the city during the period
1700-1820, its wealth, cultural achievements, and massive humane

failings, all foreshadow the changes - economic, political, social - that were to come over European and American cities in the 19c and were already under way in England in the early 18c. Its greatest writers found the city a timeless moral image: Pope, Swift, Johnson, Reynolds, Burke (the Augustan Humanists). Their dream, inherited from the classical world, was of an ordered community gathered to the form of a beautiful city, like Rome or Athens, an image of harmony and transcendence, to be placed against the equally classical form of a city of vice, like the Babylon of Revelation. Looks at "Defoe's London: 'this prodigious Thing'" (8-43). Notes (179-98). Index (199-202).

299   BYSTROM, Valerie Ann. "The abyss of sympathy: the conventions of pathos in eighteenth- and nineteenth-century British novels." *Criticism* 23 (1981): 211-31.

As the conventions of sympathetic pathos evolve through the 18c and 19c, they reflect the inconsistencies which arise simply from the effort to introduce the sympathetic program into the traditions of fiction. They also reflect the political contradictions in the sympathetic scheme itself. Since the description between heavenly and earthly politics is referred to and embraced by God's will, power may be distributed in the pathetic sense, and, ironically, the will to power, simply becomes part of the experience of pathos, or the feeling of sympathy. The moral scheme and the pathetic scene are not disturbed by the contradiction. They allow with impunity the amiable pleasures of charity, the pathetic machinations of the miserable, and the thrill of self-sacrificial glory. The economic and political inequality of the novel's reflected world, the morality of sympathy, and pathetic conventions, all persist together.

300   CAMDEN, C. (ed.). *Restoration and eighteenth-century literature: essays in honor of A. D. McKillop.* (Rice Univ. Semicentennial Pub.) Chicago and London: U of Chicago P, 1963; pp. xi, 435.

Collection of essays on 18c life and letters. Fiction is treated by Leo HUGHES, "Theatrical convention in Richardson: some observations in a novelist's technique" (239-50) and John Robert MOORE, "Daniel Defoe: precursor of Samuel Richardson" (351-70).

301   CANBY, Henry Seidel. *The short story in English.* New York: Henry Holt, 1909; pp. xiii, 386.

Overview of the development of the short story. Analysis of the development of short fiction: Italian *novella*, romance, popular literature. Notes: bibliographic and general (351-65).

302----and DAHIEL, Alfred. *A study of the short story.* New York: Henry Holt, 1913; rev. 1935; pp. iv, 375.

Provides an historical survey of the emergence of this genre, esp. the influence of the Italian *novella* and the French *nouvelle* on English short fiction in the 17c and 18c, as well as the varieties of short stories referred to as "novels of intrigue" and "true short stories". Comments on works by Behn, Congreve, Swift and Pope.

303   CANFIELD, J. Douglas and HUNTER, J. Paul (eds). *Rhetorics of order/ordering rhetorics in English neo-classical literature.* Newark, NJ: Delaware UP, 1989; pp. 200.

From the Restoration to the publication of the *Lyrical Ballads* (1798), there was a pervasive rage for order, as an age of neo-classicism, prized for its calm and confident forms and structures. Literature was seen to reflect a controlled universe in highly ordered forms, often variations on Classical genres, that embody, and inculcate social structures. The essays attempt to analyze several of the rhetorics of order. All reveal an age preoccupied with, and profoundly anxious about, the forms employed to impose metaphysical, political, ethical and epistemological stability in era and destabilized by revolutions of many kinds.

304   CARNELL, Rachel Karen. "Dominion in the household: Liberal political theory and the early English novel." Unpub. doct. diss., Boston Univ., 1995. [*DA* 55 (1995): 2400A.]

Examines the origins of the British novel in the context of late 17c political debates over monarchic succession. During and after the Parliamentary Revolution of 1688, political argument was polarized between divine right and the social contract. Calls attention to the fact that novels written in English between 1680 and 1750 frequently describe crises within the family through a vocabulary derived from this political discussion. The novel, which became so popular in this period, provided a forum through which writers could challenge the adequacy of the binary division between divine right and social contract theories by questioning whether either political paradigm addressed the needs of the individual within a household. Analyzes the major novels of Aphra Behn, Daniel Defoe, Samuel Richardson and Eliza Haywood to argue that the early British novel incorporated responses to the paradigms of the family used in political discourse from the same period. By literalizing these political metaphors, early novelists explored the inextricable connections between power in civil society and dominion in the household.

305 CARNOCHAN, W. B. *Confinement and flight: an essay on English literature of the eighteenth century.* Berkeley and London: California UP, 1977; pp. 201.

Deals with confinement in its extended sense, the psychology of confinement, that can be broken down into epistemological and metaphysical aspects. Emphasis falls more on metaphysical issues - the state of being that generates the epistemological crisis. Looks at Swift's two city poems, Denham's "Cooper Hill", Godwin's *Caleb Williams*, Beckford's *Vathek*, the islanders Robinson Crusoe, Gulliver, and Sterne's Uncle Toby (lonely figures in an enclosed and self-enclosing landscape), happy prisons in *Moll Flanders* and *Tom Jones*, the artist caught in the face of tragic events (*A Journal of the Plague Year*). Considers captive souls; islands of silence; prisons, pastorals and warders; "Which Way I Fly [...] "; Johnson in fetters; "Like Birds i' t' Cage [...] "; the poet and the happy man. "We have watched the artist-figure coming forward, whether as master of revels (*Tom Jones*), and psychic invalid (*A Journal of the Plague Year*), and criminal in the eyes of society (*Caleb Williams*). What is yet to happen after the eighteenth century is the forthright appropriation of the artist's consciousness as the central subject of art" (171). The artist has to separate his imagination from the world outside the mind, and find comfort in isolation. Texts cited (193-96). Index (197-201).

306 CARRÉ, Jacques. "Loisir et production: la villa suburbaine au 18ème siècle." *CCV* 9 (1988): 121-35.

The aristocracy and petty nobility, arbiters of the national culture, invented the suburban villa, a new architectural type specifically conceived for leisure and enjoyment. This is closely bound up with a classical frame of reference: the Whig aristocracy took Augustan Rome as its model with effects on politics, literature and architecture. The discovery of the antique villa via Pliny the Younger was a stimulus to the evolution of the landscaped garden, with wide aesthetic and practical consequences. "L'exploitation agricole reçoit de la sorte la sanction de l'art, au moment où le jardin surburbain reçoit celle de la nature [...] " (129).

307-----"La ville britannique et l'espace industrielle (1760-1829)." *Q/W/E/R/T/Y* 2 (1992): 265-72.

Looks at the impact of industrialization on the cities and the accommodation of industry: the birth of provincial urbanness in the 18c ("des usines dans le paysage: la révélation de la ville industrielle").

Demonstrates that during the whole 18c the traditional British élite preserved "une vision figée de la civilisation et du développement urbane" (271).

308-----(ed.). *The crisis of courtesy: studies in the conduct book in Britain 1600-1900*. (Brill's Studies in Intellectual History.) Leiden and New York: E.J. Brill, 1994; pp. 201.

Investigates the English conduct book from the 16c to the 20c, illustrating the role of manners in the process of civilization, showing how class structure and identity were partly defined thanks to codes of conduct, the cultural effects of prescribed femininity and masculinity, the interchange between fashionable social types at a given age, and the characters of contemporary fiction and theater. British conduct books were distinctly pragmatic, largely about the grace of authority both within the family, within the Court, within society at large. In the Augustan Age, conduct literature was still about authority. The very relationship established between author and potential reader was still one of deference. 13 essays cover the transformation of a genre, conversation and conduct, the gentleman and the man of taste, the lady and the spouse. The extended bibliography (183-95) provides a list of conduct books published in Britain between 1500 and 1993. Note on Contributors. Name Index. List of illus. (17 plates).

309   CARY, Meredith. *Different drummers: a study of cultural alternatives in fiction*. Metuchen, NJ: Scarecrow, 1984; pp. viii, 292.

By considering a long series of novels by women, the books surveys notions of 'otherness' or minority: alternative groups, international opinions, ethical alternatives, new roles in old societies, the eccentric role, escapes.

310   CASTLE, Terry. "The carnivalization of eighteenth-century English narrative." *PMLA* 99 (1984): 903-16.

With the spectacular rise of carnivalesque activity in England in the second and third decades of the 18c - marked by the institutionalization of the public, or subscription masquerade - the novel took a cue from popular culture; the carnival set-piece, or masquerade, became a standard, though highly problematical, fictional topos. 18c England escaped ambivalently from constancy and transparency, and the claims of an otherwise pervasive decorum, in the carnival.

311-----*Masquerade and civilization: the carnivalesque in eighteenth-century*

English culture and fiction. Stanford, CA: Stanford UP; London: Methuen, 1986; pp. x, 395.

Seeks to re-create the historical phenomenon of the English masquerade and to outline its literary history, particularly in fiction, between 1720-1790. It is evocative, is subject for reverie and fantasia, a utopian image, the set piece of an age. Investigates the topos, travesty and fate of the carnivalesque, literary transformations, masquerade and allegory, masked ball and utopia, the topos after the 18c. Notes (349-70). Bibliography (37-84). Illustrations. Index.

312-----*The female thermometer: eighteenth-century culture and the invention of the uncanny.* (Ideologies of Desire.) Oxford and New York: Oxford UP, 1995; pp. 278.

Series of 11 essays exploring the 'irrational' or 'Gothic' side of 18c culture, looking at the morbid, the excessive, the strange, prophetic dreams, *Doppelgänger*, primal scenes, sexual metamorphoses, disguises, estrangements and carnivalesque assaults on decorum, auras, detached body parts, inanimate objects that come to life mysteriously, optical illusions, magic lantern shows, hallucinatory reveries, corpses, tombs, warning apparitions, monomania, *folie à deux*, time travel and visionary sightings of the dead. The result is a challenge to the conventional view of the 18c as an era of unexampled social, political and philosophical progress. The venerable notion of enlightenment itself has come under ideological attack by scholars (from E. P. Thompson to Michel Foucault) who have described ways in which appeals to reason can be used 'instinctively' to control and dominate rather than to emancipate. Notes (215-52). Bibliography (253-68). Index (269-78). Illus.

313 CAWELTI, John G. *Adventure, mystery, and romance: formula stories as art and popular culture.* London; Chicago: Chicago UP, 1976; pp. 336.

While essentially a study of modern crime and detective stories, the book provides a detailed and helpful study of mystery formulas which trace terminology back to the origins of fiction: adventure, romance, mystery, melodrama, alien beings and states.

314 CENTRE AIXOIS D'ÉTUDES ET DE RECHERCHES SUR LE DIX-HUITIÈME SIÈCLE. *Images du peuple au dix-huitième siècle: Colloque d'Aix-en-Provence 25 et 26 octobre 1969.* Paris: Librairie Armand Colin, 1973; pp. 360.

In French. Series of 25 essays covering the depiction of "the people" in various aspects of 18c life and thought. Section 1) provides aspects of a definition; 2) work and popular culture; 3) the people in political and religious thought; 4) the people in literature and art (in French tragedy 1688-1715, in the *nouvelles* of the first half of the 18c, in the works of Marivaux, Prévost, Mercier); 5) the people in urban and rural images after Restif; 6) populism and poetry; 7) music and the people. The *Avant-Propos* is by Henri COULET.

315   CHANDLER, Frank Wadleigh. *The literature of roguery.* 2 vols. (The Types of English Literature.). Boston, 1907. I, 284; II, 584.

Vol. 2 ch. 8 is entitled "The Picaresque Novel in the Eighteenth Century" (285-341), and looks at Defoe, Fielding, Smollett, imitators and innovators, with an appended bibliography (340-41). Considers each of Defoe's major works, observing that "in *Moll Flanders*, and to a lesser extent *Colonel Jack*, Defoe struck the keynote of the modern novel. He had partially subordinated incident to character. His predilection for ethical studies had made his thought pivot upon the moral quality of every act. Unconsciously, he had marked out the way for the later development of the novel" (299).

316   CHARD, C. R. "Horror and terror in literature of the Grand Tour and in the Gothic novel." Unpub. doct. diss., Univ. of Cambridge, 1985. [*IT* 35 (1986): 544.]
Examines the transformations in the ordering of knowledge of the foreign, which allowed concepts of horror and terror to be formed, and to assume an important role in discussion of travel on the Grand Tour. Discusses the specific characteristics of travel writing which determined the formation of concepts of horror and terror within different areas of commentary. Comments on society, manner and religion.

317   CHEEK, Pamela Lynn. "Sexual records." Unpub. doct. diss., Stanford Univ., 1994. [*DA* 55 (1995): 3182A.]

Investigates Enlightenment pornography in France and England. Explores the process through which Enlightenment pornography both informed and put pressure on emerging institutional and scientific analyzes of human behavior and sexuality. In the course of the second half of the century, in pornographic, scientific and institutional discourses, sexuality became a privileged way of defining social difference in French and English culture. Draws on police records, travel writing, naturalist accounts, and satiric poetry to trace the development of empirical descriptions of sexuality, and ideas on the tailoring of sexual practices to the political needs of the ideal state.

318   CHERNIAVSKY, Eva. "The matrix of patriarchy: ideas of gender and community in American culture, 1640-1860." Unpub. doct. diss., Univ. of California, 1990. [*DA* 52 (1991): 1326A-7A.]

Traces the radical change in the way American culture imagines gender - the way it defines male and female identity - from the mid-17c to the mid-19c. In Puritan society the woman is thought to be morally frailer than man, prone to depravity, unless carefully restricted, yet by the middle decades of the 19c she figures as a morally superior being, an excellent influence on those around her. This is an increasingly sentimental portrait of feminine nature that accompanies the move from Puritan to republican social forms. The social and symbolic recognition of the woman in this period is an index to and product of the redefinition of American community.

319   CHOI, Julie. "The voice of common sense: Disembodiment and authority in the early English novel." Unpub. doct. diss., Stanford Univ., 1994. [*DA* 54 (1994): 4447-8A.]

The English novel achieves stability as genre with the emergence of a new narrative fiction in the latter half of the 18c. The deliberate erasure of teller/speaker is an entirely new kind of 'third' person voice marking a historically significant change. The new voice expands the reach of the novel and forges a new model of modern subjectivity. This voice presents an apparently seamless translation from the highly emotive and fashionable effusions of the first-person sentimental subject into the transparent and 'deep' other, the third person, interpreted as 'the voice of common sense', becoming a powerful and authoritative ideological tool.

320   CHRISTIE, John and SHUTTLEWORTH, Sally (eds). *Nature transfigured: science and literature, 1700-1900.* Manchester: Manchester UP, 1989; pp. 225.

Series of 9 essays which attempt to study literature and science "as a field of positive relations", attempting to recognize the potential complexity of the terrain of literature and science, once the strict and definitive boundary between them is recognized as a cultural artefact which has traditionally counterposed a humanizing literary practice to a dehumanizing scientific practice. The culture of the Enlightenment marked the ascendance of science to a position of cultural authority in the West, a privileged form, cognition and action which aided ideological liberalism and political reformation. With Enlightenment culture there is no one monolithic science, but competing versions of science: Newtonian and Cartesian, idealist and materialist, monist and dualist, realist and sceptical. But the Enlightenment was capable of emphasizing the role of imagination in science, as of empirical perceptions, and was therefore willing to see science as a product of human imagination. Scientific and literary interactions are by no means marginal, confined to idiosyncratic works, but sufficient interaction can have identifiable central effects at the level of character, plot, style, structure and genre. Refers to Defoe, Swift and Sterne. The introduction (1-120) sketches the ways in which the cultural division of literature and science was historically initiated and has been historically maintained. The essays reveal this to be selective and partial, and indicate kinds of approaches which offer the possibility of going beyond the boundaries drawn by entrenched cultural assumptions and conventional academic practice. Includes a helpful view of Defoe by Simon SCAFFER, "Defoe's natural philosophy and the world of credit" (13-44). Extensive bibliographical notes. Index (222-25).

321 CHURCH, Richard. *The growth of the English novel*. London: Methuen and New York: Barnes & Noble, 1951; pp. 179.

Using the extended metaphor of taproot, growing plant and established tree, this provides a survey and history in narrative form with clear, descriptive-critical insights, beginning with Sir Thomas Malory (1496), and carrying it into the 20c to Joyce, Lawrence and Woolf. Ch. 4 "The Tree Takes Shape" (31-40) covers the 17c, and ch. 5 "The Definition of the Foliage" (41-52) covers the early 18c until 1740. The insights are clear, concise and very helpful. Thus in speaking of Aphra Behn and the women novelists of the late 17c/early 18c, he observes: "In thus preparing the way for the gutter press, they also eased still further the trappings of prose style. Such writers as Mrs Mary Manley and Mrs Eliza Haywood carried this vogue into the following century; familiarizing the undress manner of literary style, the language of the people, but adding nothing else from which the novel might draw strength" (40). Defoe is characterized pithily as having " [...] a quality of muscular reserve in the mind at work, which gives the simple prose a kind of promissory power, for music, for anguish, subtlety of argument" (51).The perspective beyond 1740 is also succinctly captured: "After the publication of *Gulliver's Travels*, the history of the English novel becomes immediately clarified, for here was the model for blending realism with the central and propelling idea, and conveying the whole purpose in a medium that ran smoothly and economically to its goal" (52). There are no notes, and no bibliography, which limits its usefulness. Index (175-79).

322 CLARIDGE, Henry. "American literature to 1900: general." *YWES* 73 (1992): 549-55; 74 (1993): 522-26.

General discussion of new books and articles covering American literature to 1900. Of particular importance is '2. American Literature to 1825' (73:555-61); and '2. American literature to 1830' (74:526-35).

323 CLARK, Charles E. *The public prints: the newspaper in Anglo-American culture, 1665-1740*. Oxford and New York: Oxford UP, 1994; pp. xiv, 330.

Investigates the role of the newspapers in the English-speaking world of the early 18c. In 1740 the British Empire contained 60 newspapers, all but a dozen of them weekly, and probably two-thirds going to fewer than 1000 purchasers each. London alone had 17 newspapers, 6 dailies, 5 or 6 thrice-weeklies. By 1740 a more pointedly political note was developing in the newspapers. It was no longer an experiment or miscellany, but a vehicle of information and discourse about the pressing public events of the time and place. It would remain like this for the rest of the century. Looks at 1) English backgrounds; 2) America: narrative; 3) America: structures and transitions. Appendix (267-68). Notes (269-318). Index (319-30).

324 CLARK, Edith L. "The negro in fiction: a historical and critical sketch." Unpub. master's thesis, Univ. of Texas, 1902.
Abstract not available.

325 CLAYTON, Jay. *Romantic vision and the novel*. Cambridge; New York; Melbourne: Cambridge UP, 1987; pp. x, 249.

Introd. "Transcendence of the Novel" (1-26) provides important background for the emergence of the novel. Visionary power is antithetical to realistic representation. Transcendence is violent, and the fate of those who embody the absolute, like love, goodness and power, is severe.

326 CLEMENTS, Frances. "The rights of women in the eighteenth-century novel". *EE* 4:314 (1973): 63-70.

Considers a selection of novels from the years immediately following the publication of *Pamela*. These years represent the first flowering of the English realistic novel, and show that a concern for women's rights is central, and that these novels make the same demands for women which Mary Wollstonecraft was to make in 1792. The novelists' involvement with the problems of women is clear from the titles of their works; they are also alert to the heroine's problems as a victim of 18c social injustice.

327 CLIFFORD, James Lowry (ed.). *Man versus society in eighteenth-century*

Britain. Six points of view. London: Longman, 1956; pp. 175.

Collection of 6 essays in history, economics, religion, fine art, music and literature, examining aspects of the life and times.
1. Political man (J. H. PLUMB);
2. Man's economic status (Jacob VINTER);
3. The Churchman (G. R. CRAGG);
4. The Artist (Rudolf WITTKOWER);
5. The Composer (Paul Henry LANG);
6. The Writer (Bertrand H. BRONSON);
7. Commentary (J. C. CLIFFORD).
Notes (152-68). Index (169-75).

328---(ed.). *Eighteenth-century English literature: essays in criticism.* New York: Oxford UP, 1959; pp. xi, 351.

Collection of 12 critical and scholarly selections which concentrate on the literature of 18c England. "In one way or another, each challenges some deep-rooted false impression or oversimplified generalization, or provides a fresh interpretation of a major author or masterpiece" (vii). Includes the important contribution by Ian WATT, "*Robinson Crusoe* as myth" (158-79).

329   COLOMBO, Rosa Maria (ed.). *Settecento senza amore: studi sulla narrativa inglese.* Rome: Bulzoni, 1983; pp. 261.

In Italian. A collection of essays covering the period of English fiction from the late 17c to the late 18c, illustrating the bourgeois ideology of power. While the majority of the contributions are on Swift, there is coverage of the epistolary novel in the second half.

330 COLTHARP, Duane Evert. "Literary heroism and the economies of excess, 1650-1750." Unpub. doct. diss., Univ. of Michigan, 1993. [*DA* 54 (1994): 2586A.]

Students of Milton, Dryden, and Pope, and their culture, sometimes find an exaggerated faith in military heroism, while other critics discover an equally virulent anti-heroism. By interpreting epics, epic translations, panegyrics, rhymed plays and non-fiction prose, he unites these opposite evaluation of heroism by seeing the heroic idea from 1650 to 1750 as inherently a contradiction: a force that exceeds containment, must nonetheless be contained; a hero who surpasses social norms should nonetheless serve and submit to society; an excessive violence is asked to limit and cancel itself out, thus terminating in peace. Traces a shift from a 'primitivist' model of heroism, wherein the hero stands outside society in the customary position of the savage, to an 'economic' model in which the hero, or heroic poet, becomes an effect of a social conditions larger than himself.

331 CONANT, Martha Pike. *The Oriental Tale in the eighteenth century.* (Columbia Univ. Studies in Comparative Literature) New York: Columbia UP, 1908; pp. 312.

Gives a clear and accurate description of a distinct component part of 18c English fiction, in its relation to its French sources, and to the general current of English thought. That which was not original came from French imitations and translations of genuine Oriental tales. Looks at the imaginative group, the moralistic group, the philosophic group, the satiric group. Concludes with a literary estimate. Notes (257-66). Chronological Table (267-93). Books of Reference (294-306). Index. 32 such tales are listed between 1700 and 1740 (267-78).

332 CONGER, Syndy McMillen (ed.). *Sensibility in transformation: creative resistance to sentiment from the Augustans to the Romantics: Essays in honor of Jean H. Hagstrum.* Rutherford: Fairleigh Dickinson UP, 1990; pp. 235.

Collection of 11 essays which focus attention on the wide-ranging aspects of sensibility between 1690 and 1830. They depict an 'age of sensibility' that was being transformed in two interwoven senses: the sentimental ethic was transforming attitudes and forms of British culture and literature, and also undergoing considerable transformation itself by sloughing off its eccentric surfaces to gain recognition as a normative part of the human and artistic pysche, and to contribute to larger shifts in attitudes towards both public and private virtue. Important bibliographical resource: "Sensibility: a Select Bibliography of Secondary Sources" by Sydney McMILLAN CONGER and Peter V. CONROY, Jr. (208-29). Index (231-35).

333 CONWAY, Alison Margaret. "Private interests: spectatorship, portraiture, and the novel in eighteenth-century England." Unpub. doct. diss., Univ. of California (Berkeley), 1994. See Ch. 4 under HAYWOOD, **1568**.

334 COOKE, Alice Lovelace. "Fielding and the writers of heroic romance." *PMLA* 62:2 (1947): 984-94.

Mme de Scudéry and Henry Fielding propounded principles of literary theory which were in many respects identical, yet there is little resemblance between *The Grand Cyrus* and *Tom Jones*. The history of literary theory is often a study of gradual developments of different concepts of the same literary terms. "Probability", "unity" and "morality" did not mean the same thing to Fielding as they did to Scudéry.

335   COPE, Kevin L. "Satire: the conquest of philosophy." In (pp. 175-84) MARSHALL, Donald G.(ed.). *Literature as philosophy/philosophy as literature*. Iowa City: Univ. of Iowa Press, 1987; pp. x, 346.

"Satire is the only literary genre which is enthusiastically philosophical" (175). The claim of satire to philosophical rigor has seduced its major critics into misunderstanding the service it performs for philosophy. The satire of the 17c and 18c freed both philosophy and literature from the obligation to imitate truth directly. Satire directs value and beauty against evidence and disorder, and saves fact and fiction from turgid definitions. The Augustans, in search of the philosophical purpose of satire, revered it as the weapon of order and elegance against too literal an idea of the truth.

336-----"A 'Roman commonwealth' of knowledge: fragments of belief and the disbelieving power of didactic." *SECC* 20 (1990): 3-25.

Locke, Halifax, Dryden and Sprat all felt the influence of empiricist obsession with appearances. 18c dialectics challenges the Establishment, but it also establishes discourse, spurring hearers to the building of a good society. Didactic places Spartan-Roman republican desire for cooperation between self and society at the center of the foreground.

337-----*Criteria of certainty: truth and judgment in the English Enlightenment*. Lexington: UP of Kentucky, 1990; pp. viii, 224.

Late 17c and 18c writers treated explanatory systems as a kind of master genre; explaining and systematizing were a literary mode with a vitality and methodology of its own. Investigates systematizing as a technique for confronting, organizing, manipulating and subduing experience. Experience during this period becomes an "attention-getting confrontation" (3). Looks at the "Restoration of Certainty" (Rochester, Halifax, Dryden) and "Confrontation with Certainty" (Locke, Swift, Pope, Smith). Epilogue. Notes (201-18). Index (219-24).

338   COPLEY, Stephen (ed.). *Literature and the social order in eighteenth-century England*. (World and Word.) London: Croom Helm, 1984; pp. 202.
Anthology taken from periodicals, pamphlets, general and philosophical

works and more specialized economic treatises published between 1700 and 1776. They are broadly concerned with economies and related questions of social policy, part of an extensive literature on these subjects addressed to the polite reader: 1) The Second Establishment; 2) Commerce and Industry; 3) The Economy of the Social order; 4) The Poor; 5) Crime. Select Bibliography (195-7). Subject Index (200-2).

339 COUTURIER, Maurice. "La bataille du livre et la naissance du roman anglais." *Cycnos* 6 (1990): 1-15.

The novel is more than something simply printed and commercialized: it develops around itself a whole series of little conflicts between different actors: the author, the editor, the publisher, the bookseller and the reader. The novel also exposes the principal systems articulating the passions and conflicts of modern society.

340 CRAFT-FAIRCHILD, Catherine. *Masquerade and gender: disguise and female identity in eighteenth-century fiction by women*. University Park, Penn: The Pennsylvania State UP, 1993; pp. x, 190.

The adoption of disguise allowed those attending masquerades freedoms and excess of behavior they would not have customarily enjoyed. Women nonetheless perceived the ways which conformed to patriarchal structures, and in their writing attempted to outline how the apparent freedoms of the masquerade were only sophisticated forms of oppression. Female masquerade must be theorized differently from male masquerades. Unlike Castle and Schofield, this is not a literary history, or reconstruction of the cultural history of the masquerade. Reconsiders the topos as it appears in the fictions of selected Restoration and 18c women writers, and tries to trace gender formation during childhood (Aphra Behn, *The Dumb Virgin*; Mary Davys, *The Accomplished Rake*; Eliza Haywood, *Masqueraders*, *Fantomima*, *The City Jilt*; Elizabeth Inchbald; Frances Burney, *The Wanderer*). Analyzes the relationship of masquerade to the construction of femininity in 18c fiction by recourse to psychoanalytic theories which are used throughout. Posits psychological double-sidedness to masquerade: this is not simply a female-dominated sphere. Explores the art of compression and excess (overwriting and mimicry). Bibliography (175-84).

341 CRANE, Ronald Salmon. "Suggestions towards a genealogy of 'the man of feeling'." *ELH* 1 (1934): 205-30. Rpt. in *Studies in literature of the Augustan age: essays in honor of A. E. Case*. Ann Arbor, 1952.

Examines factors preparing for sentimentalism and relates them to the preaching of divines of the Latitudinarian School after the Restoration. They were anti-Puritan, anti-Stoic and anti-Hobbesian and taught: 1) virtue as universal benevolence; 2) benevolence as feeling; 3) benevolent feelings as 'rational' to man; 4) a 'self-approving' joy.

342 CRAWFORD, B. V. "The use of formal dialogue in narrative." *PQ* 1 (1922): 179-91.

This type of composition, the antiquity of which rivals that of literature itself, was a factor of real importance in England from 1600-1750. The tendency to dialogue showed itself in all fields of thought: in politics, religion, philosophy and criticism, also in the novel. Like the Character, the periodical essay, the narrative sketch, the romance, it contributed to the perfecting of the novel.

343 CROSS, W. L. *The development of the English novel.* New York: Macmillan, 1899; pp. 347.

Ch. 1 "From Arthurian Romance to Richardson" contains subsection 6 "Literary Forms that Contributed to the Novel" discussing diaries, lives, letters, characters, Character sketches.

344 CRUISE, James Joseph. "Governing scripture: authority and the early English novel." Unpub. doct. diss., Univ. of Pennsylvania, 1985. [*DA* 46 (1986): 2298A.]

This explores the origins of the early novel's authority. Bakhtin has emphasized the comic familiarity of the world of the novel in contrast with the epic stress on nationalism, generic completion and isolation from the present. From the 16c until the Restoration, exegetes often interpreted the eschatology of Christian prophecy as unfolding on a political landscape. By 1740 the Bible no longer expressed a story of simple faith, but was a text requiring critical and historical justification. The great epic of Christian history lost its narrative immediacy. This trend signaled a change in Christian hegemony to Christianity as an element of the state. It also meant a loss paternal and patriarchal authority. The burden of the novel became one of discovering authority in a world of uncertain authority, a potentially alienating process.

345 DAGHISTANY, Ann. "The *picara* nature". *Women's Studies* 5 (1977): 51-60.

The *picara* occupies a unique position in the history of literature: neither angel nor mother figure, neither siren, murderess nor evil married woman, her immorality is often the cause of both celebration and remorse. Her nature was established in Classical times by Petronius (Quartilla in *The Satyricon*, 66 AD) and Apuleius (Fotis in *The Golden Ass*, 150 AD). Their characteristics were modified by *Celestina* (1499) and later developed in Laura (Le Sage, *Gil Blas*, 1735). The standard features of the *picara* are recognized in Grimmelshausen's *Courage* (1670) and Defoe's *Moll Flanders* (1722). Also well known in *Lazarillo de Tormes* (1553), *Guzman de Alfarache* (1599) and *Simplicissimus* (1669). The *picara* tends to ascribe her misfortune to the social and physical disadvantages of her sex, rather than to any personification or universal principle.

346 DAHL, Anthony G. *Literature of the Bahamas, 1724-1992: the march towards national identity*. Lanham, MD, and London: UP of America, 1995; pp. xiii, 219.

Analyzes the literature of the Bahamas from the time of the original Arawaks until 1992. Looks at Bahamian literary production and dependency, "From Pirates to Politics: Bahamian Literature, 1724-1953). Bibliography (199-204). Index (205-19).

347 DALY, Macdonald. "Quasi-anti-vivisection in the eighteenth century." *DUJ* 81:2 (July 1990) 187-90.

The 18c remains a crucial period for the historical study of human attitudes to animals. Certain claims, e.g. that Johnson was an early champion of animal rights, are exaggerated. But a sentimental love of dogs and a fondness for cats, conjoined with an uneasiness towards deliberate acts which caused suffering, makes it a prototype of the anti-vivisection movement.

348 DAMROSCH, Leo, Jr. *God's plot and man's stories: studies in fictional imagination from Milton to Fielding*. Chicago and London: Chicago UP, 1985; pp. ix, 343.

Considers 'Doctrine and Fiction', the novelty of the novel, the significance of Puritanism, myth and the novel, the novel, consciousness and society. Also looks closely at Puritan Experience and Art, before moving on to Art and Truth in Puritan Literature, considering Bunyan, then Defoe, Richardson and Fielding.

349-----(ed.). *Modern essays on eighteenth-century literature*. Oxford and New York: Oxford UP, 1988; pp. x, 488.

Twenty essays covering the spectrum of 18c literature. Of special pertinence are contributions by Michael McKEON ("Generic Transformation and Social Change: Rethinking the Rise of the Novel") (159-80), John J. RICHETTI (*Robinson Crusoe*: the Self as Master") (201-36), G. A. STARR ("Defoe's Prose Style: The Language of Interpretation") (237-60). Others cover Richardson, Fielding, Smollett, Sterne, Johnson, Boswell, Pope, Fanny Burney, as well as theater and poetry.

350-----(ed.). *The profession of eighteenth-century literature: reflections on an institution*. Madison, WN: U of Wisconsin P, 1992; pp. 234.

Collection of eleven essays reflecting on changed approaches to the study and reading of 18c literature. Encounters the traditions of 18c studies while providing new perspectives. Essays cover 'inventing the Eighteenth Centuries', varieties of literary affection, cultural crisis and dialectical method, a new history of the Enlightenment, the resumption of authority, literary practice and theory, the hegemony of Ian Watt, ideology and the flight from history in 18c poetry, feminism, humanism. Notes on the contributors (223-36). Index (227-34). Each essay has bibliographical notes. "It seems to me that the current ambition of literary critics to reach for cultural synthesis has to be restrained, like John Bender's, by Watt's example in order to remain true to complex and particularized textual workings [...]" (John Richetti, p. 110). Watt made a generation of readers aware "[...] that the transparency and overtness of eighteenth-century fiction that Hume thinks render it uninteresting were means to socio-cultural ends rather than self-explanatory phenomena [...]. Critical understanding of the evolution of the novel is essentially indebted to this enduring example" (96-97).

351   DANZIGER, M. K. "The eighteenth-century: a comparative approach." *College Eng* 23 (May 1962): 646-48.

Proposes a course in comparative literature which would study not only English, but Spanish, French, and German novels as well. Sees *Lazarillo de Tormes* and *Don Quixote* as essential 17c background for appreciating of the picaresque novels of the 18c: Le Sage's *Gil Blas*, Fielding's *Joseph Andrews*; Smollett's *Roderick Random* and Voltaire's *Candide*. Then come the novels of feeling, or the sentimental novel: Prévost's *Manon Lescaut*, Richardson's *Clarissa*, Sterne's *Sentimental Journey*, and some side lines of the century: Diderot's *Rameau's Nephew*, Walpole's *The Castle of Otranto*.

352   DARWALL, Stephen. *The British moralists and the internal 'ought', 1640-1740*. Cambridge and New York: Cambridge UP, 1995; pp. 352.

Study of early British moral philosophy which aims to uncover the roots of *internalism* - the idea that the practical 'ought' must be based on the nature of the deliberating agent, as this developed in the thought of British philosophical writing from Hobbes to the appearance of Hume's *Treatise* in 1740. The idea was worked out in two distinct traditions. The empirical naturalist tradition (Hobbes, Locke, Cumberland, Hutcheson and Hume) argued that obligation is the practical force that empirical discoveries acquire in the process of deliberation. The other group (Cudworth, Shaftesbury, Butler, and in some moments Locke) viewed obligation as inconceivable without an autonomous will, and sought (well before Kant) to develop a theory of the will as self-determining, and to devise an account of obligation likened to that. Works cited (333-46). Index (347-52).

353 DAVIE, Donald. *Dissentient voice: Enlightenment and Christian dissent.* (U of Notre Dame Ward-Phillips Lectures in English Language and Literature [1980], 2.) Notre Dame, IN: Notre Dame UP, 1982; pp. ix, 154.
Study of English Nonconformity in the 18c taken exclusively from literature, esp. poetry. If the Enlightenment is to be understood as a triumph of the secular, infidel intelligence, then how can there be enlisted in its service a body of opinion and sentiment which is explicitly Christian: that heterogeneous body of Christian belief which because of developments peculiar to Anglo-American, gets itself called 'Dissent'? (23-24). Old Dissent must be seen serving as a vector of the Enlightenment.

354 DAVIS, David Brion. *The problem of slavery in western culture.* Ithaca: Cornell UP, 1966; pp. xiv, 505.

Historical survey of slavery, responses in medieval and early modern thought, the legitimizing of enslavement and rationalizations of it, the failure of Christianization, continuing contradictions. Part III is of particular interest in tracing the sources of anti-slavery thought in the Quakers and Sectarian Tradition, the role of 'the Man of Feeling' in the best of worlds, and the Enlightenment. Index (495-505).

355 DAVIS, J. C. *Utopia and the ideal society: a study of English utopian writing 1516-1700.* Cambridge: Cambridge UP, 1981; pp. x, 427.

Intensive study of the political thought of modern Utopias: definition of the ideal society, study of More and the European experience (1521-1619). Extensive bibliography (389-417).

356   DAVIS, Lennard J. A. "Studies in the origins of the English novel:
journalism, fiction and the law." Unpub. doct. diss., Columbia Univ.,
1976. [*DAI* 38 (1977): 276A.]

Seeks "to account for the origin of the English novel by tracing the
development of printed narrative in England from the time of Caxton
until the mid-eighteenth century". Shows how novelistic discourse was
transformed from the previous narrative discourse - whether that
narrative was factual or fictional.

357-----"A social history of fact and fiction: authorial disavowal in the early
English novel." In (pp. 120-48) SAID, Edward W. (ed.). *Literature and
society*. (English Institute Selected Papers, new ser. 3.) Baltimore, MD;
London: Johns Hopkins UP, 1980; pp. xiii, 202.

Patterns of affirmation of veracity and denial of authorship are
predictable features of early novels. This was to steer around the Puritan
sanction against non-didacticism, imaginative tales, and stories. The
author protected himself from charges of writing lies and falsehoods; it
was also part of a conventional humility. The period 1700-50 was crucial
in the separation of factual narratives from fictional ones. The revision
of the Stamp Act in 1724 finally struck a wedge between what was news
and what was fiction. Authors of English novels of the 17c and early
almost always begin their works with a preface asserting that they are
presenting not a fiction, but a factual account of some real series of
events. The author is in fact only the literary editor of someone else's
papers, journals, or oral history. Authors who denied their authorship and
insisted that their works were true, were attempting to make a statement
about the real difficulties of finding their place in the midst of a discourse
that was in the active process of rapture. As the news/novels discourse
grew into the specialized sub-discourse of journalism and fiction,
novelists saw themselves as part of a news-synthesizing and
disseminating system, but the works they were writing, for all their
recentness, immediacy, transcription, and preservation, could no longer
be seen as *news*. Extensive notes (146-48).

358-----"Wicked actions and feigned words: criminals, criminality, and the early
English novel." *YFS* 59 (1980): 106-18.

The view in the late 17c and early 18c was that novels were immoral,
criminal and dangerous because of their associations with popular culture
and the penchant for stories of pirates, whores, and pickpockets. Yet out
of the debate between wicked actions and moral ones, between feigned
words and factual accounts, between protest and repression, emerged the

troubling and profoundly criminal ambiguity that made novels both the 'official' genre of the middle classes and the illicit reading matter of idle people.

359-----*Factual fictions: the origins of the English novel.* New York and Guildford: Columbia UP, 1983; pp. 245.

Attempts to show that the novel has come into being as a form of defense against censorship, power and authority. This involves establishing a methodology of beginnings - and looking at the meaning of romance, news/novel, prose news, the law and the press, theories of fiction in early English novels, criminality and the language of print.

360-----"The fact of events and the event of facts: New World explorers and the early novels." *ECent* 32:3 (Autumn 1991) 240-55.

Certain proto-novelistic functions are seen in the attempts to write down the details of exploration and discovery. Certain discursive practices were operating, and grouping of practices occurred when later technological and material conditions created a necessity (fact and event, author, discovery, writing).

361 DAVIS, Natalie Zemon and FARGE, Arlette (eds). *A history of women in the West*: vol. 3 *Renaissance and Enlightenment paradoxes.* Cambridge, MS and London: The Belknap Press of Harvard UP, 1993; pp. x, 595.

Part of a 5-vol. coverage of the history of the West from antiquity to the present, investigating the place of women, the condition of women, women's roles and powers, how women acted, their words and silences. Looks at their many images: goddess, madonna, whore, witch. This is a rational history because the survey covers the whole of society, and by implication is necessarily a history of men too. Divided into 4 parts: 1) Works and Days; 2) So much is said about her; 3) Dissidences; 4) Women's voices, 19 essays in all. Notes (519-52). Bibliography (543-70). Contributors (571-74). Illus. credits (575-76). Index (577-95). Of particular interest to the 18c are the essays 8) Ambiguities of literature; 9) the Theater; 10) A shaping eighteenth-century philosophy; 12) From conversation to creation; 13) Female journalists.

362 DAVIS, Robert G. "The sense of the real in English fiction." *Comparative Lit* 3 (1951): 200-17.

The anti-chivalric Spanish picaresque novel, originating with *Lazarillo de Tormes*, pioneered a new form, with an individual discovering truths about a very unideal world. Surveys Nash, Cervantes, Bunyan, Behn and Defoe (who mingled history, journalism and fiction).

363 DAY, Geoffrey. *From fiction to the novel*. London; New York: Routledge & Kegan Paul, 1987; pp. vii, 223.

Critical survey through the late 17c and 18c of the shift in ideas from 'romance' to 'novel'. Each chapter is a frame for extensive quotations from some theoretical writing about fiction (Congreve, Beattie, Mrs Manley).

364 DAY, Robert Adams. *Told in letters*. Ann Arbor: Virginia UP, 1966; pp. 281.
Attempts to follow one track through a century-and-a-half of sub-literature. Of 1000 works of fiction which appeared between 1660 and 1740, 200 were epistolary fiction. This track, never entirely obliterated in the ballads of popular fiction, is the epistolary technique. Considers letters as ornaments, the importance of translations, 'familiar letters' and fiction, letter fiction, and the 'taste of the age', the arrival of epistolary fiction, before Richardson and after. Notes (212-36). Appendix A: Chronological list of English letter fiction (1660-1740) (237-58); B: Notes on Epistolary miscellanies (259-66) [203 titles]; C: A List of Letter Fiction in Periodicals [35 items] (267-70). Index (271-81).

365 DE BOLLA, Peter. *The discourse of the sublime: readings in history, aesthetics and the subject*. Oxford: Blackwells, 1989; pp. vii, 324.

Investigates the "autonomous subject, a conceptualization of human subjectivity based on the self-determination of the subject and perception of the uniqueness of every individual [...] the product of a set of discourses present to the period 1756-63, the period of the Seven Years' War" (6). Examines two powerful discourses: on debt and on the sublime which "generate the discursive milieu within which the autonomous subject becomes apparent". Bibliography (301-18). Index (319-24).

366 DE BRUYN, Frans. "Hooking the Leviathan: the eclipse of the heroic and the emergence of the sublime in eighteenth-century British literature." *ECent: T & I* 28:3 (Fall 1987): 195-215.

The 18c accorded epic and tragedy honored places, but is remembered rather for its satires and georgics, its novels, biographies and histories. The qualities and values of heroism are appropriated by the aesthetic theorist to define the experience of sublimity. 18c art turns to the sublime as a substitute for the heroic. Later the Romantic hero places himself beyond the role of society and rejects the value of its claims upon him. Like the 18c, it returns to the sublime as the defining quality of heroism, though it has become a finely understated response, asserting the absolute priority of the individual imagination, and hence the superiority of the artist as the heroic embodiment of cultural values.

367 DeRITTER, Jones. *The embodiment of characters: the representation of physical experience on stage and in print, 1728-1749* (New Cultural Studies.) Philadelphia: Pennsylvania UP, 1994; pp. xii, 172.

Examines the London stage of the 1730s and the English novel of the 1740s, exploring the representations of the human body and the attempts to enact or narrate certain physical experiences both on stage and in print during this period. Shows that the performance conventions and print narratives of this era shared a preoccupation with the relationship between certain kinds of physical experience and the processes by which individual human identities are constructed and transformed. Uses 'cultural materialism', which challenges traditional forms of literary interpretation and valuation by a type of enquiring that combines historical context, theoretical method, political commitment, and textual analysis. The shift from a post-feudal to a pre-capitalist social and economic system was accompanied by an equally disruptive shift in the way individuals conceived of themselves. Looks at the economic history of English literary production (1728-49) and the manner in which specific novelists were influenced by the drama of this era (references to Gay, Lillo, Charlotte Clarke, Richardson and Fielding). Notes (151-61). Bibliography (164-68). Index (169-72).

368 DE VOOGD, Peter J. "Recent trends in eighteenth-century studies." *DQR* 21 (1991): 71-81.

Review survey. There has been a marked increase in works that contextualize the field of 18c studies, revitalizing the history of ideas and reconstructing the social and psychological reality of the 18c, returning as they must to study of historical milieu and careful reading.

369 DHUICQ, Bernard. *Mémoire et création dans le monde anglo-américaine aux XVIIe et XVIIIe siècles.* Actes du Colloques ténu à Paris les 21 et 22 octobre 1983. [Strasbourg]: Université de Strasbourg II, [1985].

Various papers on the literary role of memory and the notion of creation and creativity in various aspects of Anglo-American life and literature on the 17c and 18c.

370   DIBELIUS, Wilhelm. *Englische Romankunst: die Technik des englischen Romans imachtzehnten und zu Anfang des neunzehnten Jahrhunderts.* (Palaestra 92, 98.) 2 vols. Berlin Mayer & Müller, 1910; pp. xv, 406; xi, 471.
Sustained survey of the history and novelistic practice of the 18c. The first volume has an introduction (1-28), laying out the premises and topics of investigation. Looks at epic and dramatic techniques, the theory of the novel: plan, construction, motivation, role devices, characters, the art of characterization, physical description, conduct of the action, objective and subjective reporting, forms of narration (autobiographical stories, letters etc.), satire and didaxis, pathos, comedy, humor, schemata of investigation, temporal and subject limitation. Ch.1 is devoted to Daniel Defoe (29-53). It examines the novel before Defoe in the briefest detail (31-33) (Lyly, Nashe) before considering Defoe's use of the adventure novel, character depiction, handling of plot, reporting, didaxis ("Es ist enge Puritanerdidaxis", 53).

371   DINGLEY, R. J. "A note on the historical sublime." *DUJ* 79:2 (June 1987): 249-56.
Sublimity both defines the nature of the viewer's response to a particular landscape or situation, and also conveys the latter's inherent property. That the concept could be employed in this dual sense had long been apparent. It is present in Longinus's seminal treatise, and when the term is extended by Addison and his successors to define certain categories of natural phenomena, critical attention is directed both to the physical characteristics of those phenomena, and to the reactions that those characteristics elicit.

372   DOCHERTY, Susan Denise. "Changing gender roles during the eighteenth century: defining the feminine in women's fiction and in Samuel Richardson's *Sir Charles Grandison.*" Unpub. doct. diss., Univ. of North Carolina at Chapel Hill, 1994. [*DA* 55 (1995): 2401A.]

At the end of the 17c women novelists consistently portrayed their female characters in what would later be considered non-traditional ways. These controversial characteristics of women would cause the work of these women to be marginalized. The dramatists Thomas Otway and Nicholas Rowe popularized a different image of femininity, the passive female. Richardson took up this passive female and placed her in the domestic world in both the sequel to *Pamela* and *Sir Charles Grandison*. These two texts prescribe, in conduct-book fashion, the proper behavior for women. In the characteristics of Harriet Byron in *Grandison*, Richardson achieves his ultimate model of the perfect middle-class housewife. Throughout this novel, he carefully delineates his definition of femininity, characterizing women as creatures confined by and to domestic space.

373 DOHERTY, Francis. *A study in eighteenth-century advertising methods: the Anodyne Necklace.* Lewiston and Lampeter: Edwin Mellen Press, 1992; pp. xiv, 464.

Shows the way in which the printed page and newspaper columns were manipulated by successful entrepreneurs in the 18c in order to promote and dignify quack medicines. Touches on topics in social history, the history of advertising techniques and promotional language. Of interest to students of 18c life and letters since it involves the plagiarisms of literary texts for advertising purposes (with literary texts occasionally borrowing back from advertising), taking writing intended for one's class and transforming it downwards for another market. Created a market through the powerful vehicle of relational deployment of language of the printed page and a whole battery of printing devices to catch the eye of the reading public. Looks at the venereal trade and its expansion, literature in the marketplace, exploiting the contemporary pamphlets, medicines and medical arts. Bibliography (447-56). Index (457-64).

374 DOLLERUP, Cay. "Heavenbound 1670-1783: some interplanetary voyages as precursors of science fiction." In (pp.573-86) LINDBLAT, Ishrat; LJUND, Magnus (eds). *Proceedings from the third Nordic Conference for English Studies, Hässelby, September 25-27, 1986.* (Stockholm Studies in English, 73-74.) Stockholm: Almquist & Wikell, 1987; pp. vii, 806.
Traces the precursors of science fiction from ancient philosophers (Plutarch), through Copernican astronomy and various works of the 17c (Francis Godwin, Cyrano de Bergerac), on to David Russell (1703), Swift, Samuel Blunt (1727) and later 18c works.

375 DONOGHUE, Emma. *Passions between women: British lesbian culture, 1668-1801.* London: Scarlet Press, 1993; New York: Harper Collins, 1995; pp. 314.

Lesbian history often has been impoverished by rigid divisions between friendship and sex, social acceptability and deviance, innocence and experience. Sets out to discuss the full range of representations of lesbian culture in Britain between 1668 and 1801 in a variety of discourses, from the poetic to the medical, from the libertine to the religious. Explores the range of meanings given to 'passion between women' in the late 17c and 18c British public. Looks at hermaphrodites, female husbands, the breeches part, a sincere and tender passion, the truest friends, seduction and sexual joy, communities. Notes (269-97). Select bibliography (298-308). Index (309).

376   DONOGHUE, Frank. *The fame machine: book reviewing and eighteenth-century literary careers.* Stanford, CA: Stanford UP, 1996; pp. viii, 213.

Literary production in the 18c existed in a kind of limbo between an age of substantial aristocratic support and the fully developed literary market of the 19c. Direct patronage of literary figures by the nobility failed to keep pace with a mushrooming population of writers, and this pattern reduced individual patronage. Its place was taken by a variety of other broader, more indirect forms of patronage, such as subscription and the open market. This transformation of the condition of literary production precipitated a crisis among aspiring authors: by the mid-18c they had neither a clear literary framework (such as affiliation with a patron once bestowed), nor a way to specify the relationship of one piece of writing to the next (since market demands so greatly influenced what they wrote). The most forceful steps taken towards making sense of these transformed conditions was by the periodical culture that increasingly came to dominate the literary scene. Excluding newspapers, there were more than 30 different periodicals published in London in 1745. By 1755 the number had increased to more than 50, and by 1765 to 75. Authorship became increasingly defined in popular criticism, and from 1750 literary careers were chiefly decided and made possible by reviewers.

377   DONOVAN, Josephine. "From avenger to victim: genealogy of a Renaissance novella." *TSWL* 15:2 (1996): 269-88.

See Ch. 4 under HAYWOOD , **1569**.

378   DONOVAN, Robert Alan. *Shaping vision: imagination in the English novel from Defoe to Dickens.* Ithaca, NY: Cornell UP, 1966; pp. viii, 272.

The inner form, or coherence that the novelist gives to his world, can describe the vision determining the structure of the 18c and early 19c novel. During this period when there was no highly developed theory or native tradition of the novel as a genre, the author's imagination supplied not only the content, but also the form of his work. If it is impossible to be sure whether a given work offers spurious history or real fiction, how is the critic to arrive at a rational judgement of it? Criticism must deal with the text that exists, and there must be an attempt to distinguish between novels as imaginative constructs and as autobiographies, histories or travel books. There must be perception of outer form, structure, and inner form. Presents a series of critiques arranged to give a representative and detailed view of the English novel's development from the 18c masters to those of the early and mid-19c (Defoe, Richardson, Fielding, Smollett, Sterne, Jane Austen, Scott, Thackeray and Dickens). Of esp. interest are ch. 2 "The Two Heroines of *Moll Flanders*" (21-46) and ch. 3 "The Problem of *Pamela*" (47-67). Speaking of *Moll Flanders,* he observes: "The novel's coherence is a product of its inner form which has succeeded in energizing and bracing up an otherwise limp and flaccid structure" (45).

379　DOODY, Margaret A. *The true story of the novel.* New Brunswick, NJ: Rutgers UP, 1996; pp. xx, 580.

Attempts to trace connections between the novels of Ancient Greece and Rome with modern fiction. Part One looks at the Ancient Novel, Part Two at the influence of the Ancient Novel, while Part Three investigates the tropes of the novel (breaking and entering; marshes, shores and muddy waters; tomb, cave and labyrinth; eros; *ekphrasis* [looking at the picture, dreams and food, the goddess]). The ancient novel is connected to the modern through a multitude of lines, through the work of the Middle Ages and the Renaissance when the surviving ancient and medieval texts became thoroughly absorbed in the bloodstream of our modern culture. Then the Enlightenment in the mid-18c created histories of fiction that cut off our view of that process. Ch. XI ("Novels in the Seventeenth Century: Histories of Fiction and Cultural Conflicts") (251-73) and Ch. XII ("The Eighteenth Century - and Beyond: The Rise of Realism, and Escape from It") (274-300) look at guiding the reader, the probable and the verisimilar, the rise of realism, realism and the foreign, escape from prescriptive realism, the survival of the novel). Bibliography (487-530). Index (555-80).

380　DOREE, C. J. "Desire with loathing strangely mixed: dreams and the English novel, 1700-1900." Unpub. doct. diss., Univ. of London, King's College, 1993. [*IT* 44:4 (1995): 1436.]

As the novel developed from 1700 to 1900, the symbolic language of the dream offered a valuable means of representing a character's inner life. Literary dreams are created to dramatize the dynamism and creative energy of the unconscious, to reveal the dangerous allure of the irrational, to expose hidden or forgotten truths within the personality, to explore taboo areas of secret, forbidden desire. Investigates the peculiar problems dreams offer to the many different genres of the novel. In the sentimental novel of the 18c, the dream reveals the dark unreason of the unconscious seething beneath the rationality of the Enlightenment.

381 DOUGHTY, Oswald. "Romanticism in eighteenth-century England." *EngS* 12 (1930): 41-44.

The 18c witnessed the beginnings and early stages of the romantic revival, which reached its culmination in the 19c. From realistic and romantic perspectives, the 18c has been subjected to close examination. There is a clearer comprehension of the variety and nature of many of the qualities of 18c art and life which combined with the great renaissance of the imagination to form the romantic revival.

382 DOWNIE, James Alan and CORNS, Thomas N. (eds). *Telling people what to think: early eighteenth-century periodicals from the 'Review' to the 'Rambler'*. London: Frank Cass, 1993; pp. 131.

The first quarter of the 18c saw the most sustained growth in newspaper and periodical publications in England. Collection of essays displaying a number of different approaches to reading 18c periodicals, what is of interest in the *Review, Tatler, Examiner, Spectator, Craftsman, Commonsense*, the *Rambler*. Bibliographic notes. Notes on contributors.

383 DOWNIE, James Alan. *To settle the succession of the state: literature and politics, 1678-1750*. (Context and Commentary.) Basingstoke: Macmillan; New York: St Martin's Press, 1994; pp. xii, 170.

In England there was a close correlation between literature and topical politics in the period between the Popish Plot and the Forty-Five Rebellion. In many works of the period, context is necessary if the reader is to understand what is going on, even at a basic level. This was the 'First Age of Party' when politics affected the church, the coffee house and the drawing room. The first political parties emerged in response to concerns about who should succeed Charles II. For the next 70 years, English politics was dominated to such an extent by the question of the succession that all other issues might be seen to be related to it. Looks at the Papist Plot, the Revolutionary Settlement, the rage of the party, public virtues, public vices, the opposition to Walpole, the 'Forty-Five'. Notes (157). Chronological Tables (158-61). Bibliography (162-65). Index (166-70).

384 DRUMMOND, Andrew L. "English non-conformity in fiction." *London Quart* 169 (1944): 310-25.

Until well into the 19c, 'the Nonconformist Conscience' was apt to relegate the reading of novels to the world, as unfit for the nourishment of awakened souls. Bunyan had written a pioneer novel in *The Life and*

Death of Mr Badman, Defoe moralized and theologized to suit the taste of his readers in *Robinson Crusoe* and other adventure stories, but the religious leader who might have encouraged the discriminate reading of novels, John Wesley, had little patience with them. All the novelists, like Defoe and Fielding, represent *natural* man in his goodness, in *instinctive* forms. All Nonconformity stands for goodness in *reflective* forms, forms that have a tendency to be self-conscious and can become Pharisaic, which is very odious to natural man, whose goodness is impulsive and instinctive.

385 DRURY, John. *Critics of the Bible 1724-1873*. Cambridge: Cambridge UP, 1989; pp. ix, 306.

English critics were brilliant initiators and exploiters of biblical criticism. The momentous exercise, whereby Scripture became the object of human critique independent of Church control, is illustrated by extracts from critics. The early 18c is covered by Anthony Collins (1724), Thomas Sherlock (1726) and Robert Lowth's influential lectures on the Psalms (1753) (69-102). Notes (193-99). Select bibliography (201-4).

386 DUCROCQ, Jean; HALAMI, Suzy and LÉVY, Maurice. *Roman et société en Angleterre au XVIIIe siècle*. (Le Monde Anglophone.) Vendome, Paris: Presses Universitaires de France, 1978; pp. 256.

Series of 16 essays exploring the novel and its relation to society in the 18c. Ch. 1 "Le monde contemporain: le temps de la confiance et des grandes expériences" (S. HALIMI) (9-28) puts the theme into perspective. Ch. 2 "Le 'petit' roman: les romancières" (S. HALIMI and J. DUCROCQ) (29-44) considers the novelists working at the same time as Defoe, and provides perspectives on Manley (40), Haywood (41), Davys (41-43). Ch. 3 "Des littérateurs populistes à Defoe" (J. DUCROCQ) (44-) situates Defoe in relation to his contemporaries and considers the place of *Robinson Crusoe*. Excellent chronology from 1688 to 1801, tabulated into political, economic, foreign policy, history of ideas, arts and literature (Europe, Great Britain, the novel) (232-47). Select bibliography (249-56).

387 DUDLEY, Edward; NOVAK, Maximillian. *The Wild Man within: an image in western thought from Renaissance to Romanticism*. Pittsburgh:Pittsburgh UP, 1972; pp. xi, 333.

Focuses on the importance of wildness and the Wild Man during a period of Western thought, which came to hold up ideals of culture and civilization as its finest accomplishment. However, the culture of the

Baroque and Rococo contained inner contradictions symbolized in the noble and ignoble savages who occur in the writings of this time. Index (321-33).

388   DUFF, Virginia M. "Woman and property, woman as property: woman, property, and law as imaged by British female novelists, 1680-1740." Unpub. doct. diss., Univ. of Colorado at Boulder, 1994. [*DA* 55 (1995): 3197-8A.]

Examines the discourse concerning women and property as it was conducted in novels by women and legal writings by men in Restoration and early 18c England, as 17c individualism challenged women's traditional roles in both public and private life. Perceptions about female nature, as well as ideas about women's property rights, underwent significant changes in the hundred years after the Civil War. Women pamphleteers publically proclaimed their dissatisfaction about domination and political oppression, females began to write novels which depicted and protested against women's lot. Male hegemony responded with material and ideological sanctions against women. Analyzes the life and works of seven women novelists: Aphra Behn, Jane Barker, Catherine Trotter, Mary Pix, Delarivière Manley, Mary Davys and Eliza Haywood. Discusses 15 novels written between 1643 and 1741. Also examines legal history from 1650 to Lord Hardwicke's Marriage Act (1753). Modifies and corrects traditional criticism of much recent feminist commentary that focuses on novels written after 1740. It was the mid-18c that males appropriated novel writing, and advanced sentimental ideology as the basis for novels for, by, and about women. Before 1740, the primary writers of the novel were female, and these females penned works about laws and customs relating to gender, marriage, divorce, adultery, rape, incest, child custody, and a myriad of property issues. The novel occupies a critical space in the discourse about women and property, and repeats a nexus from which modern ideas about these issues emanate.

389   DUFRENOY, Marie-Louise. *L'Orient romanesque en France, 1704-1789: bibliographie générale.* 2 vols. Montreal: Editions Beauchemins, 1947. I, 370; II, 502.

Large study of the role of the Orient in French thinking and literature during the 18c. Part I is divided into four sections, looking at the revelation of the Orient. Considers the 17c situation, the appearance of *Les Milles et une Nuits* and the *Mille et un Jours*, the development of Oriental fiction in France (1704-90). Part II investigates "L'Orient galant" ("histoires galantes et couleur orientale"), with special reference to Crébillon. Part III looks at Oriental satire, the imaginary voyage, Utopias and social criticism, with esp. reference to Voltaire. Part IV looks at the aspirations of the 18c and their expression in Oriental fiction, the Oriental historical novel, with reference to the followers of Fénelon, Melon and Benoit de Maillet. The Appendix provides valuable chronological lists of novels, according to their different oriental genres (342-70). Vol.II is entirely bibliographical, with lists of sources (37-88), chronological bibliography 1605-1799 of Oriental works (89-448), reference works (bibliographies and criticism, 19-20cc) (449-80).

390 DUKE, Kathleen Mary. "Women's education and the eighteenth-century British novel". Unpub. doct. diss., Univ. of Arkansas, 1980. [*DA* 41 (1980): 2119A.]

The 18c witnesses an extension of literacy to women at all levels of society, and by the century's end, the vast majority of women in the upper and middle classes were almost bound to receive some education. The whole question of the appropriate nature of women's education and its effects upon their lives and characters soon found its way into the novels of the period. The novel's treatment of learned, educated and accomplished women who find themselves outside the safe perimeters of their socially sanctioned role as daughters, wives and mothers, offer the 20c scholar a fascinating glimpse at the beginnings of the most fundamental of all the revolutions of the modern age - the vindication of the rights of women.

391 DUNLOP, J. C. *A history of prose fiction*. Rev. H.WILSON. 2 vols. Edinburgh: Longman, Hurst, Rees, Orme & Browne, 1814; pp. 504, 701.

Vol. II ch. 14 is entitled "Sketch of the Origin and Progress of the English Novel - Serious - Comic - Romantic - Conclusion".

392 DU SORBIER, Françoise. *Récits de gueuserie et biographies criminelles de Head à Defoe*. (Europäisches Hochschulschriften: ser. 14, Angelsächsische Sprache und Literatur, 117.) 2 vols. Frankfurt; New York: Lang, 1983; pp. vi, 896.

Two-volume critical history tracing the origins and development of vagabond stories and criminal biographies, how actual material is transformed into imaginative fiction. The first part is devoted to fiction and the chronicle, the second considers the emergence of fiction from various facts, the third the appearance of types of malefactor, the fourth the stories of Defoe.

393-----"Heurs et malheurs du roman anglais en France au XVIIIe siècle." In (pp. 119-31) ANON.(ed.). *Le continent européen et le monde anglo-américain aux XVIIe et XVIIIe siècles*. Rheims: Presses Universitaires de Reims for the Société d'Études Anglo-Américaine des XVIIe et XVIIIe siècles, 1987; pp. 140.

Account of the reception of the translations of English novels in 18c France (particularly Defoe and Richardson).

394   DUSSINGER, John A. *The discourse of the mind in eighteenth-century fiction*. (Studies in English Literature, 80.) The Hague: Mouton, 1974; pp. 215.
Study of the dialectal relationship between empiricism and the 'new species of writing' centered on the problem of knowledge. Readings from Richardson, Johnson, Goldsmith and Sterne attempt to account for the anxiety and ambivalence in the dynamics of representing the self in fiction. Selected Bibliography (207-12).

395-----"'The glory of motion': carriages and consciousness in the early novel." *SVEC* 263 (1989): 122-24.

Before Laurence Sterne, whose rendering of spatiality is a *tour de force* of subjective narrative, 18c fiction has nothing to match Jane Austen's fusion of the vehicle as object with the vehicle as state of consciousness. The dynamics of intimacy are curiously missing from Defoe and Richardson, despite the loneliness of their central characters. With the introduction in the 1740s of the turnpike system to preserve the roads and the lightweight steel-sprung post-chaise, the pleasures of English travel soon rivaled those of France.

396   DUTHY, Robin. "The investment file: first editions of 18th century English novels." *Connoisseur* 207 (1981): 132.

"The overall increase in value over the last ten years of the first editions of 18th-century English novels as represented by the better-known works of Richardson, Fielding, Sterne and Smollett is tentatively out at 180 per cent. This amounts, of course, to a fairly slow rate of growth in comparison to other sectors of the book market and to other alternative investments. The reason for its disappointing growth are not altogether clear [...]. Although at their best the English 18th-century novels were brilliantly funny and masterpieces of observation, the following for them has thinned out and they are seen more as amusing relics than relevant today. Investors should therefore go to livelier markets".

397 DUVAL, Gilles. "Existe-t-il des livrets de colportage du 18ème siècle?" *CCV* 9 (1988): 85-92.

Examines the role of 18c advertising at the fundamental level of door-to-door vending.

398 DYSON, A. E. *The crazy fabric: essay in irony.* London: Macmillan & Co. Ltd., 1965; pp. 233.

General examination of irony by investigation of selected texts. The 18c has Swift (the metamorphosis of irony), Fielding (satiric and comic irony), Sterne (the novelist as jester), Gibbon (discursive irony). Select Bibliography (225-28).

399 EARLE, Peter. *The making of the English Middle Classes: business, society and family life in London, 1660-1730.* London: Methuen, 1989; pp. xiii, 446.

General socio-economic survey of the period, divided into I. metropolitan economy and society, II. business life (apprenticeship, business, women and business), III. family and social life (marriage, household, civic life, expenditure and corruption, sickness and death), conclusions on the London middle class. Substantial bibliography (416-38).

400 EBIIKE, S. *A study of English novels in the eighteenth century.* Tokyo, 1950.
Abstract not available.

401 ECHERUO, Michael J. C. "The 'savage hero' in English literature of the Enlightenment." *English Studies in Africa* 15 (1972): 1-13.

Seeks to qualify some of the critical conclusions reached about the savage stereotype during the Enlightenment. The 18c, unlike the Elizabethan age, failed to achieve an effective literary representative of the savage hero because it was unable to accept the consequences of its own deep-seated imaginative attitudes.

402-----*The conditioned imagination from Shakespeare to Conrad: studies in exo-cultural stereotype.* London: Macmillan, 1978; pp. viii, 135.

Exploration of a stereotype is exploration of the character of an audience; with exo-cultural stereotypes there is no such identification. Because this type is expected to be motivated differently, it becomes impossible to assimilate him completely into the artist's culture, or write about him

other than as a type. Ch. 4 "The Exo-Cultural Hero of the
Enlightenment" (71-92) is a footnote to the history of the idea of the
'noble savage', with discussion of Defoe.

403 EDGAR, Pelham. *The art of the novel.* New York: Russell & Russell, 1933;
     pp. x, 493.

     Primary goal is "to present a systematic study of the structural evolution
     of the English novel". Begins with a discussion of the essentials: theme,
     drama and fiction, dialogue, narrative, description and analysis. The
     three men responsible for giving the novel "a strong impetus in the
     modern direction " were Defoe, Richardson and Fielding.

404 EDWARDS, Gavin. "Narrative, rites of passage and the early modern life
     cycle." *Trivium* 23 (Summer 1988): 115-26.

     Pre-19c English writing displays a "narrative idea of the moral life":
     anthropological rites of passage, ritualistic events like baptisms,
     marriages and funerals, are attempts to organize human existence into
     narrative shape. Added to these Christian rites of passage is another
     process which narrativizes life effectively: one in which young people
     normally spend the period of time between dependent childhood and
     independent married adulthood in other people's households, most
     commonly as servants or apprentices.

405 EKHTIAR, Rochelle Suzette. "Fictions of Enlightenment: the Oriental Tale
     in eighteenth-century England". Unpub. doct. diss., Brandeis Univ.,
     1985. [*DA* 46 (1985): 705A.]

     Examines Oriental fiction in England in the context of the European
     Enlightenment, focusing on politics, moral and social education. The
     genre shared numerous concerns with other 18c prose forms. Investigates
     the European image of the Orient, religious controversy, Freemasonry,
     academic Orientalism, travel literature, treatment of the Orient, authentic
     Oriental literature. Also examines the domestic Oriental narrative in
     relation to the broader literary scene, emphasizing its development as a
     response to special Enlightenment needs. Addison's use of tales to
     promote a new secular ideal had distinct political implications and set the
     tone for all the English fiction which followed. Lyttleton added an overt
     political dimension. The decline of the genre in the 1780s was caused by
     a combination of literary excesses and erosion of political Enlightenment.

406 ELLIS, Markman. *The politics of sensibility: race, gender and commerce
     in the sentimental novel.* (Cambridge Studies in Romanticism, 18.)

Cambridge and New York: Cambridge UP, 1996; pp. pp. xi, 264.

Sentimental fiction was noted for its liberal and humanitarian interests, as well as its predilection for refined feeling, for emphasizing emotion over reason, the private over the public sphere. It also consciously participated in some of the most keenly contested public controversies of the 18c, like the emerging anti-slavery opinion, discourse on the morality of commerce, and the movement for the reform of prostitutes. Investigates the significance of political material in fictional texts, and explores the way in which the novel took part in historical disputes, so illustrating that the sentimental novel was a political tool of considerable cultural significance. Bibliographic notes (222-58). Index (259-64).

407 ELISTRATOV, A. *Iz istorii angliskogo realisma.* Moscow, 1941.

In Russian. Provides a history of English realism.

408 ENGELL, James. *The creative imagination: Enlightenment to Romanticism.* Cambridge, MA; London: Harvard UP, 1981; pp. xix, 416.

The idea of the imagination, as understood in the Romantic period, and as we understand it today, was actually the creation of the 18c. During the 18c the effort to define - to create - an idea of the imagination, permitted and encouraged a critical survey of the entire creative process and of the history of literature and the arts. The creative imagination emerged as the central value of the late 18c and of Romanticism. Select bibliography (369-80). Notes (381-406). Index (407-16).

409-----*Forming the critical mind: Dryden to Coleridge.* Cambridge, MA: Harvard UP, 1989; pp. x, 322.

Explores critical ideas and concepts, especially in their development during the first explosive generation of critical thought from Dryden through Coleridge. During the 18c, many seekers after origins and originality - whether concerning language, the social contract, or aesthetic values - encountered immense frustration. But they made important discoveries and created new ideas and methods, many of which we inherit. There is a theoretical approach to language, genre, mythology, literary structure, poetic language, universal grammar, effect of composition on readers, the reaction between theory and practical criticism, and the function of literature in culture and society, all overarched by a sober consideration of the very limits of critical system and theory. Introduction "The Originating Force of Eighteenth-Century Criticism" (1-14). Notes (273-308). Index (309-22).

410   ENOMOTO, Futoshi. *Don Quixote no kage no moto ni: 18 seiki igirisu shosetsu no shoso*. Tokoyo: Chukyo Shuppan, 1981; pp. 306.

In Japanese. Aspects of the 18c novel under the shadow of *Don Quixote*.

411   ERIKSON, Robert A. *Mother Midnight: birth, sex, and fate in eighteenth-century fiction (Defoe, Richardson, Sterne)*. New York: AMS Press Inc., 1986; pp. xiv, 326.

Study of the role of 'fate' in English fiction, esp. as presented in four 18c novels, Defoe's *Moll Flanders* (1722), Richardson's *Pamela* (1740) and *Clarissa* (1747-48), and Sterne's *Tristram Shandy* (1759-67), and as experienced in the context of 17c and 18c representations and discussions of the midwife, the witch, the 'cunning woman', the bawd, and the traditional figure of fate as spinner and mover of men and women. Fate up to and during the 18c is presented purely under the dual aspect of language, spoken and written, and the procreation and termination of human life. Fate has to do with death, limitation, closure. Mother Midnight is an icon of the 17c and 18c, a dark, multifaceted literary figure, a term for midwife or bawd, or both, who exerts a profound influence on what happens to the characters in the chosen novels. Covers the period 1660 to 1760 in England, from the development of important books on midwifery by Sharp, Sermon and Wolveridge, to the publication of *Tristram*. The period 1720 to 1750, owing to the effects of an influenza epidemic, violence and the consumption of gin, was the 'age of mortality' in England, with only one in four children in London surviving. Besides social history, this is concerned with an odd assortment of things and activities: characters, names, strings, threads, clothes, houses, wombs, wallets, books, windings and turnings, midwives, thieves, bawds, and whores. Notes (261-93). Select bibliography: primary sources (294-308) and secondary sources (309-16). Index (317-26).

412-----*The language of the heart, 1600-1750*. Philadelphia: U of Pennsylvania P, 1997; pp. xxii, 273.

Studies the evolving depiction of the human heart in English narrative and culture (1600-mid 18c). Provides a map of the heart from the Greeks to the early modern period. Discusses the representation of the heart in the Authorized Version of the Bible, then traces the development of the rhetoric of the heart in four important narrative texts, each of which has something new and distinctive to say about the human heart in relation to language, gender, and the sexual body. Considers works by William Harvey (*The Motion of the Heart and Blood*, 1628), John Milton

(*Paradise Lost*, 1667), Aphra Behn (*Oroonoko*, 1688), and Samuel Richardson (*Clarissa*, 1747-49). These four narratives exemplify a movement from a strongly masculinist heroic version of the heart in Harvey, to the more feminist heroic narrative in Richardson. This is done via Milton's presentation of Satan's attack on Eve in *Paradise Lost*, and Aphra Behn's erotic-heroic figuring of the male and female heart in her fiction and poetry. Notes (229-54). Works cited (255-66). Index (267-73).

413 EVANS, William E. "New enlightenment on the eighteenth-century novel?" *CEACrit* 33:2 (1976): 37-40.

Review article of nine books over a period of 25 years, which have brought a wealth of criticism on the 18c novel. Devoted mainly to Defoe, Fielding, Richardson, Goldsmith, Austen and general background.

414 FAIRCHILD, Hoxie Neal. *The noble savage: a study in Romantic naturalism*. New York: Columbia UP, 1928; pp. 535.

Traces the convention of the Noble Savage and the Golden Age from Biblical and Classical origins, through voyages of discovery, to Montaigne and Rousseau. Ch.2 "The Noble Savage in the Pseudo-Classical Period" deals with the late 17c/early 18c, and particularly with Defoe.

415 FAUCHERY, Pierre. *La destinée féminine dans le roman européen du dix-huitième siècle 1713-1807, essai de gynécomythie romanesque*. Paris: Librairie Armand Colin, 1972; pp. 895.

The first part ("Le Massif Narratif", 25-511) presents the background to women and fiction, looking at the novel and history, mythology and truth, the fable of the young girl, family, education, offering, sacrifice, marriage and the free woman. The second part ("Itinéraires de Mythes" [512-830]) discusses the masculine-feminine polarity, efforts at unity, fluctuations in the feminine self, the woman and space, time, and the matter of destiny. The very substantial bibliography is divided into: 1) "Ouvrages de Référence" (861-62); 2) "Textes Étudiés" (French, 862-66; English, 866-68; German, 869-71; other comparative writing, 871-74]); 3) "Études": a) "Études littéraires" (French, 874-75; English 875-76; German 877-78); b) "Études historiques" (878-79); c) "Ouvrages divers" (879-80). Index of Proper Names and Works (88-95).

416 FENDLER, Susanne (ed.). *Feminist contributions to the literary canon: setting standards of taste*. (Women's Studies, 15.) Lewiston, NY and Lampeter: Edwin Mellen Press, 1997. pp. 179.

See Ch. 4 under AUBIN, **1125**.

417 FERGUSON, Frances. "Rape and the rise of the novel." *Representations* 20 (1987): 88-112.

Richardson's *Clarissa* is psychological, not because it is about the plausibility of its characters, but because it insists upon the importance of psychology as the ongoing possibility of a contradiction between what one must mean, and what one wants to mean.

418 FERGUSON, Moira. *Subject to others: British women writers and colonial slavery, 1670-1834.* New York; London: Routledge, 1992; pp. xiii, 465.

Argues that anti-slavery protest in prose and poetry by Anglo-Saxon female authors contributed to the development of feminism over a 200-year period. Their anxieties about their own powerlessness and inferiority were displaced into representations of slaves even though their texts misrepresent the very Afro-Caribbean slaves whose freedom they advocated. The condition of white middle-class women's lives, their conscious and unconscious sense of themselves as inferior, set the tone of the anti-slavery debate. Investigates the various phases of this debate, looking at: colonial slavery and protest; the birth of a paradigm in Behn's *Oroonoko*; 17c Quaker women (displacement, colonialism, anti-slavery sentiments); "Inkle and Yoriko" (an anti-slavery reading); sentiment and amelioration; emerging reluctance; the Parliamentary campaign; the radical impulse before and after the French Revolution; reaction to the rebellion in San Domingo (sentiment, suicide and patriotism); women in the provinces and across the Irish Sea; extending discourse, and changing definitions. Extensive notes (299-308). Select Bibliography (383-446). Index (447-65).

419 FIGES, Eva. *Sex and subterfuge: women novelists to 1850.* London: Macmillan & Co. Ltd., 1982; pp. 178.

Throughout the 18c, women had been writing popular novels, largely for the consumption of other women. During the last decades of the 18c a change took place: women began to write novels with a skill and authority which commanded general respect, and over the next 50 years they colonized the medium, and made it their own. Ch.1 "Background for Change" provides a study of the 18c scene, to provide the appropriate context for understanding why the quantity and quality of fiction by women increased so significantly towards the end of the 18c.

420 FLANDERS, Wallace Austin. *Structures of experience: history, society, and*

personal life in the eighteenth-century British novel. Columbia: South
Carolina UP, 1984; pp. x, 308.

Investigates the relationship between personal experience and the act of
writing which underlay the emergence of the novel as an important
literary form in 18c England, centering mainly on works of Defoe,
Richardson, Fielding, Smollett and Sterne, looking at form and language,
family, the experience of women, deviancy and crime, urban life.
Bibliographic notes for each chapter. Index.

421 FLETCHER, Anthony. *Gender, sex and subordination in England, 1500-
1800.* New Haven and London: Yale UP, 1995; pp. xxii, 442.

In the 200 years separating *Much Ado About Nothing* and *Emma*, the
relation of the sexes to each other changes dramatically. Patriarchy, the
institutionalized male dominance over women and children in the family,
and the subordination of women in society in general, was an outstanding
feature of English society in this time. This feature has been shaped and
reshaped during the long history of Western Christendom, as men have
grappled with the effective exercise of social and political power. The
structures of domination have never been inert, but have always been
adaptable and adjustable. In Tudor England gender was a cosmological
principle founded upon God's direction (biblical teaching required the
subordination of women), and women's natural physical inferiority.
There was a crucial link between the weakness of mind and conscience
which caused the first emblematic act of disobedience, and the weakness
of the body which connects to the reproductive functions, defined and
assigned women a constant public role. With the huge epistemological
shift associated with the beginnings of the 17c and with Descartes and
Newton, with the philosophical world view that has come to be called
modern, men were bound to see that women could be investigated,
designated, and thus more effectively constructed. The English Civil War
and its aftermath was far from simply a political crisis. It shook the
confidence of Englishmen and their control of the social and gender
order to its roots. The year 1660 marks a massive backlash against
change which had lasting political religious and social connotations. The
outcome was the triumph of the gentry, who by 1700 had established a
sense of class identity, based upon a set of distinct cultural and
intellectual occupations which differentiated them from the multitude.
Class consciousness became the very essence of their way of life, and it
was always gendered, taking its strength from an increasingly rigid and
elaborate scheme of gender construction by which they marked
themselves off from the masses. The rules were laid down between 1660
and 1800 in a burgeoning prescriptive literature directed at men and

women, but more specifically at women, in the upper and middling rank. Once men saw women as distinct beings, a transformation in the value of patriarchy, based upon a new reading of gender, became possible. The distinct male and female honor codes were questioned between 1660 and 1800, with the fraction of an ideological construction of gender which broke with simple didacticism of preceding years to create masculinity and femininity in something like a modern sense. Illus. (40 plates). Bibliography (414-33). Index (432-42).

422   FLETCHER, Constance Mary. "The eighteenth-century criminal in law and literature." Unpub. doct. diss., Northwestern Univ., 1975. [*DA*   36 (1976): 4506A.]

Examines the relationship between 18c criminals, law, and crime fiction, demonstrating the many connections between public attitudes to crime and those framed in law. The 18c inherited a "Bloody Code" for dealing with crime, but during the Hanoverian period it became so severe that by the end of the century many judges and juries refused to implement them. Acquittal became more common. The novel as a new and revolutionary literary form was used as a forum to debate this public issue. Defoe's essays for Mist & Applebie's weekly journals provide accurate records of increasing public interest in crime and criminals, but Moll Flanders and Colonel Jack gave a much fuller notion of the problem because Defoe put them in a complete and recognizable social milieu. The same is true of Fielding and Smollett as novelists.

423   FLINT, Christopher. "Disrupted legacies: family structure and narrative form in the eighteenth-century novel." Unpub. doct. diss., Pennsylvania, 1988. [*DAI* 50:1 (1989) 145A-146A.]

Examines the correspondence between the development of the novel in the 18c and the historical emergence of the modern nuclear family. Traces how the gradual intensification of family structure conditions narrative strategy in the works of English novelists from Defoe to Sterne, and investigates how these novels deliver and subvert myths about the privacy of family and the autonomy of individual experience. Disrupted relations manifest not only contradictions between traditional values and the disruptive values of individuals, but also modifications of existing ideologies by new ideological pressures. Examines three stages: 1) Defoe (*Robinson Crusoe*) treats family relations in a dismissive manner in order to glorify individual autonomy; 2) Richardson and Fielding use the novel to scrutinize psychological, social and political consequences of kinship; 3) later in the century, in Sterne and Wollstonecraft there is a darker vision when external factors disrupt the comfortable world of the family, threatening to undo it, or turning it into a force for repression.

424   FLÜGEL, John Clark. *The psychology of clothes.* (The International Psycho-Analytical, 18.)   London: The Hogarth Press, 1930; pp. 257.

Investigates the psychological implications of clothes used as protections, for modesty and decoration, looking at motives, individual and sexual differences, types of dress, the forces and vicissitudes, the evolution of garments, the ethics of dress (art and nature, the rationalization of fashion), the future of dress. Bibliography (106 items) (239-42). Index (243-57). Illus. (21 plates).

425 FLYNN, S. "The Scriblerus Club and the interaction of politics and literature 1710-1714." Unpub. doct. diss., Univ. of Wales, Aberystwyth, 1995. [*IT* 46 (1997): 262.]

The Scriblerus Club is viewed as a retreat from party politics into literary sociableness. However, the club was subject to politicization from both within, because of its membership, and from without, through public perception of its political allegiance. During the early 18c, a shift in the balance of power within the state from the traditional landed aristocratic to the expanding commercial and middle classes took place. This fostered an ideal of social openness which encouraged social mobility and was disseminated through the periodical writers, John Addison and Richard Steele. Scriblerian satire is a rejection of the ideology of social openness worked out through attack on the methodology of periodical writers and through attack on their target readership.

426   FOLEY, Barbara. "History, fiction, and the ground between: the uses of the documentary mode in black literature." *PMLA* 95 (1980): 389-403.

Black literature offers a broad and diverse range of materials for examining mimesis in its different modes. Because much black literature from the outset, rather like the early novel, has been challenged in its veracity, its practitioners have resorted to a diverse set of techniques for conveying their visions of historical reality and potentiality. Many writers in this tradition have effectively grounded their work in autobiographical and historical modes.

427   FOLKENFLIK, Robert (ed.). *The English hero, 1660-1800.* Newark: Delaware UP; London; Toronto: Assoc. UPs, 1982; pp. 230.
Collection of essays surveying the topic of the hero. Of particular usefulness for the general period are the chapters "England 1660-1800: an Age without a Hero" and "Concepts of the Hero in Comic Drama,

1660-1710".

428   FORD, Boris (ed.). *New Pelican guide to English literature*, Vol. 4: *From Dryden to Johnson*. Harmondsworth: Penguin, 1982. Revised and expanded from first ed. 1957; pp. 527.

Useful for Part I "Social Setting" and Part II "The Literary Scene". Defoe is given a chapter to himself: Ian WATT, "Defoe as novelist" (203-16). Other novelists are discussed by Frank BRADBROOK, Samuel Richardson" (293-312); and A. R. HUMPHREYS, "Fielding and Richardson" (313-32). An Appendix contains "For Further Reading and Reference" (445-63), a bibliography of "Authors and Works " (464-99). Index (500-10).

429   FORD, F. M. *The English novel from the earliest days to the death of Conrad*. London: Constable, 1930; pp. 148.

Ch. 2 "Towards Defoe" includes discussion of *Don Quixote* and *Guzman d'Alfarache* before moving on to Bunyan and Defoe.

430   FORSTER, E. M. *Aspects of the novel*. (Clark Lectures, 1927.) Ed. Oliver STALLYBRASS. Harmondsworth: Penguin Books, 1964, 2000.

Discussion of fiction by story, people, plot, poetry, prophecy, pattern and rhythm, conclusion. Of pertinence to the early novel is Appendix A "Extracts from Forster's Commonplace Book" which discusses Defoe's fiction briefly and negatively (163-64). "Crusoe's island differs from Prospero's because there are no real savages in it, and not a glimmer of primitive religion, and this gulf is connected with an imaginative gulf".

431   FOSS, Michael. *Man of wit to man of business: the arts and changing patronage, 1660-1750*. London: BCP, 1988; pp. 234.

Offers a social history of the arts in England in the century following the Restoration, describing the dispensers of patronage, the Royal Court, the great lords of the revolutionary period, businessmen, lawyers and county gentry. The state of the arts fluctuated with the waning influence of the king and the court, the rise of political parties, a new sense of middle-class decorum, and responsibility. Bibliography. Notes. Index.

432   FOSTER, James Otis. "Puritanism, character and narrative in the eighteenth-century novel." Unpub. doct. diss., Univ. of Virginia, 1986. [*DA* 47 (1986): 1733A.]

Puritan personal literature of the 17c often concentrates on the experiential psychology of the individual in order to reveal the fragmentation of identity, a dislocation of the self from value, order and stability. Certain writers of the 18c - Defoe, Richardson, Godwin - transform this paradigmatic Puritan psychology (exemplified in Bunyan's *Grace Abounding*) into fictional presentations of divided characters who strive against their own natures for unity in a fallen world wherein unity is unavailable. The principal mode of character development in this Puritan tradition in fiction, as in the previous autobiographical literature, is accretion, the accumulation of behavior, traits and impulses, as well as the dialectic conflict between self and society.

433 FOSTER, J. R. *History of the pre-romantic novel in England.* (Monograph Series, 17.) New York: Modern Language Association, 1949; rpt. New York; Kraus, 1966. p. 282.

Gives an account of the pre-Romantic narrative which appeared in England during the 18c, and describes the French novels influencing them. Ch. 1 "Sensibility and Deism" and Ch. 2 "Sentiment from Aphra Behn to Marivaux" includes discussion of Behn, Manley, Haywood and D'Aulnoy. Select Bibliography (277-82).

434 FOWLER, Alistair. *A history of English literature: forms and kinds from the Middle Ages to the present.* Cambridge, MA: Harvard UP; Oxford: Basil Blackwell, 1987; pp. x, 409.

Discusses the early novel in ch. 8 "Later Classicism and the Enlightenment" (170-98), in the subsection "New Types of the Novel" (189-98), which devotes pre-1740 space only to Defoe (189-98), commenting on his documentary reality, achieved " [...] by a plain style concentrating on unsensuous factual denotations [...]. Defoe imagines Crusoe's predicament so vividly that he makes involvement easy".

435 FOX, Christopher. *Locke and the Scriblerians: identity and consciousness in early eighteenth-century Britain.* Berkeley: California UP, 1988; pp. x, 174.

"'There has been very great Reason on several Accounts,' *The Spectator* tells us in 1714, 'for the learned World to endeavor at settling what it was that might be said to compose, *personal identity*'" (1). Aims to examine what the Scriblerians called "the great noise" over "this Identity"- the extensive early 18c controversy over personal identity. The second is to show how this same controversy provides a meaningful context for the Scriblerians' own masterful satire of learning, *The Memoirs of Scriblerus*.

They echo the same common concern, voiced by Butler and Berkeley and confirmed by Hume, that something significant was happening to the traditional concept of the self. Detailed bibliographical notes (131-61). Index (163-74).

436   FOXON, D. F. *Libertine literature in England, 1660-1745*. London: The Book Collector, 1965; pp. 63.

Account of the publication of prose pornography in England between 1660 and 1745, and the legal proceedings against obscene books: Aretine, Nicholas Chorier, John Cleland.

436a   FRANK, Judith. *Common ground: eighteenth-century English satiric fiction and the poor*. Stanford, CA: Stanford UP, 1997; pp. xi, 230.

Reads four 18c satiric novels "from below", exploring the ways in which the 18c poor shapes them, both thematically and formally. Work on the satire and fiction of the period has tended to focus on the transition from patrician culture to a culture dominated by the logic of the market. The story of the rise of capitalism is usually one of the middle class struggling to define itself in opposition to the aristocracy, and the poor function as a figure or allegory for the emergent middle class. Deals with the social and cultural upheavals attendant upon the development of a capitalist economy (Fielding, Sterne, Smollett and Burnes). Notes (187-212). Bibliography (213-22). Index (223-30).

437   FRIEDMANN, Edward H. *The antiheroine's voice: narrative discourse and the transformations of the picara*. Columbia: U of Missouri P, 1987; pp. xvii, 261.
Examines "a process of enunciation in narrative fiction, looking at the Spanish picaresque novel which builds on the literary tradition and the culture of the norm as it explores the bases of communication and of alienation" (xi). The feminine variations of the picaresque extended the illusion and control. Lowering the status of the speaker heightens irony and increases the distance between desire and fulfilment. The picaresque novel develops a vision of the world from below by a narrator unlike the reader. In the female variations, the complexity of the sign and the dubious authority of the picaresque narrator turn the union of author and society against the individual in an uneven battle of the sexes. Introduction, models of picaresque discourse, variations (the Spanish feminine picaresque), transformations, enlightened narrator (*Moll Flanders*), the obliging narrator (*Tristana*), the enlightened narrator (*Masta no verte Jesús mio*), the mythic narrator (*Teresa Batista*), the precocious narrator (*Fanny*). Notes (229-52). Selected bibliography (253-

58) Index (259-61).

438 FRITZ, Paul Samuel and MORTON, Richard (eds). *Women in the eighteenth century and other essays.* (Pbns of the McMaster Univ. Assoc. for Eighteenth-Century Studies, 4.) Toronto: Hakkert; Sarasota, FL: Samuel Stevens, 1976; pp. x, 343, 31 plates.

Collection of 16 papers presented to the McMaster Association for Eighteenth-Century Studies, among them: Katherine ROGERS, "The Feminism of Daniel Defoe" (3-14), F. P. LOCK, "Astraea's Vacant Throne: The Successors of Aphra Behn" (14-24), M. J. BENKOWITZ, "Some Observations on Women's Concept of Self in the 18th Century" (25-36), Robert HALSBAND, "Women and Literature in 18th-Century England" (37-54), Jean E. HUNTER, "The 18th-Century Englishwoman: According to the *Gentleman's Magazine*" (55-72), Arthur M. WILSON, "'Treated like Imbecile Children' (Diderot): The Enlightenment and the Status of Women" (73-88).

439 FROHLOCK, Richard Randall, III. "Eyes on the New World: imagining the English colony in the early Enlightenment." Unpub. doct. diss., Univ. of California (Santa Barbara), 1996. [*DA* 57 (1997): 3946-7A.]

Drawing on political, scientific and literary writings, investigates the English Enlightenment reformulations of the principles of New World appropriations. Relates cultural shifts in religion, politics and science to changes in writing about the Americas. Ch. 4 "Daniel Defoe and the Novel New World" traces in Defoe's New World fiction the argument that the New World offers possibilities of improving not only the land, but also the self and the characters of others.

440 FUCHS, Michel (introd.). "Violence(s) au siècle de la raison." *Cycnos* 6 (1990): 113pp.

Ten essays exploring the notion of violence in the Age of Reason. Considers the battle of the books and the birth of the novel; violence made into a title; tragedy and melodrama or the refusal of violence; patriotism and rebellion in Ireland; Irish reactions to English domination; violence, reason and argument; aspects of William Paleys social views; reasons for contentment addressed to the laboring part of the British public; divided selves or psychiatric violence (hysteria); final solutions, modest proposals and shortest ways. Several extended sets of references.

441 FUNGAROLI, Carole Susan. "Landscapes of life: dreams in eighteenth-

century British fiction and contemporary dream theory." Unpub. doct. diss., Univ. of Virginia, 1994. [*DA* 55 (1995): 3198A.]

Addresses the broad idea of dreaming in 18c British intellectual thought, specifically discussing the interrelationship between the idea of dreaming and representations of dreaming in British 18c fiction. Provides classical backgrounds and influential 17c dream discussions, then presents dreams either as medical and physiological phenomena, as psysiological and even precognitive events, or as a combination of these (Defoe, Richardson, Smollett, Fielding, Burney, Radcliffe, Lewis). Novelists create reasons with their fictions for the dreams that arise, supporting every literary vision with events leading up to the dream. Dreams tell the truth and they guide the reader to a deeper understanding of the characters in these complex works.

442   FÜRST, Rudolf. *Die Vorläufer der modernen Novelle im 18. Jahrhundert: ein Beitrag zur vergleichenden Literaturgeschichte.* Halle: Max Niemeyer: 1897; pp. 240.

Divided into 1) Entstehung, 2) das Übernatürliche, 3) die moralische Erzählung, 4) Revolution und Realismus. Ch. 1 (14-23) deals with the situation in England, looking at Chaucer and the English narrative, romance and novel, Italian influences, *Euphues*, narratives of life and pamphlets, short renaissance and chivalric tales, the freedom of the English stage, the novella of the present, learned society, the fourth estate and Aphra Behn, new materials, the triumph of subjects from everyday life, 'Characters', diaries and friendly letters, moralizing weekly articles, the coherence of characters, realism and Defoe, new realism and the decline of the stage, Richardson. Part II ch. 4 (95-101) traces the origins of the supernatural, linking it to French influences and the emergence of the Oriental tale before turning to the Gothic novel and the later 18c history of the novel. Notes (217-34). Index (234-40).

443   FURST, Lilian R. *Fictions of Romantic irony in European narrative 1760-1857.* Cambridge, MA: Harvard UP, 1984; pp. 276.

Attempts to come to grips with irony in order to understand modern literature. While the emphasis is on the late 18c, Ch.1 "Beware of Irony" (1-21) discusses the subject generally, and traces its use throughout the 18c. Selected Bibliography (261-71).

444   GAGEN, Jean Elizabeth. *The new woman: her emergence in English drama, 1660-1700.* New York: Twayne, 1954; pp. 193.

The belief that woman is a subordinate being with the proper sphere of husband, home and children, was entrenched in the 17c. But heterodox notions began to shake some of these assumptions. The new woman emerged into English drama during the 17c and early 18c with surprising vitality. The frequency with which the drama mirrored contemporary social modes made it inevitable that it should reflect the change in the status of women. This has an important implication for the depiction of women in the fiction of the time as several women playwrights were also novelists (esp. Behn and Manley).

445 GALBRAITH, Lois Hall. *The established clergy as depicted in English prose fiction from 1740-1800.* Doct. diss., Univ. of Pennsylvania. Philadelphia: n.p., 1950; pp. xiv, 126.

In the 18c, novelists portrayed with considerable variety and scope what historians have tended to minimize: the lower clergy, that is parish priests and their curates, with whom people were directly in touch. The study commences with *Pamela*, the piece of fiction with which the English novel may said to have reached its maturity, and continues through the novels of the century. It includes Jane Austen, whose clerical characters bear an unmistakable 18c hallmark. Considers at length all apparently firsthand representatives of the clergy by lesser writers, as well as the fictional clergymen in all the novels of the period. Valuable bibliography (120-6).

446 GALLAGHER, Catherine. *Nobody's story: the vanishing acts of women writers in the marketplace, 1670-1820.* (New Historicism, 31.) Berkeley and London: California UP, 1994; pp. xxiv, 339.

The appearance of female authorship in the late 17c and 18c coincided with the appearance of a literary marketplace. Many women writers emphasized their femininity to gain financial advantage and in the process invented and popularized numerous ingenious similarities between their gender and their occupation. Far from divulging renumerative authorship, they relentlessly embraced and feminized it, and emphasized their trials and triumphs in the marketplace. Women writers integrated the cloying concept of woman into their authorial persona, and connected it to the language of marketplace exchange. Prevalent notions of authorship were allied in the process. Looks at the prostitute and the playwright (1-48) and the 'blackness of representation' (49-87) in Aphra Behn, political crimes and fictional albis in Delarivière Manley (88-144), fiction, gender and authorial property in Charlotte Lennox, Frances Burney's universal obligation, and Maria Edgeworth's productive fiction. Index (329-39).

447   GARBER, Frederick. *The autonomy of the self from Richardson to Huysmans.* Princeton, NJ and Guildford: Princeton UP, 1982. pp 326.

The dialectic of aloofness and association runs through this book. One term of the dialectic is a hunger for autonomy, so pervasive and passionate that it has to be seen as one of the defining features of the age. What is this self-suffering like? How can I make it real? Can I bring it about? Explores a series of images of desire: what is desired, and the desiring self. The period from Richardson to Huymans is remarkably of a piece in its quest for such images. The alternative to autonomy was a submission of self, which to many was as good as its death. Charts the aspects of self-making. Bibliographical notes (297-322). Index (323-6).

448   GARCIA-TORTOSA, Francisco. "La novela inglesa del 18: sus componentes linguisticos." *Estudios sobre los géneros literarios, I* in *Acta Salamanticensia (Universidad de Salamanca)* 89 (1975): 161-72.

In Spanish. Investigates the eighteenth-century novel in its linguistic components. "Se afirma con frecuencia que la burguesía inglesa del Dieciocho es eminentemente emprendedora y dinámica, busca nuevos mercados, nuevas formas de expresión y nuevas ideas que permitan la expansíon del individuo: nuevos caminos para su indentificacíon" (170-71).

449   GARMON, Gerald M. *Tragic realism in English literature: 1720-1820.* (English Language & Literature 72.) New York: Peter Lang, 1988; pp. viii, 227.

Tries to define a concept called tragic realism, and traces the development of realism in tragic literature from 1720-1820, its formative period. Realism is a literary method which assumes a philosophical and political attitude, as well as a particular kind of subject matter. The realist is concerned with seeking out the threshold which is verified by observation and with discernible consequences. Because of his interest in specific things of everyday existence, the realist tends to center his attitudes on the individual. These become representative, but not types. Looks at literature before the 18c, seeks to define tragic realism, provides a general 18c background, and criteria for the selection of works considered. Looks at the drama, the novel and narrative poetry, with principal attention given to drama. Bibliography (215-24). Index (225-27).

450   GASCOIGNE, John. *Cambridge in the Age of Enlightenment: science, religion and politics from the Restoration to the French Revolution.*

Cambridge: Cambridge UP, 1989; pp. xii, 358.

Describes the period following the Restoration (1660 to 1768): religion and reaction in Cambridge, the Latitude-Men and the 'new philosophy', the creation and consolidation of Whig Cambridge and the establishment of Newtonian natural philosophy. From 1769 to 1800 there was an eclipse of Whig Cambridge and a revival of revealed theology, with mathematics ascendant.

451 GEORGIA, Jennifer Claire. "Polite literature: conduct books and the novel in eighteenth-century England." Unpub. doct. diss., Harvard Univ., 1994. [*DA* 55 (1995): 2402A.]

The 18c manners book is an almost unexplored genre occupying a slippery area between fact and fiction, the real and the ideal, cynicism and sermon. It partakes of genres as disparate as pietistical tract, essay, epistolary guide, periodical character, and the novel, and emerges as a unique genre. Uses a multidisciplinary approach to construct a new theory of the conduct book as a literary text, using ethical theory, gender theory, feminist theory and semiotics. It then applies this theory to the conduct book and to the emerging novel. Why was the 18c so interested in politeness? What social forces gave rise to both conduct books and novels? Examines the rhetorical similarities between the two genres, how conduct books grew out of courtesy books, how etiquette can be examined as language and related to ethics, what effects it had on gender relations, how these issues are explored in the novels of the time. Manners bring personal and social cultures into a dynamic relationship at the core of the 18c novel.

452 GEORGULIS, Christine. "'This is a true story': fiction disguised as fact in the prefaces of late seventeenth and eighteenth-century French and English prose works." Unpub. doct. diss., City Univ. of New York, 1989. [*DAI* 50:5 (1989): 1299A.]

Prefatory assertions of truth introduce many late 17c and early 18c French and English works of literary invention. Whether or not any of these works were realistically documented, the assertion of truth in the prefaces, by its inherent attractiveness, suffices initially to instil belief.

453 GERARD, Kent and HEKMA, Gert (eds). *The pursuit of sodomy: male homosexuality in Renaissance and Enlightenment Europe.* New York: Harworth Press, 1989; pp. 553.

Surveys the subject by essays divided into national groupings: France,

Germany and Scandinavia; The Netherlands; England. This is followed by overviews and book reviews. Covers history, sociology, criminal practice, and literary themes in consideration of "the differentiation of the historical and cultural forms of homosexual behavior and its social expression" (1).

454   GERIGUIS, Lora Edmister. "Bows without arrows: the role of 'native agency' in the travel narratives of Daniel Defoe and other English texts, 1668-1790." Unpub. doct. diss., Univ. of California (Riverside), 1997. [*DA* 58 (1997): 1720A.]

The travel narratives of Daniel Defoe are filled with images of heroic English travellers and the natives they encountered. These natives are portrayed in the texts in terms of the relationships between themselves (as 'agents' either of potential aid or hindrance) and the traveller (with his agenda for the construction of a heroic English identity). Examines Neville's *Isle of Pines* for its delayed production of the 'racial other' as sexually violent and rebellious. The creation of this 'native agency' from within the family of castaway descendants is used to justify the appearance of every new state apparatus down the generations. Friday is first Crusoe's dream man, and then a body to be transformed. Crusoe's early experience with Barbary slavery enables him to be transformed from the errant son of the text's opening to the revered master at the close. The transformation is ascribed to the 'in-between-ness' of the Turkish identity which is neither European nor African, neither Christian nor Cannibal. Also examines the role played by Turkish identity and its accompanying agency in *Roxana* and *Captain Singleton*.

455 GIBALDI, Joseph. "The Baroque in Europe." In (pp. 96-102) BARRICELLI, Jean-Pierre; GIBALDI, Joseph; LAUTER, Estella (eds). *Teaching literature and other arts*. (Options for Teaching 10.) New York: Mod. Lang. Ass. of America, 1990; pp. vi, 183.

General introduction to the teaching of comparative arts or interdiciplinary arts. The article provides a useful overview of many pertinent ideas in a survey of the Baroque, "a pattern of beginnings marked by brilliance, audacity and virtuosity" (98), and the principal cultural characteristic of the first half of the 18c.

456 GIBSON, Louis Rauch. "Attitudes toward childhood in eighteenth-century British fiction." Unpub. doct. diss., Univ. of Pittsburgh, 1975. [*DA* 36 (1976): 4508A-9A.]

Examines how the 18c English novelists portray children - what attitudes they exhibit, what implications they may have. These novels provide an excellent showcase for the various philosophical approaches to children, but other demands of the genre include audience interest, talent and style, degree of author interest in realistic portrayals of life in given socio-economic classes. Discusses Defoe's portrayal of children which is uniformly sympathetic, modifying picaresque convention to put forward his own desire for social reform. Smollett adheres strictly to the conventions of fiction; Richardson draws psychological complexity; Fielding uses children to illustrate theories about human motive. The thesis also examines children's fiction which grew in popularity during the 18c.

457 GILES, E. L. "Shipwrecks and desert isles." *NQ* 177 (23 Sept 1939): 218-20. Reply J. T. HARDYMAN 177 (7 Oct 1939): 268-69.

Interesting perspective on the blend of truth and fiction in the 17c and early 18c when logbook entries and explanatory footnotes were added to narrative to impart verisimilitude. HARDYMAN draws attention to other travel adventures of the late 17c.

458 GILLESPIE, Gerald. "Erring and wayfaring in baroque fiction." *RLC* 58:3 (1984): 277-99.

The master image of the labyrinth asserted itself as an alternative to the garden in the late Renaissance. The world as the place of man's erring became simultaneously a theater and labyrinth in Baroque, picaresque, educational, utopian and quest fiction. There was a need to test the suspect labyrinthine inheritances and mental processes. At the threshold of the Enlightenment Defoe linked the expanding world picture brought about by the Renaissance 'erring' with the imperative to reclaim nature as God's garden.

459 GILLIE, C. *Character in English literature*. London: Chatto & Windus, 1965; pp. 206.

Surveys the role of character in English literature: character as a role in ritual, the emergence of loneliness, character and society. Of particular pertinence is ch. 2 "The Picaresque Hero: Christian; Crusoe" (101-16). Observes that loneliness "is henceforth to be accepted as the basic human condition, and that is new. The newness arises with a new conviction that God is no longer immanent, but at best distant and inscrutable. So man seeks man, sometimes in and through, sometimes against and in spite of, Society".

460 GLADFELDER, Hal Gibson. "Criminality and narrative in eighteenth-century England." Unpub. doct. diss., Univ. of California (Los Angeles), 1993. [*DA* 55 (1994): 574A.]

Studies criminality in 18c England. The first part, a prehistory of criminality representation, examines the main strands of criminal writing from the end of the 16c to the beginning of the 18c, focusing on the trial report and criminal biography as genres which were vitally involved in the articulation of modern, contested forms of knowledge and subjectivity. The second part concerns Defoe's histories of criminals and transgressions in the 1720s. Defoe extended the materials of the criminal narrative to examine the ideological forces shaping the construction of identity under conditions of outlawry, social dislocation, and urban poverty. The third part centers on 4 texts by Henry Fielding produced during his tenure (1749-53) as a London magistrate. The roles of author and judge were completely entangled in Fielding's writings. Godwin advances an explicit critique of the law as an instrument for the enforcement of oppressive class relations.

461 GLASSMAN, Peter. "Acts of enclosure." *HR* 30 (1977): 138-46.

Looks at Patricia SPACKS, *Imagining the Self* and Fanny BURNEY, *Letters and Journals*: "[...] literature's fear of society and its suspicions about the resources of the self have increased to the point of insistency [...]. [P]recisely as humankind has felt society to have increased the complexity of its structure and the peremptoriness of its demands [...], the weight of the social has become so commanding in the enormity of the pressure against the personal as to bring into serious questioning the very actualness of human particularity" (139).

462 GOETSCH, Paul. "Linguistic colonialism and primitivism: the discovery of native languages and oral traditions in eighteenth-century travel books and novels." *Ang* 106:3/4 (1988): 338-59.

Explores the discovery and treatment of native languages and oral tradition in 18c travel books and novels, distinguishing four attitudes which had an influence on 19c regionalism: linguistic colonialism, linguistic primitivism, criticism of the stock notions of colonialists and primitivists, and cultural relativism.

463 GOLDSMITH, M. M. "Liberty, luxury, and the pursuit of happiness." In (pp. 225-51) PAGDEN, Anthony (ed.). *The language of political theory in early modern Europe.* (Ideas in Context.) Cambridge: Cambridge UP, 1987; pp.xii, 360.

The existence of "civic humanism" as a common form of British political thought in the 18c began as Country Whig ideology in the 1670s, justifying opposition to the attempt by the monarchy to introduce popery and absolutism. It provided an ideological framework for discussing politics in 18c Britain. Mandeville provided a message of scepticism about the virtues of politicians and virtue of participation. Citizens should cease grumbling. Moreover, in a commercial society, they may reject the aristocratic and classical virtues recommended in civic humanist ideology. Thus Mandeville, by showing that luxury was not "the source of every corruption in government", but that it stimulated the progress of the arts and sciences, contributed to a new conception of morality and politics in which the pursuit of happiness replaces the pursuit of virtue.

464 GOLDSTEIN, Laurence. *Ruins and empire: The evolution of a theme in Augustan and Romantic literature*. Pittsburgh, PA: Pittsburgh UP; London: Feffer & Simons, 1977; pp. 272.

18c authors habitually gave monumental ruins the role of antagonist in the drama of human salvation. Ubiquitous in literature as geographic location, ruins were a means of mortifying in the public those desires which caused the great empires, like Persepolis and Egypt, to decline and fall. The 18c had an undeniable mania for representations of decay. Pertinent application of the theme in fiction is ch. 5, "*Roxana* and Empire" (59-72). "Defoe devotes his art to the minute particulars of economy, individual and natural, because he shares Dyer's belief in the value of information: he is, however, a moral (and financial) bookkeeper of greater genius" (61). *Roxana* (1724), Defoe's last important novel, illustrates in her behavior the spiritual decay Defoe believed to be overtaking the nation; her confession is a warning to the republic whose values she endangers. Bibliographic notes (243-64). Index (265-72).

465 GÖLLER, Karl Heinz. *Romance und Novel: Die Anfänge des englischen Romans*. (Sprache und Literatur, Regensburger Arbeiten zur Anglistik und Amerikanistik, 1.) Regensburg: Carl, 1972; pp. 291.

Considers the development of chivalric romance and picaresque tale, also the use of various tropes (pilgrimage and the Fall) as structural principles. Looks at 1) "Der Ritterroman und seine Tradition"; 2) "Der pikarische Roman"; 3) "Pikarischer Roman und Ritterroman"; 4) "Der *peregrinatio* als Strukturprinzip"; 5) "Der *casus* als Strukturprinzip"; 6) "Architektonischer Roman"; 7) "Gothic Novel". Discusses Defoe's *Robinson Crusoe* in the context of the pilgrimage as structural principle. Here the journey is no longer to a heavenly Jerusalem (as in *The*

Pilgrim's Progress), but a quest in this world; the purpose of the traveller is no more directed to supernatural ends, but to earthly usefulness; the religious elevation of the *peregrinatio* is resolved in adventure (144-50). Notes (237-63). Bibliography (265-80). Index (281-91).

466   GONDA, Caroline. *Reading daughters' fictions, 1709-1834: novels and society from Manley to Edgeworth.* (Cambridge Studies in Romanticism, 19.) Cambridge and New York: Cambridge UP, 1996; pp. xx, 287.

Draws on a wide range of novels and non-literary materials from the 18c and early 19c in order to examine changing representations of the father-daughter bond. Shows that heroine-centered novels, aimed at a predominantly female readership, had an important part to play in female socialization and constructions of heterosexuality in which the father-daughter relationship had a central role. Suggests that, far from corrupting the female reader as alleged by contemporary diatribes against novels, such fictions helped to maintain rather than undermine familial and social order. Focuses on the family as *the* primary unit of social order, which makes it possible for the emerging novel to represent conscious and deliberate incest, esp. between father and daughter. Yet incestuous relationships represented by women writers earlier in the century exist as continuum with other father-daughter fictions. Looks at representations of incest in Manley, Barker and Haywood (38-65), Richardson and the limits of parental authority (66-104), *Evelina* and *Camilla*, the sins of the fathers in Gothic fiction, Elizabeth Inchbald and Mary Brunton, Maria Edgeworth. Notes (239-58). Bibliography (259-82). Index (283-87). Illus. (3 plates).

467   GONDEBEAUD, Louis. *Le roman 'picaresque' anglais, 1650-1730.* Paris: Champion, 1979; pp. x, 750.

Major survey of the picaresque novel. Looks at the Spanish models and their translations, the middle-class public readers of these works (1680-1739), autobiographical and biographical criminal adventures, from *The English Rogue* (1665) to *The Fortunate Transport* (1732), the criminal biography of the 17c (highwaymen), "Pamphlet Lives", and autobiographies of delinquency, virtuous vagabonds and sinners, Defoe and the picaresque autobiography. General Bibliography (611-71), bibliographical chronology of novels of roguery (671-89), bibliographical chronology of Spanish translations (690-96). Inventory of Private Libraries Consulted (697-707).

468-----"Le roman anglais (1700-1739): suggestions pour une étude de son public." *EA* 34 (1981): 399-412.

Investigates the nature of popular readership between 1700 and 1740. Reading was not the privilege of an elite, nor available only to few readers. But for economic reasons, the novel was hardly popular reading. The novel was absent from the successful libraries in the first half of the 18c, and absent from the popular circuits (weekly or monthly publications). It was hardly the middle class as a whole who were drawn to novels or letters in general, but rather among the cultured elite of the middle class and among the aristocrats. Indeed by the year 1740 there appeared little future for the novel. Provides tables of readership.

469   GORDON, Scott Paul. "The power of passivity: constructing disinterestedness in eighteenth-century discourse." Unpub. doct. diss., Harvard Univ., 1993. [*DA* 54 (1994): 4100-1A.]

How can individuals demonstrate the sincerity or disinterestedness of behaviors that ultimately strengthen their interests? The devastating reductive critiques of Hobbes and Mandeville leave no criteria that can free even apparently selfless or disinterested behavior from the behavior that hides self-interest. These accounts, as well as the economic and political changes that accompany them in Restoration and 18c England, precipitated a crisis of identity: individuals felt they had lost their ability to distinguish between truth-telling and rhetorical efforts to persuade. Sincerity, disinterestedness and virtue were all declared non-existent, empty terms that do not correspond to any actual behavior. The power of passivity argues that early 18c discourses deploy a strategy of passivity to resolve the crisis of security and reintegrate disinterestedness.

470 GOURNAY, Jean-François (ed.). *La justice en Angleterre du XVIIe au XIXe siècle*. Lille: Presses universitaires de Lille, 1988; pp. 254.

Collection of essays describing the function of English justice from the 16c to the 19c, analyzing its representation in the literature of the time, eventually explaining the linguistic and philosophical references to the concept. Part I looks at institutions and juridical procedures; Part II justice and its representation; Part III the just man and the image of divine justice.

471-----(ed.). *L'Érotisme en Angleterre, 17e-18e siècles*. Lille: Presses Universitaires de Lille, 1991; pp. 112, 12 plates.

Collection of essays exploring aspects of sexual love. Divided into three parts: daily eroticism (aspects of prostitution under the Georges), eroticism in literature (heroism and sexuality in Dryden), eroticism and iconography (Hogarth and Rowlandson).

472 GOVE, Philip Babcock. *The imaginary voyage in prose fiction, 1700-1800: a history of its criticism and a guide for its study, with an annotated checklist of 215 Imaginary Voyages from 1700 to 1800.* New York: Columbia UP, 1941; pp. 445.

Part One investigates the criticism of the Imaginary Voyage, the use of the term, the antiquity of the type, earlier discoverable use of the term, history of the critical discussions and bibliography, the Robinsonade, the relationship of the Imaginary Voyage to other kinds of prose fiction. Part Two provides a short- title index arranged alphabetically by author (191-97), an annotated checklist (198-402) and bibliography (403-20). The section 1700 to 1740 (198-305) contains 69 titles in English, French, German, Dutch, Danish, Swedish, Italian and Latin. Each title is given in full with details of its background, and other observations on its critical impact. Any author who removed his imaginary voyagers from the surface of the earth entered a realm of fantasy: "His style he may owe to the real voyages, but his subject rather draws upon all kinds of fiction of the past, closely allied to the imaginary voyage of their kind in the fairy tale" (174).

473 GRAHAM, Henry Grey. *Scottish men of letters in the eighteenth century.* (Philosophy of David Hume, 5.) New York; London: Garland, 1983; pp. 441.
Facsim. of edition published in London, 1908. Overview of the history of Scottish literature in the 18c. Ch. 1 looks at the dawn of Scottish literature: Allan Ramsay, Hamilton of Bangour, Robert Blair. Ch. 2 is devoted to early Scottish philosophy (Hutcheson and David Hume). Mixture of biography and commentary with portraits.

474 GRAHAM, John. "Character and description in the Romantic novel." *Stud in Romanticism* 5 (1966): 208-18.

Use of physiognomy in the novels of the late 18c indicates the establishment of the pseudo-science in the minds of writers and their public. It was no longer a bit of esoteric information tossed into the stream of the action, but had to become a primary method for determining truth about a character. Although most novelists denied that they were suggesting that man was determined by his biological composition, their interest in the impact of the environment and their acceptance of inherited exterior characteristics as evidence of interior value were not in keeping with their claimed orthodoxy. The effects of environment and other scientific/social factors on character are issues already pertinent in early 18c fiction.

475 GRANT, Douglas. *The fortunate slave: an illustration of African slavery in the early eighteenth century.* London: Oxford UP, 1968; pp. xii, 231, illus., maps.

Historico-sociological study of slavery at the end of the 17c and beginning of the 18c, providing important background material for both social and literary issues. See esp. Ch. 5 "Savage: Noble or Accursed?". Bibliography (209-12). Index (213-31).

476 GRANT, Rena Jane. "From Clarissa to Lady Chatterley: character in the British novel." Unpub. doct. diss., Yale Univ., 1985. [*DA* 47 (1985): 1344A.]

Seeks to redefine the concept of character as it changes across two centuries of the British novel, using a method informed by Jacques Lacan vis à vis Marxist concepts of the ideological production of the subject. The novel constructs not only the place of its characters, but also of its author and reader. Using *Clarissa*, shows how the 18c novel produces character in its class and gender context without reading these definitions as rigidly determinate. Questions whether descriptions of novelistic character which assume that character is directly representative of human beings, and to suggest ways in which the concept of character may be regarded as a function of ideological creations of subjectivity across different historical contexts.

477 GREEN, Catherine Sobba. "The Courtesy Novel (1740-1820): women writing for women". Unpub. doct. diss., Georgia State Univ., Coll. of Arts and Sciences, 1983. [*DA* 45 (1984): 190A.]

With the publication of *Pamela*, Richardson changed the face of the novel, with a servant girl as heroine, a true heroine, uncorrupt and concerned with feminine problems - how to move safely from the protection of parents to that of a husband. Imitations of *Pamela* may be termed the Courtesy Novel which centerd around a young lady's entry into society, the problems arising from it, and her fortunate settlement in marriage. The purpose was not merely moral instruction, but definition of a social role. Looks at Sarah Robinson Scott, Charlotte Lennox, Fanny Burney, Mary Wollstonecraft, Amelia Opie, Maria Edgeworth, Jane Austen and Susan Ferrier.

478 GREEN, Thomas Hall. *The value and influence of works of fiction in modern times.* Oxford: T. and G. Shrimpton, 1862; pp. 32. Rpt. in (pp. 20-45) *Works of Thomas Hall Green*, Vol.3. Ed. R. L. NETTLESHIP. London, 1888; pp. clxi, 479.

The novel cannot give new birth to the spirit, or imitate the effort to transcend the separations of place and circumstance, but it helps remove the barriers of ignorance and antipathy, and at least brings man nearer his neighbor, and enables each class to see itself as others see it. The novelist helps to 'level' intellects as well as situations.

479   GREGORY, P. "The popular fiction of the eighteenth-century commercial circulating libraries." Unpub. doct. diss., Univ. of Edinburgh, 1985. [*IT* 35 (1986): 1084.]

Analyzes the fictions which were the most popular during the 18c, comparing all extant commercial library catalogues from 1739 to 1801. The libraries are the best measure of the popularity of the fictions, standing as they did at the center of the book trade, commissioning, producing and supplying books to the literate elite. Analysis of interconnections between the various types of fiction suggests that of 127 stories, 34 are closely related as sequels, piracies, satires, or through borrowed characters and scenes. Popular fiction provides the index to the consciousness of the literate elite of the 18c.

480   GRIFFIN, Dustin. *Literary patronage in England, 1650-1800.* Cambridge and New York: Cambridge UP, 1996; pp. x, 317.

Aims to shed new light on literary texts, and to understand how texts function within the literary, political, and economic culture in which they were written. Underlying the argument is the assumption that to consider literary texts and writers apart from the complex system of sponsorship, financing, production and distribution is arbitrarily to abstract literature from its living contexts, and misconceive its full meaning for its original audiences. First comprehensive study of the system of literary patronage in early modern England. Demonstrates that, far from declining by 1750, as many have suggested, the system persisted, although in altered forms, throughout the 18c. The workings of patronage system is explored; authors wrote within this system, manipulating it to their own advantage, and resisting the claims of patrons with their own counter-claims. Bibliography (293-308). Index (309-17).

481   GRIMSLEY, Ronald (ed.). *The age of Enlightenment, 1715-1789.*(Pelican Guides to European Literature.) Harmondsworth: Penguin Books, 1979; pp. 505.
Collection of critical essays examining the new ideas generated during the Enlightenment, and the literature they produced in England, France, Germany and Italy: 1) the literature of ideas; 2) poetry; 3) theater; 4) the novel; 5) aesthetic ideas. The 18c was a period of intense cultural ferment

when the religious, philosophical and social ideas of the previous century were subjected to close and often hostile scrutiny. Writers were treated as the purveyors of truth and enlightenment for the happiness of their fellow men. There was a spectacular growth in interest in other cultures and civilizations. The period witnessed the rise of the bourgeoisie, the rise of the novel, and the creation of new literary genres. It sought to throw off all religious and metaphysical constraints which prevented man from exercising his essential humanity. Part 4 "The Novel" (329-84): the English section looks at Defoe, Richardson, Fielding and Smollett. Chronological Table (423-53). Bibliography (455-95). Index (497-505).

482 GRUNDY, Isobel and WISEMAN, Susan (eds). *Women, writing, history, 1640-1740*. London: Batsford, 1992; pp. 239.

Collection of 10 essays exploring the literary role of women in the history of a century. Of particular interest to fiction are Jeslyn MEDOFF, "The daughters of Behn and the problem of reputation" (33-54) and Ros BALLASTER, "Seizing the means of seduction: fiction and feminine identity in Aphra Behn and Delarivier Manley" (93-108). Each article has extensive bibliographic notes.

483 GRUNDY, Joan and JAMES, G. Ingli. "The mode of the novel." *EC* 9 (1959): 201-09.

GRUNDY maintains that a story-teller will never hold the attention of the reader without some degree of "immediacy of presentation". JAMES affirms that the novelist does not so much *tell us about* a scene as *confront us with it*, so that the novel is not a *report* of experience, but an attempt to *be* experience itself.

484 GUNNY, Ahmad. *Voltaire and English literature: a study of English literary influences on Voltaire*. (Studies on Voltaire and the Eighteenth Century, 177.) Oxford: Voltaire Foundation, 1979; pp. 309.

French writers of the 18c upheld the developing myth of a dichotomy between English thought and literature. More often than not they preferred English thought: England was the country which could teach the rest of the world how to think. Looks at Voltaire's attitude to English tragedy, English comedy, English epic, the Augustan satirists, and his use of English prose. Bibliography (291-8). Index (299-309).

485 GUTHERMUTH, Elsa. "Das Kind im englischen Roman von Richardson bis Dickens." *Giessener Beiträge* 2 (1925): 29-60.

In German. Considers the presentation of the child in the English novel from the beginning of the 18c up to the highpoint of such depiction in the first part of the 19c. Sees the child fulfilling several important functions. 1) Biographical moments: Following on the adventure novel, there are depictions of the childhood of the chief characters. The parents are sketched, and there is focus on some aspects of the hero's childhood before the sudden transition to the adult's story. Childhood is not regarded as important in itself, but simply as a stage on the way to the complete character. 2) In episodic moments, the child has several functions to fulfil, as a foil, or figure of contrast. This is present in the beginning, and increases in importance. In the 18c the child hardly emerges from this role of foil. 3) More active moments of involvement in the plot comes in the 19c, with children as dramatically effective secondary characters in Scott, and as principal agents in Dickens. Looks at the works of Defoe, Richardson, Fielding, Smollett, Sterne, Jane Austen, Scott and Dickens.

486   HAGGERTY, George E. *Men in love: masculinity and sexuality in the eighteenth century.* (Between Men - Between Women.) New York: Columbia UP. 1999; pp. xi, 214.

Investigates varieties of masculinities and the ways in which gender determines, or pre-determines, sexual behavior. Gender was a contested concept throughout the 18c, and a great deal of cultural complexity can be unraveled as questions of gender construction are answered. Sexual sensibility emerges in the 18c, and begins to have recognized contours. Masculinity became the property of males, with a great deal of unresolvable conflict about what constituted masculinity. Rewrites our understanding of male-male desire, not in terms of sodomy, but in terms of love ("Two men having sex threatens no one. Two men in love: that begins to threaten the very foundations of heterosexual culture"). Connects male-male relations and identifies various kinds: friends, both heroic and personal, fops and beaux (Restoration and early 18c comedy and satires); effeminate sodomites; mollies, sodomy trial accounts, men of feeling, sodomites, libertines, pederasts; sexual aggressors (Gothic texts). Bibliographic notes (175-202). Index (203-14). For a wider context, see FRANTZEN, Allen J. *Before the closet: Same sex love from 'Beowulf' to 'Angels in America'.* Chicago and London: Chicago UP, 1998; pp. x, 369.

487 HAGSTRUM, Jean H. *Sex and sensibility: ideal and erotic love from Milton to Mozart.* Chicago: Chicago UP, 1980; pp. xiv, 350.

Seeks to provide a comprehensive study of love in the Restoration and the

18c, with discussions of sensibility, painting and music. Ch.5 "Women in Love: The Abandoned and Passionate Mistress" (100-32) considers *The Portuguese Nun* (112-17) imitated by both Behn and Manley.

488-----*Eros and vision: the Restoration to Romanticism.* Evanston, Ill: Northwestern UP, 1989; pp. x, 290.

Art and literature from 1660-1830 have an inescapable continuity despite wrenching revolutions in politics, religion, philosophy and artistic taste. The continuity is made up of contrast and conflict of an invigorating, intense and fruitful variety.

489 HALIMI, Suzy. "Présence du paysage dans le roman anglais du dix-huitième siècle." In (pp. 45-61) ANON. (ed.). *Espace et répresentations dans le monde anglo-américaine aux XVIIe et XVIIIe siècles: actes du colloque tenu à Paris les 23 et 24 octobre 1981.* Paris: Presses de l'Université de Paris-Sorbonne for the Société d'Etudes Anglo-Américaines des XVIIe et XVIIIe Siècles, 1982; pp. 172.

While devoted essentially to the period after 1740, presents an important discussion of the place of the landscape in the growing adumbration of space in the 18c novel. Looks at the incubation period during the 1750s and 1760s when any sense of setting was a brief vignette of some man-made scene. Sees the influence of poetry (Dyer and Thomson with their vast landscapes), the Grand Tour and increasing travel literature, and a burgeoning aesthetic of nature and pictorial awareness as key factors leading to the eruption of the landscape into fiction after 1770. Considers the function of landscape in the novel, the search for aesthetic effect, the perceived relationship between ethics and aesthetics, landscape and romanesque writing. "Les paysages grandioses s'épanouiront tout à fait, de façon significative, dans la poésie romantique, au-delà du roman de dix-huitième siècle" (p. 59).

490 HALSBAND, Robert. "Lady Mary Wortley Montague and eighteenth-century fiction." *PQ* 45 (1966): 145-56.

Montague wrote prose romances and fairy tales as well as essays embodying her fictional devices. Because of her activity as a writer of fiction (none of it published) and of such essays, she brought to it a sophistication of experience. Both in her youth and maturity, she wrote distinctly old-fashioned fiction, like the already outmoded heroic romance (1705). She found her materials in extensive reading in English and French drama and fiction, and also contributed to the elaborate *histoire amoureuse* and the *conte de fée*, as well as writing for the

Spectator (1714). Later she turned her attention to criticizing the novels of the 1740s and the 1750s.

491 HAMILTON, Christopher T. "Representations of the clergyman in English literature from the fourteenth through the eighteenth century: towards defining a tradition." Unpub. doct. diss., Southern Illinois Univ. at Carbondale, 1992. [*DA* 54 (1994): 3040A.]
Examines the relationship between clerical portraits in English authors from the 14c to the 18c, and the artists' changing perceptions of their role as social reformers. Proposes that readers analyze them in terms of ancient literary traditions. Ch. 3-5 concentrate on four 18c periodical writers and three novelists: taken as a whole, this section locates an approximate historical movement where satirical portraits predominate over the more balanced delineations of earlier periods. The novels of Richardson and Fielding represent the culmination of a satirical method which, while seeking to reaffirm the traditional balance, undermined the character of the clergyman and exalted the position of the novelist.

492 HAMMER, Stephanie Bardé. *The sublime crime: fascination, failure and form in literature of the Enlightenment.* Carbondale: Southern Illinois UP, 1994; pp. xi, 224.

Within the context of hermeneutics and its insistence on the ethical dynamics of literature, 18c works dealing with crime and the criminal present a special interpretive challenge. If art and ethics are bound up together, what is the reader to make of the frequency with which crime and the criminal appear in the written texts of the period, and the manner in which they appear. Looks at the challenge of criminal literature; economy, extravagance and criminal origin (Lillo and Prévost); greatness, criminality and masculinity, the failure of satire (Fielding); criminal sin, and fear of the feminine (Schiller and Sade); the tyranny of form and pursuit of the criminal text (Godwin and Kleist); the aesthetics of failure in modern criminal literature. The modern criminal program often retains artistry and creative genius; the criminal comes to be seen as the lonely individual striking out at monstrous systems against which he is no match; the landscape/architecture of the modern criminal story changes radically, from the urban center as modern Babylon to various provincial geographies. Notes (177-200). Bibliography (201-14). Index (215-24).

493 HARRIES, Elizabeth Manwaring. *The unfinished matter: essays on the fragment in the later eighteenth century.* Charlottesville, VA, and London: UP of Virginia, 1994; pp. xi, 215.

Study of fragmentary praxis in the late 18c, how novelists, philosophies, poets and essayists, insisted on presenting their finished texts as fragmentary, the result of literary calculation or swimming along in a fragmentary tide. Notes (175-96). Selected bibliography (197-210). Index (211-15).

494 HARRIS, Jocelyn (ed). "Studies in the eighteenth century VII: papers presented at the seventh David Nichol Smith Memorial Seminar." *ECLife* 12:2 (May 1988): 1-2.

Looks at "reading the signs in the 18c", the whole endeavor, the difficult pleasure, of assigning meaning to texts. The Restoration heritage of wit put all, including language, in doubt. Signs and meanings doubling back on one another caught Defoe and Swift in their own satires. Pope dreaded the power of time over his own poetic meaning. Richardson explained and revised his words again, unsure to the end of his life whether he had said what he intended to mean. Present-day criticism builds on the very awareness of shifting words and worlds.

495 HARRIS, Wendell V. "Vision and form: the English novel and the emergence of the short story." *VN* 47 (1975): 8-12.

For an entire century, thousands of pieces of short fiction were written, but hardly a single short story as we have recognized that form since it began to emerge in the 1880s and 1890s. Before that, to write serious fiction in England was to write a species of history, to integrate. Only at the end of the 19c did fiction begin to reflect reality perceived as "congeries of fragments" (12). Delarivière Manley contrasted "Little Histories" (essentially realistic novellas) with "Romances" in a preface of 1705, and Samuel Croxall described novels (really novellas) as "Imitation of History" in the Preface to his 1720 Collection. Daniel Defoe described *Roxana* (1724) as "History" because it had a foundation in "Truth of Fact", contrasting it with the mere "Story".

496 HART, Clive and STEVENSON, Kay Gilliland. *Heaven and the flesh: imagery of desire from the Renaissance to the Rococo.* Cambridge; New York and Melbourne: Cambridge UP, 1995; pp. 237.

Examines some of the ways in which Western poets and artists have explored the connections between sexual desire and the hope of ascent to heaven. Examples are drawn from the period between the late Renaissance ("when the delicate indirections of the poetry of love had reached their full flowering"), and the late Rococo ("which culminated in a mixture of coy titillation and frank sensuality"). When erotic arts attempt to express desire rather than the consequences of desire, they have recourse to a seemingly endless series of transformations, and the same is true when they try to represent the experience of the divine. This is because both experiences can be at once so intense and so inexpressible that they are frequently coupled. Uses a variety of representative examples, from major works of art to manuals for confessors, from ecclesiastical ceiling paintings, to witty pornographic poems. The controlling framework are three divergent but actually related areas: English poetry, French and Italian easel painting, and the decorations of Baroque and Rococo churches in Southern Germany and Austria. Notes (193-215). Bibliography (216-30). Index (231-37). Illus. (50 plates).

497 HART, Francis Russell. *The Scottish novel: a critical survey*. Cambridge, MA: Harvard UP; London: Murray, 1978; pp. xvi, 442.

Investigates the Scottish novel from Smollett to Spark, incidentally addressing the problem of the dearth of Scottish fiction in the early 18c. "The Scottish novelists' problems of an audience is a real one, no less than the related problem of linguistic nationality". Perhaps "Scottish culture has featured inimical to the novel [...]. There are reasonable uncertainties as to whether the novel has a distinctively Scottish tradition" (viii). Investigates fiction from the 1760s to the 1970s, a period in which "a Scottish derivation and inspiration is not easily recognized".

498 HARTLEY, L. P. "The novelist's responsibility." *E & S* 15 (1952): 88-100.

"The novelist [...] must believe that *something matters*, or at any rate his characters must believe that something matters" (100). The measure of Defoe's success is the ambiguity of his protagonists' attitude to nature and the meaning of their experiences.

499 HARTVEIT, Lars. *Workings of the picaresque in the British novel*. Oslo: Solum Forlag A/S; New Jersey: Humanities Press International, Inc. 1987; pp. 171.

The lasting appeal of the picaresque has nothing to do with its early recognizable formula, which gives scope to the story teller, portrayer of the *comédie humaine*, and the social critic alike. It focuses on individual human interest as well as on a panoramic social canvas. Discusses: 1) its perennial appeal; 2) formulas and social models (Defoe's *Colonel Jack*); 3) picaresque formulas and the sense of socio-economic precariousness (Smollett's *Roderick Random*); 4) and the mechanism of socio-economic change (Scott's *Rob Roy*); 5) and the struggle for economic survival (Thackeray's *Vanity Fair*); 6) and socio-moral transformation (Dickens's

Great Expectations); 7) and the theme of social descent (Orwell's *Down and Out in Paris and London*); 8) reverse movement of the picaresque rhythm (John Wain's *Hurry on Down*). Bibliography (168-71).

500 HARVEY, A. D. *Literature into history*. New York: St Martin's Press, 1988; pp. vii, 207.

Attempts to examine how, why, and to what extent literature is shaped by the social and economic development of its time. Considers 1) nations and art forms; 2) literature, literary history and history; 3) types of information; 4) ideas towards a social theory of artistic change; 5) second-ratedness; 6) the audience and the artist; 7) genre and style; 8) Neo-Classicism and Romanticism in historical context; 9) another glance at Shakespeare. Notes and references (176-98). Index of personal names (199-207). Illus. (8 plates).

501-----*Sex in Georgian England: attitudes and prejudices from the 1720s to the 1820s*. London: Duckworth; New York: St Martin's Press, 1994; pp. viii, 205.

Not a history of sexual behavior in the everyday sense, but about attitudes and assumptions, and transformations of attitudes. Earnest self-righteous tones were already in evidence in the 1720s. Looks at women's bodies, the waning of female lust, seductions, rape, the desperate, the deviant, separating the spheres. Notes (170-96). Index (197-205). Illus. (28 plates).

502 HARVEY, W. J. *Character and the novel*. London: Chatto & Windus, 1965; pp. x, 222.

Introduction to the theory of the novel, looking at fiction and reality, character and narration, time and identity, freedom and causality, character, essence and existence, the end of theory. Two appendices consider the retreat from character, and the attack on character. While the focus is overwhelmingly on the 19c and 20c, it provides insights that reflect on the growing complexity of character depiction in some of the fiction of the early 18c: "the novel itself is nothing but a complicated structure of artificially formed contexts parallel to those within which we experience real people" (31). Index (219-22).

503 HASS, Robert Louis. "Reason's children: economic ideology and themes of fiction, 1720-1880." Unpub. doct. diss., Stanford Univ., 1976. [*DA* 36 (1976): 8033A-4A.]

Study of economic and psychological themes in novels and writings related to the rise of capitalism. Discusses Hobbes's *Leviathan*, Defoe's *Roxana* and *Moll Flanders*, Laclos's *Les Liasons dangereuses*, Sade's *La Philosophie dans le boudoir*, Balzac's *Le Père Goriot*, Dickens's *Hard Times* and *Our Mutual Friend*, George Eliot's *Adam Bede*, Tolstoy's *War and Peace*, Dostoyevsky's *Crime and Punishment*, Freud's *The Interpretation of Dreams*. The novel itself as an art form provided for its readers the experience of nature, dependence and interconnectedness which the economic ideology of their culture denied.

504   HAWTHORNE, Jeremy (ed.). *Narrative: from Malory to motion pictures.* (Stratford-upon-Avon Studies, ser.2.) London: Arnold, 1985; pp. xvi, 167.

Makes advances in the study of narrative available to students of fiction by way of a series of essays, theoretical discussion and practical application to texts: *écriture*, narrative composition and spatial memory, the invention of modern narrative, newspapers and popular narrative. The last three themes are of direct pertinence to the emergence of the modern novel and its relation to history, journalism, and the depiction of 'true' stories.

505   HAYDEN, Lucy K. "The black presence in eighteenth-century British novels." *CLAJ* 24:3 (1981): 400-15.

The black presence in 18c British fiction is to be found in major and minor roles from the late 17c, mirroring the economic, religious, social, political and moral milieu in which blacks lived. Investigates the contributions of Behn (*Oroonoko*), Defoe (*Robinson Crusoe*), Johnson (*Rasselas*) and Sterne (*Tristram Shandy*). Behn creates a prophetic hero, larger than life; Defoe depicts Friday as a noble savage possessed of positive virtues; Sterne tried to elicit sympathy for the plight of the blacks. Johnson's depiction is the most universal, because he deliberately depicts the black hero as Everyman in his futile pursuit of happiness.

506   HEDIN, Raymond. "The American Slave Narration: the justification of the *picaro*." *AL* 53 (1982): 630-45.

Throughout the 18c American Slave Narratives were free of outside influence: pressures and corresponding strategies came later. The first slave narrative, *Adam Negro's Tryall*, was published in 1703, two years after the first abolitionist pamphlet in America, *The Selling of Joseph*. The conjunction suggests that from the beginning the Slave Narrative was linked to the anti-slavery movement. But in the 18c this movement was not so well-defined, nor intense as it would become. 18c narrative varied in voice and emphasis: *Briton Harmonn* (1760), *Arthur* (1768), *John Marrant* (1785), *Gustavus Vassa* (1789), *Venture* (1798). In time the picaresque would lead to the non-fictional novel of manners.

507 HEIDLER, Joseph Bunn. "The history, from 1700 to 1800, of English criticism of prose fiction." *University of Illinois Studies in Language and Literature*, 13:2 (May 1928): 1-187.

Ch. 1 (1-9) studies the history of the question. Ch. 2 (17-31) looks at the state of English criticism of prose fiction about 1700, and its history to 1719. Ch. 3 (32-45) considers the history of English literature from 1719 to 1740 (criticism within the novels, stressing truth to fact coupled with ethical efficacy; pleasing instruction rather than truth to fact; comments on prose fiction in critical works). Conclusion (168-71). Chronological list of references to prose fiction in the 18c (172-76). Bibliography (177-83). Index (184-87).

508 HEILMANN, Robert B. "Two-tone fiction: nineteenth-century types and eighteenth-century problems." In (pp. 305-22) HALPERIN, John (ed.). *The theory of the novel: new essays.* New York; London; Toronto: Oxford UP, 1974; pp. 396.

Explores the phenomenon of "some inconsistency or discrepancy or variation or departure from expectation established by the apparently conventional devices employed by the novelist" (305). Examines *Moll Flanders* and *Pamela*.

509 HERRERA, C. Andrea O'Reilly. "Nuns and lovers: tracing the development of idyllic conventual writing." Unpub. doct. diss., Univ. of Delaware, 1994. [*DA* 54 (1994): 2588A.]

While the monastery ceased to be a concrete physical place in England, the idea of an exclusively female religious community continued to haunt the imagination of English writers. Investigates the Englishwoman's life conditions from the Dissolution until the 18c in order to determine the circumstances that provoked later generations of writers to feature this religious topos in their fiction. Looks at the works of Margaret Cavendish, Aphra Behn, Eliza Haywood, and Ann Radcliffe. Mapping conventual space into their fiction enabled these authors to reclaim imaginatively all of the lost possibilities that the medieval convent represented, and to comment upon and transcend the restrictions of contemporary space. The final section treats conventual literature written after the re-establishment of monasteries in England. Christina Rossetti and Charlotte Brontë prepared it as a possible, but not necessarily propitious, alternative for their heroines. Lastly looks at the social and political developments that prompted a secular transformation of conventual imagery in English fiction (Harriet Matineau and George Gissing). By the end of the 19c the monastery had outlived both its actual and symbolic function and ceased to be a radically alternative space for fiction writers.

510 HERRLINGER, Wolfgang. *Sentimentalismus und Postsentimentalismus: Studien zum englischen Roman bis zur Mitte des 19. Jahrhunderts.* Tübingen: Niemeyer, 1987; pp. xiii, 404.

While devoted mainly to the exploration of sentiment and sentimentality in late 18c and early 19c novels, this study provides a helpful survey of the origins and important concepts in early ficton, such as 'reason and sensibility', 'pity and compassion', benevolence, evil and the victimization of good, melodrama and sentimentality. Attempts to define the change in function of sentimental elements from the 18c to the 19c by analysis of the underlying issues of human nature and the concepts related to 'sentimentalism'. The central concern is the basic philosophical concepts connected to sentimentalism and their change of meaning in the 19c novel. Bibliography (367-99). Index (401-4).

511 HILL, Mary Kate. "The city of Bath in eighteenth-century English novels." Unpub. doct. diss., Univ. of Southwestern Louisiana, 1984. [*DA* 45 (1984): 1122A.]

Explores the relationship between Bath, the 18c, and novels written about Bath in the 18c. Because Bath was a microcosm of the century, novels which depict Bath also depict the values, illusions and conflicts of the century, as well as the transition of England from feudalism to capitalism. The 18c represented a break with the Classical concept of universals espoused by Plato and Aristotle, and the Medieval Scholastics. The belief in the truth of the individual's experience, born in the Renaissance, blossomed in the 18c. The novelists who came to Bath were Defoe, the Fieldings (Henry and Sarah), Charlotte Lennox, Smollett, Fanny Burney and Jane Austen. They experienced the city which was the epitome of the 18c, a place where the dualities of the time appeared in rarified form: wealth and poverty, disease and decorum, lawlessness and order, elegance and crudeness. Bath was a source of characters, images and themes. The city as it appears in the novels reveals the century's mores and ideologies in graphic detail.

512-----*Bath and the eighteenth-century novel.* Bath: Bath UP, 1989; pp. 76. Published version of the above study.

513 HILL, Rowland. "Realistic descriptive setting in English fiction from 1550 through Fielding." Unpub. doct. diss., Boston Univ., 1941.

Considers "the extent [...] of [realistic] setting as employed by the authors of the period covered, the sources of that setting, the techniques employed in using it as background or as a device for characterization, or furtherance of the narrative action, and the extent to which it makes the story of which it is a part more probable to the reader than that story would otherwise be".

514 HODNETT, Edward. *Five centuries of English book illustration*. Aldershot: Scolar Press, 1988; pp. 364.

Since the late 15c illustration has been a steadfast element in the cultural history of the English people. Presents a comprehensive, scholarly and critical record of literary illustration in England since the introduction of printing (1476). Gives a selective catalogue of illustrators and illustrated books, and lists 250 illustrators and 2700 books chosen from those reviewed. The eighteenth century is examined in two sections: 1) 1701 to 1775 (67-90), and 2) 1776 to 1800 (91-106). French artist-engravers were the leading influence in English book illustration in the first half of the 18c, although native artists were responsible for the majority of the illustrations in the books chosen for the catalogue. Publishing practices throughout the 18c tended to obscure the individuality of illustrators. Many books contain only a frontispiece. The prevalence of costumed figures and the leveling effect of engraving gave the illustrations of the 18c an interchangeable, look-alike character. Provides lists of significant illustrators and their principal works in chronological order. Index (361-64). Illus. (6 color and 200 black-and-white plates).

515 HOFFIELD, Laura Diamond. "The servant heroine in eighteenth- and nineteenth-century British fiction: the social reality and its image in the novel." Unpub. doct. diss., New York Univ., 1975. [*DA* 36 (1975): 3730A-1A.]

In the 18c the woman who serves others became the object of psychological exploration in fiction, which was continued through the 19c. Investigates the nature of the servant heroine in specific works of fiction, and the relationship between social history (the real position of the servant and the manner in which the author treats her and her aspirations). Moll Flanders and Pamela Andrews represent two views of women which form the basis of servant characterization in later novels. Moll is conceived as the erring servant, a criminal seductive and seduced. Pamela is the attractive *ingénue*, sensible, responsive, but better controlled. She is a woman perceived as moral template for man.

516   HOLLIS, Karen Anne. "Print culture and the commercialization of sexuality, 1690-1750." Unpub. doct. diss., Univ. of California (San Diego), 1993. [*DA* 54 (1994): 4450A.]

Between the 1690s and the mid-18c, a fully fledged popular print culture emerged in England, characterized by a new consumerist ideal and the burgeoning of commercial definitions of literary worth, the inflection of public and private spheres of print, the new definition of authorship, literary property and reputation. Charts how these characteristics of print culture shaped the commercial exploitation of women as readers, writers, subjects of discourse, and conversely the impact of the "femininization" of letters and the novel on the discourse of authorship, reputation, and literary property. As print both constructed and blurred definitions of public and private, the commercialization of sexuality was juxtaposed with the representation of women as redemptive of consumerism. Discusses John Dunton, Samuel Richardson and Eliza Haywood. Ch. 4 elucidates Haywood's refusal of private writing as a site of pleasure and power for women, while she exploited the commercial attractions of women's love letters in amatory prose.

517   HORNÁT, Jaroslaw. "Some remarks on fiction style, old and new." *PP* 8 (1965): 204-11.

Survey of "some syntactic features characteristic of various historical stages of the development of style" in English fiction.

518   HORNER, Winifred Bryan and BARTON, Kerri Morris. "The eighteenth century." In (pp. 114-50) HORNER, Winifred Bryon (ed.). *The present state of scholarship in historical and contemporary rhetoric*. Columbia: U of Missouri P, 1990; pp. x, 260.

Attempts to put together the wide variety of scholarship in the diverse field of rhetoric. The Classical period is included since much that follows is either a reinforcement of, or reaction against, the first canon. Rhetoric dominated the life of the Middle Ages and the Renaissance. Ch. 4, by Kerri Marris BARTON (114-40), describes the shift in focus in the 18c, traces the decline of the old rhetoric and the emergence of the new in the epistemology of the period. Also traces the new rhetoric through the 19c. Excellent bibliography of Primary Works (141-42) and Secondary Works (143-50). Index (249-60).

519   HUDSON, Nicholas. *Writing and European thought, 1600-1830*. Cambridge and New York: Cambridge UP, pp. xxv, 222.

The development of attitudes towards written language has been little studied despite a wealth of materials related to this subject and the importance of this medium in Western intellectual history. Writing is of central importance to conceptions of language, technological progress and Western civilization during the early modern era. Shows how writing became the emblem of the superiority of European culture, and how with the expansion of print culture, European intellectuals became more aware of the virtues of 'orality' and the deficiencies of literate society. Notes (167-201). Bibliography (202-17). Index (218-22). Illus. (5 plates).

520 HUFFMANN, C. H. *The eighteenth-century novel in theory and practice.* Doct. diss., Univ. of Virginia. Dayton, VA: The Ruebush-Knieffer Co., 1920; pp. 138.

Prose, esp. in the course of its development in the 18c, assumed its modern aspect at the hands of Dryden, Addison, Swift, Johnson and Goldsmith. Dryden gave directness to prose; Addison, simplicity, joined with refinement and elegance; Defoe, downright plainness; Swift, precision and clearness; Johnson, formality, regularity, elevation and poise; Goldsmith, delicacy, ease, grace and charm. Traces the history and broad outlines of the evolution of prose fiction in the 18c, but has little on the life of the novel before 1740. Looks at 1) "Types Contributing to the Novel"; 2) "The Rise of the Modern Novel: Crystallization of a Theory"; 3) "The Avowed Purposes of the Novel"; 4) "Means of Reaching the Inner Life"; 5) "The Gothic Novel and Romanticism"; 6) "The Democratic Idea". Limited bibliography (135-36). Index (137-38).

521 HUGHES, Christopher G. "Romance, probability, and politics in England, 1650-1720." Unpub. doct. diss., Univ. of Princeton, 1995. [*DA* 56 (1995): 942A.]
Examines Restoration and early 18c theories of romance. Romance is usually invoked as an archaic foil for the emergent modern and realistic forms of the novels. The term refers less to formal or generic features, but more often denotes a certain epistemology, with socio-political resonances. Romance functions as a shorthand for a shifting sense of epistemology, esp. with reference to a concept of probability which bridges literary and philosophical matters (Scudéry, Locke, Hobbes, Addison). Hobbes and Locke provide explicit theories of the romance way of knowing the world. Examines the responses of four major writers to romance - Butler, Dryden, Behn and Manley all deliberately engaged with romance in their poetry, plays, and prose fiction, but equivocally. Romance was commonly associated with a royalist interest in the period,

appealing to this group of ardent Tories. The epistemology found in romance enables a political world view that is both aesthetic and actual. Of importance to the history of the novel, the literary theory of Restoration and early 18c, and the relationship of literature to politics.

522 HUGHES, Helen Sard. "Notes on eighteenth-century fictional translations." *MP* 17 (1919): 225-31.

A conspicuous feature of the development of English fiction before the 19c is the importance of foreign models in their influence on native fiction through translation and imitation. The influence of translated fiction was strengthened and directed by the methods employed by translators of the late 17c and early 18c. Translators allowed themselves to considerable liberties that were often justified on moral and financial grounds. Such an attitude toward literary property such as license on the part of translators, both English and French, throws light upon methods of literary craftsmanship which influenced the growing fictional technique, and upon cosmopolitan relationships affecting the novel of the time.

523-----"English epistolary fiction before *Pamela*." In (pp. 156-69) *J. M. Manly anniversary studies*. Chicago: U of Chicago P, 1923; pp. 432.

Surveys the genre of epistolary fiction before Richardson, looking at various framework devices: the rifled postbag, the letter of travel with satiric comment by the foreign observer, correspondence between friends (often town and country), the correspondence of lovers. To the epistolary method already recognized as an aid to verisimilitude, and a vehicle for satire and passion, Richardson added the stuff of domestic bourgeois life.

524-----"The middle-class reader and the English novel." *JEGP* 25 (1926): 326-78.
The middle-class, with its ideals rooted in Puritanism and trade, comprised a large section of the reading public, even in the 17c. The literary needs of this class of potential readers did much to create the English novel in its image and likeness. At the beginning of the 18c, English fiction was moving from romances, both heroic and picaresque, into realistic accounts of middle-class life and manners, with the surprising adventures of heroes of the same familiar class.

525 HUGHES, Richard T. and ALLEN, C. Leonard. *Illusions of innocence: Protestant primitivism in America, 1630-1875*. Chicago: U of Chicago P, 1988; pp. xviii, 296.

Highlights the importance of the *Urzeit* in forms of Protestant primitivism, the hankering for an earlier time when all was well and man had not fallen into the guilt of history. The primordium, while never as central as the millennium (*Endzeit*), has particularly flourished in America, the New World being thought of as a newness of pristine beginnings.

526 HUNT, John Dixon. *The figure in the landscape: poetry, painting, and gardening in the eighteenth century.* Baltimore: Johns Hopkins UP, 1976; pp. xiv, 271.

Discusses the human consequences of the new designs in landscape gardening, the collaboration of poetry, painting and philosophy in a new style of gardening. Examines the psychological extensions of landscape space. Poetry itself learned fresh procedures from the new art to which it had contributed. Shows how gardening promoted and anwered imaginative experience, and how poetry emerged from the alliance of the 'three new graces'. The landscape garden provided an exciting territory in which the poet could discover in practice the poetry of introspection. A taste for the sublime turned poets outside the garden where all was unordered and unselected, where the imagination trained within landscape gardens soon formed and explained its experience of natural scenery in terms learned and tested in the great estates. Notes (251-65). Index (266-71). Illus. (75 plates).

527-----*Gardens and the picturesque.* (Studies in the History of Landscape Architecture.) Cambridge, MA; London: The Massachusetts Institute of Technology Press, 1992; pp. xviii, 388.

Six essays offer analyzes of various moments in gardening history, and esp. the relationship of gardens, garden design, and garden theory to various cultural phenomena - in particular the cult of the picturesque, verbal-visual parallels, allegorical imagery, the language of description, landscape painting and painting of gardens. See esp. ch. I.3 "Emblem and Expression in the Eighteenth-Century Landscape Garden" (75-104). Notes (337-78). Index (379-88). Copious illus.

528 HUNTER, J. Paul. "Studies in eighteenth-century fiction." *PQ* 56 (1977): 498-539.

The year's work for 1976 presented several major studies attempting some larger perspective. Mythology, psychological criticism and post-structuralism showed major weaknesses when applied to a total approach to literature, but each made an enormous contribution to the then literary context. Epistemology, ontology and linguistics in post-structuralism have brought self-consciousness to Anglo-American criticism. There is also a need for greater sensitivity to historical issues, dismissed by the old historicism, and resisted by the critical approaches of thirty post-war years.

529-----"The world as stage and closet." In (pp. 271-87) KENNY, Shirley Strum (ed.). *British theater and the other arts, 1660-1800*. Washington DC: Folger Shakespeare Library; London: Assoc. UPs, 1984; pp. 311.

This article (ch. 14) traces the concurrent decline of the English drama and the so-called rise of the novel - the emergence into prominence of a distinctly new kind of prose fiction.

530-----"'News and new things': contemporaneity and the early English novel." *CI* 14:3 (1988): 493-515.

For almost all of the early novelists, individual segments of what they wrote might easily be mistaken for the stuff of everyday popular print. Both the matters they wrote about, and the way they wrote about them, owed much to the journalistic context of the previous half-century. The novel had its origins in a popular consciousness and allegiances which are broad rather than narrow, levelling rather than hierarchical.

531-----"Novels and 'the novel': the poetics of embarrassment." *MP* 85:4 (May 1988): 480-98.

Examines the difficulty of adequately defining the nature and self-understanding of the novel. Studies the novel in the 18c, looking at the marvelous, the novel's unusual relationship with its audience, and the epistemological question that novels repeatedly ask: "How do you know?" in order to describe the novel practically. For a long time novel criticism cast aside as inferior the lively narratives of Behn, Manley and Haywood because of their 'scandalous' plots and themes, while pointedly ignoring similar episodes in canonical novels. But for 18c novels generally, the ideas of the 'horrible' and the forbidden exist side by side with everyday reality, sometimes offering a coloration of sensationalism and frenzy that threatens to associate novels with low tastes, disordered conduct and inferior characters, and always heightening the contemporary sense of ordinariness.

532-----*Before novels: the cultural contexts of eighteenth-century English fiction*. New York: W. W. Norton, 1990; pp. xxiv, 421.

Provides information on the novel, the history and theory of literary forms, 18c literature and culture. Crucial texts are being rethought, with questions about generic relationships, the assumptions of authorship and readership, interactions between cultural texts and everyday life. Looks at what was new about the novel, its readership, pre-texts (journalism, didacticism, private histories, history, biography, travel books). Bibliographical notes (357-404).

533 HYNES, Peter John. "Models of reading in the eighteenth-century epistolary novel." Unpub. doct. diss., Univ. of Toronto, 1986. [*DA* 47 (1987): 4404A-5A.]

Investigates ways in which the 18c epistolary novel displays and shapes the act of reading. Attempts to refine a formal notion of reading in the text of the epistolary novel, and then maps out the development of the sub-genre throughout the 18c century. Looks at point of view and reading strategies to facilitate the reading practices of the audience of fiction.

534 IHALAINEN, Pasi. "Language and literature in intellectual history: early eighteenth-century political literature as a historical source." In (pp. 223-44) ROBERTSON, David (ed.). *English studies and history.* (Tampere English Studies, 4.) Tampere: Univ. of Tampere, 1994; pp. 277.

Early 18c periodical essays, pamphlets, sermons, plays and poems provide fresh insights into political discourse characterized by unparalleled party conflicts and a sense of growing popular interest in politics. However, historians using political literature as a primary source with the purpose of reconstructing major arguments cannot read it in the same way as archival documents. It calls for a clarification of the methodological foundations of the work. The study of intellectual history requires sensitivity with regard to words and concepts and their use in arguments. Attention must be given to literary genres, vocabulary, neologisms, contested concepts, the interplay between politics and religion, the meanings created by the author and his audience. The historian must study the language and literature of the past. Bibliographical notes (240-44).

535 ISER, Wolfgang. *The act of reading: a theory of aesthetic response.* London and Henley: Routledge & Kegan Paul, 1978; pp. xii, 239.

Theoretical introduction to the process of reading: "[which] sets in motion a whole chain of activities that depend both on the text and on the exercise of certain basic human faculties. Effects and responses are properties neither of the text nor of the reader; the text represents a potential effect that is realized in the reading process " (ix). Investigates the situation, the reality of fiction, the phenomenology of reading, interaction between text and reader. The whole process has a double implication for reading the 18c epistolary novel where the reader subsumes the reading processes of the fictional recipient. Name and Title Index (233-35). Subject Index (236-39).

536 IVKER, Barry. "John Cleland and the Marquis d'Argens: eroticism and natural morality in mid-eighteenth-century English and French fiction." *Mosaic* 8:2 (1975): 141-48.

Their interest lies not in the quality of the writing - in both cases superior to other contemporary writings of this type - but in the use of eroticism as a vehicle for expressing basic philosophic ideas.

537 JACKSON, Mary V. *Engines of instruction, mischief, and magic: Children's literature in England from its beginnings to 1839*. Nebraska UP; London: Scolar Press, 1989; pp. xiv, 304.

Surveys the history of children's books. The early chapters cover the late 17c and early 18c: 1) "The Birth of the Children's Book Trade: Economic and Social Situation"; 2) "Puritan and Other Religious Prototypes for Juvenile Literature"; 3) "Secular Adult Forerunners of Juvenile Books and Early Audiences"; 4) "The First Innovations and Their Creation".

538 JACKSON-STOPS, Gervase. *The English country house: a Grand Tour*. The National Trust: Weidenfeld & Nicholson, 1984, 1993; pp. 240.

Gives a history of the essential components of the great homes, the rituals and etiquette which contributed to the form and decoration of the rooms. These houses have become great repositories of treasures of every description.

539-----; SCHOCHET, Gordon J.; ORLIN, Lena Cowen and McDOUGALL, Elizabeth Blair (eds). *The fashioning and functioning of the British country house*. National Gallery of Art, Washington, 1989; pp. 417.

Develops and complements the above, **538**.

540 JACOBS, Deborah A. "Göttingen and the great circle of German libraries: a comprehensive continental review of 18th-century English culture." *SNNTS* 22:1 (Spring 1990): 82-87.

Recent library research has revealed a considerable resource waiting for

18c scholars in several continental libraries. Scholars of the 18c novel in particular stand to profit from the vast reserves to be found in German repositories. Pre-eminent among them for English scholars is the massive collection of English works to be found at the Univ. of Göttingen, and developed on the basis of the Anglo-German link provided by the Hanoverian dynasty. Almost from its beginning, buyers for the library began acquiring texts by English authors in a systematic manner; by 1748 this was some 30-40 volumes per month. By 1778 Heyne had built its collection to 160,000 volumes, five times the number then housed in the Cambridge University Library. The archives are well preserved. It was the first library designed as a research facility.

541 JACQUETTE, Arlene Rita. "Vile pruriency for fresh adventures: sexuality and storytelling in selected eighteenth-century and gothic novels." Unpub. doct. diss., Vanderbilt Univ., Tennessee, 1976. [*DAI* 38:2 (1977): 783A.]

A comparison of the thematic attention to technical uses of aberrant sexuality, including rape, seduction, repression, impotence, and sadism in *Pamela, Joseph Andrews, Tristram Shandy, The Monk* and *Melmoth the Wanderer*, demonstrates the mimetic and aesthetic concerns of realistic and Gothic fiction. The relationship of literary and empirical reality - a central theme in the realistic novel - is accentuated by the ambiguities inherent in sexual desire and action. Aberrant sexuality compounds these ambiguities (like fear and pleasure). Tensions are activated and controlled by narratives, with characters' storytelling exposing the power of subjective fantasy, and displacing the fears of their victims onto their literary creations. Literary and human (sexual) concerns are found in these novels in the act of storytelling and the effect of the finished product.

542 JENKINS, Geraint H. *Literature, religion, and society in Wales, 1660-1730.* Cardiff: Wales UP, 1976; pp. 351.

Surveys Welsh printed books, authors and their works, the printing and publishing trade. Bibliography of contemporary sources, both MS and printed in Welsh and English, and modern works of reference (310-32).

543 JENKINS, Hugh David. "A fragile ideal: representations of the English country estate from Jonson to Defoe." Unpub. doct. diss., Cornell Univ., 1992. [*DAI* 53:2 (1992): 504A.]

Examines the ideology of form of the country-house poem and other literary representations of the English country house in the 17c and early 18c. Defoe's *Robinson Crusoe* marks a double shift in representation of the country house: in form, from poetry to the novel; in subject, from landed aristocracy to the mercantile classes, who increasingly made their fortunes and earned their wealth in colonial possessions.

544 JENSEN, H. James. *The Muses' concord: literature, music, and visual arts in the Baroque age.* Bloomington; London: Indiana UP, 1976; pp. xv, 259, 21 plates.

Intensively and selectively historical, concentrating on carefully chosen historical beliefs, artistic results, and the ideals in and behind art and its creation during the Baroque era, using mainly 16c, 17c, and 18c theoretical writings and works of art. Extensive notes (195-250).

545 JOHNSON, Clifford R. *Plots and characters in the fiction of eighteenth-century English authors.* 2 vols. Hamden, CT: Archon; Folkestone: Dawson, 1978. I, xx, 270; II, xxv, 243.

Designed to include plot summaries and character identifications for the narrative works of the most important 18c English novelists. Preface, chronology of events, chronology of publications, plots and characters. Vol. I includes Jonathan Swift, Daniel Defoe, Samuel Richardson; Vol. II Henry Fielding, Tobias Smollett, Laurence Sterne, Samuel Johnson, Oliver Goldsmith.

546 JOHNSON, Richard Brimley. *The women novelists.* London: W. Collins Sons & Co. Ltd., 1918; pp. viii, 299.
Sees Fanny Burney as the first woman novelist and devotes only the introduction to a brief survey of those who came before, i.e. Aphra Behn, Mary Manley, Sarah Fielding and Charlotte Lennox.

547 JONES, S. H. E. "Some literary treatments of friendship: Katherine Philips to Alexander Pope." Unpub. doct. diss., Univ. of Cambridge, 1993. [*IT* 43:3 (1994): 852-53.]

Considers the reasons for the unprecedented popularity of friendship as a topic of writing in the late 17c and early 18c, and aims to suggest why that period chose to concentrate on friendship between the sexes, as opposed to love or marriage, as a form for feeling. Friendship as an ethical quest and as a social relation met in the idea of bifocality: it is the particular achievement of Jonathan Swift and Alexander Pope to have created a literary address that may accommodate a number of passionate readers at one time without losing a sense of specificity.

548 JORDAN, Elizabeth Boyd. "Conventions of domestic realism: theory,

context, and the text." Unpub. doct. diss., Purdue Univ., 1983. [*DA* 44 (1983): 1799A.]

Explores the possibility that conventions constitute generic categories, establishing a taxonomy and methodology of conventional formation, reformation and deformation. This is investigated in terms of the development and ultimate deformation of the master conventions of domestic realism, the conventional characterization of the imaginative heroine, and the convention of 'self-referentiality', an important dimension in the concerns of the women's writing of the early 18c.

549   JORDAN, Sarah Elizabeth. "The anxieties of idleness: idleness in eighteenth-century British literature." Unpub. doct. diss., Brandeis Univ., 1994. [*DA* 55 (1994): 1266-7A.]

Examines the preoccupation with idleness present in texts by Johnson, Cowper, Thompson. The virtue of industriousness became during this period a new defining term for the nation and the individual. The newly powerful middling ranks defined themselves as the industrious members of the nation, opposing themselves to the working classes, who, it was believed, would be idle if they could, and the upper classes, whose privileged idleness the middle class increasingly criticized. At the same time, upper-class idleness was a sign of status, and often a reward for middle-class industriousness. This idleness was both a direct result of industry and a state sternly to be avoided - and therefore the cause of a profound anxiety.

550   JOST, François. "Le roman épistolaire et la technique narrative au XVIIIe siècle." *Comparative Lit Stud* 3 (1966): 399-407.

Survey of the nature, distribution and popularity of the epistolary novel in the 18c, based on the findings of Daniel MORNET who investigated the holdings of 392 Parisian libraries founded between 1740 and 1760. "[...] [E]lle donne à l'écrivain tous les avantages du roman personnel, et quelques autres par surcroît, tout en lui laissant la possibilité d'en conjurer certains périls [...]. L'histoire est narrée par plusieurs personnages paraissant successivement sur la scène. L'issue tragique, en outre, est parfaitement possible [...]. Ces deux avantages, essentiels aux préoccupations de l'époque, ne sauraient cependant à eux seuls expliquer l'ampleur et la durée d'un tel succès, ni surtout d'une influence sur l'évolution de la littérature" (401). Contains valuable tables of the most popular French examples and esp. English translations across the century.

551 JUHNKE, Janet Ann. "The prison theme in the eighteenth-century novel." Unpub. doct. diss., Univ. of Kansas, 1974. [*DA* 35 (1975): 6099A.]

Imprisonment is an important motif in the 18c. English novels of all types - picaresque, satirical, sentimental, realistic, Gothic. Surveys the uses of the prison theme in novels from Defoe to Godwin, with special emphasis on those of the latter 18c. Investigates the novelist's attitude towards crime and punishment and their contribution (or lack of it) to penal reform. Essentially concerned with the thematic and aesthetic *function* of the prison scenes (patterns of language, setting, character)

552 JUSTICE, George. "The production of literature in eighteenth-century Britain." Unpub. doct. diss., Univ. of Pennsylvania, 1994. [*DA* 56 (1995): 942A.]

After the demise of the Licensing Act in 1694, the publishing industry in London, and then the whole of Great Britain, expanded rapidly. Examines the network of material conditions of authorship and publishing during the century, with textual readings in order to explore the constitutive nature of literature, the material process that influences its production, and the social world of readers. Looks at the work of Addison and Steele, Defoe (the *Review*, debates over Union, the *Tour*), Pope, Robert Dodsley's *A Collection of Poems*, Fanny Burney. There is a movement from the 'bourgeois public sphere' of early 18c London to a modern sense of literary authorship.

553 KAHN, Madeleine. *Narrative transvestism: rhetoric and gender in the eighteenth-century novel*. Ithaca, NY, and London: Cornell UP, 1991; pp. xi, 168.

Many of the first canonical novels (*Moll Flanders, Robinson Crusoe, Pamela, Clarissa, Fanny Hill*) were written by men in the person of women. 'Narrative transvestism' is a concept to describe this use by a male author of a first-person female narrator in 18c discourse. Gender issues added to the development of narrative consciousness that became the distinguishing characteristic of the modern novel. Follows critical trends in trying to revise and modify the canon, taking into account the impact of history and politics on literature and literary criticism, and trying to reread the works in the traditional canon. Introd. (1-12). Considers transvestism and narrative structure in 18c England (13-56) before examining Defoe and *Roxana* (the reader as author) and Richardson and *Clarissa* (the author as reader). In *Roxana* the heroine struggles to escape the constraints of socially defined gender. Richardson, by posing as Clarissa's amanuensis, leads us to suspend awareness of the author outside the text in favor of the letter-writer inside the text, so heightening our reader- experience. Both Defoe and Richardson use the device of narrative transvestism to create a licence that accompanies this temporary escape from defining boundaries. Select bibliography (161-70). Index (171-72).

554 KALER, Anne K. *The picara form: from Hera to fantasy heroine*. Bowling Green, OH: Bowling Green State Univ. Popular Press, 1991; pp. 215.

Survey of the etymology and history of this literary type, looking at tapestry, picara and autonomy, the literary origins of the picara, literary characteristics, hunger, avarice and criminality, sexuality and children, marriage and prostitution, wanderer and warrior, disguise and deception, isolation and inferiority. List of works cited (204-10) covering literary theory, history of the picaro and picaresque texts (17-20cc).

555 KARL, Frederick Robert. *A reader's guide to the development of the English novel in the eighteenth century*. London: Thames & Hudson, 1975; pp. 360. Pub. in USA as *The adversary literature: the English novel in the eighteenth century*. New York: Farrar, Strauss & Giroux, 1974.
Provides an important introduction: "The Novel as Subversion" (3-54), which describes a context for the emergence of the 18c novel. Defoe was dependent on the techniques and experiments tried by people like Manley, Haywood, Blackamore, Davys. Looks at chartings, time, romance, the audience, antecedents and fulfilment. From the first, the English novel seemed to bow to the taste of the new bourgeoisie, but also stood for new and often dangerous ideas, criticized the predominant culture, and displayed subversive forms of behavior. Also looks at Don Quixote as the archetypal artist and *Don Quixote* as the archetypal novel, while examining Defoe in terms of the politics of necessity. Select Bibliography (342-50).

556 KAY, Donald. *Short fiction in 'The Spectator'*. (Studies in the Humanities, 8: Literature.) Alabama: Alabama UP, 1975; pp. 145.

A critical account of the 100 pieces of fiction scattered throughout the 555 originally issued numbers of *The Spectator* (1 March 1711 to 6 Dec. 1712). Valuable for its discussion of the storytelling tradition and periodical antecedents to *The Spectator*, and studies of character, fable, dream-vision, oriental tale and other miscellaneous forms.

557 KEENER, F. M. *The chain of becoming: the philosophical tale, the novel, and a neglected realism of the Enlightenment: Swift, Montesquieu, Voltaire, Johnson and Austen*. New York: Columbia UP, 1983; pp. x, 358.
The central genre of the Enlightenment and its best literary gift to

posterity is the philosophical tale. Explores and appreciates these tales as fiction. The tales came to prominence in the 18c both in France and England, and complement the novel. Looks at the intellectual and psychological background of the major philosophical tales (*Gulliver's Travels, Les Lettres persanes, Candide, Rasselas*), then Jane Austen (*Northanger Abbey, Persuasion, Mansfield Park*). Notes (309-44). Index (345-58).

558   KELLY, Gary G. "'Intellectual physics': necessity and the English Jacobin novel." *EA* 31 (1978): 161-75.

Blair singled out Le Sage's *Gil Blas*, Marivaux's *Vie de Marianne* and Rousseau's *La Nouvelle Héloïse* among the French, Defoe's *Robinson Crusoe*, Fielding's novels and those of Richardson among the English. By no accident these were among the novels which Holcroft and Godwin took as models when they wrote their own 'fictious histories'. The most important example had the particular weight of autobiographical authenticity to add to their exploration of individual psychology and motive.

559   KENNEDY, Margaret. *The outlaws on Parnassus*. London: The Crescent Press, 1958; pp. 214.

Survey of the novel as fiction, looking at origins, definitions, narratology, narrative forms, the language of thought, ideas and ideology, artifice, ethics, Homer, modern trends. Ch. 4 "Narrative Forms" (46-70) provides an interesting comparison between *Moll Flanders* and *Manon Lescaut*, the latter being Prévost's own version of Defoe's novel which he much admired. Discusses the influences of narrative on form, pointing out that Prévost "could not take over Defoe's form, even if he had wished to do so, since his Manon was destined to die in the Plantations, whereas Moll came back from her sojourn in good shape [...]. Manon's story, therefore, had to be handed over to Des Grieux" (49-50).

560-----"The novelist and his public." *Trans Royal Soc of Lit* 32 (1963): 72-83.

Explores a series of reader reactions to novels. If any literature survives at all, it may be admired in spite of an element of panic, dismay and guilt which to generations delivered from the fears of those bygone days, may now seem rather feeble. The self-complacency implicit in much 18c literature is now alien to us. The self-pity implicit in much 20c literature may be equally alien to posterity.

561   KENNY, Shirley Strum (ed.). *British theater and other arts, 1660-1800*.

Washington DC: Folger Shakespeare Library, 1983; London: Assoc. UPs, 1983; pp. 311.

Essays on the theater in the Restoration and early 18c London, dealing with the relationship of the theater to other facets of London life: theater, music, and dance; theater and the visual arts, theater and fiction.

562 KENNY, Virginia C. *The country-house ethos in English literature, 1688-1750: themes of personal retreat and national expansion.* Brighton: Harvester Press, 1984; pp. x, 236.

Explores the themes of individual retreat and national expansion where they occur in the same work: the 17c country-house poems are the culmination of a long tradition of literary expression of ethical views about the right use of possessions. Defoe would tap directly into these issues in *Robinson Crusoe* where the island becomes the ultimate personal retreat and a metaphor for the colonial expansion of national interests based on industriousness and the right use of 'possessions' (human and material resources).

563 KERN, Jean B. "The fallen woman, from the perspective of five early eighteenth-century novelists." *StudECC* 10 (1981): 457-68.

Women novelists of the early 18c novel moved away from the French romances towards a more realistic novel of manners. In the period 1700 to 1726 women novelists (Aubin, Barker, Davys, Haywood, Manley) were attempting to write of manners out of their own experience, turning away from French romances to write of 'facts' and 'truth'. They clearly understood that sexual mores limited a woman more than a man. Bibliographic notes.

564 KETTLE, Arnold. *An introduction to the English novel.* Vol. 1. London: Hutchinson Univ. Library, 1951; pp. 189.

Tries to indicate something of the historical development of fiction, and to question why the novel arose at all, and why it should have arisen when it did. Looks at "Life and Fiction", "Realism and Romance", before turning to the 18c where he considers the moral tale, Defoe and the picaresque tradition (52-58). "What places Defoe in the picaresque tradition is his anti-romantic, anti-feudal realism, his concern with the feel and texture of the life he conveys, and lack of pattern. It is not true to say that there is no pattern in any of Defoe's novels, but there is not the kind of concern which informs and shapes the moral fable. Defoe's novels are not illustrations" (I:52). Notes and References (179-81). Reading List

(183-85).

565-----"The eighteenth-century novel in England." *Estudios sobre los géneros literarios, I* in *Acta Salamanticensia (Universidad de Salamanca)* 89 (1975): 149-60.

The novel starts in the 16c in Spain, then shifts to France in the 17c. In the 18c the novel is English. In the 19c there are several lines of contribution - France, England, Russian, American. The English novel of the 18c is a great phenomenon. Defoe, Richardson, Fielding and Sterne were innovators of extraordinary originality. All emerged from a common situation ushered in by the English Revolutionary Settlement of 1688, undermined by the Industrial Revolution and the new stage in the democratic revolution touched off by the events in France in 1789. Defoe uses all the picaresque elements (individualism, first-person narrator, episodic construction, one person taking on a hostile environment, realism, the absence of the feudal virtues of permanence, hierarchy, modesty, idealization). His realism rests on the achievements of the Puritan Revolution. Richardson found his way closer to the human heart than any previous writer of fiction. Fielding was less bourgeois than Defoe and Richardson (*Tom Jones* is about human behavior). There is an air of complacency, a totally non-historical attitude to people and their world: human nature is there to be explored and improved. These novelists are extremely realistic and extremely humane, and belong to a generation which has come through and achieved its revolution.

566 KIM, Elizabeth Sungeun. "Exploiting rape: Women's literary representations of rape in early eighteenth-century prose fictions." Unpub. doct. diss., Univ. of Michigan, 1995. [*DA* 56 (1995): 1368A.]

The rape metaphor with its built-in issues of power, subjugation and dominance, attracted many writers of both genders in the early 18c, but understanding of its literary use derives chiefly from the rape fictions of Defoe, Richardson and Fielding. Elaborates the range of violation by examining the rape narratives of the period's most influential women writers: Manley, Haywood, and Aubin. Their varied and resourceful uses of the rape narrative allowed these women passage into largely male literary and political spaces. Manley exploited the rape narrative in her scandal fictions to charge an entire political party with the metaphorical 'rape' of Queen Anne; Haywood, in directing attack on Robert Walpole, introduced race and fear of miscegenation into the rape discourse. Aubin used the rape metaphor to dramatize themes of Anglican oppression of Catholics. Draws on a wide range of cultural artefacts (travel narratives, visual material, personal correspondence, diaries and political journals) to show how these women gained topical voice for themselves by conjoining amatory fiction with the politically subversive rape plot.

567 KINKEAD-WEEKES, Mark. "Dr. Johnson on the rise of the novel." *NRam* 24 (1983): 28-9.

The striking thing about Dr. Johnson's criticism of the novel is that there is so little of it. He praised Richardson, damned Fielding, and had a few asides on *Robinson Crusoe, Gulliver's Travels* and *Tristram Shandy*. Illuminating on the nature and quality of Johnson's sensibility. Between the 1750s and 1780s, there were few novels of note, and Johnson had no occasion to write at any length on fiction.

568 KINSELLA, Thomas Edward. "Essays on eighteenth-century dialogue." Unpub. doct. diss., Pennsylvania, 1990. [*DAI* 50:7 (1990): 2064A.]

Moves among the genres of catechism, drama, poetry, prose, essay, the novel and biography in 18c English literature, analyzing ways in which genres interact and affect one another. The common link between the works is literary dialogue - the physical representation of speech on the page. Provides insights into relationship between authors and writings which influenced authors, their printers, publishers and reading audience. At the beginning of the century, authors put little value on dialogue as a literary device. By the end, many recognized dialogue as an important technique to be used with attention and skill.

569 KLEIN, Herbert-Günther. *Der Briefroman in der englischen Literatur vom 16. bis zum 18. Jahrhundert.* (European University Studies Series 14: Anglo-Saxon Language and Literature, 154.) Frankfurt-am-Main, Bern and New York: Peter Lang, 1986; pp. 328.

In German. Substantial 8-part study of the English epistolary novel, from its emergence in the 16c to its efflorescence in the 18c. Part 1 contains an introduction, an analysis of existing research, the nature of the letter as a means of communication, the epistolary novel, the novelistic letter. Part 2 looks at the origins of the literary use of letters: in Roman times, as part of the tradition of rhetoric, non-English influences, translations from Italian and Spanish literature, the Elizabethan prose narrative, the impact of French literature. Part 3 looks at the function of epistolary novel in England from the 16c to the 18c, as lovers' correspondence, as medium of intrigue, as document, as report and satire, as travel record, the means and modes of interpretation. Part 4 examines the epistolary novel as medium of communication, as motivation for writing, senders and receivers, intention and agency of change, success and failure of letters, the effect on the reader. Part 5 examines the letter format for the whole novel form, as agent of action and characterization, as agent of completion, as communications problem. Part 6 provides a useful summary of the foregoing (226-28), and looks to the form in the 19c and 20c (229-36). Part 7 provides a catalogue of epistolary novels from the 16c to the 18c (236-92), and a checklist of English novels with epistolary interpolations from the 16c to the 18c (293-300). Part 8 is a bibliography with works and anthologies (301-4), reference works and bibliographic aids (305-7), secondary literature (308-24). The absence of an index is a serious hindrance to scholarly usefulness.

570   KLEIN, Jürgen. *England zwischen Aufklärung und Romantik: Studien zur Literatur und Gesellschaft einer Übergangsepoche.* Tübingen: Narr, 1983; pp. 206.

Studies literature and society in England in the transitional period between the Enlightenment and Romanticism, using philosophy, religion, science and literature as seismographs of change. Looks at the world view of the Augustan Age (England between rationalism and optimism), the relation between literature and society in Fielding's *Joseph Andrews*, ethics and politics in Edmund Burke, the grotesque, negativity and individualism (the destruction of the principle of hope in the Gothic novel and English Romanticism), Heinrich Christoph Jussow and the English neo-Gothic, the problem of science in Mary Shelley's *Frankenstein*, Byron's idea of democracy (investigation of the link between literature and politics). Extensive bibliographic notes. Bibliography (197-206). Illus.

571   KLEIN, Phyllis. "Impertinent itinerants: literary representations of radical Protestant evangelism in England, 1660-1775." Unpub. doct. diss., Univ. of Denver, 1994. [*DA* 55 (1995): 2842A.]

As radical Protestant evangelists confronted English society between the Restoration and the beginnings of the Reform movement, their use of the Biblical discourse of salvation was curtailed in literary representations in ways which focused the anxieties of wider cultural change and the shift of power from the ruling elite to the increasingly vocal lower classes. The Pauline model and discourse shaped 18c English evangelical activity and literary response. By looking at various figures from 1662 to 1771 (Samuel Butler, Bunyan, Foote, George Whitefield, Swift, Hogarth, Richard Graves and Smollett) demonstrates that established culture was threatened by evangelistic discourse, and attempted to deny its authority and its speakers. These literary and graphic representations struggled against the radical Protestant evangelism which mobilized the lower classes, asserted transcendence against earthly power, and transferred legitimacy from reason to emotion.

572 KLIGER, Samuel. *The Goths in England: a study in seventeenth- and eighteenth-century thought.* Cambridge, MA: Harvard UP, 1952; pp. 304.

Gothic antiquity became for England a golden age, a symbol of a successful democracy. The epithet 'Gothic' became a trope for all those spiritual, moral, cultural values contained for the 18c in the single word 'enlightenment'.

573 KLOTZ, Günther. "Roman und bürgerliche Emanzipation, 1: Das bürgerliche Individuum als literarische Figur; 2: Optimismus und Wirklichkeit im englischen Roman des 18. Jahrhunderts." *ZAA* 23 (1975): 225-38; 285-99.

In German. Shows how the English novel in 18c played an important part in the social struggle against residual feudalism, and in the construction of a bourgeois consciousness, giving impulse to the aspiration to freedom and the presentation of a natural human happiness. Defoe, standing at the forefront of this new English novel, increased awareness of a crisis of conscience between the depiction of bourgeois virtue and reality of a complex inner nature.

574-----;SCHRÖDER, Winfried and WEBER, Peter (eds). *Literatur im Epochenumbruch: Funktionen europäischer Literaturen im 18. und beginnenden 19. Jahrhundert.* Berlin and Weimar: Aufbau-Verlag, 1977; pp. 714.

In German. Massive study of the sociological (Marxist) implications of literature in the 18c and early 19c: "Zur Erforschung der historischen und literarhistorischen Bewegungen des Überganges vom Feudalismus zum Kapitalismus in Europa werden von den Gesellschaftswissenschaften der sozialistischen Länder gegenwärtig grosse Anstrengungen unternommen" (7). The 58 essays cover the territorial and regional inequalities in the transition from feudalism to capitalism; the picture of the individual and society in merchant and bourgeois emancipation; the political-operative function of literature in the war of the classes; the unfolding of the power of productivity and the autonomy of the arts in the resolution of enduring assumptions in literary theory; the evolution of the concept of world literature. Notes (617-98). Index of Names (699-710).

575 KLUGE, Walter. *Die Szene als Bauelement des Erzählens im englischen Roman des achtzehnten Jahrhunderts.* Munich: Privately printed, 1966;

pp. ii, 222.

In German. Investigates the use of the self-contained scene in the structure of 18c novels, confining the detailed analysis to the work of Defoe, Smollett, Richardson, Fielding and Sterne. "Die Abgrenzung der Szene gegenüber dem Bericht und der thematisch örtlich und zeitlich weiter gespannten Erzählphrase erwies sich bereits rein dichtungslogisch als nicht kategoriell, sondern lediglich als graduell. Diese Feststellung kam uns bei der Untersuchung der Romans Defoes and Smolletts zustatten, die Szene und Bericht und Geschehen und Erzähler, was nach unserer Definition nicht identisch sein muss, selten gegeneinander ausspielen, wie das an Richardson, Fielding und Sterne zu beobachten ist" (210). Bibliography (219-22).

576 KNAUFF, Barbara Elizabeth. "Multilingualism in French late seventeenth- and eighteenth-century imaginary voyages." Unpub. doct. diss., Yale Univ., 1994. [*DA* 56 (1995): 959A.]

Traces the shift in the philosophy of language as it is expressed in late 17c and 18c imaginary voyages, examining the representation of language in these texts, as well as the political and cultural uses of linguistic differences. The notion of linguistic difference changed dramatically in this period. Uses works by Foigny, Veiras, Lahontan, Le Sage, Defoe, Casanova, Mme de Graffigny, and Voltaire. Imaginary voyages mirror the philosophical trend away from faith in Cartesian universality towards a firm belief in insurmountable linguistic obstacles separating people and cultures. The presence of the theme of multilingualism gives a glimpse at the authors' high metalinguistic awareness, and his or her individual perception of reading and writing.

577 KNIGHT, Charles A. "Satire and conversation: The logic of interpretation." *ECent* 26:3 (1985): 239-61.

Meaning lodges philosophically in the intentions of real authors, but meaning and intentions must be public ones, intentions to communicate. Readers are parties to a contractual cooperative principle: author and reader join in giving meaning to the complexities of irony and the harshness of satire.

578 KOBAYASHI, Akio. *Chapbook - kindai igirisu no kindaika.* Kyoto: Shinshindo, 1988; pp. 389.

In Japanese. Role of chapbooks in the 17c and 18c.

579 KOCZTUR, Gizella. *Regeny es szemelyiseg. Az angol regeny születese: Defoe, Richardson, and Fielding.* Budapest: Akademiai Kiado, 1987; pp. 269.

In Hungarian. Novel and character: the birth of the English novel: Defoe, Richardson and Fielding.

580 KOENIGS, Karen Jo-Ann. "Early evaluation of the novel: periodical-reviews of mid-eighteenth-century London." Unpub. doct. diss., Loyola Univ. of Chicago, 1976. [*DA* 36 (1976): 7410A-11A.]

Considers the reviews of novels in four major periodicals to determine the concept of the novel in the mind of the reading public, from *Pamela* (1740) to *Tristram Shandy* (1767). Presents the history, contents, politics and major writings with a chronological and topical charting of critical content of the *Gentleman's Magazine*, the *London Magazine*, the *Monthly Review*, the *Critical Review*.

581 KOIKE, Sekio. *Shi to fakkatsu - beikoku dorei bungaku 1701-1865.* Nagasaki: Seibono Kishisha, 1994; pp. 294.

In Japanese. Death and rebirth: investigates black slave literature between 1701 and 1865.

582 KOLODNY, Annette. *The land before her: fantasy and experience of the American frontiers, 1630-1860.* Chapel Hill, NC: U of North Carolina P, 1984; pp. xix, 293.

Charts women's private responses to the successive American frontiers, and to trace a tradition of women's public statements about the West. Book One "From Captivity to Accomodation, 1630-1833" contains ch. 1 "Captives in Paradise" (17-34) which recounts the late 17c and early 18c experience, and is particularly important for the context it provides for the captivity narrative. Bibliography (237-82).

583 KÖNIGSBERG, Ira. *Narrative technique in the English novel: Defoe to Austen.* Hamden, CT: Archon, 1986; pp. xii, 315.

Examines the ways in which the first major English novelists developed the form of the novel, and within that form, the techniques which produced readers' responses. Defoe, Richardson, Fielding, Smollett and Sterne all extended earlier literary techniques and created new ones to establish narrative methods basic to future novelists. Looks at reader experience, perceptional psychology, visualization in the novel, with a chapter on the individual novelists. Notes (265-96). Bibliography (297-

310). Index.

584   KORSHIN, Paul J. (ed.). *The widening circle: essays on the circulation of literature in 18ᵗʰ-century Europe*. Philadelphia: U of Pennsylvania P, 1976; pp. 204.

Collection of long essays concerning literacy and the reading public in the 18c. Using original primary material, they focus on publishing, reading and diffusion of printed materials in different countries. Looks at the concept of literacy and the history of books and their 18c readers with methods of evaluating these phenomena, the diffusion of printed materials, and the growth of reading. Introduction (1-11) followed by three essays: 1) Robert DARNTON, "Trade in the Taboo: The Life of a Clandestine Book Dealer in Pre-revolutionary France" (11-84); 2) Roy McKenn WILES, "The Relish for Reading in Provincial England Two Centuries Ago"(85-116). Observes that "There is no possibility of demonstrating statistically what proportion of the population in eighteenth-century England both could and did read [...] [but] there is sufficient testimony in the newspapers alone that increasingly in successive decades multitudes of English people developed and enjoyed a relish in reading" (112-13) Bernhard FABIAN, "English Books and Their 18th-century German Readers" (117-96). Describes how "a public acquired [...] through the printed page, an impressive familiarity with a foreign literature, and [...] became [...] literate in a foreign culture" (175). Each essay carries extensive bibliographical endnotes.

585-----*Typologies in England, 1650-1820*. Princeton, NJ; Guildford: Princeton UP, 1983; pp. xvii, 437.

Studies the literary application of typology in the late 17c and 18c. Looks at the typological propensity, the possibilities and limits of typology, figural change and survival of typological traditions, typology as system, the development of abstract typologies, typology and myth, typology and the novel, satire and prophecy, typology of everyday life. Of particular pertinence is Ch.7 "Typology and the Novel" (169-268), which considers the importance of typology as interpretation of narrative. Traces the origins of prefigurative and behavioral structures inherent in the concept of the Characters in the 17c and 18c, deriving in part from the character books. Devoted mainly to 18c novels, looking at aspects of the work of Defoe, Richardson, Fielding, Aubin, Barker, the picaresque, the Gothic, Goldsmith. Views typology as present in some 18c fiction, but as something which interpreters should use sparingly and tentatively. Ch.11 "Typology: a Bibliographical Essay" (396-408) is invaluable.

586-----and ALLEN, Robert R. (eds). *Greene centennial studies: essays presented to Donald Greene in the centennial year of the Univ. of Southern California.* Charlottesville: Virginia UP, 1984; pp. xx, 489.

Collection of essays on 18c studies, including: Henry Knight MILLER, "Some Reflections on Defoe's *Moll Flanders* and the Romance tradition" (72-92); Jean HAGSTRUM, "Pictures to the Heart: The Psychological Picturesque in Ann Radcliffe's *The Mysteries of Udolpho*" (434-41).

587 KOWALESKI-WALLACE, Beth. "Tea, gender, and domesticity in eighteenth-century England." *StudECC* 23 (1994): 131-45.

In 18c popular literature, newspapers, journals and poetry, tea functions as the image of a force which simultaneously facilitated and disrupted English domesticity. Often depicted at the center of the domestic scene, tea-drinking women are similarly represented as advancing or destroying the basis of a sound English economy. In a range of texts, the tea table was the place where civilization was simultaneously promoted and undermined. What is said about the drinking of tea and the tea table has more to do with the cultural definition of womanhood, particularly with woman's place in the domestic economy, than it does with the commodity itself, and reinforces the class-bound nature of such a project. Woman is defined as a force having the ability to advance or destroy civilization, depending on the economic and social circumstances in which she finds herself. She is simultaneously a sight beautiful to behold, and also, from another angle, a vision too frightening to contemplate. Bibliographical notes (143-45).

588-----*Consuming subjects: women, shopping, and business in the eighteenth century.* New York: Columbia UP, 1997; pp. 185.

Aims to explore the ideological construction of the modern female subject in relation to the emerging consumer culture of 18c Britain. During this period the female consumer was figured as a powerfully paradoxical presence. She was sometimes depicted as supremely disciplined, at other times as disruptive or disorderly. British culture projected onto the female subject both its fondest wishes for the transforming power of consumerism, and its deepest anxieties about the corrupting influences of goods. Over the course of the 18c, two processes occurred: a cultural struggle to define the meaning of consumption and the practices of modern consumerism, and the ideological construction of the female subject. Looks at the Tea Table (tea, sugar, China), shopping (commodities, shops and shoppers, pornography), business (businesswomen, prostitutes). Bibliographical notes (159-80). Index

(181-85).

589 KRAFT, Elizabeth Ann. "Character and consciousness in eighteenth-century comic fiction." Unpub. doct. diss., Emory Univ., 1985. [*DA* 46 (1985): 1635A.]

The novel was born in a time when theories of personal identity more and more concerned process of thought. Despite assertions that the comic novels of Fielding and Smollett have no inner life, characters of this fiction are very much the products of a cultural emphasis on consciousness, even though the comic vision disallows the alienation and despair experienced in the modern world and the novel.

590-----*Character and consciousness in eighteenth-century comic fiction.* Athens, GA and London: U of Georgia P, 1992; pp. xv. 202.

In the past, comic novelists were seen to be reluctant to recognize inwardness, the absence of immersion into the psychology of an individual character served as evidence of a conservative ideology. While they avoid total involvement in the mind of any one character, they are nonetheless concerned with the nature of consciousness. Examines the *kind* of consciousness central to 18c comic fiction - the underprivileged, unauthoritative, eminently revisable narrative that forms the consciousness of the comic character. How do they reflect existence? What truths about our lives do they reveal? They 'decenter' us, call our importance into question, challenge our privilege in a variety of ways. The first part looks at the concept of character, the construct of consciousness, the identity of the narrator: 18c character and the 20c reader, character of consciousness in the 18c, narrative authority and the controlling consciousness. The second part looks at particular works of fiction, with reference to Fielding, Lennox, Sterne, Smollett, Burney. Each author questions to some degree the truth-telling capacity of the narrative, to shape the novel, appraising its readership and limitations. Bibliographical notes (159-81). Bibliography (183-96). Index (197-202).

591 KROOK, Anne Karin. "The genesis of authority: Scripture, satire, and interpretation in English literature, 1660-1760." Unpub. doct. diss., Cornell Univ., 1989. [*DAI* 50:3 (1989): 691A.]

Examines the literary representation of divine authority from 1660 to 1760. Thematic changes included a gradually increasing perception that forms of human activity have become discreet from divine authority, an increasing sense of human inability to perceive divine authority accurately. Generic changes included a move away from the heroic form to the satire. Perhaps more than at any other time since then, English history, philosophy, theology and literature were written and discussed in terms drawn from contemporary debates about the nature of Scriptural texts.

592 KROPF, Carl R. "Literary persona and role theory." *EE* 5:3/4 (1974): 14-25. Role theory puts to rest the argument that literary impersonation concerns the creation of a mythic identity which obliterates the author entirely, and at the other extreme, that the historic author and his work are accountable for the accuracy of all relevant historical and biographical data. We know ourselves and others only by the roles we play, and the same is surely true of authors and readers.

593-----*Reader entrapment in eighteenth-century literature*. New York: AMS Press, 1992; pp. xvii, 267.

Reader entrapment occurs when authors seems to force their reader into choosing among unacceptable readings, forces them into an unacceptable role, arouses expectations it does not fulfil, and otherwise causes their reader significant discomfort. In written texts it usually beguiles the reader into consenting to a proposition that is uncomfortable, self-contradictory, or turns out to have painful consequences (Swift, Pope, Fielding, drama). Centers mainly on Swift: "His prose satires are the densest the language has to offer, and in spite of the large volume of criticism devoted to them within the past decades, his poems remain fresh, enigmatic and fascinating" (xvii). Bibliography (261-62). Index (263-67).

594 KRUGER, Kathryn Sullivan. "Weaving the word: the metaphorics of weaving and female textual production." Unpub. doct. diss., Univ. of Miami, 1994. [*DA* 56 (1995): 943A.]

A culture records the symbols of its own heritage on the body of a textile, like a text encodes a page. Draws on anthropology, language, theory and analysis of Greek myths, as well as some late 18c and early 19c texts to examine scenes of weaving wherein women transform a domestic craft into a tool for signification. Weaving is related to the weaving of poetry, spells and prophecy. The stories of Arachne, Philomela, Penelope and Helen of Troy explore how different modes of weaving reflect the weaver's relationship towards the dominant culture. Also examines Blake ("The Four Zoas") and Tennyson ("The Lady of Shalott").

595 KRUTCH, Joseph W. *Five masters: Boccaccio, Cervantes, Richardson, Stendhal, Proust: a study in the mutations of the novel*. London:

Jonathan Cape, 1931. Rpt. Bloomington Indiana UP, 1959; pp. 312, illus.

History of the novel through five representative figures of primary importance. Useful for providing background on Richardson, so central to the fiction of the 18c.

596   KUBEK, Elizabeth E. Bennett. "The myth of the city: women's experiences of London in English fiction, 1660-1810." Unpub. doct. diss., The Univ. of Rochester, 1990. [*DAI* 51:2 (1990): 512A.]

Women and their culture are traditionally marginalized in urban culture. Women desire the carnal and transgressive lifestyles possible in the modern city. They acquire forbidden knowledge about male sexual values and the physical space of London.

597   KURTH, Lieselotte E. *Die zweite Wirklichkeit*. Chapel Hill: North Carolina UP, 1969; pp. 272.

In German. Investigation of German literary criticism in 18c. Part 1 considers 1) the novel in relation to society, looking carefully at the criticism and theory of the novel in the early 18c (10-25). 2) This can be seen in three parts: a new evaluation of traditional works of prose, in particular the relationship to the pseudo-historical novel of the 17c; an evaluation or critical judgement of the *galant* novel; the proliferation of novels and criticism emanating from France and England; 3) magazines and the novel; 4) the French novel; 5) the English novel (Richardson and Fielding) (50-64); 6) criticism and theory of the novel in the second half of the 18c; 7) the novel in writing and poetry. Part 2 looks at literature in the fictional world of the novel. Notes (249-58). Bibliography (259-66). Index (267-72).

598   LADEN, Marie-Paule. "Faces of the first person: the eighteenth-century novel in France and England." Unpub. doct. diss., Brown Univ., 1980. [*DA* 41 (1981): 509A.]

Studies how the self is represented in certain 18c French and English fictive memoirs (Le Sage's *Gil Blas*, Defoe's *Moll Flanders*, Richardson's *Pamela*, Marivaux's *La Vie de Marianne* and *Le Paysan parvenu*, and Sterne's *Tristram Shandy*). By examining the use of first-person in these novels, probes and challenges Benveniste's assertion that the pronoun 'I' simply designates the person who uses it. As the writer's discourse unfolds over a time span, we can discern significant differences and attitudes reflected in multiple selves. The protagonist evolves in the course of the narrative, but because of the paradoxical split in the situation of enunciation, this objectified self, even at the end of the story, cannot completely rejoin the writing 'I'.

599-----*Self-imitation in the eighteenth-century novel.* Princeton, NJ; Guildford: Princeton UP, 1987; pp. x, 192.

Explores the first-person narrative form as an alleged seal of authenticity in various 18c English, French and German fictions. Introduction (3-22); *Gil Blas* and *Moll Flanders*: imitation, disguise and mask; *Pamela, La Vie de Marianne, Le Paysan parvenu*: self-imitation, the appearance of reality; *Tristram Shandy*: imitation as paradox and joke. Bibliography (175-88). Index (189-92).

600 LANDA, Louis A. *Essays in eighteenth-century literature.* Princeton, NJ; Guildford: Princeton UP, 1980; pp. 241.

Collection of essays on Jonathan Swift, Alexander Pope, Samuel Johnson and Laurence Sterne. Devoted to the great metropolis of London, as Englishmen of the 17c and 18c viewed it. Also study of the pervasive and influential mercantile economic thought of the times, a rationalistic concept that awed men of all persuasions and found its way reverentially into the works of theologians, ethical writers and literary men. Bibliographic notes. Index (233-41).

601 LANGBAUER, Laurie. "Empty constructions: women and romance in the English novel." Unpub. doct. diss., Cornell Univ., 1985. [*DA* 46: (1985): 214A.]
Using the example of Charlotte Lennox's *The Female Quixote*, shows how the novel tries to purge itself of the perceived problems of romance by aligning the heroine with romance, then attempting to save her from it. The romance problems of disorder, rigidity of form and ambiguities of meaning, are the problems of the novel itself. Also refers to Dickens, Brontë and Eliot.

602 LANGE, Viktor. "Erzählformen im Roman des achtzehnten Jahrhunderts." In BÖCKMANN, Paul (ed.). *Stil- und Formprobleme.* Heidelberg: Carl Winter, 1959; pp. 224-29.

In German. Examines the great 18c novels, and sees the emergence of the modern concept of the interiorizing of the narrative, not always in a psychological or sentimental sense, but also in relation to a double tendency and function in the presentation. On the one side there is a progressive transformation of the world in the consciousness, and on the other the obligation of the narrator to lend individuality to this.

603　LANIER, Sidney. *The English novel: the development of personality*. New York, 1883. Rev. ed. New York: Charles Scribner's Sons, 1914; pp. xv, 302.

Derived from a series of lectures delivered at Johns Hopkins in 1881. Examples three lines of development pertaining to his subject: the "growth in personality", the "simultaneous rise of music, science, and the novel", and how "the increase of personality has required more complex forms of expression". Provides "illustrations by extracts from the novels". Discusses concepts of personality from Chaucer, Malory and Shakespeare. The earliest novels considered are by Richardson, Fielding and Smollett.

604　LAUTERMILCH, Steven James. "The marriage of realism and romance in the eighteenth-century English novel." Unpub. doct. diss., Univ. of Michigan, 1973. [*DA* 36 (1975): 1528A.]

Re-examines the theory and practice of fiction in the 18c English novel. It is characterized by realism and romance, but what is the nature of this relationship? Given the form and tradition of romance, why is realism added? *Moll Flanders*, *Clarissa* and *Tom Jones* are the main points of reference. They adapt the three modes of medieval narrative - rogue's tale, saint's life, knight's quest. Seeks to define theory and practice arising from a marriage of realism and romance, and the questions of rhetoric and religion such a union represents. *Moll Flanders* proves both picaresque and antinomian, emphasizing the ambiguity in terms of Providence. *Clarissa* becomes almost Jansenist, allowing *Liebestod* to escape in martyrdom. *Tom Jones* is epic as well as comic, portraying the attitudes of Christian humanism.

605　LAWLOR, John. "Radical satire and the realistic novel." *E & S* new ser. 8 (1955): 58-75.

Sees the triumph of Augustan verse satire as so distinctive that it became definitive: the "cool excellence of the poet always in control of his theme everywhere", the master of the comic predicament. Whether the satire is urbane or vehement, the satirist is a commanding figure, the champion of intelligence and good sense. It oversees the imposition of order, the self-possession of the artist in the face of apparent contradiction and complexity. It runs the risk of becoming merely destructive. Looks at Dryden and Swift, and considers the special character of Gulliver, who becomes the reader's own witness of the world and its folly. Considers the further contribution of realistic fiction to this mode of irony, esp. in the case of Flaubert. *Madame Bovary* is the decisive contribution to the modern art of fiction for it builds a bridge between the world of satire and the extended portrayal of character.

606 LAWSON, Jacqueline Elaine. *Domestic misconduct in the novels of Defoe, Richardson, and Fielding.* San Francisco: Mellen Research UP, 1993; pp. vii, 179.

The family is an icon of public morality, failure and hope, also in the 18c context. Using Defoe's *Roxana*, Richardson's *Clarissa* and Fielding's *Amelia*, explores the social intricacies that reflect the evolving nature of family structures. The novel used didacticism to engage the reader in the novelist's vision of society. Even though society was male-dominated, the female protagonists of these works emphasize the role of women as Eve, whether fallen from grace, or personifying redemption through virtue. The bibliography (145-72) is very useful, divided into Domestic Relations, Literary and Historical Works on the Family, Sociological and Psychological Works on the Family, and Individual Authors. Index (173-79).

607 LEAVIS, Frank Raymond. *The great tradition.* London: Chatto & Windus, 1948; pp. 266.

Discusses the 18c novelists briefly and dismissively in the opening chapter (2-4).

608 LEAVIS, Queenie Dorothy. *Fiction and the reading public.* London: Chatto & Windus, 1932; pp. xvi, 348.

Considers the contemporary situation (the book market, the middleman, author and reader); the past (the birth of journalism, the Puritan conscience, the growth and disintegration of the reading public); the significance of the bestseller (the novel, reading, reading capacity, living at the novelist's expense). Provides a list of bestsellers, books which achieved two or more editions (from 1578 to 1930), with the early 18c listed (331-32). Selected Bibliography (336-45).

609 LEE, Vernon. *The handling of words and other studies in literary psychology.* London: John Lane, The Bodley Head, 1923; pp. ix, 315.

Investigates literary construction, style, the aesthetics of the novel, the nature of the writer. Then looks at literary psychology and the handling of words. The latter two sections deal with close readings of examples, all from the 19c and early 20c.

610 LEGOUIS, Émile and CAZAMIAN, Louis. *A History of English Literature.*

The Middle Ages and Renascence (650-1660) by Émile Legouis. *Translated from the French by Helen Douglas Irvine. Modern Times (1660-1950)* by Louis Cazamian. *Translated from the French by W. P. MacInnes and the author* (1930). Rev. ed. London: Dent, 1954; pp. 1427.

Part II Modern Times (1660-1950) Ch. 4 "The Literature of the Middle Classes" (769-87) deals with Defoe (771-77). Discusses him in terms of class, his use if verisimilitude and moralizing. "The force of mental realism destroys the very principle of realism; the visionary Defoe only further develops the practical middle-class citizen" (776). In discussing *Robinson Crusoe*, observes "Defoe has written not only the instructive story of the perils which befall a frail humanity preserved by supernatural aid, but the symbolic drama of the painful patient effort by which civilization has come into being." Index (1411-27).

611 LEICHT, Kathleen Ann. "Cross-gender narration in the early English novel." Unpub. doct. diss., Univ. of Rochester, 1993. [*DA* 54 (1994): 3448A.]

Describes narrative conventions associated with the portrayal of male and female first-person narrations in English fictions of the early 18c, and examines the relationship between the sex of the writer and his or her use of such conventions. The analysis compares representations of the female narration by Daniel Defoe and Samuel Richardson to representations of male narrations by several women novelists, notably Eliza Haywood. The comparison reveals that narrative authority resides in the figure of the narrator himself when a male character tells the story, while female narrators must place their authority for writing elsewhere. The circumstances compelling the narration, the reader's judgement of it, and the truth of the sentiments expressed, are commonly cited sources of authority for female narrators. Narrations of the opposite sex are used in order to achieve a relationship to authority they cannot achieve through the voices of their own sex. The trope of masquerade works to describe the mechanism: cross-gender narration works like a mask and licences the writer to play with language in ways not ordinarily permitted by the conventions of same-sex narrators. It is used to question the conceptions of identity that arise from a society based on sexual difference.

612 LENTA, Margaret. "Form and content: a study of the epistolary novel." *UCT Studies in English* 10 (1980): 14-30.
The immense popularity of Richardson's three novels gave the epistolary mode a special status in the 19c. It allowed him to write with quasi-dramatic realism, as well as to explore the consciousness of his characters more profoundly than any earlier writer of fiction had been able to do. It

involves intimacy and a process of self-discovery.

613 LESLIE, Michael and RAYLOR, Timothy (eds). *Culture and cultivation in early modern England: writing and the land.* Leicester: Leicester UP, 1992; pp. xiii, 261.

The essays document and analyze some of the terms in which the land was conceived of and represented from the early 16c to the early 18c, how the land was written about in "a time when new conceptions of the natural world were actively and consciously created" (1).

614 LEVINE, Joseph M. *The battle of the books: history and literature in the Augustan Age.* Ithaca and London: Cornell UP, 1991; pp. xiv, 428.

Sir William Temple's essay of 1690 focused attention on the controversy about the claims for the relative merits of ancient and modern culture. Should one abide by the rules and examples of classical life in coming to grips with the modern world, or should there be some measure of freedom and invention? The discussion continued for decades, with ever more acrimonious argument on the Continent. By 1730 the argument appeared to be over. Renaissance humanism and the revival of antiquity had always generated a paradox. The Classics were resurrected for immediate use, but in order to make sense of them, scholars had to invent the techniques and methods of modern philology. Divided into two parts: 1) Literature (Wolton versus Temple; Bentley versus Christ Church; stroke and counterstroke; the *querelle*; Ancient Greece and modern scholarship; Pope and the quarrel between the Ancient and Modern; Bentley's Milton); 2) History (history and theory; Ancient; Modern; Ancient and Modern). Bibliographic footnotes. Index (419-28).

615 LEVINE, William Scott. "Towards a genealogy of English literary change: 1740-1820." Unpub. doct. diss., Indiana Univ., 1990. [*DAI* 50:12 (1989): 3962A.]

Conventional histories of English literature maintain a sharp opposition between the "Neoclassical" aesthetics of the early mid-18c and the Romantic aesthetics that began in the latter half of the 18c. As an alternative to these broadly categorical views of literary periods, a different kind of history may examine the function of past literature and criticism in constituting new works. This "genealogical" history complicates the idea of a harmonious, unified literary era because it demonstrates how writers borrow from, reinterpret, and compare the works of previous generations, esp. those in the recent past. In addition, this type of historical investigation places greater emphasis on circumstantial reasons for change than on broad temporal developments.

616 LIDDELL, Robert. *A treatise on the novel*. London: Jonathan Cape, 1947;
pp. 168.
Critical treatise on the theory of novel writing, presenting an approach
to the criticism of fiction, investigating the novelist's scope (selection and
range), the values of the novelist, the making of plot (types and models),
the making of characters (life, flat and mixed characters), background
(utilitarian, symbolic, objective and subjective). Discussion of 18c fiction
touches on Richardson and Fielding. Comments on the prevalence of
drama before 1740, observing that "we may attribute much of the tedium
of pre-Richardsonian fiction to the fact that it was the work of essentially
uncreative minds, more creative minds being in the service of the stage"
(18). Index (165-68).

617 LIDDLE, Mary Susan. "The letter and identity in eighteenth-century
fiction." Unpub. doct. diss., Stanford Univ., 1988. [*DA* 49 (1988):
1472A.]
During the 18c interest in the novel was tempered by accusations of
inauthenticity. Letters played a large role as means of communication,
and were concluded to be authentic expressions of their writers. Novels
of letters were treated as genuine, sentimental documents, the author
being no more than an editor. The period of popularity coincided with a
deepening interest in the individual and the capacity of the letter to
represent individual identity, as a metaphor for the complexity,
variability and fragility of identity. Considers Richardson, Goethe,
Rousseau, Laclos.

618 LINDQUIST, Wayne Paul. "Smollett and the structure of the novel." Unpub.
doct. diss., Univ. of Iowa, 1968. [*DA* 29 (1968): 1827A.]

Part of the work analyzes Defoe's place in the development of the English
novel.

619 LOCKHEAD, Mario. "Social history in miniature: domestic tales for
children." *Quarterly Review* 291 (1953): 516-30.

Old books for children are a source of social history. They are worth
cherishing because of their virtue as stories and their preservations of
forgotten facts of everyday life. In additional to plot and incident, the
setting of these tales with its depiction of dress, food, furniture and
possessions are vivid in detail. Traces the moralistic dimension in the
domestic tale back to Thomas Daly's "Sandford and Merton" (1783-89)
and various tales ("Moral Tales") by Maria Edgeworth. Useful as an

adjunct to BEACHCROFT (**218**) and CANBY (**301**).

620 LONDON, A. K. "Landscape and the eighteenth-century novel." Unpub. doct. diss., Univ. of Oxford, 1980.
No abstract available.

621 LONDON, April. "Placing the female: the metonymic garden in amatory and pious narrative, 1700-1740". In (pp. 101-23) SCHOFIELD and MACHESKI, *'Fetter'd or free'?* etc., **860**.

Amatory and pious novels share a concern with the fundamental issues of authority. Secular and religious were complementary responses to a world perceived as inescapably hierarchical, with characters yielding control to a superior divine or sexual force. The predominantly female protagonists use subordination of character both structurally and thematically, with gender and genre used interchangeably to realize their subject status.

622 LONGAKER, John Marsh. *English biography in the eighteenth century.* Philadelphia: U of Pennsylvania P, 1931; pp. 519.

Surveys historically and critically the nativity and growth of the English biography in the 18c. Looks at life-writing before 1700, influences which made possible the modern conception of biography, the growth of realism in the pamphlet lives, chronicles of crime, intimate memoirs and rogue lives, the 'private life' element, the advance of scholarly methods, the development of biographical lexicography in the 18c, methods of William Mason, Johnson and Boswell.

623 LONGERBEAM, Larry Simpson. "Seduction as symbolic action: a study of the seduction motif in six Victorian novels." Unpub. doct. diss., George Peabody College for Teachers, 1975. [*DA* 36 (1975): 2222A.]

Focuses on George Eliot, Hardy, Meredith and George Moore. Useful general discussion of the seduction motif, with consideration also of Fielding and M. G. Lewis.

624 LOTT, Anna Elizabeth. "Proper conduct: women teaching men in the eighteenth-century didactic novel." Unpub. doct. diss., Washington Univ., 1993. [*DA* 54 (1994): 3759A.]

Considers the figure of the woman educator in 18c writing, the paradoxical nature (both limiting and empowering) of 18c women's familial role as social and moral educator. The duties expected of women educators and the powers granted to them change between the late 17c and early 19c. Throughout the 18c, novelists and conduct-book writers confined the female educator to the house, but in late 18c and early 19c the role is expanded to establish identities as schoolteachers and educational philosophers (Richardson, Inchbald, More, Edgeworth, Austen).

625 LOVELL, Terry. *Consuming fiction.* (Questions for Feminism.) London: Verso, 1987; pp. vii, 188.

Ch. 2 "Capitalism and the Novel" (19-46) examines the attitude among Marxist and non-Marxist theorists of literature that the novel is a bourgeois form closely linked with the development of Capitalism. Ian WATT is seen as failing to integrate literary-sociological criteria in his definition of the novel. A consideration of women as members of the bourgeoisie and as writers would have forced reassessment, not only of the literary-critical standards of the 'the Great Tradition', but the whole definition of the bourgeoisie in terms of male labor and male Protestant rationality. But he was right in seeing the parenting of the novel not primarily by its literary mothers and founding fathers, but by Capitalism which is the true origin of the new form.

626 LOVETT, Robert Moss and HUGHES, Helen Sard. *The history of the novel in England.* Boston: Houghton Mifflin, 1932/ London: George Harrap & Co. Ltd., 1933; pp. 495.

Of particular interest are ch. 2 "Seventeenth-Century Fiction" (17-35) which provides succinct but cogent observations on the principal modes, genres and authors (esp. Behn and Bunyan), and ch. 3 "Eighteenth-Century Fiction" (36-51), which is divided between 'Defoe' (40-48) and 'From Defoe to Richardson' (48-51). Observations are very brief, but perceptive. Bibliography (466-79). Index (481-95). Illus.

627 LUBBOCK, Percy. *The craft of fiction.* London: Jonathan Cape, 1921; pp. 277. Rev. with new preface 1954.

Classic survey of the novel form, examining structure, the process of telling and showing. "To grasp the shadowy and fantasmal form of a book, to hold it fast, to turn it over and survey it at leisure - that is the effort of a critic of books" (1). Examines the qualities of narrative authority: Defoe produced it by the assertion of the historic truthfulness of his stories (62). Considers Richardson and his use of the epistolary form "in the attempt to show a mind in action" (152). Index (275-77).

628   LUNN, Robert Francis. "Infinite isolations: a study of self-enclosure in eighteenth-century novels." Unpub. doct. diss., Univ. of Texas at Austin, 1977. [*DA* 38 (1978): 7326A.]

It is possible to see the 18c novel as part of a progression in the development of the genre, a crucial feature of which is the isolation of the protagonist. It is to do with "self-enclosure", which implies both social exclusion and psychological isolation. The 18c was also a period conscious of a new sense of individualism and the attendant problem of reconciling the individual and the group. Hobbes and Locke show philosophical interest in this question. The novel reflects fragmentation and interiority.

629   LYNCH, James John. "Henry Fielding and the Byzantine novel: a study of romance forms in eighteenth-century prose fiction." Unpub. doct. diss., Univ. of Texas, 1980. [*DA* 41 (1981): 3118A.]

Although Fielding, like many of his contemporaries, rejects "Romances" and proposes instead to found "A new Province of Writing", the spirit of romance and some of its conventional pattern and elements still exist in *Joseph Andrews, Tom Jones* and *Amelia*. By comparing these novels to a particular romance form - the Byzantine novel - we can better define the synthesis Fielding effects in the novel and his use of literary conventions attributable to direct lines of influence. The novels imitating Heliodorus's third-century *Aetheopica*, including Cervantes's *Persites* and the French heroic novels of the mid-17c, establish the ancient romance plot as a narrative structure and use it to unify other, more contemporary, narrative concerns. Its plot concerns two lovers whose marriage is prevented by parental objections and by mysteries of identity, journeying towards a specific geographic locale, where their vows are fulfilled and the obstacles overcome.

630   LYONS, John O. *The invention of the self: the hinge of consciousness in the eighteenth century*. Carbondale: Southern Illinois UP; London: Feffer & Simons, 1978; pp. 268.

Study of 18c fiction. Ch. 9 "Rogues and Adventurers" (75-88) delineates the picaresque tradition in its importance for Defoe who "elaborates the idea that character (and presumably ideas) is not innate, but rather the sum of environment, and that actions are largely the result of the need to gratify the appetites" (81).

631   McALLISTER, Marie E. "Women on the journey; eighteenth-century British women's travel in fact and fiction." Unpub. doct. diss., Princeton

Univ., 1987. [*DA* 49 (1988): 259A.]

Explores women's travel writing in the 18c through a study of British women's non-fiction travel accounts, and women's travel in contemporary novels by women. Argues for the literary status of non-fiction travel. Studies the effects of gender, class, and audience on travel writing (Mary Wortley Montague, Elizabeth Carter), links between domestic travel writing, autobiography and establishing a female language of travel (Mary Ann Hanway, Hester Piozzi). Travel and the French Revolution freed women to enter into political discourse (Charlotte Smith, Fanny Burney). Also considers female travel as the means for feminist protest (Mary Wollstonecraft).

632 MACCARTHY, Bridget Gerard. *Women writers: their contribution to the English novel, 1621-1744.* (The Female Pen, 1.) Cork: Cork UP, 1945; pp. 288.
Traces the contribution of women to the development of the novel, and the influences which conditioned it. Ch. 7 "From 1689 to 1744" (214-62) considers the Key Novel, the Sentimental Novella, the Novel of Domestic Sentiment and of Manners, the Didactic Tale, the Picaresque Tale, and discusses Mary Manley, Eliza Haywood, Elizabeth Rowe, Jane Barker, Penelope Aubin, Mary Davys, Elizabeth Boyd, Arabella Plantin, Sarah Fielding. Ch. 8 "The Epistolary Form Prior to 1740" (263-86) looks at Margaret Cavendish, Aphra Behn, Mary Manley, Eliza Haywoood and Elizabeth Rowe. Extensive quotations from the principal works, but no critical apparatus at all. Index (287-88).

633-----*The later women novelists, 1744-1800.* Cork: Cork UP, 1947; pp. 296.

Second part of the survey of female writers, this time in the 18c and 19c. Investigates their contributions under the Oriental Novel, the Novel of Sentiment and Sensibility, the Domestic Novel (the Novel of Manners), the Didactic Novel. The Oriental Novel contains sections on Aubin and Haywood, the Novel of Sentiment on Charlotte Lennox. Bibliography (283-90). Index (291-96).

634-----*The Female Pen: women writers and novelists, 1621-1818.* Preface by Janet TODD. New York: New York UP, 1994. p. xxiv, 530.

Reprint in one volume of the original *Women writers* (1945) and *The later women novelists* (1947). The preface places McCarthy in the context of female critics of the early and mid-20c, and assesses her pioneering work in the light of feminism, and other developments in the realm of literary criticism in the late 20c. "She is a literary critic, not a modern cultural historian and she makes claims for her women in the context of her belief in the values in art. She has no interest in the women writers who do not pretend to Literature, those who have come to prominence in recent years in accordance with new theories such as New Historicism or Cultural Materialism" (xiii). Todd further points out that she ignores Quaker and Dissenting women of the 17c, the aristocratic letter writers of the 18c, cooking or conduct-book makers, makes "dated social judgements", and does not deal with the picaresque or rogue biography. Her thesis of the novel was "the daring notion that women are particularly associated with realism and verisimilitude."

635 McCLISH, Glen Arthur. "Rhetoric and the rise of the English novel." Unpub. doct. diss., Univ. of California, Berkeley, 1986. [*DA* 48:3 (1987): 1211A.]

Demonstrates the pervasive nature of the period's ambivalent attitude towards rhetoric. In a world in which the workings of Providence are for the greater part hidden from view, characters, and for that matter, narrators, must rely on their rhetorical skills to carve their meandering routes through life.

636 McCORMICK, I. D. "The monstrous and the sportive: grotesque in the early eighteenth century." Unpub. doct. diss., Univ. of Leeds, 1993. [*IT* 44:2 (1995): 514.]

Explores the classification of the grotesque and its disruptive role in natural and philosophical taxonomic systems. The grotesque served as a useful repository for the marvellous, the hybrid, and the preternatural. Looks at where the grotesque should be placed, how it manipulates different kinds of inner space, from the mental and the private spheres of representation, to the grotesque body. Also looks at the public manifestations of the grotesque in pastimes like fairs and masquerades where it reflects the evolving commercial system.

637 McCREA, Brian. *Impotent fathers: Patriarchy and demographic crisis in the eighteenth-century novel.* Newark: Delaware UP; London: Assoc. UPs, 1998; pp. 242.

Faced with the challenges of changing demography in 17c and 18c England, family life was reflected in several well established fictions. Investigates how as the patriarch became a decentered, even a marginalized figure, women in 18c novels assumed great but uncertain power. Few characters came to see the cost of representing masculine authority through the female line: the passions, needs, and rights of women who stood at the center of succession become both impossible to dismiss and yet difficult to articulate. Novels may change the social conditions, or at least change the attitude of readers to those conditions. The novel may claim to offer more than a dialectic circumscribed by the prison and the carnival, by the repressive father and the silenced daughter. Notes (195-226). Index (227-42).

638 MACCUBIN, Robert Purks (ed.). *'Tis nature's fault: unauthorized sexuality during the Enlightenment*. Cambridge, New York and Melbourne: Cambridge UP, 1987; pp. 260.

Collection of essays exploring the history of sexual advice literature. Tries to throw light on the broader contours of sexual values and practices of earlier times. Looks at tensions within the heterosexual domestic world; how mechanisms and the laws of nature affected Enlightenment thinking, and questioning of orthodox bases of judgement on masturbation and homosexuality; the role of sexual discourse in helping to undermine the old order; the diffusion of pornography and obscenity in France and Italy; the notion of libertinism, the historiography of homosexuality, homosexuality in three different cultures (England, France and Holland); analyzes of police archives and court records to explore changing attitudes to homosexuality and the existence of homosexual subcultures; censorship, erotica, the language of sexual reference, manuscript pornography. Detailed bibliographical notes.

639 McDERMOTT, Hubert. *Novel and romance: the 'Odyssey' to 'Tom Jones'*. Totowa, NJ: Barnes & Noble; Basingstoke: Macmillan, 1989; pp. xi, 257.

The English novel was not a new invention by any means, but simply a new synthesis of pre-existing modes. Fielding appears to have borrowed his theory of fiction from the French writers of heroic romance, his techniques from Paul Scarron, and his fictional structure from drama. Most importantly, he based his concept of realism on the theory of Classical comedy. Looks at: 1) ancient narrative modes; 2) medieval romance; 3) pre-18c romance (Elizabethan romance, French romance of the 16c and 17c, heroic romance in England, passionate romance, religious romance); 4) Richardson and romance; 5) Fielding's comic romances. Appendix 1 and 2 (226-29). Notes and references (230-42). Select bibliography (243-51). Index (252-57).

640 MACDOWELL, Paula Joanne. "The women of Grub Street: gender, press and politics in the London literary masterpiece, 1688-1730." Unpub. doct. diss., Stanford Univ., 1992. [*DAI* 53:1 (1992): 161A.]

See the printed version below.

641-----*The women of Grub Street.* Oxford: Clarendon Press, 1998; pp. xi, 347.

The period 1678-1730 was decisive not only in Western political history, but also in the history of the British press. Changing conditions for political expression, and the expanding book trade, enabled unprecedented opportunities for political activity. Women already at work in the London book trade were among the first to seize these new opportunities for public political expression. Examines women writers, and also printers, booksellers, and other producers and distributors of printed texts. Provides much new information about the nature, extent and complexities of women's participation in the print culture and public politics, esp. about the political-literary lives of lower-class women. Women of a large range of socio-economic backgrounds and religio-political allegiances play a very prominent role in the production and transmission of political ideas, a situation which belies claims that women had no place in public life. Bibliographic footnotes. Bibliography (302-34). Index (335-47). Illus. (5 plates).

642 MACEY, Samuel L. *Money and the novel: mercenary motivation in Defoe and his immediate successors.* Victoria, BC: Sono Niss Press, 1983; pp. 184.

Important for focusing attention on Defoe as the founder of the first prose epics of the common man and woman, motivated by the accumulation of wealth on this earth. Defoe differs from Bunyan's *Pilgrim's Progress* in his careful enumeration of earthly time and wealth. His novels allowed his readers to enjoy vicariously experiences relating directly to their own class and times: wealth was being accumulated by ordinary Englishmen and women, at home and abroad, as never before. Part I is concerned with navigation, projects and financial institutions, the middle-class amassing of money, the dangerous transition from bourgeois to gentleman. Notes (174-81).

643 McGRAW, Patricia Marie. "Ideas about children in eighteenth-century British fiction." Unpub. doct. diss., Univ. of Connecticut, 1976. [*DA* 36 (1976): 7441A.]

Studies in the history of attitudes to children have noted the importance of the 18c as the starting point for most modern ideas. 18c fiction was a powerful source of information. Examines the widely read novels of Defoe, Richardson, Fielding, Smollett, Sterne and Edgeworth. Two philosophers were particularly influential, Locke and Rousseau. Locke in *Some Thoughts Concerning Education* (1693) examined children's characteristics and children's reading, and provided an intellectual framework for future developments. 70 years later in *Émile*, Rousseau argued that children were innately good, and should be protected from corrupting social institutes. Both believed that environment was crucial to a child's development. Discusses why childhood was rarely the central study of early novels (Defoe does portray it in some detail), the nature-nurture debate, parental duties, motherly matters, educational theories, fictional accounts of schooling. In the 18c children were not yet sentimentalized.

644   MACK, Edward C. "Pamela'a stepdaughters: the heroines of Smollett and Fielding." *College Eng* 9 (March 1947): 291-301.

Fielding and Smollett were equally involved in depicting the 18c heroine, and offer an object-lesson in fruitful and sterile methods of coming to terms with popular taste. Fielding absorbed and brought the convention to life; Smollett, unable to do this, gives a pastebook caricature of an ideal.

645   MACK, Maynard (ed.). *Imagined worlds: essays on some English novels and novelists in memory of John Butt*. London: Methuen & Co. Ltd., 1968; pp. xxvi, 486.

Collection of essays from the late 17c to the 20c. Irène SIMON, "Early Theories of Prose Fiction" (19-36) provides a helpful poetics of novel-writing that links Congreve and Fielding.

646   McKEE, John B. *Literary irony and the literary audience: studies in the victimization of the reader in Augustan fiction*. Amsterdam: Rodopi, 1974; pp. 114.

Investigates the narrative voice in Augustan fiction, the basic technique of reader-victimizing irony, the process of "re-education" through its use, how this is suited to the language of prose fiction. Two appendices explore the history of irony and the formulations of irony as a critically useful term. Select Bibliography (111-14).

647   McKEON, Michael. *The origins of the English novel, 1600-1740*. Baltimore, MD: Johns Hopkins UP, 1987; pp. xx, 529.

The genesis of the novel lies in the great upheavals of secularization and reform that transformed early modern Europe. The origins of the English novel are part of the interrelated epistemological and social crises of the early modern period. By the 1740s the novel had emerged as a canonic term. Demonstrates the process in Cervantes, Bunyan, Defoe, Swift, Richardson and Fielding. Covers texts, theory and historical development such as 'news' and 'class', political absolutism and capitalism. Through a dialectical reconceptualization of the idea of genre and its relation to history enables a refiguring of the reaction of the English novel to its precursor genres. Historical analysis formulated in Marxist terms seeks to overcome the disjunction between myth and history found in Ian Watt and Northrop Frye.

648-----"Generic transformation and social change: rethinking the rise of the novel." In (pp. 159-80) DAMROSCH, Leopold, Jr. (ed.). *Modern essays on eighteenth-century literature*. New York; Oxford: Oxford UP, 1988; pp. x, 488.

Adds important elements to a fresh consideration of the emergence of the novel as a new literary genre: " [...] the volatility of the novel at this time is *analogous* to that of the middle class. But it is clear that in a certain sense, the emerging novel also has *internalized* the emergence of the middle class in its preoccupation with the problem of how virtue is signified" (177).

649-----"The origins of interdisciplinary studies." *ECS* 28:1 (1994) 17-28.

We see in Enlightenment usage a model disciplinary and interdisciplinary activity at its most illuminating: heuristic, operational, informed by a sense of utility of the epistemological project. Cultural studies can risk descent into unhistorical thinking insofar as it acts on the belief that disciplinary divisions are an impediment to knowledge. Recent approaches to Enlightenment interdisciplinary studies have shown a tendency to forget the dialectal hegemony of Enlightenment thought, to reduce it to a strict exercise in absolutist epistemology. The turn to the ontic in recent theory ('intertextuality', 'intentionality', 'canonicity') aims to bring certain cultural phenomena out into the open, to disclose as objectively systematic what was previously viewed only obscurely. To embrace a more authentically Enlightenment version of interdisciplinary studies would also facilitate a more authentic understanding of the Enlightenment. Bibliographic notes.

650 McKILLOP, Alan Dugald. "On the acquisition of minor English fiction." *Newberry Lib Bull* 4:3 (Spring 1956): 70-74.

Up until 1956, the minor fictions of the period from Samuel Richardson to Jane Austen had never been completely surveyed or studied. A principal reason for this neglect had been the inaccessibility of the novels themselves. It was impossible to make an exact evaluation of the holdings of a given library. Andrew BLACK'S *The English Novel, 1740-50* provided an authoritative listing, C. N. GREENOUGH'S card catalogue could be used only at the Widener Library in Harvard. In books acquired by the Newberry Library there are some booksellers' lists which illustrated the bibliographical situation. In 1956 there was no precise knowledge of interrelationship and influences on the area of 18c fiction comparable to what we have for 16c and 17c drama.

651-----*The early masters of English fiction.* (Kansas Paperbacks, 1.) Lawrence: Kansas UP, 1956, 1962, 1968; pp. 233. Illus.

Critical and historical survey of the major works of the principal British novelists of the first half of the 18c, extending from the publication of *Robinson Crusoe* to that of *Humphrey Clinker*. Provides an essay on Defoe: "Yet Defoe does not move exactly in the direction of the later novel of manners [...] Defoe was in a sense without successors, and because of his dubious reputation as a journalist and political agent, and because he wrote much of low life, and professed to pay little attention to literary canons, his great popularity was in large part sub-literary" (43). Notes (221-28). Index.

652 McLYNN, Frank. *Crime and punishment in eighteenth-century England.* London: Routledge, 1989; pp. xviii, 392.

Investigates crime and punishment, esp. the Bloody Code, the name given to the English system of criminal law during the period 1688-1815. In these years a huge number of felonies punishable by death were added to the statute book. From 50 offences in 1688, this had risen to 160 by 1765. The paradox was that there was a corresponding lack of executions. An act of 1706 abolished the literacy test ("benefit of clergy"). The explosion of capital statutes marked a return to Tudor severity and was the product of a mentality that saw the gallows as the only deterrent to serious crimes. Looks at London, law enforcement, homicide, highwaymen, property crime, women as victims of crime and as criminals, crimes of the powerful, high treason, smuggling, poaching, rioting, theories on crime and punishment, execution, crime and social order, the impact of war. Illus. (28 plates). Notes (347-87). Index (388-92).

653 MACPHERSON, Sandra. "Marriage acts: the eighteenth-century critique of contract." Unpub. doct. diss., Johns Hopkins Univ., 1997. [*DA* 58 (1997): 174A.]
Examines literary interventions in the debate over matrimonial law

reform between the repeal of the Civil Marriage Act (1660) and the Marriage Act of 1753. Works by such writers as Behn, Vanbrugh, Defoe, Richardson and Shebbeare are comprehensible only within the contexts of this debate. Arguments for matrimonial law reform were increasingly linked with arguments for greater state involvement with the private sphere: census-taking, public health, safety regulations, unemployed insurance, state orphanages, a poor wage. Defoe and Richardson were potentially uncomfortable with liberal consent theory - with the idea that one person's consent might absolve another for responsibility for his actions. In *Roxana* and *Clarissa* they attempt to articulate a more expansive version of legal liability that would function as an alternative to contract law and a contract-bound public policy.

654 McRAE, A. "Useful journey: travellers through life in 18th-century French and English fiction." Unpub. doct. diss., Univ. of Reading, 1986.

The scientific humanism of the Renaissance suggested new approaches to the interpretation of human experience, which questioned the validity of the Christian theocentric world view. The voyages of discovery of the previous centuries had set in motion man's self-confident discovery and reading of the diversity of his rapidly expanding world. The spread of literature and the proliferation of printed books allowed for a material unfolding of the physical world, aided by the scientific empiricism of John Locke and the scepticism of Pierre Bayle. All this found its outlet in the new and diversifying genre of the novel: the 16c Spanish picaresque novel provided a blueprint, adapted by English and French writers, allied to Lockean epistemology and the 18c travel vogue, so determining the increasing polemical and moralizing direction of prose fiction.

655 McVEAGH, John (ed.). *1660-1740: all before them.* (English Literature and the Wider World, 1.) London; Atlantic Highlands, NJ: The Ashford Press, 1990; pp. 305.

Part of a series dealing with the period 1660-1918, illustrating the British literary response to the geography and peoples of the world outside England. Each volume has a substantial editorial introduction which discusses the political events of the period, conditions of travel, the literary response to the wider world, and reaction to particular regions of the world. The essays consider the important authors of each period whose work draws on the non-English world. In this volume attention is focused on Milton, Marvell, Restoration Drama, Dryden, Pope and Defoe. See esp. "Defoe and Far Travel" (115-26). Substantial bibliography (277-85) on travel writing, travel and tourism, exploration and discovery, transport and equipment, the North, France, the Alps, Italy, Greece, the Orient, the Empire, America, Africa, racial theories. Index (291-54). Illus.

656   MAJOR, J. C. *The role of personal memoirs in English biography and novel.* Unpub. doct. diss., Univ of Pennsylvania, 1935. Facsimile. Ann Arbor: University Microfilms, 1970; pp. 176.

Provides a substantial critical view of English memoirs before 1740. Discusses the development of memoirs in France, and relations between French and English memoirs. Examines the ways in which memoirs were "a significant force" in the development of the English fiction of amorous intrigue in high society, and of the historical novel. Gives special emphasis to Daniel Defoe.

657   MANLOVE, C. N. *Literature and reality, 1600-1800.* London: Macmillan, 1978; pp. x, 238.

Investigates how much of reality the writers of the 17c and 18c found it possible to include in their work, and how the character and amount alters over the period. The entries on fiction center principally on Defoe and Fielding.

658   MANWARING, Elizabeth Wheeler. *The Italian landscape in eighteenth-century England: A study chiefly of the influence of Claude Lorrain and Salvator Rosa on English taste, 1700-1800.* New York: Oxford UP, 1925; pp. xi, 243.

Of all landscape painters, Lorrain and Rosa are named most often by the English taste in the 18c. The very contrast between them helped to establish them as examples of the two sorts of scenery which most impressed the English visitor to Italy. They were akin in possessing literary and poetic appeal. Traces the nature of their influence on 18c, what people of the time knew about them, by what means their influence spread, the conceptions of landscape beauty their influence established for 100 years in literature, in gardening, in general taste. See esp. ch. 7 "The Cult of the Picturesque" and ch. 8 "The Landscape Arts and the Picturesque in the Novels of the Eighteenth Century". Illus. (25 plates). Index (233-43).

659   MARESCA, Thomas E. *From epic to novel.* Columbia: Ohio State UP, 1974; pp. x, 238.

Attempts to trace the process whereby the novel replaced the epic as the major literary form in English. Looks closely at Dryden, Pope, Swift and Fielding.

660 MARINO, Sarah R. "'Almost infinite variation': eighteenth-century epistolary fictions." Unpub. doct. diss., Univ. of North Carolina at Chapel Hill, 1994. [*DA* 55 (1995): 3522A.]

Explores the different models of epistolary fiction. All such texts are shaped by a series of contradictory tendencies: interiority v. exteriority, privacy v. publicity, femininity v. masculinity, pedagogy v. sentimentality, individualism v. community, artlessness v. artifice. The complexity and range of these tendencies demonstrate that one model will not explain the movement of epistolary fiction in the 18c. Centers principally on work from the late 18c, but provides invaluable general insight into the nature of the plots, themes, and structure available to writers framing fiction in letters.

661 MARSHALL, David Brett. "From readers to spectators: Theatricality in eighteenth-century narratives." Unpub. doct. diss., Johns Hopkins Univ., 1980. [*DA* 40 (1980): 5043A.]

Interprets the role of the theater in a variety of 18c narratives. Texts by Defoe, Shaftesbury, Kames, Diderot, Marivaux, Du Bos and Smith are considered. Argues that rendering of these texts must be informed by an understanding of the situation of theater implicit in writing books at the time. It is not the influence of specific plays, but a figure and problem: it defines identity as role of fictive impersonation; it establishes a problematic relation between the text as spectacle and the reader as spectator.

662 MAY, Georges. *Le dilemme du roman au 18e siècle: Étude sur les rapports du roman et de la critique (1715-1761)*. New Haven, CT: Yale UP; Paris: Presses Universitaires de France, 1964; pp. 294.

In French. Taking *Gil Blas* (1715) and *La Nouvelle Heloïse* (1761) as the limits, investigates the history of the French novel in the 18c, paying special attention to the role of critical theory and reactions to the novel. The introduction defines limits and critical contours (neo-classicism, aesthetic and moral considerations). Ch. 1 looks at the critical attack on the novel in the 18c, the shadow of classicism, ch. 2 the pull between realism and idealism, ch. 3 the proscription of the novel, ch. 4 the defense of psychological realism and morality, ch. 5 the debate between the novel and history, sociological factors, the decline of the hero of the novel, feminism and the novel. Bibliography of 338 items (260-77).

Index (279-87).

663-----"The influence of English literature on the French eighteenth-century novel." In (pp. 265-80) WASSERMAN, E. R. (ed.). *Aspects of the eighteenth century*. Baltimore: The Johns Hopkins UP and London: Oxford UP, 1965; pp. 340

Part of an extensive collection of essays on all aspects of 18c life. The many translations of English novels into French in the mid-18c helped to shift the intellectual interest to the increasingly current and complex novel genre.

664 MAYER, Robert. *History and the early English novel: matters of fact from Bacon to Defoe.*(Cambridge Studies in Eighteenth-Century English Literature and Thought, 33.) Cambridge and New York: Cambridge UP, 1997; pp. xii, 246.
Argues that the novel emerged from historical writing. Examining historical writers and forms frequently neglected, shows that 17c historical discourse embraced history in the modern sense of the word, and also fiction, polemic, gossip and marvels. This is why Defoe's narrations were initially read as history. It is this claim to historicity that differentiates Defoe from Thomas Deloney and Aphra Behn. Explores the theoretical implications of this history-fiction connection. "Defoe is crucial to the history of the novel exactly because he forced history upon the novel in a way that readers have found both compelling and strange. [...]the reading of his narratives into the tradition of the novel suggests that the theory of the novel is incomplete without an account of how this form of fiction refers to historical reality" (238-39).

665 MELL, Donald, Jr. (ed. & pref.); BRAUN, Theodore E.D. and PALMER, Lucia M. (eds). *God, man and nature in the Enlightenment*. (Studies in Literature, 1500-1800 2.) East Lansing, MI: Colleagues, 1988; pp. xv, 247.
Consists of 20 essays on the Enlightenment with subjects as varied as the age itself. These subjects include: philosophy as practised in several European nations, and the relationship of philosophy to metaphysical and epistemological speculation; religion (natural and revealed), and its profound influence on literature, art and science; the social and psychological ramifications of conflicting philosophical concepts; political science in relation to economic theory and constitutional themes of governing, esp. in America; the rise of feminism as a social and moral force encompassing interpretations of history, educational theory and practice, literature and music; the impact of aesthetics on landscape gardening and architecture; changing attitudes towards language and

linguistics in their international dimension; the challenge of the newly emerging romantic aesthetic of sensibility and pathos to didactic and formalistic conceptions of art, esp. in the case of drama and the novel. Bibliographic notes. Index (239-47).

666 MELOCCARO, Lynne. "Orientalism and the Oriental tale: gender, genre, and cultural identity in eighteenth-century England." Unpub. doct. diss., Rutgers Univ., 1992. [*DA* 54 (1993): 1377A.]

The evolution of the genre of Orientalism represents an important aspect of the development of the English imperialist ideology. The Oriental tale helped to establish a sense of eurocentric cultural identity, and reveal issues of gender representation and discrimination. This contradicted the ostensible aim of opposing Oriental binary opposites, in underpinning a unified vision of English identity. 19c English culture repressed the genre because it articulated the inherent contradictions of imperialism, and its presence in literary history compromised visions of a naturally evolving imperial destiny.

667 MERIANS, Linda (ed.). *The secret malady: venereal disease in eighteenth-century Britain and France.* Lexington: Kentucky UP, 1996; pp. 269.

Collection of 15 essays seeking to present a cultural history of sexual disease in Britain and France during the 18c. Published and private responses are investigated. The disease existed in epidemical proportions, yet was the great secret malady of the time. Dissertations on and representations of v.d. appeared in visual art, operas, plays, poetry, novels, scientific essays, periodical essays, private letters and journals. Literary and figurative references were evident on the streets and in the business of everyday life. The culture of v.d. also supported related industries: advertisements for cures occupied more column space in 18c English periodicals than any other. It also entered the political arenas of both nations. The two-part structure of the book represents the historical and medical contexts of v.d. in the 18c. The second half explores how it was discussed in private conversations, written journals, as well as in literary forms and visual works of art. Index (263-69). Illus. (16 plates, 7 figures).

668 MERKEL, Ingrid and DEBUS, Allen G. (eds). *Hermeticism in the Renaissance: intellectual history and the occult in early modern Europe.* New York: Folger; London: Assoc. UPs, 1988; pp. 438.

Collection of essays providing the background to esotericism and magic in the context of the intellectual life of the Renaissance, 17c and 18c:

background and Renaissance, magic, philosophy and science, literature and art. Each essay has a specialized bibliography.

669 MEYERS, Jeffrey (ed.). *The biographer's art: new essays.* Basingstoke: Macmillan, 1989; pp. ix, 191.

Sequel to *The craft of literary biography* ([Macmillan, 1985] which consisted of 13 contemporary literary biographies). Provides a history of the genre and a substantial analysis of great biographies from the 18c to the modern period (Samuel Johnson, *Life of Richard Savage*; James Boswell, *Life of Johnson*). Notes (168-84). Index (185-91).

670 MILIC, Louis T. and SLANE, Steve. "Quantative aspects of genre in the century of prose corpus." *Style* 28.1 (1994): 42-54.

Reports on the Century of Prose Corpus, a machine-readable, half-million word compilation of British prose composed or published during the period 1680-1780. It was supposed that from this material certain genres could be found that would be recognized by the reader, that genres had an existence that could be determined statistically by the linguistic microstructure of the texts. It seems clear from the analysis that the stylistic variables employed can be used to estimate the distinctiveness of genres, and to identify the genre of a text. Obviously some genres (e.g. fiction, science) are more distinctive than others (e.g. letters, memoirs). The writers have not been able to specify ways in which each genre is unique. The results of the analysis argue not only for the existence of genres with measurable features in the Century of Prose Corpus, and by implication in other texts, but also for the possibility of identifying genre by means of the detection of these features.

671 MILLAR, J. H. *Scottish prose of the seventeenth and eighteenth centuries.* Glasgow: James Macklehose & Sons, 1912; pp. 273.

Narrative-critical account of Scottish prose over two centuries. Makes no mention of prose fiction in the first half of the 18c.

672 MILLER, Henry Knight. "Augustan prose fiction and the romance tradition." In (pp. 241-55) BRISSENDEN, R. F. and EADE, J. C. (eds). *Studies in the eighteenth century, III: papers presented at the third David Nichol Memorial Seminar, Canberra, 1973.* Toronto: U of Toronto P, 1976; pp. x, 287.

Opposes an evolutionary view of the novel and argues in favor of an "historical- or anthropological-approach" which assesses "early prose fiction in terms of later laws that it knew nothing about". Distinguishes romance from novel in terms of "epic dimension and the hierarchical and oral context".

673 MILLER, Nancy Kipnis. "Gender and genre: an analysis of literary femininity in the 18c novel." Unpub. doct. diss., Columbia Univ., 1974. [*DA* 35 (1975): 6675A.]

The 18c novel in France and England solicits the reader "by a particular valorization" of the feminine. Considers *Moll Flanders, Manon Lescaut, La Vie de Marianne, Pamela, Fanny Hill, Clarissa, La Nouvelle Héloïse, Les Liasons dangereuses, Justine.* As the titles suggest, the novels are centered on the female experience: each recounts a destiny in which the heroine is primarily defined by her participation in narrative sequences which provide the measure of her femininity. Focuses on three textual sequences: the initial seduction, the erotic situation in which the sexual imperative is confronted, the final situation where femininity is assigned positive or negative values through the resolution of polarization.

674-----*The heroine's text: readings in the French and English novel, 1722-1782.* New York: Columbia UP, 1980; pp. 180.

The book seeks to read the fictions of feminine destiny, to plot the heroine's text in eight French and English novels of the Enlightenment. Contains two sections: the First "The Euphoric Text" looks at "A Harlot's Progress" (*Moll Flanders*), "The Virtuous Orphan" (*La Vie de Marianne*), "The Rewards of Virtue" (*Pamela*); the Second "The Dysphoric Text" considers "Love for a Harlot" (*Manon Lescaut*), "The Misfortunes of Virtue" (*Clarissa, La Nouvelle Héloïse*), "The Negative Heroine" (*Les Liasons dangereuses, Justine*). Bibliography (177-80).

675 MILLER, Stuart. *The picaresque novel.* Clevelend: The P of Case Western Reserve U, 1967; pp. 164.

Tries to clarify the generic reasons for understanding and including works as picaresque by examining the 3 Spanish masterpieces and originals of the genre (*Lazarillo* 1554, *Guzman* 1599 and 1605, *El Buscón* 1626), examples from Germany (*Simplicissimus*, 1668) and England (*The Unfortunate Traveller* 1596, *Moll Flanders* 1722, *Roderick Random* 1748). Considers essentially ahistorical issues. What is uniform in the novels called picaresque? Considers: 1) plot pattern and rhythm (episodic plot, specific plot rhythms, fortune, accident); 2) character (picaresque and real characters, other literary characters, origins, picaresque education, protean forms, loneliness and love, internal instability); 3) interpretive devices (point of view, style, ending of the picaresque novel). Notes (137-56). Selected bibliography (157-62). Index (163-64).

676   MILLER, Thomas. "The formation of college English: a survey of the archives of eighteenth-century rhetorical theory and practice." *RSQ* 20:3 (Summer 1990): 261-86

College English began with the origins of the modern research university about a century ago when historical philology came to provide the rigorous specialized knowledge necessary to the creation of an academic discipline. The Dissenters were apparently the first to teach English in a systematic and concerted fashion at the college level. Extensive bibliography (277-86).

677   MISH, Charles Carol. "A note on the fiction reprint market in the early eighteenth-century market." *Newberry Lib Bull* 3:7 (1954): 201-05.

Considers the romance *Cynthia* (1687), reprinted in 1726 costing a shilling, to represent the reprint market, "that group of books which almost in defiance of polite taste, went through edition after edition, to satisfy what we must presume were the old-fashioned tastes of less culturally elevated readers" (202). By 1709 the book was back in its fifth edition, by 1750 in its tenth. When its popularity waned in England at the end of the 18c, it was unexpectedly given a boost by the appearance in America in the 1790s of three editions. The reprint market in the Age of Pope was of considerable importance. Common men and women paid no attention to the secret memoirs, the *chroniques scandaleuses*, the topical satires, the Eastern tales which were beginning to give the age its characteristic flavor in fiction. They wanted what their fathers and forefathers read and got in such reprints.

678   MOLHO, Maurice. "Picarisme des origines, ou la dialectique du maître et de l'esclave." *Caliban* 20 (1983): 5-17.

In French. Underlying the slave-master dialectic is the recognition of the consciousness of self ("la conscience n'est en soi et pour soi que si elle l'est pour autre conscience de soi, dont elle est reconnue") (13). There can be no master without the recognition from the slave, and no slave without the recognition from the master. Service is following the wishes of the other, and fulfilling them in work.

679   MONOD, Paul Kléber. *Jacobitism and the English people, 1688-1788.* Cambridge: Cambridge UP, 1989; pp. xvi, 408.

Covers history of and popular reactions to Jacobitism, popular Jacobitism, the faces of treason, Jacobitism in history (343-50). Bibliography (350-81).

680 MONTESER, Frederick. *The picaresque element in Western literature.* (Studies in Humanities, No. 5 Literature.) University, Alabama: U of Alabama P, 1975; pp. 152.

Aims to examine the picaresque novel as a genre belonging to a particular social and historical epoch, then considers *picarismo* as a continuing social phenomenon; then attempts a prognosis for picaresque elements in future literature. Looks at the origins of the *picaro*, the generic form of *la novela picaresca*, *picaro* versus picaresque, the original Spanish literature, the picaro *au français*; pre-Lazarillo picaresque elements; the picaresque in British literature, in the United States, in Latin America, modern picarismo, the picaro as anachronism. Notes (122-8). Chronological list of works (129-33). Bibliography (134-41). Index (142-52).

681 MOORE, Lisa L. *Dangerous intimacies: toward a Sapphic history of the British novel.* Durham, NC, and London: Duke UP, 1997; pp. viii, 191.

Seeks to understand the role played by the novel in the emergence of a post-Enlightenment understanding of sexual identity. The late 18c English novel was engaged in the complex process of producing identity per se in a quintessentially modern category. The modernity of this race-, class-, sex-, gender- and nation-marked categorizing lies in the characteristic movements by which the indices of particularity are erased. Sexual identity bears much of the burden for legitimizing bourgeois ascension in that the domestic novel offered powerful stories of the importance of creating and consolidating the domestic space and female virtue within it. Investigation of four chosen novels (*Millennium Hall, Memoirs of a Woman of Pleasure, Belinda, Emma*) helps to demonstrate how female homosocial spaces operated a guaranteed English moral purity. The category of female friendship is the principal syntax through which the complicated grammar of gender, sexuality, race and nation is parsed. Notes (155-80). Bibliographical (181-86). Index (187-91).

682 MOORE, P. H. "Death in the eighteenth-century novel." Unpub. doct. diss., Univ. of Oxford, 1986. [*IT* 37 (1987): 440.]

Examines the development of the novel in the 18c in relation to changing attitudes to death, and looks at how far shifting notions of the moral purpose of the novel and subsequent changes in the treatment of the deathbed scenes, murders, duels, suicides and speculation about heaven and hell reflect changing beliefs and the modification of strict Christian ideals to accommodate or combat new feelings and philosophies. Each chapter establishes the typical individuality of a particular author in relation to the period in which he was writing. Richardson is the starting point who uses the novel to question both old and new attitudes, paving the way for the novel's predominantly emotional attitude to morality and mortality.

683   MORGAN, Charlotte E. *The rise of the novel of manners: a study of English prose fiction between 1600-1740*. New York: Columbia UP, 1911; rpt New York: Russell & Russell, 1963; pp. viii, 272.

An important pioneering work in the critical investigation of the rise of English prose fiction. Ch. 3 "The Novel (1700-1740)" and ch. 4 "The Popular Fiction (Bunyan and Defoe)" are most pertinent, as is the extended Bibliography which includes works of general reference, works of special reference, sources of bibliographical information, lists of reprints and collections, an alphabetical list of the more important English writers between 1600 and 1740. While modern research has overtaken this study in many respects, it nevertheless remains of great bibliographical interest, even if the datings are often unreliable.

684   MORGAN, Peter E. "Body personal/body politic: the sexual text of eighteenth-century subjectivity." Unpub. doct. diss., Univ. of California (Riverside), 1993. [*DA* 54 (1994): 3044A.]

Explores the representation of the female subject - political, social, personal - in Restoration and 18c England in the belief that social structures and literary discourse mutually construct one another. The gendered semiotics of Aphra Behn's texts develop a characteristic vehicle for the revolutionary political aesthetic. English imperialism was a sexual enterprise which had reverberations in English society due to the attitudes it engendered in the conquerors themselves. Looks at Behn, Swift, Pope, Gay, John Michael Coetzee.

685   MORVAN, Alan. *La tolérance dans le roman anglais de 1726 à 1771*. (Études Anglaises, 88. Publications de la Sorbonne - Littérature 1, 12.) Paris: Didier, 1984; pp. 528.

In French. Looks at: 1) "L'Éclosion de la tolérance dans l'Angleterre du dix-huitième siècle: évolution historique (aspects politiques socio-culturels, religieuses"; 2) "La tolérance et sa conceptualisation (théories, roman et la valoration du concept de tolérance)"; 3) "Tolérance et contenus romanesques, le roman et la tolérance religieuse, le roman et la tolérance en matière de races et de nationalités, le roman et la tolérance morale". "Conclusion générale". "Biographie sélective" (438-510).

686-----(ed.). *Savoir et violence en Angleterre du XVIe au XIXe siècle.* (Travaux et Recherches.)   Lille: Université de Lille III, 1987; pp. 211.

In French. A collection of essays exploring the twin themes of know-how and violence over four centuries, and the complexity of their rapport. Vital background is supplied by surveys of philosophy, history of ideas and mentality, history of art, and literary criticism.

687   MOWRY, Melissa Margaret. "(Re)productive histories: epistolary fiction and the origin of the English novel." Unpub. doct. diss., Univ. of Delaware, 1993. [*DA* 55 (1994): 577A.]

Epistolary fiction was enormously popular in late 17c and early 18c, but little attention has been paid to the relations between epistolary fiction and the novel as it emerged in the mid-18c. Demonstrates how the dialectical ability to assign historical meaning to events depends upon a gendered division between the progressive movement of the father/son genealogy, and the 'dull repetition' of female reproduction. The consolidation of the novel depends on a similar embrace of patriarchal progress. Investigates gender investments of the dialectic, the collapse of the patriarchal paradigms after the Restoration, the complex relationship between the feminine and patriarchal ideology in the late 17c and early 18c (prostitution, marriage, parenting, narrative fiction), the role of early epistolary fiction in perpetuating the domestic discourse on sexuality and reproduction. The fifth chapter is devoted to a reading of Richardson, working in the light of the established historical context.

688   MUELLER, Janet and REDFORD, Bruce (ed.). "From Restoration to revision." *MP* 85:4 (May   1988): 345-609.

Introduction to a collection of essays devoted to the arts, esp. literature, from the Restoration to the late 18c. Looks at Otway, Pope, drama, opera, Dodsley, novels, Sterne, Hume, Johnson, Adam, Tinker, Newton, Gibbon. See Paul J. HUNTER, "Novels and 'the novel'" above, **531**.

689   MÜLLENBROCK, Hans-Joachim. "The British cultural context of the early eighteenth century and the changing status of the writer." *SVEC* 264 (1989): 1170-71.

British writers attained a new status during the Neo-Classical period as a result of far-reaching transformation of the cultural context. This is intimately connected with the Glorious Revolution (1688-89) where changes in norms in the political sphere caused a shift in the functions of literature which deeply affected the professional outlook of writers. A subsequent enlargement of the provinces of literature was crucial in the long-term emancipation of the writer and gave even Restoration authors a semi-independent status before the rise of a regular book market in the middle of the 18c.

690-----*Whigs kontra Tories: Studien zum Einfluss der Politik auf die englische Literatur des frühen 18. Jahrhunderts.* (Anglistische Forschungen, 104.) Heidelberg: Carl Winter, 1974; pp. 345.

In German. Provides a detailed historical-literary analysis of the influence of the great British party ideologies on the cultural life of the nation. While the emphasis is essentially on drama and poetry, the notion of the poet as historian (esp. in Thomson's *Liberty*) furnished an important concept of the ancient world both as model and warning. Bibliography (299-334). Index (335-45).

691-----and SPÄTH, Eberhard. *Literatur des 18. Jahrhunderts.* (Studienreihe Englisch, 27.) Düsseldorf: Bagel, 1977; pp. 234.

In German. Survey of the literature around the novel by reference to 1) Dryden and Swift; 2) essay criticism and other prose (journalism, pamphleteering, history writing, biography, epistolary literature); 3) drama; 4) classical poetry; 5) pre-romanticism (foundations, literary presuppositions, the Gothic novel, minor poets). Bibliography (192-218). Notes (219-28). Index (224-30). Index of topics (231-34).

692   MUIR, Edwin. *The structure of the novel.* London: The Hogarth Press, 1928; pp. 151.

General ranging and speculative introduction to the novel, covering novels of action and character, the dramatic novel, time and space, developments, conclusion. Reacts consistently to Percy LUBBOCK, E. M. FORSTER, and John CARRUTHER'S essay "Scheherazade; or the Future of the English Novel".

693   MULLAN, John. "Hypochondria and hysteria: Sensibility and the physicians." *ECent* 25 (1984): 141-74.

An examination of the functions of sensibility in 18c writing on hypochondria, hysteria and nervous disorder illuminates the contemporary cult of sensibility. In both the novel and the 'medical' text, sensibility can be a special and desirable quality, but it can also usher in the possibilities of melancholy, delirium and defeat. The very vocabulary which Richardson uses in his delineation of femininity and its resilient virtue points exactly at the 18c descriptions of hysteria: tenderness, sensibility, delicacy and disorder. Novelists designate the faculties and processes by which sentiments are composed and communicated, in the language of the physicians, to describe the conditions and workings of the body.

694 MYLNE, Vivienne. "Changing attitudes towards truth in fiction." *Renaissance & Modern Stud* 7 (1963): 53-77.

In the 17c and 18c current ideas about truth in fiction helped to provoke crucial changes in the form and content of the novel in England and France. From the picaresque came forms of autobiography (Courtilz de Sandras and Defoe). These memoir novels present fiction as fact, and yet in the fiction is some fact. By the 1720s novelists go on saying that their works are not novels, but genuine documents, yet they no longer take the pretense seriously, and give way to their own authorship at every turn (Prévost and Richardson).

695-----*The 18th-century French novel: Techniques of illusion.* Manchester, 1965; pp. 288.
Considers the development of the novel during the course of the 18c, concentrating on the novelists' methods and literary techniques rather than on the study of themes or subject matter. Looks at the theory and background, fiction, history and truth, memoirs and pseudo-memoirs, Le Sage, Prévost (the new realism), Marivaux (character in depth), Crébillon (innovations in point of view), the history and technique of letter novels, Rousseau (a new seriousness), Diderot (theory and practice), Restif de la Bretonne and Laclos (the culmination of the letter novel), Bernardin de Saint-Pierre (transitional forms). Select Bibliography (282-88).

696-----"The punctuation of dialogue in eighteenth-century French and English fiction." *The Library (Six Series)* [formerly the *Transactions of the Bibliographical Society*] 1 (1979): 43-61.

After a period of experimentation which began in the 17c, many English printers came to adopt, by the 1780s, the kind of dialogue punctuation which is now standard practice. In French novels the process began later, getting fully under way towards the middle of the 18c; the first typographical elements to be used were italics and *guillemets,* or quotation marks. The dash, introduced into French fiction in the 1760s, became generalized fairly rapidly, and by the 1780s was recognized as the commonest way of indicating a change of speaker. In both countries, the further device of putting each *réplique* on a new line seems to have caught on more slowly and was not accepted by most printers until the 19c.

697   NAPIER, Eric Rogers. "The implication of design: aspects of narrative structure in eighteenth-century English fiction." Unpub. doct. diss., Univ. of Virginia, 1979. [*DA* 40 (1979): 3321A.]

Investigates the special emphasis on form characteristic of the criticism and literature of the English Augustan Age as expressed in the novel. Plot, imagery, character and point of view often assume patterns whose meaning is crucial to the work as a whole: literary themes are frequently formalized through specific dispositions of narrative elements. Looks at eight novels: *Robinson Crusoe, Gulliver's Travels, Clarissa, Tom Jones, Peregrine Pickle, Tristram Shandy, The Vicar of Wakefield* and *Caleb Williams*. For example, in *Robinson Crusoe* formal and thematic focus on objects and order emphasize the key relationship in the novel between literal detail and the abstract principle of order which governs Crusoe's physical and spiritual movements on the island.

698   NEILL, S. Diane. *A short history of the English novel*. London: Jarrolds, 1951; pp. 340.

Systematic survey of the English novel from the earliest examples of prose fiction. Ch. 2 "Allegory, Adventure and Satire in the Seventeenth Century" (29-49) discusses Behn at some length, Manley, Barker, Rowe and Hayward very briefly, with a few critical observations. Defoe is treated more substantially (42-48), each novel given in summary, and perceptively interpreted: *Robinson Crusoe* (42-44), *Moll Flanders* (44-45), *A Journal of the Plague Year* (46), *Colonel Jack* (46). Discusses Defoe's philosophy of life, his prose style, imagination, lack of selective principle, gift for verisimilitude ("...nothing was omitted that might delight the new reading public, eager for facts, enchanted by documentary records and...the illusion of truth", 43). Selected bibliography (325-28). Index (331-40).

699   NEUBURG, Victor E. *Popular literature, a history and guide: from the beginning of printing to the year 1897*. Harmondsworth: Penguin Books, 1977; pp. 302.

The introduction (11-17) defines popular literature and traces its development until 1897, providing a critical survey of sources available for this study. Does not discuss newspapers or periodicals. Ch. 3 "1700-1800" (102-22) examines chapbooks, their characteristics and contents, suggesting why they thrived, largely at the expense of the traditional ballad sheets. Men and women were increasingly exposed to the printed word, and the printed word increasingly became part of the background, even to those not previously exposed to it. There was also a movement towards the spread of literacy. Examines the nature and content of the chapbooks, their publication and distribution, as well as the growing sophistication of the reading public. The Industrial Revolution eventually changed the public which had been content with chapbooks and simple ballads. Appendix on religious tracts (249-64). Critical bibliography (265-97) - the 18c has its own section (280-83). Index (298-302). Illus. (34 plates).

700 NEUMANN, Henry. "Villains in the English novel from Aphra Behn to Eliot: a classification and a study in the development of certain types." Unpub. doct. diss., New York Univ., 1906.
Abstract not available.

701 NEVERS, Kevin Lee. "'Immovable objects, irresistible forces': the sublime and the technological in the eighteenth century." Unpub. doct. diss., Univ. of Virginia, 1993. [*DA* 54 (1994): 3044A.]

Both historians and theoreticians have proved oddly reluctant to historicize the sublime in both their accounts of its emergence as a popular aesthetic in the 18c, and in their arguments for its applicability in the 20c. Undertakes such a historicization - first a reconstruction of the sublime and then a deconstruction - using the techniques of Foucauld.

702 NEW, Melvyn. "'The Grease of God': the form of eighteenth-century English fiction." *PMLA*   91 (1976): 235-44.

Investigates whether the world of 18c English fiction is a providential world (Defoe, Richardson, Fielding, Smollett). This literature tried to hold together two conflicting visions of life in the moment of transition.

703 NEWELL, A. G. "Early evangelical fiction." *Evangelical Quart* 38 (1966): 3-21, 81-98.

Mostly on Hannah More in the context of the Protestant religious revival of the 18c.

704 NEWLIN, Claude M. "The English periodicals and the novel, 1709-40." *Papers of Michigan Academy of Science, Arts & Letters* 16 (1931): 467-

76.

Englishmen of the first part of the 18c inherited a large library of prose fiction for light reading: prose versions of romances of chivalry, 17c French romances and English translations of them, Italian, French and Spanish novellas. Prose fiction was also sentimentalized in the drama of the same period. The periodicals made an important contribution to this development, both in criticism of fiction and in publication of stories. Investigates and provides an interpretation of this movement as revealed in the *Tatler*, *Spectator*, *Guardian* and in later periodicals. The period writers who followed Addison and Steele showed substantially the same attitude and continued the process of moralizing the novel. Novel-reading was persistently attacked. For 30 years English periodical writers had called for a moralized English novel based on English life, adapted to middle-class readers. Richardson was seen to be in harmony with these efforts, and the English public had been well prepared to receive his work. In *Pamela* gallantry is defeated and virtue is rewarded. Richardson divested the novel of its objectionable features, while preserving the essential features of the plot.

705   NEWTON, Sarah Emily. "'An ornament to her sex': rhetorics of persuasion in early American conduct literature for women and the 18c American seduction novel." Unpub.doct. diss., Univ. of California (Davis), 1976. [*DA* 37 (1976): 1550A-1A.]

Investigates the literature of advice, both European and American, designed for the instruction of young women in novels, and read in America primarily during the 17c and 18c. Both overt and masked patterns of approved female conduct were adapted by early American writers in the novels of didacticism and seduction which marked the post-Revolutionary debut of the American novel. To enforce approved paradigms for women, conduct writers use three principal rhetorics of persuasion: religion, reason and fiction.

706   NICHOLSON, Colin. *Writing and the rise of finance: capital satires of the early eighteenth century.* (Cambridge Studies in Eighteenth-Century Literature and Thought, 21.) Cambridge and New York: Cambridge UP, 1994; pp. xv, 219.

Reads such familiar texts as *Gulliver's Travels*, *The Beggars' Opera* and *The Dunciad* as 'capital satires', responding to the social and political effects of the installation of capitalist financial institutions in London. The founding of the Bank of England and the inauguration of the National Debt permanently altered the political economy of England: the South-Sea Bubble disaster (1721) educated a political generation into the money markets. While Swift, Pope, and Gay invested in stocks and shares, they conducted a campaign against the civic effects of these new financial institutions. The conflict between these writers' commitment to reviving an inherited discourse of civic humanism, and the transition being undergone by their own society, reconstituting those values radically, affected a number of English literary texts. Bibliography (202-11). Index (212-19).

707 NICOLAY, Theresa Freda. "Transforming the traditional: gender roles, literary authority, and the American woman writer, 1620-1850." Unpub. doct. diss., Univ. of Rochester, 1993. [*DA* 54 (1993): 1367A.]

Demonstrates the formation and expansion of the role of New England women of letters by examining three of the most important women writers between 1620 and 1850: Anne Bradstreet, Margaret Fuller, Mercy Warren. Their societies looked upon these women as cultural authorities, serious commentators on literary, social, political and moral concerns.

708 NOKES, David. *Raillery and rage: a study of eighteenth-century satire.* Brighton: Harvester Press, 1987; pp. 211.

Tries to enhance the understanding and enjoyment by modern readers of 18c satire with all its teasing paradoxes and allusive parodies. Describes the range of theoretical justifications formulated by the satirists, the practical synergy of rhetorical techniques which contribute to the creative vitality of the satires. The literature of the century from Charles II to George III is dominated by satire, so rather than providing a comprehensive coverage of the most celebrated satires, the book tries to offer new perspectives on satirical themes and contextual issues (themes and forms, Pope, Gay, Fielding and Swift). Notes (197-206). Index (207-11).

709 NORTON, James Harris, III. "Confession in seventeenth- and eighteenth-century Protestant literature." Unpub. doct. diss., Indiana Univ., 1994. [*DA* 55 (1995): 3200A.]

The English first-person novel (beginning with Bunyan's *The Pilgrim's Progress* and Defoe's *Robinson Crusoe*) has been seen as a recycled form of the older genre of the autobiography, like St Augustine's *Confessions*. A broader study of confessional language will give a clearer understanding of how early modern English authors developed and used these genres. The social and discursive practices of the confession in early modern England, particularly those involving religion, law, and rhetorical theory, constitutes models for the invention of the twin genres of English confessional autobiography and the first-person novel.

710 NORTON, Robert E. *The beautiful soul: aesthetic morality in the eighteenth century.* Ithaca and London: Cornell UP, 1995; pp. xi, 314.

Many during the 18c considered the beautiful soul (after the Hellenic ideal of *kalokagathia*) to be the very symbol of enlightened humanity and devoted substantial amounts of energy to discovering how to attain this. The 18c saw the most explicitly articulated and ambitious attempts to realize the ideal of moral beauty in two-and-a-half thousand years of its recorded existence. In the early 1700s, inaugurating a development that closely parallels the chronological progression of the European Enlightenment as a whole, several thinkers in England, France and Germany began to employ terms referring to moral and aesthetic excellence to address contemporary problems of ethical philosophy. After the 1750s some versions of moral beauty appeared in almost every 18c discussion of morality, whether in works of high philosophical seriousness, or in literary texts meant for the popular market. The amalgamation of abstract moral and aesthetic qualities became personified by the notion of the 'beautiful soul'. Bibliography (291-307). Index (308-14).

711 NOVAK, Maximilian E. "Some notes toward a history of fictional forms: from Aphra Behn to Daniel Defoe." *Novel* 6 (1973): 120-33.

Defoe did not create his fiction in a literary vacuum: it can be accounted for in terms of literary origins, influences and forms rather than by recourse to broad social theories. Nationalism in the study of literature has little place in the period 1660-1730. We should not try to read back values the authors would not have admired, but should be continually aware of the influence of the past. What is needed is a history of fictional forms. References to Mary Manley and Penelope Aubin.

712-----"The extended movement: time, dream, history, and perspective in eighteenth-century fiction." In (pp. 141-66), BACKSCHEIDER, P. (ed.). *Probability, time and space in eighteenth-century literature.* See above, **189**.

From the beginning of the 18c, writers such as Swift remarked on the paradoxes inherent in choosing to perceive in one way or another - too deeply or too superficially. Analyzes works by Defoe, Richardson and Radcliffe who had the idea that what they perceived was not exactly the mirror image of the phenomenal world, and each recognized the need to create an autonomous reality within their fiction. Behind the realism of Defoe and the landscapes of Gothic fiction there is the same kind of daemonic agency that haunts allegory. The intricacies of realism, particularly the relationship between fantasy and realism in the same work, needs more exploration. Bibliographic notes (164-6).

713-----*Eighteenth-century literature.* (Macmillan History of Literature.) London: Macmillan, 1983; pp. ix, 227.

Survey of the century looking at the kinds of people who wrote, the forces which acted upon them, the history, political, philosophical, economical, cultural background. Writers both accepted and rejected the literary conventions of the time, and developed them into new kinds of literary expression. Looks at the interaction between literature and art, music and architecture, whether writers were affected by their contemporaries or not. During the 18c literary forms once regarded as crude, like the novel, came into the highest fashion, while genres like the epic and tragedy tended to take second place. It was an age of contradictions, and intensely aware of them. Looks at transitions, the age of disguise, Pope and the poetic art, sublime nature and corrupt civilization, and the emergence of a new literary ideal (Daniel Defoe), Scriblerian satire, the era of sincerity, mid-century fiction and drama (Richardson, Fielding and Sterne), the age of sensibility, Samuel Johnson (times and circles), the century's end. Chronological table (208-18). Bibliography (219-21). Index (222-27). 19 plates.

714 NOYES, Robert Gale. *The Thespian mirror: Shakespeare in the eighteenth-century novel.* (Brown Univ. Studies, 15.) Providence, RI: Brown UP, 1953; pp. 200.

English novels of the 18c contain a body of criticism of drama and the stage which has been virtually unexplored. In the hundreds of novels published between *Pamela* (1740) and 1780 (the year after Garrick's death), one can find criticism of repertory, acting, and audiences of a much more lively and informal nature than one discovers in the professional dramatic criticism of the age of Johnson. Introductory chapters devoted to the comedies, the histories, the tragedies, the romances. Illus. Index (193-200).

715-----*The neglected Muse: Restoration and eighteenth-century tragedy in the novel.* Providence: Brown UP, 1958; pp. 187.

This is a sequel to the above. Considers the topic of tragedy as viewed by the 18c novelists, based on 750 novels written between 1740 and 1780. Looks at the novelists' examination of tragedy: Restoration heroics, pathos and sentiment, Augustan tragedy, domestic tragedy (Lillo), pseudo-Roman tragedy. Index (181-87). 10 illus.

716   NUSSBAUM, Felicity A. and BROWN, Laura (eds). *The new eighteenth century: theory, politics, English literature*. New York; London: Methuen, 1987; pp. viii, 320.

The essay "Heteroclites: the Gender of Character in the Scandalous Memoirs" (144-67) provides perspective on early 18c fiction.

717   NUSSBAUM, Felicity A. *Torrid zones: maternity, sexuality, and empire in eighteenth-century English narratives*. (Parallax: Revisions of Culture and Society.) Baltimore, MD: Johns Hopkins UP, 1995; pp. x, 248.

Analyzes the connections between 18c women in England and women in the emergent British empire. Discovery/invention of the 'other' women of empire enabled the consolidation of the cult of domesticity in England, and, at the same time, the association of the sexualized women in love with the exotic and 'savage' non-European women. There was a kind of national imperative to control women's sexuality and fecundity when the increasing demands of trade and colonization required a large able-bodied citizenry, and women's reproductive labor was harnessed to the task. Connects the perception of women at home and abroad during the expansion of commercial and imperial authority in order to analyze the interrelationship that evolved among sexual, racial and class hierarchies. Explores the interpenetration of the domestic and exotic, civil and savage, political and sexual, centering on reproductive and sexual issues, literature, travel, narrative, medical documents, visual artefacts and legal records, excluding infanticide, prostitution, the seraglio, and the homoerotic. Notes (211-54). Index (255-64).

718   OAKLEAF, David Arthur. "Solitary voices: aspects of theme and form in eighteenth-century and Romantic fiction." Unpub. doct. diss., Univ. of Toronto, 1977. [*DA* 39 (1979): 4246A-7A.]

As a recurring theme, solitude or isolation offers a useful approach to 18c and Romantic fiction. Obvious in the individualism of *Robinson Crusoe* and *Clarissa*, this theme is also central to self-conscious formal experiment in fiction. The detached observation of isolated systems characteristic of empirical thought can oppose moral and social action. The chamber of the mind becomes the distracting prison or madhouse. The skepticism demanded by empiricism and the assumption that personality is prior to social ties, gives a new urgency to questions of solitude and communication. Examination of particular works reveals the importance of Locke's account of the subjectivity of language in exploring how acutely writers felt the problem.

719-----"Marks, stamps and representations: character in eighteenth-century fiction." *SNNTS* 23:3 (Fall 1991): 295-311.

The tension between distinct conceptions of character energizes 18c fiction. Defoe's protagonists work as hard to create and support characters not inscribed from without, as Sterne later struggles to heighten the burden of his public character. The subjects of 18c narratives are often deprived of social identity. An autonomous external character is a common experience in the 18c. They fight for and over representation; they experience reading and interpretation because character is a representation of potential contradictions. When they challenge the isolated integrity of text and self, they are instantly intertextual, appealing to other texts or contexts to ground their authority on shared extratextual signs rather than the writer's integrity.

720   O'DRISCOLL, Sally. "Rethinking realism: Early women novelists in England and France." Unpub. doct. diss., City Univ. of New York, 1991. [*DA* 52:9 (1992): 3274A.]

Examines the definitions of realism in England and France during the 17c and early 18c, and introduces the concept of 'female realism' as a way to rethink the boundaries of the novel as genre, and integrate the contribution of women into its history.

721 OGDEN, Daryl Scott. "Re-visioning female vision: the novel, women and scopo-cultural production in England, 1740-1925." Unpub. doct. diss., Univ. of Washington, 1994. [*DA* 55 (1995): 2844A.]

Traces an interdisciplinary history of 'scopo-cultural' texts - texts which articulate or theorize vision, particularly female vision. These include conduct books, illustrated periodicals, scientific writings, art criticism and particularly novels. Freud's theory of scopophilia, or exhibitionism, has dominated the terms of critical debate about vision in the 20c, excluding female vision from its discourse. Considers the question of the female domestic gaze in 18c England. Through readings of Richardson, Burney, and Austen shows how, leading into the Victorian Age, the female domestic gaze became an important feature of cultural ageing for women, and yet at the same time marginalized female vision from contemporary scientific and philosophical debate. Later chapters investigate the situation from Victorian and 20c angles (Darwin, Pushkin, Sarah Ellis, Eliot, Hardy, Forster, Woolf).

722 OKAMOTO, Seikei. *Igirisu kindai shosetsu no keisei*. Tokyo: Kirihara Shoten, 1976; pp. 462.

In Japanese. The growth of the modern English novel.

723 OLIVE, Barbara Ann. "The eighteenth-century family and Puritan domestic literature: a study of the origins and development of fictional domestic themes." Unpub. doct. diss., Southern Illinois Univ. at Carbondale, 1979. [*DA* 40 (1980): 4610A.]

Puritan domestic conduct manuals, one genre of the mass of Puritan literature that inundated 16c and 17c England, had established a definite form and content by the early 17c which served as model for domestic instruction until the latter part of the 18c. These manuals prescribed the reciprocal duties in the major familial relationships, between husband and wife, parent and child, master and servant. They contained other familial concepts such as the close connection between the various duties, rewards and punishments attached to their performance. These prescriptions for domestic life influenced fiction through the novels of Richardson, Fielding and Jane Austen. As the manuals lost their popularity, these themes became less predominant in fiction. The family became increasingly withdrawn and isolated.

724 OLSEN, Kristen. *Daily life in 18th-century England*. (The Greenwood Press 'Daily Life Through History' Series.) Westport, CT and London: Greenwood Press, 1999; pp. xiv, 395.

Survey of the daily life and times of 18c England, looking at politics, class and race, the family, London, the Provinces, housing, clothing, the passage of time, worker wages, entertainment, transportation and communication, the economy, law and order, education, food and drink, behavior, health care and hygiene, religion, science and ethnology, Notes (293-306). Glossary (307-48). Bibliography (293-56). Index (357-95). Many illus.

725 OLTEANU, Tudor. *Morfologia romanului european in secolul al XVIII-lea*. Bucharest: Univers, 1974; pp. 516.

In Rumanian. The morphology of the European novel in the eighteenth century.

726 O'NEAL, John C. "Review essay: Eighteenth-century female protagonists and the dialectics of desire." *ECL* 10:2 (1986): 87-97.

The explicit presence of active sexual desire seems crucial to the literary form of the 18c. It is, moreover, feminine desire which helps to structure these texts. Considers how Nancy K. MILLER, Janet TODD, Peggy KAMUF and Rita GOLDBERG analyze women from a woman's perspective, and evaluate the representation of feminine desire in a patriarchal society. In each case a reading of the actions and words reveal a protagonist's conscious and unconscious desires.

727 O'NEILL, John H. "The experience of error: ironic entrapment in Augustan narrative satire." *PLL* 18 (1982): 278-90.

A traditional narrative strategy of the Restoration and the 18c is the use of the reader's identification with a central character as a means of teaching a moral lesson. The use of this strategy in the novel begins with *Moll Flanders*. In such narration, the reader finds a human being, like ourselves, reflecting errors common to us all.

728 OSTER, Elisabeth. *Das Verhältnis von Mutter und Kind im englischen Roman von 1700-1860*. Bonn: Privately printed, 1923; pp. 99.

In German. Looks at: 1) the heroic mother; 2) the wicked stepmother; 3) various types of shrew (cultural-historical overview and attitude to women: the mother who wants to see her child married, mother as society lady, mother as agitator); 4) dissolution of the types (mother types without special characteristics, the wife in conflict between spouse and mother love, passionate love between mother and child, mother and abnormal child, mother as housewife, the mother's struggle for the soul of her child, the fallen woman as mother, attitude of the mother to the problem of free love). The 18c examples are drawn from James Shenley, Daniel Defoe, Samuel Richardson, Tobias Smollett, Henry Fielding, Horace Walpole, Oliver Goldsmith, Fanny Burney, Ann Radcliffe, Matthew Lewis, Jane Austen, Maria Edgeworth.

729 OSTERGAARD, Claus Bratt. *Romanens tid: om kon og civilisation i det 18. og 19. arhundredes fiktion*. Copenhagen: Basilsk, 1987; pp.598.

In Danish. The period of the novel: on sex and civilization in the 18c and 19c.

730 OTTEN, Karl. *Der englischen Roman vom 16. bis zum 19. Jahrhundert.* (Grundlagen der Anglistik und Amerikanistik, 4.) Berlin: E. Schmidt, 1971; pp. 184.

In German. General critical survey of major prose works. Looks at the beginnings of prose fiction in England, the arrival of the 'novella', the novel of the English Renaissance, the novel in the 17c and 18c. Bibliography provided in the notes.

731   PABST, Walter. "Literatur zur Theorie des Romans." *Deutsche Vierteljahrschrift*. 34:2 (1960): 264-89.

In German. Surveys important texts on the theory of the novel, with extensive coverage and analysis of each book. Principal attention given to: - R. KOSKIMIES, *Die Theorie des Romans* (Helsinki, 1935); - W. FLEMMING, *Epik und Dramatik: Versuch einer Wesensdeutung* (Munich, 1955); - E. M. FORSTER, *Aspects of the Novel* (London, 1927); - M. LAWSON, *Spannung in der Erzählung* (Bonn, 1934); - K. R. MEYER, *Zur erlebten Rede im englischen Roman des zwanzigsten Jahrhunderts* (Bern, 1957); and - E. LÄMMERT, *Bauformen des Erzählens* (Stuttgart, 1955).

732   PAKNADEL, Félix. "Discussions dans l'Angleterre du dix-huitième siècle sur la correspondance des arts." In (pp. 491-9) ROUSSEAU, André-M. (foreword). *Art et littérature*. Aix-en-Provence: Univ. de Provence, 1988; pp. 363.
In French. At the beginning of the 18c, England saw great achievement in its poetry, philosophy and music, but not in painting. "Il faut attendre une ou deux générations après 1740 pour que la peinture anglaise ait sa place dans l'art européen. Mais bien avant d'avoir une école anglaise de peinture [...] les Anglais surent créer un art que joignait couleur, mouvement, forme, évocation du passé: je veux dire le jardin paysager [...] .Mais en dehors des arts de la scène, les Anglais créaient un art total, celui des jardins, art qui correspondait mieux à leur sensibilité, à leur éthique, à leur philosophie politique" (498). Notes and bibliography (499).

733   PALMER, Nancy B. and PALMER, Melvin D. "The French *conte de fée* in England." *SSF* 11 (1974): 35-44.

Between 1691 and 1729 there was a vogue for fairy tales from France, some 62 appearing in translation. The genre, however, exerted little specific influence on developing English fiction.

734   PARADISE, Nathaniel Joseph. " Poetry and the early novel: Negotiations in British literary culture." Unpub. doct. diss. Univ. of Pennsylvania, 1996. [*DA* 57 (1997): 4757A.]

Identifies the literary, cultural and economic contexts for 18c novel's interpolation of verse, revealing interpolated poetry to be a window on the evolution of the 18c literary culture - a culture in which emergent genres were linked to emergent classes of readers and writers, and in which challenges to literary and social hierarchies coincided. The novel uses poetry to establish legitimacy for a new class of writers and writing. Uses Bakhtinian understanding of the novel as a polyglot genre to conclude that, through its interpolations of poetry, the novel displays the various discourses of the era, and tests poetic discourse against narrative prose.

735   PARK, W. "Fielding and Richardson." *PMLA* 81:2 (1966): 381-88.

Discusses their similarities with John Shebbeare, Charlotte Lennox et al.

736   PARKER, Alexander A. *Literature and the delinquent: the picaresque novel in Spain and Europe, 1599-1753*. Edinburgh: At the Univ. Press, 1967; pp. x, 195. 10 illus.

Examines the subject from a new angle, with the primary aim of calling attention to historians and students of English and French literature to the value of certain Spanish and German novels in the period before Defoe and Le Sage. Survey concludes with Smollett because it is still possible in 1753 to distinguish in his work a clear novelistic tradition constituting a definable section of literary history. Looks at: 1) the genesis of the picaresque; 2) the delinquent emerges; 3) zenith and nadir in Spain; 4) Grimmelshausen and the Thirty Years' War; 5) the picaresque tradition in England and France. Appendix on the alleged unorthodoxy of *Guzman d'Alfarache*. Bibliographic notes (143-84). Index (185-95).

737   PARKER, Todd Christopher. "Engendering consistency: identity and the rhetoric of sexual difference in British literature, 1700-1750." Unpub. doct. diss., Cornell Univ., 1994. [*DA* 54 (1994): 3760A.]

Examines the literary emergence of heterosexual difference as the dominant cultural paradigm for categories of personal and political identity in British literature from the late Restoration to the mid-18c. "Natural" heterosexuality replaces other more diverse expressions of socially determined sexual identity, such as 17c aristocratic libertines, or youthful sodomites, because fundamental shifts in the representation of sexuality, esp. male sexuality, make these identities untenable. Outlines the transition from the late 17c understanding of the sexuality as context-specific and relational to 18c conceptions of male sexuality as innate and intimately heterosexual orientation. Moves from 17c consciousness of human nature as a function of sin to the predominant 18c notion of human nature as a function of inherent biological urges. Looks at Pope, Swift, Cleland.

738 PASCAL, Roy. "The autobiographical novel and the autobiography." *EC* 9:2 (1959): 134-50.

It is not possible to use the terms 'fictional' and 'true' to distinguish between autobiography and the autobiographical novel. An autobiography is written by one who has a position or reality known to the reader in advance. Autobiographical novels center in experiences which transform and mold a fictional character, and do not revolve around a single outstanding 'real' event.

739-----"Tense and novel." *MLR* 57 (1962): 1-11.

A cursory glance at the tenses used in the modern novel, particularly those which use the stream of consciousness technique, will reveal an almost bewildering variety of situations in which they are used, and to which the logic of grammar is inadequate to provide a clue. The meaning of the tenses cannot be equated with the temporal functions they have in normal discourse. Their function in fiction cannot be judged out of context: they take their meaning from the context.

740 PASHIGOREV, V. N. "Filosofskie i literaturnye predposylki nemetskogo romana vospitaniia." *FM* 2 (1990): 36-43.

In Russian. Investigates the philosophical and literary premises of the German *Bildungsroman*. Eliza Haywood provides one of the most arresting prototypes of the kind of novel in *Betsy Thoughtless*.

741 PATEY, Douglas Lane. *Probability and literary form: philosophic theory and literary practice in the Augustan age*. Cambridge: Cambridge UP, 1984; pp. xiii, 380.

Attempts to make available to the student of 17c and 18c literature a largely neglected body of thought that was crucially important to Augustan literary theory and practice. Examines: 1) the historical development and applications of the concept of probability until the 18c; 2) the role of this concept in Augustan literary theory in its general accounts of nature and the structure of literary works; 3) and the more specific way in which literary and philosophical concepts of probability affected literary practice in giving shape to particular works. It is also about change: the shift from Renaissance to Augustan notions of the probable; the ways in which a theoretical term changes its meaning in migrating from one concept to another, and within the Augustan period when the kinds of interrelationships enjoyed by literature and philosophy remained fairly stable; the ways in which shifts in philosophical theory alter literary practice. Detailed bibliographical notes (282-335). Extensive bibliography (336-63). Index (364-80).

742 PATTERSON, Craig. "Horrible roberys [*sic*], high-way men, and murders: Defoe, Gay, Lillo and Fielding and the popular literature of crime." Unpub. doct. diss., Univ. of Toronto, 1994. [*DA* 55 (1995): 3854A.]

Popular literature of the late 17c and early 18c England represents a vast body of material that circulated in a complex network of cultural exchange. Composed from an array of sources, reprinted with variants and additions in anthologies, they were inconsistent and unstable, and there was a difficulty representing vice in an era that distrusted all potentially fictionalized representations, esp. where any account of crime could be construed as a glorification of criminality. The popular literature of crime was subject to the pull of opposing forces. The work of Defoe, Gay and Lillo represent disparate forms of popular criminal literature, although they participate in the same network of exchange. Defoe's criminals, like the popular depiction of the highway man as a shabby gentleman, also change categories; but instead of dying at the gallows like most reformed criminals, Moll Flanders and Colonel Jacques are allowed to become the people they once strove to be. Defoe allows for social mobility and social impostures that are outside the boundaries of criminality. In Gay, criminals have absorbed the corrupt manners and mores of their betters. Lillo presents the dire consequences of a revolt that is both civil and religious, a deviation from obedience and a disregard of the dangers of sexuality.

743 PATTERSON, Malcolm Howie. "Early English novelists imitating *Don Quixote*." Unpub. doct. diss., Univ. of Oklahoma, 1975. [*DA* 37 (1976): 286A.]

Investigates English imitations of Cervantes's novel during the 18c and 19c when 10 such works were written:
1. Charlotte Lennox's *The Female Quixote*;
2. Henry Fielding's *Joseph Andrews*;
3. Tobias Smollett's *Sir Launcelot Greaves*;
4. Robert Graves's *The Spiritual Quixote*;
5. the anonymous *The Philosophical Quixote*;
6. Jane Purbeck's *Sir George Warrington*;
7. Charles Lucas's *The Infernal Quixote*;
8. George Buxton's *The Political Quixote*;

9. the anonymous *The Amicable Quixote*;

10. John William Cunningham's *Sancho, or the Proverbialist*.

All these authors had various purposes in adapting characters, places, adventures and structures of the original. Lennox, for example, was attacking a foolish literary type of her day, the French romances. Adaptations often resulted in a masquerading and warping of the character of Don Quixote, Sancho Panza and Sanson Carrasco. Most authors saw Don Quixote's vision as selfish, foolish, worthless. The authors whose writings were didactic appear ridiculous, even evil. Other novelists attempted dissections of the Spanish knight's character; they created two or more heroes, each representing one facet of Don Quixote.

744   PAULSON, Ronald. *Satire and the novel in eighteenth-century England.* New Haven and   London: Yale UP, 1967; pp. viii, 318.

Mostly about Fielding and Smollett, satire and sentimentalism and the novel of manners. Aims at tracing the satiric strain that went into the making of the novel in 18c England. What happened to the novel when satire entered, and what happened to satire? Ch. 1 "Satire and the Conventions of Realism" (3-51) looks at satire, realism, the evolution of anti-romance, and England: the examining of conventions. The last part (41-51) examines the non-satiric branch of the picaresque, and how Defoe brought forth the first bloom of the English novel. This genuinely English picaresque "is decidedly centrifugal, interested in the hero's life rather than the society through which he passes" (41). Looks at 17c examples (Nash, Bunyan, Carleton), early 18c (Defoe, Davys). Also observes that "the accomplishment of the French was to break away early from the realism-satire partnership in works like Mme. de La Fayette's *Princesse de Clèves* (1678) and De Préchac's *Illustre Parisienne* (1679) and in the eighteenth century to develop the novel of psychological analysis through Marivaux, Crébillon *fils*, and Choderlos de Laclos" (51).

745-----"Life as journey and as theater: two eighteenth century- narrative structures." *NHL* 8 (1976): 43-58. See below.

746-----"Life as pilgrimage and theater." In (pp. 181-200) DAMROSCH, Leopold, Jr.(ed.). *Modern essays on eighteenth-century literature.* New York: Oxford: Oxford UP, 1988; pp. x, 488.

Addison uses the metaphors of pilgrimage and theater as alternative models of providential design. The pilgrimage stresses teleology: whether Christian pilgrimage or epic journey, it must have a destination. Aspects of divine providence in the theatrical metaphor were apparent arbitrariness, inscrutibility and incalculable distance from everyday concerns. Refers to Defoe, Hogarth and Gay.

747-----*Breaking and remaking: aesthetic practice in England, 1700-1820.* New Brunswick, NJ: Rutgers UP, 1989; pp. xiv, 363. 49 plates.

English aesthetics in the 18c consisted of a succession of theories promulgated by the third Earl of Shaftesbury, Joseph Addison, William Hogarth, Edmund Burke, Richard Payne Knight and Uvedale Price which focused on the response of the spectator to the world around him. The problem they addressed was how to extend the sense of the beautiful to certain natural objects not ordinarily considered beautiful, how to explain as aesthetic those experiences and objects that deviated from the beautiful. One way was to apply a second term, the great (or later sublime), then to explain phenomena that fitted neither category. Addison added the term the uncommon or novel (which later became the picturesque). Part I looks at: 1) the aesthetics of iconoclasm (Swift and Gray); 2) the aesthetics of Georgic renewal (Pope); and 3) the aesthetics of revolution (Byron and Wordsworth). Part II investigates: 1) the aesthetics of modernity (Hogarth); 2) the aesthetics of mourning (Wright and Roubiliac); and 3) the aesthetics of possession (Reynolds, Stubbs and Constable). Notes (331-56). Index (357-63).

748-----*The beautiful, novel, and strange: aesthetics and heterodoxy.* Baltimore, MD, and London: Johns Hopkins UP, 1996; pp. xix, 369.

Aims at filling a gap in studies of aesthetics at its point of origin in England. The scholarly sense of 'aesthetics' tended to focus either on the refinements of taste, or on the aspect of beauty that came to be known as the sublime, excluding both the Beautiful and Addison's third term, the Novel, or New, or Uncommon (until it merges with the Picturesque). Attempts to conceive aesthetics as many contemporaries did - not as theory, but as a poetics of practice, to show that the most popular of modern literature had a crucial relevance to those who contributed to the high-cultural pursuit of philosophical goals, and so both to fuse the Novel and the novel, and to distinguish one from the other. Illus. (42 plates) (267-310). Notes (311-56). Acknowledgements (357-58). Index (359-69).

749 PAVLOVA, T. A. "On the role of revolutionary ideology in the formation of the English Enlightenment." *SVEC* 263 (1989): 223-7.

The ideas of the English enlighteners, esp. John Locke, had tremendous influence on the French and American Enlightenment. The Glorious Revolution not only gave rise to new ideas, but also made them popular with the masses. Complete freedom in interpreting religious truths and an overwhelming pantheism, which sometimes turned almost into materialism or deism, were typical trends. The ideological influence of the Revolution on mass consciousness must be taken into account.

750 PAYNE, Linda R. "Genre and gender: women as writers of prose fiction and drama in Restoration and early eighteenth-century England." Unpub. doct. diss., Univ. of Delaware, 1990. [*DAI* 51:11 (1991): 3757A.]

Women writers like Mary Delarivière Manley, Mary Pix and Catherine Trotter were marginalized personally and professionally. In order to publish and sell their work, they developed mediatorial strategies in their writing which in many cases anticipated broader generic developments in drama and fiction. Their subversive acts of writing embedded revolutionary sentiments and anarchic impulses beneath the surface of their works, covertly disrupting the ideology they ostensibly reflect.

751 PAZICKY, Diana Loercher. "The orphan and the other: wanderings through American imagination, 1620-1855." Unpub. doct. diss., Temple Univ., 1995. [*DA* 56 (1995): 2240A.]

Interprets the orphan trope as a social and cultural metaphor representing a response to historical events that threaten the identity of domestic culture. Specifically examines why an identification with childhood took place within the context of three major historical episodes in American history: the Great Migration, the Revolution, and the rise of capitalism. The interpretation of orphanhood as a response to historical events unfolds within the broader context of psychoanalytical theory, the dynamism of intersubjectivity. Blame for the threat that change posed to the identity of the dominant culture was displaced onto groups of marginalized racial, religious, and ethnic outsiders - mainly Native American, African-Americans, and immigrants. As victims of various forms of socio-economic oppressions, these groups also assumed the role of cultural orphans, thereby enabling the dominant culture to preserve its hegenomy. Uses René Girard's theory of scapegoat.

752 PERRIN, Noel. *Dr Bowdler's legacy: a history of expurgated books in England and America.* New York: Atheneum, 1969; pp. xvi, 296.

Useful for putting the whole issue of expurgation into historical context. See esp. ch. 1 "The Causes of Bowdlerism" (3-24), ch. 2 "Bowdlerism Before Bowdler" (25-59). Discusses the effects of expurgation on 18c novels during the 19c. From the beginning of 1806 the flow of Bowdlerized prose became a flood, with the practice lasting throughout the century. Defoe's *Moll Flanders* and *Roxana* illustrate aspects of this

Victorian attitude (238-43). Both novels effectively disappeared, in the manner of *Fanny Hill*. *Moll Flanders* came out in 1722 and had three editions in its first year, and another every few years for the next 60. This was followed by a blank. A lone 19c edition appeared in 1896, published in Holland. The novel entered the literary mainstream again only in the 1920s, with three editions in 1924, and nine during the rest of the decade, none of them expurgated. *Roxana* repeated the pattern on a lesser scale. The first five editions appeared between 1724 and 1775, but the sixth was a joint one with *Moll* only in 1907; the seventh through the tenth were all in the 1920s. These novels were, however, included, unexpurgated, in expensive sets of the complete works, when regarded as out of reach of the ordinary classes, as in the collective Defoe begun by Hazlitt in 1841, in the 20-volume set begun by Sir G. C. Lewis at the same time, and in the complete novels by George Aitkin in 1895. A fourth 'popular' collection, *The Works of Defoe* (Edinburgh and New York, 1869) omitted them both; this was an edition for 'weaker' people, as John Keltie stated in his preface. References (271-87). Index (288-96).

753 PERRY, Ruth. "Women, letters and the origins of English fiction: a study of the early epistolary novel." Unpub. doct. diss., Univ. of California (Santa Cruz), 1974. [*DA* 35 (1975): 5358A.] See published version below.

754-----*Women, letters, and the novel.* New York: AMS Press, 1980; pp. 218.

Studies the English epistolary novel as it existed prior to the publication of *Pamela* (1740), sifting through most of the letter novels published between 1660 and 1740, including translations. Establishes the characteristics of the genre, different aspects of the social context (place of women, use of the letter in public and private writings). Examines the relationship between the position of women in genteel society and their standard problems in the fiction of the day. Discusses the phenomenological questions of letter-reading and letter-writing. Epistolary method resulted in certain characteristics of modern fiction, esp. isolation and self-scrutiny. Notes (169-90). Bibliography (191-207).

755-----"De-familiarizing the family; or, writing family history from literary sources." *MLQ* 55:4 (1994): 415-27.

Fiction in the 18c saw a renewed interest in the meaning of consanguinity. The recycling of this ancient topos in sentimental fiction may be a clue to profound changes in the practice and meaning of kinship in English 18c culture, changes brought about by new economic policies and social practices, changes not apparent from parish records, demographic statistics, or even conduct manuals. Read in the changing tropes and formulas of popular fiction, literary evidence can influence the archival sources of the historians by bringing to life attitudes about marriage, sexuality, and lineage that are very different from our own. Literature can be used to de-familiarize the family and suggest alternatives for the organization and meaning of human relations in the cultures that produced and consumed these texts.

756   PETERS, Jan Eden and STEIN, Thomas Michael (eds). *Scholastic midwifery: Studien zum Satirischen in der englischen Literatur 1600-1800.* Tübingen: Narr, 1989; pp. ix, 209.

In German. A collection of essays surveying the role of satire in English literature from 1600-1800. While it covers mainly accounts of drama and poetry, it also examines political satire present in English fiction as depicted in the interplanetary voyages made popular by Cyrano de Bergerac. See esp. the contribution by Roland BORGMEIER (113-28).

757   PETRICONI, Hellmuth. *Die verführte Unschuld.* (Hamburger Romantische Studien, Reihe A, 38.) Hamburg, 1953; pp. 137.

Investigates the theme of seduced innocence, from the Classical models of Lucretia and Virginia through Richardson, Laclos and Sade, to Goethe's Gretchen.

758   PICKERING, Samuel F. "The cheap repository tracts and the short story." *SSF* 12:1 (1975): 15-21.

The short story was the stable of 18c periodicals. Societies like "The Society for Promoting Christian Knowledge" and "The Society for the Propagation of the Gospel in Foreign Parts" published tracts throughout the 18c, but tract publishing became a major feature of the English literary landscape only with the growth of the Sunday School Movement in the 1780s and 1790s, and the eruption of the French Revolution and the Napoleonic Wars. Short stories in the *Cheap Repository* established the form as a familiar and respected genre. Because of the popularity of their short narratives, some pietistic writers became celebrities.

759-----"The evolution of a genre: fictional biographies for children in the eighteenth century." *JNT* 7 (1977): 1-23.

Investigates the growth in children's books in the latter half of the 18c which was phenomenal, and thought by contemporaries to be one of the most important developments of the age. The growth of the popularity of the novel focused attention on the dangers of fiction which was addressed by the writers of children's books.

760-----*John Locke and children's books in eighteenth-century England.* Knoxville: Tennessee UP, 1981; pp. xiii, 286.

Study of children's literature and the ideas of John Locke who, for the 18c educator, provided "a theoretical umbrella for all seasons". Looks at the animal creation, the dangerous world of fairy tales, biographies of animals and the inanimate, chapbooks and religious tracts, natural theology, disciplining natural temper.

761-----"The 'ambiguous circumstances of *Pamela*': early children's books and the attitude towards *Pamela.*" *JNT* 14:3 (Fall 1984): 153-71.

For 18c educators, Pamela's circumstances were ambiguous. Whatever the attitude towards that ambiguity, Pamela and her history provided matter for early children's books, and served as a touchstone for contemporary belief about reading and education. As prosperity spread at the end of the 18c, making society more mobile and seemingly more Lockean, many critics thought that wealth was corrupting the middle classes. Instead of providing children with an education which schooled them for life and eternity, parents, critics believed, were misled by the promises inherent in Locke's educational views. References to *The History of Little Goody Two-Shoes* (1765), *The Renowned History of Primrose Prettyface* (1780?), Hannah More's *The Two Wealthy Farmers.*

762-----*Moral instruction and fiction for children, 1749-1820.* Athens, GA and London: U of Georgia P, 1993; pp. vii, 214.

Looks at Allegory and the Eastern Tale, School Stories, *Robinson Crusoe*, the Foundling, *Pamela*, Servants and Inferiors, Liars and Tell-Tales. Provides an appendix of emblems in early children's books and extensive bibliographic notes (195-208).

763 PIERCE, R. B. "Moral education in the novels of the 1750s." *PQ* 44 (1965): 73-87.

The decade after the publication of *Tom Jones* in 1749 was a bleak period for the English novel. Neither Richardson nor Fielding equalled their early masterpieces, and the lesser novelists were even less able to rival the great decade of the 1740s. The popular novel of sentiment lacked the potential for development until Rousseau's *La Nouvelle Héloïse* (1761) and *Émile* (1762). Most sentimental and scandal novels were desperate attempts to capture the emotion of Richardson's novels and French tales of sensibility. The novels of the 1750s were interested in the depiction of moral education, less in the portrayal of character development. Morality came to the picaresque novel in great doses, and set a pattern that was to last into the 19c.

764 PIPER, Wiliam Bowman. *Common courtesy in eighteenth-century English literature*. Newark and London: Assoc. UPs, 1997; pp. 200.

Common courtesy allowed 18c society to improve common sense. The 18c absorbed the understanding of courtesy to attend to the feelings and positions of fellow members at court, to avoid the use of any term or mention of any topic that might cause offence, shock or embarrassment. It governed the early poems of Pope and pervades 18c fiction. The 18c also practised an ambitious courtesy - one which provided ladies and gentlemen with an environment in which they might avoid confronting serious and vexatious topics. Common sense was held to be the best and most useful intellectual achievement of humankind. 18c authors were determined both to establish a community of experience and construct a community of opinion. Looks at Berkeley's philosophy, Pope's poetry, Sterne's fiction, Johnson's criticism, Boswell's biography. Notes (185-92). Bibliography (193-96). Index (197-200).

765 PITCHER, Edward W. "On the conventions of eighteenth-century British short fiction. Part 1: 1700-1760; Part 2: 1760-1785." *SSF* 12 (1975): 119-212, 327-41.

In the first half of the 18c, short prose fiction had a significant place in the literature of both the polite and vulgar reading public. Polite society apparently doted on "amours" and "scandals" that poured from the pens of Mrs Manley, Mrs Aubin, Mrs Barker, Mrs Grainger and the prolific Mrs Haywood. The man in the street knew a different culture, and street literature consisted of tales of rogues and whores, crime and lechery, retribution for sins symbolized by the scaffold and implicit in the "confessional" form of many such narratives. In the early 18c authors deliberately sought to fuse a new narrative style and fictional content with a new narrative purpose: there was a marriage of realism to didacticism. Because readers were rational beings, they were expected to profit without the pain of their fictional counterparts. The domestic tale, the didactic fictional epistle, the oriental apologue were to survive long after 1760, but each genre was to be affected by short tales in the "sentimental manner". The age of sensibility is examined in Part 2.

766-----"A reconsideration of magazine serials in *The Town and Country*

Magazine." Library 5 (1983): 44-52.

The prose essays and tales in this magazine (1769 to 1796) are of interest to literary history, partly because the magazine contributors included Thomas Chatterton and Thomas Holcroft, and partly because the magazine specialized in thinly veiled 'scandal' tales, parodic 'oddities', and satirical narratives, while publishing a conventional and copious selection of moral, sentimental and factual compositions such as were typical of magazine proliferation.

767 PLUMB, J. H. and DEARING, Vinton A. *Some aspects of eighteenth-century England: papers read at a Clark Library Seminar, March 7, 1970.* With an introduction by Maximilian E. NOVAK. Los Angeles: William Andrew Clark Memorial Library, U of California, 1971; pp. vi, 64.

The two papers attempt to map out certain areas of English life in the 18c. PLUMB'S "Reason and Unreason in the Eighteenth Century" (1-26) draws clear distinctions in the spirit of the age between 1680 to 1720, and 1760 to 1800. In contrast to the earlier period when rational inquiry was given encouragement by the social and political establishment, after 1760 the court and society tended to distrust scientists and *philosophes*. DEARING'S "A Walk through London with John Gay and Run with Daniel Defoe" (27-59) provides a literary map of London as known to Gay in *Trivia* and Defoe in *Colonel Jack*, investigating the places that both authors might still recognize. Bibliographic notes.

768 POLITI, Jina. *The novel and its presuppositions: changes in the conceptual structure of novels in the 18th and 19th centuries.* Amsterdam: Hakkert, 1976; pp. 269.

Focuses on the changing structures of thought in fiction. The concept of mimesis and the transformations which it underwent through the ages suggest that these changes were grounded on the permanent structures of language and experience. Novels share a common structure of a physical world-model and a mind-model interacting with it. Defoe constructs a revolutionary world-model in *Moll Flanders* which is based on the philosophy of such thinkers as Hobbes and Mandeville. His oppositions do not derive from metaphysics, but from nature and culture. Fielding's world view in *Tom Jones* admits the operation of law in the universe as it had come to be defined by the science of his day. Richardson's world-model in *Pamela* is an appeal for the preservation of an orthodox, Christian model of the world. His inspiration comes from mystical thought based on ethical dualism, cosmic and expressive of fallen nature. Defoe anticipates the 19c by opposing character to society. Major bibliography (251-69).

769   POPKIN, Richard H. (ed.). *Millenarianism and messianism in English literature and thought, 1650-1800: the Clark Library Lectures 1981-2.* Leiden: Brill, 1988; pp. vii, 210.

Collection of essays focusing on the relevant developments in English literature, philosophy, politics, science, and theology between 1630 and 1800 on the theme of 'the end of days', which is the conviction that the climax of providential history predicted in the Bible will occur, transforming the human scene into a paradise on earth.

770   POPKIN, Susan Marsha. "The aesthetics of narrative self-consciousness in eighteenth-century fiction, biography, and history: a study of the narrator and the reader." Unpub. doct. diss., New York Univ., 1986. [*DA* 47 (1987): 1337A.]

Investigates the aesthetics of narrative self-consciousness in 18c fiction, biography and history. Examines the 'chattiness' of the narrator, and the function, in epithets and address, of the reader, and investigates the difference between authorial intrusion and self-conscious narration. Conversations help to unify narration; self-consciousness is bound to the very idea of narration. Refers to Fielding, Sterne, Gibbon and Johnson.

771   PORTER, Ray. *English society in the eighteenth century.* (The Pelican History of Britain.) London: Allen Lane, 1982; pp. 424.

Between 1700 and 1800 England was still comparatively empty. Competition for living space, national resources and livelihood was not so pressured and dictated by impersonal economic laws. Runaway population rise and tumultuous industrial change built up in the last third of the 18c, but came to peak only in the 19c. Ch. 1 offers a flavor of Georgian society, its peculiarity and diversity. Ch. 2 and ch. 3 depict the different social groups and their interrelationships, hierarchical inequalities, but fundamental stability. Ch. 4 emphasizes how social solidarity was internalized by inherited patterns of reproduction and continuity. Ch. 5 and ch. 6 explore the generation of change and its impact on the economy and in society. Ch. 7 considers processes of cultural consensus and cultural atomization. Ch. 8 and ch. 9 scrutinize the acceleration of industrialization. Ch. 10 considers how the endorsement of capitalism in fact spelt the demise of Georgian society, and saw the rise of industrialization, its self-confident manufacturing bourgeoisie, a desperate proletariat, and political dissatisfaction. Statistical Tables (381-92). Further Reading (393-403). Index (405-24).

772   PORTER, Susan Speer. "Domination and dissent: Gendered duality and patriarchal authority." Unpub. doct. diss., Claremont Graduate School, 1995. [*DA* 55 (1995): 3845A.]

Shakespeare, Milton, Defoe, Hawthorne and Melville are chosen as representative of an analysis of gendered structures of authority. All have an Augustinian tradition of individualism. Analysis is built on three aspects of Augustine's concept of human nature: inwardness, the natural and original authority of the father, and a contrast between patriarchal authority in the family and authority in the state. Defoe's Roxana belongs to Milton's Puritan stream of Augustinianism. She is a strong and independent woman who poses a threat to the patriarchal order. The conflict between Milton's intolerance of dissent in the patriarchal family and his atomistic individualism is further reworked by Defoe who can be seen as his heir.

773   PORTNOY, Jeffrey A. "The transition to print: editorial presence and literary community." Unpub. doct. diss., Emory Univ., 1988. [*DAI* 49:6 (1988): 1464A-1465A.]

The printing press was an agent of change in politics, religion, science, social and economic structures. Printed material and printing technology engendered a subjectivity and individuality, and threatened a shared world view. The writer's task thus included educating the reader who no longer listened and responded as part of a community, but now evaluated and interpreted a text independently. Ben Jonson, John Dryden and Samuel Richardson all used editorial techniques to direct the interpretation of their texts and to establish a relationship with the reader.

774   PRESCOTT, S. H. "Feminist literary theory and British women novelists of the 1720s." Unpub. doct. diss., Univ. of Exeter, 1997.

See Ch. 4 under AUBIN, 1127.

775   PRESTON, John. *The created self: the reader's role in eighteenth-century fiction*. New York: Barnes & Noble; London: Heinemann, 1970; pp. 220.

By looking at *Moll Flanders, Clarissa, Tom Jones* and *Tristram Shandy*, seeks to interpret essential features of the novel form, and characteristic procedures, particularly the rhetorical aspects. All four authors are interested in creating a text which will give instruction to the reader. They wish to keep the form open, and so think of the novel as a process, not a product, and as a situation for the reader, not a received text. They want to create readers, just as the readers want to create writers. This is the created reader, the 'created self', and the work he is given to do in reading the text. See esp. ch. 2 "*Moll Flanders*: 'The Satire of the Age'". Select Bibliography (212-17). Index (219-20).

776 PRINSEN, J. D. *De roman in de 18e eeuw in West Europa*. Groningen and Den Haag: J. B. Walters UM, 1925; pp. viii, 540.

In Dutch. Wide-ranging survey of the 18c and the novel. The Introduction (1-183) provides an overview of political and social conditions in the century, French classicism, science and at the beginning of the 18c, influences of the new sciences and on art and commerce, the turn to the past and historical studies; Lessing and Winckelmann; aesthetics and discovery of Shakespeare; the transition to romanticism. The account of the 18c novel (165-512) is divided into the novel before 1740: 1) Le Sage and Defoe; 2) Sandras, Marivaux, Prévost; and the novel after 1740:1) *Pamela* to *René*: Richardson, Rousseau, Goethe, De Chateaubriand; 2) from Fielding to Jane Austen: Fielding, Smollett, Sterne, Goldsmith; 3) the novel of terror; 4) the influences of the English and French novels in Germany and Holland; the effects of Richardson and Rousseau in France; 5) the didactic novel after 1740. Index (535-40). While there are only minimal footnotes, and no bibliography, there are some very interesting perspectives on selected secondary reading in French, German and Dutch.

777 PRIOR, Mary (ed.). *Women in English society, 1500-1800*. London; New York: Methuen, 1985; pp. xvi, 267.

Collection of essays looking at various aspects of women's life and social functions: marital fertility, the remarrying widow, women and the urban economy, recusant women. Provides a checklist of women's published writings, and statistical analysis of women's printed writings.

778 PROBYN, Clive T. *English fiction of the eighteenth century, 1700-1789*. (Longman Literature in English.) London: Longman, 1987; pp. xii, 244.

The novel in the 18c was characterized by diversity, formal instability, mixture of modes and techniques. By 1767 the early novelists had established all the techniques of narrative prose fiction, and a variety of definitions of the novel was first encountered. Looks at novels and readers (1692 to 1785), then at Defoe, Richardson, Fielding, Smollett and Sterne, and finally at society, sentiment and self in the novel (1764 to 1789). Provides a chronology (189-210), detailed bibliographic notes and general bibliography of fiction in the 18c (211-19), biographical and bibliographical information on individual authors (220-39).Index (240-44).

779 PROPER, Coenraad Bart Anne. *Social elements in English prose fiction between 1700 and 1832*. New York: Haskell House, 1965; pp. 302.

Surveys the period 1700 to 1832 in investigating the political background of contemporary fiction. The period was characterized by optimism and repose, which is typical of periods between constitutional and social upheavals of the first magnitude. The middle class, though raised socially, was not to attain its political majority until the Reform Bill of 1832. Contemplates the gradual widening of the social area of prose fiction before the birth of the social novel proper, and points out the features in its predecessors as may be said to have paved the way for its creation. Looks at many comparatively neglected minor writers. See esp. ch. 1 "From 1700 to Richardson" (22-44) (Steele, Addison, Defoe, Swift, Richardson, Arbuthnot). Bibliography (291-302).

780 PUNTER, David. "Fictional representation of the law in the eighteenth century." *ECS* 16 (1982): 47-74.

Fiction in the 18c is obsessed with the law, its operation, its justifications, with all its limits. This was one of the most important sets of changes heralded by Defoe. The universe of the 17c romances was bounded and controlled by cosmic justice, reflected in already given and quasi-mythic narrative structures. The universes of Defoe and Fielding, Godwin and Radcliffe are limited by various manifestations of human law. Discusses some of the ways in which novelists of the 18c represented the law, legal characters and legal processes, and seeks to uncover a set of attributes which lie below the fictional surface.

781 RACAULT, Jean-Michel. *L'Utopie narrative en France et en Angleterre: 1675-1791*. (Studies on Voltaire and the Eighteenth Century, 280.) Oxford: Voltaire Foundation, 1991; pp. xii, 830.

In French. Part II looks at the utopian genre, its sociology and displacement, novels of desert isles, Robinsonades and imaginary voyagers (215-90), before moving on to canonized forms and adapted models, human nature and the century of reason (Foigny and Swift). The conclusion considers micro-Utopias and small societies in the novel of the Enlightenment. Bibliography (783-810).

782 RACEVKIS, Inese. "True and false delicacy: conflict and balance in the eighteenth century." Unpub. doct. diss., New York Univ., 1995. [*DA* 56

(1995): 1797A.]

Delicacy is one of the key words of 18c culture and functions in psychological, moral, social, gender and literary contexts. Its meaning is unstable, leading to debate about 'true' or 'false' delicacy. With the popularization of Shaftesbury's philosophy, it became associated with the feminine vocation of sensibility and sentimentality. In the mid-18c Hume and his contemporaries recaptured the critical meaning of delicacy as the integration and construction of a new balance of opposites, esp. between reason and feeling, sense and sensibility, reason and virtue. True delicacy is an adherence to social decorum in taste and conduct, false delicacy an imbalance of feeling and judgement, often producing foibles and comic errors in judgement and conduct.

783 RADCLIFFE, David Hill. "Meditations and literary history, 1600-1750." Unpub. doct. diss, Univ. of Virginia, 1989. [*DAI* 50:1 (1989): 149A.]

Literary genres change by incorporating, resisting or merging with other genres in ways which articulate changing values in religion, philosophy and social history. Studies the importance of meditational genres in articulating philosophical, religious and social positions in the years between 1600 and 1750. Looks closely, among other subjects, at Restoration Theater, Defoe, comedy, prisons and the picaresque, serious reflections, religious practice, commercial relations and fictional techniques.

784 RALEIGH, Walter. *The English novel: a short sketch of its history from the earliest times until the appearance of 'Waverley'*. London: J. Murray, 1894. Rev. 1929; pp. xii, 298.

Ch.5 "The Beginnings of the Modern Novel" (110-39) describes the work of the 17c, the preparation for the modern novel, character writing, autobiographies, diaries, letters, French parodies of romance, the new prose, the *Tatler* and *Spectator*, their detached sketches, their educating of the public, Daniel Defoe, his *Shortest Way with Dissenters*, the turning point of his career, *The Apparition of Mrs Veal*, his realistic method, *Robinson Crusoe*.

785 RANSOME, Arthur. *A history of story-telling: studies on the development of narrative*. London: T.C. & E.C. Jack, 1909; pp. xviii, 318.

General survey of the development of prose fiction: influences, narrative technique. Discusses the contribution of the essayists to story-telling (esp. Addison and Steele) (107-21), and the role of Bunyan and Defoe in the emergence of the classic 18c novel. Index (313-18).

786 RAWSON, Claude. *Order from confusion sprung: Studies in eighteenth-century literature from Swift to Cowper.* London: George Allen & Unwin, 1985; pp. xv, 431.

Large study of Swift, Pope and Augustan verse satire, Fielding, Cowper and Christopher Smart. Bibliographical notes. Index (419-31). Useful for the wider literary background of prose fiction.

787-----*Satire and sentiment, 1660-1830.* Cambridge and New York: Cambridge UP 1994; pp. xviii, 309.

Examines the evolution of satirical writing in the period 1660 to 1830, focusing on English writers from Rochester to Austen. Describes European conduct of this period as part of a tradition deriving from classical and 16c humanism, and leading to later writers like Flaubert and Yeats. Within the given period, satire moved from an unusually dominant position to a relatively modest one, softened by the cult of 'sensibility' or 'sentiment'. This transition was connected with large social and cultural changes, culminating in the French Revolution. Concentrates on evasions and internal contradictions, on continuities and discontinuities with earlier and later periods, and with literature and modes of thought outside Britain. Bibliographic footnotes. Index (299-309).

788 RAY, William. *Story and history: narrative authority and social identity in the eighteenth-century French and English novel.* Cambridge, MA: Blackwell, 1990; pp. viii, 362.

In the mid-18c French and English fiction suddenly emerged in the critical discourse as the primary vehicle for representing contemporary social reality, and even shaping that reality. The importance of fiction for the morals of its readers received substantial re-examination and refinement at the hands of the proponents and detractors of the novel. Covers the whole century. The first half centers on private lives and public stories (*La Princesse de Clèves*), personal ordering and providential ordering (*Robinson Crusoe*), negotiating reality (*Moll Flanders, Roxana*), individualism and authority, the seduction of the self (*La Vie de Marianne* and *Le Paysan parvenu*), from private narration to public narration (*Pamela*). Bibliography (351-57). Index (358-62).

789 REED, Joel. "Academically speaking: Language and nationalism in seventeenth- and eighteenth-century England." Unpub. doct. diss., Univ.

of California (Irvine), 1991. [*DAI* 52:12 (1992): 4341A.]

In the 17c and 18c numbers of writers proposed the formation of a state-supported academy for the reform and supervision of the English language and culture (Daniel Defoe and Jonathan Swift in the early 18c). Uses the texts of their proposals and essays on language reform as a focal point to consider how these authors contributed to the promotion of English national discourse.

790 REED, Walter. *An exemplary history of the novel: the Quixotic versus the picaresque*. Chicago: Chicago UP, 1981; pp. viii, 334.

Presents a poetics of the novel, discussing its origins (going back to Classical and romance source, the effect of the Reformation and the Council of Trent on European literature, with the emergence of the picaresque tradition in Spain.

791 REES, Christine. *Utopian imagination and eighteenth-century fiction.* (Studies in Eighteenth- and Nineteenth-Century Literature.) London and New York: Longman, 1996; pp. vi, 296.

Utopian fiction was a particularly rich and important genre in the 18c. Utopian writing became mingled with other fictional genres, like the increasingly dominant novel. Seeks to interpret and locate these innovative fictions in the tradition of utopian writings, which stretches back through the Renaissance to the Ancient World. How a society disciplines and punishes its citizens is an index of its ideology. Punishment also calls into question the relativity of standards of civility and barbarism. This kind of challenge runs right through utopian fiction. Looks at the classical origins and Renaissance locations, 17c utopias, utopian discussions in the 18c, utopias overseas (connecting Defoe [*Robinson Crusoe* and *A Grand History of the Pyrates*]), Gaudentini di Lucca, Peter Wilkins) (73-122), Utopia and satire (Swift), domestic utopia (Fielding and Richardson), women's Utopias (Delarivière Manley and Mary Astell) (205-40), Utopia and the philosophical tale (Johnson). Each chapter has notes and references. Bibliography (272-89). Index (290-96).

792 REEVE, Clara. *The progress of romance. Through times, countries and manners, with remarks on the good and bad effects of it, on them respectively in a course of evening conversations by Clara Reeve, author of The English Baron, The Two Mentora etc. in 2 volumes.* Colchester, 1795. Rpt. New York: The Facsimile Society, 1930; pp. xvi, 136.

Presents an 18c view of the history of romance from ancient times (Homer, Diogenes), Eastern (Arabian) and late Medieval works (Geoffrey of Monmouth, Amadis de Gaul, Chaucer), through figures of the 16c and 17c (Lyly, Sidney, Cervantes, Scudéry, De Lafayette, Le Sage, Behn), right into a survey of 18c works (Manley, Marivaux) (53-54). Contains her famous distinction between 'romance' and 'novel' (I, 110-11).

793   REID, Richard. *The Georgian house and its details.* London: Bishopgate, 1989; pp. 190.

The 18c was the golden age of English house building, of a quality of craftsmanship and design that had not been seen before. For the rising middle class of the period, handsome rectangular, symmetrically planned houses were the most modern design. In the 18c, for the first time, many smaller houses could be conceived along either architectural or vernacular lines. Collection of essays based on the readings and sketches of a practising architect concerned with the relationship of building to architecture, a relation made so poetic in 18c England. Looks at the construction, convenience, furniture and fittings of both larger Georgian houses, and particularly the smaller houses and cottages of the period. Important introduction "Eighteenth-Century England" (9-13). Bibliography (180-83). Index (184-90). Profusely illus.

794   REILLY, Elizabeth Carroll. "Common and learned readers: shared and separate spheres in mid-eighteenth-century New England." Unpub. doct. diss., Boston Univ., 1994. [*DA* 55 (1995): 2334A.]

Explores print and reading in mid-18c New England in order to shed light on relationships among different social and cultural groups. Most previous studies have concentrated on the sermons and libraries of learned ministers and social leaders. This seeks to provide a fuller picture of how various layers of society and culture interacted in the world of print. The reading of the learned and wealthy members of society is studied through the records of two booksellers, who imported matter from England - Jeremy Condy and Henry Know who worked in Boston from the mid-1750s through 1774.

795   REILLY, Patrick. *The literature of guilt: from Gulliver to Golding.* Iowa City: U of Iowa P, 1988; pp. viii, 178.

Defines a recurrent situation found throughout literature which he defines as 'the Judas moment', "when the self gags at its own corruption has become a salient, almost defining characteristic of modern literature. It is especially interesting, because here, as in so much else, our century has shockingly challenged the assumptions and pieties of our predecessors" (1).

796   REIMANN, K. A. "On their own account: Pirate narratives and pirate writers of the long eighteenth century." Unpub. doct. diss., Univ. of Oxford, 1996. [*IT* 45 (1996): 3269.]

Analyzes the elements of pirate narrative which have contributed to their enduring popularity. A. O. Exquemelin's *Bacaniers of America* (1684) and Defoe's *A General History of the Pyrates* (1724) survived into the 20c and suggest some quality in these texts which transcended their period in a way unusually associated with 'literary' works. Focuses on the late 17c and early 18c, offering a close reading of these texts to enhance understanding of both internal structures and political motivations that in part determined these structures.

797   REINHOLD, Heinz. *Der englische Roman im 18. Jahrhundert: Sozialistische, geistes- und gattungsgeschichtliche Aspekte.* (Sprache und Literatur, 104.) Stuttgart: Kohlhammer, 1978; pp. 206.

In German. Presents a series of essays on the major figures of the 18c: Swift, Defoe, Richardson, Fielding, Smollett, Sterne, Goldsmith, and the Gothic novelists. Puts the novel in context in "Der englische Roman am Anfang des 18. Jahrhunderts" (14-16), describing the transition from Behn to Manley, Haywood and Aubin, and mentioning the growing Puritan emphasis. Select bibliography (184-97) provides both background on the novel and the period, and works on each author dealt with individually. Chronology 1688 to 1826 (198-99).

798   REITZ, Ann L. "Sawbones to saviour to cynic: the doctor's relation to society in English fiction of the eighteenth, nineteenth, and twentieth centuries." Unpub. doct. diss., Univ. of Cincinnati, 1985. [*DA* 46 (1986): 2701A.]
The doctor has always been seen as a man with special powers which arouse awe and suspicion, and often derision. All three facets - hero, villain and clown - have received literary acknowledgement in a long procession of wise men, poisoners, scientists and quacks. Investigates why different periods have chosen to emphasize one of these, from comic bungler of the 18c, through the Victorian doctor-hero, to the alienated intellectual of the 20c.

799   RENWICK, W. L. "Comic epic in prose." *E & S* 32 (1946): 40-43.

In the early 18c *comic* did not mean 'funny' and *epic* did not mean 'exciting and dangerous'. By 1742 the terms had not suffered their modern degradation. Nor was *in prose* merely a tag to fill out the phrase. Each word carried the full weight of the critical tradition from which it derived the force of established authority. The continuity of this tradition was broken by 1800. 'Comic' partakes in the nature and purpose of comedy, 'epic' demands narrative.

800   RIBEIRO, Alvaro and BASKER, James G. (eds). *Tradition in transition: women writers, marginal texts, and the eighteenth-century canon.* Oxford: Clarendon Press, 1996; pp. xviii, 360.

Collection of 18 essays written by the pupils of Prof. Roger Harrison Lonsdale on 18c English literature. Divided into 1) Women writers (Elizabeth Carter, Mrs Thrale, Mary Wollstonecraft, Jane West, Maria Edgeworth); 2) Marginal texts (Defoe, Swift, Boswell, Samuel Patterson, oral tradition, Sir Joshua French, Capt. Bligh); 3.) The eighteenth-century canon (Parnell, Pope, periodical poetry, William Collins, literary sources, Dodsley, Warton). Index (359-60).

801   RICHETTI, John J. *Popular fiction before Richardson: narrative patterns 1700-39.* Oxford: Clarendon Press, 1969; pp. xxix, 274.

Defoe was a man of practical realism, serious beliefs and commitments, but his novels are best understood in terms of a broadly conceived theory of the kind of satisfaction that fiction uniquely delivers to its willing readers: *Robinson Crusoe* (the self as master), *Captain Singleton* (revision of popular legend), *Moll Flanders* (dialectics of power), *Colonel Jacques* (the self enters history), *Roxana* (nature, knowledge and power), *A Journal of the Plague Year* (epitome).

802-----"The portrayal of women in Restoration and eighteenth-century English literature". In (pp. 65-97) SPRINGER, *What manner of woman* etc., **931**.

Woman as moral topic becomes woman as metaphor: the literary tradition moves to examining female experience as a revealingly intense version of human experience.

803-----"Popular narrative in the early eighteenth century: formats and formulas." In (pp. 3-39) ARMISTEAD (ed.), *The first English novelists* etc., **29**.

Society and psychological realism, moral complexity and narrative self-consciousness of the 18c English novel represent for modern criticism a sort of evolution, a pinnacle of narrative achievement. Defoe, Richardson and Fielding transmit and transform their crude contemporaries and

immediate predecessors, and dramatize the profound originality of the
minor novelists (Falconer, Gildon, Manley, Haywood, Davys). Suffering
and confused female characters in 18c popular fiction enact a cultural
crisis and enormous ideological transition, the privatization and
fragmentation of experience for men and women. The major writers
accept and attempt to revise this by means of the technical control and
moral coherence they bring to bear on the formulas of popular fiction
(33). Detailed notes (33-39).

804-----"Recent studies in the Restoration and the eighteenth century." *SEL* 30:3
(Summer 1990): 517-54.

Review/discussion looking critically at some 75 texts on the 18c, esp. in
the context of the anxiety that the research on the 18c had perhaps failed
to keep up with new methods and perspectives that have characterized
critical work on the Renaissance and Romanticism. The list of books
surveyed shows a lively variety of subject matter and approach, with
traditional scholarship and unreconstructed literary criticism flourishing
side by side with feminism and the new historicism.

805-----(ed.). *The Cambridge companion to the eighteenth-century novel.*
Cambridge, New York and Melbourne: Cambridge UP, 1996; pp. xiii,
283.
The past 20 years have seen understanding of the emergence of the novel
in the 18c change dramatically. Presents 12 essays based on new research
in social and political history which challenge and refine the traditional
view of the origins and purpose of this fiction. The novel is not primarily
defined by realism of representation, but by new ideological and cultural
functions in the emerging modern world of print culture. The essays
cover fiction by women, sentimental and Gothic fiction, and detailed
readings of works by Defoe, Swift, Richardson, Fielding, Sterne,
Smollett, and Burney. Provides a comprehensive guide to the 18c novel
and its place in the culture of its time. Of particular general interest are
the introduction (John RICHETTI) (1-8), the novel and social/cultural
history (J. Paul HUNTER) (9-40), women writers and the 18c novel (Jane
SPENCER) (212-35). Each article has detailed notes and its own
bibliography. Chronology (xi-xiii). Index (277-83).

806-----*The English novel in history, 1700-1780.* (Novel in history.) London and
New York: Routledge, 1999; pp. x, 290.

18c fiction is an important stage in the fashioning, and a key tool for the
understanding of, the evolving entity of the socially constructed self.
Even in the early years of the century, narrative in Britain was

increasingly (if implicitly) concerned with the problem of what it was to be an individual. Narratives of all kinds return consistently to the largest of questions: where is the authority that can judge subjectivity? Novelists pretend to cede authority in the search for a center, deferring to correspondents or fictional narrators to make whatsoever sense they can of social diversity and a multiplicity of relationships and negotiations for power and pleasure. Interest in social change and social representation means a wide sample of texts. Looks at fiction and society in 18c Britain, amatory fiction (Behn, Manley, Haywood), Defoe (mapping social totality), Richardson (passion to suffering and the transformation of amatory fiction), Fielding (age and satire), Smollett (resistant knowledge and action), women novelists (and the transformation of fiction), sentimental narrative (philosophy and fiction). Bibliographic notes. Index (282-90).

807 RICHMOND, Herbert. "The naval officer in fiction." *E & S* 30 (1944): 7-25.

Survey of the type of the naval officer in fiction from the latter 17c to the early 20c. Investigates the changing historical role and perception of the officer, the recurrent emergence of the type in literature. "It was with this background that the sea officer made his appearance in the drama and the dawn of the novel. The stage preceded the novel as the mirror of life" (10). Considers the type in the 18c at length, looking at Defoe's pioneering role in pressing for naval reform, the type in Shadwell, the satire of Ned Ward, Smollett, Fanny Burney and Jane Austen.

808 RICKWORD, E. "A note on fiction." In (pp. 294-305) *Towards standards of criticism* (1933). Rpt. in O'CONNOR, W. V. (ed.). *Forms of modern fiction.* Bloomington, IN: U of Indiana P, 1959; pp. ii, 305.

Important for the discussion of the emergence of realism in the novel. "[...] it is the problem of objectifying and setting in disciplined motion the subjective narrative that has occupied nearly all English novelists of importance since Fielding and Richardson [...]" (302).

809 RIDLEY, Hugh. *Images of imperial rule.* London: Croom Helm; New York: St Martin's Press, 1983; pp. vii, 181.

Attempts to give a picture of the literature which was produced in France, Britain and Germany describing and praising the achievements of the colonial expansion in the late 19c. Important for the Introduction: "*Robinson Crusoe* and the Reading of Colonial Literature" (1-13). Defoe's novel stands in direct descent from the great voyages of discovery in the late 16c and 17c, yet shows, like the whole genre of the imaginary journey, how readily the exploration of new worlds became a pretext for the demonstration of the qualities of the old (5).

810   RIGAUD, Nadia and DENISOT, Paul (eds). *La violence dans la littérature et la pensée anglaises*. Aix-en-Provence: Univ. de Provence, 1989; pp. 176.
      In French. Eleven essays provide a survey of the theme of violence in British literature from the Jacobean theater to the 20c (Bertold Brecht, Angus Wilson, D. M. Thomas). Claude SOUPEL considers "Modalités de la violence dans *The Life and Strange Adventures of Robinson Crusoe, of York, Mariner* (1719)" (31-46). "Le livre de Defoe fait écho à son temps et affirme la vitalité turbulente du peuple anglais marin et commerçant, lui proposant une image de lui-même hautement réfléchie dans un héros symbolique qui le fascine" (31). Bibliography (46).

811   RIVERO, Albert J. (ed.). *Augustan subjects: essays in honor of Martin C. Battesin*. Newark: Delaware UP; London and Toronto: Assoc. UPs, 1997; pp. 311.
      See Ch.4 under DEFOE, **1411**.

812   RIVERS, Isobel (ed.) *Books and their readers in eighteenth-century England*. Leicester: Leicester UP, 1982; pp. xi, 267.

      Collection of essays on writers, books and readers intended as a contribution to the literary and cultural history of 18c England. The approach is historical, investigating significant kinds of 18c writing and how they were designed, for and received by, different audiences. Covers 1) publishers and writers; 2) classics and chapbooks; 3) politicians, peers and publication by subscription (1700-50); 4) classical poetry and the 18c reader; 5) bibliographic and critical literature and the 18c reader; 6) dissenting and Methodist books of practical divinity; 7) philosophical literature; 8) science books and readers in the 18c. Each essays has extended bibliographic notes. Index (257-67).

813----*Reason, grace and sentiment: A study of the language of religion and ethics in England, 1660-1780*. Vol. 1: *Whichcote to Wesley*. (Cambridge Studies in Eighteenth-Century English Literature and Thought, 8.) Cambridge; New York: Cambridge UP, 1991; pp. xiii, 277.

      Studies changes in the ways in which the relationship between religion and ethics was perceived in the period from the mid-17c to the later 18c by different religious and secular movements, and the kinds of language in which these changes were expressed. There is an emphasis in Anglican thought on the capacity of human reason to cooperate with divine grace; and on an attempt to divorce ethics from religion to find the springs of human action in human nature alone. Of particular interest to 18c studies are the sections on affectionate religion, Watts, Dodderidge and the tradition of old dissent, John Wesley and the language of Scripture, reason and experience. Bibliography (254-66).

814   RIVINGTON, Charles A. *'Tyrant': the story of John Barber, 1675-1741: Jacobite Lord Mayor of London and printer and friend of Dr Swift*. York: William Sessions, 1989; pp. viii, 311.

Study of the Lord Mayor of London whose ability and single-mindedness made him an invaluable assistant to various leaders: during Queen Anne's reign to Swift and Bolingbroke; in 1722 to the Jacobite leaders; and later to Pulteney and Bolingbroke in their opposition to Walpole. His Jacobitism was genuine, and an expression of discontent with the corrupt and sometimes tyrannical government of Walpole, which was supported by the Hanoverian monarchs. Notes (260-305). Index (306-11). Illus. (14 plates).

815   RIZZO, Betty. "The English author-bookseller dialogue." *AJ* 2 (1989): 353-74.
The author-bookseller dialogue of the 18c is a particular subgenre of the dialogue. Collected more than 30 examples and many analogues, ranging from 1727 to 1779, examples showing great similarities and many differences. Can be verse or prose, exchange of letters, stage dialogue, and formal dialogue. Common overriding feature that identifies them all as part of a single tradition is the subject matter, which always involves the booksellers' interference, for financial gain, with the evil bookseller an important factor in the metonymic meaning of the dialogues. Booksellers act as the corrupting force: money and the lust for it distort morality and art. The trade of bookselling controls the profession of authorship. Full bibliographic notes (368-70). Annotated bibliography of author-bookseller dialogues (370-74).

816-----*Companions without vows: relationships among eighteenth-century British women*. Athens,   GA: Georgia UP, 1994; pp. x, 439.

Studies women's relationships with one another in 18c England, focusing particularly on a network of middle- to upper-class women who produced a significant body of writing, in letters, memoirs, and fiction. Focuses on women and their lives, their discourse about themselves, each other, and the conditions in which they lived - social, economic, and psychological. Considers the depth, richness, diversity, and occasional perversity of some such relationships which often cut across economic and social lines.

Most interested in investigating the institutionalized and compassionate relationship between employer and humble companion, and to a lesser extent, the relationship of marriage; also parent and child, deputy laborers, agents, rivals and spies, business partners, the domestic triangle, romantic friendship, friends and reformers. Notes (320-28). Bibliography (389-406). Annotated index (407-39).

817 ROBERTS, Marie Mulvey and PORTER, Roy (eds). *Literature & medicine during the eighteenth century.* London and New York: Routledge, 1993; pp. x, 293.

Thirteen essays explore the dialogue between the history of medicine and literary history and criticism - the close, complex relationship between culture, natural knowledge and the imagination. Looks at the meanings of health and sickness, the moral place of medicine in the social economy, investigation of the ways in which medicine and the bio-medical sciences created fields of meaning serviceable to 18c culture and its literary expression. Medical accounts of the mechanisms of sickness and the processes of health constituted the ideal natural language for exploring emotion, personality and social intercourse. A central Enlightenment claim was that literature, the culture of the word, should serve a healing function. Therapeutically, literature was to conform to the rule of utility. Medicine is as much a cultural construct as literature, and in need of scrutiny with the tools of literary criticism, as with those of the surgeon, whether they be for the purpose of dissection or deconstruction. Illus. (8 Hogarth prints). Bibliographic notes appended to each essay.

818 ROBERTSON, C. W. "Relative choices: choice of partner in some eighteenth-century novels." Unpub. doct. diss., Univ. of Oxford, 1994. [*IT* 44:3 (1995): 954.]

Examines the choice of marriage partner in the works of selected 18c and 19c British and American novelists, esp. Defoe, Richardson, Burney, Inchbald, Brunton and Brockden Brown. Their heroines reject the dangerous passions of suitors - who may resemble their own unworthy fathers - in favor of the unthreatening esteem of a fraternal suitor. The heroines set out to exercise their right of choice, yet they often encounter familial pressure that redefines choice as mere consent or even submission.

819 RODNEY, Paul Wayne. "Travel and maps of identity in English narrative, 1719-1850." Unpub. doct. diss., Univ. of Michigan, 1996. [*DA* 57 (1997): 4757A.]
In 18c improvements of roads and the increasing availability of maps

fostered significant growth in British travel. Explores how representations of travel developed and complicated ideas of national and individual identity. Literal maps define possessions of space by imposing border lines upon a landscape. A similar figurative process occurs through narrative accounts of travel. Mental maps define both space and relationships in civil society. In a discussion framed by Spinoza's metaphysics, sees how liberty of travel also incorporated forms of mental and literary imprisonment. Aesthetic discourses of the sublime and picturesque provided codes whereby travel writers rationalized their own tastes as superior to that of others. The Gothic novel was eventually to juxtapose freedom of travel with the sublime threat of imprisonment. Although representations of travel appeared in diverse literary forms, they aestheticized Britain as an aesthetic unity in spite of often sublime threats to social harmony.

820   ROGERS, Deborah D. "The commercialization of eighteenth-century English literature." *Clio* 18:2 (Winter 1989): 171-78.

Discusses the role of copyright law in the book trade. During the Restoration and 18c, as private artistic patronage became less obtainable, booksellers became more important. Throughout the 18c, while the financial basis of literature was being transformed, systems of patronage and pay were not discreet. The passing of the Copyright Act, advances in the technical production of literature, the rise of literary journalism and the novel characterize the early decades of the century. These developments would eventually create the situation in which those who controlled the means of production, who can be seen as representative of the middle class, were finally able to subsidize a literature that would address their tastes needs, desires, and concerns. Excellent bibliographic notes.

821-----"Guiding blight: the soap opera and the eighteenth-century novel." *CenR* 34:1 (Winter 1990): 73-91.

The particular fantasies and anxieties of the modern soap opera relate directly to the 18c sentimental novel (e.g. seduction and the reformed-rake plots). The novel shifted attention of readers to the lives of ordinary people who reflected a new middle-class audience of readers. Increased amount of feminine leisure time which came with economic specialization was a major contributing factor to the growth of 18c literacy, and was encouraged by the establishment of the circulating libraries. The sentimental novel became a form of women's fiction. A multitude of details slowly unfolded in a realistic time scheme. Realism distinguished it from previous fiction. The family was central to the 18c novel: domesticity, emotional ties, love, sex, romance and marriage, all in relation to the nuclear family, received unprecedented emphasis. The family was valued obsessively, and also was a cause of anxiety. Women were reconciled to traditional feminine roles and relationships, reinforcing patriarchal stereotypes and structures.

822   ROGERS, Kathleen M. "Fantasy and reality in fictional convents of the eighteenth century." *CLS* 22 (1985): 297-316.

From the time of the Dissolution of the Monasteries in England (1535), convents played an active part in English fantasy, reflecting writers' assumptions about "Popery" and women living without men. In popular literature it appears as an odious alternative to marriage, but others idealized it into a place where women could develop their intellectual and spiritual potential more fully than they could in actual society at the time.

823   ROGERS, Nicholas. *Whigs and cities: popular politics in the Age of Walpole and Pitt.* Oxford: Clarendon Press, 1989; pp. xi, 440.

Looks at London politics in the age of Walpole and Pitt, and includes a section on provincial politics. Considers the city of London in national politics, the rise of the Whig oligarchy, the struggle for control in the city (1728 to 1747), the city, patriotism and empire (1747 to 1763), the social configurations of metropolitan politics, the provincial perspective (esp. Bristol and Norwich), the role of the crowd in urban politics (1710 to 1760). Bibliography (407-31). Index (433-40).

824   ROGERS, Pat [John Patrick William][Bristol, UK]. *Grub Street: studies in a subculture.* London: Methuen & CP. Ltd., 1972; pp. 430.

Investigates the historical and physical reality of Grub Street, and its metaphorical meaning in literary circles through the centuries. Looks at the Suburban Muse, the Plagues of Dulness, the Criteria of Duncehood, Swift and the Scribbler, Life Studies (esp. Defoe as dunce, 311-26), the Grub Street Myth. Detailed bibliographic notes at the end of each chapter. Appendices. Index (421-30). Also see below, *Hacks and dunces* etc., **826**.

825-----(ed.). *The eighteenth century.* (The Context of English Literature.) London: Methuen & Co.Ltd., 1978; pp. xvi, 246.

Part of a series that presents the literature of the age in its political, historical and cultural context, stressing the importance of events and ideas to the works of English literature. Gives the literary classics an

intelligible place in history. The essays cover the achievements of men like Hume, Walpole, Chippendale, Newton, and Reynolds, and show how writers were affected by exciting developments in psychology, aesthetics, and medicine. Literary works are shown to have emerged from a rich and diverse culture.
1) Introd.: the writer and society (Pat ROGERS) (1-80);
2) Politics (W. A. SPECK) (81-119);
3) Religion and ideas (John Vladimir PRICE) (120-52);
4) Science (G. S. ROUSSEAU) (153-207);
5) The visual arts (Peter WILLIS) (208-39).
Each essay is divided into thematic subsections with its own select bibliography (sometimes annotated). Table of dates (ix-xvi). Index (240-46). Illus. (32 plates).

826-----(ed.). *Hacks and dunces: Pope, Swift, and Grub Street*. London: Methuen, 1980; pp. 239. (Abridgement of *'Grub Street': Studies in a subculture*. London: Methuen, 1972.)

Study of early 18c literary London, examining hack writers, their haunts and their cultural significance. Also concerned with literary masterpiece exploring the Grub Street milieu, esp. *The Dunciad* and *The Tale of a Tub*. Shows the presence and use of London in imagery in the work of Pope and Swift. Esp. important for social history, London life, 17c and 18c urban development, and Augustan literature in general.

827-----"Classics and chapbooks." In (pp. 27-45) RIVERS, Isabel (ed.). *Books and their readers in eighteenth-century England*. Leicester: Leicester UP, 1982; pp. xi, 267.

The tradition of chapbook publishing went on alongside the conventional literary productions of the 18c. Investigates the treatment of some classic works of literature in popular abridgements and adaptations. The texts which did enjoy real currency at the lower end of the market are *The Pilgrim's Progress, Robinson Crusoe, Moll Flanders* and *Gulliver's Travels*. Bunyan's masterpiece became a chapbook classic. In the case of *Robinson Crusoe* a secular work establishment itself as a modern legend.

828-----*Eighteenth-century encounters: studies in literature and society in the age of Walpole*. New York: Barnes & Noble Books; Brighton: Harvester Press, 1985; pp. x, 173.

Series of 10 essays covering a spectrum of literary-historical themes from the 18c. Particularly useful for two books by Defoe: ch. 9 "The

Guidebook as Epic: Reportage and Art in Defoe's *Tour*" (115-50); and ch. 10 "'The Calamitous Year': *A Journal of the Plague Year* and the South Sea Bubble" (151-68). "Although there is so much shrewd observation of contemporary Britain in the pages, the inner momentum of the book derives from an astonishingly clear sense of history" (145). "For this task he [Defoe] needed all his literary art, acquired not just as a great reporter, but as a great imaginative writer. So Defoe achieved the true English epic [...]. Some of the deeper imaginative currents of the book must have been set in motion by his recent experiences in witnessing - and chronicling for the press - the traumas of the Bubble year" (164-65).

829-----*Literature and popular culture in eighteenth-century England*. Brighton: Harvester Press, 1985; pp. xiv, 215.

Explores a phase of cultural history in which leisure was being organized and sold on a commercial basis in an entirely fresh way, and during which new boundaries were defined for elite and mass art forms. Looks at high and low art, rise of the impresario, invention of publicity, showmen and statesmen, masques and operas, coronations, Grub Street biography (Defoe on Jonathan Wild), classics and chapbooks, *Moll* in the chapbooks. Bibliographic notes. Index (211-15) with detailed listing of persons, places and topics.

830 ROGERS, Pat [Trinity College, CT]. "North and South". *ECLife* 12:2 (May 1988): 101-11.

The Enlightenment used a persistent quasi-geographical map to forward certain ideas. The disjunction between North and South turned space into moral contrast, with a southern indulgence compared unfavorably with a northern austerity. This potent myth rested on feeble ethnography and mistaken history. A putative geographic scheme was a way of getting points across. North and South are metaphoric counters meant to express certain human characteristics only tangentially related to human qualities. They articulated current phobias and dreams and helped to energize some literature of lasting interest.

831 ROMBERG, Bertil. *Studies in the narrative techniques of the first-person novel*. Stockholm: Almquist & Wiskell, 1962; pp. xii, 379.

Discusses theories of the first-person novel and of narrative technique. Analyzes 'the epic situation', 'the memoir novel" (38-46), 'the diary novel' (43-46), and 'the epistolary novel' (46-55) before going on to the narrator and his narrative.

832 ROPPEN, G. and SOMMER, R. *Strangers and pilgrims: an essay on the metaphor of journey.* Bergen; Oslo: Norwegian Universities Press, 1964; pp. 388.
Discusses the recurrence of the journey in world literature (17-24) and the meaning of this metaphor (75-112). Includes a section on the journey in the picaresque novel (64-68), looking at the social and fictional implications of the picaro's loneliness and roguery, with reference to Mendoza's Lazarillo (1554), Alemán's Guzman (1599), Le Sage's Gil Blas (1715) and Defoe's Moll (1722). Bibliographic notes (355-81). Index (385.-88).

833 ROSENHEIM, James M. *The Townshends of Raynham: nobility in transition in Restoration and early Hanoverian England.* Middletown, CT: Wesleyan UP, 1989; pp. xxi, 265.

Provides vital background to an understanding of English society at a key time of social transition, by examining the fortunes of two generations of an aristocratic family between 1650 and 1740, and so illustrating the transformation of England's provincial elite into a truly national ruling class, a development essential for the emergence of modern English society.

834 ROSS, Ian Cambell. "Rewriting Irish literary history: the case of the Irish novel." *EA* 39:3 (1986): 385-89.

Castle Rackrent is generally regarded as the first Irish novel, but the article proves the contrary by surveying the history of the form in the 18c, going back to Sarah Butler's *Irish Tales: Or, Instructive Histories for the Happy Conduct of Life* (1716). He discovers an entertaining, accomplished and varied body of Irish fiction, which, however, often rejects the notion of "essential Irishness".

835 ROSS, Trevor. "Just when *did* 'British bards begin t'immortalize'?" *SECC* 19 (1989): 383-98.

Discusses the formation of the canon. Contests the claim by Howard WEINBROT that the English began to make and celebrate a canon of their literature only sometime in the 18c. There is no real increase in affection for national letters in the 18c, but an expansion of the canon to include the works of Chaucer, and popular forms like the novel and ballads. Shakespeare increases in popularity, Waller declines. There is not so much an increase on approval for the canon, but a gradual removal of conflict in how it is defined. With the publication of Johnson's *Lives*, canon-making in England seems to become ordered and systematic, but also more flexible and open to change.

836 ROSTON, Murray. *Changing perspectives in literature and the visual arts 1650-1820*. Princeton: Princeton UP, 1990; pp. xv, 454.

Survey of the interrelationship between art and literature in the late Baroque, Rococo, Pre-Romantic and Romantic periods. The first two sections focus on Milton, Dryden, Pope and the emergence of the novel (ch. 4, 151-92). Notes, profuse illustrations.

837 ROTHSTEIN, Eric. "A novel path to Pentonville." *ECent* 31:1 (Spring 1990): 81-90.

Considers the evolution of the prison theme in literature. Discusses John BENDER'S *Imagining the Penitentiary*, and finds the chapters on Defoe and 18c realism the most helpful parts.

838 ROUSSEAU, G. S. and PORTER, Roy (eds). *Sexual underworlds of the Enlightenment*. Manchester: Manchester UP, 1987; Chapel Hill: U of North Carolina P, pp. x, 288.

Series of essays, looking in Part I at sex as discourse (erudition, medical erotica, modern prostitution, pregnancy and monsters, anti-clericalism and homosocial desire); in Part II at sex and society (the culture of travesty [sexuality and masquerade], prosecutions for rape, man-midwife as sexual predator; in Part III at sex at the margins (gender boundaries, sex and shamanism). All essays have bibliographical notes. Index (281-8).

839-----(ed.) and PORTER, Roy (introd.). *The languages of Psyche: mind and body in Enlightenment thought*. (Pbns from the Clark Library Professorship 12.) Berkeley: U of California P, 1990; pp. xix, 480.

Part I discusses theories of mind and body; Part II looks at mind and body in practice; Part III considers the politics of mind and body: radical practitioners and revolutionary doctors; Part IV investigates the Jewish question.

840 RUBIN, Abba. *Images in transition: the English Jew in English literature, 1660-1830*. (CSWL 4.) Westport, CT: Greenwood, 1984; pp. 157.

Traces the history of Jews in England from their readmission until 1830 (3-46), and looks specifically at the Jew in English literature from the Restoration to the mid-18c (47-68). Important Bibliographical Note (149-

52).

841   RUDÉ, George. *Hanoverian London, 1714-1808*. London: Secker & Warburg, 1971; pp. xvi, 271.

Hanoverian London was unique among the cities of the world, and by 1801 acquired the largest population. Throughout the century Londoners formed a larger proportion of the national population than the inhabitants of any other city. A consequence of this concentration was that it formed a vast consumers' market and was able to exercise a disproportionate influence on the economy of Britain as a whole. London became the greatest point of exit and entry for a large portion of the world trade, and became the money market of the world. Examines the merchant and aristocratic classes, the prevailing aristocratic patronage and culture. Another unique feature was the emergence of a genuine citizens' democracy. Investigates growth, economy, prosperity, social life, the arts and entertainment (164-81), the 'other' London, religion and churches, the government of London, London radicalism, social protest from below, the political riot, London and the French Wars. Bibliography (256-62). Index (263-71).

842   RUDOLF, Jo-Ellen Schwartz. "The novels that taught the ladies: A study of popular fiction written by women, 1702-1834." Unpub. doct. diss., Univ. of California (San Diego), 1972. [*DA* 33 (1972): 169A.]

Eliza Haywood, Maria Edgeworth, Jane Austen and Susan Ferrier all wrote novels in a particular genre of popular literature, the "tea-table novel". This is characterized by the didactic purpose of teaching young, unmarried women how to manoeuvre the intricacies of 18c moral and social rules. The plot revolves around minor social embarrassments and dilemmas, rather than sensational or exciting adventures. The center of interest is a young upper-class woman, unoccupied but intelligent, whose goal is the security, comfort and affection assured by marriage to a good, responsible and solvent male. These novels also contain evidence of dissatisfaction with the status quo and introduce a self-assertive self-sufficient female character.

843   RUNGE, Laura A. ""Bold expression and exquisite sensibility: Gender in British literary criticism, 1660-1790." Unpub. doct. diss., Emory Univ., 1993. [*DA* 54 (1993): 1379A.]

During the 18c in England, the regulation of literary and sexual difference surprisingly occupied the same textual spaces, preoccupied the same authors and audiences, and relied on the same language and tropes.

Analyzes the intersections of the discourse of literary criticism and gender, suggesting the effects and significance of the many relationships between the two. During the formative years of British criticism, literary values assumed the powers or limitations of the gendered associations and this had pronounced effects on the production and reception of various works by men and women. From 1660 to 1790, the dominant understanding of sexual difference changes from one of fundamental similarity, when difference was only a matter of degree, to a paradigm of utterly separate and distinct sexual characteristics. This can be seen in the imagery and language used to represent the different genders. The use of gender in criticism changes from 1660 to 1790, and varies from genre to genre. Each chapter analyzes a different way that the ideology of gender informs the critical judgement of the 18c.

844 RUSSELL, Ann Zimmerman. "The image of women in eighteenth-century English novels."Unpub. doct. diss., Brandeis Univ., 1974. [*DA* 35 (1975):1122A.]

The development of the idealized heroine in 18c didactic fiction, beginning with *Pamela*, suggests that a high degree of censorship was considered necessary for the novel to reach its audience, most of whom were from the middle class. The rigid standards for the heroine was based on the morality of conduct books. Because the heroine always acted as she should, there was little internal conflict. The characters accept the structures of the feminine ideal, and find ultimate fulfilment in marriage. But were actual women in 18c England happy with this? Examines the attitudes of women to their social position in letters, diaries and memoirs. They had no legal, economic or human rights, and there was no vocabulary available to them to discuss their frustrations and sense of degradation.

845 RUSSELL, H. K. "Unity in eighteenth-century episodic novels." In (pp. 183-96) CHAMPION, Larry Stephen (ed.). *Quick springs of sense: studies in the eighteenth century.* Athens, GA: Georgia UP, 1974; pp. 254.

Collection of original essays by 18c scholars, including Benjamin BOYCE, "The Shortest Way: Characteristic Defoe Fiction" (1-14); Robert B. WHITE, "The Rivalry of the *Female Tatler*: Periodical Piracy in the Early Eighteenth Century" (51-60); A. S. KNOWLES, "Defoe, Swift and Fielding: Notes on the Retirement Theme" (121-36); M. K. RUSSELL, "Unity in Eighteenth-Century Episodic Novels" (183-96). Detailed bibliographic notes.

846 RUTHERFORD, A. "Quest patterns in English, American and Australian literature." *RLV* 38:4 (1972): 380-91.

Man's dual role as a finite being inhabits a definite season of time, and as an infinite extension of certain human attributes (modified by landscape, climate and historical experience). Man is the archetypal pilgrim and visionary, fighting forces of materialism, and seeking a reality beyond the material even when it fails. No matter what happens, man continues to seek and hope for the Promised Land. Pain is a necessary preliminary to a new existence: initiation rites are reminders of this; to achieve immortality we must rid ourselves of material dross.

847 SABOR, Peter. "Harold Bloom on eighteenth-century fiction." *ECF* 3:2 (Jan. 1991): 153-63.

Review of the Chelsea House collections of critical essays on 18c fiction published between 1986 and 1988: volumes on Defoe, Swift, Richardson, Fielding, Smollett, Goldsmith, Burney and Austen. Harold Bloom was responsible for editing and introducing them. He presents his chosen author or work in a global context, with abundant generalizations that cut across centuries, genres, and national boundaries. These introductions, replete with quotations, average 4 or 5 pages. They are primarily of value, not for insights into 18c fiction, but what they reveal about Bloom. Other readers of these 18c volumes have been very critical, not only of the selections of critical opinion provided, but because of the policy of cutting footnotes and parenthetical references from every essay in the series.

848 SACKS, Sheldon. *Fiction and the shape of belief: a study of Henry Fielding, with glances at Swift, Johnson and Richardson.* Berkeley and Los Angeles: U of California P, 1964; pp. viii, 278.

The six chapters provide a detailed theoretical and practical analysis of 18c fiction and satire. While chs. 2-5 are devoted to close reading of Fielding's novels, ch. 1 "Toward a Grammar of the Types of Fiction" (1-69) and ch. 6 "The Great, Useful and the Uncommon Doctrine" (230-72) discuss literary theory which is of interest to the novel generally, and to 18c studies particularly. "Apart from any moral intention, he [the novelist] *must*, if he is to write a good novel, judge characters, acts and thoughts as part of his representation. It is not sufficient for him, as it is for the satirist, to show us what he does not like in the external world" (271).

849 SAINTSBURY, George Edward Bateman. *The English novel.* London: J. M. Dent & Sons, 1913; pp. vi, 319.

The early origins of the novel are discussed, developments in the 17c and early 18c covered in ch. 2 "From Lyly to Swift" (32-76).

850   SAMBROOK, James. *The eighteenth century: the intellectual and cultural context of English literature 1700-1789.* (Longman Literature in English Series.) London and New York: Longman, 1986; 2nd ed. 1993; pp. xii, 328.
Provides a critical introduction to the major genres and their historical and cultural context. Chapters on science, religious ideas, philosophy, political ideas and historiography, aesthetics, visual arts (architecture, sculpture, painting, landscape gardening), models (Roman, Grecian, Gothic, Ritual, Savage). Conclusion (exploration, empiricism and evolution, perception and imagination). Chronology (244-49). Bibliographies (270-92): 1) general background (270-71); 2) science (271-73); 3) religious ideas (274-75); 4) philosophy (276-77); 5) aesthetics (281-82); 6) visual arts (283-89); 7) models (290-92); 8) authors (293-316). Index (317-28).

851   SAMPSON, George. *The concise Cambridge history of English literature* (1941). Third rev. ed. Cambridge: Cambridge UP, 1970; pp. 976.
Ch. 9 "From Steele and Addison to Pope and Swift" includes 'Defoe: the Newspaper and the Novel' (377-81) which surveys his life and work in tandem, giving a brief description of the novels (380). "It should be enough that Defoe was not only the author of *Robinson Crusoe* and *Moll Flanders*, but that he had in him something of the uncalculating love of liberty which is the real work of a tribune of the people" (381). There is no discussion at all of the emerging English novel by other authors of the early 18c. Behn and Manley are mentioned in passing as playwrights. Index (939-76).

852   SAMS, H. W. "Anti-Stoicism in seventeenth- and early eighteenth-century England." *SP* 41 (1944): 65-78.

Perhaps the most important development in 17c England was the growth of individual liberty. Along with liberty of conscience and freedom of enterprise grew a respect for the dignity of human emotion. The Stoics were unpopular on the score of emotional apathy, but it is mistaken to call the burgeoning spirit which condemned them 'anti-Stoical'.

853   SANDERS, Andrew. *The short Oxford history of English literature* (1994). Rev. ed. Oxford: Clarendon Press, 1996; pp. ix, pp. 718.

Ch. 5 "Eighteenth Century Literature 1690-1780" (273-333) discusses fiction in the subsection 'Defoe and the Rise of the Novel' (301-06), looking at his major novels, but very thin on the wider context of minor fiction. Aubin and Haywood are not mentioned: Manley as novelist is not discussed. The important French translations are referred to in passing (Prévost). Defoe's "prose fiction [...] sprang from an experimental involvement in other forms [...]. Nor was he the only begetter of a form which it is now recognized had a long succession of both male and female progenitors" (302). Chronology (641-61). Guide to Further Reading (663-701). Index (705-18).

854   SCHELLENBERG, Betty A. *The conversational circle: rereading the English novel, 1740-1775.* Lexington: UP of Kentucky, 1996; pp. 165.

Study of mid-18c fictions that experiment self-consciously with conversational structures as a means of embodying socially conservative (or anti-individualistic, anti-conflictual) ideology. These fictions do not fit the criteria of plot and character generalized as characteristic of the 'classical' novel. The chosen texts have a formal and thematic commitment to the conversational circle (Richardson's *Pamela II, Sir Charles Grandison*, Fielding's *Amelia*, Smollett's *Humphrey Clinker*). Notes (137-60). Index (161-65).

855 SCHEUERMANN, Mona. *Social protest in the eighteenth-century English novel.* Columbus: Ohio State UP, 1985; pp. ix, 247.

There is much social protest but little revolution in 18c novels. Novelists as early as Defoe saw the need for much change in English society, but advocate the reform of existing structures, rather than the destruction of basic institutions. Their protest was essentially against the corruption and debasement of sound institutions. Considers works by Henry Fielding, Henry Brooke, Thomas Day, Fanny Burney, Thomas Holcroft, William Godwin, Elizabeth Inchbald, Robert Bage. Bibliographic notes.

856-----*Her bread to earn: women, money and society from Defoe to Austen.* Lexington: The UP of Kentucky, 1993; pp. x, 284.

Examines the representations of women in the work of some of the major novelists, both male and female, of the 18c: esp. Defoe, Richardson, Fielding, and Austen. Each author specifically addresses the situation of women in society, as do the radical novelists of the Godwin circle (but not Smollett or Sterne). Comparing the image of woman presented by these novelists presents surprising patterns. Defoe has the most positive view of women and their capabilities: a woman's talent is limited only by society's definition of what avenues are open to her. Fielding and Richardson do less well when what they actually say and show about women and her capacities and place in society are examined. Austen seems more conservative when her images of women are compared with those of Wollstonecraft, Bage and Holcroft. Examines themes related to women, the most ubiquitous being money, finances, and financial status. The vast majority of 18c women characters are very active in living their lives, and there is much concern with making a living. Marriage is widely depicted, but mother-child relationships are virtually ignored. There are alarming rates of mortality. Females from all social classes are depicted. The horrible real-life legal restrictions on women are also investigated, to redefine perceptions of how women are seen in the 18c English novel. Bibliographical notes (252-80). Index (281-84).

857 SCHLAEGER, Jürgen. "Die Robinsonade als frühbürgerliche 'Eutopia'." In (pp. 279-98) VOSSKAMP, Wilhelm (ed.). *Utopieforschung: interdisziplinäre Studien zur neuzeitlichen Utopie*. Vol. 2. Stuttgart: Metzler, 1982; pp. 386.

In German. Utopias do not seek uncompromising transference into praxis made by the 'eutopian' Robinsonade, but always make the compromise that what exists may be less complete and more contradictory than the projected ideal. *Robinson Crusoe* builds a bridge between the old idealizing systems of world interpretation and the new dimensions of practical experience.

858 SCHMIDT, Johann N. "Von Restauration zur Vorromantik." In (pp. 149-216) SEEBER, Hans Ulrich (ed.). *Englische Literaturgeschichte*. Stuttgart: Metzler, 1991; pp. x, 461.

In German. Presents an extended descriptive/critical account of the period 1660-1790, contextualizing the age, discussing terms of description and self-understanding, the emergence of literary openness, the influence of science and philosophy, poetry and parody, criticism and satire, perception of nature, the development of the novel (Bunyan, Defoe, Richardson, Fielding, Smollett, Sterne, the sentimental novel), satire (Pope and Swift), pictorial and verse satire, moral periodicals, Restoration comedy, the sentimentalization of comedy and tragedy. There is a sensitive focus on essentials, a sharp critical edge to discussion. Numerous illus. Bibliography (439-46). Index (447-60). Picture sources (461).

859 SCHNORRENBERG, Barbara Brandon. "A paradise like Eve's: three eighteenth-century English female Utopias." *Women's Studies* 9 (1982): 263-73.
Points out that Utopias are satires of current conditions, blueprints for

how a society might be better structured, or descriptions of a dreamland that can never really be achieved. All these variations share a desire for improvement in the human condition. In the late 17c and 18c three proposals with plans for an ideal society were formulated: by Mary Astell, *A Serious Proposal to the Ladies for the Advancement of Their True and Greatest Interests* (1694, 1697); by Sarah Robinson Scott, *A Description of Millennium Hall, and the Country Adjacent* (1763); and by Clara Reeve, *Plans for Education, with Remarks on the Systems of Other Writers* (1792).

860 SCHOFIELD, Mary Anne and MACHESKI, Celia (eds). *Fetter's or free? British women novelists, 1670-1815.* Athens, OH; London: Ohio UP, 1986; pp. 441.

Series of 23 essays examining how women wrote during the early and late decades of the 18c, detailing and reacting to their subordination and exploitation under the cover of their fictions. Examines Jane Barker, Mary Davys, Eliza Haywood, Mary Manley, Elizabeth Inchbald, Sarah Fielding, Charlotte Lennox, Hannah More, Charlotte Smith and Mary Brunton. Looks at gender and genre, feminine iconography, love, sex and marriage, moral and political revolution, fictional strategies, critical assessments. Detailed bibliographical notes.

861 SCHOFIELD, Mary Anne. *Masking and unmasking the female mind: disguising romances in feminine fiction, 1713-1799.* Newark: U of Delaware P, 1990; pp. 217.

Seeks to present a more accurate view of the 18c reading and publishing world, moving the focus away from studies written by male scholars which focus on a "canon". Sees a problem of two plots: masculine and feminine. Male writers tend to favour "happy", whitewashed, patriarchally approved endings, whereas female writers subvert happy, satisfying closures, and instead present unfulfilling, nagging, wearisome, tragic endings which underscore the sense of separateness in which women exist and write. Looks in Part I at "Romancing the Masquerade" (Elizabeth Boyd, Penelope Aubin, Elizabeth Haywood, Jane Barker, Mary Davys, Mary Collyer). Part II "Masquerading the Romance" (later Haywood, Sarah Fielding, Charlotte Lennox, Charlotte Smith, Elizabeth Inchbald, Jane West). Bibliography (201-12). Extensive Notes (192-200).

862 SCHORER, Mark. "Technique as discovery." *Hudson Rev* 1:1 (Spring 1948): 67-87.

Technique is the means by which the writer is able to attend to experience, his subject matter. It is the means of discovering/ exploring and developing his subject, of conveying its meaning, and finally of evaluating it. The writer capable of the most exacting technical scrutiny of his subject matter will produce works with the most satisfying content, works with thickness and resonance, works which reverberate with maximum meaning. Feels that Defoe's *Moll Flanders*, for example, is not the true chronicle of a disreputable female, but the allegory of an impoverished soul - the author's; not an anatomy of the criminal class, but of the middle class. Because Defoe had no adequate resources and technique to separate himself from his material, thereby to discover and to define the meaning of his material, his contribution is valuable not so much to fiction, but rather to the history of fiction and to social history. The book has no moral life; everything is external.

863-----"Fiction and the 'matrix of analogy'." *Kenyon Rev* 11:4 (Autumn 1949): 539-60.
The novel, like a poem, is not life, it is an image of life. The critical problem is first of all to analyze the structure of the images. Metaphorical language reveals to us the character of any imaginative work in that, more telling than any other element, it shows us what conceptions the imagination behind the work is able to entertain, how fully, how happily. It is style which first conceives then expresses the themes, subjects and kinds. Symbolism is both an end and an instrument.

864-----*The world we imagine: selected essays.* New York: London: Chatto & Windus, 1969; pp. vi, 402.

"Modern criticism, through its exacting scrutiny of literary texts, has demonstrated with finality that in art, beauty and truth are indivisible and one" (3). Part 1 looks at technique as discovery and the "analogical matrix" (3-48). Looks at the base of language, figurative structures, rhetorical style. Of 18c novels, only *Moll Flanders* is analyzed. Part 4 examines the "burden of biography" (221-42), and investigates the essential difference between the writer of fiction and biographer. There is no index to the multifarious literary allusions.

865 SCHÖWERLING, Rainer. *Chapbooks: zur Literaturgeschichte des einfachen Lesers. Englische Konsumliteratur, 1680-1840.* (Sprache und Literatur: Regensburger Arbeiten zur Anglistik und Amerikanistik, 18.) Frankfurt; Bern; Cirencester: Peter Lang, 1980; pp. 354.

In German. Surveys the history and popularity of chapbooks, from the point of view of production and reception, and the chapbooks themselves and their categories. Bibliography (340-54).

866 SCHULTE, Edvige. *Origine e tendenze del romanzo inglese dalla metà del seicento alla metà del settecento.* Naples: Ligouri, 1977; pp. 232.

In Italian. Provides a detailed history of the emergence of the English novel. The introduction traces the movement from heroic romance to the reality of facts. Section 1 (31-40) looks at verisimilitude and aesthetic theories at the end of the 17c and the beginning of the 18c, and their influence on narrative. Section 2 (41-69) investigates the fictional world of Mary Manley and Mary Davys among others, while section 3 (70-95) explores the origins of the historical romance, particularly in the 18c. Section 4 (95-108) examines the birth of the epistolary novel, esp. the contribution of Cavendish and Manley. The greater part of the book is devoted to 18c studies. Notes (207-25).

867-----*Scritti minori di letteratura e lingua inglese.* (Univ. di Napoli, Quaderni della Facolta di Scienze Politiche 33.) Naples: Giannini, 1989; pp. 368.

In Italian. In the second half of the 17c many works of French and Spanish prose fiction were translated into English and formed the taste of authors who helped shape the great narrative art of the 18c.

868 SCHULTZ, Dieter. *Studien zur Verführungsszene im englischen Roman (1660-1760).* Marburg: Privately published, 1968; pp. 314.

In German. Explores the seduction theme in its technical implications, regarding the scene as a narrative form. A major objective is to see how a number of writers from the Restoration to the 1750s, with differing ideological backgrounds and technical abilities, came to terms with the charge of lasciviousness brought against erotic scenes. In the 18c there was an ever-increasing religious attitude to the problem of seduction. Bibliography (291-314).

869-----"'Novel', 'Romance', and popular fiction in the first half of the eighteenth century." *SP* 70 (1973): 77-90.

No period in English literature appears to demonstrate the validity of the critical distinction between romance and novel more convincingly than the first half of the 18c. Defoe, Richardson, Fielding, and Smollett considered their fiction as an alternative to the chivalric and heroic romances still read in the 18c, but when they explicitly mentioned the heroic romance as their target, their notion of 'romance' was profoundly influenced by the productions of such writers as Aphra Behn, Mary Manley and Eliza Haywood.

870-----*Suche und Abenteuer: die 'Quest' in der englischen und amerikanischen Erzählkunst der Romantik.* (Reihe Siegen, 25.) Heidelberg: Winter, 1981; pp. 376.

In German. Analyzes the recurrence of the quest pattern in English literature from Spenser to Melville. Introd. (5-24) discusses the recurrence of this topos, concentrating on the phases of the journey, the dualism of the determining characters and symbols, the goal, the hero, the historical occurrences. Looks at the early stages (Spenser, Bunyan, Johnson) before concentrating on the Gothic novel, Scott, Cooper, Poe, Hawthorne, Melville. Defoe is discussed as part of the recurrent phenomenon (*Robinson Crusoe*, 223, 241). Bibliography (352-69). Index (371-76).

871 SCHULZ, Max F. *Paradise preserved: recreations of Eden in eighteenth- and nineteenth-century England.* Cambridge: Cambridge UP, 1985; pp. xviii, 384.

The idea that one can construct the lost Eden has been secularized and historically realized in the ways the English of the last two centuries have tried to mirror paradise in their gardens, art, literature, technology, engineering and urban centers. Introduction "The Continuing Mystique of Paradise" (1-8). Looks at "Eighteenth-Century Landscape Garden Paradises", "Romantic Paradisal Bowers, Valleys and Islands" and "Victorian Heavenly Cities and Blessed Demozels". Notes (326-61).

872 SCOTT, Robert Francis. "The reinvention of the eighteenth-century novel in contemporary British and American fiction." Unpub. doct. diss., Michigan State Univ., 1994. [*DA* 56 (1995): 948A.]

By looking closely at nine modern works, demonstrates that the impulse towards reinventing the 18c is a strong and varied one in recent British and American fiction. Discusses reasons behind the contemporary interest in reinventing the 18c novel by returning to the roots of the form.

873 SCOTT, Sir Walter. *The lives of the novelists.* 10 vols. London, 1821-24. Rpt. in World Classics as *The Lives of the Novelists.* With an introduction by Austin DOBSON. London, New York & Toronto: Henry Frowde, 1906; pp. x, 342.

These 'Lives' were first published as a series of prefaces to the *Novelist's Library* (10 vols, 1821-24). Provides critical biographies of Fielding, Smollett, Le Sage, Charles Johnstone, Sterne, Goldsmith, Johnson, Mackenzie, Walpole, Reeve, Richardson, Bage, Cumberland, Mrs Radcliffe. Minor errors are rectified and additional information provided in a general note at the end of each chapter by Austin DOBSON.

874 SCOTT, William. "Mottoes from the English poets as chapter-headings in the novel." *NQ* 202 (Nov. 1957): 478-80.

It was no doubt Sir Walter Scott's example which led a number of later 19c novelists to provide mottoes. It is difficult to trace its history in the 18c. Mottoes, usually in Latin, were frequently attached to periodical essays, a custom popularized by the *Spectator*. The sporadic appearance of mottoes in a number of 18c novels suggests that the idea came independently to a few writers in the 1750s. Scott was certainly familiar with the romances of Charlotte Smith and Ann Radcliffe, in which English verse was quoted at the head of chapters.

875 SEAMON, Roger. "Narrative practice and the theoretical distinction between history and fiction." *Genre* 16 (1983): 197-218.

The distinction between history and fiction is fundamentally one between works which make a claim to truth and works which do not. Poetry is about universals, not about particular historical names and places. Both can take the form of a narrative. History can be presented in a figurative fashion, narratives as figurative history. Historical narrative can partake of the forms of fiction. Important for Defoe's fiction.

876 SEBBAR-PIGNON, Leila. "Le mythe du bon nègre: ou, L'idéologie coloniale dans la production romanesque du XVIIIe siècle." *Temps Modernes* 29e année 336 (July 1974): 2352-69; 337-38 (Aug.-Sept. 1974): 2588-2613.

In French. Concerned principally with the influence of the notion of the good negro in 18c French fiction. Considers slavery under all the stages of its unfolding, from abduction, through exile and cultural imprisonment, to settlement and liberation.

877 SEEBER, Edward D. "Ideal languages in the French and English imaginary voyage." *PMLA* 60 (1945): 586-97.

Authors of imaginary voyages showed particular preoccupation with the virtues and possibilities of superior languages, based either on logical conceptions, or deriving their elements from natural tongues. These reveal a modern problem which has emerged in the universal language movements of the 19c.

878 SEIFERT, Lewis C. *Fairy tales, sexuality and gender in France 1690-1715: nostalgic utopias.* Cambridge and New York: Cambridge UP, 1996; pp. xii, 276.

Between 1690 and 1750 well over 100 literary fairy tales appeared in

France, two-thirds of them written by women. Explores why fashionable adults were attracted to this new literary genre, and considers how it became a medium for reconceiving literary and historical discourses of sexuality and gender. Integrating socio-historical, structural and post-structural approaches, argues that these fairy tales used the marvellous (or supernatural) to mediate between conflicting cultural desires, particularly between nostalgia and utopian longings. Bibliographic notes (224-60). Selected bibliography (261-70). Index (271-76).

879 SENEFELD, James Lowell. "The novel as life-history: an analysis of the British autobiographical novel in the eighteenth century with particular emphasis upon Laurence Sterne's *Tristram Shandy.*" Unpub. doct. diss., Ball State Univ., 1977. [*DA* 38 (1977): 1417A.]

In the 18c the English novel derived its purpose, structure and theory of characterization from the life-history in the form of biography and autobiography. The novel and the life-history emerged in recognizably modern forms, the novel maintaining its purpose both to instruct and entertain. Fictional and life-story elements shared the same structure, as each novel purported to be the biography or autobiography of the title character of the work. Finally, both adopted the same theories of characterization for major and minor characters, within their works. The sources of the 18c novel lay in the dynamic biography and autobiography of the Restoration and the 18c, and in the Classical, Medieval, Renaissance life-writings (Plutarch, Josephus, Seutonius, St Augustine, Dante, Benvenuto Cellini).

880 SHANKLIN, Tip Harrison. "Thresholds, boundaries, crossings: reading liminality in the English novel." Unpub. doct. diss., State Univ. of New York at Binghampton, 1995. [*DA* 56 (1995): 1372A.]

Studies thresholds and boundaries and their agency as contingent places of passage and crossing in the narrative themes and structures of four English novels: *Robinson Crusoe*, *Frankenstein*, *Wuthering Heights*, and *Heart of Darkness*. Drawing on Victor Turner's work in liminality and rites of passage, investigates patterns of transition and transformation, exile and outsiderhood, either as interim aspects of the individual self, suspended between social and communal structures, or as permanent states of anti-liminal exclusion and outsiderhood from which a return is foreclosed. Thresholds and boundaries are depicted as the structured essence of limned spaced bordering two places and times, the crossing of which serves, in the case of Robinson Crusoe, as a symbol of a secularized rite of passage - detachment, exile, return. Threshold and boundaries implicitly are about problems of space and distance and eventual return, or anti-liminal places of displacement and exclusion.

881 SHAPIRO, Charles (ed.). *Twelve original essays on great English novels.* Detroit: Wayne State UP, 1960; pp. xii, 281.

Set of essays surveying the English novel by way of great representative works. The 18c is represented by Defoe, Fielding and Sterne. Harvey SWADOS provides "*Robinson Crusoe*: the Man Alone" (1-21), studying the effects of human loneliness. Shows how Defoe re-imagined the story of an actual neurotic castaway, and came up with one of the great tales of all time, producing a novel which, by normalizing the abnormal, reaches us today in our contemporary doubts, isolation, and everpresent loneliness. Irvin EHRENPREIS writes on "Fielding's Use of Fiction: the Autonomy of *Joseph Andrews*" (23-41), demonstrating how the novel progresses by shuttling the structure of the story. The structure of the story depends upon small oscillations of emotion which gather as a large design into massive waves of reversal, a process of demasking, so producing a symbolic comedy, without regard to the principles of consistency many contemporary critics demand of a novelist.

882 SHAVIT, Zohar. "Cultural notions and literary boundaries: on the creation of the systematic opposition between children's literature and adult literature in the eighteenth century." In (pp. 416-22) BAUER, Roger (et al eds). *Proceedings of the XIIth Congress of the International Comparative Literature Association*, Vol. 4. Munich: Iudicium, 1990; pp. 651.
During the 18c chapbooks became the most important reading material for children. The more important a child's education and reading matter became, the less the educational establishment was ready to accept what children read, namely chapbooks. A new industry of the child and childhood emerged into social consciousness with a new and previously unknown demand for books. It took more than 100 years for cultural consciousness to become aware of the existence of new borders. Various establishments involved in the production of books for children declared war on chapbooks, tried to prohibit their reading, and offered children alternative reading material. The systematic opposition between children's literature and adult literature continued to be one of the most prominent factors in the literary poly-system, even if the boundaries and elements were constantly being reshuffled. Bibliography (421-22).

883 SHEPPERSON, A. B. *The novel in motley: a history of the burlesque novel in English.* Cambridge, MS: Harvard UP, 1936; pp. 301.

In the 18c and early 19c when satire was a spontaneous form of expression, parody and burlesque occupied a place in literature that was far from insignificant. High-quality literary satire appeared in the form of fiction, and as a critique of fiction. In the 18c, with Richardson's view of literature as a moral instrument, there was a lack of formal critical reactions. In this absence, it is hardly surprising that parody and burlesque became agents in controlling the excesses of this literary form. Important appendix with a list of burlesque and parody-burlesque novels (1830-1900) with descriptions (249-83). Index (289-301).

884 SHERBO, Arthur. *Studies in the eighteenth-century novel*. East Lansing: Michigan State UP, 1969; pp. 213.

Seeks to account for the uniqueness of Richardson, Fielding, Smollett, and Sterne. Richardson and Smollett wrote epistolary novels and have the advantages of a shifting point of view. Fielding and Sterne gain from having self-conscious narrators.

885-----"A postscript to *Studies in the eighteenth-century novel*." *JNT* 4 (1974): 226-32.
Investigates identifying, qualifying and disclaiming parenthetical statements as part of a long narrative tradition in prose and poetry, and hence almost formulaic in nature. Looks esp. at Defoe and Fielding.

886 SHERBS, Randall L. "The function of the teacher in selected eighteenth-century English novels (1742-1796)." Unpub. doct. diss., West Virginia Univ., 1980. [*DA* 41 (1980): 1067A.]

The 18c was a didactic age which valued learning in all its branches, but nonetheless a time of "unparalleled inferiority in education". In both the schools and universities, unproductive methods and curricula governed the behavior of teachers. Consequently, in the fiction of the time, the teacher is usually an object of satire. Examines contemporary attitudes to teachers in 10 respectable novels by Fielding, Smollett, Coventry, Shebbeare, Johnson, Burney.

887 SHERMAN, Stuart. *Telling time: clocks, diaries, and English diurnal form*. Chicago and London: U of Chicago P, 1996; pp. xv, 323.

Traces the relations between clocks, which tell time, and narratives, which tell what transpired in time, in a place and period critical to the development of both clocks and narratives in England from the late 17c through the late 18c. Clocks not only tell time, but articulate meaning in and for the culture that produces them. Just as every report also entails interpretation, every clock proposes a temporality, a way of conceiving time, using it, inhabiting it. Looks at chronometric invention and prose form, Pepys and his predecessors, the diary as time keeper, correspondence and containment in the *Spectator* and its predecessors, travel writing and the dialectic of diurnal form, diurnal dialectic in the Western Islands, Defoe and Burney, the unmasking of the diurnal in the making of the novel. Bibliographic notes (279-312). Index (313-23).

888 SHERWOOD, Irma Z. "The novelists as commentator." In (pp. 113-25) *The age of Johnson: essays presented to C. B.Tinker.* New Haven, CT: Yale UP, 1949; pp. 426.

While focusing on the period after 1740, the essay is an important consideration of the vital role of the novel as a social commentator. In the historical novels of the 18c, the commentary does not smother the story: the author knows where he is going and does not permit his novel to degenerate into a commonplace book. Yet even in unified novels (like *Clarissa* and *Tom Jones*), the author's shadow keeps intruding between the reader and the imaginative world of the novel. To achieve a complete fusion between the critic-moralist and the creative artist was beyond the 18c novelist's capacity.

889 SHIN, Hyun-Kyu. "18 seki yeongguk soseol gwa yeongguk humor wa pungya eui jeontong." *BIHS* 10 (1984): 77-100.

In Japanese. Examines the 18c English novel and the tradition of humor and satire.

890 SHORTLAND, Michael. "Setting murderous Machiavel to school: hypocrisy in politics and the novel." *JEurS* 18:2 (1988): 93-119.

The politics of the 18c was a never-ending treadmill of dissimulation, treachery and deceit. Hypocrisy is assigned the role of an organizing device - a metaphor as well as a concrete phenomenon. The novelist, by showing that apparently unrelated aspects of interests are closely linked and governed by a unique set of (hypocritical) concerns, assumes a more coherent role and can appear as a moralist.

891 SHOWALTER, English, Jr. *The evolution of the French novel, 1614-1782.* Princeton: Princeton UP, 1972; pp. vi, 372.

Provides a detailed account of the unfolding of French narrative fiction, defining *roman* and *nouvelle*, discussing the purposes of the novel, and in ch. 3 the "Technique of Realism in Early Fiction", both comic and serious (67-196).

892 SHROFF, Homai J. *The eighteenth-century novel: the idea of the gentleman.* New Delhi; London: Arnold-Heinemann, 1983; pp. 299.

Investigates the preoccupation of many 18c writers to apply the term 'gentleman' to their personal conception of the ideal man who embodies the fine qualities which society regards as ideal. Studies the attitude of the leading novelists of the 18c to the contemporary class system, and to contemporary trends in philosophy and education. Select Bibliography (291-94).

893 SHUMAKER, Wayne. *English autobiography: its emergence, motives and form.* Berkeley; Los Angeles: U of California P, 1954; pp. ix, 262.

Describes the development of the modern autobiographical convention as part of the discovery of the individual. The confessional mode and descriptions of contemporary conditions of living were important elements in the emergence of prose fiction. Bibliography (245-55). Index (259-62).

894 SIDORCHENKO, L. V. "Literaturno-esteticheskie spory ob ostroumii v Anglii pervoi chetverti XVIII veka." *VLU* 3 (July 1989): 33-42.

In Russian. Treatment of wit, and its relationship to Classicism.

895 SIEBER, Harry. *The picaresque.* (The Critical Idiom, 33.) London: Methuen & Co., 1977; pp. viii, 85.

Provides a succinct general account of the picaresque tradition: some definition, an account of the origins and definitions in Spain (*Lazarillo de Tormes*, the epistolary beginnings of the picturesque, Mateo Aléman, the picaresque as genre, Spanish descendants, the picaresque novel after Cervantes). The third section surveys the genre in Europe: a literary itinary of the *picaro* (Italy, Germany, France, England). The picaresque as genre and myth. The epilogue considers the *picaros* in the promised land. The picaresque in England (50-8) looks mainly at Defoe and Smollett. Defoe's fiction has a basic similarity to the Spanish picaresque. The only fully picaresque novel of the 18c is Smollett's *The Adventures of Ferdinand Count Fathom.* Bibliography (75-80). Index (81-85).

896 SILL, Geoffrey M. *Defoe and the idea of fiction, 1713-1719.* Newark, NJ: Delaware UP, 1983; London: Assoc. UPs, 1984; pp. 190.

In the period 1713 to 1719, Defoe established himself as a writer more or less free of political connection, while negotiating the extremely treacherous passage from the Stuart to the Hanoverian monarchies. This was a formative period containing many valuable clues to his development as maker of fictions. It was a process whereby he came to accept fiction as a legitimate means for regarding human experience. He began using fiction not merely to illustrate moral or political ideas, but as the very form of those ideas. His fictions served as organizing principles around which men and women became aware of themselves in relation to the dominant and emerging ideas of their times. In accepting these ideas and acting on them, Defoe's readers imposed on themselves the hegemony of the new Whig culture, and at the same time, the restraining virtues of moderation, experience and tradition, thus contributing to the establishment of the new order. Detailed bibliographic notes (177-86). Index (187-90). Illus.

897 SIMONDS, William Edward. *An introduction to the study of English prose fiction.* Boston: Heath, 1894; London: Isbister, 1895; pp. x, 240.

Provides an overview of the rise of the English novel. Examines the patterns of storytelling as handed down from the earliest sources (like Beowulf) which led to the development of the novel. In "The Rise of the Novel" he discusses the 17c situation before commenting on Manley, Defoe and Swift, as well as several other writers of the 18c. Examines how aspects of their work prefigured the "perfection of the novel in the mid-18c".

898 SIMMONS, Ernest J. *English literature and culture in Russia (1553-1840).* (Harvard Studies in Comparative Literature, 12.) Cambridge, MA: Harvard UP, 1935; rpt. New York: Octagon, 1964; pp. 357.

Covers the subject of Anglo-Russian contact from Ivan the Great, through Boris Godounov, Peter the Great and Catherine II (1553 to 1796). Of particular pertinence are ch. 5 "English Literature in the Eighteenth-Century Russian Journals" (102-33) and ch. 6 "The English Novel in Eighteenth-Century Russia" (134-60). Shows how the growth of Russian literature and the emergent intelligentsia were encouraged by extensive translations from English periodicals. The bibliography (126-33) lists the Russian periodicals and the translations from English ones. "The journal, however, was not the most popular literary genre in Russia in the eighteenth century. This distinction belongs to the novel [...] which was a powerful force in the cultural growth of the younger generation between the years 1775 and 1800" (135). Translations of Prévost and Marivaux, with their emphasis on character development and plot, set the stage for the appearance of the English novel which swept all before it for the remainder of the 18c and the early 19c. Defoe, Richardson, Fielding and Sterne effected a revolution in European letters by their accurate studies of contemporary society. Bibliography (159-60). Looks also at sentimentalism, Shakespeare, Scott and Byron in the Russian Romantic movement. Notes (309-38). Indices (339-57).

899 SIMON, Irène. "Le roman féminin en Angleterre au xviiie siècle." *EA* 27 (1974): 205-13.

In French. Review of Philippe Séjourne's *Aspects généraux du roman féminin en Angleterre de 1740 à 1800* [Aix-en-Provence, 1966; pp. 568]. While this is concerned with fiction from the later 18c, it remains important for a general understanding of the female contribution to the novel. Séjourn "a voulu mettre en relief leur contribution à l'émancipation de la femme, dégager cet effort, 'infiniment émouvant, de tout un sexe que, dans l'évolution de la société, cherchait à créer un genre littéraire qui deviendrait son mode d'expression propre' [...] .le roman est écrit par des femmes pour de femmes, qui sont principales abonnées des bibliothèques circulantes'" (p. 14).

900 SIMONSUURI, Kirsti. *Homer's original genius: eighteenth-century notions of the early Greek epic (1688-1798).* Cambridge: Cambridge UP, 1979; pp. 219.
Studies the mechanism of gradual delays in the history of the classical tradition, the complex development that characterizes the 18c discussion of the Greek epic, as well as the nature and interrelation of the reasons why Homer was preferred as the model of the original genius. Considers ancients and moderns, primitivism and realism. Notes (157-94). Bibliography (195-214). Index (215-19). Illus.

901 SINGER, G. F. *The epistolary novel: its origin, development, decline and residuary influence.* Philadelphia: U of Pennsylvania P, 1933; pp. x, 266.

Surveys the epistolary novel, looking at the development of the literary epistle, the letter writer, the vitalization of the letter. Of particular importance is ch.4 "The Fictional Outposts and the Pre-Richardsonian Letter Story" (40-59) which considers Gildon, Manley, Defoe and Montesquieu. Extensive bibliography: works of reference (217-20) and list of epistolary texts (220-55).

902 SINGH, Sarup. *Marriage: the eighteenth-century English novel.* New Delhi: Manohar, 1995; pp. x, 238.

Investigates the status of women in 18c England, concentrating on their status in marriage, exploring what some authors have had to say on the subject. Begins with a discussion of Mary Astell's views on contemporary marriage, *A Serious Proposal to the Ladies* and *Reflections upon Marriage* which are seminal works. Looks esp. at Defoe and his contradictory views, with *Moll Flanders* and *Roxana* showing him wholly realistic in presenting two women who use whatever methods are available to survive in a difficult world. Also looks at Richardson, Fanny Burney, Susan Ferrier and Jane Austen. Index (233-38).

903 SINGLETON, Robert R. "English criminal biography, 1651-1722." *HLB* 18 (1970): 63-83.

Investigates the characteristics of the genre and its representative works, their fictional features and links with the jestbook tradition. Provides "A Chronological Finding List of Criminal Biographies" (80-82).

904 SITTER, John. *Literary loneliness in mid-eighteenth-century England.* Ithaca, NY; London: Cornell UP, 1982; pp. 230.

The middle of the 18c between the Age of Pope and Swift (to 1740) and the Age of Johnson (from 1750 onwards) is an interesting, confusing and relatively neglected literary period. It was a conspicuous time of literary experiments, and was underlined by the assumption and its variants that authors were solitary writers for solitary readers. It seems clear that the narrative problems experienced by Richardson and Fielding in their best works are closely related to the impasses confronting mid-18c poetic conventions. While poetry attempts to dissociate itself from history, and the novel presents itself as history undistorted by romance, there is a similarity of poetic intention in achieving 'pure poetry', and what Richardson calls 'sentiment'. Index (227-30).

905 SKILTON, David. *The English novel: Defoe to the Victorians.* Newton Abbott: David & Charles; New York: Barnes & Noble, 1977; pp. 200.

Points out the great contrast between the unselfconscious realism of Defoe's fiction and the highly self-conscious Neo-Classical mode of satire used by the poets; a celebration of the revolutionary-capitalist virtues of work and profit on the one hand, and the aristocratic myth of hierarchy and obedience on the other. "The emergence of realistic prose fiction as a major literary form in England is inextricably involved in the social and cultural conflict this contrast reveals" (7). Looks at Defoe and the Augustan Age, Richardson and Fielding. Select Bibliography (192-93).

906 SLAGLE, K. C. *The English country squire as depicted in English prose fiction from 1740 to 1800.* Philadelphia: Diss. Univ. of Pennsylvania,

1938.

Examination of a large number of 18c novels finds that most agree as to the character, opinions, and manner of life of the typical squire. A minority was concerned with representing him as decadent in comparison with his robust 17c predecessor. The image was not a flattering one: he was regarded as "morally and emotionally unstable, striving to stem and divert the natural course of progress". The cause of this hostility lay in a growing revolt of the urban middle class against the snobbishness and the squirarchy, and partly in the development of radical social theories.

907 SMEDMAN, M. Sarah. "A portrait of the ladies: Women in popular English fiction, 1730-1750." Unpub. doct. diss., Indiana Univ., 1975. [*DA* 36 (1976): 5328A.]

In some 60 popular English novels of the period 1730 to 1750, selected because the protagonists are women, the plots detail the trials which these heroines confronted and through which they triumph (or are defeated). Three prominent classes of heroine emerge: the virtuous innocent anxious to preserve her virginity until she marries in accord with parental approval; the sexual libertine who lives outside approved social mores, usually because it is more economically feasible; and the androgyne who disguises herself as a male to achieve her goals, social, sexual, military or political. Few of the authors were concerned with processes of characterization, but employed conventional patterns of description, point of view and dialogue to delineate fictional character.

908 SMITH, Grahame. *The novel and society: Defoe to George Eliot*. Totowa, NJ: Barnes & Noble, 1984; pp. 235.

Important background is provided in ch. 1 "Problems in the Relationship of Literature to Society" (9-45) and ch. 2 "The Eighteenth Century: Defoe, Smollett and the Rise of the Novel" (46-71). "Among the many formal discoveries made by the pioneers of the novel, the most important was their realization of the possibility of achieving secular dignity for their characters by embedding their lives in the wider life of human relationships that came to be known as society" (70-71). Select bibliography (234-35).

909 SNELL, Michael Patrick. "Antebellum histories: the apocalyptic narrative of ethicity and nationhood before the Civil War." Unpub. doct. diss., Univ. Oregon, 1993. [*DA* 54 (1994): 3439/40A.]

Contrary to the principles they declare, antebellum Americans of various backgrounds and beliefs derive their versions of natural history from the repetitive, apocalyptic narrative of biblical typology. God identifies the chosen nation as an ethnically distinct, unified people. The victories of the chosen over the 'heathen' prefigure the apocalyptic end of ethnic difference, and hence of conflict. But it also repeats history, and promises the future repetition of history. Just as the Israelites prefigure Christians, any subsequent chosen people may prefigure another that prefigures another. American Calvinists succeed English Protestants who have succeeded Roman Catholics as the true Christian millennial people. Various people are chosen: Protestants of different sects, Irish-American Catholics, slaveholders, African-American and non-sectarian humanity (Emerson, Melville, Whitman, Afro-American abolitionist David Walker, apologist for slavery Thomas Deid, naturalist Lyman Beecher, Irish Catholic John Hughes).

910 SOCIÉTÉ D'ETUDES ANGLO-AMÉRICAINES DES XVIIe ET XVIIIe SIECLES. *Mémoire et création dans le monde anglo-américain aux XVIIe et XVIIIe siècles: Actes du Colloque tenu à Paris les 21 et 22 octobre 1983*. Strasbourg: Université de Strasbourg II, 1983; pp. 171.

In French. Collection of essays covering various aspects of life and literature from the late 17c through the 18c: nature according to Hobbes (Frank LESSAY); Hobbes and Hume on the burden of the past and the power of innovation (François TRICAUD); the creative memory in England (Marie-Madeleine MARTINET).

911 SOKOLOLYANSKY, Mark G. "The noble primitive in English fiction, 1674-1796: A current and potential radicalism in eighteenth-century literature." Unpub. doct. diss., Univ. of Exeter, 1977.
Abstract not available.

912 SOLIDAY, Mary Anne. "High life below stairs: Servants and masters in eighteenth-century fiction." Unpub. doct. diss., Univ. of Illinois at Urbana-Champagne, 1990. [*DAI* 51:4 (1990): 1242A.]

Examines how servants invert and reverse two symbolically opposed realms, above and below stairs, that order the domestic space of many 18c fictional houses. Because servants may confuse the normal vertical distance between high and low characters, they have the potential to revitalize the emotional, social and linguistic hierarchy that structures domestic relations. Liminal or hybrid figures temporarily negate distance between ruler and ruled: servants thus suggest moments in the text where characters experience class struggles. This invocation between dominant and subordinate characters creates reciprocal identities, thus temporarily parodying the idea of a private narrative self in the 18c. Looks at works by Defoe, Richardson, Fielding, Sterne, Smollett, Godwin and Edgeworth.

913   SOUPEL, Serge. "La joie: Étude de quelques aspects dans le roman anglais du milieu du dix-huitième siècle." *EA* 32 (1979): 272-82.

In French. Manifestations of happiness are found as much in the novels Richardson, Fielding, Smollett and Sterne as in the works of other novelists of their time, in depicting the differences of subject, tone and sensibility which distinguish their works one from the other.

914-----*Apparence et essence dans le roman anglais de 1740 à 1771: L'Écriture ambigue.* (Études Anglaises, 84.) Paris: Didier, 1983; pp. 306.

In French. Looks at: 1) "Le personnage: son milieu, son corps et son esprit"; 2) "Connaissance, verité et mensonge"; 3) "Apparences et essence de l'écriture romanesque (harmonies, modes de l'ambiguité, procédés d'expression)". Bibliographic footnotes.

915-----"Le roman anglais au milieu du XVIIIe siècle: De la connaissance à la conscience de soi." In (pp. 193-203) ELLRODT, Robert (ed.). *Genèse de la conscience moderne: Étude sur le développement de la conscience de soi dans les littératures du monde occidental.* (Publications de la Sorbonne, série 'Littératures II', 14.) Paris: Presses Universitaires de France, 1983; pp. 424.

The article is part of the "Quatrième Partie: Du Classicisme au siècle des lumières", and investigates the growth of interiority, the movement from knowledge to consciousness of oneself in the fiction of the 18c. Looks at 'self-exposure', 'self-characterization', 'remorse' as psychological motivation, permanence of identity, egoism, the implications of third-person narration, and first-person autobiography. "Cette conscience de soi faite roman est une conscience souple et généreuse, nourrie de sympathie pour les hommes aspirant à comprendre et à partager" (202). "La sagesse consiste à se savoir fou (' [...] plus fou, et par conséquent plus heureux,' dit Erasmus). Cette conscience éclairée et charmée de son humeur ne peut procéder d'un sens aigu de l'humeur" (203).

916   SOUTHALL, Raymond. *Literature and the rise of capitalism: critical essays mainly on the sixteenth and seventeenth centuries.* London: Lawrence & Wishart, 1973; pp. 175.

There are 13 essays which share a common concern for the way in which the rise of capitalism made itself felt in English literature. Between the prologue (on Thomas More) and the epilogue (on Samuel Johnson), the essays are grouped naturally around the initial enthusiasm, the subsequent questioning, the final despair and resolution with which the literature of the period responded to social change. Reference notes (163-70). Index (173-75).

917-----*Literature, the individual, and society: critical essays on the eighteenth and nineteenth centuries.* London: Lawrence & Wishart, 1977; pp. 184.

Series of 10 essays considering how, once capital was established as a social system, it created its own conditions of consciousness. Looks at "The Novelist and the Isolated Individual" (7-10). Explores some of the consequences in literature of the simultaneous elevation and isolation of the private individual which follow from the development of industrial capitalism. An awareness of the community of human interests is common in all great writers. Also covers the politics of sensibility; pastoral poetry and rural life; the villagers of Gray, Goldsmith and Crabbe; the natural world of Wordsworth; the social world of Jane Austen; the romanticism of Coleridge; Mill and *laissez-faire*; fantasy and reality in *Middlemarch*. Index (183-84).

918 SORENSEN, Janet Linda. "The grammar on (*sic*) empire, the figure of the nation: Language and the cultural identity in eighteenth-century Britain." Unpub. doct. diss., State Univ. of New York at Buffalo, 1994. [*DA* 55 (1995): 3525A.]

The constellation of political, economic, and social conditions in 18c Britain increasingly organized capital and culture into a centralized national block. The resulting culture was in deep conflict because of the mutually dependent movements - yet mutually exclusive claims - of nation and empire. Investigates British identity which seeks to bond generations across time within an empire claiming to unite diverse peoples as it expands in space. Focuses on the development of a national language, that works intimately with them within the frame of empire, through reading dictionaries, novels, language theories and historical documents. There is a development of an 'imperial grammar' (Scotland features as the training ground for the enforcement of English language usage). 'Cultural nationalism' saw language play a central role in the establishment of British national identity. Compares the exchange economy depicted in Defoe's *Roxana* (1724) to the semiotic economy of empire. Both processes diminish difference through exchange across space. These exchanges participate in a spatial semiotic which suppresses the temporal, historical and contingent factors involved in meaning.

919 SPACKS, Patricia Meyer. "Early fiction and the frightened male." *Novel* 8 (1974): 5-15.

Complications in 18c novels derive from the diverse meanings of sexual interchange, which usually involves money, and always demands physicality. Sex is a social as well as an individual concern, containing dynastic possibilities or threatening the destruction of family stability. How should emotion be properly expressed and controlled? Novels deal with money, bodies, families, feelings and reveal the problem of power which underlies them all.

920-----*Imagining a self: autobiography and novel in eighteenth-century England.* Cambridge, MA; London: Harvard UP, 1976; pp. 342.

The spacious novels of the 18c, with the names of their central figures as titles, are equally preoccupied with character and with human identity. Their stories focus on the intricacies, the paradoxes and the difficulties of human development. Looks at Defoe, Cibber, Richardson, Fielding, Cowper, Gibbon, Sterne, Fanny Burney, Boswell. Notes (317-38). Index.

921-----"The dangerous age." *ECS* 11 (1978): 417-38.

Novelists glorify maturity in the great mythology of age, yet try to imagine a mature mode which would neutralize the dangers of youth and the energies of this dangerous period of immaturity.

922-----and CARNOCHAN, W. B. *A distant prospect: eighteenth-century views of childhood. Papers read at a Clark Library Seminar, 13 October 1979.* Los Angeles: William Andrews Clark Memorial Library, 1982; pp. v, 50.

Humanistic studies have turned increasingly to inquire into the life of the child. Two essays pursue the inquiry into the domain of 18c English literature. SPACKS considers relationships between young and old in a family context (1-24). CARNOCHAN considers the imagery surrounding the relationship of the adult to the childhood self (25-48). Introduction. Bibliographic notes.

923-----*Desire and truth: functions of plot in eighteenth-century English novels.* Chicago: U of Chicago P, 1990; pp. ix, 262.

Investigates the kinds of truth conveyed in the 18c, and how fiction conveys them, concentrating less on truths of verisimilitude than on those of desire. Fiction creates and conveys its truths through plot. 18c fiction is both profoundly realistic, voicing the realities of the culture from which it emerges, and also consistently daring in its exploration of formal, psychological and social possibility. Further delineates the struggles between 'masculine' and 'feminine' values, since gender terms loom large in 18c discourse, and underlie the action of many novels. Also examines the critical problems several writers (incl. novelists) found inherent in the developing genre. Tries to sketch a history of the English novel and its transformation in the 19c by concentrating, esp. on the working out of sexual assumptions in novelistic plots. Preoccupation with how the vicissitudes of phallic power shape major fictions in the 1740s and 1750s. Consists mainly of other people's quotes in an argument that reflects the feminism of the 1980s. Notes (241-43). Bibliography (245-54). Index (255-62).

924 SPADAFORA, David. *The idea of progress in eighteenth-century Britain.* New Haven and London: Yale UP, 1990. 1990.pp. 464.

Investigates the ideas of progress in 18c British thought. What were the most prominent of these notions, esp. in the period 1730 to 1789? How did they arise, develop, become widespread? During the Age of Enlightenment the idea of progress was a characteristic and important part of the world view of the educated, literate citizens of Britain. Identifies the intellectual and social factors which led to the development and prevalence of the idea of progress. Also considers the goal and methods of traditions adopted by intellectual historians and historians of ideas. Looks at the Ancients and Moderns in arts and sciences, the Christian vision of history, medicine of the mind, language and progress, the progress of human culture, the sources of belief. Appendix (417-24). Bibliographic essay (425-56). Index (455-64).

925 SPÄTH, Eberhard. "Das private und das öffentliche Tagebuch: zum Verhältnis von Fiktion und Journalismus im englischen Roman." *Poetica* 19:1-2 (1987): 32-55.

In German. The first part considers the theme of 'the truth' and 'fiction', and the importance of the concept of 'the truth of nature'. The early 18c saw correspondences between journalism and the novel: writer and journalist were often combined in one person (like Defoe).

926 SPEARMAN, Diana. *The novel and society.* London: Routledge & Kegan Paul, 1966; pp. 256.

Part I "The Novel as a Literary Form" (17-60) considers the theory of the middle-class novel, looking at the political systems, economic activities, class attitudes, authors and their audiences, the 18c view of social structures. Part III "The Literary Background of the Eighteenth-Century Novel" (103-17) investigates the theory of the prose epic, the Spanish picaresque tale, realistic elements in the heroic novel, the influence of the drama. Index (251-56).

927 SPECK, W. A. *Society and literature in England, 1700-1760.* Dublin: Gill & Macmillan, 1983. See the expanded version below.

928-----*Literature and society in eighteenth-century England, 1680 - 1820: Ideology, politics and culture.* London and New York: Longman, 1998; pp. vii, 224.

Considers the historical and literary contexts of the 18c, dividing the century into three: 1) the First Age of Party (1680-1720) considering the political alignments, poems on the affairs of state, party ideology and society; 2) the Classical Age of the Constitution (1721-88), looking at Jacobitism and Patriotism, the emergence of the novel, literature, law and order; 3) the Age of the French Revolution (1789-1820) investigating the breakdown of the constitutional consensus, novels and the war of ideas, poems on the state of affairs. Select bibliography (210-13). Index (215-24).

929 SPECTOR, Robert Donald (ed.). *Essays on the 18th-century novel.* Bloomington; London: Indiana UP, 1965; pp. 205.

Collection of 9 essays on the five principal novels of the mid-18c. Ch. 1 is on *Moll Flanders* by Dorothy VAN GHENT (3-17). The introduction makes it clear that it was Defoe, Richardson, Fielding, Smollett and Sterne "who were primarily responsible for giving it [the novel] the fundamental purposes and significance, form and content which have characterized it from their day to the present" (vii). Demonstrates the relationship of "form and function" to the novel genre. Notes (185-94). Select Bibliography (195-205).

930 SPENCER, Jane. *The rise of the woman novelist: from Aphra Behn to Jane Austen.* Oxford: Blackwell, 1986; pp. 256.

Major study of the emergence of the novel in the 18c and the fate of professional women writers whose writings were deeply marked by the "femininity" demanded of them by their culture. The 18c critical establishment accepted the woman novelist, but their works treated certain themes differently from their male counterparts, and may be called "women's traditions". Considers the women novelist as heroine (Behn, Manley, Barker), heroines by women novelists (Manley,

Haywood, Sarah Fielding), reformed heroines: the didactic tradition (Trotter, Davys, Haywood), romance heroines: the tradition of escape (Lennox, and the Gothic novelists). Bibliographic notes to each chapter. Index.

931 SPRINGER, Marlene (ed.). *What manner of woman? Essays on American life and literature.* New York: New York UP, 1977; pp. xx, 357.

Essays dealing with the social and literary role of women. In the 17c and 18c images of women are often accounts of real people, but brief and fragmented.

932 STADLER, Eva Maria. "Addressing social boundaries: dressing the female in early realist fiction." In (pp. 20-36) HIGONNET, Margaret R. and TEMPLETON, Joan (eds). *Reconfigured spheres: feminist explorations of literary space.* Amherst: Massachusetts UP, 1994. pp. x, 212.

Shows how the varied functions of clothing figured in the realist novels from the beginning of the 18c. Defoe, Marivaux and Richardson all used the language of dress to construct and define a woman's social, sexual and psychological identity by manipulating a cultural system. Through her creative selection, composition, and disposal of attire on her person, the heroine may succeed in crossing class and gender boundaries, asserting her own individuality and sense of personal value, and gaining entry into reserved areas where she can find security and power. Bibliographic notes.

933 STAFFORD, Fiona J. *The last of the race: the growth of a modern myth from Milton to Darwin.* Oxford: Clarendon Press; New York: Oxford UP, 1994; pp. 326.

An attempt to describe and analyze the perennial interest in the last of the race through study of varied treatments by writers of the 18c and 19c. Discussion focuses on literary expressions, but analysis is influenced by extensive reading among the diaries, historical accounts, and newspaper reports of men and women who have been seen to represent the last of their kind. Comparisons between 'fictional' and 'real life' accounts of last men and women are mutually illuminating. All the works used have contributed something to the collective myth of the last of the race. Traces the growth of these ideas from the Restoration, when traditional Christian views of mankind began to wane, to the late 19c, when new patterns of racial ending had emerged in the wake of evolutionary and thermodynamic theories. Of particular interest is ch. 3 "Towards the Last of the Race: Robinson Crusoe as Sole Survivor" (56-82). "Defoe's novel can [...] be seen as a positive response to the great seventeenth-century sense of change. The myth of the sole survivor provides structure through which to reappraise old values and assumptions and balance tradition with innovation" (81). Select bibliography (308-20). Index (321-26).

934 STAMPER, Donald Rexford. "Success and openness in English fiction from Richardson through Jane Austen." Unpub. doct. diss., Univ. of Arkansas, 1973. [*DA* 34 (1973): 2656A-7A.]

Study of nine novelists and 22 novels, stressing the relationship between the success the characters in these novels pursue as viable goals and how this success contributes to the artistic merit of the work. They have the power to alter the reader's understanding of the psychological, phenomenological or theological organization of reality (Richardson, Fielding, Smollett, Goldsmith, Fanny Burney, Mackenzie, Sterne, Godwin, Jane Austen).

935 STANZEL, Franz. "Die typischen Formen des englischen Romans und ihre Entstehung im achtzehnten Jahrhundert." In (pp. 243-48) BÖCKMANN, Paul. (ed.). *Stil- und Formprobleme*. Heidelberg: Carl Winter Universitätsverlag, 1959; pp. 524.

In German. Examines the preponderance of the first-person narrative mode in the novels of the early 18c. " [...] seit dem Beginn des 18. Jahrhunderts [besteht] eine deutliche Tendenz [...], hauptsächlich typische Formen zu schaffen, d. h. Romane, deren Erzählsituation derjenigen eines der drei Typen sehr nahe kommt [...] " (245). "Eine klare Linie zeigt die Entwicklung des Ich-Romans bis zur Mitte des 18. Jahrhunderts. Die Ich-Form wurde zunächst fast ausschliesslich mit der Absicht, das Erzählte als 'wahr' auszugeben, verwendet. So erklärt sich, warum gerade die unglaubhaftesten Erzählungen, die phantastischen Reisen zu utopischen oder exotischen Welten, immer nur in der Ich-Form dagestellt werden. Auch die Nachahmung des heroisch-galanten Romans mit seinen unglaubwürdigen Helden und seinen fremden Schauplätzen drängt zur Ich-Form hin, weil in ihm häufig einer der Helden sehr ausführlich seine eigne Geschichte erzählt" (247).

936-----(ed.). *Der englischen Roman von Mittelalter zur Moderne*. 2 vols. Düsseldorf: August Bagel, 1969; pp. 432, 399.

In German. Collection of essays on individual works covering the history of the English novel. The editor has an introduction "Gedanken zur Poetik des Romans" (9-22). The early 18c is represented by Robert WEIMANN, "Defoe, *Robinson Crusoe*" (I, 108-43). Covers various topics: Der Autor: Soziologie und 'sensibility'; *Robinson Crusoe*: Stoff und Idee; Der Aufbau des Helden: Wirklichkeit und Utopie; Charakterisierung und Erzählkunst; Erzählperspektive und Romanstruktur; *Robinson Crusoe*: Wirkung und Romanstruktur; *Robinson Crusoe*: Wirkung und Geschichte. "*Robinson Crusoe* ist nicht nur ein geschichtliches Werk, es hat selbst Geschichte gemacht" (139). Looks also at criticism and reception history.

937-----*Narrative situations in the novel: 'Tom Jones', 'Moby Dick', 'The Ambassadors', 'Ulysses'*. Trans. James P. PUSAK from *Die typische Erzählsituationen im Roman*. Bloomington and London: Indiana UP, 1971; pp. 186.

Introd. (3-21) discusses the importance of narrative for the structure and comprehension of the novel, showing how narrative situation determines the structure. "It determines the order in which the narrator or author can unfold the fictional world before the eyes of the reader. At the same time the narrative situation and its specific guise bring the reader to expect a definite consistency of illusion from the narrative" (21). Ch. 2 "The Authorial Novel: *Tom Jones*" (38-58) discusses the nature of epic narration by particular reference to Fielding. Ch. 3 "The First-Person Novel" (59-91) is also very important for 18c fictional types, even though the focus of investigation is Melville; reference to the 18c is limited to Defoe's *Moll Flanders*. Ch. 6 "Excursus: The Rendering of Consciousness" (145-57) and Ch. 7 "A Typology of the Novel" (158-69) provide enduringly important introductions to narrative modes and the interplay of epic, dramatic and lyrical modes.

938 STARN, Randolph (introd.). "Seance and suicide: the media of somatic history." *Representations* 22 (Spring 1988): 1-59.

Considers the handling of these subjects in periodicals: the treatment of the human body, and its perceived relationship to society.

939 STAUFFER, Donald Alfred. *The art of biography in eighteenth-century England*. 2 vols. Princeton: Princeton UP, 1941; pp. 572.

Investigates biography and the drama, biography and the novel (65-130, summary 131), biography and the romantic spirit, knowledge infinite (eccentrics and antiquarians), the life within, the great names, the trend of biography (constant currency, foreign influence, democratization of biography, didacticism replaced by new concepts of entertainment and truth, interest in style and structure, practices in writing, theories of biography). Index. Ch. 2 which focuses on the novel investigates the principal relations between the two forms, various types of fictional biography: 1) life and amours: D'Aulnoy (69-71); Manley (72-74); Anthony Hamilton (74-76); 2) life and adventures: Defoe (77-80), James Wyatt (1748)(81-84); Edward Browne (1739) (84-85); William Rufus Chetwood (1736) (85-88); 3) biography and individual novelists (Richardson, Fielding, Smollett, Sterne); individual successes in novelizing actual life.

940 STAVES, Susan. "*Don Quixote* in eighteenth-century England." *CL* 24:3 (Summer 1972): 193-215.

No national literature assimilated the idea of *Don Quixote* more thoroughly than the English. During the 18c this novel came into its own: not only was it good to read and enthusiastically appreciated, but it also found many imitators. In this process of assimilation, the knight underwent a fascinating metamorphosis. First we see Don Quixote as a buffoon, a madman who belongs in a farce. Then ambiguity crept in and a figure emerged who is still ridiculous, still a buffoon, but who at the same time is beginning to look strangely noble, even saintly. Then finally, towards the end of the century, the Romantic Don Quixote can be glimpsed, an idealistic and noble hero. Is he a buffoon whose delusion reveals only his bizarre pride and the absurdity of the literature which has provoked his quest? Or is he an exemplary figure who refuses to allow his high ideals to be sullied by the filthy reality of a fallen world?

941-----"Studies in eighteenth-century fiction, 1978." *PQ* 58 (1979): 429-68.

Critical review of books and articles on the 18c, from the mid-1970s: centers on Bunyan, Defoe, Richardson, Fielding, Smollett, Sterne, Goethe.

942-----"Fatal marriages? Restoration plays embedded in eighteenth-century novels." In PATEY, Douglas Lane and KEEGAN, Tim (eds). *Augustan studies: essays in honor of Irvin Ehrenpreis*. Newark: Delaware UP: London: Assoc. UPs, 1985; pp. 270.

The novels of the 18c often evoke the late 17c by a representation of action from Restoration drama, juxtaposing Restoration stage representations against the depiction of later 18c life. The novel represents the real-life activities of its contemporaries and reveals a fictional appropriation by bourgeois women of sentiments and entitlements that had formerly been the dramatic property of aristocratic men.

943 STEEGE, David Kriek. "Golden dreams: Treasure-hunting in American literature to 1843." Unpub. doct. diss., Univ. of North Carolina, Chapel Hill, 1991. [*DAI* 52:10 (1992): 3605A.]

Treasure-hunting texts have their origins in the non-fictitious accounts of exploitation of mineral and other resources in the New World. Texts involving treasure-hunting reveal much about their authors' attitudes towards social mobility, the proper way to wealth, and the 'magic' world view.

944 STEEVES, Edna. "Pre-feminism in some 18c novels." In (pp. 222-32) BROWN, Cheryll and OLSON, Karen (eds). *Feminist criticism: essays on theory, poetry and prose.* Metuchen, NJ and London: Scarecrow Press, 1978; pp. 369.

Discussion of the "woman question" before 1800, with reference to Mary Astell, Addison, Defoe, Manley, Haywood, Richardson, Burney, Mary Wollstonecraft. In the program of the novel there is, from Defoe to Austen, a growing interest in the improvement of women's situation. Fiction nonetheless reflects little practical or organic effort by society to better their postion.

945 STEEVES, Harrison R. *Before Jane Austen: the shaping of the English novel in the eighteenth century.* London: George Allen & Unwin; New York: Holt, Reinhart & Winston, 1965; pp. xii, 399.

Deals with the years in which the novel was still an experiment. The novel may be regarded as an assembled rather than an invented artistic form. It had been too long, too didactic, too stiff in style, too punctuated, too commonplace, too uninteresting. But once its importance became clear, the perfecting of method and technique made rapid progress. Considers Nashe, Behn and Bunyan in ch. 2 (6-21), before focusing on Defoe, Swift, Richardson, Fielding, Smollett and later 18c writers. Ch. 5 "Sex in the Eighteenth-Century Perspective" (88-102) and ch. 9 "Sentimentalism" (160-66) provide useful perspectives up to 1750. Profuse and interesting illus. Index (395-99).

946 STEINTRAGER, James Alvin. "Stages of cruelty in eighteenth-century France, England and Germany." Unpub. doct. diss., Columbia Univ., 1997. [*DA* 58 (1997): 1269-70A.]

Examines the possible enjoyment of another's pain as a troublesome aspect of sentimental discourse. The Enlightenment proclaimed that cruelty would end with the spread of reason, but rather than turning its back on cruelty, the Enlightenment as a system found itself engaged in the production of images and texts depicting acts of inhumanity. These texts and images played various roles: eliciting proper affective response, creating forms of group identity, and determining sites and modes of intervention against malevolence. Sources range from dramas, philosophy and libertine novels to theatrical reviews and everyday periodicals. Concentrates mainly on the emergence of the horror drama in France (Crébillon) as a point of reference to explore audience observation of cruel spectacles. The *Sturm und Drang* used violence to indicate a break with social systems, including the theater itself. Provides analyzes of philosophical, aesthetical and journalistic discussions of the scientific gaze and voyeuristic gaze.

947 STEPHENSON, Peter. "Three playwright novelists: the contribution of dramatic techniques to Restoration and early eighteenth-century prose fiction." Unpub. doct. diss., Univ. of California (Davis), 1970. [*DAI* 30:7-9 (1970): 3920A.]

Many novelists of the experimental period 1660 to 1740 also wrote plays. Provides detailed analysis of the plays and novels of Aphra Behn, William Congreve and Mary Davys: their experiments with comedy led to improved characterization and increased realistic detail.

948 STEVENSON, John Allen and SUSSMAN, Herbert (eds). *The British novel, Defoe to Austen: a critical history.* (Twayne Critical History of the Novel.) Boston: Twayne, 1990; pp. xiii, 153.

Considers where the novel comes from and its great diversity, with surveys of heroism in *Robinson Crusoe*, power in *Clarissa*, language in *Tom Jones*, laughter in *Tristram Shandy*, courtship in *Emma*. Crusoe's heroism (5-20) becomes an occasion for exploring the heroic possibilities of the genre in general. Chronology (xi-xiii). Notes and references (132-41). Select bibliography (142-48). Index (149-53).

949 STEVENSON, Lionel. *The English novel: a panorama.* London: Constable & Co., 1961; pp. 539.

History of the novel from its earliest forms. Ch. 3 "The Discovery of Realism (1700-1740)" (54-78). Discusses the 18c literary scene, looking at Ned Ward and Tom Brown, the work of Steele (*Tatler*) and Addison (*Spectator*), Manley (58-61), Defoe (61-76), looking at *Robinson Crusoe, Moll Flanders, Memoirs of a Cavalier, Captain Singleton, Colonel Jack, Roxana, A Journal of the Plague Year.* Examines Defoe's handling of generic models and themes in some detail, comparing him with Swift. "If

Defoe never achieved a full-scale novel because his books lacked interpretation of life, *Gulliver's Travels* falls outside of the canon for the opposite reason. Its greatness resides in its meaning not in its story" (76). Also discusses Manley and Haywood briefly, with passing reference to Barker, Rowe, Aubin, Davys, Plantin and Boyd. Extensive bibliography covers general bibliographies, histories, criticism, studies, themes and specific topics, with items on each chapter (495-99). Useful chronological summary of the English novel (16c-20c) (518-34). Index (535-39).

950-----"Varieties of the novel." *SBHT* 13 (1972): 2251-59.

Ever since Richardson and Fielding established a new mode of prose fiction as realistic representation of contemporary experience, novelists have provided countless details of mores which might never have been recorded by graver chronicles.

951 STOCK, R. D. *The holy and the daemonic from Sir Thomas Browne to William Blake*. Princeton, NJ: Princeton UP, 1981; pp. 395.

Concerned with certain kinds of religious experience as recorded in 17c and 18c literature. The chapter "The Witch of Endor and the Gadarene Swine: The Debate over Witchcraft and Miracles in the Seventeenth and Eighteenth Centuries" (61-116) contains an extended discussion of Defoe's *Robinson Crusoe* (109-16), as one of the happiest attempts in the 18c to reinvigorate a sense of the miraculous and the providential. Defoe lies between the polemical anthologies of the Restoration (in the mode of Joseph Glanvill), and the sensational appeal of the Gothic novel. In *Robinson Crusoe* and *A Journal of the Plague Year* Defoe dramatizes a providential world, and while eschewing the overtly miraculous, his use of omens, visions and coincidences strongly suggests a watching Deity rather than a celestial watchmaker, much involved in his creation. Index (387-95).

952 STONE, Lawrence. *The family, sex and marriage in England, 1500-1800*. London: Weidenfeld & Nicolson, 1977; pp. 446; plates 16 pp.

Historico-sociological survey of three centuries, looking at: the open lineage family from 1450 to 1630; the restricted patriarchal family from 1500 to 1700; the closed domestic nuclear family from 1640 to 1800; sex (upper-class behavior in the 16c and 17c); behavior of 'the quality' in the 18c; gentlemanly sexual behavior (Pepys and Boswell); plebeian sexual behavior.

953 STOUT, Janis Diane Pitts. "Sodoms in Eden: the city in American fiction before 1860." Unpub. doct. diss., Rice Univ, 1973. [*DA* 34 (1973): 1257A.]

Fictional treatment of urbanization and urban society in America before 1860 generally reflects the anti-urban feelings prominent in American social thought since the time of Jefferson, and even before. Although the city is occasionally depicted as an arena of opportunity with material and cultural advantages, the overwhelming tendency is to regard the city with strong ambivalence or distrust. Special reference to Cooper, Melville, Hawthorne.

954 STRATMANN, Gerd. "Life, death and the city: the discovery of London in the early eighteenth century." *JSBB* 4:1-2 (1997): 63-72.

It is a paradox of 18c British culture that, although obsessed with the excitements of discovery (geography, science, psychology), it appears to exclude London, its undisputed center, from its overt focus. Most of the canonical authors of the age define London negatively. The 18c debate on the meanings of modern city life was begun by a number of poplar 'travelogues' which offered a kind of subversive account of the new (i.e. post-Fire) city of London. Polite authors were partly inspired by the intention to invalidate popular interpretations of the city, to 'undiscover' the dangerous attractions they had so temptingly displayed.

955 STRATTON, Jon. *The virgin text: fiction, sexuality, and ideology.* Brighton: Harvester Press; Norman: Oklahoma UP, 1987; pp. xvii, 237.

A rewriting of the history of the novel, covering sexuality and confinement, fetishism and marriage, repression and pornography, desire and worldliness, reality and replacement, rape and virtue, love and death.

956 STREATFIELD, David C. and DUCKWORTH, Alistair M. *Landscapes in the gardens and the literature of eighteenth-century England.* (Clark Library Seminar, 18 March 1978.) Los Angeles: William Andrews Clark Memorial Library, Univ. of California, 1981; pp. 128.

From the beginning to the end of the 18c, there was a dramatic shift from one end of the spectrum to the other, from the rigidly formal to the romantic, from the geometric to the irregular, from an artificial style (of French, Dutch and Italian influences), to the indigenous, artfully artless back-to-nature style of the English landscape garden. The change was a turning point in the development of landscape architecture, and enduring landmark in Western attitudes towards "the good life". Its historical and symbolic impacts are still felt in our own time, and are addressed in the two long essays presented: 1) STREATFIELD looks at art and nature in the English landscape garden (1700 to 1818) (1-87); 2) DUCKWORTH looks at fiction and some uses of the Country House setting from Richardson to Scott (89-128). Both essays have extensive bibliographical notes.

957 STRIEDTER, Anna Kuntz. "Women writers and the epistolary novel: gender, genre, and ideology in eighteenth-century fiction." Unpub. doct. diss., Univ. of California (San Diego), 1994. [*DA* 54 (1994): 4435A.]

Traces the French and English women's epistolary novels from 1745 to 1803, a period during which women authors increasingly popularized and appropriated the genre. Women authors used the genre to express different views on the rights, education and social roles of women: female independence and legal equality, the ideal of domesticity, the criticism of domesticity, the increasing criticism of the French Revolution and the cult of virility, the cultural pessimism resulting from the enormous disappointment the Revolution represented for women. All these are examined from the perspectives of gender, culture and social class.

958 STRONG, Suasn Clancy. "Countries of the mind: the Oriental 'topoi' in eighteenth-century English and French literature." Unpub. doct. diss., Univ. of California (Berkeley), 1979. [*DA* 40 (1980): 4022A.]

In the 19c and 20c Orientalism is a negative projective fantasy (SAID, 1978). But in the early 18c a radically different Orientalism flourished. Characterized by positive identification and rhetorical manipulation, the most important literary form of this phenomenon, the Oriental *contes philosophiques* of England and France, shows eastern topoi controlling the rhetorical system of these works. The topoi form an extended analogy between East and West in which the latter is clearly the true subject. Distinct national analogies first appeared in English and French Oriental tales in the *Spectator*, and the innovations of Montesquieu are studied in this light. The permutations and contributions of possible topoi (Oriental travellers or fairy tales) are examined in the work of Voltaire and Johnson.

959 SUHR, Heidrun. *Englische Romanautorinnen im 18. Jahrhundert: Ein Beitrag zur Entwicklung des bürgerlichen Romans.* (Anglistische Forschungen, 169.) Heidelberg: Carl Winter Universitätsverlag, 1983; pp. 309.
In German. Major study of women writers of fiction in the 18c. Ch. 1 "The Fair Triumvirate of Wit" (19-35) considers Aphra Behn (22-24), Mary Delarivière Manley (25-29), and Eliza Haywood (30-35). Ch. 2 "The Moral Censors of the Age" looks at Penelope Aubin (36-40) and

Jane Barker (40-50). Ch. 3 (50-86) investigates the novel in 18c England from an historico-theoretical perspective, aspects of its development, conditions for the emergence of the novel, the novel as a medium of self-expression for women. Ch. 4 "Eliza Haywood - revisited" (87-103) resumes the analysis of her work after her reappearance in 1741. The rest of the book looks in depth at women's writing in the last 60 years of the century. All the novelists are investigated in detail with copious quotations from their works, and a thorough involvement with the secondary literature on them and their times. The bibliography (285-308) is of great importance.

960 SUNSHINE, Kathleen. *Early American literature and the call of the wild: nature, the Indian and the woodsman in fiction.* (Harvard Dissertations in American and English Literature.) New York; London: Garland, 1987; pp. 329.

Sets out to determine the characteristics of the early American novel before the appearance of Cooper's first novel, *The Spy* (1821), and to ascertain the elements that distinguish it from the British fiction which spawned it.

961 SUTHERLAND, James Robinson. "Some aspects of eighteenth-century prose." In *Essays on the eighteenth century presented to David Nichol Smith.* Oxford: Clarendon Press, 1945; pp. vi, 288.

The clear stream of writing which had its rise at the end of the 17c, to which Addison, Steele, Swift, Fielding, Chesterfield and Horace Walpole contributed, was joined in the middle of the century by another style usually associated with Johnson and Gibbon. Johnson's prose carries with it a deposit of learning which distinguishes it from the writing of Addison. The later was the perfect model for the average man with average thoughts and feelings. The styles of Johnson, Gibbon and Burke were too powerful, too emphatic. By the end of the 18c, the engaging simplicity of Addison and Steele had evaporated from prose writing. In literature, as in painting and sculpture, the grand manner was all the fashion.

962-----*On English prose.* Toronto: U of Toronto P, 1952; pp. 123.

Considers the ways in which 18c English prose was written at different periods, tracing the most important developments. Looks at the problem of prose; "apes and peacocks" (the movement towards a more conscious and artificial prose style in the 16c); the imitation of Cicero, the ages of prose (Elizabethan, Jacobean, Caroline, the 18c, the 19c and after).

963 SWAN, Beth. *Fictions of law: an investigation of the law in eighteenth-century English fiction.* (Anglo-American Studies, 9.) New York and Frankfurt: Peter Lang, 1997; pp. 231.

Seeks to interpret legal discourse and practice from a literary perspective, clarifying aspects of legal history which have been largely ignored or misunderstood, and which have led to problems in interpreting 18c fiction. Many fictional predicaments that have been taken as romantic or melodramatic are often grounded in the precise, actual practices of 18c law. Commentary has failed to show how 18c fiction, by both men and women, traced the manifold difficulties women encountered under the law, and just how detailed and precise women's understanding was of the predicaments in which the law could place them. Looks at 18c fiction and contemporary marriage laws, property, finance, virtue as a moral concept in a legal context, criminal law. Bibliography (209-22). Index (223-31).

964 SWARTZ, Richard G. "Patrimony and the figuration of authorship in the eighteenth-century literary property debates." *Works and Days* 7:2 (Fall 1989): 29-54.

Investigates the history of copyright law and of literary property debates in 18c England where authorship was defined as a series of historically, socially, and economically governed roles, forms and conventions. The history of copyright makes it clear that the options of the self-defining, self-validating author, who serves as the final source of the text's internal coherence and its aesthetic, cultural, and moral value, was not always the case, and that this notion of authorship was contested at the moment of its emergence. Critical attention to copyright further challenges the belief that the aesthetic, intellectual and cultural dimensions of cultural and literary production have no determinate relationship to the economic world of the book trade. Copyright law by its very nature defines the text as a product and the author as a kind of producer. Any interpretation of copyright and its history challenges traditional literary criticism by revealing the degree to which socio-economic considerations are intrinsic to the notions of authorship, aesthetic merit and literary value inherited from the mid- to late-18c, the era of the great English copyright debates.

965 SWEET, R. H. "The writing of urban histories in eighteenth-century England." Unpub. doct. diss., Univ. of Oxford, 1993. [*IT* 44:2 (1995): 523.]
Urban history developed as a distinctive genre of literature in its own right. Examines the different literary traditions which shaped urban histories: antiquarianism, urban chronicles, travel literature. Such histories are related to wider literary and intellectual movements such as

the interest in the medieval past stimulated by the Gothic revival. Urban histories were part of a thriving provincial urban culture, with a dynamic and identity of their own.

966   SYPHER, Feltus Wylie. "The anti-slavery movement to 1800 in English literature, exclusive of the periodical." *Harvard University Summaries of Theses, 1937*, 1938. See expanded published version below, **968**.

967-----"The West-Indian as a 'character' in the eighteenth century." *SP* 36 (1939): 503-20.

During the 18c the Irishman, the Scotsman, the Nabob, or South-Sea Islander, were all frequently portrayed as 'characters' in the Theophrastian manner. The West Indian, or 'Creole', was likewise a type in the novel, drama, and verse of the late 1700s. The traits allegedly West-Indian are unmistakable, and the 'Creole' is a not inconsiderable literary figure of the period. Plantation life marked the West-Indian character, and however distorted by the negrophile writers, there was throughout the later 18c in the mind of the common Englishman a combination of traits definitely 'creolian'.

968-----*Guinea's captive kings: British anti-slavery literature of the XVIIIth century*. Chapel Hill: U of North Carolina P, 1942; pp. x, 340.

Provides an overview of the British slave trade, the protest against it, and the literature inspired by both. Includes commentary on travel narratives which discuss the slave trade.

969   TAINE, Hippolyte Adolphe. *The history of English literature*. Paris, 1863. Trans. H. Van Laun. With a preface by the author. 2 vols. Edinburgh: Edmonston & Douglas, 1871; pp. 531, 550.

Ch. 4 in vol. 2 is devoted to "The novelists", looking at: 1) characteristics of the English novel; 2) Defoe; 3) circumstances which gave rise to the novels of the 18c; 4) Richardson; 5) Fielding; 6) Smollett; 7) Sterne; 8) Goldsmith; 9) Samuel Johnson. Defoe is discussed in terms of his life, energy, devotion, politics, spirit, differences of old and modern realities, works, career, aims; *Robinson Crusoe*: how this character is English, his inner enthusiasm, his obstinacy and patience in work; his methodical common sense, religious emotion, final piety. General index (544-50).

970   TAVOR, Eve. *Scepticism, society and the eighteenth-century novel*. New York: St Martin's Press, 1987; pp. 273.

18c fictions which 20c criticism has characterized as 'novels' and 'good novels' all grow out of the 18c sceptical tradition represented by Locke, Mandeville, Hume and Shaftesbury which determines the concerns and formal features of the novel. Explores these common formal features and the common socio-historical 'provenance' using adapted sociology of literature developed by George Lukács and Lucien Goldmann. Looks at Defoe's boundaries of middle-class understanding, Richardson's dogmatic scepticism, Fielding's 'nothing for everyone', Sterne's beginnings of genteel realism. Detailed bibliographical notes (243-60), Select Bibliography (261-65).

971 TAYLOR, Houghton W. "Modern fiction and the doctrine of uniformity." *PQ* 19:3 (July 1940): 224-36.

The conception of character which by and large controlled the novelist of the 18c, and which stands in almost complete contrast to the essential preoccupations of the 20c, is that of uniformity: that human nature is basically the same in every time and place. This nation was already being modified in the 18c, and a change was noticeable by the start of the 19c.

972-----"'Particular character': an early phase of literary evolution." *PMLA* 60:1 (1945): 161-74.

Shows fundamental ways in which the idea of particularity assumed explicit form in the 18c in respect to characterization. Affects all kinds of writing in which character is portrayed. Modern psychology ordered by concern for the individual consciousness is responsible for the furthest extremes, as is naturalism with its implications of particularity arising from the theory that a character must be influenced or molded by specific environment.

973 TELTSCHER, Kate. *India inscribed: European and British writing on India, 1600-1800.* Delhi; Oxford and New York: Oxford UP, 1995; pp. 280.
Draws on a wide range of texts, some ignored by scholars, to depict writing about India in 17c and early 18c. All texts are unified in their production of an India for a domestic and expatriate audience. European texts are preoccupied with a wide set of questions about authority in India which provide a discursive framework particularly amenable to later colonial use. Many of the texts are determined by national and religious rivalries, by domestic concerns - both cultural and political. In this period it is possible to speak of a European tradition in writing about India. Bibliography (259-74). Index (275-80). Illus. (7 plates).

974   TEMPLE, Kathryn Doris. "The author in public: literary scandals, legal reputation, and national identity in eighteenth-century Britain." Unpub. doct. diss., Univ. of Virginia, 1994. [*DA* 55 (1994): 1268A.]

Focuses on the intersection of authorship, law and popular culture, examining how 18c literary scandals provided a public arena for mediating problems of national identity. Literary scandals embraced aspects of both print and popular culture, and found popular voice in caricature, ballad operas and theatrical productions (Richardson and the Irish book pirates, Johnson and Macpherson over Ossian, the theft of Catherine Macaulay's private correspondence). All three reveal the highly politicized origins of a literary property system thought to be apolitical. Both critical discourse and popular representations of literary scandals emphasized regional difference as part of a larger effort to consolidate national identity.

975   TENGER, Zeynep. "Inventing the writer and the reader: Eighteenth-century literary theory." Unpub. doct. diss., New York Univ., 1991. [*DAI* 51:12 (1991): 4113A.]

Examines the development of a new poetics of the reader and writer in late 17c and 18c France and England as manifested in critical treatises of the period. Ch. 1 provides an overview of Neo-Classical criticism as it flourished approximately between 1620-1670 (Chaplain, D'Aubignac, Scudéry, La Mesnardière, Davenant). The success of this theory was based on its utilization of the rules and precepts of art as tools for categorization and analysis of literary works. Ch. 2 and 3 cover the years 1670-1715, and record how critics of the period come to question the efficacy of assigning the regulation of the readers and writers to the rules (Rapin, Boileau, Saint-Evremond, Dennis, Shaftesbury, Addison, Pope). Method was no longer perceived as adequate to enable the writer to produce socially useful works to affect the audience. The last two chapters chart the further development of these discourses of the writer and the reader in the critical theory between 1715-70 (Dubos, Batteux, Hume, Young, Duff, D'Alembert, Burke). They presented their analyzes of the processes of reading and writing as models that actual writers and readers should emulate.

976   TERRY, Richard. "The circumstances of eighteenth-century parody." *ECLife* 15:3 (Nov. 1991): 76-92.

The Augustan Age was the first great age of parody. This was of unique relevance to an age where the greatest writers affected intimacy with their predecessors (through imitation) and hostility to their contemporaries (through satire). Defence and indignation, imitation and the grotesque, fell within the ambit of parody. Tries to place parody in relation to a complex of material conditions and tendencies that were formative. The circumstances of literary production, the propinquity of parody to other aesthetic techniques, the debate about the conditions of the language, and esp. the rise of the viewpoint that writing styles reflect psychological traits possessed by their authors, all constituted a cultural syndrome, fostering an efflorescence of parodic activity.

977 THACKER, Christopher. *The wildness pleases: the origins of Romanticism.* London: Croom Helm, 1983; pp. vi, 282.

In the last decades of the 17c, the "aesthetic of Versailles", if not the political domination, was widely accepted and imitated. But in the 18c there was a general weariness with the regime of Louis XIV, a tiredness with formality. The classical ideal of Molière, Corneille, La Fontaine and Boileau was a mighty force existing beside newly born and strengthening impulses of romanticism. The classical ideal was contained in a fairly "pure" form, and we may see it as the alternative, or even opponent, of the new romantic ideal of the 18c. It is above all established in the 18c view of the *citizen*, a bourgeois man, hard-working and responsible. Looks at the status quo and reaction, the notion of Primitivism, Man-in-Nature, Primitive Man, the holiday, Ossian, the Noble Savage, the Wildness Pleases. Bibliography (273-75). Index (276-82). 50 plates.

978 THOMAS, David. *Theater in Europe: Restoration and Georgian England, 1660-1800.* Cambridge: Cambridge UP, 1989; pp. xxx, 460.

Detailed account of the world of Restoration theater (1660 to 1737), a useful background to the unfolding of prose fiction. Provides details of control, contractual and company documents, playhouses, stage presentation, actors and acting, audiences, repertoire, morality debates, criticism.

979 THOMPSON, James. *Models and value: eighteenth-century political economy and the novel.* Durham, NC and London: Duke UP, 1996; pp. viii, 271.

The 18c saw the transformation in the early modern concept of money from treasure to capital and the consequent refiguration of money from species to paper. Where is value or worth to be located - in silver or paper, thing or name, or in different genres? Two literary forms preeminently handled this crisis. Political economy and the novel are at the same time produced by this crisis and inseparable from it. Both can be understood as essentially solutions, and each describes value, and is charged with exploring it. Finally looks at the generic or discursive consequences: tries to throw a new light on the history of the novel. Looks at models of value, representation and exchange, money and sign, Defoe and the narrative exchange, Fielding and property, Burney and debt, Austen and the novel. Notes (199-250). Bibliography (251-66). Index (267-71).

980   THOMSEN, Christian W. *Das Groteske im englischen Roman des 18. Jahrhunderts: Erscheinungsformen und Funktionen.* (Impulse der Forschung, 17.) Darmstadt: Wissenschaftliche Buchgesellschaft, 1974; pp. 350.
In German. Investigates Jonathan Swift's *Gulliver's Travels* as grotesque satire and satirical grotesque, then Fielding (burlesque, grotesque, caricature), Smollett (picaresque inheritance, odd characters, the grotesque of wounded humanity), Sterne (grotesque world view and experiential novel form). Survey of the grotesque from Swift to Sterne with a view of the Gothic. Bibliography (331-44). Index (345-50).

981   THOMSON, J. A. K. *Classical influences on English prose.* London: George Allen & Unwin, 1956; pp. 271.

Useful for linking the emergence of the various prose and fictional forms to classical models: simple narrative, the mature narrative style, the short story, the romance, the novel, characters, the literature of travel, the letter. The chapter on the romance (67-80) underlines the importance of Apuleius on Nash and Defoe (77-80).

982   THURIN, Susan Molly Schonbauer. "Marriageability: a study of the factors entering marriage choice in English novels." Unpub. doct. diss., Univ. of Wisconsin-Milwaukee, 1979. [*DA* 40 (1980): 2080A.]

The typical ending of the English novel up to the end of the 19c is the happy marriage. Up to Jane Austen the central plot usually revolves around some obstacle to marriage, with the actual marriage of the protagonist treated cursorily at the end. In the 18c marriage is often allied to the development of democratic values and individualism, so that traditional values are challenged in some ways, although the resolution of the plot essentially supports the traditional values.

983   TIEJE, Arthur Jerrold. "The expressed aim of the long prose fiction, 1579-1740." *JEPG* 11 (1912): 402-32.

Even before 1579 there was a considerable amount of critical comment upon prose fictions as distinguished from poetical. Authors sought to delight, but there were many serious aims: a desire for social reform, a return to nature, idealizing and controversial fictions of religion. By the allurement of fiction, people were won to listen to philosophy, history, economics, geography, physical science, criticism, fashion, and the depiction of life.

984-----"A peculiar phase of the theory of realism in pre-Richardsonian prose fiction." *PMLA* 28 (1913): 213-52.

One of the aims of pre-Richardsonian fiction was to gain the implicit credence of the reader. With this end in view, the authors assailed the reader with assertions of veracity. It affected structure, characterization, setting and style in narrative. It let loose a flood of moral characters, and called the attention of writers to the close portrayal of human beings of every age, rank and appearance. It aided the introduction of spatial and temporal 'local color', and suggested that the style of a book is dependent on the individuality of its characters' personae.

985-----"The problem of setting in pre-Richardsonian fiction." *PMLA* 29 Appendix (1914): xxvi.

There were five uses of setting: to provide variety, information, vividness, to express love for nature, to show the influence of scenery upon man.

986-----*The theory of characterization in prose fiction prior to 1740.* (Univ. of Minnesota Studies in Language and Literature, 5.) Minneapolis: U of Minneapolis P, 1916; pp. 131.

A survey of the literature prior to Richardson, centering on romance practice and its changes, the practice of realists, the personality of heroes and heroines. Bibliography (115-31).

987 TILLYARD, E. M. W. *The epic strain in the English novel.* London: Chatto & Windus, 1958; pp. 208.

Continues his *English epic and its background*. By the 19c, the real course of the epic had forsaken the traditional verse form for the novel. Considers those novels he sees fulfilling the requisites of epic. "Introductory" (9-24) considers and defines his terms. Ch. on Defoe (25-50). "I believe *Robinson Crusoe* to be an epic having some of the limitations of the middle-class ethos whose choric expression it was " (50). Index (205-8).

988 TINKLER, John F. "Humanist history and the English novel in the

eighteenth century." *SP* 85:4 (1988): 510-37.

Approaches the novel from the perspective of history-writing, esp. as it emerges from the Renaissance into the 17c and 18c, arguing that novelists took over and extended the rhetorical history of the humanists.

989 TODD, Dennis. *Imagining monsters: miscreations of the self in eighteenth-century England*. Chicago and London: Chicago UP, 1995; pp. xvii, 339.

Examines in detail ideas about the imagination, monstrosity, and personal identity in the 18c, particularly a conception of self-identity shared by a number of artists and thinkers of the period, but articulated most strikingly by the Scriblerians, esp. Swift and Pope. When formulating the conception of selfhood, these artists and thinkers turned repeatedly to the notion of the imagination, and to the figure of the monster. Attempts to uncover some of the historical determinates and provocations that explain why they did: this covers contemporary philosophical assumptions about the psychology of the imagination, contemporary philosophical arguments about personal identity and the body-mind relationship, theoretical embryology, teratological debates, the staging of monster exhibitions, and stereotypes about the deformed. Bibliographic notes (269-330). Index (331-39). Illus. (3 plates).

990 TODD, Janet. *The sign of Angellica: women, writing and fiction*. London: Virago, 1989; pp. vii, 328.

Literary history of the Restoration and the 18c, focused entirely on women. Considers in detail dozens of female writers from Margaret Cavendish to Ann Radcliffe, locates them in a changing political, social and economic scene, and demonstrates the variety of attitudes, concerns and techniques employed by women during a century and a half. The sophisticated activity of Aphra Behn was never duplicated by her successors: women's novels move from concerns with social sign and sexual manipulation, to an increasingly sentimental kind of moralism, and finally, at the end of the 18c, asserting claims of moral authority.

991 TOMLINSON, Richard S. "Pornography and propaganda: personal libel and revolution." *EER* 1:2 (Winter 1991): 181-96.

By the time of the Revolution, the French had used the pornographic pamphlet to develop a political mythology which echoed one theme: the despotism of the ancient order was the certain fruit of its moral malignancy. While much more than this was required to bring down the most absolute monarchy in Europe, the events of 1792 would have been unlikely without the propagandists who used pornography during the 18c to strip it of its sacramental legitimacy. The Bourbons who came after the Sun King failed, much like the *philosophes* of the Enlightenment, to respond to foulest smut directed against them. Nothing suggests that such a climate existed in the England of the 1790s.

992 TSCHACHER, Walter G. "Orte der Literaturkritik in der Frühaufklärung: London - Zürich - Leipzig." Unpub.doct. diss., Univ. of Wisconsin-Madison, 1990. [*DAI* 50:12 (1991): 3968A.]

Investigates the *Tatler* and the *Spectator* and their influence on *Die Discourse der Malern* and *Der Biedermann*.

993 TUCKERMAN, Bayard. *A history of English prose fiction from Sir Thomas Malory to George Eliot.* New York: G. P. Putnam & Sons, 1882, 1891; pp. 332.
General discussion of the development of prose fiction through its different periods. Ch. 5 looks at the Restoration and early 18c, with consideration of Aphra Behn and Mary Manley (112-55). Index (329-32).

994 TUMBLESON, Raymond Dana. "Catholicism in the Protestant imagination: nationalism, religion, and literature in seventeenth- and eighteenth-century England." Unpub. doct. diss., Univ. of Washington, 1993. [*DA* 55 (1994): 286A.]

Analyzes anti-Catholic rhetoric in the 17c and 18c, surveying a broad range of familiar and obscure texts. Repeatedly, contending parties in religion and politics attempted to identify each other with the Catholic menace, until ultimately fear of Popery became a principal guarantor of Enlightenment oligarchism. Investigates neglected relationships between poetry and prose, religion and polemic. The threat of Catholicism is Marvell's political bogeyman, Milton's sinister stand-in for Anglicanism, Dryden and Swift's "error", and finally Defoe and Fielding's "enemy of an imperial domestic virtue".

995 TURNER, Cheryl. *Living by the pen: women writers in the eighteenth century.* London and New York: Routledge, 1994; pp. ix, 261.

Based on a substantial listing of novels, authors and publication details from 1696 to 1796, traces the pattern and growth of women's fiction and offers an explanation for the remarkable rise of women authors during this period. Explores esp. dealings with the world of publishing, looking at 17c antecedents, the occupational structure for women, writers' relationships with their publishers, methods and levels of payment, readership, access to women's fiction through libraries and magazines, use of other genres to support literary careers. Contains very important statistical figures, a catalogue of women's fiction published in book form between 1679 and 1796 (152-211) and a chronological list of women authors (212-14). Bibliographical notes (215-33). Bibliography (234-48). Index (249-61).

996 TURNER, James Grantham. "Sex and consequence." *Rev* 11 (1989): 133-37.

Review article, investigating books on sexuality and the Enlightenment (Alice BROWNE, *The eighteenth-century feminist movement*; ROUSSEAU and PORTER, *Sexual underworlds of the Enlightenment*; Peter WAGNER, *Eros revisited: Erotica of the Enlightenment*). New social history tries to rescue sexuality from the realm of biology, or invariable 'human nature', and establish it as a phenomenon that varied in time and place. Did sexuality change in the 18c between the Age of Libertinism and the Age of Sensibility? Sex must never be studied in isolation, but always in its complex relationship to discourse (ideas, languages, representations, genres, conventions) and to society, a society mapped out by power, divided into underworlds and dominant groups, peripheries and centers. 18c women's voices generated a welcome debate because they spoke on both sides of the discussion of sexual freedom. Scholars neglect the complex relationship between high and low culture, the 'secret nexus' between canonical literature and libertine or scandalous texts.

997 TURNER, Margaret. "A note on the standard of English translations from the French, 1685-1720." *NQ* 199 new ser. 1 (1954): 516-21.

Examines translations from the French during this period, and concludes that the public was indifferently served. Many translators provided barely tolerable versions of the works they attempted. Yet the public was ready to buy their works, which illustrated the extent of English interest in contemporary French literature.

998 TYLER, Paula Eyrich. "Fiction as wisdom: the moral heritage of the eighteenth-century English novel." Unpub. doct. diss., Texas Christian Univ., 1986. [*DA* 47 (1987): 3052A.]

Studies genuine moral values in the early 18c novel, focusing on the narrative voice in Defoe's *Robinson Crusoe* and Richardson's *Pamela*. In spite of genetic explanations, this concentrates on the moral intentions of 18c literature. This wisdom of the detached narrator, praised in Jane Austen, has been overlooked in these two novels where there is a simple ethos drawn from English pragmatic philosophy, which is also conveyed in the characters' attempts at being analytical, self-controlled and discerning.

999 TYTLER, Graeme. *Physiognomy in the European novel: faces and fortune.* Princeton, NJ; Guildford: Princeton UP, 1982; pp. xx, 436.

Investigates the subject of physiognomy, esp. familiar to students of literature because of the abundance of reference to it in 18c and 19c fiction. Lavater's theories (and those of his successors) have had a more obvious relevance to the development of modern literary portraiture than much physiognomical theory of the Classical, Medieval, and Renaissance eras. Looks at the historical background (3-122) and the literary background (123-315). Notes (323-92). Select bibliography (393-420). Index (421-36). Illus. (17 plates).

1000 UPHAUS, Robert W. *The impossible observer: reason and the reader in eighteenth-century prose.* Lexington: Kentucky UP, 1979; pp. 168.

Investigates prose and its readership by looking at Swift and the problematical nature of meaning, Mandeville and the force of prejudice, Defoe and dissimulation, as well as aspects of Richardson, Fielding, Johnson, Sterne, Godwin. Bibliographic notes (143-56).

1001-----(ed.). *The idea of the novel in the eighteenth century.* London: Colleagues Press, 1988; pp. x, 143.

The six essays address two interrelated questions: how was the novel conceived, read and understood in the 18c? What kind of critical approach or methodologies (new and traditional) lead to a better understanding of the idea(s) of the novel in the 18c? Considers fashion and the force of example; story and its reform in the 18c; the novel and society (Daniel Defoe); the dilemmas of gender; the language of 'real feeling'. The 18c novel features an enormous diversity of social representations, and individual books present a varied canvas in which comic chaos seems a deliberate parody of orderly plenitude. That same ambiguity as Hogarth depicted seems to operate in 18c fiction. Bibliographic notes. Index (141-43).

1002 UTTER, Robert Palfrey. "Studies in the origins of the English novel: with special reference to the influence of the periodical essay." Unpub. doct. diss, Harvard Univ., 1906. Abstract not available.

1003-----and NEEDHAM, Gwendolyn Bridges. *Pamela's daughters.* London:

Lovat Dickson Ltd., 1937; pp. xiii, 512.

Study and analysis of the diverse species of heroines in English fiction. "If every woman in life is a daughter of Eve, so is every heroine in fiction a daughter of Pamela. If Eve were alive today, we should rejoice to analyze her soul, mind, and body, as a basis for a biological and psychological study of her daughters" (1). Considers *Pamela* and its effect, the love plot with economic obstacles, the heroine's fear of men, the history of gloom, family, and the figure of fashion, the delicate air, the old maid, Clarissa: her story and its lesson, the virtuous working girl, Victorianisms, impulses on the 20c scene. Notes (481-91). Index (493-512).

1004   VAIL, Marilyn Irene. "Transformations of narrative structure in relation to the role of the female protagonist in the 18c novel." Unpub. doct. diss., Cornell Univ., 1978. [*DA* 39 (1978): 313A.]

Investigates the role of the female protagonist in relation to the transformations of narrative structure. Considers Defoe's *Moll Flanders* (1722), Prévost's *Manon Lescaut* (1731), Tencin's *Mémoirs du Comte de Comminge* (1735), Marivaux's *La Vie de Marianne* (1742) and Diderot's *La Religieuse* (1760). These texts attest to the disintegration of the romantic solution and of the prosperity of a fundamentally paternal, masculine authority. Nameless and unclassified, the female protagonist bears no relationship to a father: she lacks money, power, lineage, land, resources. Unable to progress beyond the limitations of her sex, the female-loser status, she seeks immanence, comfort, sympathy, abundance, a return to maternal care. Mme de Lafayette had already treated the inevitability of unhappiness and the retreat which follows on the failure of the romantic adventure.

1005   VALLONE, Lynne. *Disciplines of virtue: Girls' culture in the eighteenth and nineteenth centuries.* New Haven, CT, and London: Yale UP, 1995; pp. x, 230.
The girl's journey from marriageable to married, maiden to matron, is the focus and fascination of many literary texts in the 18c and 19c. Explores this moment of concentrated attention from the angle of cultural critique, refocusing on the significance of aestheticized girls' culture. Investigates girlhood with the evidence supplied by 18c and 19c British and American literature, conduct manuals, conduct novels written to guide and reform, religious tracts, institutions for 'girlhood gone wrong', including 18c asylums for penitential prostitutes, and rescue houses in late 19c America, the social and legal practices such as the dowry system that allowed for economic transfer of value. It is also a book about much-

loved girl characters: depicts girls falling into adulthood with all its sexual, commercial and social concerns. Notes (159-210). Bibliography (211-26). Index (227-30).

1006 VANDE BERG, Michael James. "The struggle between oral and script cultures and its effect on narrative development." Unpub. doct. diss., Univ. of Illinois at Urbana-Champaign, 1984. [*DA* 45:11 (1985): 3345A.]

Several 18c and 19c narrative techniques are manifestations of the last stages of an oral culture: the rise and fall of intrusive narrators, mock readers, rhetorical typography, and epistolary fiction. The appearance of free indirect style and multiple narration within individual works marks the victory of script culture.

1007 VAN DEN VEEN, H. R. S. *Jewish characters in eighteenth-century English fiction and drama*. Groningen, 1935. Rpt. USA: Ktav Publishing House, 1973; pp. 474.

Preceded by Edgar ROSENBERG, "Tabloid Jews and Fungoid Scribblers" (1972) (7-88), which has notes on the 18c drama. The Introduction (89-99) sets the scene, and discusses previous research and bibliography. Part I "Prose Writers and the Jews" has the important ch.1 "The Early Eighteenth Century Prose Writers" (99-116). This examines contributions by Addison, Defoe, Shaftesbury, Swift, Pope and Fielding - but incredibly not Eliza Haywood (*The Fair Hebrew*, 1729). "The share which Defoe had in the literary persecution of the Jews is considerable. The influence of *Roxana* [...] in which he paints a Jew in the blackest colors [...] is difficult to estimate" (99-100). Other chapters deal with Smollett, and later 18c novelists, Cumberland and the Humanitarian movement. Part II is devoted to "The Dramatists and the Jews". There are extensive appendices, esp. III (Jews in a checklist of English and continental plays, 1769 to 1815) (447-52) and IV (Jews and the Enlightenment: some 18c documents from Locke to Goethe (453-57). Bibliography (57-60). Index (461-74).

1008 VAN GHENT, Dorothy. *The English novel: form and function*. New York: Holt, Reinholt & Winston, 1953; pp. xi, 276.

Surveys the history of the English novel, with essays on prominent works. The introd. (3-7) discusses the judgement and evaluation of novels. The early 18c is represented by *Moll Flanders* (33-43). Discusses Defoe's use of realism, irony, emotional variety, criminality and the moral sermon. Concludes that the book is more than a patchwork of scandal-sheet anecdotes, indeed a great novel, coherent in structure, shaped and nuanced by a complex system of irony.

1009   VAN SANT, Ann Jessie. *Eighteenth-century sensibility and the novel: the senses in social context.* Cambridge, New York and Victoria: Cambridge UP, 1993; pp. xv, 1993.

Discusses literary representations of suffering and responses to it in the social and scientific context of the period. Defines and discusses the concept of 'sensibility' and the related terms sentiment/sentimental and delicacy, centering first on sight, secondly on touch. Looks at philanthropic organizations, pathetic and investigative observation of suffering, *Clarissa* as a pathetic narrative and experiment in sensibility; touch as resulting from sensationalist epistemology and psychology; the body of the man of feeling, a 'feminized and physiological body'; the implication of readers' reports of their reading; an understanding of the cultural significance of sensibility in examination of the physical; scientific in relation to various traditional elements: the rhetorical strategy for creating pity; problems of traditional narratives of suffering; physiologically based ways of describing psychological responses. Footnotes. Bibliography (126-36). Index (137-43).

1010   VAN TIEGHAM, Paul. "La sensibilité et la passion dans le roman européen au 18e siècle." *RLC* 6 (1926): 424-35.

In French. Explores the religious, moralizing and educational origins of the sentimental novel during the 18c. Sentiment was first used as a moral addition, as an expression of virtue, then cultivated for itself as a sign of the beautiful soul. Next came egoistical sentiment, then passion, the heavy burden of moralism, the social and moral problems, the exultation of passionate solutions, the reflection of a proud and desolated soul. From this sentimental form emerged the modern novel of the family and the individual, psychological and social, devoted to the study of conscience or a moral conflict. The psychological-sentimental novel of the 18c, disengaged from the novel of adventure, of gallant heroism and of bourgeois realism, opened up a way to the modern novel. The sentimental element further opened the way to romantic passion, and widened the capacity for expressing tenderness, emotion and the pathetic, in short sensibility and passion.

1011-----"Le roman sentimental en Europe de Richardson à Rousseau." *RLC* 20 (1949): 129-51.

In French. Looks at the history of the novel from the appearances of *Pamela* (1740) to that of *La Nouvelle Héloïse* (1761), tracing most esp.

the place of sentiment in the psychological analysis and the moral teaching offered by the authors concerned. Even if the term 'preromantic' is not justified, it nevertheless concerns literary attitudes which Romanticism would only accent further. Discusses the importance of Richardson, the situation in England (131-36), in Germany (136-40), in France (140-51).

1012 VARANKA, Dalia. "Editorial and design principles in the rise of English world atlases, 1606-1729." Unpub. doct. diss., Univ. of Wisconsin-Milwaukee, 1994. [*DA* 55 (1995): 2948-9A.]

Summarizes research on the rise and transformation of the English world atlases in the 17c and 18c. The analysis of atlases was done in view of two major intellectual transitions in scientific thought and the way knowledge was presented. Corresponding changes in style have been identified as ranging from Elizabethan to a plain utilitarian style. The philosophy of change rooted in the broader social context can be seen in atlas maps as well - a transformation from 'art' to 'science', although both styles were ones of realism. This view was identified in the close contemporary ties between geography and astronomy. During the transition into the modern era, text was dropped from the atlas in recognizable layers. Important for the background to the themes of exploration and the imaginary voyage.

1013 VAREY, Simon. *Space and the eighteenth-century English novel.* (Cambridge Studies in Eighteenth-Century English Literature and Thought 7.) Cambridge: Cambridge UP, 1990; pp. xi, 220.

Studies space in 18c Britain. Falls into three sections: 1) conceptions of space expressed mainly by architects and writers about architecture, as well as divine design by philosophers and theologians; 2) spatial thinking in practice, in the city of Bath; 3) spatial concepts in the major novels of Defoe, Richardson and Fielding. Andrea Palladio interpreted Vitruvius's *De Architectura* for the modern Western world (1570). Attempts to locate in contemporary spatial discourse some of the most important and popular writing which have been considered important in the 20c. Considers narrative as spatial design; the language of architecture used to describe people; the exploitation of personal spaces (such as experiences of imprisonment, isolation and alienation); the constitutive control of human activity that occurs when a particular function is assigned to a social space. Spaces created by architects and novelists express specific ideology and are therefore political. For one who resents the pressure to conform, as for one who does not, the self is defined space. Index (209-20). Illus. (16 plates).

1014   VAUGHAN, Alden T. "Early English paradigms for New World natives."
       PAAS 102:1 (1992): 33-67.

Unfortunately for the colonial experience in general and the Indians in
particular, the initial Old World reaction to the 'untreated strangeness' of
the New World was to demonize it, applying pejorative paradigms - wild
men or monsters - to its inhabitants. The countertrend, which saw
America as a Garden of Eden and the natives as undefiled primitives,
was to lie fallow until resurrected by the 18c *philosophes*. The paradigms
often reinforced the Europeans' own expectations and, in their eyes,
justified conquest and conversion.

1015   VERMILLION, Mary. "Capricious testators and marriageable women: Last
       wills in eighteenth-century novels." Unpub. doct. diss., Univ. of Iowa,
       1993. [*DA* 55 (1994): 579A.]

Considers the relationship between the 18c English novel and inheritance
practices. The last will and testament is an important genre for the
development of the novel. Richardson, Burney, Smith, Hays, and
Inchbald contributed to the legal reformation of aristocratic inheritance.
Novels that portray the conflicts between male will-makers and
marriageable women revise literary and legal practices that concern
property, and identify through time and great individual men the power
to impose their wills on women, children and succeeding generations.
Only the Marriage Act and the Thelluson Act (1800) promoted a freer
circulation of property that championed the rights of the living over wills
of the dead.

1016   VICKERY, Amanda. *The gentleman's daughter: women's lives in
       Georgian England.* London and New York: Yale UP, 1998; pp. xi, 436.

Presents letters, diaries, and accounts books of over 100 individuals from
commercial, professional, and gentry families, a group one could call
'genteel'. The central focus is the hopes and fears of the women of these
families, the merchants' daughters, the solicitors' wives, gentlemen's
sisters. Offers a narrative of decline and fall, using women's manuscripts
to illustrate a tale of increasing female passivity and ever-tightening
domestic encirclement. The experience of Elizabeth Shackleton (1726-
1781) dominates the book because of the richness of her manuscripts,
unparalleled in range and detail, esp. the 39 diaries she wrote (1762-
1781) which document her life over a 19-year period. Looks at gentility,
love and duty, fortitude and resignation, private economy, elegance,
civility and subjectivity, property. Select bibliography (397-414). Illus.
(66 plates). Index (418-36).

1017   VON MÜCKE, Dorothea. *Virtue and the veil of illusion: generic innovation and the pedagogical project in eighteenth-century literature.* Stanford, CA: Stanford UP, 1991; pp. xiii, 331.

Beginning with primers and collections of fables, books in the second half of the 18c sought a much closer fusion of reading and seeing, beyond the traditional decorative vignettes or allegorical pictures as frontispieces. Rousseau was the great theorist of the new pedagogy, and chose Gravelot to illustrate *Julie*, giving him detailed instructions for the 12 plates which follow the narrative closely. This marked a new approach to book illustrations, one in which the pictures collaborate with the reader's imaginary involvement in their fiction. Such pictures frequently exceeded their specific relevance to the plot, encapsulating 'primal scenes' for the mid-18c cultural program of combining literary practice and moral improvement. Looks at the project of *Anschaulichkeit* in the mid-18c, the epistolary novel and bourgeois tragedy, Rousseau, *Bildung* in German Classicism and neo-humanism, Classical tragedy and the *Bildungsroman*. Notes (277-316). Bibliography (317-26). Index (327-31). Many illus.

1018   WACKWITZ, Beate. *Die Theorie des Prosastils im England des 18. Jahrhunderts.* Hamburg: Cram, de Gruyter & Co., 1962; pp. 184.

In German. Provides a systematic survey, looking at the foundations of 18c prose style (Swift, Addison, Steele, Shaftesbury, Pope, Chesterfield), educational writing (Hume, Edwards, Temple, Shenstone, Sheridan, Baker), Samuel Johnson on his own, conflict of opinion, systematizers (Ogilvie, Campbell, Knox, Blair), critical retrospective. Bibliography (178-84).

1019   WADE, Toshihide. *Igirisu 18 seiki shosetsu ron.* Tokyo: Kaibun, 1987; pp. xx, 304.
In Japanese. Essays on 18c British novels.

1020   WAGENKNECHT, Edward. *Cavalcade of the English novel.* New York: Holt, 1943; rev. ed. New York: Holt, 1954; pp.686.

Survey of the history of the English novel. Rpt. has minor corrections and supplementary bibliography (620-60).

1021   WAGNER, Peter. *Eros revived: erotica of the Enlightenment in England and America.* London: Secker & Warburg, 1988; pp. 498.

Historico-sociological survey of erotica and pornographic literature in the late 17c and 18c. Sees the 18c as the turning point in the history of erotica. Shows the whole spectrum of bawdy, obscene, erotic and pornographic works that flourished during the Enlightenment, comprising not merely fiction, poetry, and drama, but also scientific treatises, para-medical works, satire and erotic art. Uses over a hundred illustrations to reveal not only the sexual art of the times, but the society it reflected, and the telling effect they had on the economic and political thought and deeds of the time. Shows what was found erotic, the reasons for pornography, the riotous flourishing during these years, and why France was seen as the source of so much sexual invention and scurrility. Ch. 7 "Erotic Prose" (201-62) is of particular pertinence, covering short prose fiction and the novel (the erotic novel, the French erotic novel, the amatory novel and *chronique scandaleuse*, the whore biography, the pornographic novel, erotic magazines and plays). Illus. (93 plates). Bibliographic notes (321-88). Extended bibliography (bibliographies, histories, anthologies, book catalogues, sources and critical materials) (390-478). Index (478-98).

1022 WALKER, Marshall. *Scottish literature since 1707.* (Longman Literature in English.) London and New York: Longman, 1996; pp. xvi, 443.

Discusses Scottish literature in English and Scots from 1707, the year of new beginnings for Scotland. From then on, Scottish Calvinism was compounded by paranoia; Scotland has either acknowledged England's supremacy in a nominal Britain, or resented forces which seemed to have sabotaged an ancient nation, and has functioned in terms of awareness that it is peripheral to the cultural and economic center of the union. Scottish female sensibility has been doubly peripheral, marginalized by both place and sex. For the 18c, looks at patriotism and change: Scottish identity and tradition, Union and Enlightenment; satire, sentiment and the Scots. Very extensive chronology (351-82), general bibliography (383-96) which covers: 1) bibliographical and reference guides; 2) literary, historical and cultural backgrounds; 3) history and criticism; 4) anthologies; 5) individual authors (notes on biographies, major works and criticism) (399-436). Index (437-43).

1023 WARD, A. W. and WALKER, A. R. *The Cambridge history of English literature.* 14 vols. Cambridge: Cambridge UP, 1912; Vol. 9, *From Steel and Addison to Pope and Swift*; pp. xv, 609.

Ch. 1 "Defoe - The Newspaper and the Novel" (1-25) gives an account of Defoe's life and work, and briefly considers his 'Evolution as a Novelist' (19-22). No reference is made to any other developments or figures in early 18c English fiction. Bibliographies (486-574). Table of Principal Dates (575-78). Index of Names (579-609).

1024 WARNER, William B. and McKEON, Michael (reply). "Realist literary history: McKeon's new origins of the novel." *Diacritics* 19:1 (Spring 1989): 62-96.

The origins of the novel is evidence of a vast and decisive modern cultural shift from aristocratic to middle-class norms and audience. The affinity of Marxist thinkers and critics (like Marx and Engels, Lukács and Bakhtin, Watt and Jameson) demonstrates the way the novel anticipates at a cultural level those achievements towards which Marxism aspires at the level of knowledge and politics. Reading McKeon suggests a social role for the novel which requires terms and oppositions outside those he develops.

1025 WARNER, William B. "The social ethos of the novel: McKeon's not so social allegory of the novel's origins." *Criticism* 32:2 (Spring 1990): 24-53.

Power has become the politically urgent question to which ethics, epistemology, sexuality and aesthetics are subjected and referred. For McKeon, the years 1600 to 1740 mark the boundaries of that early modern period where the novel and other concomitants of modernity originate.

1026-----"Taking dialectic with a grain of salt: a reply to McKeon. *Diacritics* 19:1 (Spring 1990): 104-07.

Seeks to rescue many valuable findings of McKeon's literary history from the confining dialectical method which structures and defends it.

1027-----"Social power and the eighteenth-century novel: Foucault and transparent literary history." *ECF* 3:3 (April 1991): 185-203.

McKeon and Damrosch have demonstrated the serious and responsible role played by the novel in the early modern crisis of secularization. McKeon's study allows the novel to be understood as narrative practice which enables the cultural agency of its practitioners and readers. By contrast, Armstrong and Bender, thinking of social power along the lines provided by Foucault, describe the insidious fashion in which the novel promotes systems of social control.

1028 WASSERMAN, Earl R. (ed.). *Aspects of the eighteenth century.* Baltimore: The Johns Hopkins UP; London: Oxford UP, 1965; pp. 346.

Various essays examine the Age of Reason; the malleability of man in 18c thought; Herder and the Enlightenment; the concept of Classicism;

Diderot and historical painting; imitation, eclecticism and genius; taste, style and ideology in 18c music; uses of retirement by Pope; the English poet and the burden of the past (1660 to 1820); knowledge and science (Goethe and *Faust*); the Enlightenment and the French Revolution; divergent loyalties to Newton in the 18c. Georges MAY, "The Influence of English Fiction on the French Mid-Eighteenth-Century Novel" (265-80) observes that " [...] the most truly beneficial effect of the English novel in France was that it added its tremendous weight to the scale which was then only slowly tipping in favor of the novel genre" (280). Index (335-46).

1029   WATSON, George. *The story of the novel.* New York: Barnes & Noble, 1979; pp. xiii, 166.

A poetics of the novel, very pertinent for the chapters on memoirs, letters and dialogue. Considers titles and devices, beginnings and endings, tense and time, history in its place, scene-making, how novelists write. Provides notes for further reading and a glossary of European terms.

1030   WATSON, H. F. *The sailor in English fiction and drama, 1550-1800.* New York: Columbia UP, 1931; pp. 241.

Of particular relevance is ch. 6 "The Sailor in Fiction: 1600-1760" (98-134): "[...] the maritime novel of the hundred years following the Restoration, regardless of minor variations, such as [Brunt's] *A Voyage to Cacklogallinia*, remained close to the model set by the narratives of real voyages. That these did provide the standard is indicated not only by similarities of technique, such as the journal method of telling the story, but in most cases by the actual borrowing of details and phraseology. With Fielding and Smollett came a different method of presentation, leading to more stress on character and the inclusion of a different kind of sailor" (133-34). Notes (204-19). Bibliography (220-30). Index (231-41).

1031   WATT, Ian. "The naming of characters in Defoe, Richardson and Fielding." *RES* 25 (1949): 322-38.

In most fiction until the 18c, names used were quite different from those used in real life, artificial and conventional designations suited to half-generalized types of the romance and the pastoral. It was only in the later developments of fiction - the professedly non-fictional "true histories" and biographical memoirs - that names could possibly be mistaken for those of real people. Defoe's names for his heroes and heroines all sound real, but although realistic, are rarely the true, full, permanent name ratified by baptism and legal record (the exception being Robinson Crusoe). Defoe is esp. casual about naming his secondary characters. Apart from the 'I' of his autobiographical narratives, all Defoe's characters are treated as secondary, and almost without exception, lack the elementary requirement of a full name. His economy in the use of names is appropriate to the genre he promoted and the society he described. Richardson had no theoretical bias toward the representative. Fielding's use of names illutrates his interest as a novelist in those aspects of character that are representative of all mankind.

1032-----*The rise of the novel: studies in Defoe, Richardson and Fielding.* London: Chatto & Windus, 1957. Rpt. Harmondsworth: Penguin, 1963; pp. 319.
Ties the emergence of the English novel to that of the middle class, and to 18c philosophical and political currents of empiricism and individualism. Detailed links are drawn between the formal characteristics of early novels and these social and philosophical ideas. There is extensive treatment of Defoe, Richardson and Fielding, with contextual density of historical, intellectual and sociological scholarship. Index (303-19).

1033-----*Myths of modern individualism: Faust, Don Quixote, Don Juan, Robinson Crusoe.* Cambridge and New York: Cambridge UP, 1996; pp. xiv, 293.
Examines four myths of the modern world, all created in the 16c to 18c as distinctive products of a historically new society. All four figures reveal the problems of individualism in the modern period: solitude, narcissism, and the claims of the self versus the claims of society. None of them marries, or has lasting relations with women; rather each has as his closest friend a male servant (Mephistopheles, Sancho Panza, Catalinan, Friday), who are devoted to the end to their subordinate role - the perfect personal servant. Each figure embodies self-centeredness, and pursues his own view of what he should be, raising strong questions about his character as a hero, and about the society whose ideals he reflects. The initial unflattering portraits of Faust (1587), Don Quixote (1605), and Don Juan (1620) were re-created in the Romantic period as admirable, even heroic. Robinson Crusoe (1719) is seen as representative of the new religious, economic, and social attitudes. Footnotes. Index (285-93).

1034 WEBB, Igor. *From custom to capital: the English novel and the Industrial Revolution.* Ithaca, NY; London: Cornell UP, 1981; pp. 219.

The novel, esp. written between 1780 and 1850, is necessarily an expression of a response to the Industrial Revolution, demonstrating a fundamental interconnection between social consciousness and forms of fiction. The 17c saw the emergence of the scientific method and mentality fundamental to the industrial developments and economies of the 18c.

1035 WEBER, Donna-Lee. "Fair game: rape and sexual aggression on women in some early eighteenth-century novels." Unpub. doct diss., Univ. of Toronto, 1980. [*DA* 42 (1981): 233A.]

Considers novels by Penelope Aubin, Jane Barker, Mary Davys, Eliza Haywood, Mary Manley. Rape and sexual aggression on women are common themes and circumstances in 18c prose fiction. Investigates the crime, social and legal attitudes towards men and women, sexual mores and courtship behavior. Looks at 18c laws relating to rape, conduct books and moral treatises with prevailing moral codes, and literary portrayal of the theme in works of the five popular female novelists writing in the early 18c. Various attitudes are discussed towards portrayal of men, women and social violence. Appendix recording 18c reports on rape. Attempts to clarify often contradictory ideas both in fiction and real life informing these themes.

1036 WEHRS, Donald Roger. "Irony and story: the emergence of the realistic novel, 1740-1829." Unpub. doct. diss., Univ. of Virginia, 1986. [*DA* 48 (1988): 2638A-9A.]

The relationship between 18c and 19c fiction becomes explicable when one views the novel as shaped by a conscious effort to reconcile ironic suspicion of the evidence of experience, with a story whose 'truth' derives from a fictional representation of experience. Richardson and Fielding created stories whose events and characters would appear 'as if they were 'historical'. They attempt to legitimize morality by demonstrating that a 'realistic' observation of experience discloses a moral, providential order, and this proves that a moral basis for irony arises 'naturally' from the course of everyday life.

1037 WEIMANN, R. "Erzählkunst und 'point of view': zu Geschichte und Ästhetik der Perspektive im englischen Roman." *ZAA* 10 (1962): 369-416.

In German. The nature of perspective in narration constitutes a central problem in both the history and aesthetics of the novel. The artistic form of the middle-class novel replaced the all-embracing 'we' of epic narration with individual consciousness, so constituting humanly significant and socially pertinent narrative personalities by means of exploratory perspectives, and ends with the destruction of such personalities. Eventually this means not only a loss of human perspective, but a retraction of humanism and the very destruction of the art of narrative.

1038-----"Romanheld und Wirklichkeit." *ZAA* 8 (1960): 254-71.

In German. Explores the gradual diminishment and withdrawal of the hero as an aspect of structural change in the modern English middle-class novel. Increase of subjectivity in the modern novel has meant the displacement of 'point of view', and has necessitated new modes of presentation (like 'stream of consciousness') which oppose narrative generalization and are aimed at the experience, rather than the acknowledgement, of reality.

1039 WEINSTEIN, Arnold. *Fictions of the self: 1550-1800*. Princeton: Princeton UP, 1981; pp. x, 302.

The novel offers a full interplay between person and setting. Each fiction is a drama of self-realization, a life story in which both the self and the fiction come of age. This study charts the interaction between the self and the world through four major stages: the self initially has marginal status (the picaresque) before it begins to flourish, tries to impose its will on society, and finally takes a prophetic inward turn. It is divided into sections: 1) the Marginal Self (*Lazarillo de Tormes, La Veda del Buscón, Simplicissimus, La Princesse de Clèves*); 2) Orphans (*Moll Flanders, La Vie de Marianne, Joseph Andrews*); 3) Collision (*Manon Lescaut, Die Leiden des Jungen Werthers, Clarissa, Les Liaisons dangereuses*); 4) the Life as Book (*Le Neveu de Rameau, Tristram Shandy, Les Confessions*). Notes of Original Languages (263-300). Index (301-2). Claims that Defoe's Moll "is one of the most fully realized individuals in literature" (85).

1040 WEISENHEIMER, Joel C. *Eighteenth-century hermeneutics: philosophy of interpretation in England from Locke to Burke*. New Haven, CT and London: Yale UP, 1993; pp. xii, 275.

18c Britain produced many thinkers from Locke to Burke who gave the problems of interpretation intense and fruitful scrutiny. Interpretive schisms from the Restoration to the mid-18c violently divided Deists from Dissenters, Anglicans from Catholics, High Churchmen from Low Churchmen, and gave the need to understand understanding a special urgency. The turmoil in biblical hermeneutics was merely the most evident manifestation of a much more widespread crisis in understanding that plagued and invigorated intellectual, political and all common life. Opens with Locke's epistemological denigration of hermeneutics, and ends with Burke's hermeneutic denigration of epistemology, exploring, through Gadamer's 'philosophical hermeneutics', Swift, Locke, Toland, Bolingbroke, Hume, Reid, Blackstone, and Burke. Notes (235-58). Bibliography (259-72). Index (273-75).

1041 WEITZMANN, Arthur Joshua. "The influences of the Middle East on English prose fiction, 1600-1725: an eighteenth-century perspective." Unpub. doct. diss., New York Univ., 1964.

Discusses how the 17c fable of Bidpai and French and English romances contributed to the taste for Oriental tales which became so popular in the early 18c.

1042 WENDORF, Richard. *The elements of life: biography and portrait-painting in Stuart and Georgian England.* Oxford: Clarendon Press, 1990; pp. xxi, 309, 41 plates.

Study of verbal and visual portraiture in the 17c and 18c, looking at representation of historical character, iconic biography, ironic pictures, brief lives and miniatures, double agents, Hogarth's dilemma, biography at mid-century (as conversion, romance and redemption), Reynolds and 'The Genius of Life', Boswell's Flemish picture.

1043 WESTON, Peter J. "Some images of the Primitive before 1800." *History of European Ideas* 1:3 (1981): 215-36.

For two centuries, the standard model for describing the natives of North America was the sentimental-exotic model from which grew the thread of potential radicalism implicit in the cult of the primitive in the 18c.

1044-----"The Noble Primitive as bourgeois subject." *Literature and History* 10 (1984): 59-71.

The progressive discovery by Europeans of the indigenous peoples of the Americas in the 16c and 17c was a significant part of the profound challenge to the Medieval Christian world view and the Renaissance. What was born of the cultural upheaval was the bourgeoisie: but the 'conception' was mediated by names, customs and illusions from earlier discourse of European history. The story of discovery is thus uneasy in its imperfect accomplishment: in the late 17c misrepresentation of the 'noble savage' was followed by the brutality of colonialism in the 18c, and marked *en route* by the sentimentalism of terror and nostalgia.

1045 WHEATLEY, Philip. "The form, meaning, and context of sensibility, in eighteenth-century Britain, with particular reference to the literature of the period 1740-94." Unpub. doct. diss., Univ. of Oxford, 1987. [*DAI* 51:5 (1990): 1624A.]

Explores the reasons for the practice of literary and intellectual history in the light of the application of the theories of Hans-Georg GADAMER, *Wahrheit und Methode* (1960); also explores the genealogy of sensibility. Passes through emergent (Medieval), ascendant (Renaissance), and critical (Enlightenment) stages. By reference to Locke, shows how the factors contributing to the development of 'individualism' - Protestantism, empiricism, the emergence of new financial and commercial practices - provide the characteristic language of sensibility. In Richardson the conflict between sensibility and power generated a 'critical' meaning for sensibility. Also looks at the problem of personal identity, and passion in relation to its psychological and political expression. There are connections between poetry, epistemology and the economics of commercial society. Sexuality within sensibility may generate a discourse which can transcend but not transform a dominant culture. Sensibility expressed a critical and finally pessimistic relationship between self and society in the middle of the 18c.

1046 WHITE, Robert B., Jr. (ed.). *The dress of words: essays in Restoration and eighteenth-century literature in honor of Richmond P. Bond*. Lawrence: Univ. of Kansas Libraries, 1978; pp. vi, 220.

Series of 14 essays looks at: 1) English Literature and Culture (justice and reconciliation [Milton], Pope's *Illiad*, Lady Mary Wortley Montagu, Defoe and 'doing good', dialetic and symbolism in Gulliver, Goldsmith and anti-sentimentalism, Stowe, Cowper and satire); 2) The Periodical (Able Boyer as Whig journalist, Dunton's *Post-Angel*, Steele and his answerers, Hawkesworth's *Adventurer*, late 18c spectatorial essays [William Roberts]). Bibliographic notes.

1047 WHITEFORD, Robert Naylor. *Motives in English fiction*. New York: Putnam, 1918; pp. 390.

Discusses the style and influence of major authors. Arranges the English novel from Malory to Mitford according to publication dates of first novels, presenting the material not only as a history of English fiction, but also as a view of its variations in atmosphere, motivation and characterization, to determine leading motives, distinctively English in origin, which were formative in the creative process. Ch. 2 "From Bunyan to Jonathan Swift" (52-85) and ch. 3 "Samuel Richardson, Henry

Fielding, Sarah Fielding and Tobias Smollett" (86-118) cover the period in question. Defoe is discussed by reference to his major novels (65-75), considering his moralizing and use of a vernacular style. Apart from fleeting reference to Manley and Haywood (88-89), the other novelists of this period are not treated. Haywood is seen as an imitator first of Manley and Defoe, and then of Richardson. Index (367-78).

1048 WICKLEIN, Ernst. *Das 'Ernsthafte' in dem englischen komischen Roman des 18. Jahrhunderts.* Inaugural dissertation, Univ. of Jena. Dresden: Max Emil Fischer, 1908; pp. 98.

Investigates the theme of high seriousness in the 18c novel: 1) Foundations of examination (the realistic novel in France in the 17c; the literary-critical approach of the *Spectator*; seriousness in the novels of Fielding, Smollett and Sterne); 2) Cervantes and the French realists of the 17c (Sorel, Scarron, Furetière, Le Sage); 3) Marivaux and the transformed presuppositions of the English novel 4) Smollett, Fielding and Sterne in relation to French theory and the *Spectator*; preface to *Roderick Random*; Fielding and the prose epic, his relation to Antiquity; Addison's essay on Milton; the critic's brief, the moral tendency in the epic and comic novel; the fable, characters, diction. "Eine enge Verbindung knüpft sich zwischen dem französischen Roman, dem *Spectator* und dem englischen Roman durch die Forderung der Darstellung lebenswahrer Charaktere" (98).

1049 WICKS, Ulrich. "Picaro, picaresque: The picaresque in literary scholarship." *Genre* 5 (1972): 153-92.

Investigates trends in scholarship on the picaresque tradition over 70 years. The term 'picaresque novel' still remains a problematic literary concept. It can be either an historico-literary phenomenon tied to a particular race, moment and milieu, or it can be a loose novelistic form. Surveys scholarship, finding dominant and sometimes overlapping trends. Looks at historically oriented approaches, and ahistorical trends, seeing picaresque fiction in terms of narrative forms and types in general (a generic and modal approach). Finds Claudio Guillén's genre study most helpful, distinguishing four interrelated topics: 1) the picaresque genre; 2) the picaresque in the strict historical sense; 3) the picaresque in the broader sense of the term; 4) picaresque myth, an essential situation or structure of meaning deriving from the novels themselves.

1050-----"The nature of picaresque narrative: a modal approach." *PMLA* 89 (1974): 240-49.

Establishes the characteristics of the picaresque narrative in terms of structure, character, point of view, protagonist, setting, types, parody, themes and motifs.

1051-----*Picaresque narrative, picaresque fictions: a theory and research guide.* New York; Westport, CT and London: Greenwood Press, 1989; pp. xvi, 367.

Describes picaresque narrative with careful attention to its historical development as a genre and its persistent appeal as an archetypal narrative structure; to propose a genre construction of generic awareness in the act of reading by describing a number of specific fictions that collectively illustrate the full narrative spectrum of the picaresque novel. Part I "A Theory of Picaresque Narrative" (1-84) looks at the picaresque genre, its presence in literary scholarship, the picaresque mode, the nature of the picaresque narrative, basic studies on picaresque narrative/works (69-84) [bibliographies, critical anthologies and collections, books and articles, genre theory, narrative technique, literary history and other related studies]. Part II "A Guide to Basic Picturesque Fictions" (85-352). Looks at a comprehensive series of works arranged alphabetically. Each chapter quotes from primary texts, with quotations from other critical sources, and lists its editions and own selected bibliography. Chronology of basic picaresques (353-55). Index (357-67).

1052 WILDEBLOOD, Joan. *The polite world: a guide to English manners and deportment from the thirteenth to the nineteenth centuries.* Oxford, New York and Toronto: Oxford UP, 1965; pp. xiv, 291.

Outlines the development of the English ideals of behavior, with descriptions of the homes and furniture which surrounded the polite world in order to illuminate the contemporary manners of each period. The central portion gives technical descriptions of the deportment and salutations in each period and the accompanying etiquette. Ch. 9 "The Eighteenth Century" (209-36). Illus. (16 plates). Illus. (12 figures). Index (281-91).

1053 WILES, Roy M. *Serial publication in England before 1750.* Cambridge: Cambridge UP, 1957; pp. xv, 391.

Surveys the history of periodical literature in ch. 1 and ch. 2, and then considers the earliest 'number books' (1678 to 1731) (35-194). Provides a List of Booksellers and Printers who took part in the production of number books before 1750 (Appendix C), and a bibliography (367-70).

1054 WILLEY, Basil. *The eighteenth-century background: studies in the idea of* *nature in the thought of the period.* London: Chatto, 1940; pp. viii, 302. Rpt. 1962.

Whereas for the 17c 'Truth' seemed the key word, in the 18c it was 'Nature'. Not an outline history of 18c thought in general, but an illustration of the importance of the idea of nature in religion, ethics, philosophy and politics, and an indication of some stages in the divinization of nature which culminates in Wordsworth. Considers the turn of the century, the wisdom of God in creation, cosmic Toryism, natural morality (Shaftesbury), natural morality (Joseph Butler), nature in satire, David Hume - defender of nature against reason, David Hartley and nature's education, Holbach's *Système de la Nature,* Joseph Priestley and the Socinian moonlight, nature in revolution and reaction, nature in Wordsworth. Index (292-302).

1055 WILLIAMS, Harold Herbert. *Two centuries of the English novel.* London: Smith, Elder & Co., 1911; pp. 340.

Ch. 1 "Prose Romance and the Birth of the Novel" (1-11) provides the briefest of introductions, with consideration of the picaresque novel and the contribution of the *Tatler* and the *Spectator.* Index (331-40).

1056 WILLIAMS, Ioan M. *The idea of the novel in Europe, 1600-1800.* London: Macmillan, 1979; New York: New York UP, 1979; pp. xii, 253.

During the 18c there was a chance of focus which brought the novel closer to the texture of individual and social experience. This change did not amount to the evolution of a new literary form, but rather the development of an existing one. The development of the novel through the previous 200 years in Europe may be seen as continuous though irregular. Traces this process by looking at 1) "The Novel as Romance: Cervantes' *Don Quixote*; 2) "After Cervantes: Romance and Reason in the 17c"; 3) "The Fall of Romance: the Development of French Fiction after 1670" (includes discussion of Le Sage's *L'Histoire de Gil Blas de Santelane*); 4) "Progress and Compromise: the Novel in England and France 1715-1758"; 5) "The Age of Rousseau, 1760-1800". Bibliography (242-49). Index of Names (250-51). Index of Titles (252-53). Ch. 3 (133-200) is of direct pertinence to the early 18c, and includes provocative critical essays on Le Sage, Marivaux, Defoe and Prévost (e.g. "Between Truth and Lie; the Problematic Case of Defoe", 146-53).

1057 WILLIAMS, Jeffrey James. "Narratives of narrative." Unpub. doct. diss., State Univ. of New York, Stony Brook, 1990. [*DAI* 51:11 (1991): 3760A.]

Delineates various poetic or formal features of several canonical novels in the English tradition (*Tristram Shandy, Joseph Andrews, Tom Jones, Wuthering Heights, Heart of Darkness* and *Lord Jim*) that are explicitly reflexive. The reflexive plot of narrating calls into question the hierarchical relation of plots and their referential or literal grounding in a narrator's statements, or in an assumed author's voice. Explicitly reflexive narratives "thematize the art of narrative, thereby signaling an allegorical narrative of narrative".

1058 WILLIAMSON, George. *The Senecan amble: a study in prose form from Bacon to Collier.* London: Faber & Faber, 1951; pp. 377.

This is not a history of prose style in the 17c, but an account of its most incisive pattern. As it deals with one of the extremes that serve to define contemporary styles, it becomes more than the story of a fashion. Ch. 11 "Pert Style in Neo-Classic Times" (336-70) is of direct bearing on 18c perceptions of prose style. This style discovers a mean between brevity and prolixity - the extremes of Seneca and Cicero. The relaxed Senecan style, which adopted a conversational form, prevailed after the Restoration. This style naturalized a pattern which English prose assumes from time to time, commonly with the impulse to brevity, or epigram, or smart expression. Index (371-77).

1059 WILSON, Kathleen. *The sense of the people: politics, culture and imperialism in England, 1715-1785.* (Past and Present.) Cambridge and New York: Cambridge UP, 1995; pp. xiv, 460.

Investigates how the politics and culture of 18c English cities came to occupy central roles in the political life of English towns between the Hanoverian Succession and the American War. Using provincial newspapers, prints, pottery, commemorative sculpture and parliamentary speeches, argues that the ideologies and practices of extra-parliamentary politics in provincial towns and London attuned ordinary men and women to the implications of state power and imperial expansion. Also defines the relationship between the state and the citizen in terms of gender, class, and racial differences. 'The sense of the people' thus came to mean a rational libertarian political public to which the state was held to be accountable, and an exclusionary conception of political subjectivity that shaped notions of national belonging into the 19c. Appendix (Women's Occupations) (441-42). Select Bibliography (443-49). Index (450-60).

1060 WILSON, Penelope. "'High Pindaricks upon stilts': a case-study in the eighteenth-century classical tradition." In (pp. 23-41) CLARKE, G. W. and EADE, J. C. (eds). *Rediscovering Hellenism: The Hellenic heritage* *and the English imagination.* Cambridge: Cambridge UP, 1989; pp. xiii, 264.

Traditionally the 18c has been represented as owing its classical allegiance to Rome rather than to Greece, but recent scholarship has also demonstrated the existence of a specifically Hellenic impulse in English culture throughout the so-called 'Augustan' period and contributed to a new awareness of the variety of classical impulses which went into the making of what was intellectually a notably eclectic age.

1061 WOLFE, Susan J. and PENELOPE, Julia (eds). *Sexual practice/textual theory: lesbian cultural criticism.* Oxford and Cambridge, MA: Blackwell, 1993; pp. xii, 388.

Nineteen essays explore the construction and deconstruction of Lesbian identity and voices in everyday life and within the complex framework of feminist, postfeminist, postmodern and poststructuralist theories. Essays divided into: 1) the need for lesbian feminist literary criticism; 2) texts as sources for a lesbian sense of self; 3) lesbian feminist (re-)visions of the canon; 4) (op-)positional aesthetics: creating lesbian culture(s). References (355-78). Index (379-88). Particularly pertinent is Diana L. SWANSON, "Subverting closure: compulsory heterosexuality and compulsory endings in middle-class British women's novels" (150-63). Examines the necessities of the marriage ending as a connecting thread through the middle-class British women's novels from the 18c to early 20c, a history of women writers making their way out of or across the closure demanded by the novel form itself. There have always been women who resisted male dominance and compulsory heterosexuality. Women have always told subversive stories directly or indirectly for us to search out and interpret. Action is in literary plot, and sentiment is centerd in female friendship. Also important is Linda GARBER and Vilashini COOPPAN, "An annotated bibliography of lesbian literary critical theory, 1970-1989" (340-54).

1062 WOLFF, Erwin. *Der englische Roman im 18. Jahrhundert: Wesen und Formen.* Göttingen: Vanderhoeck & Ruprecht, 1964; pp. 140.

In German. Survey by broad theme of the principal novelists of the 18c: 1) the world as "wilderness" and world allegory (John Bunyan); 2) the world as subject of experience (Daniel Defoe); 3) the social world as experience (Samuel Richardson); 4. the picaresque world and its transformation (Henry Fielding); 5) Fielding and the "world theater"; 6) the world as the ultimate instance of individual experience (Laurence Sterne); 7) the world as panorama (Tobias Smollett); 8) the ambivalence of the fabulous (Walpole, Dr Johnson, Goldsmith). These are essays with few notes, no bibliography, and no index.

1063 WOMACK, Peter. *Improvement and romance: constructing the myth of the Highlands.* Basingstoke: Macmillan, 1989; pp. xii, 211.

Describes the process whereby the formation of the Highland romance as an historical event began with the military defeat of the Jacobite clans in 1715 and 1746, and can be regarded as complete by 1810 to 1811 when several publications (esp. Scott's *The Lady of the Lake*) depended on and confirmed a settled cultural construction of the Highlands as "a romantic country" inhabited by a people whose ancient manners and customs were "peculiarly adapted to poetry". Looks at converting the uncouth savages, warriors, the land, ghosts, social tribes, holidays, the structure of the myth. Notes (181-206). Index (207-11).

1064 WONDERLEY, A. Wayne. "The concept of seclusion in German literature and its cultural background in the eighteenth century." *JEGP* 49 (1948): 245-65.

Seclusion was a poetic revery or mental attitude. Although seclusion was much spoken of, people did not seclude themselves physically: it was experienced mentally or emotionally. People sought seclusion to forget bitter reality. The experience could result in an aesthetic or philosophical contemplation of beauty and truth. It might lead to deeper appreciation of the value and dignity of human personality, or could assume the form of religious exaltation, contemplation of death and immortality, or of medicine and hypochondria.

1065 WOOD, Robin. "Solitary confinement: the criminal in popular literature." Unpub. doct. diss., Univ. of California (Berkeley), 1991. [*DAI* 52:4 (1992): 1346A.]

Studies criminal stories from the 18c to 20c. The treatment of criminals in popular literature reflects the way in which a culture deals with issues of criminality. Popular crime texts betray a fear that crime is both physically threatening and morally contagious. They attempt to silence the criminal voice and sequester the criminal. The success of this effort coresponds with society's efforts to apprehend the criminal and remove him from public gaze.

1066 WOODCOCK, George. "The deepening solitude: notes on the rebel in literature." *Malahat Review* 5 (Jan. 1968): 42-62.

Gives an overview of the rebel figure in literature from the 17c through the 20c. A new found individualism had followed the Reformation, and middle-class man began to forge his own literary forms: autobiography, biography, and novel, all concerned with the individual standing out from his world, rather than being contained within it.

1067 WORTH, C. G. "Techniques and uses of landscape description in the British novel, 1700-1830, with special reference to Scott." Unpub. doct. diss., Univ. of London (Birbeck Coll.), 1981. No abstract available.

1068 WRIGHT, Terence. "'Metaphors for reality': mind and object and the problem of form in the early novel." *DUJ* 38 (1977): 239-48.

The English novel began to evolve a special form in the 18c, a form related to man and his world. This is an empirical one, the world is known and observable from evidence drawn from everyday observations of reality. Metaphoric structures emerge from this empirical approach, which is examined in the relationship between mind and object in the work of Defoe (*Robinson Crusoe*) and Richardson (*Clarissa*). The English novel has never since dealt with human beings in such social nakedness as did Defoe with his prostitutes, castaways, criminals, lonely children and plague victims. This basic vision has made it impossible for many readers to accept Defoe's fiction as novels at all. Richardson is concerned with moral reflection, analysis and deduction as these problems face man in society, and such concerns have constituted one of the most important themes of English fiction. Richardson's concern with reflection meant that the balance shifted from the object to the mind that views it. Defoe refused to complicate his vision with such matters.

1069-----"The imperfect ideal of the novel." *MLR* 73 (1978): 1-16.

The real strength of the early novelists' work lay in their 'imperfect' , 'unideal' features. By missing the optimum, and being concerned with the casualness and triviality of life, they made 'unideal' features the speciality of realism, the aesthetic of 'the imperfect ideal'.

1070 WRIGHT, Walter Francis. *Sensibility in English prose fiction 1760-1814: a reinterpretation. Illinois Studies in Language and Literature* (Urbana) 22:3-4 (1937); pp. 158.

Examines the prose fiction of the later 18c, looking at the influences from the previous generation, the common emotions after 1760, nature and foreign influences, Sophia Lee, Charlotte Smith, Ann Radcliffe, terror and horror, sensibility in political and social philosophy. Bibliography (154-56). Index (157-58).

1071   WÜRZBACH, Natascha. "Die Struktur des Briefromans und seine Entstehung in England". Unpub. doct. diss., Munich, 1964.

See ANTHOLOGIES, Ch. 2, **149**.

1072------"Wandlung in der Struktur der englischen Prosaerzählung vor Defoe (Ein Beitrag zur Entstehungsgeschichte des Romans)." *Die Neueren Sprachen* 17 (1968): 585-601.

Wherever a greater number of narrative forms exist as opposed to the form transmitted, there occurs a greater attempt at justifying the veracity of what is narrated. It is in this respect particularly that the novel before Defoe, which has been too little regarded, made its by no means negligible contribution to the development of the English novel.

1073   WYNNE, Edith Jane. "Good nature and prudence: Moral concepts of character in eighteenth-century fiction." Unpub. doct. diss., North Texas State Univ., 1976. [*DA* 37 (1976): 3658A.]

To appreciate the ethical dimension inherent in the literature of the 18c, it is necessary to understand the moral bias of an author, a bias best ascertained by a study of the treatment he accords good nature and prudence. Establishes the significant guides to these concepts in later 17c by theologians, esp. Latitudinarians and the Cambridge Platonists (Barrow, Collier, Clarke, Butler, Tillotson). These theologians influenced ethical philosophy. Further, interpretation of good nature and prudence by Locke, Shaftesbury, Hutcheson and Hume is explored, as it is in the periodicals (Addison and Steele). The birth of the novel is studied as a response to the demands of a middle-class reading public for moral and social institutions presented in an entertaining context. The novel in fact emerges as a book of ethics.

1074   YANG, Yu-Mi. "The novelistic anomaly: origins of modernity's narrative forms." Unpub. doct. diss., Univ. of California (Santa Cruz), 1996. [*DA* 57 (1997): 4385A.]

Proposes to wrest the term 'origin' from essentialist usage and recast it in terms of the eccentric rhythm of *Ur-sprung* or 'originary leap' which gives rise to the twofold process of de-territorialization and re-territorialization marking the transitional situation. Unlike capital which proceeds by attacking and disclaiming the 'patriarchalist' symbolic link based on territorial integrity and hierarchical affective bonding, the novel functions to revitalize, recode, or override the 'de-territorialized ' flows, not by waging war against the patriarchal despot, but paradoxically by laying siege to and 're-territorializing' the bodies of women (Richardson's *Clarissa*) and of the colony (Defoe's *Robinson Crusoe*). The result is a new perverse tapestry on which the split between the imaging fantasy of the heterosexual masculine ego and the pure reason of the white capitalist superego is superseded by the 'phantasmatic opacity of the re-territorialized bodies'. The novel thus propels the modern symbolism of capitalism, "inexorably determining it as capitalistic patriarchy".

1075 YEAZELL, Ruth Bernard. "Podsnappery, sexuality and the English novel." *CI* 9 (1982): 339-57.

The intense effort not to talk about sex is really a mode of heightened attention to it, and the very insistence on silence is a form of the compulsion to transform sex into discourse.

1076 ZEITZ, Lisa Margaret. "The physico-theological tradition in eighteenth-century prose literature in English." Unpub. doct. diss., Queen's Univ. at Kingston (Ont.), 1987. [*DA* 48 (1988): 2017A.]

The range and variety of physico-theological traditions in prose literature has not been adequately appreciated. Demonstrates the importance of a knowledge of the tradition to both writers of the 18c and those who study them. Physico-theology appears in the prose fiction of the 18c in 3 contexts: as subject, as methodology (the employment of narrative "experimental method"), and as structure (through the active interventions of Providence in the plot). The clearest example of fiction employing natural theology are "desert island narratives" about children who acquire (independently) a knowledge of Nature and Nature's Creator.

1077 ZELLE, Carsten. "Ästhetischer Neronismus: zur Debatte über ethische oder ästhetische Legitimation der Literatur im Jahrhundert der Aufklärung." *DVLG* 63:3 (Sept. 1989): 397-419.

In German. The attitude of ethics and aesthetics were separated in the 18c Enlightenment as a result of reflections about the reasons for the pleasure deriving from terrifying subjects (d'Aguesseau, Dubos, Gottsched, Mendelssohn, Moritz). The interpretations of delightful horror as feeling of oneself anticipates the Nietzschean aesthetics. Valuable bibliographic notes.

1078 ZELLE. Hildegard. *Die Ich-Erzählung im englischen Roman.* (Sprache- und Kultur der germanischen und romanischen Völker, A14.) Breslau:

Priebatsch's Buchhandlung, 1933; pp. viii, 99.

Considers first-person narration as a formal element of epic presentation. Ch. 2 looks at the beginnings of this mode in English literature: the historical foundation, cultural situation and taste that gave rise to it (picaresque adventures, the Puritan sense of the self). Bibliography (97-99)

1079 ZIONKOWSKI, Linda Joan. "The value of words: writing and the eighteenth-century commerce in letters." Unpub. doct. diss., Northwestern Univ., 1988. [*DAI* 49:11 (1989): 3373A.]

Scholars have begun to investigate how structures of social and economic order shape textuality. The system of commodified print and authors' responses to that system help determine the course of literary practice in the first half of the 18c. While commercial publishing transformed literature by endowing it with exchange value, authors' awareness of this value enabled them to reimagine and restructure their craft. Moving from the opening years of the 18c to its middle decades, proposes a model for a materialist history of literature - one that examines debates and tensions shaping literary culture by viewing writing as it became a mode of commodity production.

1080 ZIPES, Jack. "The rise of the French fairy tale and the decline of France." In (pp. 1-12) *Beauties, beasts and enchantment* etc., **150**.

Provides a survey of the fairy tale, as it arose in the context of the growing political, social and economic stresses of Louis XIV's reign at the end of the 17c. Given the stringent censorship of the régime, the *conte de fée* served as a medium for venting criticism of the times while also projecting hope for a better world. "The salon tales were marked by the struggles within the upper classes for recognition, sensible policies, and power" (6). Examines the phenomenon of *préciosité*, and investigates the tale in its various generic guises: the salon fairy tale, the Oriental fairy tale, the comic and conventional fairy tale. The enduring captivation of these tales lies in an ability to rise above contemporary topicality to embrace the future. "They anticipate hopes and wishes that we ourselves have yet to fulfil" (12).

1081 ZOMCHICK, John Paul. "The public conscience: fictions of law, authority and personal identity in the later eighteenth-century novel." Unpub. doct. diss., Columbia Univ., 1985. [*DA* 48 (1988): 2017A.]

The law is a familiar subject of representation in the 18c novel. It is a social institution with which rogues and criminals must contend. Non-criminal protagonists must learn to govern their desires and impulses so that propertied independence can protect them from the worst effects of competition in a non-cooperative society. Examines plots of comic individualism (Smollett, Fielding, Goldsmith), tragic individualism (Richardson, Goldsmith), tragic individualism (Richardson, Godwin). All represent a dialectal relationship between fictional subjectivity and what Hobbes calls the "public conscience" in society's juridical authority. By demonstrating the necessity of subordinating social and individual passions to individual or familial interests, the legal institution offers a practical standard of behavior that humanizes the protagonist's newly acquired juridical calculus. Novelists tend to create metaphysical escape or nostalgic retreat as the ultimate response to the often cruel effects of social life.

1082-----*Family and the law in eighteenth-century fiction: the public conscience in the private sphere.* Cambridge, New York and Victoria: Cambridge UP, 1993; pp. xviii, 210.

Offers challenging new interpretations of the public and private faces of individualism in 18c English novel. Surveys the social, historical and ideological functions of law and family in 18c England's developing market economy. Examines in detail their part in the fortunes and misfortunes of the protagonists in novels by Defoe (*Roxana*), Richardson (*Clarissa*), Smollett (*Peregrine Pickle*), Goldsmith (*The Vicar of Wakefield*), Godwin (*Caleb Williams*). These novels attempt to produce a 'judicial subject': a representation of the individual identified with principles and aims of the law (esp. its respect for property), and motivated by an inherent need for affection and human community fulfilled by the family - which offers a motive for internalizing the law. A critique of the law emerges in a nostalgia for less competitive social relations and the law's operation in the service of elites. Bibliography (193-206). Index (207-10).

Part II

INDIVIDUAL AUTHORS
AND SPECIFIC WORKS
OF FICTION 1700-1740

4

Alphabetical List of Individual Authors, Titles, and Translations 1700-1740

ANONYMOUS

An account of some remarkable passages in the life of a private gentleman, with reflections thereon (1708, 1711, 1715 [as *An abstract of the remarkable passages*], pp. 304)

NCBEL II 985[17]; McBurney 31
Autobiographical; much realistic self-analysis; anticipates Defoe.

STUDIES

1083 STARR, G. A. *Defoe and spiritual autobiography.* Princeton, NJ: Princeton UP, 1965; pp. xiii, 203.

Suggests that Defoe in *Robinson Crusoe*, and to a lesser extent *Moll Flanders* and *Roxana*, is strongly influenced by a long tradition of spiritual autobiography. Focuses on those aspects of the genre that bear on Defoe, and investigates a number of different autobiographies to illustrate certain themes. Spiritual autobiography was the common property of English Protestantism. Ch. 2 "The Transition to Fiction" (51-73) closely examines *An Account of Some Remarkable Passages.* The Private gentleman suffers spiritual decay by casting off superior rule and guidance, paternal and divine. But he does not become entirely alienated from God, for it proves impossible to escape his omnipresence. Spiritual dissatisfaction is suggested in the language of physical distance, and indicates through bodily wandering that the hero is spiritually astray. The Private Gentleman, like all autobiographers before him, dwells at length on the spiritual significance of his every action, sometimes to the virtual exclusion of actual narrative. Defoe, on the other hand, by leading his hero through a series of conventionally meaningful activities, fuses a great deal of interpretation and comment into the narrative itself. Bibliographical footnotes. Index (199-203).

The adventures of Lindamira, a lady of quality (1702, 1703, 1713 [as *The lover's secretary*] etc., pp. 228)

NCBEL II 984[17]; McBurney 7; ECSTC 416A22
Epistolary domestic novel of excellent quality; ascription to Thomas Brown unjustified.

EDITIONS

1084　*The Adventures of Lindamira, A Lady of Quality*. Ed. Benjamin BOYCE. Minneapolis: U of Minneapolis P, 1949; pp. xvii, 167.

Introd. (v-xv) explores the origins of the novel, its background, its possible author, its style and structure. "For it is the social attitude and the moral tone of Lindamira as much as the story and form that make the book notable. There is an innocence of mind in our narrator, an ethical standard for herself and others that separate the book from [...] the fiction of Mrs. Behn and Mrs. Manley. Mme. de Scudéry may be partly responsible [...]" (x). As this "was a pioneering effort drawing on two kinds of literature, we need not be surprised to discover that the style is somewhat unsteady" (xi). Note on editing practice, books printed for the original publisher, S. Wellington. Fasc. title page. modernized text. Textual emendations (167).

STUDIES

1085　KLEIN in (pp. 278-79) *Der Briefroman in der englischen Literatur* etc., **569**.
Tabulates the epistolary exchange in *Lindamira*.

———

Amadis de Gaul (1665 [5th part]; 1702)

STC 541-2; ECSTC 946A1
Orig. trans. Anthony MUNDAY (1590-92/95) from the French *Amadis* (trans. Herberay des ESSARTS et al, 1540-48).
The prototype of the the the popular chivalric romance.

———

The amours of Edward the IV: an historical novel (1700; pp. 120)

WING M565; NCBEL II 984[17]; Morgan 413
Perhaps a trans.
Follows the pattern of French romanticized histories; introduces Richard III.

Bateman's tragedy: or the perjur'd bride justly rewarded [1700? pp. 13]

NCBEL II 984[11]; SALZMAN 377 - Folger Lib.
Lurid tale of revenge, with urban setting and bourgeois characters.

EDITIONS

1086 Ed. MISH, Charles Carol. In (pp. 276-89) *Restoration prose fiction 1666-1700: an anthology of representative pieces.* Lincoln, NE: U of Nebraska P, 1970; pp. xv, 289.
With facs. title page and introduction. "*Bateman's Tragedy* is a ghost-story written for popular consumption. For all its apparent crudeness, it has a good deal of strength [...]. The story has obvious popular appeal" (275).

___

The brothers, or treachery punish'd (1730, pp. 166)

NCBEL II 992[14]; McBurney 247; Morgan 597; ECSTC 4506B4
Spanish setting; romance plot with interpolated stories.

STUDIES

1087 KLEIN in (p. 245) *Der Briefroman in der englischen Literatur* etc., **569**.

Analyzes the epistolary exchange in *The brothers*.

___

Celenia: or the history of Hyempsal king of Numidia (1736, 1740. Pt 1 had appeared with *The Persian letters continued* [1735], 2 vols; pp. 1-319, 321-642)

NCBEL II 994[3]; McBurney 314; Morgan 639; ECSTC 1304C2
May be trans. of LEVESQUE, *Célénie* (1732)
Allegorical apologue.

___

The compleat mendicant or unhappy beggar: being the life of an unfortunate gentleman (1699, 1700 etc., pp. 156)

WING C5646B; NCBEL II 984[7]; Morgan 411
By DEFOE?
Realistic pseudo-autobiography.

———

The Court of Atlantis (1714, 1717, 1732 [in *Court Tales*], pp.153-78)

NCBEL II 987[5]; McBurney 69
May be by John OLDMIXON.
Scandal-chronicle; short tales of court amours and political intrigues.

———

Cynthia: with the tragical account of the unfortunate loves of Almerin and Desdemona (1687, 1700; over 19 edns in the 18th century, pp. 207)

WING C7710A; NCBEL II 981[5]
Nouvelle galante; episodic and moralizing.

STUDIES

1088 MISH, "A note on the fiction reprint market in the early eighteenth century," **677**.

———

The double captive: or chains upon chains (1718, n.p.)

NCBEL II 988[4]; Morgan 489
Epistolary tale, ostensibly by a prisoner in Newgate; realistic picture of prison life.

EDITIONS

1089 *The Double Captive; or Chains upon chains, containing the amorous poems and letters of a young gentleman, one of the Preston prisoners in Newgate. To which is added the execution dream, with a preface to the ladies and an introductory novel.* Ed. WÜRZBACH in (pp. 91-101) *The novel in letters* etc., **149** .

Introd. (93). Combines the tradition of gallantry with a realistic treatment of background reminiscent of the literature of roguery. Daydreams as the narrative, with varying success, tries to escape his actual surroundings.

———

The English nobleman: or peasant of quality (1735, pp. 88)

> NCBEL II 993[17]; McBurney 302; Morgan 630; ECSTC 1674E1
> Trans. of *My lord ---* (1702), profiting from the vogue of MARIVAUX, *LePaysan parvenu*. Morgan ascribes it to Westminster.

———

The fair concubine: or the secret history of the beautiful Vanella (1732 [3 edns], pp. 17-49)

> NCBEL II 993[3]; McBurney 267
> Scandal history of Miss Vane, mistress of Frederick, Prince of Wales.

———

The fatal effects of arbitrary power and the dangerous conditions of Court favourites (1715, n.p.)

> NCBEL II 987[11]; McBurney X12
> Secret history of Philip II of Spain in the form of a memoir by a minister.

———

The finished rake: or gallantry in perfection (1733, pp. 59)

> NCBEL II 993[8]; McBurney 277; ECSTC 782F1
> Unusually realistic autobiographical narrative; semi-picaresque; sympathetic treatment of the hero's childhood.

———

The generous rivals: or love triumphant. A novel (1711, 1713, 1716, pp. 270)

> NCBEL II 986[11]; McBurney 62 (gives 1713); Morgan 485 (gives 1716)
> Comedy; misunderstanding of lovers; colloquial style; set in London.

———

The German Atalantis (1715, 1719, 1721 [as *Hanover tales*], pp. 143)

> NCBEL II 987[12]; McBurney 76; ECSTC 650H1
> Scandal-chronicle of German and English Courts of George I.

———

The German rogue (1720, pp. 111)

> NCBEL II 988[16]; McBurney 116; ECSTC 667G1
> Trans. of a contemporary version of Till Eulenspiegel.

The history and proceedings of the mandarins and proatins of the Britomartian empire (1712, 1713, pp. 3-78)

> NCBEL II 986[15]; McBurney 59
> Pretended secret history of the manoeuvres of chief Whigs and Tories.

The history of Autonous (1736, pp. 117)

> NCBEL II 994[4]; McBurney 308; ECSTC 2269A1
> Account of an autodidact living on a desert island; one of many borrowings from IBN AL-TUFAIL, 1674.

The history of Menuthia; with an account of the chief transactions in that kingdom (Nottingham, 1715, pp. 3-52)

> NCBEL II 987[13]; McBurney 77; ECSTC 2057M1
> Hanoverian politics, disguised as a letter from Madagascar.

The history of Prince Mirabel's infancy, rise and disgrace; with the sudden promotion of Novicus (1712, 1712; 3 pts, pp. 1-90, 3-80, 3-80)

> NCBEL II 986[14]; McBurney 58; ECSTC 2683M1
> Political satire on Marlborough and Harley.

The illegal lovers: a true secret history (1728, n.p.)

> NCBEL II 991[21]; Morgan 583; ECSTC 3204L5
> Unusual anticipation of the psychological novel. The sister turns out to be an unfortunate orphan adopted by the hero's family. The story is the same as that in *Love Letters between a Nobleman and his Sister* (Morgan, p. 226).

STUDIES

1090 DAY in (pp. 174-75) *Told in letters* etc., **364**.

> The story is outlined reflectively by a 'friend of the family' with 7 long letters carrying most of the narrative burden: "The twists and turns of

mental anguish perhaps have passion as their ultimate cause, but the proximate cause is a Protestant conscience, and the casuistry and scrupulous views are Levitical, not *précieux* [...]. It may owe something to the general ideas behind *La Princesse de Clèves* and its imitators, but it is clear that epistolary fiction had come a long way since *Love Letters between an Officer and his Sister* in which a similar situation was tossed off with amoral abandon" (175).

1091 KLEIN in (p. 273) *Der Briefroman in der englischen Literatur* etc., **569**.

Tabulates the epistolary exchange in *The illegal lovers.*

———

The infernal congress: or news from below (1713, 1713, n.p.)

NCBEL II 986[17]
Letter from the dead to the living; social and political satire.

———

The jilted bridegroom: or the London coquet (1706, pp. 55)

NCBEL II 985[8]; McBurney 20; ECSTC 4025B2
Domestic epistolary tale; London middle-class life; unusual realism.

STUDIES

1092 KLEIN in (p. 274) *Der Briefroman in der englischen Literatur* etc., **569**.

Provides a breakdown of the epistolary exchange in *The jilted bridegroom.*

———

Johnny Armstrong (1700?, pp. 24)

WING P2531
Popular non-chivalric fiction.

EDITIONS

1093 Ed. MISH in (pp. 257-72) *Restoration prose fiction* etc., **1086**.

With facsimile title page and introduction. " [...] the story, anonymously as the ballad which follows the prose text, has the quality of a legend [...], everything is larger than life. The prose story is [...] economically told, the whole [...] pointed towards the dramatic and tragic climax" (259).

———

The ladies tale, exemplified in the virtues and vices of the quality (1714; 3 edns by 1741; pp. 264)

NCBEL II 987[6]; McBurney 70
Short stories in a frame narrative.

———

A letter from Mrs Jane Jones, alias Jenny Diver (1737, pp. 11)

NCBEL II 994[11]
Ironic autobiography and advice to courtesans.

EDITIONS

1094   Ed. WÜRZBACH, in (pp. 53-64) *The novel of letters* etc., **149**.

Introd. (pp. 55-56). The story of of Jane Jones represents the limit of realistic portraiture in 18c fiction.

STUDIES

1095   ANON., Review article. *TLS* (25 Sept 1969): 1107.

In criticizing Würzbach's *Novel of letters*, the reviewer points out that she fails to identify several London places and the various lovers mentioned in *A letter from Mrs Jane Jones*, let alone the notorious procuress herself. The identity of these lovers is of some importance as it brings this epistolary piece nearer to the scandalous memoir than the realistic-didactic type of fiction where Würzbach is inclined to place it. If her skimpy annotation detracts a little from the value of her book, she is to be commended for the short critical commentaries with which she introduces each of the stories, and for her making of very scarce texts available.

———

Letters from a Moor at London to his friends at Tunis (1736, pp. 274)

NCBEL II 994[5]; McBurney 309; ECSTC 1424L12
24 letters combining travelogue with satire on English manners.

———

The life and adventures of Capt. John Avery, the famous English pirate (1709, pp. 64)

NCBEL II 986[5]; McBurney 43; Morgan 454

Fictitious biography, in the manner of DEFOE. Morgan gives the title as *The King of Pirates, being an account of the famous Captain Avery, the Mock King of Madagascar [...] .Written by a Person who made his Escape from thence.*

———

The life and adventures of Mrs Christian Davies, commonly call'd Mother Ross. Who in several campaigns under King William and the Duke of Marlborough, in the quality of a foot-soldier and dragoon, gave many signal proofs of an unparall'd courage and bravery. Taken from her own mouth when a pensioner of Chelsea-Hospital. And known to be true by many who were engaged in those great scenes of action (1739, pp. 104)

NCBEL II 994[18]; McBurney 332;ECSTC 471D1

Fictionalized biography of Mrs Christian Davis (1667-1739) who served in disguise as a soldier.

STUDIES

1096 DUGAW, Dianne. Introduction to *The Female Soldier; or, The Surprising Life and Adventures of Hannah Snell (1750)*. (Augustan Reprint Society.) U of California P; pp. xiii, iv, 42.

Remarks on the "surprising [...] frequency of eighteenth-century female soldiers and sailors [...] not only in fiction but in history as well".

———

Love letters between a certain late nobleman and the famous Mr Wilson (1723, pp. 49)

NCBEL II 989[17]; McBurney 138

Epistolary scandal-chronicle.

STUDIES

1097 DAY in (pp. 142-43) *Told in letters* etc., **364**.

Discusses the technique of double narrative, and the justification of the twice-told tale. It begins with 20 letters which are confusing in the extreme. Examines the confusion and attempts at resolving it. "But a literary puzzle is hard to evaluate with an art form, and unless we wish to see Beau Wilson's story as a forerunner of detective fiction, we may dismiss it as a curiosity of literature, an unusual variant of the scandal-novel" (143).

———

Love upon tick: or implicit gallantry (1724, 1725, pp. 143)

NCBEL II 990[3]; McBurney 150; ECSTC 3152L42
Foolish fop duped by feigned love letters; clever satire; style and details suggest Mary MANLEY as the author.

STUDIES

1098 DAY in (pp. 140-41) *Told in letters* etc., **364**.

Explains the technique where 43 letters sustain the story, since the interlinking passages do little more than comment on and prepare the reader for the text. Yet the reader is constantly curious to know by what strategems the lady will keep the farce of disguise going, and avoid discovery. "*Love upon Tick* may be the work of Mrs. Manley. The author is a woman who writes with an unusually masculine, ironic style, and knows it" (140).

———

Love without artifice: or the disappointed peer (1733, 1734, 1736, pp. 47)
NCBEL II 993[9]; McBurney 279

Based on contemporary scandal; blend of fact and fiction; uses supposedly authentic letters as documentation.

———

Memoirs of love and gallantry (1732; also issued as *Love in all shapes*; pp. 3-74)

NCBEL II 993[4]; McBurney 270; ECSTC 2006M15
Secret history of extreme complexity; vivid characters.

———

A narrative of all the robberies, escapes etc. of John Sheppard (1724 [8 eds], pp. 31)
NCBEL II 990[4]; McBurney 151; ECSTC 2075S6
Feigned autobiography of famous highwayman.

———

A new voyage to the island of fools, representing the policy, government and present state of the Stultitians (1713, 1715; 2 pts, pp. 1-58, 59-62)

NCBEL II 986[19]; McBurney 63; ECSTC 800V4
Ramble through London; satire of manners. Attributed to Edward
WARD; resembles his manner in *The London Spy*.

———

Passionate love-letters between a Polish princess and a certain chevalier (1719,
pp. 3-72)

NCBEL II 988[9]; McBurney 105
Epistolary novel; purports to be a correspondence of the Old Pretender
and Maria Clementina of Poland, who married in May 1719.

STUDIES

1099 DAY in (p. 172) *Told in letters* etc., **364**.

Treats of love in high places. Describes the complex and absurd plot of
separation, imaginative emotion, abduction and escape. "The high-flown
language of the letters is made all the more ridiculous by the absurdity of
the situation, but the expectations aroused by the book's title no doubt
assured an adequate sale".

———

The perfidious P**: being letters from a nobleman to two ladies (1702, 1704, pp.
143)
NCBEL II 985[1]; McBurney 9
Dramatic epistolary novel; excellent technique and characterization.

———

The perjur'd citizen: or female revenge (1732, pp. 55)

NCBEL II 993[5]; McBurney 271
Sensational but realistic plot; pictures of bourgeois life which seem based
on actual events.

———

*The pleasant intrigues and surprising adventures of an English nobleman at the
last carnival at Venice* (1707, pp. 156)

NCBEL II 985[10]; McBurney 24
Complex plot of adventure; anticipates the modern novel of espionage.

———

The rover (*British Mercury*, 1714)

NCBEL II 987[7]; ECSTC 1984R1
First long fiction to have first publication in instalments; picaresque.

STUDIES

1100 JONES, Claude E. "*The Rover*, 1714." *NQ* 201 (May 1956): 206-10.

One of the most interesting of the precursors of Defoe's novels is the anonymous *Rover*, the first longer English prose fiction to be published in periodical instalments. Appeared in the *British Mercury* (July-Sept. 1714). It follows the regular, long-established picaresque pattern, with a 17c Spanish setting. Alonzo, the protagonist, has an adventurous and peripatetic career told in a series of incidents loosely tied together by his identity. His companions experience considerable shifts of fortune motivated by chance. Although there is no attention paid to setting, he travels throughout Spain. The review includes a summary of 7 chapters. The plot is typical of the late picaresque novel, with the most interesting part, from both a folkloristic and literary point of view, being Alonzo's "Adventure with the Witch", reproduced in full.

––––

The secret history of Mama Oella, Princess Royal of Peru (1733, pp. 51)

NCBEL II 993[10]; McBurney 280; Morgan 621; ECSTC 852M1
Roman à clef based on the marriage of Anne, daughter of George II.

––––

The secret history of the Prince of the Nazarenes and the two Turks: The fatal amour between a beautiful lady and a young nobleman (1719, 1721 [3rd edn]; 2 pts, pp. 1-25, 27-66)

NCBEL II 988[10]; McBurney 94; Morgan 509; ECSTC 194N1
The first tale is a political satire; the second an epistolary, realistic tale of adultery.

––––

The secret of Pythagoras: Part I. Translated from the original copy lately found at Otranto in Italy (1721, 1722, pp. 7-36)

NCBEL II 989[5]; McBurney 118; ECSTC 4122P1
Trans. Dr James WALKER.
The subtitle may have inspired WALPOLE'S title *The Castle of Otranto*.

———

A select collection of novels in six volumes (1720, 1725, 1729 [with 9 novels added]; 6 eds by 1740; n.p.)

NCBEL II 988[17]; McBurney 117
Ed. Samuel CROXALL: 26 titles, mostly trans., of the most popular short fiction of the previous century; authors include CERVANTES, MACHIAVELLI, Mme DE LAFAYETTE, LESAGE, BRÉMOND, SCARRON, SAINT-RÉAL, ALMÁN, Mlle DE LA ROCHE-GUILHEM, FÉNELON. HUET'S essay on romance was included in vol. 1.

STUDIES

1101 HUET, P. D. "Essai sur l'origine des romans" (1670). Trans. and rpt. in (pp. 140-59) ELLEDGE, S. and SCHIER, D. (eds). *The continental model: selected French critical essays of the seventeenth century in English translation.* Minneapolis; Ithaca, NY and London: Cornell UP, 1960.

The famous and influential essay outlines the history of romance from classical times to the topical situation of 17c France.

———

Some memoirs of the amours and intrigues of a certain Irish dean (1728, 1730 [3rd edn]; pp. 68)

NCBEL II 992[1]; McBurney 225
An attack on Swift and the Blount sisters combined with a tale of extravagant passion.

STUDIES

1102 DAY, Robert Adams. "An anonymous attack on Swift." *NQ* 200 (Dec 1955): 530-32.

The appearance of this anonymous book in London 1728 and in Dublin 1730 throws light on the practices and authors of the early 18c. There is considerable reason to suppose that the *Memoirs* were by Eliza Haywood, "the Abitress of Passion". In 1728 she was in financial straits, since after 1726 her production fell off, mostly because the public was tiring of her work, and she was doubtlessly ready to seize on any expedient for money. She could have had no kind feelings for the hostile literary set surrounding Pope and Swift, whom she had atacked in *Memoirs of a certain island* (1725). A book saleable because of its scandalous hints could be turned out with maximum speed and profit to both author and bookseller.

———

The Spanish libertines: or the lives of Justina, Celestina and Estevanillo Gonzales (1707, 1709; n.p.)

NCBEL II 985[11]; ECSTC 4319S24
Trans. of 3 famous Spanish novels by Capt. John STEVENS.

———

The tell-tale: or the invisible witness (1711, pp. 3-67)

NCBEL II 986[12]; McBurney 53; ECSTC 490T3
Whimsical satire on beaux and belles; the invisible narrator spies on events.

———

The unfortunate Dutchess: or the lucky gamester; a novel founded on a true story (1739, pp. 78)

NCBEL II 994[19]; McBurney 333; Morgan 648; ECSTC 2460D3
Rpt of the second tale of D[AVID] CR[AWFURD]'S *Several letters*, 1700.
Epistolary fiction in the manner of the French romances.

———

The unnatural mother and ungrateful wife. (1727/1730?, pp. 107)

NCBEL II 992[14]; McBurney 221a; ECSTC 3627M14
Domestic-realistic tale of family treachery; epistolary.

———

The velvet coffee-woman (1728, pp. 46)

NCBEL II 992[2]; McBurney 228; ECSTC 1541R1
Supposed biography of the notorious Mrs Anne Rochford, but apparently a composite plagiarism.

STUDIES

1103 DAY, Robert Adams. "How to write a shilling biography." *Newberry Lib Bull* 6 (1970).
Examines how this work is composed entirely of plagiarisms from works

of popular fiction.

———

A view of the beau monde: or memoirs of the celebrated Coquetilla (1731, pp. 60)

NCBEL II 992[17]; McBurney 256
Picaresque secret history; detailed setting at Bath.

———

A voyage to the new island Fonseca, near Barbadoes (1708, pp. 44)

NCBEL II 985[18]; McBurney 34
Imaginary letters by 2 travellers satirizing life in England and the colonies.

———

Winter evenings tales (1731, Dublin 1733-4, 1737 [6th edn], 1738 [3 of tales as *French novels*]; pp. 284)

NCBEL II 992[19]; McBurney 261; Morgan 615
17 stories told by members of a group, as in Madeleine de GOMEZ'S *La Belle Assemblée* (1724).

———

A., Ma.

The prude 3 pts (1724-6 [4 eds], pp. 87)

NCBEL II 990[5]; McBurney 153; ECSTC 28A1
Interesting mixture of character and adventure; girl a secret libertine.

STUDIES

1104 KLEIN in (p. 238) *Der Briefroman in der englischen Literatur* etc., **569**.

Tabulation of the epistolary correspondence in *The prude*.

———

ABELARD AND HELOISE

Letters of Abelard and Heloise; to which is prefix'd a particular account of their lives, amours and misfortunes. 1713, 1714 etc; 10 edns by 1765; serialized 1734-35.

NCBEL II 986[18]

Trans. by John HUGHES of DUBOIS, *Histoire des amours et infortunes d'Abelard et d'Héloise.*

Romanticized account with versions of their letters. Highly popular.

EDITIONS

1105 *The Love Letters of Abelard and Heloise.* Ed. H. MORTON. (Everyman's Library.) London: J. M. Dent, 1937. 10th ed. by 1987.

This is a rpt of John HUGHES'S paraphrase of 1714.

1106 The 1722 edn rptd in Temple Classics (London, 1904).

1107 *The Letters of Abelard and Heloise. Now Translated from the Latin by C. K. SCOTT MONCRIEFF.* London: Guy Chapman, 1925; pp. xix, 211.

Preface by way of a correspondence between Scott-Moncriff and George Moore (ix-xix). Text of 8 letters, each preceded by an 'argument', but without notes or scholarly apparatus.

1108 *The Letters of Abelard and Heloise. Translated with an introduction by Betty RADICE.* Harmondsworth: Penguin Books, 1974; pp. 309.

The introd. (9-55) provides a comprehensive history, background, previous editions, and particularities of translation. Select bibliography (296-99). Maps and Plans (300-2). Index (303-9).

———

ALEMÁN, Mateo

Guzman de Alfarache (1708; pp. 308)

NCBEL II 985[19]; ECSTC 675A1
Archetypal picaresque novel.
Trans. initially by James MABBE (1622) from *Guzman de Alfarache*, 1599-1600.

EDITIONS

1109 *The Rogue, or The Life of Guzman de Alfarache. Written in Spanish by Matheo Aleman and into English by James Mabbe. Anno 1623. With an Introduction by James Fitzmaurice-Kelly.* Ed. James FITZMAURICE-KELLY. London: Constable & Co. Ltd. and New York: Alfred A. Knopf,

1924. 4 vols. I, xx, 269; II, 291; III, 358; IV, 353.

Introd. (ix-xx). Dedication in Spanish and English (1-11). The Spanish picaresque novel differs vitally from the English novel of the same type. With the exception of Thomas Nash's *Jack Wilton* (1594), the English tales of roguery were either autobiographies of repentant criminals themselves, or they were the work of authors intent on social reform. It is quite otherwise in the *novelas picarescas* of Spain, which form a distinct branch of literature.

1110 Preface ed. C. E. JONES. In *Prefaces to three eighteenth-century novels (1708-1751-1797)*. (Augustan Reprint Soc., 64.) Los Angeles, 1957.

Introd. (i-iv). Any serious study of developments during the critical 17c and 18c, of the form and aesthetic of prose fiction in English, requires access to many dedications, prefaces, periodicals and other essays and pamphlets. The first part of Aleman's *Vida del picaro Guzman de Alfarache* was published in Madrid in 1599. Despite its immediate international popularity, Aleman was forced to emigrate to Mexico to improve his circumstances. There he wrote the second half of *Guzman*. The first English translation was published by James MABBE (as *Don Diego Puede - Ser*) in 1623, and was avidly received by English readers. The Age of Anne, like Mabbe's period, was notable for translations. One of the group of authors frequently so occupied include, in addition to John SAVAGE, the celebrated Tom BROWN. It was probably this group of "several hands" who were responsible for the 1705 translation of *Guzman* from Gabriel de BREMOND'S 1699 French translation. *Guzman* is prolix, and despite occasional flashes of character and situation, dull to the modern reader. Its importance as a precursor of such fiction as *The English Rogue* and the Defoe novels is considerable. Fragments of it and other Spanish picaresque tales comprise the first serially published English "novel", *The Rover* (1713). The "English Translator's Preface" provides apologies for prose fiction current in English throughout the 18c and 19c. It is occasionally ironic, pleas for the "low" estate as allegory of mankind in general, justifies interpolated tales to relieve the novel's tediousness, all familiar in spirit to the readers of early prose fiction, echoed in prefaces by Defoe, Fielding and their successors. Reprints title page, frontispiece, dedicatory epistle (iii-iv), and preface (vii-xiii).

STUDIES

1111 BENSADON, Michel Emile. "Transformations of the self in the European picaresque novel: *Guzman de Alfarache, Moll Flanders, Gil Blas de Santillane*," **231**.

1112 GONDEBEAUD, Louis. "*Guzman d'Alfarache* en Angleterre: 1622-1708." *Caliban* 20 (1983): 19-27.

> Surveys the influence of the translation of Alemán's *Guzman* (1656) on the history of the English novel. 'Rogue stories' and 'criminal biographies' have been unjustly neglected, yet they reveal a care for characterization and an elaboration of narrative technique. They form a 'missing link' in the history of the novel. The diffusion of *Guzman* in the second half of the 17c contributed to the elaboration of narrative technique and helped to shape the English picaresque novel.

1113 SIEBER, Harry. "Mateo Alemán: the picaresque as genre". In (pp. 17-23) *The Picaresque* (The Critical Idiom, 33.) London: Methuen & Co., 1977; pp. viii, 85.

> Alemán eschews critical commentary on abuses in the Church. Owing to its emphasis on the doctrines of original sin, the saving power of grace and the concept of free will, Maurice Mohlo has described the novel not as the 'life' of a criminal, but as the 'life of a criminal soul'.

1114 STARKIE, Walter F. "Miguel de Cervantes and the English novel." *Essays by Divers Hands*, new ser., 34 (1966): 159-79.

> There is a vast difference between Cervantes and his great contemporary, Mateo Alemán, whose picaresque novel, *Guzman d'Alfarache* (1599) rivalled *Don Quixote* in popularity (one year after its publication it was printed in France, Portugal and Flanders, and by 1605, twenty six editions and 50,000 copies had been sold). Both Cervantes and Alemán influenced the entire history of the novel: they marked two parallel paths along which that literary genre would develop as a mirror of modern life. But if Guzman, the arch-mentor of rogues and picaroons, had remained in lone supremacy as the model, and had not given way to public favour in the late 18c and 19c, to Quixote, the Knight of the Rueful Figure, and his squire Sancho Panza, the English novel might never have known the work of Fielding, Sterne and Defoe.

———

ARMENO, Cristoforo

The travels and adventures of three Princes of Sarendip. Interspersed with eight delightful and entertaining novels translated from the Persian into French and thence into English (1722; 2 pts, 1-260, 261-76)

NCBEL II 989[11]; McBurney 132; Morgan 524

Trans. from the French version by MAILLY, 1719.
Fantastic adventures; a favourite of Horace Walpole.

EDITIONS

1115 *Serendipity and the Three Princes. From the 'Peregrinaggio' of 1557. Edited by Theodore G. Remer. With a Preface by W.S. Lewes.* Norman, OA: U. of Oklahoma P, 1965; pp. xi, 199. 2 illus.

Part I *Serendipity* discusses Walpole and his letters, definitions and usage. Part II presents the *Peregrinaggio*, providing a history (35-50), the imprimatur of 1557 (51-3), the dedication of 1557 (54) and the text itself, translated by Augusto G. and Theresa L. BORSELLI (57-63). 3 appendixes look at the nature of Serendipity, the origins of the *Peregrinaggio*, editions and translations of the *Peregrinaggio*. Bibliography (191-95). Index (196-9).

STUDIES

1116 SCHAAR, Bernard E. "Serendipity." *NQ* 205 (1960): 387-9.

Discusses Horace Walpole's propagation of misconceptions about Armeno's book (letter of 1754). He gets the title and several details about the book wrong, and his use of the word "serendip" is the source of another error carried on in dictionaries. It is open to question whether lexicographers would have associated "Sarendip" with Ceylon if Walpole had not used that name. The tale seems to rule out Ceylon. "Serendipity" in the dictionaries has not travelled too far from Walpole's original definition of the word despite his erroneous interpretation of the princes' experiences. There is no validity in the current application of the term to scientific investigation in which some unlooked-for event has speeded discovery and opened a new line of investigation, resulting in a discovery along an entirely different avenue.

———

AUBIN, Penelope

1. *The life of Madam de Beaumont, a French lady, who lived in a cave in Wales above fourteen years undiscovered [...]. Also her Lord's adventures in Muscovy* (1721, 1728; several other eds c.1770 [as *Belinda*]; pp. 9-143)

NCBEL II 989[6]; McBurney 119; Morgan 507; 2154A10
Adventure, romance, religion.

2. *The strange adventures of the Count de Vinevil and his family. Being an account of what happened to them whilst they resided at Constantinople* (1721, 1728 etc, 1739 [in *A collection of entertaining histories and novels*]; pp. 9-138)

 NCBEL II 989[7]; McBurney 120; Morgan 510; ECSTC 2154A12
 Sensational adventures in a Turkish setting.

3. *The life and amorous adventures of Lucinda, an English lady* (1722, 1739; 2 pts, pp. 1-260, 261-76)

 NCBEL II 989[12]; McBurney 126
 Autobiography; heroine captured by Barbary pirates.

4. *The noble slaves: or the lives and adventures of two lords and two ladies whoe were ship-wrecked* (1722, 1729; numerous edns through the century; pp. 202)

 NCBEL II 989[13]; McBurney 127; Morgan 521; ECSTC 2154A11
 Similar in plot to *Lucinda*.

5. *The life of Charlotta Du Pont* (1723, 1733; 6 eds by 1800; pp. 282)

 NCBEL II 989[18]; McBurney 140; ECSTC 2154A9
 Abduction and adventure in North and South America.

6. *The life and adventures of the Lady Lucy, daughter to an Irish Lord* (1726, 1728, 1729 [in collection]; pp. 131)

 NCBEL II 991[1]; McBurney 189; Morgan 569; ECSTC 2154A7
 Separated spouses, fantastic adventures; historical matter involving the Irish rebellion under James II.

7. *The life and adventures of the young Count Albertus [...] Son of Count L. A. by Lady Lucy* (1728).

 Reprinted in "an undated edition of Mrs Aubin's works in the Col. Libr." (Morgan, p. 225 § 2), perhaps indentical with No. 8 below.

8. *Collection of entertaining histories and novels* (1739)

 Contains:
 1) *The Noble Slaves*;
 2) *The Life and Adventures of Lucinda*;

3) *Conjugal Duty Rewarded or the Rake Reformed*;
4) *Life and Amorous Adventures of Lucinda;*
5) *Fortune Favours the Bold;*
6) *Count de Vinevil;*
7) *Lady Lucy;*
8) *Life and Adventures of Young Count Albertus*;
9) *Life of Charlotte du Pont;*
10) *Madame de Beaumont.*

EDITIONS

1117   *The Life of Madam de Beaumont, a French Lady and The Strange Adventures of the Count de Vinevil and his Family.* Ed. Josephine GRIEDER. (Foundations of the Novel.) New York: Garland Publishing, 1973.

1118   *The Strange Adventures of the Count de Vinevil and His Family.* Ed. BACKSCHEIDER and RICHETTI in (pp. 113-52) *Popular fiction by women, 1660-1730* etc., **119**.

BIBLIOGRAPHY

1119   SCHOFIELD, Mary Anne. "Aubin, Penelope". In (pp. 1-8) SAAR and SCHOFIELD, *Eighteenth-century Anglo-American novelists: a critical reference guide* etc., **93**.

Annotated criticism from 1900 to 1992 (39 items).

SELECTED PRE-1992 STUDIES

1120   DOOLEY, Roger B. "Penelope Aubin: forgotten Catholic novelist." *Renascence* 11 (1959): 65-71.

Anti-Catholic feeling infiltrated every branch of English literature in the early 18c. Of the four traditional founders of the novel, only Richardson refrained from attacks on Catholics. The presence of Aubin, a woman who was not only a Catholic and a novelist, but who actually dared to write as a Catholic novelist, is astonishing. Using Turks and infidels for her villains, she presented the most attractive Christian virtues in her Continental Catholics, and unlike Defoe, presented them simply as good people, without apology or defence. In *Count Albertus* she created the only character in the 18c fiction who took religion seriously enough to die for it. She showed extraordinary independence of mind in presenting Catholic themes with honesty and understanding. "Except for

Richardson's two in *Grandison*, Penelope Aubin's were the last admirable priests to appear in the English novel for more than fifty years. If her literary skill as a novelist was no more than average for her day, her moral courage as a Catholic was to remain unmatched among English writers for the remainder of the eighteenth century" (71).

1121 KLEIN in (p. 240) *Der Briefroman in der englischen Literatur* etc., **569**.

Provides a breakdown of the literary correspondence in *The life of Madam de Beaumont* and *The life and adventures of the Lady Lucy*.

1122 McBURNEY, Wiliam H. "Mrs Penelope Aubin and the early eighteenth-century English novel." *HLQ* 20 (1957): 245-67.

Account of life and works. In 1729 Aubin established herself in her own oratory in the York Building near Charing Cross. Her career as an oratrix was not the last phase in her literary progress as poetess, novelist, editor, translator and dramatist (1730), but it was the most eccentric. Her novels are her only claim to fame today. As the boldest and most productive imitator of Defoe's works, particularly *Robinson Crusoe*, she contributed to the first important cycle of 18c English fictional publication which reached its peak in 1727. Her original novels helped to fuse the narrative tradition of Defoe with continental fictional genres. Her translations are themselves interesting studies in the divergencies of English and French tastes, and through both original and derivative works, she exerted influence upon the novels of Abbé Prévost and Richardson, whose vogue in France Prévost was later to initiate as translator. Although they cannot be classified as historical novels, Aubin's works take place against the exciting political and religious backgrounds of the great Anglo-French populations of the late 17c - the emigration of the Huguenots after the revocation of the Edict of Nantes in 1685, and the flight of the Jacobites to France with the last Stuart kings and after the Battle of the Boyne.

1123 WEBER, Donna-Lee. "Fair game: rape and sexual aggression on women in some early eighteenth-century prose fiction," **1035**.

1124 ZACH, Wolfgang. "Mrs Aubin and Richardson's earliest literary manifesto (1739)." *ES* 62:3 (June 1981): 271-81.

The preface to the *Collection of Entertaining Histories and Novels* (quoted, 281-85) is attributed to Richardson. There is substantial evidence in Richardson's novels and letters that he read far more widely than he was prepared to admit. His fervent parodying of earlier amatory novels and heroic romances suggest a firsthand knowledge of them. He also refers to the pernicious tendencies of Behn, Manley and Haywood's novels, which implies that he was familiar with the earlier tradition of the novel. Mrs Aubin is esp. reminiscent of Richardson in the high moral tone of her novels, very unusual for the time. She is preoccupied with virtuous heroines in distress who are exposed to all kinds sexual dangers, only to be saved by Providence and receive their due reward in the end. Her novels were reprinted posthumously in 1739 with an annotated preface, very likely by Richardson. He poses as a lawgiver to all the novelists, insisting on purity of style and manners, a recommendation of all the duties of social life, and the preservation of an air of probability so that the didactic effect will not be lost on the reader.

STUDIES (1992-1999)

1125 FENDLER, Susanne. "Intertwining literary histories: Women's contribution to the rise of the novel." In (pp. 31-64) FENDLER, Susanne (ed.). *Feminist contributions to the literary canon: Setting standards of taste.* (Women's Studies, 15.) Lewiston, NY and Lampeter: Edwin Mellen Press, 1997; pp. 179.

The aim is to search for a development in character, realism, and moralistic content that provides the 'missing link' between romance and Richardson's kind of novel. The secondary aim is to examine the justification of the enduring rejection of these early novels on the grounds of a compromised morality. Examines chosen texts, with plot summaries, in order to concentrate on aspects relevant to these questions under consideration.
The Aubin text selected from is *The Life of Madam de Beaumont* (1721) (49-53) in which she strives to create an image of herself as a 'moral didacticist'. Her characters are either evil and pay no heed to other people, or they are virtuous, ready to die to keep this virtue, or dying because of it.

1126 KIM, Elizabeth Sungeun. "Exploiting rape: women's literary representations of rape in early eighteenth-century prose fictions," **566**.

1127 PRESCOTT, S. H. "Feminist literary theory and British women novelists of the 1720s." Unpub. doct. diss., Univ. of Exeter, 1997. [*IT* 46 (1997): 12165.]
Considers four women writers of the early 18c who published novels in one decade: Aubin, Barker, Haywood, Rowe. Emphasizes the contemporaneity of these women and argues against a literary-historical model which sees two traditions of female authorship in this period: one shaped by the 'disreputable' image of Aphra Behn, the other emulating

the 'chaste' reputation of Katherine Philips (Orinda). Examines the work and reputation of Haywood and Aubin, comparing their fictions and their common use of romance conventions, the seduction narrative, and the Christian fable. Usage is remarkably similar, and not aimed at different audiences.

1128 RILEY, Esther Powell. "Resisting writers: Four eighteenth-century female novelists in search of a literary voice." Unpub. doct. diss., Univ. of Tennessee, 1992. [*DA* 53 (1993): 3923A.]

Discusses novels by four women writers (Aubin, Davys, Lennox and Charlotte Smith) who were forced to support themselves by writing when patriarchy failed them. Using psychoanalytic theory of reading, reveals how each woman's work amounts to a critique of patriarchy and an attempt to reconstruct female subjectivity in order to counter patriarchal ideology. Looks at the position of middle-class females in 18c society, Aubin's reiterated images which emphasize the precarious plight of the female in a male-dominated world; death may be preferable to being trapped in a woman's body. Davys's plots and characterizations interrogate accepted courtship practice in order to negotiate a more honest relationship between men and women. Depicting failed marriages and the destructive effects of depriving ambitious and capable women of power, the novels suggest that a revolution in behaviour is required for both men and women. Traces of these writers' resistance to unjust male forms remain.

———

AULNOY, Marie Catherine Jumelle de Berneville, Comtesse d'

1. [?] *The novels of Elizabeth, Queen of England* (2 pts. 1680-81, pp. 135)

WING A4221; NCBEL II 979[12]
Trans. Spencer HICKMAN from *Nouvelles d'Elisabeth*, 1674.
Romanticized pseudo-history, loosely connected tales of court amours.

2. *The ingenious and diverting letters of the lady --'s travels into Spain* (1691, 1692; 10th edn by 1735; 3 vols I, 149; II, 162; III, 228)

WING B2038/40/41; NCBEL II 982[13]
Trans. of *Relation du voyage d'Espagne*, 1691.
Highly popular, initiates the genre of lively epistolary travel-narratives.

3. *Memoirs of the Court of France* (1692, 1697; pp. 160)

WING A 4218A; NCBEL II 982[17]
Trans. from *Mémoirs et aventures singulières de la cour de France*, 1692.

4. *Memoirs of the Court of Spain* (1692, 1701; pp. 379)

WING A4220; NCBEL II 982[18]
Trans. Thomas BROWN from *Mémoirs de la Cour d'Espagne*, 1690.
Nouvelle historique.

5. *The present Court of Spain* (1693, 1698; pp. 379)

WING A4223; NCBEL II 983[3]
Trans. from *Nouvelles espagnoles*, 1692.
Several novels of varied content. *The enamoured Teresa* is both epistolary and psychological.

6. *Memoirs of the Countess of Dunois* (1699, pp.185)

WING A4218
Orig. unknown.

7. *Tales of the fairys* (1699, 1716 [new trans.]; at least 15 edns by 1800)

NCBEL II 984[6]
First appearance in English of several famous fairy tales.

8. *The diverting works of the Countess d'Anois* (1707; at least 4 edns by 1749, varying from 1 to 3 vols.; pp. 648)

NCBEL II 985[12]; McBurney 27; Morgan 443
Includes her fairy tales, a fictionalized autobiography, Spanish histories:
1) *Memoirs of her own life;*
2) *Marquis of Lemos and Dona Eleonora of Montelon;*
3) *Dona Eugena of St Angelo;*
4) *Marquis of Leyva;*
5) *Dona Camella D'Arellano;*
6) *Hortense of Ventimiglia;*
7) *Marquis of Mansera and Teresa of Castro;*
8) *Her Letters;*
9) *Tales of the Fairies.*

9. *The history of the Earl of Warwick, sirnam'd the Kingmaker* (1707, 1708; 3 pts, 1-199, 1-175 + 3-78)

NCBEL II 985[13]; McBurney 29
Trans. of *Le comte de Warwick.*
Love story with slight historical interest.

10. *Memoirs of the Court of England* (1707, 1708; 3 pts, 1-220, 353-518 + 521-616)

NCBEL II 985[14]; McBurney 28
Trans. by J. C.
Amorous history of the Court of Charles II.

11. *Hypolitus Earl of Douglas. Containing some memoirs of the Court of Scotland, with the secret history of Mack-Beth. To which is added the amours of Count Schlick* (1708; 5 edns by 1768; 1768 [another trans.]; 3 pts, pp. 256, 97, 63

NCBEL II 985[20]; McBurney 35; Morgan 449
Count Schlick is a new version of AENEAS SYLVIUS (Pope PIUS II), *Historia de duobus amantibus* (*Euryalus et Lucretia,* 1444), a Renaissance *roman à clef.*

EDITIONS

1129   *Relation du voyage d'Espagne.* Ed. R.FOULCHÉ-DELBOSC, Paris 1926. Trans. *Travels into Spain.* (Broadway Travellers.) London: George Routledge & Sons Ltd, 1930; pp. 447.

Adaptation of FOULCHÉ-DELBOSC'S introd. and notes for the English edition. Introd. (i-lxxiii) presents a very detailed account of her life and works. Part 1 life (iii-xii), Part 2 the *Memoirs of the Court of Spain* (xii-xiv), Part 3 the *Memoirs of Villars,* Part 4 the *Travels into Spain* (xxvii-lxvi), conclusion (lxi-lxxiii). Bibliography of the works of Mme d'Aulnoy (lxxv-lxxxv). Facs. of the title page of the English edition. The text is a reprint (with modern spelling and a few slight alterations) of the second edition of the *Relation du voyage d'Espagne* (1692) (1-399). Notes to the introd. (401-21), to the bibliography (422-24), to the text. Index.

1130   A selection of fairy tales. In (pp. 261-598) ZIPES, Jack (trans. and introd.). *Beauties, beasts and enchantment: Classic French fairy tales* etc., **150.**

Contains:
1) "The Island of Happiness";
2) "Beauty with the Golden Hair";
3) "The Blue Bird";

4) "The Good Little Mouse";
5) "The Golden Branch";
6) "The Ram";
7) "Finette Cendron";
8) "The Bee and the Orange Tree";
9) "The Babiole";
10) "The Yellow Dwarf";
11) "The Green Serpent";
12) "The Princess Rosette";
13) "The White Cat";
14) "The Benificent Frog";
15) "Belle-Belle, or The Chevalier Fortuné".

Introd. (1-12) discusses Mme d'Aulnoy as a writer of *contes de fées* in the context of the efflorescence of this genre in late 17c and early 18c France.

STUDIES

1131 BALLASTER, Ros. "Watching Women: Marie d'Aulnoy." In (pp. 123-31) BALLASTER, *Seductive forms* etc., **199**.

Mary Manley's scandalous fictions consistently address and rework the fiction of the French travel and scandal writer, Marie d'Aulnoy, who appears to have been her consciously chosen heroine. D'Aulnoy insists on the authenticity and contemporaneity of her stories, whereas Manley locates hers in the ancient past or imagined worlds. D'Aulnoy represents herself as an 'amatory spy' amassing information, details and facts. She used an allegorical structure, but not so obscure that her readers could not recognize her fiction for the party-political propaganda it was.

1132 BARCHILON, Jacques. "*Précieux* elements in the fairy tales of the seventeenth century." *L'Ésprit créateur* 3 (1963): 99-107.

Although Mme d'Aulnoy uses traditional fairy tale motifs, she endows them with sophistication, the tales dealing with animals esp. revealing refined *précieux* elements.

1133 BEELER, James R. "Madame d'Aulnoy: historical novelist of the late seventeenth century." Unpub. doct. diss., Univ. of North Carolina, 1964.

While this study does not deal with the English reputation and influence of the authoress, it does provide illuminating discussion of her historical works, as well as bibliographical material.

1134-----"An interesting use of genealogy in historical romance." In (pp. 31-40)

DANIEL, George Bernard, Jr. (ed.). *Renaissance and other studies in honor of William Leon Wiley*. Chapel Hill: U of North Carolina P, 1968; pp. 282.
Discusses Mme d'Aulnoy's use of the device.

1135 DAY, Robert Adams. *Told in Letters* etc., **364**.

The Present Court of Spain is a double narrative monster created by the accomplished and prolific Mme. d'Aulnoy, which went through 2 editions in 5 years in English translation, and demonstrates plainly the magical sales powers which love letters were thought to have, and the difficulties which the epistolary novel was undergoing in breaking free from the trammels of convoluted narrative (142). Also discusses *Memoirs of the Court of England*. In this short 'novel' of 39 pp., containing 26 letters of varying length, the slight plot is given in double narrative, either side of which would have been sufficient to convey its essentially. The narration in letters is filtered through the Countess's personality, while the Duke's story lacks emotional overtones, and concentrates on events rather than their impact.

1136 HUBERT, Renée Riese. "L'amour et la féerie chez Mme d'Aulnoy." *RF* 75 (1963): 123-29.

Her style is tinged with the urbanity, sophistication and gentle irony of the salon.

1137 McLEOD, Glenda. "Mme d'Aulnoy: writer of fantasy." In (pp. 91-118) WILSON, Katharina M. and WARNKE, Frank, J. *Women writers of the seventeenth century*. Athens, GA: London: U of Georgia P, 1989: pp. xxii, 545.
Provides a biography, critical account of her works, the text of the tale "The Bee and the Orange Tree", select bibliography.

1138 PALMER, Melvin D. "Madame d'Aulnoy in England." *CL* 27 (1975): 237-53.
Account of life and works. In view of the remarkable popularity of Mme d'Aulnoy in England in the four or five decades after 1690, and the general neglect of her work since then, the lack of a study of her reputation and influence in England seems a gap worth filling - even though her works, with some exceptions, merit the neglect they have received. But there are works of sufficient merit which deserve attention. An investigation of her work should also prove an important index to the translating practices and reading tastes in the years just before Richardson and the great mid-18c novelists in England. Bibliographic

appendix of works and later editions divided into 17c, 18c, 19c and 20c.

1139-----"*The History of Adolphus* (1691): the first French *conte de fée* in England." *PQ* 49 (1970): 565-67.

This tale was originally inserted into the sentimental romance *Histoire d'Hypolite* (1690), but because the translator gave the story a remarkably English flavor, it was regarded as a native English work until quite recently.

1140 PALMER, Nancy B. and PALMER, Melvin D. "The French *conte de fée* in England." *SSF* 11 (1974): 35-44.

Between 1691 and 1729 there was a vogue for fairy tales from France, with 62 appearing in translation (18 of them by Mme d'Aulnoy).

1141 STORER, Mary Elizabeth. *Un épisode littéraire de la fin du XVIIe siècle: la mode des contes de fées (1685-1700)*. (Bibliothèque de la *Revue de Littérature Comparée*, 48.). Paris: Librairie Ancienne Honoré Champion, 1928; pp. vii, 289.

Comprehensive study of the vogue for fairy tales in late 17c France. Provides an introd. (1-16) placing the vogue in context. Then devotes a chapter to each of the major figures who worked in the genre, including Mme d'Aulnoy (9-17) and Perrault (76-181). Looks at biography and gives a critical survey of the works. Bibliography (261-83).

1142 ZIPES, Jack. "The rise of the French fairy tale and the decline of France." Introd. (pp. 1-12) to *Beauties, beasts and enchantment* etc., **150**.

Provides a survey of the genre, as it arose in the context of the growing political, social and economic stresses and hardship of Louis XIV's reign at the end of the 17c. Given the stringent censorship of the régime, the *conte de fées* served as a medium for venting criticism of the times while also projecting hope for a better world. "The salon tales were marked by the struggles within the upper classes for recognition, sensible policies, and power" (6). Examines the phenomenon of *préciosité*, and investigates the tale in its various generic guises as the salon fairy tale, the Oriental fairy tale, the comic and conventional fairy tale. Their enduring captivation lies in an ability to rise above contemporary topicality to embrace the future. "They anticipate hopes and wishes that we ourselves have yet to fulfill" (12).

1143-----"Marie-Catherine d'Aulnoy." In (pp. 295-97) *Beauties, beasts and* *enchantment* etc.

Succinct critical introd. to the life and works. Points out how d'Aulnoy initiated the great fairy tale vogue with the story "L'Île de la félicité" intercalated in her novel *L'Histoire d'Hippolyte, comte de Douglas* (1690). She paid close attention to details of dress, architecture, speech and the manners of her day, giving her stories the ring of authenticity. She rebelled against constraints, the ways in which women were treated and compelled to follow patriarchal codes, and filled her stories with violence and violations that have to be resolved. This is a nightmarish world where the only saving grace is love, or *tendresse*.

AVALLANEDA, Alonso Fernandez de

A continuation of the comical history of the most ingenious knight Don Quixote
(1705, pp. 437)

NCBEL II 985[5]; McBurney 19
Trans. of a version by LE SAGE of the Spanish original.

BARKER, Jane

1. *Love's intrigues: or the history of the amours of Bosvil and Galesia* (1713; at
least 4 edns by 1750 [in *Entertaining novels*], pp. 71)

NCBEL II 987[1]; McBurney 66; ECSTC 753B5
Moralizing romance.

2. *Exilius: or the banish'd Roman; written after the manner of Telemachus* (1715,
1719-50 [in *Entertaining novels*]; I, 172; III, 142)

NCBEL II 987[14]; McBurney 78; Morgan 481; ECSTC 753B3
Short romance, with inserted histories; modest, moralizing tone.

3. *The entertaining novels of Mrs Jane Barker* (1719; 3 edns by 1736; 1750; 2
vols, pp. 310)

NCBEL II 988[11]; McBurney 95; ECSTC 753B2
Consists of *Exilius, Bosvil and Galesia*.

4. *A patch-work screen for ladies; or, love and virtue recommended in a
collection of instructive novels* (1723; 2 pts, pp. 38, 143)

NCBEL II 989[19]; McBurney 141; Morgan 534; ECSTC 753B6
Stories in frame, with poems; mild romances of country life.

5. *The lining for the patch-work screen* (1726, pp. 201)

NCBEL II 991[2]; McBurney 190; ECSTC 753B4
Tales as a sequel to *The patch-work screen* (1723); one continues the story of a Portuguese nun.

6. *The entertaining novels of Mrs Jane Barker* (1726, advertised by Bettesworth as the 2nd ed. The earliest known ed. is that of 1736, rpt. 1743; n.p.)

NCBEL II 991[2]; ECSTC 735B2

Contains:
1) *Exilius*;
2) *Clelia and Marcellus; or the constant lovers*;
3) *The reward of virtue: or the adventures of Clarenthia and Lysander*;
4) *The lucky escape; or the fate of Ismenius*;
5) *Clodius and Scipiana; or the beautiful captive*;
6) *Piso: or the lewd courtier*;
7) *The happy recluse: or, the charms of liberty*;
8) *The fair widow or false friend*;
9) *The amours of Bosvil and Galesia.*

EDITIONS

1144 *Love Intrigues*. Ed. BACKSCHEIDER and RICHETTI in (pp. 81-112) *Popular fiction by women, 1660-1730* etc. See ANTHOLOGIES, Ch. 2, **119**.

BIBLIOGRAPHY

1145 SCHOFIELD, Mary Anne. "Barker, Jane." In (pp. 9-17) SAAR and SCHOFIELD, *Eighteenth-century Anglo-American novelists: a critical reference guide* etc., **93**.

Annotated criticism from 1900 to 1992 (48 items).

SELECTED PRE-1992 STUDIES

1146 KLEIN in (p. 240) *Der Briefroman in der englischen Literatur* etc., **569**.

Provides a breakdown of the epistolary content of *A patch-work screen for ladies.*

1147 McBURNEY, W. H. "Edmund Curll, Mrs Jane Barker and the English novel." *PQ* 37 (1958): 385-99.

In the early 18c the novel was still a matter of financial speculation. More than 250 booksellers and printers crowded Grub Street by 1700, and controlled the large body of professional translators, compilers, hack writers and aspiring authors. Edmund Curll was found among them, and published works by Mrs Manley and Mrs Haywood. The latter, a Royalist Catholic, was gifted in imitation of the Scudéry romances. She engaged in clandestine political intrigue, although her featured works do not reflect any of the Pretender's troubles, but rather a placid, if impecunious, rural existence. Her aim was "to reform the world and restore Heroic Love to its ancient Justification". Her defence of romance showed an awareness of the financial appeal of this type of fiction. She showed a genuine, but rarely exercised, gift for realistic description, and was influenced by Behn, the periodical essays by Addison and Steele, and the moralizing of Mrs Aubin. She certainly avoided the moral licence of the 1720s. The taste for short romances characterized much of the fiction published between 1700 and 1740, a taste directly ascribable to Curll and his literary ladies.

1148 WEBER, Donna-Lee. "Fair game: rape and sexual aggression on women in some early eighteenth-century prose fiction," **1035**.

———

BEAUCHAMPS, Pierre-François-Godart de

The history of King Apprius, translated from a Persian manuscript. By a gentleman who served in   the Persian armies (1728, 1728, 1739; pp. 7-116)

NCBEL II 992[3]; McBurney 236; Morgan 582
Trans. of *Histoire du Prince Apprius* (1728)
Obscene account of sexual matters using anagrams: Apprius is Priapus etc.; a key to the disguised personages was published in 1764

———

BERINGTON, Simon

The memoirs of Sigr. Gaudentio di Lucca (1737, 1738; 8 edns by 1800; pp. 335)

NCBEL II 994[12]; McBurney 323; Morgan 633; ECSTC 1855B3

Not a trans.; original Utopian voyage.

EDITIONS

1149 *The Adventures of Signor Gaudentio di Lucca. Being the Substance of His Examination before the Fathers of the Inquisition at Bologna, in Italy. Giving an Account of an Unknown Country in the Midst of the Deserts of Africa. Compiled from the Original Manuscripts in St Mark's Library at Venice. With Critical Notes by the Learned Signor Rhedi. Translated from the Italian.* (The Phoenix Library: A Series of Original and Reprinted Works bearing on the Restoration and Progress of Society in Religion, Morality and Science. Selected by J. M. Morgan.) London: Charles Gilpin, 1850; pp. xxviii, 297.

Reprints the preface: "The Publisher to the Reader".

STUDIES

1150 ELLISON, Lee Munroe."*Gaudentio di Lucca*: a forgotten Utopia." *PMLA* 50 (1935): 494-509.

Coming at a time when prose fiction was casting about for its appropriate subject matter, and was still in the experimental stages of its art, *Gaudentino* is almost the only specimen of the novel in English between *Robinson Crusoe* and *Gulliver* on the one hand, and *Pamela* on the other. On its appearance in 1737, the work found favour immediately, coincident with the growth of interest in the Utopian novel. The book was not only intended to controvert the arguments of Deism, but was the apotheosis of the patriarchal theory of government, along with the corollary principle of strict primogeniture and the proposition that the state is but the family on a vastly greater scale. It was further intended to serve the cause, permanently lost 8 years after its appearance, of the abortive efforts of Charles Edward to regain the throne of his fathers.

1151 HARVEY, A. D. and RACAULT, Jean-Michel. "Simon Berington's *Adventures of Sigr Gaudentio di Lucca*." *ECF* 4:1 (Oct. 1991): 1-14.

Explores Berington's narrative technique. English novelists of the 18c attempted most of the permutations of narrative form, yet one of the most innovative and accomplished, and in its day one of the most popular of 18c novels, has been virtually forgotten since the 1850s. The core of Berington's novel is a description of Utopia, with Campanella and Veiras as the principal inspiration. The hero, after many adventures, is eventually liberated from the Inquisition. The text is decorated with weightily learned footnotes which are attributed to an editor, Signor Rhedi, and give the real author an opportunity to show off the extent and profundity of his scholarship. The narrative itself is essentially a series of narratives within narratives: there are successively or alternatively no less than six narrative voices within the novel, each serving to give the semblance of credibility and authority to the successive narratives they introduce. Berington, a priest of the outlawed Catholic Church, and not on the best of terms with his superiors, was not allowed, for professional reasons, to acknowledge his most successful literary creation in his lifetime.

BIGNON, Jean-Paul

Adventures of Abdalla, son of Hanif, sent by the Sultan of the Indies to make a discovery of the island of Borico [...] translated into French from an Arabick manuscript [...] by Mr. de Sandisson [...] done into English by William Hatchett (1729; 4 edns by 1733; pp. 169)

NCBEL II 992[8]; McBurney 243; Morgan 590; ECSTC 2459B1
Trans. W. HATCHETT.
Fantastic adventures, with inserted histories in the manner of romances.

EDITIONS

1152 "Princess Zeineb and King Leopard." In (pp. 145-50) ZIPES (trans. and introd.), *Beauties, beast and enchantment* etc., **150**.

A tale extracted *Les Aventures d'Abdalla, fils d'Anif* (1712-14). Each episode of the book is a self-contained story in the exotic adventures of Abdalla.

STUDIES

1153 ZIPES, Jack. "The rise of the French fairy tale and the decline of France." Introd. (pp. 1-12) to *Beauties, beasts and enchantment*, **150**.

1154-----"Jean-Paul Bignon." In (pp. 143-44) *Beauties, beasts and enchantments* etc.
Brief critical introd. to the life and works, pointing out how Bignon combined Oriental motifs with French folklore. His use of first-person narrative set an important example for the Beauty and the Beast tradition developed by Gabrielle-Suzanne de Villeneuve and Jeanne-Marie Leprince de Beaumont.

—

BLACKAMORE, Arthur

1. *The perfidious brethren: or the religious triumvirate, displayed in three ecclesiastical novels* (1720, pp. 104)

   NCBEL II 988[18]; McBurney 109
   Attacks priests, Presbyterians, Anabaptists.

2. *Luck at last: or the happy unfortunate* (1723, 1737 [as *The distress'd fair*]; pp. 112)

   NCBEL II 989[20]; McBurney 139
   Decorous and domestic; heroine disguised as a servant.

EDITIONS

1155 *Luck at last: or the happy unfortunate.* Ed. McBURNEY in *Four before Richardson* etc. See ANTHOLOGIES, Ch.2, **133**.

STUDIES

1156 DAVIS, Richard Beale. "Blackamore: the Virginia colony and the early English novel." *Virginia Magazine of History & Biography* 75 (1967): 22-34.
If it could be shown that the novels of Blackamore were composed in the colony of Virginia, the date for the first "American novel" would be set back at least half a century. The 1723 work is a significant precursor of Samuel Richardson; the 1720 one is a thinly veiled attack, in the dedication and in each of the 3 novellas of which it is composed, on personages, parties and perhaps sects in the colony, though the settings as such are not American. Both were written by an educated gentleman who had recently returned to England after many years in the New World. Both are dedicated in fulsome praise to living Virginians. One has a major character modelled on a Williamsburg matron. The other is concerned with a religio-political struggle going on in the Old Dominion. Blackamore was a Londoner, educated at Oxford, who was sent to Virginia in 1707 as a schoolteacher. As a confirmed alcoholic, he appears frequently in personal, academic and gubernatorial records as a significant local problem. If he had stayed in Virginia he would have been the American Swift or Defoe.

—

BLAND, Captain

The northern Atalantis: or York spy (1713, 1713; pp. 70)

NCBEL II 987[2]; McBurney 67; ECSTC 2881B1
Scandal-chronicle of Yorkshire gentry.

———

BOCCALINI, Traiano

Secretaria di Apollo: or letters from Apollo (1704, n.p.)

NCBEL II 985[3]; ECSTC 3076B3
Trans. Martin BLADEN.
Early example of letters from the dead to the living.

STUDIES

1157 BRODERSON, G. L. "A Boccalini translation identified." *NQ* 198 (1953):
154-55.
Discusses Bladen and his translation. He was a typical early 18c jack-of-
all-trades, a soldier, a party hack, and minor writer. His addresses to the
reader in each volume contain examples of would-be aristocratic Grub
Street bickering, with Hughes and his colleagues, and there are a few
"worthless verses" of commendation.

———

BORDELON, Laurent, Abbé

A history of the ridiculous extravagances of Monsieur Oufle (1711, 1754; pp. 303)

NCBEL II 986[13]; McBurney 56; ECSTC 3341B1
Trans. of satirical account of an adept deluded by magic.

———

BOURSAULT, Edmé

Letters from a lady of quality to a chevalier (1721, 1724 [also in *Works of Mrs
Haywood*]; pp. 86)

NCBEL II 989[8]; McBurney 122
Trans. Eliza HAYWOOD from *Lettres nouvelles*, 1699.
Sentimental-psychological epistolary novel: little action.

STUDIES

1158 LANCASTER, H. C. "Calderon, Boursault, and Ravenscroft." *MLN* 51 (1936): 523-28.

Boursault's *Ne pas croire qu'un void, histoire espangnole*, a satirico-romantic novel published in 1670, 1672, 1677, and 1739 provides an example of French literature acting as an intermediary between Spain and England. It is based on Calderon's *Casa con dos puertas* and was translated into English, not only by the author of *Deceptio visus*, but also by Ravenscroft in his *Wrangling Lovers*.

———

BOYD, Elizabeth

The happy-unfortunate: or the female-page (1732, 1737 [as *The female page*]; pp. 340)

NCBEL II 993[6]; McBurney 275; ECSTC 3686B3
Highly romantic work of disguise and adventure; written entirely in blank verse rhythm.

STUDIES

1159 KLEIN in (p. 248) *Der Briefroman in der englischen Literatur* etc., **569**.

Provides a breakdown of the literary correspondence in *The female page*.

———

BOYER, Abel

1. *The wise and ingenious companion* (1700, pp. 232)

WING B3918; ECSTC 3704B38
Bilingual English and French jest-book.

2. *Letters of wit, politicks and morality* (1701, n.p.)

Epistolary collection.

EDITIONS

1160 "Captain Ayloffe's Letters" from *Letters of wit, politics and morality*. Ed. WÜRZBACH in (pp. 23-36) *The novel in letters* etc., **149**.

Introd. (25-26). What makes these 14 letters of this correspondence interesting is the way in which the style of each letter is suited to the recipient.

STUDIES

1161 GUSKIN, Phyllis J. "Some animal versions and observations of wit, politics and morality in the life of Abel Boyer." *ECL* 12:3 (Nov. 1988): 118-38.

After 40 years in England, and a major contributor to the literature, politics and culture of his age, Boyer still felt himself an alien, friendless and rootless, vulnerable to the blows of fate. However, it may have been his very marginality itself that enabled him to look closely and clearly at the English political scene, and capture the complex material and motives of the volatile years he documented for posterity. Detailed bibliographical notes (134-38).

1162 SYNDER, Henry L. "The contribution of Abel Boyer as Whig journalist and writer of the *Protestant Post-Boy*." In (pp.139-50) Robert B. WHITE (ed.), *The Dress of Words* etc., **1046**.

Boyer was one of the most prolific and important of the early 18c journalists working in England. He is remembered as the editor of a pioneer French-English dictionary that went through 41 editions between 1702 and 1841. By others he is remembered as a translator and editor. His greatest achievement lies in his *Political State of Great Britain*, a monthly which he edited from Jan. 1711 until his death in 1729. It carried on the summaries of Parliamentary debates begun in his *History of the Reign of Queen Anne Digested into Annals* (11 vols, 1703 to 1713). He also contributed to the *Protestant Post Boy*, a strong Whig, pro-Marlborough publication which appeared semi-weekly from 4 July. - 12 Sept.1712.

BOYER, Jean-Baptiste de

See **D'ARGENS**

BROWN, Thomas

Amusements serious and comical, calculated for the meridian of London (1700; at least 10 edns by 1760; pp. 160)

NCBEL II 984[13]; ECSTC 4640B30
Uses ingénu device for social satire.

EDITIONS

1163 *Amusements Serious and Comical and Other Works [Letters on Several Occasions, Letters from the Dead to the Living].* Ed. Arthur L. HAYWARD. London: George Routledge & Sons Ltd., 1927; pp. xvii, 476. 15 illus.

Introd. (xiii-xvii). "Tom Brown was, without question, one of the best of Grub Street literary hacks - scholarly, witty, scurrilous, and unscrupulous, and excellent journalist, with a sure instinct for a good 'story', and a ready pen to serve it up as his public would have it [...]. [H]e carried his readers with him by an assumption of honest conviction. He is inevitably compared with Ned Ward since both their principal works have the same scope in their description of contemporary life in London. Yet Brown has a finer touch, and though his fictions are not as true to life as Ward's, they form, on the whole, a pleasanter picture" (xvii).

STUDIES

1164 ANON. "Defoe, Ward, Brown, and Tutchin, 1700-1703." *NQ* 162 (1932): 418-23.

After a long period of repression and persecution, the English Press gained its freedom in 1695 when the Licencing Act was first abrogated. Several newspapers, issued 2 or 3 times a week, arose in London and disseminated news: *Flying Post, Post Boy, Post Man, London Post, English Post, London Gazette.* By consulting the advertisements to obtain accurate information on any subjects, new light can be shed on the many difficulties surrounding Defoe, Brown, Ward and Tutchin in their journalistic work. The extracts are all taken from 1700 to 1703.

1165-----"The life and works of Thomas Brown, 1663-1704." *Harvard University Summaries of Theses, 1933*: 278-81. See below, **1169**.

1166-----"Two debits for Tom Brown, with a credit from Joseph Addison." *PQ* 14 (1935): 263-69.

Brown's *Amusements*, one of the cleverest developments in English of the 'citizen of the world' device, was a free and amplified translation of Charles R. Dufresny's *Amusements sérieux et comique* (1699). But those portions of Brown's *Amusements* which remain in the memory of the modern reader - the crowded, brightly colored street scenes and the vividly etched interiors - are for the greater part either not as impressive in Dufresny's book, or not there at all. But when one turns to the witty sallies and sarcastic allusions, the rapid account of what his Indian saw in the shops and ordinary churches of London, one sometimes finds not Brown's own work, but numerous phrases, sentences, paragraphs which had previously appeared in Quevedos's *Suenos*. When Addison described his visit to Westminster Abbey in No. 26 of the *Spectator*, much of his observations were based on those of Brown.

1167 BOYCE, Benjamin. "Milton and Thomas Brown's translation of Gelli." *NQ* 171 (1936): 328-29.

In 1702 Brown translated "The Circe of Signor Giovanne Battista Gelli", a rationalistic attack on the orthodox belief that man is the perfect summit of creation. Gelli's coldly rational story is transformed into something Christian. The poetic diction is the most interesting feature of Brown's Miltonic rendering of these lines by a 16c naturalist.

1168-----"Tom Brown and Elia." *ELH* 4 (1937): 147-50.

That Charles Lamb read Brown appears in 2 specific references to him. That he copied Brown's characteristic facetious simile at least once is also evident. There is a resemblance, too, in the kind of comic phrases used by both authors. But these are minor matters: the important likeness is less tangible, and rests in the method and tone of the treatment of London life by both writers. It is the blending of swift, realistic description, sharp and even acid wit, and a faint undertone of disillusionment and melancholy.

1169-----*Tom Brown of facetious memory: Grub Street in the Age of Dryden.* (Harvard Studies in English, 21.) Cambridge, MA: Harvard UP, 1939; pp. ix, 215.
Although Brown is a secondary figure, students of the period of William and Mary, and of Anne have realized that his works are a storehouse of vivid sketches and witty comment upon London in his day. Covers youth and education, early satires and adventures in journalism, history and literature of Grub Street (1692 to 1698), prose translations, the letter as popular entertainment, paper pellets (1699 to 1700), news from France and from Hell (1700 to 1702), the end of his career (1702 to 1704), death. Bibliography (189-208) lists published works with contribution by Brown, and works to which he probably contributed. Index (209-15). Of esp. interest is ch. 7 "*Amusements Serious and Comical*" (134-47) which discusses the origins and nature of the book. Bibliographical notes. "The casual reader of Brown will unquestionably find his greatest pleasure in the profuse, disorderly spectacle of London life and the mordant

observations upon the scene" (209).

1170   EDDY, William A. "Tom Brown and *Tristram Shandy*." *MLN* 44 (1929): 379-81.

Sterne is another of those famous humorists who turned to the relatively obscure Tom Brown for concrete incident. The famous passage of "The Dwarf" in *The Sentimental Journey* is copied from Brown almost verbally. Sterne is closer to Brown's translation of Scarron's *Le Roman comique* than to the French original.

1171-----"Tom Brown and Partridge the astrologer." *MP* 28 (1930): 163-68.

Tom Brown was the earliest and most persistent of Partridge's tormentors, and his mock predictions, published in 1700, anticipated almost every point in Bickerstaff's later attack, except for Swift's gravity and pseudo-seriousness. It is Brown's predictions rather than the activities of Partridge himself, which were the principal inspiration for the role of Bickerstaff. The Partridge affair is another proof of what so far has been hardly investigated: that the disreputable Brown furnished a good deal of material for the satire of his more conventional contemporaries.

1172   POTTER, Mabel. "A letter of Tom Brown." *NQ* 20 (1973): 393.

The Dobell MS (*Dob*) containing poetry and prose of John Donne contains a humorous exchange between Tom Brown and WB. The opening lines are based in an epigram by Martial, and continues with a reference to a "woollen-Draper" found elsewhere in Brown's work. The recipient can be identified with Dr William Balam (1651-1726), an Ely lawyer and Donne enthusiast.

1173   SCHULTE, Edvige. *Thomas Brown e le origini del saggio de costume*. Napoli: Ligouri, 1969.

In Italian. Account of life and works.

1174   WEBSTER, Clarence M. "Tom Brown and *The Tale of a Tub*." *TLS* (18 Feb. 1932): 112.

Brown used a theme of satire which is like one made famous by Swift in *The Tale of a Tub*. Brown wrote *The Men and Women Saints in an Uproar: or the Superstitions of the Romish Church Expos'd, 1687*. Both authors mocked the infallibility of papal decrees, and both represent the Pope as irascible and tyrannical. Swift changes the theme to ridicule the theory of transubstantiation, but the same fundamental idea - satire of papal insistence that things are what they are proclaimed to be - is the same in both writers. If we accept the likeness between the two passages as evidence of conscious imitation and adaptation of Brown by Swift, there is more than additional proof that Swift was indebted to his fellow satirist.

'BRUNT, Samuel, Captain'

A voyage to Cacklogallinia (1727, pp. 167)

NCBEL II 991[8]; McBurney 205; ECSTC 4827B1
Satire imitative of Swift.

EDITIONS

1175 *A Voyage to Cacklogallinia. With a Description of the Religion, Policy, Customs and Manners of that Country. By Captain Samuel Brunt. Reproduced from the Original Edition, 1727, with an Introduction by Marjorie Nicolson.* Ed. Marjorie H. NICOLSON. (Facsimile Text Society Publications, 48.) New York: Columbia UP, 1925; pp. xv, 167.

Complete facsimile reprint with frontispiece and title page. The introduction presents the work and its meaning. "It lives [...] because of its satiric reflection of the background of the age. It is republished both because of its historical value and because of its peculiarly contemporary appeal today. Its satire needs no learned paraphernalia of footnotes; it can be readily understood and apprehended by readers in an age dominated [...] by economics [...] and science" (vi).

STUDIES

1176 BORGMEIER, Raimund. "*Memoirs of Sundry Transactions from the World in the Moon* - drei satirische Mondreisen von Zeitgenossen Gullivers." In (pp. 113-27) PETERS and STEIN (eds.). *Scholastic Midwifery: Studien zum Satirischen in der englischen Literatur 1600-1800* etc., **756**.

On Brunt, Defoe and McDermot. Investigates three satirical journeys to the moon:
1) Defoe's *The Consolidator: Or, Memoirs of Sundry Transactions from the World in the Moon* (1705) (115-22);
2) Capt. Samuel Brunt's *A Voyage to Cacklogallinia: With a Description of the Religion, Politics, Customs and Manners of that Country* (1727) (122-24);

3) Murtagh McDermot's *A Trip to the Moon: Containing Some Observations and Reflections, made by him [the Author] during his Stay in that Planet , upon the Manner of the Inhabitants* (1728) (124-27). Brunt's story is based on the 'great orgy of speculation, the South Sea Bubble', with thinly veiled satire describing a country remarkably similar to England under Walpole. Shows how in all 3 stories the more 'realistic' kinds of satire are always just on the verge of falling over into the symbolic mode, despite the satiric claims to literal truthfulness.

BUSSY-RABUTIN, Roger de

The amorous history of the Gauls (1725, 1727; pp. 232)

NCBEL II 990[16]; McBurney 184.
New trans., probably by Samuel HUMPHREYS.

BUTLER, Sarah

Milesian tales: or instructive novels for the happy conduct of life (1719, 1727; pp. 130)

NCBEL II 988[11]; McBurney 96; ECSTC 5634B1
May have appeared in 1716 as *Irish tales*; perhaps by Charles GILDON.

[CAMPBELL, John?]

The polite correspondence: or rational amusement. (1730?, n.p.)

NCBEL II 992[15]
6 series of letters; the first, a domestic novel of intrigue with complex plot.

EDITIONS

1177　The first series of letters ed. WÜRZBACH, in (pp. 149-96) *The novel in letters* etc., **149**.

Introd. (149). The author [Campbell] takes a critical view of heroic and scandalous novels. This piece of literary theorizing within the novel is symptomatic of a trend at the beginning of the 18c when the novel was passing through a stage of experimentation.

CASTILLO SOLÓRZANO, Alonso de

La picara: or the triumphs of female subtilty (1665, [1700?], pp. 304)

WING C1231A; NCBEL II 976[7]
Trans. John DAVIES of Kidwelly.
Clever anti-heroine Rufina; inserted romantic tales.

OTHER VERSIONS

- *The life of Donna Rosina* (1703-8);
- *Three ingenious Spanish novels* (1712) (ECSTC 1071C4);
- *The Spanish pole-cat* (1717) (ECSTC 1071C2);
- *Spanish amusements* (1727).

CERVANTES SAAVEDRA, Miguel de

1. *The famous history of Don Quixote de la Mancha* (1686; 5 edns by 1699; pp. 616)

   WING C1772; NCBEL II 981[3]
   Various versions of an abridgement.

2. *The second part of the history of Don Quixote of the Mancha* (1672-5; 2 pts, pp. [8] 137, 138-273)

   WING C1777; NCBEL II 977[18]
   "Newly corrected and amended" by Thomas SHELTON.

3. CERVANTES and CASTILLO SOLÓRZANO. *The Spanish Decameron: or ten novels* (1687, 1720; pp. 587)

   WING H2599; NCBEL II 981[7]
   Trans. Sir Roger L'ESTRANGE; 10 novellas selected from both authors: "The rival ladies"; "The mistakes"; "The generous lover"; "The libertine"; "The virgin captive"; "The perfidious mistress"; "The metamorphos'd lover"; "The impostor out-witted"; "The amorous miser"; "The pretended alchemist".

SELECTED STUDIES

1178 CORDASCO, Francesco. "Smollett and the translation of the *Don Quixote*: a critical bibliography." *NQ* 193 (1948): 383-84.

List of 18 titles for the convenience of the antiquarian who wishes to review the critical notices.

1179 ENOMOTO, Futoshi. *Don Quixote no kage no moto ni: 18 seiki igirisu shosetsu no shoso* etc., **409**.

1180 KNAPP, Lewis M. "Smollett's translation of *Don Quixote*: data on its printing and its copyright." *NQ* 201 (1957): 534-44.

Examination of original and whatever other translation Smollett might have known. Believes that Smollett knew no Spanish, and his text was the result of a commission from a hack school.

1181 KNOWLES, Edwin B. "*Don Quixote* abridged." *PBSA* 51 (1957): 19-36.

The standard editions of *Don Quixote* before 1700 are well-known: Thomas Shelton's trans. 1612 and 1620, folio reissue in 1652, 1675, 1677; John Philips's trans. 1687. Almost unknown are the 4 short chapbook versions published in London in 1686, 1689, 1699 and an undated vol., c. 1700. In these 4 cheap little abridgements we see a combination of the typical first English reactions to Cervantes's novel - first, that it was a hilarious book, but without depth or serious worth; second, a clear foreshadowing of the typical 18c view - that it was a great satire, comic to be sure, but universal in its common applicability, with its serious function (in Fielding's words) "to expose and extirpate those follies and vices which chiefly prevail".

1182 LINSALATA, Carmine Rocco. *'Smollett's Hoax': 'Don Quixote' in English.* (Stanford Univ. Publications, Language & Literature, 14.) Stanford, CA: Stanford UP, 1956; pp. ix, 116.

Smollett's translation of Cervantes has always been controversial. It has never been determined conclusively whether "Smollett's *Quixote*" (1755) was done independently or with the aid of existing translations. It has been alleged that his was a reworking of Charles Jarvis's rendition. Tries to disentangle the issues, looking at 1) the possiblity of Smollett's having relegated the translation to a hack school, 2) the date of Jarvis's composition, 3) the Spanish text employed in its rendition. Shows that Smollett's translation is "a gem in the realm of fraudulent acts".

Interesting for ch.1 "Spanish literature in English translations, 1484-1755" (1-2), ch. 2 "*Don Quixote* in English translation, 1612-1755" (3-12). Various comparative appendices. Bibliography (113-4). Postscript (115-6).

1183 NOWAIRA, A. H. A. "Irony in the Quixote novel of the eighteenth century, 1742-1773." Unpub. doct. diss., Univ. of Birmingham 1980.
Abstract not available.

1184 PARKER, A. A. "Fielding and the structure of *Don Quixote*." *Bulletin of Hispanic Studies* 33 (1956): 1-16.

Cervantes was transferred into *Joseph Andrews*, and there are numerous parallels between characters and incidents. But there are also dissimilarities, and bringing out the contrast between the two different approaches throws light on the problems of constructing a novel. The Spanish novelists of the 16c and early 17c (Alemán, Quevedo, Cervantes) are not interested in epic structure, but rather in the question of moral responsibility in pinning down the evils in society to the self-assertion and the deliberate choices made by individual human beings and the influences that we exercise upon each other. They devise a novelistic structure in which casuality connects episodes to character, that is to say, human actions to human motives. The structure of *Tom Jones*, on the other hand, has an ordering of a different kind, which gives to the novel only the purely external and superficial quality of formal neatness. This is the mark of the 18c which in its quest for rational order accepted and promulgated rules for composition. The age of Cervantes was less interested in outward form regulated by fixed precepts, and more interested in the universal significance that could be given to the literary representation of human characters and their actions. The age presented a freedom of construction, indeed gave the imagination of great writers much wider scope, enabling them to range the breadth of human experience in a way the 18c could not emulate.

1185 PATTERSON, Malcolm Howie. "Early English novelists imitating *Quixote*,"**743**.

1186 STARKIE, Walter F. "Miguel de Cervantes and the English novel." *Essays by Divers Hands*, new ser., 34 (1966): 159-79.

Don Quixote, the first modern novel in the world, was created out of the disillusion, frustration and poverty by a maimed ex-soldier. It is one of those rare novels in which the hero and the author are so closely related to one another that it is not possible to study them apart. Provides a close account of Cervantes's life. Part 2 looks at England, the 17c and transition, and considers the history of *Don Quixote* in translation and imitation. After the Revolution of 1688 and the reign of William and Mary, came the era of Queen Anne, which was one of transition, leading into the Augustan Age (1740-80). It was then that the deep message of Cervantes's spiritual autobiography reached responsive hearts. Looks at Fielding, Smollett, Charlotte Lennox and Laurence Sterne. When one considers the evolution of the novel - the epic of modern life - through the centuries to our own days, it is instructive to note how many tendencies that are now considered modern already existed in *Don Quixote*, the first novel. A parallel can be drawn between it and the epoch-making *Ulysses*: just as Joyce's novel has been an elusive, eclectic *Summa* for the 20c, so was Cervantes's work the *Summa* for the age of the Renaissance, and the Baroque Age of the Counter Reformation.

1187 STAVES, Susan. "*Don Quixote* in eighteenth-century England." *CL* 24 (1972): 193-215.

No national literature assimilated the idea of *Don Quixote* more thoroughly than the English. During the 18c it was read and enthusiastically appreciated, and found many imitators. In this process of assimilation the knight undergoes a fascinating metamorphosis in 3 stages. First he is a buffoon, a madman in a farce. Then ambiguity begins to creep in, and although he is still ridiculous, he begins to look strangely noble, even saintly. Towards the end of the 18c we begin, thirdly, to glimpse the romantic Don Quixote, an idealistic and noble hero. Treatment of the Quixote idea in the English novel changes in ways which are quite parallel to the critical responses to Don Quixote himself. The literary Quixote comes full circle when Sir Walter Scott can use it not to destroy romance, but to create the romance which he sees as the most authentic realism.

———

CHAMBERLEN, Paul

Love in its empire, illustrated in seven novels (1721, pp. 180)

NCBEL II 989[9]; McBurney 121; ECSTC 1422C7
The first is original, the others trans. from LA ROCH-GUILHEM, LA FOIRE DE BEAUCAIRE, 1708 etc.
Novels of intrigue.

———

CHASLES, Robert

The illustrious French lovers (1727, 1739 [one episode as *The unnatural mother*];
2 vols: I, 1-267; II, 3-347)

NCBEL II 991[9]; McBurney 221; ECSTC 1718C1
Trans. Penelope AUBIN from *Les illustres Françoises*, 1722.
7 interlinked realistic tales.

EDITIONS

1188 *Les Illustres Françoises: Édition critique publiée avec des documents
inédits par Frédéric DELOFFRE.* (Les textes Français.) Paris: Société
d'Éditions 'Les Belles Lettres', 1959, 1967. 2 vols. I, iv, 280; II, 281-613.

Introd. (vii-lv) gives a detailed account of Chasles's life and the book
itself, the critical text. Fasc. title page. In vol. II there is an appendix
containing detailed bibliography (555-66), documents from the author's
life (567-88), criticism (589-92), variants. Index of names and themes
(609-13).

CHETWOOD, William Rufus

1. *The voyages, dangerous adventures and imminent escapes of Capt. R. Falconer*
(1720; 6 edns by 1769; 3 pts, pp. 76, 136, 176)

NCBEL II 989[1]; McBurney 110; ECSTC 1887C14
In the manner of Defoe.

2. *The voyages and adventures of Captain Robert Boyle* (1726, 1727; at least 13
edns by 1800; pp. 374)

NCBEL II 991[3]; McBurney 191; ECSTC 1887C15
Extremely popular; adventure, sentiment, hazard; resembles the manner
of Defoe, but lacks his moral tone; partly set in America.

[CIBBER, Colley?]

*The secret history of Arlus and Odolphus, ministers of state to the Empress of
Grandinsula* (1710 [3 edns]; pp. 40)

NCBEL II 986[9]; McBurney 48

Thinly veiled political satire, pro-Harley, anti-Godolphin. One of several similar works in a controversy using the same names.

BIBLIOGRAPHY

1189 ASHLEY, Leonard R. N. "Colley Cibber: a bibliography." *RECT* 6:1 (1967) 1-27; 6:2 (1967): 51-57.

Part A: The most modern and complete listing of Cibber's work. 1) Plays; 2) Plays attributed to Cibber; 3) Romantic Prologues and Epilogues; 4) Attributions; 5) Non-Dramatic Works. Part B: Writings about Cibber. 1) Books; 2) Anonymous Pamphlets; 3) Other Pamphlets; 4) Unpublished Manuscripts; 5) Periodicals; 6) Theses and Dissertations; 7) Biographies and Critical Essays.

STUDIES

1190 ASHLEY, Leonard R. N. *Colley Cibber.* (Twayne English Author Series, 17.) New York: Twayne, 1965; pp. 224.

Account of life and works, looking at chronology, youth, the actor, the playwright, Drury Lane, the management, the theater and the company, the laureate, the *Apology*, the literary quarrel with Pope, old age. Notes and references (171-204). Select bibliography (205-20). Index (221-24). Thinks that *The Secret History* is probably not by Cibber. The only 'evidence' is the fact that this work, published anonymously in 1714, was advertised by a publisher as "By Mr. Cibber" (79).

1191 BLOCK, Raphael H. "Without contempt: some new observations on the life and works of Colley Cibber." Unpub. doct. diss, Denver, 1972. [*DAI* 33 (1972): 1674A.]

Although Cibber is today remembered negatively, his plays as a body do not deserve the usual critical contempt, while his *Apology* is a most valuable source of information regarding the theatre of his day. His position in his own time was respected, and he was a leader in the movement from the comedy of manners to the early comedy of sentiment. A study of his plays convinces one that he is worthy of better appreciation.

1192 EAVES, T. C. D. and KIMBEL, Ben D. "Edward Young's comment on Colley Cibber." *NQ* 219 (1974): 256-57.

In Henry Pettit's edition of Edward Young's correspondence, he comments on a letter by Cibber to Richardson of 26 March 1751. The two were friends, but the letter, and Young's comment on it, nonetheless reveal their strikingly contrasting personalities.

1193 EVANS, John M. "A critical edition of *An Apology for the Life of Mr Colley Cibber, Comedian* [Including the facsimile edition of 1740 with author's notes]." Unpub. doct. diss., Yale, 1967. [*DA* 27 (1967) 3044A.]

As the result of the publication of his *Apology*, Cibber became a symbol for what the Opposition saw as the degeneration of English culture under the reign of the Hanoverians and the domination of Sir Robert Walpole. He had become, as the result of his own failures of character and the accidents of history, a ludicrous figure in the 1730s. After 1740, when the *Apology* appeared, he acquired a larger and more tangible significance. For his enemies he became at once the cause, victim and emblem of the decay of morals and taste in his own age. Pope fully exploited this symbolic potential in *The Dunciad*.

1194 FRUSHAL, Richard C. "Cibber's 1743 Birthday Ode and some 'Advice to the Laureate'." *NQ* 19 (1972): 374-75.

Cibber's "Ode on his Majesty's Birth-Day" appeared on George II's birthday (30 Oct. 1743) and in Nov. in *The Gentleman's Magazine*, one month after the publication of Pope's *Duciad*. Cibber's poem must have seemed to its 18c readers worthy of its author and of Pope's enthronement of him as chief dullard.

1195 GILMORE, Thomas B., Jr. "Colley Cibber's good nature and his reaction to Pope's satire." *PLL* 11 (1966): 361-71.

Pope's dislike of Cibber had a long history, but manifested itself appreciably in *The Dunciad* when Cibber became an inviting target as laureate. Cibber took no public notice of it until his *Apology* (1740), in the first 2 chapters of which he remonstrated with his critic. He frequently praised Pope's poignant wit and poetic skill as a poet who had attained real mastery of his art. Cibber's blithe and easy banter, his most characteristic weapon, was attractively new, but he used it to wound Pope. He further published 3 letters to Pope (1742, 1743, 1744) and a pamphlet *The Egoist* (1743) in which Pope features prominently.

1196 NEW, Melvyn. "The dunce revisited: Colley Cibber and Tristram Shandy." *SAQ* 72 (1973): 547-49.

It is just possible that Sterne had convinced Diderot that the writings of

Cibber and Pope could help him towards an understanding of *Tristram Shandy*. Cibber chose to play the clown in his *Apology*: the first chapter, where he etablishes himself before the reader, contains several passages which foreshadow the Shandian style. Cibber consciously sets his style of life and literature against another way of thinking. At the heart of Pope's attack on bad writing, or more generally bad taste, is precisely that prideful indulgence of self so evident in the passages from Cibber. The moral failure imitated by Cibber's self-indulgence, and made obvious in the parodist's attack on Cibber's moral relativism is, in Sterne's hands, the center of a subtle and complex examination of the respective roles of religion, reason, and feeling in the moral life.

1197 PEAVY, Charles Druery, III. "'Cibber's crown of dullness: a re-examination of the Pope-Cibber controversy." Unpub. doct. diss., Univ. of Tulane, 1964. [*DA* 25 (1964): 454A.]

The chief reason for Pope's hostility to Cibber was based on aesthetic and moral values. From 1717 until 1742, Pope's letters and published work are full of references to the innumerable offences Cibber committed as actor, dramatist, manager and poet laureate. Since Pope believed that literary and aesthetic crimes have implications on a higher, moral level, affecting not only the welfare of nations, but also the conditions of men's souls, he naturally excoriated the man whose career epitomized the corrupting elements in England's culture. Cibber became a symbol of the disintegration of the moral fibre and decay in good taste portrayed in *The Dunciad*.

1198-----"The Pope-Cibber controversy: a bibliography." *RECT* 3:2 (1964): 51-55.

List of 34 items with brief annotations, arranged chronologically (1717 to 1744), with the various items (plays, poems, satires, letters) tracing the various stages of the controversy.

1199 ROGAL, Samuel J. "Pope's treatment of Colley Cibber." *LHR* 8 (1966): 25-30.
Cibber was for Pope the epitome of artistic corruption: as actor, comic playwright, and finally poet turned court jester. Pope played an important role in relegating Cibber to eventual obscurity: his works were not of sufficient quality to stand on their own merits, and through Pope's satire he became the universal symbol of the universal spineless fop.

1200 SHESGREEN, Sean. "Cibber in Fielding's *Jonathan Wild*." *AN&Q* 12 (1974): 88-90.

Critics of Fielding's novels have done a thorough job of recovering the names of the real people the novelist satirized. One such instance is in *Jonathan Wild* (1754) where the assistant bailiff was probably suggested by Cibber's brief, bloodless and abortive military career under the Earl of Devonshire for William of Orange. Fielding's detestation of Cibber and all his work and deeds is proverbial, and one of Cibber's most vulnerable areas was his renowned *Apology*. Fielding had already used Cibber's autobiography to attack him in *Shamela* and *Joseph Andrews*, and continued the tradition in *Jonathan Wild*.

1201 SHUMUTA, Natsuo. "Colley Cibber." *EigoS* 118 (1972): 146-47, 194-95, 278-79.

In Japanese. Account of life and works.

1202 SITTER, John E. "Cibber and Fielding's Quintessential Ode." *NQ* 25 (1978): 44.

Suggests that Fielding's satire applies to a juvenile exercise, and has little to do with the grown man.

1203 WOODS, Charles B. "Cibber in Fielding's *Author's Farce*: three notes." *PQ* 44:2 (1965): 145-51.

Cibber is one of the major satirical targets of Fielding's *The Author's Farce*. He was portrayed as "Keyber", a Germanic-sounding appellation to ridicule his loyal support of the Hanoverian family. He is also cast as "Marplay" because he was said to cobble old plays and mangle new ones; he is made out to have written the offensive parts of Vanbrugh's play *Journey to London* (1728) in his own *The Provok'd Husband* (1729). All are part of Fielding's campaign against Cibber.

———

CORDONNIER [DE SAINT-HYACINTHE], Hyacinthe

The history of Prince Titi, a royal allegory (1736, pp. 7-204)

NCBEL II 994[6]; McBurney 315; Morgan 641; ECSTC 3962C1
Trans. Eliza STANLEY; another trans., *The royal memoirs and history of Prince Titi*, in the same year by Ralph JAMES.
Scandal novel concerning Frederick Prince of Wales.

STUDIES

1204 IMBERT-TERRY, Henry. "An unwanted Prince." *Essays by Divers Hands*, new ser., 15 (1936): 135-60.

Considers the life of Frederick, Prince of Wales. There is a discussion of *The History of Prince Titi* in the context of the royal quarrel (135-40). The fact that a curious state secret, the intention of George II to separate the Crowns of Hanover and England, and to bequeath the former to his second son, the Duke of Cumberland, shows that the author must have been possessed of certain knowledge of the royal intention, and to some extent, provides the reason for introducing the subject to the notice of the Royal Society.

1205 SHIPEY, John B. "James Ralph, Prince Titi and the black box of Frederick, Prince of Wales." *BNYPL* 71 (March 1967): 143-57.

Hyacinthe Cordonnier de Saint-Hyacinthe (also known as Thémiseul de Saint-Hyacinthe) was born in Orleans (24 Sept. 1684), led a varied literary and amatory career on the continent, eloped to London with Suzanne de Marconnay. Married in July 1722, remained in London for 12 years, and was admitted to the Royal Society (Oct. 1728). Decided to capitalize on a family quarrel in the Royal Family. He had perceived the monetary possibilities of exploiting the royal dispute, and because of his aversion to George II, who in the early months of 1730 had cut off the pension given to French converts to Protestantism. In his book he described a young man tried by unhappiness, subject to shocking injustice from those from whom he least expected it, heroically overcomes the perils, and punishes his enemies only by overwhelming them with gifts. The book appeared in 1735 as the *Histoire du Prince Titi. A[llegorie] R[oyale]*. A ridiculous, far-fetched tale, it sought and achieved obvious notoriety as a *roman à clef*.

COSTEKER, John Littleton

The constant lovers; being an entertaining history of the amours and adventures of Solenus and Perrigonia, Alexis and Sylvia (1731; 2 pts, pp. 3-94, 97-248)
NCBEL II 992[20]; McBurney 257; Morgan 605; ECSTC 4115C1
2 old-fashioned romances.

EDITIONS

1206 The second romance, *Alexis and Sylvia* Ed. WÜRZBACH in (pp. 105-48)

The novel in letters etc., **149**.

Introd. (105-6). Contains a rudimentary domestic background and a certain amount of psychological realism.

STUDIES

1207 KLEIN in (pp. 248-49) *Der Briefroman in der englischen Literatur* etc., **569**.

Analyzes the epistolary exchange in *The constant lovers*.

———

COURTILZ DE SANDRAS, Gatien de

1. *The French spy: or the memoirs of John Baptist de la Fontaine [...]. Translated from the French original* (1700, 1703; pp. 371)

   WING C6597A; NCBEL II 984[14]; McBurney 3; Morgan 417; ECSTC 4302C3
   Trans. of *Mémoirs de Messire J.B. de la Fontaine* (1698).
   Ostensibly an autobiographical memoir of a soldier of fortune; purports to reveal secret history.

2. *The unfortunate marriage* (1722, pp. 296)

   NCBEL II 989[14]; McBurney 134
   Trans. of *Mémoires de Mme la marquise de Fresne* (1701).
   Tale of separated spouses and Turkish captivity.

———

CR[AWFURD], D[avid]

Several letters, containing: The unfortunate Dutchess, Love after enjoyment, The unhappy mistake (1700 [first tale reprinted separately, 1739; second separately, 1735]; n.p.)

   WING C6863A; NCBEL II 984[15]; ECSTC 3153L13
   Epistolary fiction in the manner of French romances.

STUDIES

1208 MACAREE, D. "Three early 18th-century prose romances." *Book Collector* 11 (1962): 215-16.

Three romances by David Crawfurd (1665-1726), identified as:
1. *Several Letters Containing the Amours of the Unfortunate Dutchess: Or, the Lucky Gamester*;
2. *Love after Enjoyment; Or, Fatal Constancy*;
3. *The Unhappy Mistake; Or, The Fate of Cross'd Lovers. Written by M.D.Cr--rd, Gent.* (London, 1700).

1209------"Crawfurd: a forgotten man of Scottish letters." *Stud in Scottish Lit* 5 (1967): 28-45.

Account of Crawfurd's life and works, giving details of his prose fiction. In the three novels that make up the collection, Crawfurd, following the example of the author of the *Portuguese Letters*, demonstrates his interest in female psychology by probing the motives and actions of his central female characters in considerable detail. He pays less attention to his young men; only one of them is described in any detail. The three tales may be considered as exercises in two modes of narration, for *Love after Enjoyment* and *The Unhappy Dutchess* are essentially the two sides of the same coin, consisting as they do in the account of Timindra's experiences in love sent in a letter to her friend Sirena, and of the latter's reply in similar terms, giving her story. *The Unhappy Mistake* is the story of what is alleged to be a recent scandal in high society, told in a long letter by an observer of the comedy to the lady he has been wooing unsuccessfully.

1210 R[OY], G. R. "David Crawfurd - an unrecorded broadside." *Stud in Scottish Lit* 6 (1969): 190-91.

A broadside in the possession of the National Library of Scotland gives the precise date of Crawfurd's death as 16 Jan 1708.

———

CRÉBILLON, Claude-Prosper-Jolyot de, *fils*

1. *Letters from the Marchioness de M*** to the Count de R**** (1735, pp. 304)

NCBEL II 994[18]; McBurney 304
Trans. Samuel HUMPHREYS.
Epistolary novel of extreme sensibility, action almost suppressed; psychological analysis.

2. *The skimmer: or the history of Tanzai and Néadarné (a Japanese tale) translated from the French* (1735, 1742, 1748; 2 vols: I, i-xiii, 15-271; II, 1-44)

NCBEL II 993[19]; McBurney 305; Morgan 635
Fantasy with 'Japanese' setting; wit, eroticism, political and religious satire.

STUDIES

1211 BROOKS, Peter. *The novels of worldliness: Crébillon, Marivaux, Laclos, Stendhal.* Princeton: Princeton UP, 1969; pp. ix, 295.

Studies the concept of worldliness: real, moral, psychological and imaginative, the correspondence between representation and social reality. The 18c inherited a creation of society's image of itself in the great worldly and literary salons of the 17c. This is both a real and imaginative concept. The choice of novelists, from the late 17c to the early 19c, provides a selective study of the most important events and transformations of the period, in terms of an intellectual structure. The sociability of 17-18c France was rich because of social closure: it produced one of the most elaborately systematized orders of "being together" the world has known, and the writers who turned their attention to it occupy a privileged position in the range of the novel. Looks at Crébillon, Laclos, and the experience of worldliness, the proper study of mankind, Marianne in the world, Alceste-Julie-Clarissa, *Les Liasons dangereuses*, Stendhal and the style of worldliness. *La Vie de Marianne* is successful in depicting imagination: human emotions, the progress of the individual's life, personal relationships, are profoundly examined in relation to the demands made by the exigencies of society: what are people together like, what do they expect of each other, what do they do to one another? (94-141). Brief footnotes. Index (288-95).

1212 CHERPACK, Clifton. *An essay on Crébillon fils.* Durham, NC: Duke UP, 1962; pp. xvi, 190.

The 7 chapters describe the writer and his problem, the ways of love, men and women, the Oriental Tale and a discussion of *Les Egarements du coeur et de l'Esprit* and *Les Heureux Orphelins*, three epistolary novels, two dialogues and a conclusion. Selected Bibliography (171-83). Crébillon *fils* is hardly remembered, and then only as an 18c purveyor of frothy salaciousness. Tries to encourage a reassessment, undertakes a phenomenological and topographical description of his works, and discusses them individually. Tries to provide a more intimate and concentrated sense of Crébillon's creative mind as revealed in his fiction. Endeavours to isolate and group Crébillon's most characteristic and important themes and preoccupations. His satirical inclination as an artist led him to a form of expression regarded as somewhat bizarre.

1213 DAY, Douglas A. "Crébillon fils, ses exils et ses rapports avec l'Angleterre."
RLC 33 (1959): 180-91.

In French. While certains stages of Crébillon's life are poorly
documented, there are some papers which suggest that the role he played
in Anglo-French relations during his exile was not negligible. He did not
hestitate to address himself to political figures, and there are two
unedited letters he wrote to John Wilkes between 1765 and 1767.

1214-----"On the dating of three novels by Crébillon fils." *MLR* 56 (1961): 391-92.

Several big errors have slipped into the account of Crébillon's career. The
obscurity of certain episodes in his life also extends to the dates of
publication of three of his novels: *Tanzai et Nódarné* and *Le Sopha* which
earned him prison and exile respectively, and *Ah! Quel conte!*. *Tanzai*
came out in Dec. 1734, while eight parts of the Oriental novel *Ah! Quel
conte!* appeared between Dec. 1754 and April 1755; a ninth did not
appear. *Le Sopha* was published in early Feb. 1742.

————

D'ARGENS, Jean-Baptiste de Boyer, Marquis

The Jewish spy: being a philosophical, historical and critical correspondence
(1739-40, 1744; 5 edns by 1766; 5 vols)

NCBEL II 994[20]; McBurney 337; ECSTC 3705B3
Trans. of *Lettres juives*, 1736.
Imitated correspondence on the manners of several European countries.

STUDIES

1215 FRIEDMAN, Arthur. "Goldsmith and the Marquis d'Argens." *MLN* 53
(1938): 173-76.

The anonymous essay "A Dream", describing the author's visit to the
Fountain of Fine Sense was ascribed to Goldsmith by Thomas Wright
(1760). It appears to be closely imitated from the "Dix-neuvième Songe"
in *Songes philosophiques* by Jean-Baptiste de Boyer, Marquis d'Argens.

————

D'AULNOY, Marie Catherine Jumelle de Berneville, Comtesse

See AULNOY

————

DAVYS, Mary

1. *The amours of Alcippus and Leucippe* (1704, n.p.)

    NCBEL II 985[4]
    Domestic comedy of manners; commonsense realism.

2. *The fugitive* (1705, 1725 [in *Works*]; pp. 204)

    NCBEL II 985[6]; McBurney 16; ECSTC 609D1
    Humorous, loosely organized tale, based on her own life.

3. *The reform'd coquet. A novel* (1724, 1725; at least 8 edns by 1785; pp. 171)

    NCBEL II 990[7]; McBurney 154; Morgan 545; ECSTC 609D4
    Exemplary novel; humour, good characterization, plotting.

4. *The works of Mrs Davys* (1725 [1704, 1705, 1724 with *The cousins* and
    Familiar letters betwixt a gentleman and a lady]; 2 vols: I, 272; II,308)

    NCBEL II 990[17]; McBurney 171; ECSTC 609D1

5. *The accomplish'd rake: or modern fine gentlemen* (1727, 1756; pp. 196)

    NCBEL II 991[10]; McBurney 207; ECSTC 609D2
    Satiric, realistic, humorous; much indebted to Restoration comedy.

EDITIONS

1216 *Familiar Letters betwixt a Gentleman and a Lady.* Ed. Robert Adams DAY.
    (Augustan Reprint Society, 54.) Los Angeles: William A. Clark
    Memorial Library, 1955.

    Introduction (i-iv). Notes (iv). Bibliography (v-x) [186 items, epistolary
    novels]. Reprinted text (265-308). Although *Familiar Letters* shows that
    epistolary fiction of considerable merit had been produced long before
    Pamela, it fails to convey a notion of the variety and importance of the
    works in that field, or of their significance to the history English prose
    ficton, and the devlopment of taste (iii).

1217 *The accomplish'd rake.* Ed. McBURNEY in (pp. 232-373) *Four before
    Richardson* etc. See ANTHOLOGIES, Ch. 2, **133**.

1218 *The Reformed Coquet.* Ed. BACKSCHEIDER and RICHETTI in (pp. 251-

322) *Popular fiction by women, 1660-1730* etc. See ANTHOLOGIES, Ch. 2, **119**.

1219 *Familiar Letters* (1725). New York: Garland, 1973. Facsimile reprint.

BIBLIOGRAPHY

1220 FIELDS, Polly. "Davys, Mary." In (pp. 118-31) SAAR and SCHOFIELD, *Eighteenth-century Anglo-American women novelists: a critical reference guide* etc., **93**.

Annotated criticism from 1900 to 1992 (76 items).

SELECTED STUDIES

1221 KLEIN in (pp. 250-51) *Der Briefroman in der englischen Literatur* etc., **569**.
Provides a breakdown of the epistolary exchange in *The accomplish'd rake* and *The reform'd coquet*.

1222 McBURNEY, William H. "Mary Davys: forerunner of Fielding." *PMLA* 74 (1959): 348-55.

Account of life and works. After scores of 'secret histories', 'authentick memoirs' and 'true relations' produced by Eliza Haywood and other female novelists of the 1720s, the four volumes written by Mary Davys manifest a "cheerful, sunshiny, breezy" effect (such as Coleridge attributed to Fielding's work as opposed to the "close, hot, day-dreamy continuity of Richardson"). The double emphasis is more than subjectively valid, for Mrs Davys stands in much the same relation to Fielding's ebullient masculine genius that Mrs Haywood's distressed damsels do to Richardson's heroines -- both as a forerunner and as an influence upon the early 18c reading public. She is interesting as one of the few writers before 1740 to formulate a conscious theory of the novel, to show how realistic comedy might be adapted to the new genre, to place emphasis upon characterization and setting rather than upon simple variety of action, and to bring sturdy common sense and humour to a literary form that had been dominated by the extravagant, the scandalous, and the sensational.

1223 STEFANSON, Donald H. "The works of Mary Davys: A critical edition: vols. I and II." Unpub. doct. diss., Univ. of Iowa, 1972. [*DAI* 32 (1972) 5203A.]

Provides an unmodernized, critical edition based on the 1725 version of Davys's collected works that includes all of her published novels, with the exception of *The Accomplish'd Rake* (1727), which did appear in the *Works*, has only one authoritative text, and is available in a modern reprint. Discusses her works, and explains the choice of texts and principles of emendation.

1224 STEPHENSON, Peter S. "Three playwright-novelists: the contribution of dramatic techniques to Restoration and early eighteenth-century prose fiction." Unpub. doct. diss., Univ. of California (Davis), 1970. [*DAI* 30 (1970): 3920A.]

Many novelists of the experimental period 1660-1740 also wrote plays. Illustrates, by examining the work of selected playwrights-novelists, how drama stimulated new capabilities in fiction, thereby preparing the way for the modern novels of Richardson and Fielding. Detailed analysis of the plays and novels of Aphra Behn, William Congreve and Mary Davys shows how their experience with drama, particularly comedy, led to improved characterization and increased realistic detail in their novels. Soon after 1660 the novel displaced the prolix romance in popularity, and became the basis for the modern novel. Drama was one of the forces causing the novella to grow in length. Some drama of the time shared the artificiality of romantic fiction, whereas the comedy of manners, which drew on contemporary and realistic observation, was the effective influence.

1225 WEBER, Donna-Lee. "Fair game: rape and sexual aggression on women in some early eighteenth-century prose fiction," **1035**.

STUDIES (1992-1999)

1226 BOWDEN, Martha F. "Mary Davys: self-presentation and the woman's reputation in the early eighteenth century." *WWr* 3:1 (1996): 17-33.

Davys provides an interesting case study on the pressures and expectations of a woman writer experienced in the first quarter of the 18c. By examining Davys's writings, particularly her prefaces and dedications, demonstrates the way in which she moulded her attempts to present an acceptable persona: despite being a professional writer and Irishwoman, she insists that she is a respectable member of society, loyal to the king, and the Church of England, and although she is a woman, she represents herself as a competent and adept writer. In the contradictions, as well as the excessive flattering of the early dedications, she reveals the pressures of a profession/private dichotomy.

1227 FENDLER, Susanne. "Intertwining literary histories: women's contribution to the rise of the novel." In (pp. 31-64) *Feminist contributions to the literary canon* etc. See above under AUBIN, **1125**.

Discusses Davys's *The Reform'd Coquet* (1724) (53-57). She improved the concept of the didactic novel by connecting the story with the didactic purpose. Apart from their literary merit, Davys's novels are the last step in the development to Richardson's novels. There is no hint on the woman's side of immoral behaviour or thought.

1228 RILEY, Esther Powell. "Resisting writers: four eighteenth-century female novelists in search of a literary voice." etc. See above under AUBIN, **1128**.

1229 RILEY, Lindy. "Mary Davys's satiric novel *Familiar Letters*: refusing patriarchal inscription of women." *TSL* 37 (1995): 206-21.

Familiar Letters represents not only Davys's repudiation of the falsely glamorized position of women as depicted in female characters in the romance genre, but also represents her satiric exposure of the dangerous and uncomfortable position of women in 18c social structure. Davys's use of the traditional male genre, albeit gentle, exposes the double standards of patriarchy. Bibliography (221).

1230 SAJÉ, Natasha. "'The assurance to write, the vanity of expecting to be read': deception and reform in Mary Davys's *The Reform'd Coquet*." *ELit* 23:2 (1996): 165-77.

The coquette figure appears in literature at the moment when the novel as we know it was being invented, also the moment when women started writing in greater numbers, first in France and then in Britain. The recurrence of the coquette "provides a site for the critique and regulation of women's self-expression and economic power" (165). Mary Davys's *The Reform'd Coquet* (1724) is the first of several novels by writers such as Haywood, Burney, Inchbald and Austen in which a coquette heroine's 'reform' is initiated and monitored by a male character who loves and subsequently marries her. Davys makes her male protagonist a dual character, a virile lover disguised as an aged guardian. By "reinscribing" the dynamic coquette figure in their novels, women writers like Davys "produced plots whose implausibilities tell us about the writing conditions of their own writing lives" (176).

———

DANIEL DEFOE

WORKS

COLLECTIONS

1231 *Romances and Narratives*. Ed. George A. AITKENS. 16 vols. London, 1895.

1232 *Novels and Selected Writings*. 14 vols. Oxford, 1927-8.

1233 *Letters*. Ed. G. H. HEALEY. Oxford, 1955.

1234   List of writings in NCBEL II, 495-514.

INDIVIDUAL TITLES OF PROSE FICTION

1. *The life and strange adventures of Robinson Crusoe, of York, mariner, written by himself* (1719, pp. 364)

NCBEL 900[9]; McBurney 99; Morgan 494

SELECTED EDITIONS

1235   4 edns in 1719: 25 April, 9 May, 4 June, 7 August; 1720, 1722 etc.

1236 - ed. A. DOBSON 1883 (facs.).

1237 - Everyman's Library, 1906; latest ed. 1991.

1238 - ed. with introd. Angus ROSS. Harmondsworth: Penguin 1965, 1985.

1239 - ed. Donald CROWLEY. Oxford English Novels, 1972.

1240 - ed. Michael SHINAGEL. *Robinson Crusoe: an authoritative text, contexts, criticism*. (A Norton Critical Edition.) New York and London: Norton, 1975. Second ed. 1994; pp. vii, 436. Fasc. title page.

Provides a detailed critical apparatus (227-434): contexts (227-56) contemporary accounts of marooned men, autobiography, the Puritan emblematic tradition (J. PAUL HUNTER); eighteenth-and nineteenth-century opinions (257-82) (Gildon, Pope, Cibber, Rousseau, Johnson, Blair, Beattie, Chalmers, Coleridge, Lamb, Wordsworth, Poe, Hazlitt, De Quincey, Borrow, Macaulay, Marx, John Stuart Mill, Leslie Stephen); twentieth-century criticism (283-432) (Virginia Woolf, Ian Watt,

Maximilian Novak, Frank Budgen, James Joyce, George A. Starr, J. Paul Hunter, James Sutherland, John J. Richetti, Leopold Damrosch Jr., John Bender, Michael McKeon, Carol Houlihan Flynn). Defoe chronology (433-34). Selected bibliography (435-36).

Translations:
- French 1720, 1721, 1722 etc.
- German 1720, 1721 etc.
- Dutch 1720, 1721, 1735.
- Italian 1731, 1738 etc.
- Danish 1774.
- Slovenian, 1982.
- Bulgarian 1985.

2. *Memoirs of a cavalier: or a military journal of the wars in Germany, and the wars in England, from the year 1632 to the year 1648* (1720, pp. 338)

NCBEL 901[9]; McBurney 113

SELECTED EDITIONS

1241 - Edinburgh 1759

1242 - London 1766, 1788.

1243 - Everyman's Library.

1244 - ed. James T. BOULTON. Oxford English Novels, 1970; with new introd. by John MULLAN, 1991; as World's Classics (Oxford and New York: Oxford UP, 1996), pp. xxxv, 356.

Translations:
- German 1785-86.

3. *The life, adventures and pyracies of the famous Captain Singleton, containing an account of his being set ashore in the island of Madagascar as also of his many adventures and pyracies with the famous Captain Avery and others* (1720, pp. 344)

NCBEL 901[10]; McBurney 112; Morgan 499

SELECTED EDITIONS

1245 - 1721, 1737, 1768, 1800 (abridged), 1810, 1887.

1246 - ed. James R. SUTHERLAND. Everyman's Library, 1963.

1247 - ed. Shiv K. KUMAR. Oxford English Novels, 1969. With a new introd. by Penelope WILSON, 1990.

4. *The fortunes and misfortunes of the famous Moll Flanders, written from her own memorandums* (1721 [for 1722], pp. 424)

NCBEL 901[19]; McBurney 128

SELECTED EDITIONS

1248 - 1722, 1722 (rev.), 1723, 1740, 1741, 1759 etc.;

1249 - 1723 (abridged with added chapter);

1250 - 1730 (as *Fortune's fickle distribution*, with continuation of the lives of her husband and governess);

1251 - 1776 (as *The history of Laetitia Atkins*);

1252 - chapbooks c. 1750, c. 1770.

1253 - 1896 (printed in Holland).

1254 - 1907 (with *Roxana*).

1255 - 1924 (3 editions, with 9 further edns during the decade).

1256 - ed. H. DAVIS. Oxford English Novels, 1961.

1257 - ed. Edward KELLY. *Moll Flanders: an authoritative text, background and sources, criticism.* (A Norton Critical Edition.) New York and London: W. W. Norton & Company, 1973; pp. ix, 444. Facs. title page.

Contains a detailed critical apparatus (287-444): backgrounds and sources (287-320) (Hall, Defoe, Alexander Smith, T. Read, John Robert Moore, Gerald Howson); eighteenth- and nineteenth-century opinions (321-34) (Swift, Gay, Addison, Gildon, Pope, Johnson, Coleridge, Lamb, Hazlitt, William Lee, Leslie Stephen); twentieth-century criticism ((335-434) (Virginia Woolf, E. M. Foster, James Joyce, William Faulkner, A. D. McKillop, Ian Watt, Terence Martin, Wayne C. Booth, Martin Price, Arnold Kettle, Robert Alan Donovan, Michael Shinagel, Maximilian Novak, G. A. Starr). Defoe chronology (435-37). Map of Moll Flanders's

London (438). Bibliography (441-44).

1258 - Introd. Pat ROGERS. (Everyman's Library.) London, Melbourne and Toronto: Dent, 1982; pp. xxviii, 295. Rpt. of old Everyman's Library ed. (1930) with a new introd. Latest ed. 1992.

1259 - introd. Erica JONG. In *Three Eighteenth Century Novels*. New York: New American Library, 1982. (Printed with *Joseph Andrews* and *The Vicar of Wakefield*).

1260 - ed. and introd. David BLEWETT. Harmondsworth: Penguin, 1989; pp. 454.

Translations:
- German 1723, 1745;
- Dutch 1752;
- French 1761.
- Hebrew 1980.

- Bulgarian, 1983. Introd. Julia STEFANOVA.

5. *A Journal of the Plague Year: being observations or memorials of the most remarkable occurrences, as well publick as private, which happened in London during the last great visitation in 1665, written by a citizen who continued all the while on London* (1722, pp. 287)

NCBEL 902[1]; McBurney 130; Morgan 519

SELECTED EDITIONS

1261 - 1754 (as *The history of the great plague in London*);

1262 - 1795 (abridged);

1263 - 1824, 1832, 1835, 1840, 1863, 1886;

1264 - ed. Anthony BURGESS and Christopher BRISTOW, with an introd. by A. BURGESS. Harmondsworth: Penguin, 1966.

1265 - ed. Louis LANDA. Oxford English Novels, 1969. With new introd. by David ROBERTS, 1991.

1266 - ed. Paula R. BACKSCHEIDER. *A Journal of the Plague Year: Authoritative Text, Backgrounds, Contexts, Criticism.* (A Norton Critical Edition.) New York and London: W. W. Norton & Company, 1992; pp.

xiii, 361. Map of H. F.'s London. Fasc. title page.

Contains detailed critical apparatus (195-355): backgrounds - the Plague of 1665 and the threat of 1720-21 (various documents and contemporary reports); contexts - reflexions on plagues and their effects (231-64) (Thucydides, Boccaccio, Dekker, Camus, Foucauld, Susan Sontag, George Whitmore, material on AIDS); criticism (265-355) (essays by Sir Walter Scott, Louis A. Landa, Everett Zimmermann, John J. Richetti, Maximilian E. Novak, John Bender, Michelle Brandwein). Defoe chronology (356-59). Selected bibliography (360-61).

1267 - ed. John MAN. (Everyman's Library.) London: Dent; Rutland, VT: Tuttle, 1994; pp. xxiv,   240.

Translations:
- Bulgarian, 1983. Introd. Julia STEFANOVA.
- Rumanian, 1985. Introd. Antoaneta RALIAN.

6. *The history and remarkable life of the truly honourable Colonel Jacque, commonly call'd Colonel Jack* (1723 [for 1722], pp. 399)

NCBEL 902[4]; McBurney 129; Morgan 515

SELECTED EDITIONS

1268 - 1723, 1724, 1738, 1809 (abridged), 1810, 1813.

1269 - ed. Samuel Holt MONK. Oxford English Novels, 1965. With new introd. by David ROBERTS, 1989.

Translations:
- Dutch 1729;
- German 1740.

7. *The fortunate mistress: or a history of the life and vast variety of fortunes of Mademoiselle de Beleau, afterwards call'd the Countess de Wintselsheim, in Germany, being the person known by the name of the Lady Roxana, in the time of King Charles II* ([1724], pp. 407)
Commonly abbreviated:
Roxana: the fortunate mistress, or, A history of the life and vast variety of fortunes of Madamoiselle Beleau. 1724.

NCBEL 902[6]; McBurney 155; Morgan 538

SELECTED EDITIONS

1270 - [1745?], 1750 (with an anonymous continuation, partly from Eliza HAYWOOD'S *British Recluse*), 1755, 1765 (abridged), 1766.

1271 - 1907 (with *Moll Flanders*);

1272 - 1923;

1273 - ed. W. CATHER (New York, 1924);

1274 - ed. R. B. JOHNSON [1926];

1275 - ed. J. JACK. Oxford English Novels, 1964.

1276 - postsc. K. ROGERS. New York and London: New English Library, 1979; pp. vi, 296.

1277 - ed. David BLEWETT. Harmondsworth: Penguin, 1982; pp. 404.

1278 - ed. John MULLEN. (Worlds Classics.) Oxford and New York: Oxford UP, 1996; pp. xxxv, 356.

Translations:
- German 1736.

BIBLIOGRAPHIES 1719-1994
(in chronological order)

1279 BURKH, C. E. "British criticism of Defoe as a novelist, 1719-1860." *ES* 67 (1932): 178-98.

1280 PAYNE, William L. "An annotated bibliography of works about Daniel Defoe, 1719-1974." *BB* 32 (1975): 3-14, 27, 32, 63-75, 87, 89-100, 132.

Divided into bibliographies; biographies; collected works; selections; letters; general studies, criticism and reviews; Defoe and other authors; individual works. *Robinson Crusoe* has its own bibliographies; sources; studies, criticism and works. Points out the central idea of shorter works in a sentence or two, and lists reviews of longer works.

1281 HAMMERSCHMIDT, Hildegard. "Daniel Defoe: articles in periodicals (1950-1980)." *BB* 40:2 (June 1983): 90-102.

Lists over 400 items.

1282 STOLER, John A. *Daniel Defoe: an annotated bibliography of modern criticism, 1900-1980.* (Garland Reference Library of the Humanities, 430.) New York; London: Garland, 1984; pp. xiv, 424.

Lists 1,569 items, almost all of which (except for dissertations and foreign-languages items) are descriptively annotated.

1283 HAHN, H. George and BEHM, Carl III. *The eighteenth-century British novel and its background: an annotated bibliography and guide to topics* etc.
Lists over 200 items on Defoe with brief descriptions of their salient theme.

1284 PETERSON, Spiro. *Daniel Defoe: a reference guide (1731-1924).* (Reference Guides to Literature.) Boston: Hall, 1987; pp. xxxiv, 455.

Illustrates the "history and development of Defoe's reputation" by listing 1,565 copiously annotated items. This volume is designed to supplement STOLER.

1285 DÉTIS, Elisabeth. "*The Life and Strange Surprising Adventures of Robinson Crusoe, of York, Mariner*: a selective critical bibliography." *BSEAA* 33 (Nov. 1991): 7-33.

1286 LOVETT, Robert W. *'Robinson Crusoe': A bibliographical checklist of English language editions.* New York: Greenwood, 1991; pp. xii, 303.

Introd. (xii). Bibliographical checklist (1-294) lists 1,198 items. Index of publishers (295-303). The purpose "is to list, describe, and comment on as many English language editions as I can find or about which I have sufficient bibliographical information". Each entry lists title and publication details, and a description of pages, illustrations, and publisher advertisements.

1287 PETERSON, Spiro. "Daniel Defoe: Supplement to annotated bibliography, 1731-1924." *BB* 49 (1992): 215-33.

Adds 34 items to Peterson's 1987 bibliography.

1288 BLAIM, Arthur. "Recent works on Defoe." *USt* 4:2 (1993): 150-61.

Review article.

1289 LETELLIER, Robert Ignatius. *A bibliography of the English novel from the Restoration to the French Revolution: A checklist of sources and critical materials with particular reference to the period 1660-1740* etc., **61**.

In section IX: DANIEL DEFOE (159-93) provides a list with some brief annotations of 411 critical items which appeared between 1980 and 1990, presented alphabetically by author. XII. THEMATIC INDEX cross-references each article alphabetically by theme, with specific themes listed under each of Defoe's individual works.

1290 PETERSON, Spiro; CHO, Sungku; COTTON, Hope; ODA, Minoru; XIAN-FANG, Huang and KIM, Sung-Kyoon. "Bibliography of Defoe studies in the Far East: China and Taiwan, Japan, and Korea." *ECF* 8:1 (1995): 95-142.

Presents 162 items between 1905 and 1993. Introduction and extensive annotation. This bibliography has the power to startle by its insights into very different cultures and into what readers and critics find in close professional study and leisure reading. Divided into sections on China, Taiwan, Japan and Korea. Scholars in the Far East have had difficulties in obtaining copies of 20c critics, even those written in the Far East. Leads one to discover how persistent Defoe's appeal was at certain periods and in certain countries. In *Robinson Crusoe* we are engaged in comprehending a cultural phenomenon, European and worldwide, psychological and historical, mythic and generic. This is what Far Eastern states and readers have found.

1291 STOLER, John A. "Daniel Defoe: A partly annotated bibliography of criticism, 1981-1994 (Parts 1 and 2)." *BB* 53:1 (1996): 11-22; 53:2 (1996): 125-37.

Continuation of the major STOLER (1984) and PETERSON (1987 and 1992) bibliographies. "It is meant to be a thorough, but far from exhaustive, listing of materials. Dissertations are not annotated [...]. No attempt was made to obtain and translate foreign-language materials [...]" (11). Contains 495 items, divided as:
   1. Bibliographies (items 1-7);
   2. Editions (8-12);
   3. Canon (13-32);
   4. General works on Defoe's life, thought, and art (33-93);
   5. The major novels:
      a) General (94-134);
      b) *Captain Singleton* (135-138);
      c) *Colonel Jacques* (139-40);

d) *Journal of the Plague Year* (141-154);

e) *Memoirs of a Cavalier* (155-156);

f) *Moll Flanders* (157-204);

g) *Robinson Crusoe* (including *Farther adventures* and *Serious reflections*) (205-307);

h) *Roxana* (308-328);

6. Miscellaneous Writing (329-382);

7. Foreign language items (383-459);

8. Dissertations (460-495).

CANON
(partially annotated)

1292 DeLUNA, D. N. "*Jure divino*: Defoe's 'whole Volume in Folio, by Way of Answer to, and Confutation of *Clarendon's* History of the Rebellion." *PQ* 75:1 (1996): 43-66.

1293-----"Yale's poetasting Defoe." *1650-1850* 4 (1998): 345-62.

1294-----"'Modern *Panegyrick* and Defoe's 'Dunciad'." *SELit* 35:3 (1998): 419-35.

1295 DOWNIE, J. A. "Defoe's early writings." *RES* 46:182 (1995): 225-30.

1296 MOORE, Robert. *Checklist of the writings of Daniel Defoe* (1960). Bloomington: Indiana UP, 1962.

Lists 570 items. Later added 140 new ones.

1297 FURBANK, P. N. and OWENS, W. R. *The canonisation of Daniel Defoe*. New Haven, CT: Yale UP, 1988.

Investigate the complexities of Defoe attributions, and challenge the formation of a Defoe canon. Set up rules for the establishment of a canon, suggest how Defoe can be recognized, and urge a fresh start to form a vastly reduced and more probable bibliography of Defoe's writings.

1298-----*Defoe de-attributions: a critique of J. R. Moore's 'Checklist'*. London and Rio Grande, OH: Hambledon Press, 1994; pp. xxxiv, 161.
Introd. (xi-xxxi). Argue that 252 items assigned by MOORE were questionable attributions. Index of titles (151-51).

1299-----"Daniel Defoe and *A Letter from a Gentleman at the Court of 'St Germains'* (1710)." *EA* 48:1 (1995): 61-66.

1300-----"The dating of Defoe's *Atalantis Major*." *NQ* 44:2 (1997): 189-90.

1301-----"Defoe's de-attributions: A critique of J. R. Moore's *Checklist*." *HLQ* 59:1 (1997): 83-104.

1302-----"The myth of Defoe as 'Applebee's man'." *RES* 48:190 (1997): 198-204.

1303-----"On the attribution of periodicals and newspapers to Daniel Defoe." *PubH* 40 (1996): 83-98.

1304-----(eds). *'The True-Born Englishman' and other writings*. (Penguin Classics.) London and New York: Penguin, 1997; pp. xxix, 296.

1305------"Defoe and the sham *Flying Post*." *PubH* 43 (1995): 5-15.

1306-----*A critical bibliography of Daniel Defoe*. London and Brookfield, VT: Pickering & Chatto, 1998; pp. xxxvii, 319.
Introd. (xiii-xxx) considers:
1. The history of Defoe attributions;
2. Bibliography and biography;
3. The principles of author attributions;
4. The presentation of entries.
The critical bibliography lists 276 items:
1. Collected works (items 1-2);
2. Books, pamphlets, and broadsheets (3-249);
3. Periodicals (250-256);
4. Contributions to books and periodicals (257-262);
5. Works left in manuscript (262-271);
6. Letters (272-276).

1307 KENNEDY, Lawrence. "*The Jubilee Necklace*: a new Defoe attribution?" *Scriblerian* 29:1 (1996): 1-7.

Thinks that "The Jubilee Necklace" (1703) may be a previously unrecognized poem by Defoe.

1308 NOVAK, Maximilian. "Whither the Defoe canon?" *ECF* 9:1 (1996): 89-91.

1309-----"The Defoe canon: attribution and de-attribution." *HLQ* 59:1 (1997): 83-104.
Review article.

1310 OWENS, W. R. and FURBANK, P. N. "Sir Alexander Cumming and Defoe's *Mercator*." *NQ* 42:4 (1995): 454-55.

STUDIES (1995-1999)

GENERAL STUDIES

1311 ADAMS, Stephen. "Daniel Defoe's *Review* and authorial issues in the early English periodical." Unpub. doct. diss., Univ. of Missouri-Columbia, 1996. [*DA* 57 (1997): 4747A.]

Defoe's *Review* (1704 to 1713) was a tri-weekly journal of political opinion written solely by Defoe, each issue featuring a single essay on current political issues. It has long been recognized as important for its wealth of detail about political life in the reign of Queen Anne and for its contribution to our knowledge of Defoe's political involvement. Less attention has been given to its importance in the development of the opinion-journal, and more specifically, to the use of the genre of the essay as a form of comment. Defoe emphasizes external reality and presents political comment as based on the solid reality of public affairs, rather than on the interpretation or interest of the author. A deterioration of the objectivist position occurs when Defoe discloses his identity as author and pursues self-vindication within the essays. He adopts a third authorial perspective, that of political moderation. Connects his career and periodical with the restraint and inclusiveness of Robert Harley's moderate Tory ministry.

1312 ARMSTRONG, Katherine A. *Defoe: writer as agent.* (ELS Monographs, 67.) Victoria, BC: English Literary Studies, Univ. of Victoria, 1996.

Investigates Defoe's desire to take part in the political and economic life of his country. By setting aside the preoccupation with the veracity of Defoe's prose narratives (and of Defoe himself by extension), and by examining them instead as conscious interventions in various contemporary political debates, one can transform the readings of them. Considers the *Cavalier* (memoir or memorandum?), political theory in *Captain Singleton*, Moll Flanders as urban guerrilla, the productions of history in *Colonel Jack, Robinson Crusoe* and the value of labor. Defoe had more impact on literary history than on affairs political, economic and social, but without the urge to influence contemporary events, his achievements as a novelist would have been far fewer. Notes (131-48). Works cited (149-56).

1313 AUSTIN, Michael. "Saul and the social contract. Constructions of 1 Samuel 8-11 in Cowley's *Davideis* and Defoe's *Jure Divino*." *PLL* 32:4 (1996): 410-36.

During the 17c the Bible served both as an agent for radical change and as a basis for preserving the status quo. Both Cowley and Defoe used the choice of Saul for king to emphasize their opinion that kingship is conferred by men and not invested with any special power from God. Both authors came from different religious and social backgrounds, lived at different times, and responded to different events. What is instructive is the almost identical way in which they incorporated the biblical narratives into their own historical epics. The secret of this sacred historiography was not just to quote from the Bible, but to merge text and context into a single unified and rhetorically compelling historical narrative capable of accounting for every aspect of contemporary culture.

1314 BACKSCHEIDER, Paula R. and COTTON, Hope D. "Spiro Peterson (1922-1992) and Defoe studies." *ECF* 8:1 (1995): 89-94.

PETERSON'S work on Defoe is valuable for many reasons, but is esp. unusual because of its global sweep and constant attention to the world's readings of Defoe.

1315 BAINES, Paul. "'Able mechanick': *The Life and Adventures of Peter Wilkins* and the eighteenth-century fantastic voyage." In (pp. 1-25) SEED, David (ed.). *Anticipations: essays on early science fiction and its precursors,* **195**.

1316 BIGAMI, Marialuisa. *Daniel Defoe: dal saggio al romanzo.* (Milan, 1984.) Second edition (Biblioteca di cultura, 183.) Florence: Nuova Italia, 1993; pp. xi, 125.

Account of life and works, examining the Puritan tradition in Defoe's work. Ch. 1 looks at Milton who was a strong influence in demonological writings and characterization. Moll Flanders has affinities with Eve in *Paradise Lost*: both have great energy, awareness of human dignity, their nature as autonomous social subjects. Ch. 2 looks at links with Swift, while ch. 3 traces the formation of the new gentleman in treatises, and the birth of the bourgeois thief whose role is analogous to the villain in Jacobean tragedy. Also looks at the new movement introduced by the representation of the merchant as a dynamic character. Ch. 4 deals with the narrator's utopias. The *Farther Adventures* introduces thetemporal dimension with a progressiveness that adheres to its inhabitants changing needs. Ch. 5 shows Defoe using the traditional topics of occultism and demonology, showing an interest in the relation of man with the forces of evil. Occultism becomes functional to narrative needs and the psychology of characters (in *Moll Flanders* and *Roxana*). There is an updated bibliography of over 500 items.

1317-----(ed.). *Wrestling with Defoe: approaches from a workshop on Defoe's prose*. (Quaderni di Acme, 30.) Bologna: Cisalpini, 1997; pp. 200.

Collection of 8 essays devoted to Defoe and the rise of the novel. Introduction (pp. 7-10).

1318-----"Daniel Defoe's military autobiographies: history and fictional character." In (pp. 91-108) BIGAMI, Marialuisa (ed.), *Wrestling with Defoe* etc., **1317**.

In the final phase of his life, Defoe showed an interest in the lives of strong men who acted on the battlefield, thereby trying to find and give political and moral meaning to the history of the previous troubled century.

1319 BOWERS, Terence Noel. "Rites of passage: inventions of self and community in eighteenth-century British travel literature." Unpub. doct. diss., Univ. of Chicago, 1994. [*DA* 55 (1995): 2399-400A.]

The 18c witnessed an explosion in the production of travel literature, whose output was second only to theology. Considers the cultural needs fulfilled by travel writing. It structured the way people understood themselves and their habitat took on heightened importance as England changed its own borders (becoming 'Great Britain') and as an international presence. Such writing functioned as a medium for the construction of new national, social and civic identities. Part I analyzes the travel narratives of Defoe, Fielding and Smollett, Part II the works of female travellers (Lady Mary Wortley Montague and Mary Wollstonecraft). These narratives constitute radical acts of self-assertion that invent novel concepts of personhood, citizenship and community, all of which are explored in depth in *Robinson Crusoe*.

1320-----*The politics of motherhood: British writing and culture, 1680-1760*. Cambridge, New York, Melbourne: Cambridge UP, 1996.

Investigates "Unnatural motherhood in two novels by Daniel Defoe" (98-123): - Incest and maternal identity in *Moll Flanders*; - 'For Decency's Sake': *Moll Flanders* and the mystification of natural economy; - 'Dreadful Necessity': motherhood and death in *Roxana*; - Maternity and the necessity of infanticide in *Moll Flanders* and *Roxana*.

1321 BRANTLINGER, Patrick. "Cashing in on the real: money and the failure of mimesis in Defoe and Trollope." *SLI* 29:1 (1996): 9-21.

The realist novel is a 'form of frustration' because the closer it appears to come to effacing the distinction between itself and reality, the more duplicitous it becomes. Thematic and metaphoric connections between money/commodification and realistic fiction go back at least as far as Defoe. In contrast to the more or less aristocratic 'romance', Defoe's decidedly bourgeois novels depict the gaining and losing of 'fortunes' in the most basic monetary sense. Just as *Robinson Crusoe* deals with money, *Roxana* reads like an account book in which the heroine precisely tallies up the story of her life in pounds, shillings and pence. The Dutch Merchant's opening of his account books to Roxana may be taken as an analogue for the novel as a whole.

1322 BROWN, Homer. "The institution of the English novel: Defoe's contribution." *Novel* 29:3 (1996): 29-318.

Defoe became a major novelist when professional readers were able to read him as a novelist of character rather than of incident, or a novelist who used incident to reveal character. When the novel of psychological analysis fell out of favor, to be replaced by the well-made novel, Defoe's plotlessness, his lack of a structured sequence and clear resolution, counted against him. Then there is the opposition, marked in every Defoe preface, between the imperative of explicit moral dedication and the pleasure in the well-made plot. Hypocritical didacticism is contradicted by the narrator's singular pleasure in moral activities, and the values expounded by a quest for money and position. Arguments about Defoe's use or lack of irony center around this question.

1323 CARNELL, Rachel Karen. "Dominion in the household: Liberal political theory and the early British novel," **322**.

1324 CARRÉ, Jacques. "La Ville britannique et l'espace industriel (1760-1829)." *Q/W/E/R/T/Y* 2 (1992): 265-72.

Looks at the impact of industrialization on the cities and the acommodation of industry: the birth of provincial urbanness in the 18c ("des usines dans le paysage; la révélation de la ville industrielle"). Demonstrates that the traditional British élite preserved during the whole of the 18c "une vision figée de la civilisation et du développement urbaine" (271).

1325 CHESLEY, Laurie. "The place of *Mrs Veal* in Defoe's fictions about women." *ELit* 22:1 (1995): 3-16.

Defoe's ghost story "A True Relation of the Apparition of One Mrs Veal"

(1706) became enormously popular, in fact one of the best ghost stories ever written. By claiming historicity and empirical premise, such narratives were important for the genesis of the novel. Apparition narratives were not only forerunners of the novel, but participate in the same literary and socio-cultural milieu as the novels. Defoe intended all his works - fiction an nonfiction - to teach a moral lesson, to help readers to behave better, and receive an eternal reward. Although in this work Defoe does not wear a female mask, the story exposes a malevolent patriarchy and provides proof that women need not adapt to the ways of the world or learn the tricks and manners of their immoral and spiritually degenerate oppressors to triumph. This triumph will eventually be spiritual and eternal.

1326 CHEUNG, Kai-Chong. "Maxine Hong's non-Chinese man." *TamkR* 23:1 (1992/3): 421-30.

In *China Men*, Maxine Hong Kingston synthesized mythical figures from various classical and popular Chinese sources into her own family background. One chapter of the novel appropriates *Robinson Crusoe*, transforming him into a Chinese figure. Kingston's use of this character (whose British identity she conceals) to reinforce her praise in the novel of the perseverance of Chinese-American men who suffered oppression in 19c American society, is inappropriate. Not only was Defoe a British racist who spoke of the inferiority of 18c Chinese culture, the primary qualities of Kingston's exemplary 'China men' - patience, endurance, ability to overcome hardships through social solidarity - are quite different from Crusoe's (Western male's) scientific ingenuity, self-reliance and extreme individualism.

1327 COPELAND, Edward. "Defoe and the London Wall: mapped perspectives." *ECF* 10:4 (1998): 407-28.

The small insignificant figures, so common in 17c Dutch art, are the more typical inhabitants of Defoe's urban space. Defoe's nameless little people -- the shopkeepers, jades, pickpockets and honest merchants of his novels -- hold on to space and existence solely by their right to the map of London. They owe their fictional lives, and our perspectives of them, to the mapping operation of Defoe's camera obscura, a remorseless catalogue of visual reality.

1328 CURTIS, Laura A. "A rhetorical approach to the prose of Daniel Defoe." *Rhetorica* 11:3 (1993): 293-319.

Previous attempts to account for Defoe's stylistic versatility have failed to consider the important role played by his training in rhetoric. Argues that a useful taxonomy of styles can be generated by examining traditional and rhetorical principles of sentence composition, prose rhythms, and *clausulae* construction, the use of various figures of speech, and the frequency of tropes. Analyzing Defoe's prose shows deliberate rhetorical choices in his lesser-known essays and pamphlets, as well as in his better-known fiction. A rhetorical approach to Defoe's style can be more fruitful than a grammatical one.

1329 DURRANT, Samuel. "Bearing witness to apartheid: J. M. Coetzee's inconsolable works of mourning" *ConLit* 40:3 (1999): 430-63.

Freud's insight is that we are destined to repeat that which we fail to work through. Interrogates the idea that literature offers a way through a collective history by examining three of J. H. Coetzee's novels (*Waiting for the Barbarians* [1980], *The Life and Times of Michael K.* [1983], *Foe* [1986]). His novels resist the process of verbalization, and relentlessly force us to confront the brute, indigestible materiality of suffering engendered by apartheid. Each of them extends the historico-colonial discourse initiated by Defoe in *Robinson Crusoe*.

1330 DUTHEIL, Martine Hennard. "The epigraph to *The Satanic Verses*: Defoe's Devil and Rushdie's migrant." *SoRA* 30:1 (1997): 51-69.

Salman Rushdie's novel exemplifies the process of reinscription characteristic of postcolonial writing. The novel's intertextual relations with *Robinson Crusoe* and *The True-Born Englishman* clearly signal this strategy. But *Satanic Verses* also comments on Defoe's lesser-known *The Political History of the Devil* excerpted in its epigraph. Rushdie's critique of religious myth shares many traditional traits with Defoe's pamphlet, and focuses on the discursive construction of migrancy as in Defoe's text. Rushdie in fact uncovers and de-familiarizes a commonplace in the Western literary tradition. The epigraph thus provides a useful key onto the complex fictional world of *Satanic Verses* as a parody of the demonization of cultural difference.

1331 FALLER, Lincoln B. *Crime and Defoe: a new kind of writing.* (Cambridge Studies in Eighteenth-Century English Literature and Thought, 16.) Cambridge and New York: Cambridge UP, 1993; pp. xix, 263.

Seeks to recover something of the original excitement, challenge and significance of Defoe's four novels of criminal life by reading them with and against the conventions of the early 18c criminal biographies. Crime raised deeply troubling questions in Defoe's time, a sign of the breakdown of traditional social authority and order. Defoe's novels provided ways of facing, working through as well as avoiding certain of the moral and intellectual difficulties that crime raised for him and his readers. 'Literary' and 'aesthetic' qualities of fiction contribute to these ends. Analyzes the various ways in which Defoe's novels exploited, deformed and departed from the genres they imitate. *Moll Flanders*, *Colonel Jack* and *Roxana* are given extended readings, with consideration of Defoe's realism, his own theory of reader response, the structural imitation of providential design in the novels, and his recurrent effort to deny the notion that trade was equivalent to theft. Extended bibliographic footnotes. Index (259-63).

1332 FROHOCK, Richard Randall, III. "Eyes on the New World: imagining the English colony in the early Enlightenment," **439**.

1333 FULK, Mark Kenneth. "Pious readers, polemical fictions: Christian thought in the later careers of Daniel Defoe and Henry Fielding." Unpub. doct. diss., Miami Univ., 1997. [*DA* 58 (1997): 882A.]

Examines the influence of Christian ideals on the fiction of the 18c, particularly Defoe and Fielding. Many such fictional works made claims about improving the 'virtue' of their readers. Method combines reader criticism (Stanley Fish and Wolfgang Iser), formalist criticism, and recent advances in historiography and feminist concerns. *Roxana* and *Amelia* are at the center. Both are polemical and show signs of irony and inconsistency; both conclude ambiguously. All this shows that tutoring virtue through fiction is not simple didacticism, but something more complex. Both contain struggles with the application of their faith in 18c Britain. Even those believe in Christianity cannot easily or dogmatically resolve conflicts inherent in the social mores of the era. Both texts raise more questions than they provide answers.

1334 GEERTSEMA, Johan. "Inventing innocence: allochronism and the politics of the novel." *JLS* 13:1/2 (1997): 38-61.

Allochronism is "the denial of the simultaneity of the ethnographic other with the representing subject and the consequent placing of that other in another time". The collision of allochronism with Empire is examined in terms of both the historicist project and the appearance of the novel. The allochronic invention of the innocence of people 'discovered' by European explorers in the New World is a sign of the inaccessibility experienced by the European explorers at what they found: "this invention of innocence is an attempt to account for alterity within the epistemology of Empire (this has important bearing on the experiece of *Robinson*

Crusoe). Such an insistence on epistemological innocence may be related to the constitutive ambivalence and resultant duplicity of the (early) novel in relation to its fictionality. *Moll Flanders* can be understood as a tension between fact and fiction that is to be explained in terms of the tension between identity and invention within an autobiographical narrative which is not, after all, autobiographical.

1335 GERIGUIS, Lora Edmister. "Bows without arrows: the role of 'native agency' in the travel narratives of Daniel Defoe and other English texts, 1668-1790," **454**.

1336 HOPES, Jeffrey. "L'évolution historique des définitions génériques des 'romans' de Daniel Defoe." *La Licorne* 22 (1992): 57-68.

In French. The ideological heritage of the novel has exercised a great influence, notably in the affirmation of qualities of imagination and creativity in the work of Defoe ("qualités qui continuent à distinguer le 'littéraire' du 'non-littéraire'").

1337-----"Scottish unionism and the beginnings of Defoe criticism." *Études Écossaises* 4 (1997): 159- 65.

Defoe's visit to Scotland to promote the economic interests of Union marks a decisive moment in his career as a public writer.

1338 KAHN, Madeleine. *Narrative transvestism: rhetoric and gender in the eighteenth-century novel,* **553**.

1339 KING, Kathryn R. "Spying upon the conjurer: Haywood, curiosity, and 'the novel' in the 1720s." *StudN* 30:2 (1998): 178-93. See below under HAYWOOD, **1579**.

1340 KNAUFF, Barbara Elizabeth. "Multilingualism in French late seventeenth- and eighteenth-century imaginary voyages," **576**.

1341 KUCZYNSKI, Ingrid. "A discourse of patriots: the penetration of the Scottish Highlands." *JSBC* 4:1/2 (1997): 73-93.

Defoe travelled extensively in the Lowlands. In his tour he supplied a survey of the state of commerce and trade since the Union of 1707 which he had actually promoted as a means of progress. He was concerned that the impatiently expected economic takeoff seemed rather slow in coming, and indulged in the fantasy of boundless natural resources and commercial opportunity in Scotland and the Highlands which needed the initiative of the inhabitants to be tapped.

1342 LARSSON, Björn. "La fiction n'est plus ce qu'elle était: quelques remarques sur les théories pragmatiques du concept de fiction." *OL* 49:6 (1994): 317-37.
In French. New theories have deemed the criterion of referential truth as irrelevant. But this is the only essential and distinguishing criterion of a fictional text versus a non-fiction text. A theory which does not include this criterion will not stand up to empirical data of real readers. Referential truth is also the only argument that can be put to those who choose to treat fictional texts as factual ones, or to those who treat the horrors of this world as fiction. Discusses the *Mémoires de Robert Drury*, *A General History of the Pyrates* and the complex factual and fictional interpretation of authorship (Capt. Johnson, Defoe, Misson). "Defoe réussit non seulement le tour de force de tromper ses contemporaines, mais il a également défié les efforts de la posterité, y inclus ceux des specialistes, pour faire la part entre vérité et fiction dans son oeuvre" (322).

1343 LAWSON, Jacqueline Elaine. *Domestic misconduct in the novels of Defoe, Richardson, and Fielding*, **606**.

1344 LOGALDO, Mara. "*Memoirs of a Cavalier* and *Memoirs of an English Officer*: new narrative forms and the legacy of literary genres." In (pp. 109-30) BIGAMI, Marialuisa (ed.). *Wrestling with Defoe* etc., **1316**.

Irony creeps into Defoe's novels as a determining element of its generic alchemy.

1345 LUND, Roger D. *Critical essays on Daniel Defoe.* (Critical Essays on British Literature.) New York: G. K. Hall; London: Prentice Hall, 1997; pp. xii, 290.

Collection of 13 essays which stress Defoe's attraction to the realities of life in his day. His fictional work combines the concern expressed in his essays for morality, practical advice, travel, crime, economics (including the slave trade), pirates, and the exotic. The essays were all written during the 1990s, and cover the range of Defoe's prose, including his essays, historical fictions and the novels *Robinson Crusoe*, *Moll Flanders* and *Roxana*. "*Roxana*, once the most neglected of Defoe's major fictions, has become a novel for our times, and we are now in the position of seeing how deeply embedded it is in the history of the novel" (Paula Backscheider) (240). Bibliographic notes. Index (285-90).

1346 MACPHERSON, Sandra. "Marriage acts: the eighteenth-century critique of contract," **653**.

1347 MAYER, Robert. *History and the early English novel: matters of fact from Bacon to Defoe*, **664**.

1348 MULCAIRE, Terry. "Public credit: or, The feminization of virtue in the marketplace." *PMLA* 114:5 (1999): 1029-47.

'Cato' was the pseudonym of the Whig polemicists John Trenchard and Thomas Gordon. *Cato's Letters* was inspired by the South Sea Bubble. This and the ensuing financial and political crisis seemed to sum up for the Tory critics like Defoe the dangers of an economy built on paper properties and a political system that had cast in its lot with the new economy.

1349 NORTON, James Harris, III. "Confession in seventeenth- and eighteenth-century Protestant literature," **709**.

1350 NOVAK, Maximilian. "Defoe and the art of war." *PQ* 75:2 (1996): 197-213.
Defoe never ceased to admire the courage of the soldier, and, along with the rest of contemporary Europe, considered the state of war the natural condition of relations between nations.

1351-----"Picturing the thing itself, or not: Defoe, painting, prose fiction, and the arts of describing." *ECF* 9:1 (1996): 1-20.

Explores the relationship between Defoe's fiction and painting. Underscores Defoe's interest in painting, argues that Defoe drew much from the contemporary artistic form that best represented the real; he only gradually came to understand some of the advantages of prose fiction over the established form of realist painting. For Defoe painting and prose fiction embodied methods of deception that could be turned to useful ends. Considers Defoe's sense of scene, his sense of the visual mainly in terms of realist painting as it developed during the 17c, and esp. the realistic reading of scene in Dutch painting.

1352 PARKINSON, John M. "Daniel Defoe: Accomptant to the Commissioners of the Glass Duty." *NQ* 45:5 (1998): 455-56.

Defoe was recruited by his friend Dalby Thomas to be Accomptant to the Commissioners of the Glass Duty (1695-1700). Draws attention to various details in this report, Defoe's salary, the five reports referring to

Defoe, and the variant spellings of his name.

1353 PATTERSON, Craig. "Horrible roberys [*sic*], high-way men, and murders: Defoe, Gay, Lillo and Fielding and the popular literature of crime," **742**.

1354 PORTER, Susan Speer. "Domination and dissent: gendered duality and patriarchal authority," **772**.

1355 REED, Joel. "Nationalism and geoculture in Defoe's history of writing." *MLQ* 56:1 (1995): 31-53.

In arguing for the divine priority of Hebrew writing and Judaic culture, Defoe shifted the alphabet's history from the sacred Scriptures to a profane and modern context in which its letters write the history of England as a chosen nation and people. Fascinated with world exploration and travel literature, Defoe, the famous dissenter at times in his debates with Toland, supported the national church and criticized tolerance of non-Christian religions in defense of a unifying myth of national origins.

1356 REIMANN, K. A. "On their own account: pirate narratives and pirate writers of the long eighteenth century," **796**.

1357 ROGERS, Pat (ed.). *Daniel Defoe: The cultural heritage.* (The Critical Heritage Series.) London and New York: Routledge, 1972, 1995; pp. xiv, 228.
Collection of contemporary and later responses to the writer (1703-1879), showing the formation of the critical attitudes to his work and its place within a literary tradition. Two appendices: 1) a selective list of contemporary comments on Defoe's work; 2) Defoe's literary career. Bibliography (222-24). Index (225-28).

1358 RUMMEL, Kathryn. "Defoe and the Black Legend: the Spanish stereotype in *A Voyage around the World*." *RMRLL* 52:2 (1998): 13-28.

European, and esp. English, negative attitudes towards Spain were already firmly entrenched by Defoe's day. Spain was suffering from what historians call the 'Black Legend', the idea that Spaniards are somehow crueller and inferior to other Europeans. On 23 July 1711 Defoe outlined a proposal to his patron Robert Harley for the establishment of an English colony in Chile. The scheme is remarkably thorough even if it failed to win government support, and Defoe held to his idea, which he embodied in his 1724 travel fiction, *A New Voyage Round the World*. Here he enlarged upon his ideas, asserting that the Spaniards are unfit to colonize. His manipulation of the Spanish stereotype in order to further his own colonial designs raises interesting questions about the nature of the Black Legend itself, which served as a convenient scapegoat for European justifications of colonialism.

1359 SASSI LEHNER, Christina Maria. "An annotated noncritical edition of Daniel Defoe's *The Storm* (1704), including a historical introduction and a critical commentary placing it in the context of the author's works." Unpub. doct. diss., City Univ. of New York, 1997. [*DA* 58 (1997): 176A.]

Reproduces without alterations the 1704 text of Defoe's *Storm* by means of photographic facsimile. The text of this otherwise rare and difficult-to-locate work has a critical introduction that demonstrates the ways in which this long overlooked work has significant connections with Defoe's late novels. Establishes the historical background of the unprecedented storm which devastated the south of England and Wales. For months it was the subject of numerous newspaper reports, sermons, calamity pamphlets, scientific journals and poems. Defoe produced the only authoritative chronicle of the event, analyzing it from both providential and scientific perspectives. While working within the tradition of the providence guide, the calamity pamphlet, science booklet, Defoe created his own pseudo-history by combining these forms and using innovative narrative strategies. Explores the relationship between a history, a political pamphlet, and a historical poem, its lasting importance in relation to Defoe's work as a novelist, its narrative organization, identification of persons, mythical, historical and contemporary allusions, name places. Gains insight into Defoe's method of composition in identifying passages he culled from other works.

1360 SCHONHORN, Manuel. "Defoe and the limits of Jacobite rhetoric." *ELH* 64:4 (1997): 871-86.

Defoe's historical examples show the acceptance of diversity in both Catholic and Protestant countries, and his demand for diversity penetrates the political discussions. Despite his lifelong plea for unity, for one interest in matters of state, Defoe saw the need for a similar tension. Principled Whigs and principled Tories guaranteed a healthy tension of opposites.

1361 SCOTT, Paul H. *'Defoe in Edinburgh' and other papers*. East Linton, East Lothian: Tuckwell Press, 1995; pp. 252.

Collection of 34 essays that address subjects often alluded to but not adequately explained. The first considers Defoe in Edinburgh, where he was during the long debate on the Treaty of Union. What did he do there and why? His real achievement went beyond any journalistic contribution he might have made to the approval of the treaty. He was an enthusiast for the idea of union which was to be more than a political arrangement. He believed that England and Scotland ceased to exist in 1707 and were replaced by a new enlarged entity of Britain. He appealed for mutual tolerance and understanding between the two ancient enemies: this is commonplace enough, but it is difficult to find any sign of it before Defoe.

1362 SHANKLIN, Tip Harison. "Thresholds, boundaries, crossings: reading liminality in the English novel," **880**.

1363 SHERMAN, Sandra. "Commercial paper, commercial fiction: *The Compleat English Tradesman* and Defoe's reluctant novels." *Criticism* 37:3 (1995): 391-411.

In this work Defoe develops the didactic format so popular during the late 17c/early 18c, into an anti-didactic subversion of marketplace knowledge. The text reifies generic irony. While it inhabits the genre of updated Protestant guidebook, it misguides the tradesman, offering a type of accounting that was susceptible to error, and that induced the assumption that fiction and truth were hard to keep apart.

1364-----"Credit, simulation, and the ideology of contract in the early eighteenth century." *ECL* 19:3 (1995): 86-102.

The discourse of early modern finance lacked a vocabulary that was 'purpose-built', sufficient to describe phenomena whose rapid, radical progress outpaced linguistic invention. The financial crisis of the early 18c, culminating in the South Sea Bubble of 1720, literally beggared the imagination. After the Bubble burst, discussions of contract became crucial to the restoration of public credit, and hence to the reputation of Parliament itself. In *The Compleat English Tradesman* (1725-27) Defoe portrayed a credit environment in which individuals were not autonomous. Their promises were implicated in a web of promises not traceable to anyone's volition. Such commitments operated as simulacra, floating in the market without the sanction of an original capital fund.

1365------"Lady Credit no lady: or, The Case of Defoe's 'coy mistress', truly stat'd." *TSLL* 37:2 (1995): 185-214.

For 24 years beginning in 1689, England was at war with the continent, precipitating an escalation in the National Debt, with the institution of public credit becoming the subject of debate. Defoe embodied in a 'Lady' the indisputable but mercurial pleasure of financial credit, an oxymoron, since a female narrator subject who embodies credit eschews ladylikeness. Both Lady Credit and Roxana are brilliant forays into Defoe's own sense of the possibilities of a narrative that aspires towards non-resolution, toward the suspension of contraries. In both cases Defoe conceptualizes his work in terms that implicate a woman's sexual deportment, displacing his honesty as an author with the gendered honesty of the female body. Such a displacement is possible because Lady Credit, Roxana and Defoe configure a single topic: narrative elusiveness on the market.

1366------"Servants and semiotics: reversible signs, capital instability, and Defoe's logic of the market." *ELH* 62:3 (1995): 551-73.

Defoe was suspicious of servants; the 'servant problem' discussed in late tracts reflects his absorption with macro-economics, particularly the credit-based market where notes stood for cash. Defoe's barbs aimed at servants thus domesticate a concern with signifying practice, with a market in which remote participants are linked through texts.

1367------*Finance and fictionality in the early eighteen century: accounting for Defoe.* Cambridge and York: Cambridge UP, 1996; pp. xii, 222.

In the early 18c the increasing dependence of society on financial credit provoked widespread anxiety. The texts of credit -- stock certificates, IOUs, bills of exchange -- were denominated as potential fictions, while the polemical fictions of other texts was reassured in terms of the 'credit' they observed. Argues that in this environment finance is like fiction, employing the same tropes. Defoe understood the market's capacity to unsettle discourse, demanding and evading 'honesty' at the same time. Defoe's work, straddling both finance and literature, theorizes the disturbance of market discourse, elaborating strategies by which an author can remain in the market, perpetrating fictions while avoiding responsibility for doing so. Extensive bibliographic notes (179-220). Index (221-22).

1368-----"'New nothings', neologisms, and the recoinage of 1696." *1650-1850* 3 (1997): 189-210.

Defoe's "An Essay Upon Projects" (1697) is an early remarkable text addressing financial conditions following the national state of war. Defoe's concatenation of coins and words applies to language the contest over valuations that arose during the 'recoinage crisis' of the 1690s when

Parliament finally recalled clipped, devalued coins that, along with counterfeits, had debased the money supply. Defoe urges that 'custom' be suppressed, words implanted with a value unmediated by a devaluing consensus. Related to Defoe's animus toward the 'custom' of non-signifying speech is *The New Text of the Sense of the Nation* (1710) where the sweeping and meaningless oaths of allegiance are related to politeness (swearing meaningless expletive oaths).

1369-----"Promises, promises: Credit as contested metaphor in early capitalist discourse." *MP* 94:3 (1997): 327-49.

The late 17c/early 18c witnesses a new disconcerting faith in financial credit. Defoe credit's archetype, concatenating finance and imaginations, real and unreal, into a marketplace epistemology, rationalized by counter-intuition. Defoe's calibrations of honesty to market demands reflects the episteme of the South Sea Bubble, but also may reflect his chronic financial woes, his imaging a commerce of self in *Moll Flanders* and *Roxana* (whose heroines perversely invoke necessity), and his productions of commercial fictions (*Crusoe, Moll, Roxana*) that exploit public interest in amazing but 'true' accounts. His arguments are produced through engagement with history, most likely sharpened by self-interest and deepened by personal reflection. All this is a dexterous escape from Protestant convention.

1370 SORENSON, Janet Linda. "The grammar on (*sic*) empire, the figure of the nation: Language and cultural identity in eighteenth-century Britain," **918**.

1371 STADLER, Eva Maria. "Addressing social boundaries: Dressing the female body in early realist fiction." In (pp. 20-36) HIGONNET, Margaret R. and TEMPLETON, Joan (eds.). *Reconfigured spheres: feminist explorations of literary space*, **932**.

1372 SWANN, Charles. "Hardy, Defoe, and Leslie Stephen." *NQ* 42:2 (1995): 203-04.
Discusses Hardy's reference to Defoe's fictional style can be traced to an essay on Defoe by Leslie Stephen (1868).

1373-----"Mark Rutherford's ambiguous deliverance: Bunyan, Defoe, Spinoza, and secular history." *RES* 49:193 (1998): 23-39.

In *Robinson Crusoe* Defoe was aware not only of the two meanings of 'deliverance' but that they were related, and it is arguable that he was consciously drawing on the same tradition as Bunyan (Crusoe's 'Load' parallels Christian's 'Burden'). Defoe gives primacy to the religious, the Christian, rather than the legal meaning of 'deliverance'. William Hale White was later to juxtapose and contrast Bunyan and Spinoza's moral vocabularies and to explore the ambiguities and history of a term.

1374 TUMBLETON, Raymond D. "'Family religion': Popery in Defoe's domestic regime." *Genre* 28:3 (1995): 255-78.

Examines how Defoe impresses Protestant religious anxieties into the service of coercive narrative of domesticity in his didactic quasi-novel, *Religious Courtship*, as an exemplification of how the two interrelate in the development of modern sexual and political regimes. These regimes present themselves as emancipatory continuations of the Reformation, but it is no longer easy to be confident that one can know exactly what constitutes progress.

1375 TURLEY, Hans. "The homosocial subject: Piracy, sexuality, and identity in the novels of Daniel Defoe." Unpub. doct. diss., Univ. of Washington, 1994." [*DA* 56 (1994): 1373A.]

Emphasizes the transgressive nature of Defoe's protagonists, and demonstrates that Defoe continues to explore the possibilities of fiction after his first great novel, *Robinson Crusoe*. Using piracy as the cultural trope to re-read *Captain Singleton*, *The Farther Adventures of Robinson Crusoe* and *The Serious Reflections of Robinson Crusoe*, suggests that they would be significant in the context of an alternative history of the novel. Emphasizes transgressions from sexual 'reality' and legal trade based on middle-class depictions of the self. Piracy was culturally important for early 18c England. This study seeks to reconstruct the 'real' pirate through trial records, confessions, and other primary sources. The pirate is both heroicized and vilified by 18c writers, and this dual reaction makes him an unstable character who challenges normative sexual and economic conventions. Also looks at the fictional reality of the pirate depicted in Defoe's *A General History of the Pyrates*, one of the most important but overlooked works of the 18c. Defoe suggested alternative forms of social structures that privilege an identity based on homosocial transgressive norms. In *Captain Singleton*, Defoe repeats the search for identity that differs from the normative subjectivity which emerges in early 18c England. *Robinson Crusoe* takes on a different meaning when read with its two sequels, *Captain Singleton* and in the historical context of piracy. Read as a trilogy, all three Crusoe novels represent a search for identity that Crusoe loses on his return to England after years of isolation. Connections between Crusoe's wandering inclination and his stay on the island are stressed. Religious zeal is the only way to stabilize a sense of self-based desire, be it homosocial, economic or homoerotic.

1376 VAUTIER, Marie. "Les métarécits, le postmodernisme et le mythe postcolonial au Quebec: Un point de vue de la 'marge'. " *Études littéraires* 27:1 (1994): 43-61.

In French. Examines the post-modernist commentary on mythic situation through the medium of meta-texts. Looks at Tournier's examination of *Robinson Crusoe* in his *Vendredi, ou les Limbes du Pacifique*. Defoe lends support to the two pillars of western civilization in the 18c and 19c - the Christian religion and the capitalist system.

1377 VICKERS, Ilse. *Defoe and the new sciences.* (Cambridge Studies in Eighteenth-Century English Literature and Thought, 32.) Cambridge and New York: Cambridge UP, 1996; pp. xvii, 196.

Defoe always advocated the value of personal observation and experience: his conviction was that it is man's duty to explore and make productive use of nature. Studies Bacon's legacy to Defoe, showing that the ideas and concepts of Baconian science were a significant influence on Defoe's way of thinking and writing. Outlines the 17c intellectual milieu and discusses the prominence of Charles Morton, a major Baconian thinker and Defoe's teacher. Considers a wide range of Defoe's work from the point of view of his familiarity with the ideas of experimental philosophy, and throws new light on the close link between his factual and fictional works. Shows that Defoe was not only a thorough Baconian but a more consistent writer than has been recognized. Footnotes. Bibliography (182-92). Index (193-96). Illus. (3 pl.).

1378 WALL, Cynthia. "Grammars of space: the language of London from Stow's *Survey* to Defoe's *Tour*." *PQ* 76:4 (1997): 387-411.

Before the Great Fire, the few descriptions of London (textual topographies) were modelled almost exclusively on John Stow's 1598 *Survey of London* which conceptually pursues and narratively reflects a comparative sense of urban fixity. Defoe's London Line marks spaces and changes: it establishes records and crosses boundaries. As in the novels, the *Tour*'s line of topography merges with the line of narrative: the Line of boundary merges with the author or agent who defies the boundaries.

1379-----"Details of space: Narrative descriptions in early eighteenth-century novels." *ECF* 10:4 (1998): 387-405.

Defoe's narrative world, and the world of early 18c narratives in general, have far more familiar contours than we are used to noticing, given our expectation of Dickensian detail, our disconcertedness with gestures and glimpsed detail. In a narrative pattern that includes *The Pilgrim's Progress* in its lineage, Defoe's novels quite often supply very rich, warm, sensuous details. His novels not only abound with windows and doors, but are also profuse in colors and texture. Description itself opens metaphysical windows, indicates interpretation, hints at boundaries, and frequently creates the space for narrative possibility.

1380 WARNER, John M. *Joyce's grandfathers: myth and history in Defoe, Smollett, Sterne, and Joyce.* Athens, GA, and London: Georgia UP, 1993; pp. xiii, 193.

Evokes a double perspective on the literary tradition of three 18c novelists. Defoe, Smollett and Sterne can function in some ways as models, if not precise sources, for Joyce's later achievement. Joyce's dialectal response to history and myth can yield for us a deeper appreciation of artistic and intellectual strategies which have been overlooked in these three 18c novelists. Ch. 2 "Mythic and Historic Time in Defoe" (23-) shows that Defoe was able to use the idea of belief as a way to give shape to his novels. The central creative thrust for his fiction was the tension between diachronic and synchronic vision. Deeply attracted to the sense of shape found in mythic repetition, Defoe was nonetheless too much a modernist not to give priority to history. In the Judeo-Christian conception of time he had a tradition that allowed him to bring together linearity with some of the sense of form found in myth. As Christian *telos* gave shape to history, so repentance could give form to fiction. Linear history without a sense of transcendental purpose becomes a nightmare. Bibliographic notes (163-75). Bibliography (177-87). Index (189-93).

1381 WEST, Richard. "If in doubt, chuck out." *TLS* (21 March 1997): 16.

In the context of a discussion of the devastation of some of Britain's local libraries through the ideological actions of leftwing librarians, reflects on Defoe's observations in *The Compleat English Gentleman*, his book of etiquette, that a good library can compensate for a lack of good education. He followed his own advice in countless fake memoirs, histories, and records of overseas travel, as well as in the *Tour*.

1382-----*The life and surprising adventures of Daniel Defoe.* London: Harper Collins, 1997; pp. xvi, 427.

Biography dealing with Defoe's life and work in tandem, although it claims that it is "not intended to be a definitive, academic or even scholarly analysis of Defoe's writing." He worked for the secret service and enjoyed mystery, deception and 'disinformation'. Uses Defoe's minor books, pamphlets and journalism (esp. the 22 vols. of the *Review*), emphasizing his brilliance as journalist, reporter and travel writer. Notes for further reading (409-10). Index (413-27).

1383 WOLFF, Larry. "When I imagine a child: the idea of childhood and the philosophy of memory in the Enlightenment."*ECS* 31:4 (1998): 377-401.

Discusses Defoe in the context of childhood in the Enlightenment. Defoe fills the head of the young Robinson Crusoe without any epistemological qualifications concerning the character of memory. Moll Flanders is provided with a more uncertain account of her origins. When Defoe describes the mind of Moll, gradually emerging from darkness, straddling the threshold of memory, he carries out Locke's philosophical experiment.

1384 YANG, Yu-Mi. "The novelistic anomaly: origins of modernity's narrative forms," **1074**.

1385 ZANDER, Horst. "Die verheiratete Frau als Dienerin und Sklavin: zur Ehrenproblematik bei Mary Astell und Daniel Defoe." *AAA* 21:3 (1996): 239-53.
Mary Astell and Defoe prove to be antagonists in several respects: they hold quite different, or rather contrary, views on politics, religious matters and marriage. In *Roxana* Defoe opposes his own conceptions of marriage to those of Astell. The result is a text in which the probable situation of the married woman in the early 18c is more profoundly elucidated than in either Astell's or Defoe's expository writings.

PARTICULAR STUDIES (1995-1999)

Robinson Crusoe

1386 ANDRIES, Lise (ed.). *Robinson.* (Figures mythiques.) Paris: Autremont, 1996; pp. 159.

Collection of 9 items discussing reactions to *Robinson Crusoe* and the trope of marooning and castaway through 2 centuries. - Introd. (Lise ANDRIES) (9-25); - *Naissance du mythe* (Claude GAIGNEBET, Frank LESTRINGANT); - *Le récit au XVIIIe siècle* (Michel BARIDON, Haydn MASON); - *Les Robinsons modernes* (Jean-Michel RACAULT, Jacques

MEUNIER, Michel TOURNIER, Christopher PILLING).

1387 BERTRAND, Didier. "Order and chaos in Paradise: Colonial and 'postcolonial' constructions of religious identity through the Robinson Crusoe story." *ReLit* 27:3 (1995): 29-51.

Concentrates on *Robinson Crusoe* as a progressive myth that keeps on looking for adequate formulations to address present-day experiences of the God-world relation, therefore combining both economic and spiritual concerns. With the help of more recent Cultural Criticism, which deals with the colonial aspects of the novel, shows that Tournier in *Vendredi* questions the order of colonial Protestantism established by Defoe. Where Defoe grounds his religious feeling on a Protestant concept of God's transcending and immanent nature, Tournier assimilates his to that of the Oriental religion enthusiast Romain Rolland. As a 20c writer convinced of the damage done by the Christian order upheld by the Crusoes of colonial power, Tournier reduces that order to the point of absurdity and finally promotes the notion of a divine essence which ultimately frees him from that order.

1388 BIONDI, Carminella. "Naufragio con bagalio appresso: Gli oggetti di Robinson." In (pp. 375-83) BACCOLINI, Raffaella; FORTUNATI, Vita and MINERVA, Nadia (eds). *Viaggi in utopia.* (Forme dell'utopia: sezioni studi, 6.) Ravenna: Longa, 1996; pp. 450.

In Italian. Takes the topos of the oppressive baggage saved from shipwreck to examine various important Robinsonades: Johann David Wyss, *Die Schweizerfamilie Robinson* (1814); the anonymous *Robinson de Jean-Jacques Rousseau* (1834); Jules Verne, *L'Oncle Robinson* (1888, pub. 1891); the anonymous *La scuola di Robinson* (1882); St-John Perse, *Images à Crusoé* (1909); Giraudoux, *Suzanne et le Pacifique* (1921); Paul Valéry, *Robinson, pourvu, oisif, pensif* (post 1950); Tournier, *Vendredi, ou Les limbes du Pacifique* (1967); Gaston Compère, *Robinson 86* (1986); Coetzee, *Foe* (1986).

1389 BLEWETT, David. *The illustration of 'Robinson Crusoe', 1719-1920.* Gerrards Cross: Smythe, 1995; pp. 235.

Studies the illustrations of *Robinson Crusoe*, primarily the editions of the novel proper (vol. 1, or vols. 1 and 2 together), only partially examines illustrated editions of rewritten or severely abridged versions, and scarcely any of the Robinsonades. Independent prints and paintings designed to be sold apart from the text have been considered. The extraordinary power of the image of Robinson Crusoe, his status as one of the enduring mythical figures in Western culture, is reason enough for this study, but the relationship between image and text in the history of book illustration is complex, and raises important questions. What is the value of illustrations? What do they imitate? What qualities should one look for? The evaluations of the Crusoe myth depends as much on power of the illustrations as on Defoe's text. Illus. (103 plates). Appendix A: A Select Checklist of Illustrated Editions of *Robinson Crusoe* (191-227). Appendix B: Independent Illustrations of Scenes from *Robinson Crusoe* (227-28), Index (229-35).

1390   BOEHRER, Bruce. "'Men, monkeys, lap-dogs, parrots, perish all!': Psittacine articulacy in early modern writing." *MLQ* 59:2 (1998): 171-93.

The growing popularity of pet parrots in early modern England and its consequnces for literary representation is important because of the way in which it is rendered trivial in the 16c and 17c. Dismissive references to parrots inform a larger discursive pattern developing out of the culture of early modern exploration. Parrots became popular objects for painterly display and increasingly associated with servants or inferior men. One of the most famous parrots in English literature, Poll in *Robinson Crusoe*, is described in terms of anthropomorphic subordination. The history of Crusoe's relationship with parrots is the history of a twofold transformation: as he takes on the character of a monarch, he turns Poll into a servant or person who mirrors and confirms his own self-announced sovereignty. This metaphor prepares the way for his later acquisition of a human servant.

1391   CARTER, Margaret Anne. "Spiritual rebirth in *Robinson Crusoe*: the Western religious search and its effect upon Friday." Unpub. doct. diss., The Claremont Graduate Univ., 1995. [*DA* 55 (1995): 3849A.]

Explores a cultural reinterpretation of reality and its incorporation into the novel, which can be used to justify foreign invasion and the subjugation of captive people. *Robinson Crusoe* promotes a social and ethical order generated from Biblical mythology. Genesis 1-3 determines the landscape of the novel and its moral architecture. It justifies Crusoe's characterization as lord of the island, with his assumption of superiority and unquestioned dominion over the land and over Friday as the unpaid labourer of the island. The unveiling of the biblical construct challenges its reputation as solidly built on reality. Levi-Strauss's structured anthropology provides the theoretical foundation for the investigation of the logic underlying the cosmological representation of Genesis, with its mythic structural logic being appositional, polarized and antagonistic. It informs a broad range of social activity, esp. a search for paradise on the one hand and a transformation of the wilderness through spiritual elevation on the other. Genesis determines the landscape of the novel and serves as the intellectual foundation for Crusoe's awakening, his self-proclaimed ownership of the island, and his enslavement of Friday. The text ultimately becomes a rationale for the conquest of the New World and the subjugation of the American natives. Realism is underpinned by a selective integration of cultural perceptions.

1392 CHANDLER, David. "Borrow's *Robinson Crusoe*." *GBB* 15 (1998): 7-27.

The 1850s children's edition is probably the copy of *Robinson Crusoe* that so impressed the young George Borrow.

1393 CLOWES, Edith W. "The Robinson myth reread in postcolonial and post communist modes." *Crit* 36:2 (1995): 145-59.

Postmodernism topples 'totalities', undermining absolute truths, including the meta-narratives of emancipation and enlightenment, gladly departing from a 'modernist' nostalgia for some kind of ultimate certainty. All has become a commodity that can be traded for the right price. The danger may be that a widespread enthusiasm for semiotics, ideological politics and other fragmentation might turn into a new claim of Western cultural hegemony in which the specific character of any given culture is easily ignored. Compares and contrasts Coetzee's *Foe* and the Stalin-era parody by Ilia Ilf and Evgeny Petrov, "How Robinson Was Made" ("The New Robinsons"). The narrative voice in both is female, which draws attention to the maleness of Defoe's concept of economic individualism. An act of liberation is confronted in both that is ultimately not liberating. In both works there is an inability to negotiate between the self and others, while the 'other' represents the persecutor and the persecuted (as in *Foe*). An awareness of the impossibility of communication can merge into the undesirability of communication, a pathological aspect of post-modernism, and the beginning of a global development of mini-totalities.

1394 COPE, Kevin L. "All aboard the ark of possibility: or, Robinson Crusoe returns from Mars as a small-footprint, multi-channel interdeterminacy machine." *StudN* 30:2 (1998): 150-63.

No critical approach can encompass so big, so elusive and protean an author as Defoe. His taste for strong topics encourage critics to try out every possible approach. *Robinson Crusoe* is the epitome of the 'Defoe problem', the problem of an author who is simply too big and diverse for any literary approach, theoretical or otherwise. Any attempt at narratological, ideological, psychological and even explicative approaches to his work is doomed to fail. There are simply too many dimensions to Crusoe's character, too many variations, variabilities and irregularities. Suggests that *Robinson Crusoe* is a sort of multi-channel indeterminacy machine, a perverse if wonderful device generating alternatives, diversions and counter-interpretations.

1395 CROWLEY, John E. "The sensibility of comfort." *AHR* 104:3 (1999): 749-82.

Robinson Crusoe romanticized the new 18c notion of comfort. Confronted with having to provide for himself from scratch, Crusoe demonstrates in detail what it meant to be comfortable in early modern England. The importance of these details lies in the sheer existence of a fictional narrative in which an ordinary person's daily activities are the center of continuous literary attention. Isolation on the island leads Crusoe to learn that he had come to take his physical comforts for granted as natural, when in fact they were deeply historical. The development of a popular culture of fashionable consumption in the 18c coincided with a new language to describe the physical basis of material need.

1396 DONOGHUE, Frank. "Inevitable politics: rulership and identity in *Robinson Crusoe.*" *StudN* 27:1 (1995): 1-11.

During his stay on the island, Crusoe resorts to several political expedients through perplexing impersonations. He dearly wishes to be self-sufficient, but is repeatedly confronted with the unsettling sense that he is connected to the European world. England's expanding empire, defined by an emergent mercantile ideal, forced Defoe to furnish Crusoe with more complex answers to questions about his political identity than would have been required of an Englishman of an earlier age.

1397 EGERER, Claudia. "Hybridizing the zero: Exploring alternative strategies of empowerment in J. M. Coetzee's *Foe.*" In (pp. 96-101) NYMAN, Jopi and STOTESBURY, John A. (eds). *Postcolonialism and cultural resistance.* (Studia Carelica humanistica, 14.) Joensuu, Finland: Univ. of Joensuu, 1999; pp. 259.

Highlights the complexities, contradictions and difficulties of the cultural encounter. Coetzee illustrates how the very symbol of subjection, Friday's tongueless silence, can be seen as a means to resist and undermine that subjection by usurping the story, growing in potency until it finally overwhelms the narration.

1398 ENGÉLIBERT, Jean-Paul. *La postérité de Robinson Crusoé: un mythe* *littéraire de la modernité, 1954-1986.* (Histoire des idées et critique littéraire, 362.) Geneva: Droz, 1997; pp. 352.

In French. Discusses literary myth and the mytho-critique of *Robinson Crusoe*, looking at:
1) the genesis of the Robinsonade (prehistory of the genre, the arrival of *Robinson Crusoe*);
2) "Le social et le religieux: la rupture des liens" (Robinsonades since Golding, the quest for "l'altérité - hétérotopies, entropies" - the representation of the world);
3) "Le travail littéraire du mythe" (subjects in question, the death of the hero, the impossible ethical question in Golding, the elaboration of the 'I' in literary myth);
Conclusion (birth of the Robinson myth, structure and metamorphosis of the myth, Robins - literary myth of modernity). Bibliography (343-50).

1399-----"Reécrire *Robinson Crusoé*: mythe littéraire et deuil de la modernité." *RLC* 70:1 (1996): 52-71.

In French. This modern literary myth captures the grief and alienation of modern man.

1400 FAUSETT, David. *The strange surprizing sources of 'Robinson Crusoe'.* (Text: Studies in Comparative Literature, 3.) Amsterdam and Atlanta, GA: Rodopi, 1995; pp. viii, 229.

Examines the literary and historical background of *Robinson Crusoe* and reassesses some views traditionally held both by literary historians and the general public. A Dutch novel of marooning by Hendrik Smeek, *The Mighty Kingdom of Krinke Kesmes* (1708), may have been its model. The sources extend across the literary, religious and economic history of the age, and to events not only in Britain, but around the world. Focuses on the religious background and critical problems it poses, the social background, and their interrelations. The specific sources are traced, from the perspective of an incipient realism and the decline of the utopian ideal. Evidence regarding the sources of the work is reviewed and some conclusions are reached. Bibliography (205-24). Index (225-29).

1401 FIELDING, Penny. "'No pole, nor pillar': imagining the Arctic with James Hogg." *SHogg* 9 (1998): 45-63.

Hogg's interest in meaning of cannibalism is most striking in *The Three Perils of Man* (1822). The character Allan Gordon looks closely at the strange reciprocal relationship between cannibalism and the rejection of it. Disgust is both cannibalism's opposite (as recognized in *Robinson Crusoe*) and its mirror image -- the excorporation, as opposed to the incorporation, of taboo matter.

1402 HOEGBERG, David E. "'Your pen, your ink': Coetzee's *Foe, Robinson Crusoe*, and the politics of parody." *Kunapipi* 17:3 (1995): 86-101.

Coetzee's novel *Foe* presents itself as a 'source' or earlier version of *Robinson Crusoe*. Explores how *Foe* functions as a critique not only of *Robinson*, but also of broader ideological formations of which Defoe's novel is only one manifestation. Coetzee sees *Robinson Crusoe* as a powerful myth of colonialism: it encourages belief in the justice and profitability of colonialism. In the final analysis, is Coetzee doing anything more than demonstrating *his* benevolent concern for colonial victims? The most valuable treasure lies in the effort to recover Friday's voice and perspective.

1403 HOPES, Jeffrey. "Real and imaginary stories: *Robinson Crusoe* and the *Serious Reflections*." *ECF* 8:3 (1996): 313-28.

Serious Reflections has been much neglected, but it constitutes a reply to attacks on the fictional and moral status of *Robinson Crusoe*, in particular to the accusation that behind a specious 'claim to history', Defoe has written an implausible romance that articulates suspect religious views. The reply more generally demonstrates Defoe's concerns to establish not only the book he intended *Robinson* to be, but the way in which he considered it should read.

1404 JENKINS, Hugh. "Crusoe's country house(s)." *ECent* 38:2 (1997): 118-33.

Robinson Crusoe represents Defoe's fictive exploration and celebration of the psychological and social orientation of economic individualism. Crusoe returns again and again to the country house ideal to describe and celebrate his island estate. The good colonial son, once removed from his native setting, becomes, because of his undeniable otherness, simply the unavoidable reminder of the processes through which the father established himself. Yet it is these very processes that the novel, like the country-house poem a hundred years earlier, has constantly sought to mask. Similarly, in Friday's disappearance, his 'magical extraction' from the text, the dynamics of racism and colonialism are uncovered at the moment when they are most effaced.

1405 KEANE, Patrick J. *Coleridge's submerged politics: 'The Ancient Mariner' and 'Robinson Crusoe'*. Columbia and London: Missouri UP, 1994; pp. xiii, 419.

Explores Samuel Taylor Coleridge's role in and response to several crucial issues of the revolutionary and post-revolutionary age: the tragic question of slavery and the Atlantic slave trade, and the rise and suppression of English radicalism during the decade of the French Revolution. Relates *The Ancient Mariner* to the slave-trading of *Robinson Crusoe* and to the failure of the French Revolution, and connects them to the *counter*-revolution in England. This is a historical as much as literary study, born out of analysis of what Coleridge did and did not say in annotations of *Robinson Crusoe*. The extended notes of the marginalia celebrate Robinson Crusoe as humanity's 'Universal Representative' even though his slave-trading activities are not mentioned. Explores the attitude not only of Coleridge but also of Defoe towards slavery and the slave trade, both in their best known works. Also looks at treatment of the Crusoe-Friday story, considering what both Defoe and Coleridge never say. Bibliography (377-402). Index (403-19). See also POWELL below, **1415**.

1406 MARAIS, Mike. "Colonialism and the epistemological underpinnings of the early English novel." *EngA* 23:1 (1996): 47-66.

The relation of travel writing to the novel is conventionally construed in terms of the distinction between fact and fiction, a distinction which conceals the interplay pertaining between fact and fiction in travel writing prior to the 18c. Discusses *Robinson Crusoe* to show the degree to which the form of the novel was affected by the discursive ruptures, linguistic changes and epistemological shifts of the 17c and 18c. In response to these changes, the novel as genre developed realism as its distinguishing feature, a representational strategy that colludes with a mode of knowledge implicated in imperialism. Contends, therefore, that the history of the rise of the novel cannot be separated from the history of European imperialism.

1407----- "'One of those islands without an owner': The aesthetics of space in *Robinson Crusoe* and J. M. Coetzee's *Life and Times of Michael K.*." *Current Writing* 8:1 (1996): 19-32.

The apparent difference between Crusoe's island and Europe is systematically reduced as he domesticates the wilderness and transforms it into a replica of England. Despite the realist illusion of immediacy, the representation of the subject's encounter with colonial space unconsciously reveals that the former's knowledge of the latter is mediated by European discourse, and not determined by the actual terrain. In Coetzee's *Michael K.*, the decolonization of the farm reverses the process of colonization which the island undergoes in Defoe's novel. The transformation of the island from wilderness to property to colony is concomitant with Crusoe's composition of self, which expresses itself in his development from castaway to proprietor to governor in the course of the novel. Conversely, in Coetzee's text, K.'.s decomposition of self and eventual fusion with the land lead directly to the decolonization of the farm, the revelation of its 'being there'.

1408 MEDALIE, David. "Friday updated: *Robinson Crusoe* as sub-text in Gordimer's *July's People* and Coetzee's *Foe*." *Current Writing* 9:1 (1997): 43-54.

The movement in Defoe's novel from shipwreck and despair to the contentment of the reconciled and resourceful self on the island, and then to rescue it from it, marks a specific trajectory of progressivist discovery and self discovery. *July's People* in its refusal to affirm either a completed revolution or a definite conclusion of liberating understanding, refuses the teleology of *Robinson Crusoe*. *Foe* suggests the extent to which the island myth is a myth of control and authority, based on vigorous exclusion. Coetzee's Friday points to the limitations inherent in the enterprise of narrative itself. In this novel it is not only the Adamic authority, but also the Adamic author, who, as another kind of castaway, haunts the world in search of a place from which to speak and bestow utterance.

1409 MORRISSEY, Lee. "*Robinson Crusoe* and the South Sea trade, 1710-1720." In (pp. 209-15) DIGAETANI, John Louis (ed.). *Money: lure, love, and literature*. Westport, CT and London: Greenwood Press, 1994; pp. xix, 268.

In *Robinson Crusoe* Defoe advances an argument similar to that found in his South Sea trade pamphlets. The 'novel' form, which includes narrative and allusive elements of autobiography, could reach a different audience than the pamphlets' 'familiarizing' theme. Suggests the contextual and historical similarities of *Robinson Crusoe* and the trade pamphlets, urging that the issue is not that Defoe could 'transform' the South Sea pamphlets into a small resounding commercial success, but rather how and why. Crusoe dramatizes the possibility of a South Sea trade, an exemplar of the Protestant and bourgeois virtues. For this reason it is important that Defoe divert his agents for a South Sea trade to a different audience. References (214-15).

1410 NEILL, Anna. "Crusoe's farther adventures: discovery, trade, and the law of nations." *ECent* 38:3 (1997): 197-213.

The *Farther Adventures* begins where *Robinson Crusoe* left off, setting the relationship between patriarchal government and colonial plantation and settlement in the context of larger questions about sovereignty and the law of nations. The *Farther Adventures* explores this violent scene of contact where the law of nations has little or no jurisdiction. Crusoe discovers that his authority is determined by his weak sense of national identity. To subjugate people and set up as their absolute ruler is to become denationalized and dangerously removed from commercial culture. To make war on isolated savages and pagans in the name of cosmopolitan right and the freedom of trade is at once to be profitable, and in the modern sense of the world, English.

1411 NOVAK, Maximilian. "Friday; or , The power of naming." In (pp. 110-22) RIVERO, Albert J. (ed.). *Augustan subjects: Essays in honor of Martin C. Battesin*. Newark: Delaware UP; London and Toronto: Assoc. UPs, 1997; pp. 311.

Examines Crusoe's transforming his island world through the agency of language and particularly his proclivity to create a world through a creative process of naming. Despite his isolation, Crusoe is a maker of laws. As monarch of his island, he creates the rules by which he lives as well as the names that demarcate his territory. He creates all and possesses all as much by the power of naming as by his labor. The true values of discerning for Crusoe lay in the economic exploitation of new lands we know as colonialism.

1412 NOWAK, Helge. *'Completeness is all': Forsetzungen und andere Weiterführungen britischer Romane als Beispiel zeitübergreifender und interkultureller Rezeption*. (Sprache und Literatur: Regensburger Arbeiten zur Anglistik und Amerikanistik, 39.) New York, Bern and Paris: Peter Lang, 1994; pp. 446.

In German. Considers the completion and continuation of certain English novels as examples of cross-temporal and intercultural reception. Looks at the relevance of this phenomenon, the inclusion of literary-theoretical concepts before considering the process in relationship to Defoe, Jane Austen, the Brontës, Dickens, and some of the popular novels of the 19c. Ch. 3 "Weiterführungen zu Defoes *Robinson Crusoe* (115-76) looks at Michel Tournier's *Vendredi* (1967), Adam Mitchell's *Man Friday* (1972-75), Derek Walcott's *Pantomime* (1978), Gaston Compère's *Robinson 86* (1986) and J. M. Coetzee's *Foe* (1986). Appendix considers issues of typology. Bibliography (409-42). Index (443-46).

1413 O'CARROLL, John. "The island after Plato: a 'Western' amnesia." *SoRA* 31:2 (1998): 265-81.

Pacific islands are often associated with paradoxical rhetorics of paradisalism and monstrosity. Even writers offering a critique of these 'myths' confine themselves to British or post-Enlightenment island narratives, but it is more properly associated within a fractured heritage of ancient Greek cosmology. This involves considering the island as an exemplary site of civic analysis, which raises other suggestive issues about the conception of the city, the island, and memory systems. All these things are traced in terms of Plato's work. In the Enlightenment the island utopia lost its place as a privileged grid of state, urban formation, individual boundary of thought and site of sacred defiance. It became central to numerous forms of utopias set on isolated islands, the Robinsonade island from then on until the present becomes the site of foundational epistemological activity.

1414 PESSINI, Elena. "Hervé et Compère: ou, L'Histoire de Robinson sans Vendredi." In (pp. 385-93) BACCOLINI, FORTUNATI and MINERVA (eds). *Viaggi in Utopia* etc., **188**.

In French. Considers the modern Robinsonades by Alain Hervé, *Robinson* (1985) and Gaston Compère, *Robinson 86* (1986), and in particular the implications of the absence of Friday in both these re-writings. For Hervé " [...] contrairement à Tournier, le sauvage n'as pas un influence directe sur le héros qui ne le rencontre qu'après avoir subi lui-même une profonde transformation" (390); Compère "n'admet qu'une seule relation, celle de l'individu avec lui-même [...]" (392).

1415 POWELL, Raymond. "Coleridge's debt to Defoe: *The Ancient Mariner* and *The Farther Adventures of Robinson Crusoe*." *ELN* 33:2 (1995): 48-52.

Robinson Crusoe made an impression on Coleridge, and the sequel also seems to have impressed itself on Coleridge's imagination, leading him to draw on it while composing *The Ancient Mariner*: the account of a servant girl and the whole ship's company facing slow death from starvation, and the ideal of raising the reader's eye above the distinctions of Christian denominational division. Coleridge owes to Defoe a sense of the universalist spirit: "he makes me forget my *specific* class, character, and circumstances raise me into the Universal *Man*". See also KEANE above, **1405**.

1416 RANKIN, Walter P. "Autobiographical fiction *vs* fictional autobiography: Christa Wolf's *Kindheitsmuster* and J. M. Coetzee's *Foe*." *CLS* 36:4

(1999): 306-19.

The 'reality' of *Robinson Crusoe* hinges upon the assumption that the author can choose to separate himself from the text and grant it his authority. The post-modern relationship between the author and text is decidedly more ambivalent and less peaceful. No longer is it assumed that the author controls the text in creating it. Both Wolf's *Kindheitsmuster* and Coetzee's *Foe* transcend autobiographical traditions outlined in literary handbooks. Focused on the ontology of writing itself (as well as the self), these are works which not only reflect the authors' concepts of writing, but actually come to reflect upon themselves as written texts.

1417 RITCHIE, Daniel E. "Robinson Crusoe as narrative theologian." *Ren* 49:2 (1997): 95-110.

Demonstrates that the terms of recent narrative theology give the reader a way of understanding why Defoe's *Robinson Crusoe* has pleased more readers than its sequel, the *Farther Adventures*. Crusoe finds that the truths of Biblical narrative are validated in his own narrative. The three volumes of *Robinson Crusoe* appeared at a time of great change in Biblical hermeneutics, the strongly realistic literal and historical, and the historical-critical, where historical readings of Scripture began to split off from the edifying. The first and best-known volume reflects an earlier reading of Scripture: Crusoe comes to recognize the authority of the Bible for the purpose of reinterpreting his past life, and shaping his future one. The second and third volumes (esp. their prefaces) give evidence of the hermeneutical shift taking place. Here Defoe becomes extremely concerned about the 'truth' -- the historically verifiability - of the narrator and his fictional character. Defoe's reading of his own novels begin to separate their 'edifying' meaning from their historically unverifiable fictions.

1418 ROGERS, Shef. "Crusoe among the Maori: translation and colonial acculturation in Victorian New Zealand." *BH* 1 (1998): 182-95.

Print culture played a significant role in the establishment of the vast British Empire, esp. in the settlement of New Zealand. Among the early European translators into Maori, pride of place goes to Henry Tracy Kemp, who was part of an explicit government policy of Maori acculturation. Among his fictional translations was *Robinson Crusoe*. The texts themselves, and the historical and social contexts surrounding Kemp's selection, tell us much about European and Maori attitudes towards print. In the light of Kemp's views on the Maori understanding of capitalism, it makes sense that the government should resort to a fictional embodiment of the same values in *Robinson Crusoe*.

1419 ROMMEL, Thomas. "Aspects of verisimilitude: temporal and topographical references in *Robinson Crusoe*." *LLComp* 10:4 (1995): 279-85.

Analysis of temporal and topographical references in *Robinson Crusoe* shows that the text is designed to create the impression of verisimilitude. Two different sets of references are correlated in an attempt at creating a plausible report of Crusoe's life on the island. One set of references belongs to the world of empirical facts known to contemporary readers of the novel, and the other set refers to the material frame of reference established in the text. Contributions of both temporal and topographical references were identified, tagged and mapped using TUS and TEP to collate a variety of different word-lists. The result of the computer-assisted analysis shows that Defoe emphasizes the impression of verisimilitude by establishing a plausible network of internal references. The computer-assisted identifications of 'approximation' further enhance the impression of a report based on facts (as Defoe claims at the beginning of the novel) rather than a work of fiction.

1420 ROTHMAN, Irving N. "Coleridge and the semi-colon in *Robinson Crusoe*: problems of editing in Defoe." *StudN* 27:3 (1995): 320-40.

Coleridge equated the ironies of the passage when Crusoe pockets the gold in the cabin to the creditable psychological responses which equate Defoe with England's most profound writing. He well appreciated Defoe's religious sentiments and his powers as a narrative artist, but he did not have the best text available to him when he read *Robinson Crusoe*.

1421 SAARILUOMA, Lisa. "Hinaus mit der Zivilisation: Tourniers *Vendredi* et Rousseaus Zivilationskritik." *GRM* 47:1/1 (1997): 133-49.

Tournier's novel turns around the opposition between 'civilization' and 'barbarism' used in the subtext, Defoe's *Robinson Crusoe*. While Defoe's Crusoe maintains civilization on the desert isle, and integrates Friday into it, presuppositions brought from civilization are called into question for Tournier's Robinson as a result of the encounter with loneliness and the 'barbarian'. Friday has the function of the abstract savage in Rousseau's critique of civilization which Tournier continues. In contrast to Rousseau, Tournier neither has the choice of returning to an unadulterated 'state of nature', nor is it possible for his characters to develop from a natural state into members of civilization, as in *Émile*. Tournier's Robinson remains inside a subjectively constructed reality, outside of the human community. Unlike Rousseau, Tournier only denies the society, and does not offer a utopian model of it.

1422   SANTESSO, Aaron. "A note on goats: Defoe on Crusoe's 'devil'." *Scriblerian* 30:2 (1998): 48-49.

Refers to *Scriblerian* 16:2 (1984): 184 where James MEANS suggested that Defoe was influenced by a passage in the *Philosophical Transactions*. Defoe's impatience with those who would see the Devil in a goat allows us to reinterpret Crusoe's discovery of the dying goat as one more in a series of misguided episodes designed to show a foolish sinner still unclear as to the true nature of God - or Satan.

1423 SCHLAEGER, Manuel. "Literature and national identity." *JSBC* 5:1 (1998): 67-80.

National identity is close to what some would call 'patriotism'. Uses *Robinson Crusoe* to illustrate how Defoe fosters this. It took only one generation of readers to establish the hero as a mythical figure resonant of all the major characteristics attributed to the English race (i.e. the middle classes): self-reliance, entrepreneurial astuteness, a distinct sense of superiority. The novel moves from a discourse of exploration and national self-assertion to an exemplaristic story that fuses external and internal exploration, and from that fusion arrives at a renewed and theologically fuelled impulse to construct a forceful national ideology of economic expansion.

1424   SILL, Geoffrey M. "A source for Crusoe's tobacco cure." *ELN* 32:4 (1995): 46-48.
The cure for Crusoe's distemper may have first come to Defoe's attention in an abstract of a medical text that appeared in *The History of Learning: or, An Abstract of Several Books* edited by Jean Cornand de la Crose in 1691. Defoe is deliberately ambiguous about whether the tobacco or the Bible is to be credited for Crusoe's deliverance, consistent with his usual practice of admitting of both natural and supernatural explanations for observed events.

1425-----"Neurology and the novel: Alexander Monro *primus* and *secundus*, *Robinson Crusoe*, and the problem of sensibility." *LitMed* 16:2 (1997): 250-65.
On the evidence of Benjamin Rush's journal we have Defoe's novel *Robinson Crusoe* to thank for the continuation of one of the great medical dynasties in modern history. Munro's senior's selection of *Robinson Crusoe* as the text with which to stimulate young Alexander's

curiosity about human nature provides a new opportunity to study the connections between neurology and the emergence of the novel of sensibility in the 18c. The sensibility of the nervous system moved from being considered at the periphery to the center of human social activity. The British novel may have helped to initiate this movement.

1426-----"The source of Robinson Crusoe's 'sudden joy'." *NQ* 45:1 (1998): 67-68.

Crusoe thanks for his deliverance are taken from Robert Wild's poem "Wild's Humble Thanks for His Majesties Gracious Declaration for Liberty of Conscience, March 15, 1672", a broadside. Defoe uses Wild's line to warn readers of the danger of excessive passions, even those aroused by favorable circumstances.

1427 SONCINI, Sara. "The island as social experiment: a reappraisal of Daniel Defoe's political discourse(s) in *Robinson Crusoe* and *The Farther Adventures*." In (pp. 11-44) BIGAMI, Marialuisa (ed.). *Wrestling with Defoe* etc., **1316**.

Hobbes, Locke and Defoe share a common attribute and aims. All three transfer the power relations shaping their contemporary reality into a more or less fictional discourse hidden behind the patina of history, primitivism or theoretical speculation.

1428 SOUHAMI, Diana. *Selkirk's island*. London: Weidenfeld & Nicholson, 2001; pp. 246.

Investigation of the story of the original model for Robinson Crusoe, Alexander Selkirk, who was marooned on the island of Juan Fernandez for four years (1704-8). Examines the two contemporary accounts by Captain Woodes Rogers and Richard Steele, as well as unpublished manuscripts. Considers the detail of Selkirk's battle for survival, including the psychological struggles, and the physical effects of his habitation, the destruction of wild nature by man.

1429 SOUPEL, Serge. "D'un archétype à l'autre: *The Mysteries of Udolpho* et *Robinson Crusoe*." *BSEAA* 43 (1996): 51-61.

In French. Points out that in the confrontation with isolation and fear, in the exploration of the psychology of fear, and in many other details of experience and imagery, *Robinson Crusoe* can be seen as the atavistic ancestor of Mrs Radcliffe's novel, which established itself as another generic prototype in its own right. " [...] [la] thème particulière de la terreur chez les deux auteurs, qui conduira à certains approfondissements du psychisme des terrorisés dans leur cadre de vie."

1430 SPAAS, Lieve and STIMPSON, Brian (eds). *Robinson Crusoe: myths and metamorphoses*. Basingstoke: Macmillan; New York: St Martin's Press, 1996; pp. xvii, 328.

Collection of 23 essays considering various aspects of the enduring popularity of *Robinson Crusoe*, analyzing links between the Puritan ethic and the spirit of capital enterprise, and the various adaptations, imitations and critiques that have appeared in its wake. Considers works by Pixérécourt (1805), Giraudoux (*Suzanne et la Pacifique*) (1921), Tournier (1967), Walcott (1978) and Coetzee (1986).

1431 STABLEFORD, Brian. "The descendants of Robinson Crusoe." *Million* 6 (1991): 49-53.

Robinson Crusoe was the first best-selling English novel, and has been in print in England for over 270 years, and nearly as long in other languages. It stands at the head of a whole sub-genre of 'Robinsonades' which has produced many other best-sellers. The most successful include *The Swiss Family Robinson* (1812) by J. R. Wyss, *The Coral Island* (1858) by R. M. Ballantyne, *The Mysterious Isle* (1875) by Jules Verne, *The Blue Lagoon* (1908) by H. de Vere Stacpoole, and *Lord of the Flies* (1954) by William Golding. This line of literary descent presents to the modern reader a sequence of very interesting variations rung upon a central theme: that of the castaway from civilization forced to build his own microcosm from scratch.

1432 STOTESBURY, John A: "Constructions of heroic resistance: Crusoe, Mandela, and their desert island." In (pp. 244-52) NYMAN, Jopi and STOTESBURY, John A. (eds). *Postcolonialism and cultural resistance*. (Studia Carelica humanistica, 14.) Joensuu, Finland: Univ. of Joensuu, 1999; pp. 259.

Nelson Mandela's own life narrative has been structured by the Crusoe myth, forming another Robinsonade with all that this entails as far as its Western origins are concerned. Our post-apartheid reading of the myth, reinforced to varying degrees by the emerging plethora of Island narratives, must take critical account of the contradictory forces of myth and countermyth. In the process of resistance, Robben Island itself casts off the potentially ambivalent Crusoesque symbolism of the West, and becomes transformed as the heroically redemptive location for the gestation of a new civilization.

1433 SVILPIS, Jänis."Bourgeois solitude in *Robinson Crusoe.*" *ESCan* 22:1 (1996): 35-43.

In Jules Verne's *L'Ile mystérieuse* the castaway Aryton becomes feral, loses all traces of civilization and becomes scarcely more than an animal. Verne offers a critique of Robinsonades generally, and particularly Defoe's construction of his hero. Crusoe is an unnatural figure but he is a figure central to Western European culture, one who appears and reappears through a long series of texts, and the impossibility that he represents has a continuing value for us. Together with his spiritual experience, his labour authenticates him as an exemplary individual, not merely a laborer. His is a scene of heroic labor - appropriating territory, dominating nature, and improving human life in a compelling variant of the grand narratives of liberation and enlightenment. His labor becomes a symbolic representation of capitalist production, a ghostly image of the entire society demanded by such productions. And he, the integrated, spiritually cultured, skilled and industriously economic man imagined by capitalism, can be fully himself only when he is alone.

1434 TOLEDANO BUENDÌA, Carmen. "Translation as palimpsest." *RCEI* 38 (1999): 195-202.

Discusses the Spanish translation of *Robinson Crusoe.*

1435 WATT Ian. *Myths of modern individualism: Faust, Don Quixote, Don Juan, Robinson Crusoe* etc., **1033.**

1436 WHEELER, Roxann. "'My savage', 'my man': racial multiplicity in *Robinson Crusoe.*" *ELH* 62:4 (1995): 821-61.

A dynamic of race relations between Crusoe and Friday informs the whole novel. Bringing racialized difference and multiplicity to bear on *Robinson Crusoe* allows analysis of ways in which categories other than color were racialized, but as flexible and permeable categories. *Robinson Crusoe* helps to demonstrate that colonialism was not simply staged between white and black men, nor even between Europeans and Amerindians, and brings to the foreground the way that the desire for clearer boundaries of difference has always informed both the writing and subsequent readings of *Robinson Crusoe.*

1437 WITTENBERG, Hermann. "Imperial space and the discourse of the novel." *JLS* 13:1/2 (1997): 127-50.

Uses recent theories of space as basis for investigating the relationship between imperialism and the discourse of the metropolitan novel. Coetzee's *Foe* is a critical engagement with spatialized structures of power, such as imperialism, which seek to establish the dominance of a Western, rational, male subjectivity over colonized domains. Novelistic narrative is a key discursive feature of this dominance, and in this sense the metropolitan novel is complicit with imperialism. The critique of imperial spatial arrangements found in *Foe*, therefore, takes the form of an intervention in the archive of the novel: a rewriting of *Robinson Crusoe* in a radically different register.

Captain Singleton

1438 DE MICHAELIS, Lidia. "'A Tale-Gathering in those Idle Desarts': movement as improvement in Defoe's *Captain Singleton*." In (pp. 45-90) BIGAMI, Marialuisa (ed.). *Wrestling with Defoe* etc., **1316**.

Defoe simultaneously endorses and disavows his own stories while ultimately deferring both responsibility and judgement to the reader. Reading is a dangerous epistemological undertaking.

1439 RUSHBY, Kevin. *Hunting pirate heaven: a voyage in search of the lost pirate settlements of the Indian Ocean*. London: Constable, 2001; pp. 294.
Explores the pirate-socialist utopia established along the African coast, investigating the surprising elements of the election of pirate captains, men disabled in battle receiving compensation, and strongly held beliefs opposing slavery. Provides important background and context for *Captain Singleton*.

1440 TURLEY, Hans. "Piracy, identity, and desire in *Captain Singleton*." *ECS* 31:2 (1997/1998): 199-214.

Captain Singleton is the most important of Defoe's pirate works, and particularly significant in a history of the novel that emphasizes psychological realism and domestic subjectivity. Usually ignored or dismissed in Defoe studies and histories of the novel, this work portrays a fictional hero quite different from *Robinson Crusoe*. Singleton seems difficult to pin down for 20c readers precisely because depictions of transgressive sexuality have been ignored in Defoe criticism. The standard view of the novel as lacking realistic psychological detail fails to take into account the unspoken desires of the central figures as they exist within the framework of practical transgression explained in Defoe's metaphor of trade and mercantilism. Singleton finds a home, but it is a secret transgressive world within the boundaries of heterocentric English society. Defoe's closed ending challenges the standards by which individuality must be integrated with, and defined by, social norms.

Moll Flanders

1441   BANDRY, Anne and DECONNICK-BROSSARD, Françoise. "On peut compter sur Moll Flanders." *BSEAA* 45 (1997): 171-90.

In French. Report of a computer analysis of the language of *Moll Flanders* helps to throw light on the thematic unity of the novel, the sincerity of the final repentance, and the semantic groupings "qui font apparaître l'organisation du texte".

1442   BONY, Alain. "' [...] and takes it as he pleases': l'étrange contrat de lecture de *Moll Flanders*." *BSEAA* 45 (1997): 91-115.

In French. Discusses the authorial strategies encoded in the preface to *Moll Flanders*, a "contrat de lecture et récit de transmission". Focuses on 'novel and romance', 'a private history', typology and empiricism.

1443   CATON, Lou. "Doing the right thing with *Moll Flanders*: a 'reasonable' difference between the *picara* and the penitent." *CLAJ* 40:4 (1997): 508-16.
The thematic conventions of the conversion narrative (or spiritual autobiography) in *Moll Flanders* help both to organize and disrupt the episodic and worldly expectations of the female rogue (*picara*) narrative. The novel further moves in two directions because of the application of two forces: the ambiguous use of reason, and the image of transportation. Reason symbolizes both a worldly logic and sacred belief. The heroine's journey to the material riches of the 'New' World becomes an emblem of her newly discovered 'penitent' conversion.

1444   CONNOR, Rebecca E. "'Can you apply Arithmetick to Every Thing?': *Moll Flanders*, William Petty, and social accounting." *StudECC* 27 (1998): 169-94.
Although himself dogged by the consequences of ill-kept finances, in Defoe's fiction and nonfiction alike exact financial documentation always pays off. But accounting in Defoe is no means confined to money: everything in his writings is counted. Defoe may in fact be located within a movement of social accounting. This sensibility of quantification is useful in explaining the rich trope of accounting in *Moll Flanders*. It is related to the cultural need to fix identity. While quantification may emphasize acquisition, in Defoe's novel it is neither inherently nor axiomatically self-restricting: indeed it offers undeniable liberation.

1445 DENIZOT, Paul. "De Moll Flanders à Moll Hackabout: tolérance et/ou rigueur." *BSEAA* 45 (1997): 191-200.

In French. Ten years separate the publication of *Moll Flanders* (1722) and the engraved series by Hogarth "The Harlot's Progress" (1732). These two major testimonies, literary and iconographic, distil a popular tradition of 'gueserie' which stretches from Richard Head's *English Rogue* (1665 to 1671) to Cleland's *Fanny Hill* (1749). "Les deux Moll – celle de Defoe, celle de Hogarth - s'inscrivent dans la ligne des Long Meg of Westminster, Mary Carleton, Jenny Voss, Sally Salisbury, Moll Catpurse, et autre heroïnes populaires qui ont défrayé la chronique à le fin du xviie et au début du xviiie siècle". Illus. (2 plates).

1446 DÉTIS, Elisabeth. *Daniel Defoe: 'Moll Flanders'*. (Collections CNED-Didier concours.) Paris: Didier Érudition, 1997; pp. 197.

In English. Discusses the major issues of irony, repentance, and narrative structure, with an approach consistently inspired by Genette's school of criticism. Identifies complex figures of speech, examining the novel's rhetorical features, and investigating the neglected aspect of body language. The work is not a rogue/criminal biography, nor a picaresque tale, nor a spiritual biography, although it draws on all three traditions. Questions Moll's repentance, and discusses the ironic ambiguity of the text. Selected bibliography.

1447 DROMART, Anne. "Moll Flanders l'heroïque." *Q/W/E/R/T/Y* 7 (1997): 51-57.
In French. Moll gains the sympathy of the reader because "elle intègere au même temps son récit des voleurs sûrs auxquelles adhère le fond commun de l'humanité. [...][S]es exploits n'ont rien de dérisoire à la façon des anti-héros. Moll est une héroine moderne car elle n'est pas infaillible: elle se différencie du personnage intouchable, invulnérable, surdoué auquel le réalisme de la modernité a fait perdre sa credibilité."

1448 DUNN, Tony. "Moll Flanders: Body and capital." *Q/W/E/R/T/Y* 7 (1997): 59-67.
It seems unlikely that Defoe intended us to read Moll as a self-deceiving heroine whose capacity for analysis is not equal to the information we as readers receive about her. Defoe has constructed too precise a pattern of coincidence between his ideological ideals, the eventual outcome of Moll's life, and a number of linguistic clusters (business, trade, industry are applied to theft and temptation at the height of Moll's criminal career) to afford us as readers the space for an ironic appropriation of the text.

1449 DUPAS, Jean-Claude. "Le coq d'Orbaneja: *Moll Flanders*, entre *exemplum* et *fabula*." *BSEAA* 45 (1997): 117-35.

In French. Considers the notions of storytelling and moral teaching which achieved a natural synthesis in Defoe's work. This combination accounts for the success of his fiction against the comparative neglect of his other writings.

1450 HÉROU, Josette (ed.). Daniel Defoe: *Moll Flanders*. Paris: Ellipses, 1997; pp. 125.

In French and English. "Ce receuil d'articles, concernant le roman de Daniel Defoe, *Moll Flanders*, ne prétend pas traiter tous les sujets de discussion possibles à propos d'un livre qui reste énigmatique. Il cherche à aider des candidats en éclairant certaines aspects précis comme la justice, les practiques commerciales, à presenter des èmes récurrents comme l'argent, le sexe, la symbolique, les prcécés d'écriture." Essays by:
1) Jean-Claude DUPAS, "Pro-logue" (9-16);
2) Jeffrey HOPES, "Moll Flanders: femme des affaires (17-34);
3) Joëlle HAREL, "L'argent dans *Moll Flanders*" (35-46);
4) Sophie MENNESSON, "Sexe et argent dans *Moll Flanders*" (47-54);
5) Rosemary KMIECIK, "The passage from dependence to independence in *Moll Flanders*" (55-64);
6) GeorgesLEMOINE, "*Moll Flanders* et la justice de son temps: quelques aspects" (68-76);
7) Josette HÉROU, "*Moll Flanders*: aspects religieuses et moraux" (77-88);
8) Raphaëlle COSTA DE BEAUREGARD, "*Moll Flanders*: a 'picaresque novel' vs a 'modern novel'" (89-101);
9) Josette HÉROU, "L'art de l'écrivain dans *Moll Flanders*" (101-12);
10) Raphaëlle COSTA DE BEAUREGARD, "The masks of fortune: women and truth in *Moll Flanders*" (113-26).

1451 HUGUET, Christine. "*Moll Flanders* et la tradition picaresque." *BSEAA* 45 (1997): 67-90.

In French. *Moll Flanders* may be considered as post-picaresque romance, part of a process whereby the chivalric hero and the picaresque rogue are brought into a working compromise. The same is true of Colonel Jack, whose destiny is strikingly similar to Moll's: one the abandoned son of a nobleman who turns to crime, the other a thief who attains gentility. They are like twins, one a 'semi-picaro', the other 'semi-noble'.

1452 HUMMEL, William E. "'The gift of my father's bounty': patriarchal patronization in *Moll Flanders* and *Roxana*." *RMRLL* 48:2 (1994): 119-

41.
Should primacy be accorded to class or gender divisions? Enters into the debate between feminists and Marxists by taking a new look at a feminist analysis of *Moll Flanders* and *Roxana* in terms, not of market economies, but rather as ethnographic studies of gift-based economies. Defoe's critique of the social, political, and economic rights accruing to males and the deprivation of the same for women is not so much dependent on the systematic consequences of the relations of production. The types of material and symbolic transactions that take place between Defoe's male and female characters are more fully explained by a theory of gift exchange. Moll and Roxana are gifted and capable women who are 'gifted' by men: the physical endowments they receive help to confer their identity and to subsume their subjectivity. The giving is a sex-role embedded in subjugation, and it is the tendency of Defoe's male characters to turn a gift transaction into a market transaction by demanding profit that most fully reveals the 'gender of the gift'.

1453 IANNÀCCARO, Giuliana. "Predestinarian doctrine in *Moll Flanders*: a controversial presence." In (pp. 145-68) BIGAMI, Marialuisa (ed.). *Wrestling with Defoe* etc., **1316**.

The search for an overall theological meaning in the story engenders moral confusion in the reader unless he stops looking for a unifying pattern altogether.

1454 KIBBIE, Ann Louise. "Monstrous generation: the birth of capital in Defoe's *Moll Flanders* and *Roxana*." *PMLA* 110:5 (1995): 1023-34.

Part of a study of images of capital in the early modern period. The legacy of the analogies between biologist and monetary generation is evident in Defoe's *Moll Flanders* (1721) and *Roxana* (1724), novels in which biological reproduction is explicitly bound up with capital increase. Defoe has almost become a personification of capital. Seeks to reopen the role of the anti-usury tradition in the evolving discourse of capitalism, and to discover Defoe's attitude toward the self-generating power of money. These two novels are treated as companion pieces: a comedy and a tragedy of capital. These heroines indicate that the fate of the anti-usury doctrine of the 18c is not so much extinction as metamorphosis, and at the center of the transformation is the woman whose body becomes the body of capital.

1455 KIETZMAN, Mary Jo. "Defoe masters the serial subject." *ELH* 66:3 (1999): 677-705.

Picaras like Mary Carleton and the young Moll Flanders conduct themselves by manipulating their appearance in a male culture that dissipates the orginal and attenuates the author. *Moll Flanders* and the reformation of its protagonist depend on the discursive formation of serial subjectivity that pervaded late 17c and 18c culture. Defoe resolves Moll's story by replacing serial subjectivity with a prototypical model in which Moll and Jemmy acquire real gentility only after they claim their diverse productions and assume authorial control over subjectivities which are constituted most profitably as histories.

1456 LAMOINE, Georges (ed.). *Lectures d'une oeuvre: 'Moll Flanders' de Daniel Defoe*. Paris: Éditions du Temps, 1997; pp. 156.

In French and English. Collection of essays exploring various aspects of the novel. 1) Gilles DUVAL, "Defoe face au roman: vielles questions, certitudes nouvelles" (15-28); 2) Jean-François BAILLON, "Moll Flanders et le hasard" (29-40); 3) Sylvie LAFON, "La parole est d'argent, le silence est d'or: lecommerce des mots dans *Moll Flanders*" (41-50); 4) Jeffrey HOPES, "Labyrinth of trouble: exploring narrative structures in *Moll Flanders*" (51-72); 5) Jacques CARRÉ, "Les territoires de Moll Flanders" (73-90); 6) Joëlle HAREL, "L'Amerique dans *Moll Flanders*" (91-108); 7) Joëlle HAREL, "Pièges de l'argent et corruptions dans *Moll Flanders*" (107-36); 8) Raphaëlle COSTA DE BEAUREGARD, " Life 'à vif' in *Moll Flanders*" (119-36); 9) Georges LAMOINE, "La dimension religieuse de *Moll Flanders*" (137-54). Bibliography (155-56).

1457 MICHAEL, Steven C. "Thinking parables: what *Moll Flanders* does not say." *ELH* 63:2 (1996): 367-95.

The apparent absence of a moral center or controlling lesson about goodness constitutes the very presence of the center or lesson of Moll Flanders. The ambiguous operation of goodness can be minimally clarified by a brief look at Defoe's moral psychology. Language resonates for Moll because it becomes part of her economy of accumulations: it is constantly associated with capital, in the sense that capital is a resource for Moll's continued identity as a 'gentlewoman'. Language *becomes* capital for Moll: as narrator and character, she withholds and spreads information as either suits and profits her.

1458 MILLER, Louise M. "Moll Flanders: the fortunate female Houdini." *Q/W/E/R/T/Y* 7 (1997): 69-77.

There is, according to Moll, a symbiotic relationship between her converted conscience and her gratitude for her material rehabilitation. Readers are left to assume the tacit persistence of her repentance. There is a happy congruence between the image of Fortune and Moll, the prosperous recorder of her own famous 'History'. The narrative serves its usual function as a medium of exchange.

1459 SIMMS, Norman. "A plain conviction to the contrary: Moll Flanders' name and other lies." *Q/W/E/R/T/Y* 7 (1997): 79-88.

The period of the late 17c/early 18c is an age of deep duplicity among the very people who would otherwise be expected to stand as exemplars of innocence and purity, namely the adherents to a reforming Puritan set of faiths (whether Protestant, Catholic, or Jansenist) who find themselves in situations where their true identities seem forced upon them. The playing off of text and context in Behn's *Oroonoko* partly matches with the double narrator in *Moll Flanders*. The penitent sinner who warns her readers of moral pitfalls and prays for her own forgiveness jars against the voice of an energetic entrepreneur who has succeeded as a woman against all odds in a men's world, and who boasts of her financial gain and manipulation of bourgeois society. Perhaps her life of crime was continued out of the sheer pleasure in the creativity of deception. What percolates through the text, whether the interested persona, the editorial censor, or the author himself, is that identity cannot be accorded to the categories of confusion or fictional exposé.

1460 SOUPEL, Serge. "*Moll Flanders*: conditions et labyrinthe." *BSEAA* 45 (1997): 138-50.

In French. Moll's frenetic experiences underline the importance of the archetypally recurrent novelistic trope of prison, cave, tomb, labyrinth. Her repentance is a static penance.

1461 SUAREZ, Michael F. "The shortest way to Heaven? Moll Flanders' repentance reconsidered." *1650-1850* 3 (1997): 3-28.

A spiritual chaos or void subverts Moll's shallow pursuit of true security. Throughout her narrative Defoe demonstrates that a life of moral turpitude exacts a dear price. While her sins bring her material riches, they necessarily effect her moral impoverishment. Her chronicle shows that she has gained the world, but the account of her repentance establishes that she has lost her soul.

1462 SWAN, Beth. "Moll Flanders: the felon as lawyer." *ECF* 11:1 (1998): 33-48.

It is difficult for modern readers fully to grasp Moll's discourse, to identify and appreciate its rhetoric because it functions as part of an intricate juridical context. She draws the reader into the narration of her criminal life by way of her language. Her characteristic discourse, esp. pleading, is appropriate to her attempts at self-vindication. Moll's personal text is a counter-text to contest the public record: it is a plea in the investigation made by the court of her readership.

1463 TADIÉ, Alexis. "Sex, lies and no videotapes: les fictions du secret dans *Moll Flanders*."*BSEAA* 45 (1997): 151-70.

In French. Examines the tension between public and private realisms, an essential apposition, applying this to Moll's sliding strategies, fictions of her proliferations of appearances and the multiplicity of her surfaces.

1464 TERRIEN, Nicole. *'Moll Flanders', un roman de l'équilibre et de la démesure*. Paris: Messène, 1997; pp. 119.

In French. Provides a reading of the novel, "une héroïne consciente mais faible". Sees it offering "une sérieuse critique de la société. La forme de l'autobiographie fictive donne à voir les causes de cette attitude en mettant en scène les peurs et les désirs les plus intimes de l'héroïne, et présente au lecteur un personnage doté d'une profondeur ontologique qui annonce le roman psychologique." Looks at: 1) "l'intégration en question (un univers instable; une critique sociale)"; 2) "un personnage prisonnier? (la quête; la conquête, défaite et rédemption)"; 3) "la résolution des contraires (une reconstruction; le théâtralisation)". Notes (113-16). Bibliography (119).

1465 VESCOVI,. "*Moll Flanders*: The cohesion of the discourse." In (pp. 131-44) BIGAMI, Marialuisa (ed.). *Wrestling with Defoe* etc., **1316**.

A sort of organization can be found in the relationship between character and plot. The first pages proleptically present the whole novel *in nuce*, with the semantic code of ch. 1 becoming a proairetic code which dominates the rest of the work.

1466 VIVIÈS, Jean. "' [...] a private drawer in my chest': la vie à tiroirs de *Moll Flanders*." In (pp. 173-80) LEDUC, Guyonne (ed.). *Vie, formes et lumières(s): Hommage à Paul Denizot*. Villeneuve-d'Ascq: Société d'Études Anglo-Americaines des XVIIe et XVIIIe Siècles, 1999; pp. 304.

In French. Explores the mentality and ramifications of secrecy.

A Journal of the Plague Year

1467 BRODSLEY, Laurel. "Defoe's *The Journal of the Plague Year*: A model for stories of plagues." In (pp. 11-22) NELSON, Emmanuel S. (ed.). *AIDS: the literary response*. New York: Twayne; Toronto and Oxford: Maxwell Macmillan, 1992; pp. ix, 233.

Collection of 16 essays. Defoe's innovative work of fiction provides a model for the way literature can give insight into private and public responses to major epidemics -- both in its content (a depiction of London life during the bubonic plague of 1665), and in its form (a first-person memoir narrated by a survivor). Defoe's depiction of the daily life of London citizens during this time of pestilence, his enumerations of government policies to contain the spread of the disease, and to care for its victims, and his evaluations of the efficacy of edicts and practices, provides a paradigm for both fiction and non-fiction on the social effects of devastating infectious diseases. Individual experiences are placed within the context of public health policies. In small inset stories, the protagonist H. F. reports stories of people's behaviour under the terror of the plague. Notes and references (204-18). Selected bibliography on the literary treatment of plague and AIDS by Emmanuel S. NELSON: non-literary texts, fiction, drama, poetry, memoirs/testaments, criticism (219-24). Filmography by Kevin J. HARTY (225-7). Index (231-33).

1468 DAVIS, Lennard J. "The dreadful gulph and the glass cadaver: decomposing women in early modern literature." *Genre* 23:2/3 (1990): 121-33.
Defoe locates the Plague emblematically in the female body. Like many plagues in classical and biblical literature, the Plague is an assault against fertility, against the female function as defined in male terms and interpreted (or misinterpreted) by the male. The plague/grave has a kind of connection to the female genitalia, representing the locus of desire and at the same time the stress point for repulsion.

1469 GREGG, Stephen. "Godly manliness: Defoe's good men in bad times." In (pp. 141-59) WILLIAMS, Andrew P. (ed.). *The image of manhood in early modern literature: viewing the male.* (Contribution to the Study of World Literature, 95.) Westport, CT, and London: Greenwood Press, 1999; pp. xv, 286.

The culture of moral reformation on the 1690s, aimed esp. at male behaviour, is projected against the backdrop of the Great Plague and the Restoration period, which offered Defoe a paradigmatic moment: against this backdrop of confusion and disorder, the 'bad times' of the 1665 pestilence, *A Journal of the Plague Year* offers ideas of unsuitability through the disciplinary efforts of the moral reformers. Godly manliness is promoted as an ideal behaviour through the identification and exclusion of irrational and impious men, the qualities of godly man, an unswerving religious faith, an active, almost martial courage, and a rational world view, emerged as a new standard of masculine self-deportment. 'Reformation' became the crucial rhetorical underpinning of the book; it is the catalyst for imaging an ideal masculinity that ultimately finds its foundation on the 'godly' fortitude of the urban working class. Bibliographic notes.

1470 JUENGEL, Scott J. "Writing decomposition: Defoe and the corpse." *JNT* 25:2 (1995): 139-53.

The disruptive force of the impure and expelled is a powerful agent in Defoe's *A Journal of the Plague Year* (1722), a rigorous examination of the impact of the 1665 bubonic plague on the citizenry and collective psyche of early modern London. Explores what the epidemic leaves behind: the problematic corpse that exists as the supplement of the plague's coming. This work explores the textual element of 'decomposition' implicit in the writing of the plague by making the management of the corpse a precondition for the narrator's emergent subjectivity. Confrontation with contemplation of textual and corporeal deterioration ultimately reflects a larger, more disturbing threat: the breakdown of the composition of verbal reality in the presence of epistemological crisis.

1471 WALL, Cynthia. "Novel streets: the rebuilding of London and Defoe's *A Journal of the Plague Year*." *StudN*. 30:2 (1998): 164-77.

Although *A Journal* is carefully set in the year before the Great Fire of 1666, the spatial desolation to come haunts the streets of this text, as it haunts much of Restoration and early 18c literature. This and particularly Defoe's urban novels attempt to reoccupy a rebuilding city, a city dramatically divorced from its past topographical patterns, which had to refind and redefine its lines of urban space. The urban 'novel' was a distinct generic transformation.

Colonel Jack

1472 ARMSTRONG, Katherine A. "'I was a kind of an historian': the productions of history in Defoe's *Colonel Jack*." In (pp. 97-110) RIBEIRO, Alvaro and BASKER, James G. (eds). *Tradition and transition: women writers, marginal texts, and the eighteenth-century canon* etc., **800**.

In *Colonel Jack* Defoe offers two competing models of the relationship between society and the individual, or history and historical persons. The first is a more conventional and simplistic model in which the individual is a victim of historical and social forces beyond his or her control, and is finally overtaken by the second, which acknowledges the contribution of the individual to the course of history. Although Jack would like the reader to subscribe to the first model, since this would absolve him of responsibility for his many crimes and deceits, his narrative nonetheless reveals his agency, his direct role in the creation of his times.

1473 HUGUET, Christine. "*Moll Flanders* et la tradition picaresque." etc. See above, **1451**.

1474 O'BRIEN, John. "Union Jack: amnesia and the law in Daniel Defoe's *Colonel Jack*." *ECS* 32:1 (1998): 65-82.

Jack frequently worries about the questions of being "the same man". In scenes where he exchanges money or tears for the confirmation of his identity, he seems intent on revealing, but then also denying, that a conflict exists between the assumptions underpinning contract and those supporting penal law, the former demanding that persons be stable and predictable, and the latter insisting that the radical breaks in personal identity are possible, desirable, necessary. Recent criticism has detailed how Defoe participates in both the reform of penal law and the development of the market in 18c Britain. He therefore offers a helpful framework for unfolding the implications of this conflict.

Roxana

1475 BOARDMAN, Michael M. "Defoe's *Roxana*: structure and belief." In (pp. 20-58) *Narrative innovation and incoherence: ideology in Defoe, Goldsmith, Austen, Eliot, and Hemingway*. Durham, NC, and London: Duke UP, 1992; pp. 226.

From Crusoe to Moll to Colonel Jack, Defoe's great fictional narratives do not seem to present the same set of problems that later actions do. For Defoe the choice of form - the imitation of a true story - led to an implicit recognition that the form has moral liabilities that must be avoided, eliminated by a new form. Notes (209-14). Bibliography (215-21). Index (223-26).

1476 BRANTLINGER, Patrick. "Cashing in on the real... " etc. See above, **1321**.

1477 BURKE, Helen. "*Roxana*, corruption, and the progressive myth." *Genre*

23:2/3 (1990): 103-20.

In *Roxana* it is the dual and contradictory capacity of the new economy to create both excess and lack represented in the history of Roxana and her pimping servant. The succeeding episodes in Roxana's life, her affairs with the Prince, the King, and the Lord, may be read as successive narratives elaborating a contradiction, a disclosure of moral and economic order empty of principle and simultaneously characterized by accretion. As Roxana accumulates more and more wealth and power, the instability and alienation first represented in the opening scenes become more and more profound, a reflection of capitalism's fear of its own irrationality and excess.

1478 CANAVESI, Angelo. "*Roxana: The Fortunate Mistress*. Orchestration of contexts and escape of words from their literal meaning." In (pp. 179-89) BIGAMI, Marialuisa (ed.). *Wrestling with Defoe* etc., **1316**.

Defoe's position as author is purposely ambiguous or flexible. Any claim to the 'truth of fact' (preface) undermines the tenets of formal realism and the illusion of reality. The reader's concern is centered not so much on the responsiveness to facts and report as on language and words.

1479 HUMMEL, William E. "'The gift of my father's bounty': patriarchal patronization in *Moll Flanders* and *Roxana*" etc. See above, **1452**.

1480 KIBBIE, Ann Louise. "Monstrous generation: the birth of capital in Defoe's *Moll Flanders* and *Roxana*" etc. See above., **1454**.

1481 NEW, Peter. "Why Roxana can never find herself." *MLR* 91:2 (1996): 317-29.
Defoe's characters are attracted equally to freedom and to security. A recurrent problem is that although sometimes complementary, they are often mutually exclusive. Security may be a means of ensuring independence, freedom a means of achieving security; but in many civilizations, security can be bought only through loss of freedom, or freedom at the expense of security. For Defoe, a person is what he/she does. Roxana cannot fully decide what she wants, freedom or security, an owned self or a disowned self, and consequently an *ad hoc* decision is taken for her by a temporary self, who desires freedom. She is condemned to search for an identity in the story of herself, and to be unable ever to find it.

1482 O'BRIEN, John F. "The character of credit: Defoe's 'Lady Credit', *The Fortunate Mistress*, and the resources of inconsistency in early eighteenth-century Britain." *EHL* 63:3 (1996): 603-31.

Aims to interrogate how credit and character were reciprocally constituted in Defoe's writings of the first quarter of the 18c, how the characters deployed in these texts serve as vehicles to condense or displace inconsistencies between gender, property and politics in what we can think of as the period's commercial imagination. Drawing particularly on Defoe's last work of fiction (1724), suggests why it is that women, who were normally enjoined from *possessing* credit, were called upon to *represent* it.

1483   PAGETTI, Carlo. "Deceiving Roxana." In (pp. 169-78) BIGAMI, Marialuisa (ed.). *Wrestling with Defoe* etc., **1316**.

The history of Roxana is an ambivalent lie, speaking of the nature of women and men, a tale of deception simulating the absolute sincerity of an autobiography, the representation of the illusionistic substance of life.

1484   TERRIEN, Nicole. "Roxana: Une femme perdue pour les hommes?" *Imaginaires* 2 (1997): 75-90.

Discusses Roxana's powerful but fateful attraction for men.

OTHER WORKS

A Tour Through the Whole Island of Great Britain

1485   FELDMANN, Doris. "Economic and/as aesthetic constructions of Britishness in eighteenth-century domestic travel writing." *JSBC* 4:1/2 (1997): 31-45.

Aims to explore some of the modes of textual representation through which travel writing helped to fashion the nation as an imagined homogeneous community made up of various ethnic groupings. Pays particular attention to the assimilation of Scotland and Wales into the British nation. Focuses particularly on Defoe's *Tour* (1724-26), a work whose successive editions were progressively updated and which remained popular until the 1770s. In Defoe's account of Great Britain, the nation acquires an abstract existence.

1486 IRIMIA, Michaela. "Defoe and Cantemir: eighteenth-century explorers, West and East." *1650-1850* 3 (1997): 239-49.

Makes use of contemporary critical methods to open a discussion of the dialogue between 18c 'eastern' texts and western conceptions of 'Enlightenment', considering Defoe and Cantemir as explorers in time and space. Considers the *Tour* (1722 to 1726) (a Domesday *redivivus* which by the mid-century had acquired the qualifications of a palimpsest and is no less an illustration of the life as journey metaphor) and Cantemir's *The History of the Growth and Decay of the Othman Empire* (1714 to 1716) (which is nothing short of a fullscale philosophy on the fate of power). In both works one finds the century's *Weltanschauung* with its melioristic penchant. Both codify 18c reality, and do this in philosophic concepts that bring them close to the meditative literature produced at the time. Respect for the writers' worth is obvious. Both venerate codifications. Both tried to decode the code of power.

1487 PARKER, Christopher, "'A true survey of the ground': Defoe's *Tour* and the rise of thematic cartography." *PQ* 74:4 (1995): 395-414.

On the whole critics have remained blind to Defoe's cartography, and have used the text of the *Tour* as a means of bolstering his reputation as literary craftsman. But in the *Tour* he actually displays an expert's ability to put into practice the procedures of map surveying and construction.

1488 ROGERS, Pat. *The text of Great Britain: theme and design in Defoe's 'Tour'*. Newark: Delaware UP; London: Assoc. UPs, 1998; pp. 247.

Aims to provide a basis for reassessing Defoe's *Tour* by describing the elements that went into its making. Puts it in the historical context of travel writing and the development of a rhetoric of tourism. Also locates the book within Defoe's wider *oeuvre*, how some of its findings can be applied to his novels. Considers aspects of its ideology, its political bearings, and treatment of the South Sea Bubble of 1721. Attempts to illustrate its 'design', its formal structure along with the intellectual attitudes supporting and supported by that structure. Notes (213-31). Bibliography (232-33). Index (234-47).

1489 SCHELLENBERG, Betty A. "Imagining the nation in Defoe's *A Tour thro' the Whole Island of Great Britain*." *ELH* 62:2 (1995): 295-311.

Defoe's plan appears to have been that in reading regularly revised editions of the *Tour*, the reader will reassert membership on a national community, while a uniform image of that community will be reinforced. The *Tour* indicates that this constructed nation is as much a reflection of Defoe's need to impose some organizing principle upon the chaotic detail of his (or his reader's) experience of Britain, as it is a confident 'Whig' departure from traditional ordering structures. Ironically, the public participation that Defoe invites in imaging Great Britain leads in fact to the dissolution of his vision. The portrait of the all-consuming, ruthlessly public nation is never fully realized, its outlines dissolving into private participants once again.

———

DELERAC, François-Paulin

Polish manuscripts (1700, pp. 290)

WING D127; McBurney 4
Trans. from *Les anecdotes de Pologne*, 1699.
Nouvelle historique.

———

DESFONTAINES, Pierre-François-Guyot

The travels of Mr John Gulliver, son to Capt. Lemuel Gulliver (1731, 2 vols: I, 212, II, 198)

NCBEL II 992[21]; McBurney 263
Trans. John LOCKMAN from *Le Nouveau Gulliver* (1730).

STUDIES

1490 MORRIS, Thelma. *L'Abbé Desfontaines et son rôle dans la littérature de son temps.* (Studies on Voltaire and the Eighteenth Century, 19.) Geneva: Droz, 1961; pp. 390.

In French .The five chapters consider his life and career, his work as a journalist, his literary doctrine, his curiosity of foreign things [*étrangères*], his role as translator. An Appendix contains letters written by Desfontaines. Bibliography (369-89). Looks at manuscript documents, memoirs, correspondence, newspapers, periodicals and contemporary books to present a more detailed picture of Desfontaines, man and writer.

———

DuNOYER, Anne Marguerite Petit

Letters from a lady at Paris to a lady at Avignon (1716, 1716, 1717; pp. 239)

NCBEL II 987[18]; McBurney 83
Trans. from *Lettres historiques et galantes.*
Lively fictional correspondence, imitated from Court gossip and with

good characterization.

———

E., G.

Authentic memoirs of the life and surprising adventures of John Sheppard (1724, pp. 82)

NCBEL II 990[8]; McBurney 156; Morgan 539; ECSTC 9E2
Rogue biography in a series of letters. Sometimes ascribed to Defoe.

———

FÉNELON, François de Salignac de la Mothe

The adventures of Telemachus the son of Ulysses (1699 [incomplete], 1700; numerous edns through the century; pp. 152)

WING F674; NCBEL II 984[8]
First English trans. of *Les Aventures de Télémaque* (1699), by LITTLEBURY and BOYER.
Didactic fiction; highly esteemed.

EDITIONS

1491   GORÉ, Jeanne-Lydie (ed.). *Les aventures de Télémaque; Fénelon, chronologie et introduction par J.-L. Goré.* Paris: Collection Garnier. Flammarion, 1968; pp. 508.

Chronology (5-23) provides a succinct and useful overview of Fénelon's life and work. The Introduction (25-55) describes the intellectual background to the novel, and its design and structure, its relation to Antiquity, its place in Western intellectual history. Bibliography (57-59). Text in 28 Books (65-506)

SELECTED STUDIES

1492 CADBURY, Henry J. "Fénelon and the Quakers." *NQ* 180 (1941): 122.

Further evidence of the influence of Fénelon upon the Quakers may be found in the fact that Josiah Martin translated into English and supplied additional material to Fénelon's *Dissertation on Pure Love*, which Luke Hinde published in 1735.

1493 CORDASCO, Francesco. "Smollett and the translation of Fénelon's *Telemachus.*" *NQ* 193 (1948): 563.

A careful reading of the 1776 edition ascribed to Smollett demonstrates that it is actually the translation of John Hawkesworth, which had appeared in London in 1768. This translation was issued as Smollett's with even Hawkesworth's dedicatory epistle retained. In the edition of 1786, the dedication is omitted, but the text remains the same.

1494 FACTEAU, Bernard. "An unpublished *Mémoir* of Fénelon with emended letter." *PMLA* 57 (1942): 116-32.

The Versailles edition of the Works and Correspondence of Fénelon (1820-30), reproduced with modifications in the Paris edition (1848-52), is incomplete and imperfect. In recent years numerous additional works and letters have been published in books and periodicals, which with revisions made of the Correspondence, have rectified knowledge of Fénelon and his activities. This exercise further modifies the situation, esp. by reproducing for the first time a *Mémoire* written by Fénelon, concerned with the progress of Jansenism, which appears unknown to the editors.

1495 GORÉ, Jeanne-Lydie. *La notion d'indifférence chez Fénelon et ses sources.* (Univ. de Grenoble Publications de la Faculté des Lettres, 16.) Paris: Presses Universitaires de France, 1956; pp. 316.

In French. Considers the ideas making up Fénelon's spirituality. I. "Indifférence et Révolte", which considers the genesis of the concept (19-86); II. "Fénelon et l'Indifférence", examines his view of the concept (91-186). An Appendix provides extracts from spiritual writers (187-296). Bibliography (297-306).

1496-----*L'itinéraire de Fénelon: humanisme et spiritualité.* (Univ. de Grenoble Publications de la Faculté des Lettres, 17.) Paris: Presses Universitaires de France, 1957; pp. 756.

In French. Substantial study of the life and works, looking at the years of formation (33-320), *Les Espoirs du mystique et de la l'humanité* (325-612), the Solitude of Cambrai (615-729). Bibliography (731-44). Index of Names.

1497 KNAPP, Lewis M. "Smollett's translation of Fénelon's *Télémaque.*" *PQ* 44 (1965) 405-07.

This novel had an extraordinary appeal for 18c readers for its poetic and Homeric quality, and because of its moral instruction. It inspired imitations, abridgements and complete translations: Littlebury and Boyer (1700) (16 editions by 1739); John Ozell (1720); J. Kelly (1743); John Hawkesworth (1743). One in 1776 has the name of Smollett, which can confidently be placed in the canon of his works [? -- see CORDASCO above, **1493**].

1498 LOMBARD, Alfred. *Fénelon et le retour à l'Antique du XVIIIe siècle.* (Mémoires de l'Université de Neuchâtel, 23.) Neuchâtel: Secrétariat de l'Université, 1954; pp. 144.

In French. Divided into nine sections: 1) "La survivance des Dieux"; 2) "La Fable à l'époque classique"; 3) La Philosophie et l'Antiquité"; 5) "Les Jugement littéraire et artistique"; 6) "Le religion et la poésie"; 7) "La poète du *Télémaque* (i. La culte de Fénelon; ii. La Regne de l'Antique", iii. "L'Antique galante"); 8) *Télémaque* et le xviie siècle; 9) La mythologie romantique.

1499 SCHINZ, Albert. "Fénelon, critique littéraire précurseur." *Revue des Cours et Conférences* 27:1 (1926): 587-601.

Points out that Fénelon understood the menace posed by the absolutism of Louis XIX. He made efforts to disengage himself from the critical ideas formulated in the 17c. His attitude to the *Querelle des ancients et des modernes* illustrates the critical pull in his thoughts, as do his ideas for the Académie. " [...] Fénelon a demandé dans son *Mémoire* (1713) que l'Académie puisse se reconstituer comme elle l'entendait pour examiner librement, sans les entraves de sa première constitution, les problèmes intéressant la langue et la littérature[...]" (601).

———

FONTANIEU, Gaspard Moïse de

Rosalinda: a novel. Containing the histories of Rosalinda and Lealdus, Dorisba and Leander, Emilia and Edward, Adelais, Daughter of Otho II, and Alerames, Duke of Saxony. With a most remarkable story of Edmund, the gallant Earl of Salisbury [...] By a man of Quality. Tr. from the French (1733, 1741; pp. 347)

NCBEL II 993[11]; McBurney 285; Morgan 620; ECSTC 1193F1
Trans. of a French version of a work by Bernardo MORANDO.
Mixed texture, numerous interpolated histories: moralizing romance, somewhat between *Telemachus* and the heroic romance.

GALLAND, Antoine

The Arabian nights entertainments: consisting of one thousand and one stories
(1706-8; 8 edns listed by 1736; numerous edns through the century in 3-
12 vols; 3 vols, pp. 592)

> NCBEL II 985[9]; McBurney 23; ECSTC 153G1
> Pts 1-6 of the French version had appeared by 1704, the remainder by
> 1717. The English translation was by an unknown hack writer, and was
> known as the 'Grub Street version'.

EDITIONS

1500 Trans. Henry TORRENS (1838).

This was a literal translation of the first 50 Nights.

1501 Trans. W. E. LANE as *The Arabian Nights' Entertainment* (3 vols., 1839-
41). With famous illustrations by William Harvey.

A bowdlerized selection for the drawing room. Contains valuable notes.

1502 Trans. John PAYNE (9 vols, 1882-84).

First complete translation published in a limited edition of 500.

1503 Trans. Richard BURTON (10 vols, with five supplementary vols, 1885-86).

Most celebrated version of the direct translations, eccentric but stylish.

1504 *Tales from the Thousand and One Nights. Translated with an Introduction
by N. J. DAWOOD. Engravings on Wood from Original Designs by
William Harvey.* Harmondsworth: Penguin Books, 1973; pp. 407.

Collection of 38 tales, originally published separately as *The Thousand
and One Nights* (1954) and *Aladdin and Other Tales* (1957). The two
were combined with revisions and editions.

STUDIES

1505 DAWOOD, N. J. Introduction. In (pp. 7-12) *Tales from the Thousand and
One Nights* etc.

Discusses the origin of the *Arabian Nights* in the context of the folk-tale genre and the Medieval Middle East. Examines the various translations, the selection of tales chosen for translation, and details of the rendition. Particularly helpful for insights into the Galland version, pointing out that, while not always faithful in a literal sense, he "selected his materials and skilfully adapted them to contemporary European tastes, emphasizing the fantastic and the miraculous and carefully avoiding the candid references to sex" (9). Also important for the light it throws on the 'Grub Street' translation which "established the popularity of the *Arabian Nights* with successive generations of Englishmen and was read with delight by the English Romantics in their childhood."

———

GILDON, Charles

1. *The post-boy rob'd of his mail: or the pacquet broke open* (1692-93, 1706; pp. 386)

   WING G735A; NCBEL II 982[21]; ECSTC 890G8
   Derived from PRÉCHAC, *La valize ouverte* and PALLAVICINO, *Il corriere svaligiato.*
   Variety of characteristic letters, some in narrative sequences.

2. *The new metamorphosis: being the golden ass of Lucius Apuleius* (1708; 5 edns by 1733; 2 pts,   pp. 380 + 325)

   NCBEL II 986[1]; McBurney 40; ECSTC 890G34
   May be original or trans.; popularized adaptation, under the pseudonym Carlo MONTE SOCIO.

3. *The golden spy: or a political journal of the British nights entertainments* (1709-10, 2 vols; 1 vol. [1724?]; pp. 304)

   NCBEL II 986[6]; McBurney 44; ECSTC 890G15
   Inanimate spy; an anthropomorphized gold piece explores many social levels; early example of a popular genre.

4. *The post-man robb'd of his mail: or the packet broke open* (1719, pp. 340)

   NCBEL II 988[13]; McBurney 102; ECSTC 890G30
   Epistolary miscellany containing psychological novel, *The lover's sighs.*

5. *Miscellanea aurea: or the golden medley* (1720, n.p.)
   NCBEL II 989[2]

Epistolary miscellany, moral in tone; contains two utopian imaginary voyages and a psychological novel in letters.

STUDIES

1506 ANDERSON, G.L. "Charles Gildon's Total Academy." *JHI* 16 (1955): 247-51.

Considers Gildon's educational theories. The idea of British academy to regulate the language played some part in the fierce political battle that made Addison a politician, Pope a Tory, and sent Swift into exile in the last years of Queen Anne's reign. The idea of an academy had developed in the mind of Gildon at least by the date of his tragedy, *Phaeton* (1698), In 1710, in a letter to Harley, Gildon outlined his plan for an academy. In 1719, in a volume of carelessly assembled miscellaneous prose pieces called *The Post Man Robb'd of His Mail*, Gildon sets forth in detail the scheme which he thought would do justice to English letters. His academy is "total", elaborate and extremely authoritarian, seeks to regulate all phases of literary life, not merely language. Accordingly, Gildon's academy is part of his continuing war on the new Neo-Classicism that characterizes the works of Rowe and Pope, and distinguishes this classicism from that of the age of Dryden. Harassed by illness and hindered by blindness, Gildon became more and more repetitious in his literary labours as his life went on. He was incapable of seeing that no poet could survive the regulations of his academy. Yet his proposal is not the dreamy fantasy of a retired pedant, but the down-to-earth plan of a critic in creative competition with fellow critics for the minds of men.

1507 BOYCE, Benjamin. "Pope, Gildon, and salamanders." *NQ* 194 (1949): 14.

The Post-Boy Robb'd of His Mail as a possible source of the machinery in Pope's *The Rape of the Lock*. In the second volume of the novel, as Letter VI, there appears "An Answer to a Letter concerning a Cabbalistical Opinion of Zilphs and Salamanders, a sort of Aerial Ladies and Gallants, or a species betwixt Angels and Men".

1508 DAY, *Told in letters* etc., **364**.

The Post-Boy Robb'd of his Mail had furnished examples of the elaborate devices of verisimilitude thought appropriate and necessary in an epistolary collection. Many of the letters in *The Post-Man Robb'd* are actually essays, some obviously modelled on the successful example of the *Spectator*. This brings together a miscellaneous collection of odd fragments, giving the appearance of unity. Some are letters from type characters, commenting on vice and follies; two series of long letters are addressed to a noble lord, and are essays on projects concerning a proposal for founding a royal academy of arts and sciences. Others are variations on the stock theme established by the Bretonian letter collection. He writes letters to himself, commending his own works and criticizing contemporaries like Pope. The collection also includes a psychological novel in letters, *The Lover's Sighs*.

1509 HONORÉ, Jean. "Charles Gildon et la grammaire de Brightland." *EA* 18 (1965): 145-65.

In French. Gildon published a pamphlet, *Bellum Grammaticale*, on 25 March 1712. "Malgré des formules piquantes et des passages amusants (comme la prosopopée de Dame Prosodie indignement abandonée par Greenwood), ce pamphlet de Gildon ne dépasse guère le niveau du libelle. Mais il nous renseigne plus complètement que la Préface (1712) sur les multiples erreurs de méthode et de terminologie que Gildon croit pouvoir reveler chez ses rivaux."

1510 MAXWELL, J. C. "Charles Gildon and the quarrel of the ancients and moderns." *RES* new ser. 1 (1950): 55-57.

Gildon was certainly an accurate mirror of the intellectual fashions of the moment. It is a reasonably accurate summary to say that he championed the Moderns against the Ancients, but his interests were narrower than this suggests. Gildon was writing just at the time when the controversy in England had almost waned, and esp. scientific learning for that of art and poetry. The conventional Royal Society brought accusations against the Greeks for preferring words to things, linked not with the name of Bacon, but that of Descartes. It is odd for a patriot in the criticism of poetry to invoke a French rather than an English patron for the new philosophy.

1511 MOORE, John Robert. "Gildon's attack on Steele and Defoe in 'The Battle of the Authors'." *PMLA* 64 (1951): 534-38.

In 1720 a long nameless tract, *The Battle of the Authors*, appeared. The identification of Gildon as the author of the tract and as 'Anonymous' in the mock battle described in it should have been made long ago. The mention of a 'young Author' was only a mask which served its purpose well.

1512 SCHEURWEGHS, G. "Brightland's or Steele's Grammar." *ES* 40 (1959): 136-41.

Evidence for Gildon's authorship.

——

GOMEZ, Madeleine, Dame de

1. *La Belle Assemblée: or the adventures of six days; a curious collection of some remarkable incidents which happened to Persons of Quality* (1724, 1725; 1728; 1735-36; 8 edns by 1765; 3 pts, pp. 138, 105, 119)

   NCBEL II 990[9]; McBurney 167; ECSTC 1414H6
   Trans. Eliza HAYWOOD from *Les journées amusantes*.
   Collection of novels in a frame story.

2. *L'entretien des beaux esprits* (1734; 2 vols: I, 272; II, 264)

   NCBEL II 993[15]; McBurney 292; Morgan 622; ECSTC 1414H7
   Trans. Eliza HAYWOOD from *Les cent nouvelles nouvelles*, 1732.

STUDIES

1513 MISH, Charles Carol. "Mme de Gomez and *La belle assemblée*." *RLC* 34 (1960): 212-25.

Madeleine-Angelique Poisson (1648-1770) is much neglected, yet her 15 titles were popular, and ran into several editions, like *La Belle Assemblée* which was exceeded in popularity only by *Gulliver's Travels*, *Robinson Crusoe*, Fénelon's *Telemachus* and the *Arabian Nights*. The sort of material in her book represents what readers of fiction wanted at the time, for, the appeal of Mrs Haywood's translation notwithstanding, the content was basically responsible for the success. It is a piece of fiction representative of the 1720s: it is serious, romantic, and the work of a woman. Indeed the fiction of the 1720s was dominated by female novelists: Aubin, Barker, Haywood, with reprints of Behn, Manley and D'Aulnoy. *La Belle Assemblée* marks the endpoint of a long line which runs back through Roch-Guilhem, Scudéry and D'Urfé, and behind them to the chivalric and metrical romances (Marie de Medici). The characteristic devices and concerns of the romances all appear: the love-and-honor theme, the intercalated tales, refined sentiments, stock motifs. Gomez also looks forward. Although Richardson and Fielding drove the romance from the field, there is a large measure of common feeling between her *précieuse* ladies, and Pamela and her descendants: delicacy of feeling matters. The work is also of intrinsic worth. In an age given to *chroniques scandaleuses*, political allegories, and topical commentary dressed as fiction. *La Belle Assemblée* stands out as a well-done imaginative writing, its stories interesting and well-managed, the frame interesting and lively. She could tell a good story.

———

GUEULETTE, Thomas-Simon

1. *A Thousand and One Quarters of Hours: being Tartarian Tales. Done from the Paris Edition* (1716, pp. 9-254)

    McBurney 84

2. *Chinese tales: or the wonderful adventures of the mandarin Fum-Hoam translated from the French* (1725, 1740; 4 edns by 1800; 2 vols: I, 275; II, 264)

    NCBEL II 990[18]; McBurney 186; Morgan 550; ECSTC 2497G1
    Trans. J. MACKY. 2 other versions recorded in the same year.

3. *Peruvian tales, related in one thousand and one hours* (1734, Dublin 1734, London 1735; at least 6 edns by 1800; pp. 187)

    NCBEL II 993[16]; McBurney 294; ECSTC 2497G2
    Trans. Samuel HUMPHREYS and John KELLY from *Les mille et une heures*, 1733-4.
    Variation on Arabian nights theme.

4. *Mogul tales: or the dreams of men awake. Now first translated into English with a prefatory discourse on the usefulness of romances* (1736, 1743; 2 vols: I, 288; II, 238)

    NCBEL II 994[7]; McBurney 316; Morgan 640; ECSTC 2497G3
    Trans. of *Les Sultanes de Guzarate*, 1732; had already appeared in *Appleby's Weekly Journal* 1733-5.

EDITIONS

1514 *The Thousand and One Quarters of an Hour (Tartarian Tales)*. Trans. and ed. Leonard C. SMITHERS. London: H. S. Nicholas & Co., 1893; pp. vi, 308.
Preface (v-vi). Discusses Gueulette's life and work briefly: "He imitated the tales of Count Hamilton and, though his style is less brilliant, and his incidents have less of what the French call *bizarrerie*, the numerous stories which he has produced abound in interesting situations, and are, in general, true pictures of what they are intended to represent." The text

presents the introduction and five tales.

1515 *The Transmigrations of the Mandarin Fum-Hoam (Chinese Tales)*. Trans. and ed. Leonard C. SMITHERS. London: H. S. Nicholas & Co., 1894; pp. viii, 251.

Preface (v-vi). "Commenting on these stories, Mr. W. A: Clouston, a well-known 'storiologist', remarks: 'Much of the groundwork of the clever imitations of the *Arabian Nights* has been directly or indirectly derived from Eastern sources." The text comprises 17 tales.

STUDIES

1516 ROVILLAIN, Eugène E. "Jonathan Swift's *A voyage to Lilliput* and *The thousand and one quarters of an hour, Tartarian tales* of Thomas Simon Gueulette." *MLN* 44 (1929): 362-64.

The composition of *Gulliver's Travels* was well advanced by 1720. The work of Gueulette was published in 1712, and it attracted such attention that 5 editions followed between 1712 and 1723. Swift was fond of tales of wonder, and may well have read those of the French author, one of the great masters in this particular field. Swift's proficiency in French meant that he did not have to wait for the first English translation of Gueulette's book in 1725.

———

HAMILTON, Anthony

Memoirs of the life of the Count de Grammont (1713, 1719; at least 4 edns by 1760; pp. 356)

NCBEL II 987[8]; McBurney 74; ECSTC 426H4
Trans. Abel BOYER.
EDITIONS

1517 *Mémoirs du chevalier de Grammont*. Ed. Claire-Eliane ENGEL. Monaco: Edition du Rocher, 1958.

1518 *Count Grammont at the Court of Charles II*. Ed. and trans. Nicholas DEAKIN. London: Barrie & Rockliff, 1965; pp. xi, 212.

Precise and informative introd. (vii-xi). " [...] Sir Walter Scott considered [it] to be one of the most entertaining [books] ever written. Part fact, part imagination, the two are so closely interwoven that the most ponderous of scholarly analysis has sometimes failed to disentangle them. Hamilton's book is a classic not in any scholarly sense, but because it still has the power now, as when it was written, to make its readers laugh" (xi). It is a masterpiece, the supreme example of a work written in a language not the author's own. There is a "Translator's Preface" which gives a short but helpful introduction to the life and world of the author, a postscript (201-2) which provides observations on the translation, and an appendix of the characters who appear in the work (203-12).

STUDIES

1519 DE LA TORRE, Lilian. "Forged 'Hamilton' letters." *NQ* 198 (1953): 163.
Genuine letters of Elizabeth, Duchess of Hamilton, differing completely in content, character and prose style, dating and significance exist to reinforce the suspicion that the letters published by M. CORDASCO (*NQ* 193 [1948]: 363-64) are forgeries.

1520 DRION, H. "Des *Mémoires du chevalier de Grammont*." *Tirade* 8 (1964): 602-14.
In Dutch. Account of origins and contents. This is "een merkwaardig lichtzinnig boek. Merkwaardig lichtzinnig als men bedenkt welke dramatische jaren Engeland en de schijver zelf had doorgemaakt tussen de tijd waarin de *Mémoirs* spelen en de tijd dat hij het boek schreef. Het is geen boek van burgerdeugden, en de burger die het prijst zou de schijn kunnen wekken dat hij voor lichtzinniger door wil gaan dan hij is: de kinderachtigste vorm von huichelarij" (613-4).

1521 ENGEL, Claire-Eliane. "Le véritable chevalier de Gramont." *Revue des Deux Mondes* (15 May 1960): 298-315.

In French. "Antoine Hamilton à cette date [1708], avait terminé son roman. Il l'avait écrit avec amour, pour amuser sa soeur et son beau-frère, pour s'amuser lui-même. Il allait rendre à ses héros leur beauté et leur jeunesse. Charles II restait pour lui le roi le règne duquel lui et sa soeur avaient eu vingt ans, sous lequel l'inimitable Grammont les avaient eus pour la seconde fois" (315).

1522 FILTEAU, Claude. "Le burlesque 'aristocratique' dans les *Mémoirs du Comte de Grammont* d'Antoine Hamilton." *DSS* 110-111 (1976): 93-103.
Discusses the novel of 'noble' reaction to the Restoration of Charles II who has a role to play, like a feudal monarch of heroes of myth, on his return. The second half of the novel shows Grammont exiled in England and bringing with him influences from the Court of Louis XIV. The exile

is changed into an heroic quest of a popular tale, and the epic style of the first part is over, a burlesque of the aristocracy. The exile of the Stuarts was the death of feudalism, and a new burlesque scenario emerges. Piece of Court writing which approximates factual intrigue and gallantries to the form of the *nouvelle galante*.

1523 FOSTER, James R. "*Peregrine Pickle* and the *Memoirs of the Count of Grammont.*" *MLN* 66 (1951): 469-71.

Smollett may have taken hints for the types like his clergyman, old man, usurer, and poet from 17c literature of roguery. The story of Lord Rochester's playing the role of a German fortune-telling doctor in Anthony Hamilton's *Memoirs* was also drawn on by Smollett for the fashionable scandal and satire of women so prominent in *Peregrine Pickle*. The fortune-telling adventure of Perry and Crabtree is similar in tone and conception if not in detail. Peregrine and Rochester are inquisitive, proud, daredevil incarnations of the spirit of satire. Did Smollett indeed model his hero in some measure after Rochester?

———

HAYWOOD, Eliza

1. *Love in excess: or the fatal enquiry* (1719; at least 9 edns by 1750; pp. 56)

    NCBEL II 988[14]; McBurney 103; ECSTC 1414H26
    Sensationally popular; melodramatic romance of passion and intrigue.

2. *The British recluse: or the secret history of Cleomira, suppos'd dead* (1722; 4 edns by 1732; pp. 138)

    NCBEL II 989[15]; McBurney 138; Morgan 511; ECSTC 1414H10
    An imitation of Mrs AUBIN'S romances.

3. *Idalia: or the unfortunate mistress. A novel* (1723; 4 edns by 1732; 3 pts, pp. 1-74, 1-66, 67-135)

    NCBEL II 989[21]; McBurney 142; Morgan 528; ECSTC 1414H20
    Amorous misadventure. Trans. into French in 1770.

4. *Lasselia: or the self-abandon'd. A novel* (1723; 4 edns by 1732, pp. 80).

    NCBEL II 990[1]; McBurney 144; Morgan 541; ECSTC 1414H23
    Amorous misadventure.

5. *The fatal secret; or constancy in distress* (1724; 4 edns by 1732; pp. 61)

> NCBEL II 990[10]; McBurney 158; Morgan 551
> Novel of passion; melodramatic psychology.

6. *The masqueraders: or fatal curiosity* (1724; 6 edns by 1732; pp. 47)

> NCBEL II 990[11]; McBurney 159
> Intrigue in high life.

7. *The works of Mrs. Eliza Haywood* (1724, 4 vols: I, 323; II, 138; III, 1-74, 1-66, 67-135; IV, 128)

> NCBEL II 990[13]; McBurney 163; ECSTC 1414H8
> 8 novels together with poems and plays, rptd in 4 vols.

8. *A spy upon the conjurer* (1724-1725 [several issues], pp. 259)

> NCBEL II 990[12]; McBurney 161; ECSTC 1414H51
> Secret history, largely epistolary, of Duncan Campbell, a famous soothsayer of the period.

9. *Bath-intrigues; in a Collection of Original Letters to a Friend in London* (1725 [3 edns], 1727 [in *Secret histories*]; pp. 51)

> NCBEL II 990[19]; McBurney 172; Morgan 549; ECSTC 1414H33
> Lively epistolary scandal chronicle.

10. *Fantomina: or love in a maze* (1725, 1732 [in *Secret histories*]; pp. 257-91)

> NCBEL II 990[20]; McBurney 174; Morgan 551; ECSTC 1414H33
> Clever story of amorous strategems.

11. *Memoirs of a certain island adjacent to the kingdom of Utopia* (1725, 1726; 2 vols: I, 77; II, 92)

> NCBEL II 990[20]; McBurney 177; Morgan 558; ECSTC 1414H28
> Scandal chronicle of politics and amours in high life, in the manner of Bacon's *New Atalantis* (1627).

12. *Secret histories, novels and poems written by Mrs Eliza Haywood* (1725; 4 edns by 1742; 4 vols: I, 259; II, 114; III, 162; IV, iii, 5-45, 7-93, 3-50)

> NCBEL II 990[22]; McBurney 179; Morgan 560; ECSTC 1414H33

Reissue of the 1724 edition. There was also a shorter collection published in two vols in 1725. The longer ed. was reprinted in 1732. It is a reissue of 11 novels, including:
1) *Fantomina*
2) *The British Recluse*;
3) *Idalia* in 3 parts;
4) *The Injured Husband*;
5) *Lasselia*;
6) *The Rash Resolve*;
7) *The Fatal Secret.*

13. *The city jilt: or the alderman turn'd beau* (1726 [3 edns], 1727 [in *Secret histories*]; pp. 60)

   NCBEL II 991[4]; McBurney 193; ECSTC 1414H33
   Clever plot; realistic depiction of middle-class life.

14. *The mercenary lover: or the unfortunate heiresses, being a true secret history of a city amour, in a certain island adjacent to the kingdom of Utopia. Written by the author of the said island* (1726, 1726, 1728; pp. 9-62)

   NCBEL II 991[5]; McBurney 196; Morgan 572; ECSTC 1414H29
   Primitive psychological novel.

15. *Cleomelia: or the generous mistress* (1727, 1727; pp. 104)

   NCBEL II 992[11]; McBurney 208; ECSTC 1414H43
   Passion, adventure, intrigue.

16. *Letters from the palace of fame* (1727 [also in *Secret histories*], pp. 24 [incomplete])
   NCBEL II 991[13]; McBurney 210; ECSTC 1414H33
   Epistolary scandal chronicle of political figures.

17. *Love in its variety* (1727, pp. 250)

   NCBEL II 991[15]; McBurney 220
   Six novels, said to be translations from Matteo BANDELLO; more probably original or freely adapted.

18. *The fruitless enquiry* (1727; 5 edns by 1800; pp. 274)

   NCBEL II 991[13]; McBurney 209; ECSTC 1414H16

Stories, linked by a framework, of a search for happiness.

19. *The life of Madame de Villesache, written by a lady, who was an eye-witness*
    of the greatest part of her adventures, and faithfully translated from her
    manuscript by Mrs E. H. (1727, pp. 63)

    NCBEL II 991[5]; McBurney 218; Morgan 575; ECSTC 1414H24
    Probably trans. of an unidentified French source.
    Unusually good analysis of heroine's feelings, motivations.

20. *The perplex'd Dutchess, or treachery rewarded: being some memoirs of the*
    Court of Malfy (1727, 1727, 1728; pp. 60)

    NCBEL II 991[16]; McBurney 211; ECSTC 1414H50
    No connection with Webster's play; intrigues of a scheming parvenue.

21. *Philidore and Placentia: or l'amour trop délicat* (1727; 2 pts, pp. 1-46, 3-48)

    NCBEL II 991[17]; McBurney 212; Morgan 576
    Highflown tale of love and adventure.

22. *The secret history of the present intrigues of the Court of Caramania* (1727,
    1727; pp. 348)

    NCBEL II 991[18]; McBurney 213; Morgan 578; ECSTC 1414H34
    Love and politics at the English court; *roman à clef.*

23. *The agreeable Caledonian: or memoirs of signiora di Morella, a Roman lady*
    (two pts. 1728, 1729; one vol. 1768 [as *Clementina*]; pp. 93)

    NCBEL II 992[4]; McBurney 231; ECSTC 1414H9
    Intrigues and adventures in Italy; heroine abducted from a convent.

24. *Irish artifice: or the history of Clarina* (1728, pp. 17-24)

    NCBEL II 992[5]; McBurney 232; Morgan 584; ECSTC 1414H22
    Grimly realistic story of a fortune-hunter and his victim.

25. *The fair Hebrew, or a true but secret history of two Jewish ladies who lately*
    resided in London (1729, 1729; pp. 53)

    NCBEL II 992[9]; McBurney 242; Morgan 591; ECSTC 1414H44
    Use of Jewish characters for exoticism; realistic plot becomes sensational.
    A story with a somewhat similar title, *La Belle Juive*, was included in a

collection of current novels called *Histoires tragiques et galantes* published in Paris in 1731.

26. *Love-letters on all occasions lately passed between persons of distinction* (1730, pp. 224)

NCBEL II 992[16]; McBurney 249; Morgan 598; ECSTC 1414H27
Collection ranging in scope from single narrative letters to short letter novels.

27. *Adventures of Eovaai, Princess of Ijaveo* (1736, 1741 [as *The unfortunate Princess*]; pp. 244)

NCBEL II 994[8]; McBurney 313; Morgan 638; ECSTC 1414H52
Pretended trans. Secret history attacking Walpole.

EDITIONS

COLLECTIONS

1524 *Masquerade novels of Eliza Haywood. Facsimile Reproductions with an Introduction by Mary Ann SCHOFIELD.* (Scholars' Facsimiles & Reprints, 412.) Delmar, NY, 1983.

Provides the facs. texts of:
1) *The Masqueraders* (1724-5) (pp. 45 + 45);
2) *Fantomina* (1723) (pp. 257-91);
3) *The Fatal Secret* (1723) (pp. 207-54);
4) *Idalia* (1724) (pp. 162).
Introd. (5-20) presents the life and work of Haywood. "Not only the sheer number of her works, but her continued reputation of romance patterns (e.g., love in excess, persecuted virtue) together with the symbolic matrixes propounded in these tales (i.e., imprisonment, escape, confinement, masquerade) make her one of the leading spokeswomen of her age. Haywood's fiction, like most of the feminine novels of the early and mid-years, encodes the woman's position in the 18c. Through the use of gender-specific language, archetypal situations, metaphors and other literary figures, Haywood delineates what it is to be female during these years of the eighteenth century" (5). Individual critical account of each novel. Extensive bibliographic notes (18-20).

1525 *Four novels of Eliza Haywood: 'The Force of Nature', 'Lasselia', 'The Injur'd Husband', 'The Perplex'd Dutchess'.* Photoreprints. Introd. M. A. SCHOFIELD. (Scholars' Facsimiles & Reprints 376.) Delmar, NY:

Scholars' Facsimiles & Reprints, 1983.

Introduction (5-17).

1526 *Three Novellas*. Ed. Earla A. WILPUTTE. (Early English Women Writers, 1660-1800, 5.) East Lansing, MI: Colleagues Press; Woodbridge, Suffolk: Boydell & Brewer, 1995; pp. vii, 141.

      Provides the texts of:
      1) *The Distressed Orphan* (25-64);
      2) *The City Jilt* (65-104);
      3) *The Double Marriage* (105-41).
      Critical ed. with introd. (1-15). A Note on the Text (16). Chronology of Eliza Haywood (17-20). Selected bibliography of critical studies (21-22). Introd. divides Haywood's career into two distinct periods and corresponding genres: the amatory novels of the 1720s and 30s, and the moralistic, didactic works of the 1740s and 50s (7). The amatory novellas depict the erotic possibilities and the social realities for both sexes as they instruct, delight and attempt to reform the age (15).

1527 BACKSCHEIDER, Paula R. (ed. & introd.). *Selected fiction and drama of Eliza Haywood*. New York and London: Oxford UP, 1999; pp. xlvi, 313.

      Provides the texts of:
      1) *A Wife to be Lett; A Comedy* (1727) (1-82);
      2) *The City Jilt; or, The Alderman Turn'd Beau: A Secret History* (1726) (83-120);
      3) *The Mercenary Lover; or, The Unfortunate Heiresses* (1726)(121-62);
      4) From *The Fruitless Enquiry* (1727) (163-70);
      5) *The Operas of Operas; or, Tom Thumb the Great* (1733) (171-220);
      6) From *The Adventures of Eovaai, Prince of Ijaveo* (1736) (221-42);
      7) From *The Invisible Spy* (1755) (243-98);
      8) From *The Wife* (1756) (299-313).
      18c orthography has been retained. Haywood's notes are incorporated into the footnotes. Approximations of titles pages with annotations. Foreword (ix-x). Introd. (xiii-xliii). Selected bibliography (xliv-xlv). The extensive introd. covers 'Life', 'Career', 'Contributions', 'This Volume's Selections', with detailed bibliographical footnotes.

1528 *The Injur'd Husband* and *Lasselia*. Ed. Jerry BEASLEY. Kentucky: U of Kentucky P, 1999; pp. xliii, 162.

      Critical ed. List of illus. (3 plates, portrait and frontispieces) (vi). Preface (vii). Chronology (xxxix). Note on the text (xliii).

Texts: *The Injur'd Husband* (1-102); *Lasselia* (103-50). Notes to the Novels (151-58). Sel. Bibliography (159-62).

INDIVIDUAL TITLES

VARIOUS

1529 *Philodore and Placentia*. Ed. McBURNEY, in *Four before Richardson* etc. See ANTHOLOGIES, Ch. 2, **133**.

1530 *Love in excess: or, The fatal enquiry*. Ed. David OAKLEAF. (Broadview Literary Texts.) Peterborough, Ont.: Broadway Press, 1994; pp. 273 Critical ed., with annot. text. Introd. (7-24). A Note on the Text (25-27). Chronology (28-31). Selected bibliography (32-35). Text (41-273). This novel is "exuberantly various. It also celebrates sexual desire, a topic its competition fastidiously avoids. [...] [S]he elaborates her basic narrative situation, the love triangle, to present an impressive variety of female roles and fates" (11).

1531 *The adventures of Eovaai*. Ed. Earla A. WILPUTTE. (Early English Women Writers, 1660-1800.) East Lansing, MI; Woodbridge, Suffolk: Boydell & Brewer, 1996; pp. 243.
Critical ed. Introd. (9-34). Chronology of Eliza Haywood (35-38). A Note on the Text (39). Annotated text (41-166). Appendix A: Selected Literary Portraits by Eliza Haywood (167-75); B: Selections from *The Country Gentleman* (176-90); C: *The Secret History of Mama Oello, Princess Royal of Peru* (191-238). Bibliography (239-43). "Haywood exploits the analogy between sexuality and political relationships, as she plays with the idea of power lust through images of physical lust: both deny reason and extol appetite for personal satiety." (31).

1532 *The British Recluse*. Ed. BACKSCHEIDER and RICHETTI in (pp. 153-226) *Popular fiction by women, 1660-1730* etc. See ANTHOLOGIES, Ch. 2, **119**.

1533 *Fantomina*. Ed. BACHSCHEIDER and RICHETTI in (pp. 227-50) *Popular fiction by women, 1660-1730* etc. See ANTHOLOGIES, Ch. 2, **119**.

The History of Miss Betsy Thoughtless

1534 ELWOOD, John Robert. "A critical edition of Eliza Haywood's *The History of Miss Betsy Thoughtless* [with] text of the first edition in four volumes." Unpub. doct. diss., Univ. of Illinois, 1963. [*DA* 24 (1963): 2462.]

This is sometimes referred to as the first domestic novel in English (1751). The present editor provides textual and explanatory notes and an introduction which seeks to determine its contribution to the development of the English novel. It provided Fanny Burney with some of the pattern for *Evelina*, and was popular in England, France and Germany. Investigates its reputation among commentators to the present, and analyzes Haywood's development as novelist from her scandal chronicles of the 1720s to her creation of *Betsy Thoughless* in 1751.

1535 *The History of Miss Betsy Thoughtless, 1751.* Ed. M. A. SCHOFIELD. (Facsimile.) (The Novel, 1720-1805, 4.) 2 vols. New York, London: Garland. 1979; pp. xii, 1175.

The Introduction provides a serious critical revaluation of Mrs Haywood: "Throughout her writing, and throughout *The History of Miss Betsy Thoughtless*, Eliza Haywood holds up to scrutiny the values of her day, and she does not hesitate to focus on sexual double standards and their inherent injustice. And because Betsy Thoughtless seeks to be an independent woman -- and because Eliza Haywood endorses that stand -- the novel is still relevant and illuminating today [...]. That Eliza Haywood should have been erased from the literary records [...] is not only surprising, it is also sad. For this woman writer (and the characters she creates) occupies a central place in women's literary history" (xii).

1536 SPENDER, Dale (introd.). *The History of Miss Betsy Thoughtless.* (Mothers of the Novel.) London: Pandora, 1986; pp. xii, 594.

The novels themselves, both for literary and historical reasons, merit reprinting, but some of the contributors confuse uncritical chattiness with accessibility. The introductions do not always provide the wider historical explanations of the novels.

1537 *The History of Miss Betsy Thoughtless.* Ed. Beth Fowkes TOBIN. (World Classics.) Oxford and New York: Oxford UP, 1997; pp. xi, 580.

Introd. (ix-xxxv). Annotated crit. text (9-568). Notes (569-80). Major investigation of the life and the importance of Haywood and of this novel: "The rise of bourgeois morality was inextricably linked with the ideology of domestic femininity" (xxvii) [...] [The novel] represents Haywood's successful negotiation of the contemporary moral climate without abandoning the hallmarks of her earlier fiction: sexual passion and social critique. Using the plot of the reformed coquette, she was able to develop a character and a narrative that could represent female sexuality without appearing immodest, and in doing so, could provide a subtle critique of bourgeois conceptions of femininity and propriety" (xxxv).

BIBLIOGRAPHY

1538 BLOUCH, Christine. "Haywood, Eliza." In (pp. 263-300) SAAR and SCHOFIELD, *Eighteenth-century Anglo-American women novelists: A reference guide* etc., **93**

Annotated criticism 1900 to 1992 (195 items).

SELECTED PRE-1992 STUDIES

1539 BLOUCH, Christine. "Eliza Haywood and the romance of obscurity." *SEL* 31:3 (Summer 1991): 535-51.

Investigates accurate biographical parameters for Haywood's often obscured career, and suggests ways that biographical questions intersect with critical issues. Little is known about her life, and much received detail is inaccurate. Establishes new possibilities for her birth date, family origins; corrects accounts of her marriage, and confirms that she had children. Her life and works are defined in terms of marginality. There are inevitable considerations of canon formation and critical context raised by her work, but it is still surprising that the author of more than 70 pieces in six genres over four decades, and one who played a key role in the evolution of the novel, and defined central issues in the portrayal of 18c female subjectivity, should have elicited so little critical interest. Extensive bibliographical notes (546-52).

1540 BOWERS, Terence Noel. *The politics of motherhood: British writing and culture, 1680-1760* etc., **265**.

Looks at "Dreams of maternal autonomy: scandalous motherhood in three tales by Eliza Haywood" (124-46): - Maternal autonomy and patriarchal authority: *The Rash Resolve* (1724); - Imagining publicly authoritative motherhood: *The Force of Nature* (1725); - Maternity, community, and subversion in *The Female Spectator* (1744-46); - Maternal failure and socioeconomic difference: *The Unnatural Mother* (1734).

1541 DAY, *Told in Letters*, etc., **364**.

Discusses *Fantomina*. In some epistolary novels the inserted letters adumbrate so much of the action that the story is in fact told twice over -- once in the bare narrative of events, and once through what the reader can pick up from the characters' reporting on them in correspondence. "Mrs Haywood allows the reader to discover for himself from Beauplaisir's own pen the state of his mind and the motivations which sway him" (139).

1542 EINHOFF, Eberhard. *Emanzipatorische Aspekte im Frauenbild von 'The Review', 'The Spectator' und 'The Female Spectator'*. (Europäische Hochschulschriften, 75.) Frankfurt: Peter Lang, 1980; pp. 171.

Considers the emancipation of women from the prescribed formulas (*Vorstellungen*) which characterized the perception of women in the early decades of the 18c. Looks at the features characterizing the image of women from an historical perspective (Renaissance, 17c, early 18c), emancipatory aspects of the image of women in Daniel Defoe's *Review* (1704-13), in *The Spectator* (1711-12/1714), and in Eliza Haywood's *Female Spectator* (1744-46). Concentrates on marriage and education. Bibliography (165-71).

1543 ERIKSON, James P. "*Evelina* and *Betsy Thoughtless.*" *Texas Studies in Literature and Language* 6 (1964): 96-103.

Although there is no proof that Fanny Burney ever read *Betsy Thoughtless*, and internal evidence is inconclusive, there are important similarities of plot and character, and even more significantly, similarities of theme. Both novels teach the necessity of conforming to society's customs and mores, and both illustrate this through a young woman's entering London society, and suffering an unwarranted reputation for wantonness and the loss of an ideal lover because of her failure to observe expected forms. The threadbare conventions of romance are less essential to *Evelina* than to *Betsy Thoughtless*. Burney is not primarily concerned with telling a love story, whereas every chapter of Haywood is about romantic relations between the sexes. Burney is much more scenic throughout than Haywood, reflecting the lessons learned from Richardson, who had shown that fiction is not just a story to be told, but an experience to be felt and shared.

1544 FIRMAGER, Gabrielle M. "Eliza Haywood: some further light on her background?" *NQ* 38 (June 1991): 181-83.

Although George WHICKER went to great lengths to uncover the facts of Haywood's life, he was perhaps ignorant of a couple of undated letters to unknown prospective patrons which throw further light on her background [Birch Collection in the Manuscripts Dept of the British Library.]

1545 FLETCHER, E. C. "The date of Eliza Haywood's death." *NQ* 166 (1934): 385.
Discusses the two reports from the *Gentleman's Magazine* and the *London Magazine* which have given rise to confusion about the actual date.

1546 KENT, John P. "Crébillon fils, Eliza Haywood and *Les heureux orphelins*: a problem of authorship." *RomN* 11 (1969): 326-32.

The *Heureux Orphelins* (1754) was thought to be an imitation of an English work, but it was not until 1919 that Helen Hughes noticed that the work imitated was a novel by Eliza Haywood, *The Fortunate Foundlings* (1744). The work ought to be excised from the canon of Crébillon's works, since in avowing authorship he may well have been protecting his wife, Henriette Marie Stafford Howard, from possible censure.

1547 KISHI, Eiro. "Female writers and morality: Eliza Haywood." *TCEL* 53 (1980): 57-77.
Abstract not seen.

1548 KLEIN, *Der Briefroman in der englischen Literatur* etc., **569**.

Provides a breakdown of the epistolary exchanges in *Betsy Thoughtless* (262-64), *Love in excess* (268-69), *Memoirs of a certain island* (269-70), *The mercenary lover* (270-71), *The rash resolve* (271), *The secret history* (271-72).

1549 KOON, Hélène. "Eliza Haywood and the *Female Spectator*." *HLQ* 42 (1978): 43-55.

In 1744 Haywood began the first magazine by and for women, which lasted for 24 issues. It has been ignored, patronized and belittled, but occupies a unique position in the history of periodical literature. Both *Spectators* were written in an easy colloquial style, although the *Spectator* essays are brief and sparkle with aphoristic argumentative wit. One uses male exemplary characters, the other female. The *Spectator* gracefully acknowledges women, but discusses politics, Parliament, foreign affairs, aesthetics, art, literature, criticism. The *Female Spectator* is strictly devoted to women's affairs, and men are only peripheral, a viewpoint which probably affected the presentation of every subject. Haywood was more than a moralist: she was a fine journalist with excellent narrative powers, and her work deserves more critical attention. She brings great insight to the substructures of the 18c society in which women lived, thought and perceived experience quite differently from their male counterparts.

1550 LOCKWOOD, Thomas. "Eliza Haywood in 1749: *Dalinda, and Her Pamphlet on the Pretender.*" *NQ* 36:4 (1989): 475-77.

There is now documentary proof that a one-volume duodecimo novel of romance, deception and suffering (July 1749) is by Eliza Haywood.

1551 MITRA, Madhuchhanda. "Educating the eighteenth-century heroine: the lessons of Haywood, Lennox, and Burney." Unpub. doct. diss., Kent State Univ., 1990. [*DAI* 51:1 (1990): 170A.]

The rise of the novel in 18c England is bound up intimately with the ideology of domestic relations. The early English novel was part of an immense field full of discourse that reformulated the sexual and filial relations based on the new economic criteria of the imminent Industrial Revolution. Along with education manuals and popular periodicals, the conduct literature re-defined the concept of 'femininity'. Recent feminist criticism has drawn attention to the ways in which the ideal of domestic femininity simultaneously empowered and contained the literary representation of women in the 18c. Examines how this ideal influenced the works of Haywood, Lennox and Burney.

1552 MORVAN, Alain. "*The Fair Hebrew* d'Eliza Haywood: contribution à l'étude du thème judaique dans le roman anglais du dix-huitième siècle." *BSEAA* 6 (June 1978): 21-36.

In French. Investigates Haywood's bold treatment of the Jewish theme. "Si l'assimulation est inéluctable - l'historien Hyamson considère ainsi que, pour les Juifs d'Angleterre, le dix-huitième siècle représente une véritable émancipation du ghetto - elle ne se fait pas soubresauts [...] (21). D'une lecture qui se veut édifiante, et engage les jeunes gens à se défier des traquenards d'une passion trop nourrie de sensualité, le roman d'Eliza Haywood est en même temps une variation sur le thème de la jeune Juive qui s'enfuit avec un amoureux chrétien [...] (23). Sous couleur de réserve et d'objectivité, elle trouve en effet moyen d'insinuer que, même lorsqu'ils agissent bien - et c'est assurément bien agir que d'embrasser la 'vraie' religion - il n'est pas évident que les Juifs le fassent pour les meilleures raison [...] (32). Pourtant, alors qu'elle ne peut s'empêcher de requérir en sous-main contre ceux-là mêmes qu'elle semblait défendre, la romancière - qui n'en a peut-être pas clairement conscience - contribue à sa manière à ébranler les certitudes totalitaires du manichéisme raciste [...]" (33).

1553 RICHETTI, John J. "Voice and gender in eighteenth-century fiction: Haywood to Burney." *SNNTS* 19:3 (Fall 1987): 263-72.

Gender must affect speech. Given their distinct positions in the hierarchy of social power, men and women must have different relationships to language and use it in different ways. The British 18c novel bears out this analysis since the achievement of female practitioners were recognized by contemporaries as based quite specifically on their limited access to the resources of language. Haywood makes intelligence and verbal ability such as she obviously possessed, completely subordinate to rendering the absolute limits of female experience, in a subtle suffering quite beyond words. A measure of education, a superior understanding are, if anything, intensifiers of this female suffering. Despite its formulaic crudity, Haywood's specifically female refutation of language, or her insistent dramatization of its inadequacy, is an accurate rendition of the relationship most female characters have to language -- invented as they are by men in 18c fiction. Even Defoe among the male novelists who dominate fiction in the mid-18c tend to dramatize the female speaking as a comic or dangerous loquacity, and deprive the women they represent of a distinct voice.

1554-----"The awakening of the eighteenth-century heroine: Eliza Haywood's new woman." *CEACrit* 43:3 (March 1981): 9-13.

The abundance and popularity of Haywood's work provides a comprehensive treatment of the question of women as a social and moral issue for the period. She presents a pattern of feminine behaviour, centered around a characteristic fable of feminine distress. In her stories, certain recurring motifs emerge. There is a pervasive pattern of virtue in distress and persecuted innocence, while her heroines reveal an interior ambivalence and unconscious unrest. These are intimately related to pervasive questions of order and disorder, harmony and chaos, the typical milieu of the 18c novel. Her brand of increasing feminine awareness comments importantly on the position and role of women in the 18c.

1555-----*Quiet rebellion: the fictional heroines of Eliza Fowler Haywood.* Washington DC: UP of America, 1982; pp. x, 137.

Haywood was the author of scores of racy, titillating novels and amorous romances, and was one of the most widely read fiction writers of her day. Her first novel, *Love's Excess: Or, The Fatal Enquiry* (1719) rivalled *Robinson Crusoe* and *Gulliver's Travels* in popularity. The sheer abundance and familiarity of her work (over 60 works - romances, novels, secret histories, translations of continental romances, and her plays) made her a significant figure in the development of the novel in England. Her theme is always "love in excess", making her the pre-eminent chronicler of female passion and distress for the early part of the 18c. She was also an aggressive writer, commenting upon the position and role of women in the early century, and an able story teller of tales of passion and intrigue which captured the imagination of the new popular audiences.

1556-----"Exposé of the popular heroine: the female protagonists of Eliza Haywood." *Stud ECC* 12 (1985): 93-103.

While the women protagonists of Defoe, Richardson and Fielding are widely acclaimed and admired, this is not the case with the heroines of the popular minor novelists of the period. *Love in Excess* (1719) challenged *Robinson Crusoe* and *Gulliver's Travels* as the most popular English fiction of the 18c before *Pamela*. Haywood had intimate knowledge of the women's problems of her time, and supported herself and her two children by her literary efforts. Each of her novels concerns itself with the heroine and her problem of self-identity. She provides the most comprehensive contemporary treatment of the 'woman question', and looks at the impact of the popular novel on the traditional concepts of 'woman', 'wife' and 'mother'. In probing the dictates of a male-dominated society, she created 4 distinct types: the supporter of the status quo, the independent woman, the models of extreme feminine disorder, and conventional moralistic femininity.

1557 WALMSLEY, D. M. "Eliza Haywood: a bicentenary." Corr. in *TLS* (24 Feb. 1956): 117.

Confirms the date of her death as 25 Feb. 1756, observed in the *Whitehall Evening Post.*

1558 WEBER, Dona-Lee. "Fair game: Rape and sexual aggression on women in some early eighteenth-century prose fiction," **1035**.

1559 WHICHER, George Frisbie. *The life and romances of Mrs Eliza Haywood.* (Columbia Univ. Studies in English and Comparative Literature.) New York: Columbia UP, 1915. p. xi, 210.

Eliza Haywood deserves wider recognition as an important link between Aphra Behn and Fanny Burney. Her earliest romances and fictitious chronicles have historical interest, as English counterparts of French models, and her plays are not entirely negligible. Much of her work was of a journalistic nature, and has connections with Defoe's writings. She was the first woman to edit a periodical, following Addison and Steele, and the first to attempt a publishing venture. *Jemmy and Jenny Jessamy* is highly praised in *Old Mortality*, while *Miss Betsy Thoughtless* is a remarkable precursor of *Evelina*. The book provides an account of her life, short romances of passion, the Duncan Campbell pamphlets, secret histories and scandal novels, the heroine of *The Dunciad*, letters and essays, later fiction, the domestic novel. Bibliography (176-200). Chronological list of writings with contemporary works (1719-78): list of writings (collected works, single works [67], attributed works) (201-4). Index (205-10).

1560 WOODCOCK, George. "Mary Manley and Eliza Haywood." *Room of One's Own* 2:4 (1977): 49-65.

Important introductory article to these two women writers. Haywood had neither Behn's varied talents nor the peculiar and often ironic vivacity one encounters in Manley at her best. She was intelligent and industrious, and almost always imitative. Her early work was modelled on Behn's passionate romances and Manley's political *romans à clef*, as well as on contemporary French fiction. In her middle period she took to Defoe's kind of journalism, while her long novels *Betsy Thoughtless* and *Jemmy and Jenny Jessamy*, her best and historically most significant works, are indebted to Richardson and Fielding.

1561 WOODRUFF, James F. "The authorship of the *Tatler Revived*, 1750." *NQ* 30 (1983): 524-55.

Cautiously accepts the authorship of Mrs Haywood.

STUDIES (1992-1999)

1562 BACKSCHEIDER, Paula R. "The shadow of an author: Eliza Haywood." *ECF* 11:1 (1998): 79-102.

There is a difficulty working with Haywood's texts. She creates exceptionally complex narrators and narrative perspectives, and there always seems to be more in her writing than even the most experienced interpreter sees. Her topical allusions are myriad, her engagement with the political and social issues continuous, her fictions complex and subtle. Debate continues about whether her novels are shallow, trivial and repetitious, whether they provide significant social commentary, an important part of the literary history of the novel, or simply erratic writing. It seems indisputable that she has come to stand for the nexus and point of tension between a number of things - transgressive, outspoken women and the moral, admonishing woman writer, between amatory fiction and the new novel.

1563 BAER, Cynthia Marie. "Wise and worthier women: Lady Mary Wroth's *Urania* and the development of women's narrative", **192**.

1564 BENEDICT, Barbara M. "The curious genre: female enquiry in amatory fiction." *StudN* 30:2 (1998): 194-210.

Curiosity, esp. sexual curiosity, is an impulse traditionally attributed to women (Eve, Pandora, Alice). In the late 17c and 18c, Behn, Manley and Haywood found a cultural space for this spying in the novel. They were the contemporary equivalent of inquiry in the New Science, exploiting new kinds of visual lust and new representations of peeping, and providing an ideology for the publication of sexual novels, works vaunting empirical exploration of semantics and novelty itself. These amatory writers present this enterprise as experimentation in love. All three endow female or feminine narration with a scientific posture of objective analysis to lend public authority to previously censored exploration of a physical nature, both sensual experience and the material items like literature that include them. Popular empiricism as threat and power infused the novels of the early 18c. The three most widely sold works of the early 18c, Defoe's *Robinson Crusoe* (1719), Haywood's *Love in Excess* (1719-20), and Swift's *Gulliver's Travels* (1720), all play with the border between legitimate and illegitimate curiosity. *A Journal of the Plague Year* treats the reivention of popular curiosity through literature as Lockean empiricism.

1565 BURTON, Kathryn Mary. "'An Addison in petticoats': Eliza Haywood and the political essay." Unpub. doct. diss., Florida State Univ., 1993. [*DA* 54 (1994): 2585A.]

Because of the work as a novelist, Haywood 's impact on the 18c periodical is virtually unnoticed. She was author of the first periodical written by a woman for women, the monthly *Female Spectator* (1744-46). Her other periodical works included *The Tea-Table* (1724), *The Parrot* (1728), *The Parrot with a Compendium of the Times* (1746), and *The Young Lady* (1756). The essays display a wide range of knowledge, interests and concerns, and offer the modern reader an insight into 18c life. Surveys her periodical works, focusing on their contribution to the history of the periodical essays, a reconsideration of her periodicals, and her role as an early feminist.

1566 CARNELL, Rachel Karen. "Dominion in the household: liberal political theory and the early British novel." etc., **304**.

1567-----"It's not easy being green: gender and friendship in Eliza Haywood's political periodicals." *ECS* 32:2 (1998-99): 199-214.

While scholars have recently begun to recognize the political overtones of Haywood's scandalous domestic fiction from the 1720s, few have considered the political import of her periodicals from the 1740s, both of which she describes as political commentary. Argues that in *The Female Spectator* and *The Parrot* she protests against the nascent gendered split in the 1740s between literary genres perceived of as political, and those perceived as domestic. She articulates her objection to this split through a refiguration of the forms of friendship that Derrida describes as being traditionally excluded from the political realm.

1568 CONWAY, Alison Margaret. "Private interests: Spectatorship, portraiture, and the novel in eighteenth-century England." Unpub. doct. diss., Univ. of California (Berkeley), 1994. [*DA* 55 (1995): 2839-40A.]

Why did the English 18c novel invest so much energy in the representation of vision and its effect? Looks at the role of portraiture in Manley's *New Atalantis*, Richardson's *Clarissa*, Fielding's *Amelia*, Haywood's *The History of Miss Betsy Thoughtless*. The portrait defines questions of subjectivity in relation to competing modes of spectatorship. The portrait's complex nature and the response it elicits render novelistic modes of spectatorship and representations of character paradoxical. Can the portrait function as a metaphor for incorruptible personality when it remains so closely tied to the workings of the commodities of desire? Personality participates in configurations of desire that are simultaneously private and public. The erotic interrupts the novel's attempts to isolate the private sphere as the site of ideal virtue. Characters find themselves for better or worse implicated in social structures of fetishism and commodification.

1569 DONOVAN, Josephine. "From avenger to victim: genealogy of a Renaissance novella." *TSWL* 15:2 (1996): 269-88.

Discusses the plot of a popular Renaissance tale which had numerous retellings and variants: a seduced and abandoned lower-middle-class woman who avenges herself by killing her treacherous aristocratic lover. Unlike the sentimental heroine's text which became an important 18c fiction where the betrayed woman dies in disgrace, here the woman has a moment of triumph in which she takes a feminist stand against exploitation. Conducts a comparative study of this genealogy from 16c

Italy to 18c England which formulates important new theories about women's literary history of the early modern period. The primary plot is to be found in novella 42 of Matteo Bandello's *Novelle* (1554). English versions of the tale include Manley's "The Wife's Resentment" (novel 3 in her *The Power of Love: In Seven Novels* [1720]) and Haywood's "Female Revenge: or, the Happy Exchange" (in *Love in its Variety* [1727]). Manley's work is discussed at length (276-80): "Rodrigo is set up as much more offensive a character than he is in the sources, and much more deserving of his fate. Manley's sympathies are clearly with the woman". Haywood's story is also discussed in detail (281-83). "Haywood tames a powerful story of female agency and feminist revenge, turning it into a misogynist tale of male ascendancy and female powerlessness, disgrace and death." Her version of the novella accords with the changing ideological climate of the time, in which, many historians claim, women's economic and social power was in eclipse, "suggests a reason for Haywood's capitulation." Manley restores the feminist thesis and adds important socio-economic details that link her work to the emerging realist novel. Haywood sentimentalizes the novella, recasting the story in terms of a male supremacist ideology.

1570 ELLIS, Lorna Beth. "Engendering the *Bildungsroman*: the *Bildung* of Betsy Thoughtless." *Genre* 28:3 (1995): 279-301.

Examination of *Betsy Thoughtless* (1751), a novel of a young woman's development, offers a more complex understanding of the genre of *Bildungsroman* as a whole, and of the culture and material circumstances that produced it. In part, the female protagonist's manipulation of appearances to gain autonomy exposes the socially constructed nature of her own development. Furthermore, evidence that the *Bildungroman* began in the mid-18c with a woman's text, rather than with Goethe's *Wilhelm Meister* (1749) as is commonly assumed, raises questions about the genre's traditional tie to Romanticism, and about how we construct Romanticism itself.

1571 FENDLER, Susanne. "Intertwining literary histories: women's contribution to the rise of the novel." In (pp. 31-64) FENDLER, *Feminist contributions to the literary canon: setting standards of taste*, etc..See above under AUBIN, **1125**.

Examines *Love in Excess* in detail (42-49). Most of Haywood's characters show more than one side, and possess more than one quality. The women are the truly loving characters here, while the male character is immoral, denying the possibility of love, and looking for his own pleasure. Instead of rakishness, she describes weakness. She uses the romance patterns of the life at court, the stage of lonely peril, grief and exertion, and the final stage where heart and object are joined. The only thing that has changed is the nature of the adventures. The demands made on the hero are more domesticated: he has to prove his virtue as a loving man. Haywood provided the most comprehensive treatment of women characters in the period, achieving popularity and influencing others.

1572 FIELDS, Polly Stevens. "High drama at the Little Theatre, 1730-1737: Henry Fielding, Eliza Haywood, Charlotte Clarke, and company." Unpub. doct. diss., Louisiana State Univ. and Agricultural and Mechanical College, 1992. [*DA* 54 (1993): 530-1A.]

Staging works unaccepted and unacceptable to the establishment, Fielding, Haywood, Clarke and company produced a series of protest dramas at the Little Theatre in the Haymarket between 1730 and 1737. The playwrights deliberately ruptured theater tradition and boldly presented plays challenging not only the mainstream theater, but also the current social system. They used both tragedy and comedy to enlarge the province of the drama to include the ordinary human with real problems. In this way they displaced the aristocratic concept of the theater based on class distinction, and brought in its place a realistic appraisal of systematic exclusion by class and gender.

1573 GIBSON, Suzanne. "The eighteenth-century Oriental tales of Eliza Haywood, Frances Sheridan and Ellis Cornelia Knight." Unpub. doct. diss., McMaster Univ., 1996. [*DA* 58 (1997): 2224A.]

Oriental tales were very popular in the 18c, a fact which has been ignored until recently. Women contributed to this popular but marginalized form. Looks at Haywood's *Adventures of Eovaai*, Frances Sheridan's *History of Nourjahad*, and concludes with Ellis Cornelia Knight's *Dinarbas: a Tale, being a continuation of Rasselas, Prince of Abissinia*. Follows the use of the domestic woman in the decidedly undomestic Oriental Tale as these authors negotiate genre, their culture and gender through the writing of these tales. They represent an opposing voice to developing literary realism so beloved of the middle-classes. Capitalism relies not only on an ethic of saving, generally associated with realism, but also on an ethic of spending. These tales contain sumptuous description and luxury, reinforce expenditure with women absolutely central in the development and construction of their culture through their writing and through their gender associated with consumption.

1574 HICKS, Stephen J. "Eliza Haywood's technique in three early novels (1721-27)." *PLL* 34:4 (1998): 420-36.

Haywood's work in the epistolary form proved pivotal to the development of prose fiction. Analyzes three works (the translated *Letters from a Lady of Quality to a Chevalier* [1721], *Bath-Intrigues* [1725], *Philadore and Placentia* [1727]) to show that Haywood had the narrative acuity of other canonical authors, and further developed the novel by using the letter format in varying ways in different works, manipulating the technique in a manner beyond any contemporary prose writer. She possessed ingenuity and perspective, and formed her material to help the varied needs of a popular prose writer. Without her, the development of the epistolary novel would not have been so advanced when Richardson decided to adopt the form in the late 1730s.

1575 HOLLIS, Karen. "Eliza Haywood and the gender of print." *ECent* 38:1 (1997): 43-62.

Haywood has been relegated by critical posterity to a decidedly third place in the 'fair Triumvirate'. Her work continues to occupy an indeterminate place in the literary market, shifting between her early amatory and later moral fiction, between popular and academic editions. She would have been the first to appreciate the significance of this public history, since her extraordinarily long-lived and multifaceted career is marked by an extended engagement with the sexual politics of private and public writing, with the cultural values associated with script and print. Acutely aware that gendered forms of power are at issue not only within the text, but also in the world of textual production and circulation, her texts and her publishing strategies continually interrogate relations between gender, genre, the marketplace, and the politics of literary reputation.

1576 INGRASSIA, Catherine. "Additional information about Eliza Haywood's arrest for seditious libel." *NQ* 44:2 (1997): 202-4.

Haywood's level of involvement in the material aspects of production, the frequency and intensity of her political writings, are certainly greater than previously realized. She had a complicated and sustained relationship with other booksellers as a distributor of politically oriented publications, and a reputation as a political writer.

1577------"Fashioning female authorship of Eliza Haywood's *The Tea Table*." *JNT* 28:3 (1998): 287-304.

Haywood's *The Tea Table* (1725) interrogates the binaries of public and private spheres, male and female writers, authors and 'scribblers'. She made the culturally distinct categories of woman writer and professional author reinforcing rather than mutually exclusive, and constructed a specific hybrid - the professional *female* author. She made this gesture in various texts, but *The Tea Table* particularly deserves attention because of its commentary on contemporaneous literary discourses, its renegotiation of gendered literary space, and its interrogation of the public and private spheres.

1578 KIM, Elizabeth Sungeun. "Exploiting rape: women's literary representations of rape in early eighteenth-century prose fiction."etc., **566**.

1579 KING, Kathryn R. "Spying upon the conjurer: Haywood, curiosity, and 'the novel' in the 1720s." *StudN* 30:2 (1998): 178-93.

Seeks to complicate the merging feminist storyline of novel-writing by returning to one of its original sources. Circulating scandal was woman's work, as it was woman's matter. Behn, Manley and Haywood wrote during a moment of troubling, if ill-understood, cultural change, change bound up with the new culture of print, new ideologies of gender, new ways of commodifying literature. Their fictions, obsessed with things indecorous, smutty and impertinently inquisitive, delivered new kinds of reading pleasure and bred new kinds of irreverently curious readers. Haywood's scandalous fiction, and more particularly her *A Spy upon the Conjurer* (1724-25), may have done the dirty work of scripting for her generation its worst scenario about where reading, writing and women were going.

1580 LEICHT, Kathleen Ann. "Cross-gender narrative in the early English novel," **611**.

1581 MACEY, J. David Jr. "'Where the world may ne'er invade'? Green retreats and garden theater in *La Princesse de Clèves, The History of Miss Betsy Thoughtless*, and *Cecilia*." *ECF* 12:1 (1999): 75-100.

The bower scene provides Mme. de Lafayette, Haywood and Burney with a unique opportunity to explore the complex interplay of desire, duty, and self-consciousness in their heroines' lives because of the bower's ambiguous position at the intersection of the domains of 'nature' and 'culture'. The bower or summer house play an important part in the process of mediation because it is neither 'inside' nor 'outside', and therefore figures in both the domestic and extramural affairs of the household.

1582 NELSON, T. G. A. "Stooping to conquer in Goldsmith, Haywood and

Wycherley." *EC* 46:6 (1996): 319-39.

Several characteristics of the type of man described by Freud prove applicable to the Restoration rake, like compulsive repetition, or the preference of married women as love objects. A radical 'stooping' is carried out by the protagonist of *Fantomina* (1725), a novella by Haywood that Goldsmith may have known. Here in a story written half a century earlier than *She Stoops to Conquer*, the shadowy, sinister, unrealized intrigue which lurks behind Goldsmith's play is plainly visible.

1583 NESTOR, Deborah Jean. "Women's discourse and the constructions of the English novel, from Eliza Haywood to Jane Austen." Unpub. doct. diss., Univ. of California (Los Angeles), 1993. [*DA* 54 (1994): 3044A.]

Neither of the two most notable attempts to construct a history of 18c fiction offers a paradigm that can adequately account for the rise of the English novel. McKeon hardly questions the limited canon mapped out by his predecessor Watt. Nestor wishes to show that the English novel rose out of 18c women's discourse. Women through their authorship of plays, periodicals and novels, created a discursive sphere in which they addressed issues affecting the domestic space of private life. These women also developed the complex narrative structures Bakhtin later identified in the dialogue novel. Haywood is central here: her novels show development of the novel from the racy romances of the 17c to a form whose stated purpose is to reocommend bourgeois morality. She structures her later works around a covert resistance to this new fictional model, and interpolates anti-Richardsonian tales within larger structures. She reveals how from being a form which enables women to create powerful fantasies, the novel begins to serve as a conduct book. Austen's playful ambivalence towards all social ideologies is a direct inheritance from 18c women's discourse.

1584-----"Representing domestic difficulties: Eliza Haywood and the critique of bourgeois ideology." *Prose Studies* 16:2 (1993): 1-26.

The Female Spectator was popular enough to be reprinted in a collection that went through nine editions between 1746 and 1775. Haywood's periodical problematizes the notion that women who follow the patterns of virtuous behavior established by social authorities will be rewarded with positions of authority and power within their own households. She continued this critique in texts like *The Wife* (1756) and *The Husband* (1756), works she attributed to her Female Spectator Club. Although she never openly opposed the ideology of marriage presented by her influential predecessors (Addison and Steele), she does reveal the difficulties it creates for women, and the novelistic form she uses to present this perspective enables her to reveal the unresolvable complexities that arise out of woman's paradoxical role as the powerless center of the domestic sphere. Extensive bibliographic notes.

1585 OAKLEAF, David. "The eloquence of blood in Eliza Haywood's *Lasselia.*" *SELit* 39:3 (1999): 483-98.

In *Lasselia* (1723) Haywood places blood at the center of her text. She insists that blood embodies private desire as well as public lineage, maternal labor as well as paternal honor, intimacy as well as ambition. In the blood, patrilineal constraint struggles with individual sexual desire as the body defies gender constraints on female assertion. By recovering the significance of blood for the early 18c writers, we can feel the historical contradictions out of which emerged the novel and the characteristically modern sexual relationships it often represents.

1586 PITCHER, E. W. "The reprinting of Eliza Haywood's stories in *The Weekly Entertainer.*" *NQ* 42:1 (1995): 73-75.

Provides a list of 17 shorter fictions by Haywood published in Sherbourne's *Weekly Entertainer* (1783-1819). Aside from instalment reprinting of four of her translations of Mme de Gomez, the magazine spread her fiction over 30 instalments between the third and 136th numbers (1783-85), a deliberate and extraordinary concentration.

1587 PRESCOTT, S. H. "Feminist literary theory and British women novelists of the 1720s" etc. See above under AUBIN, **1127.**

1588   RICHARDS, Cynthia. "'The Pleasure of Complicity': sympathetic identification of the female reader in early eighteenth-century women's amatory fiction." *ECent* 36:3 (1995): 220-33.

Women's amatory fiction offers a version of identification and alliance which a reliance on modes of sameness and difference tends to obscure. The possibilities of female identification were always structurally overdetermined and politically volatile. In the 18c this overdetermination often took the form of a still familiar binary: women were endowed with an unregulated sensibility, a passive and presumably automatic display of sentiment, against which an active, socially useful and 'masculine' sympathy was increasingly defined. Haywood's novel *The British Recluse* (1722) is remarkable for being one of the very few early novels 'resolved through the friendship of women', and thus one of the very few suggestive of sustaining connections between women. It promotes an identification between women that is neither painful nor alienating.

1589 RICHETTI, John J. "Amatory fiction: Behn, Manley, Haywood." In (pp. 18-51) *The English novel in history, 1700-1780*, **806**.

There is a sophisticated self-consciousness about the moral and social relevance of fictional extravagance in the spirited novellas of Behn, Manley and Haywood, a current of subversive intelligence which offers readers a pertinent commentary. Feminist criticism has illuminated this aspect of English amatory fiction by finding in the works of the 'Fair Triumvirate of Wit' a political resistance to masculine constructions of the feminine. There is a gendered struggle over interpretation, as a competition between men and women for control of the means of seduction becomes the central theme. Male (and sometimes female) seducers present sexual passion as a liberation, a reproach to the unnatural constraints of society and religion. But even at its most lubricous, the amatory novel often exposes such libertine rhetoric as a rationalization for exploitative sexuality which is ultimately related to male domination and privilege. Behn's mixture of romantic subtext and cynical worldliness sets a tone for such fiction that endured in her most famous successors, Manley and Haywood. Manley, in opposing the libertine personality and its innocent victim, offers a pattern that articulates a new and disturbing reality in the political climate of the time. Haywood's fiction shifted from the exposure of moral imbalance in the upper reaches of society and the spectacle of suffering innocence, to the exaltation of female passion, which is almost invariably provoked by restrictive circumstances in a social sphere in which men and women have nothing to do but desire one another in unsanctioned or illicit ways. Haywood's romances discard the lingering resonance of romance and nostalgia; and ironic disparagement of the present, such as Behn and Manley exploit, is exchanged for the focused immediacy of sex and suffering. In spite of the superficial exoticism of her stories, she provokes the present, the here and now with a new vividness.

1590 STARR, G. Gabrielle. "Rereading prose fiction: lyric convention in Aphra Behn and Eliza Haywood." *ECF* 12:1 (1999): 1-18.

Writers such as Behn and Haywood sought ways to accomplish the affective dimensions of their narratives, the substantial affinity between the province of the lyric and the demands of their writing led them to the use of lyric conventions. In *Love in Excess* (1719) Haywood reinterprets the metaphysical tradition of amatory poetry, esp. that of Donne, to create her own figures of emotional excess. She uses lyric implications in her novels, expanding upon usual use of lyric in letters as a first-person form to suffuse entire scenes with sensual power.

1591 WARNER, William B. "Formulating fiction: romancing the general reader in early modern Britain." In (pp. 279-305) LYNCH, Deirdre and WARNER, William B. (eds). *Cultural institutions of the novel.* Durham, NC and London: Duke UP, 1996; pp. vi, 488.

The 'hegemonic account' of the rise of the novel loses out by disregarding the 18c vogue for the novels of amorous intrigue authored by Behn, Manley and Haywood which began in the 1680s and culminated in the institution of formula fiction in the early 1720s. This alternative 'institution' of another kind of novel precedes, and helps to motivate the cultural elevation of the novel in Britain in the 1740s around the reception of Richardson and Fielding. But this later 'finally hegemonic' institution of the novel erases the earlier novel and coopts and detours the reading pleasures it had defined. The new formula fiction of Haywood achieved its distinctive popularity and scandal by appealing not to any particular kind of reader, but the 'general reader' -- those not limited in scope. The popularity of her bestseller depended on her formulation of fiction with traits appealing to this general reader.

1592 WILPUTTE, Earla A. "The textual architecture of Eliza Haywood's *Adventures of Eovaai.*" *ELit* 22:1 (1995): 31-44.

This is a hybrid novel in which political satire, woman's romance, imaginary voyage, oriental fantasy and semi-pornography are incorporated in a "wild blend of genres" to accentuate the fragmentation of traditional hierarchical government and to exploit the analogy between sexual and party politics. It manifests a concern for exposing social and sexual injustices from many perspectives, and emphasizes this through the use of many genres and editorial intrusions This invites a questioning and a critique of governmental and social authority (playing on the idea of author-ity), with various 'editors' of the text (author, translator, commentator, historian and 'cabal') depicted at odds, and the reader left to formulate his own conclusions. This fascinating format includes a literal subtext in the form of footnotes. Despite this unique narratological form, previous criticism has focused only on specific, esp. feminist, themes within the novel.

1593-----"Wife pandering in three eighteenth-century plays." *SELit* 38:3 (1998): 447-64.
Behn, Haywood and Fielding employ wife-pandering to expose the political, social and personal crimes of their era. More than feminist

statements about the injustices of marriage, these plays show how the willingness to sell something which one has in principle agreed to protect and care for manifest a darker urge in society to sacrifice anything for money. All three use this titillating image to comment on politcal and social irresponsibility and the declining power of the individual to combat it or to make a difference.

HEARNE, Mary

1. *The lover's week: or the six days adventures of Philander and Amaryllis* (1718, 1718, 1720 [in *Honour the victory and love the prize*], 1724 [serialized in the *Original London Post*]; pp. 56)

   NCBEL II 988[5]; McBurney 90; ECSTC 1459H2
   Epistolary autobiographical tale; excellent characterization.

2. *The female deserters. A novel. By the author of the lover's week* (1719, 1720 [with *The lover's week*], 1731 [in *A collection of curious novels*]; pp. 109)

   NCBEL II 988[15]; McBurney 104; ECSTC 1459H1
   Sequel to *The lover's week*. Inserted histories.

EDITIONS

1594 *The lover's week.* Ed. WÜRZBACH. In (pp. 65-90) *The novel in letters* etc., **149**.
Introd. (67). Typical example of a hybrid between autobiographical narrative and epistolary story.

'JOHNSON, Capt Charles'

1. *A general history of the robberies and murders of the most notorious pyrates* (1724, 1724; 6 edns by 1734 [combined with SMITH'S *History of highwaymen*, 1713]; pp. 17-320)

   NCBEL II 990[14]; McBurney 164; ECSTC 724J1
   Often reissued adapted and abridged.

2. *The history of the life and intrigues of that celebrated courtezan and posture-mistress, Eliz. Mann* (1724, pp.49)

NCBEL II 990[15]; McBurney 165
Hack biography hastily compiled; plagiarism from jestbooks.

STUDIES

1595 BARNES, J. Paul. "The life of Charles Johnson (1679-1748)." *NQ* 35:2 (June 1988): 183-84.

Details of life are scarce and ambiguous. Several of his 17 plays (1709-32) were succesful. He had a legal training and exercised the profession in the decades before he started writing plays in earnest. On his retirement he set up a tavern in Bow Street.

1596 RYMER, Michael. "Another source for Smollett's Lismahago." *NQ* 21 (1974): 57-59.

The influence of the adventurer Robert Strabo on Lieutenent Obadiah Lismahago in *Humphrey Clinker* was supplemented by Smollett's reading of a popular contemporary novel, *Chrysal, Or The Adventures of a Guinea* (1760-65) by Charles Johnson, in which there appears a character whose adventures among the American Indians are markedly similar to those Lismahago.

L., S.

The amours of Philaris and Olinda: or the intrigues of Windsor (1730; also undated edn as *Windsor tales*; pp. 70)

NCBEL II 992[17]; McBurney 246; ECSTC 66L5
Short romance in domestic setting; inserted letters.

LA CHAPELLE, Jean de

The adventures of Catullus, and history of his amours with Lesbia (1707, 1708; pp. 400)

NCBEL II 986[15]; MacBurney 30; ECSTC 111L1
Trans. of romanticized biographical novel of 1680-81, interspersed with CATULLUS'S poems.

LEDIARD, Thomas

The German spy, in familiar letters (1738, 1740; pp. 436)

> NCBEL II 994[15]; McBurney 326; ECSTC 965L1
> Said to be a trans.; more likely Lediard's own letters, enlarged and including anecdotes and fiction.

———

LEGUAT, François

See **MISSON, François**

———

LE NOBLE, Eustache, Baron de Saint Georges et de Tennelière

1. *Abra-Mulé: or a true history of the dethronement of Mahomet IV* (1696, pp. 132)

> WING L1051; NCBEL II 983[16]
> Trans. 'J.P.' from *Abra-Mulé*.
> Romanticized oriental history.

2. *Pure love, a novel: being the history of the Princess Zulima* (1718, 1719 [as *Zulima*], 1725, 1750 [as *Pure love*]; pp. 257)

> NCBEL II 988[6]; McBurney 91
> Trans. 'M.B.' from *Zulima*, 1694 or 1718.
> Sentimental novel in the French historical mode.

3. *Ildegerte, Queen of Norway; or, Heroick Love, a novel. Written originally in French by the author of the Happy Slave and tr. into Eng. by a gentleman of Oxford* (1721, 1722; 2 pts, 1-56 + 3-166)

> NCBEL II 989[10]; McBurney 124; Morgan 506; ECSTC 1233L5
> Trans. John CAVENDISH from *Histoire de d'Ildegerte*, 1695.
> Romanticized history, ultimately derived from Saxo Grammaticus.

———

LE SAGE, Alain René

1. *Le Diable boiteux: or the Devil upon two sticks* (1708; 6th edn 1729; numerous edns through the century; pp. 278)

NCBEL II 986[2]; McBurney 38; ECSTC 1318L1
Early example of non-human spy genre.

2. *The history and adventures of Gil Blas of Santillane* (1716; 5 edns by 1744 [2-4 vols], n.p.)

NCBEL II 988[1]; McBurney 85; ECSTC 1314L1
Trans. of *Histoire de Gil Blas* (1715-35); superseded by SMOLLETT'S trans., 1749.

3. *The bachelor of Salamanca: or memoirs of Don Cherubim de la Ronda* (1737-9, 1767, Dublin 1784; 2 vols, pp. 259)

NCBEL II 994[13]; McBurney 324; ECSTC 1316L1
Picaresque.

SELECTED STUDIES

1597 BENSADON, Michel Emile. "Transformations of the self in the European picaresque novel: *Guzman de Alfarache, Moll Flanders, Gil Blas de Santillane*" etc., **231**.

1598 KENT, John P. "Smollett's translation of *Gil Blas*: a question of text." *ELN* 5 (1967): 21-26.

Smollett inevitably based his translation on the 1732-37 version of *Gil Blas*. Whether he had the 1747 revised version to hand, and for aesthetic reasons preferred the earlier, is not possible to ascertain. He may have spent longer on the translation than is thought.

1599 KNAPP, Lewis Mansfield. "Smollett and Le Sage's *The Devil upon Crutches*." *MLN* 47 (1932): 91-3.

Whether Smollett had a hand in this version published for J. Osborn in 1750 is rather a matter of conjecture. There are similarities between this translation and Smollett's *Gil Blas*, a considerable freedom in transposing ideas from French into English. There is also a good chance that Smollett was responsible for the first appearance of the translation which he corrected some 10 years later.

1600 MYLNE, Vivienne. "Structure and symbolism in *Gil Blas*." *French Stud* 15 (1961): 134-45.

The twin issues of form and significance seem likely to push *Gil Blas* back among the novels which are read only as part of literary history. The book does nonetheless have a timeless and universal quality: Lesage has zest, vigour and gaiety, incisive wit and a keen eye for the foibles of humanity. He can make the most of a short story.

1601 SAGARRA, Eda. "*Gil Blas*: Geschichte und Abenteuer eines Romanhelden auf dem europäischen Buchmarkt." In (pp. 1-15) FRÜHWALD, Wolfgang; MARTINO, Alberto; FISCHER, Ernst and HEYDEMANN, Klaus (eds). *Zwischen Aufklärung und Restauration: sozialer Wandel in der deutschen Literatur (1700-1848).* (STSL 24.) Tübingen: Niemeyer, 1989; pp. x, 471.

Traces the history and imitations of the work into the mid-19c."*Gil Blas* ist aber nicht nur als ein Roman der Weltliteratur Lieblingswerk von Autoren vom Rang eines Stendhal oder Scott bekannt, sondern auch Gegenstand langwieriger Kontroversen, die weit über die Nationalgrenzen hinausreichen" (1). "Gerade das, so könnte man mit Scott meinen, haben nun die neuen Leserschichten durch die Begegnung mit einer ihnen fremden Welt in ihrer Lektüre der Gilblasiaden erreichen dürfen" (15).

1602 WILLIAMS, Ioan. "Le Sages's *Further Adventures*; the Failure of *Gil Blas*". In (pp. 133-36) *The idea of the novel* etc., **147**.

—

LOCATELLI, Francesco

Lettres moscovites: or Muscovian letters (1736, pp. 190)

NCBEL II 994[9]; McBurney 317; ECSTC 2184L1
Trans. William MUSGRAVE.
11 long letters of travel and adventure in Russia, mingling facts and fiction.

—

LONGUEVILLE, Peter

The hermit: or the unparalleled sufferings and surprising adventures of Mr Philip Quarll, an Englishman (1727 [2 versions]; 13 edns by 1800; pp. 264)

NCBEL II 991[19]; McBurney 216; ECSTC 3022L1
Highly successful exploitation of the Crusoe idea; extreme variety of adventures; many versions, including chap-book abridgements.

STUDIES

1603   HARKINS, Patricia. "From *Robinson Crusoe* to *Philip Quarll*: the transformation of a Robinsonade." *POMPA* (1988): 64-73.

The Hermit was one of the most successful imitations (or 'Robinsonades') to appear in the wake of the vast success of Defoe's novel. It is similar in theme to *Robinson Crusoe*, but different in spirit. Its preface analyzes popular trends in literature, criticizing Defoe for appealing to vulgar taste, and maintains that the book is merely an edition of the papers of Philip Quarll, an island recluse. This article gives an account of the plot and an analysis of Longueville's originality, esp. his three-dimensional characterizations, earthy depictions of London life, and imaginative recreation of an island setting which secured the novel popularity for over a hundred years. Indeed in its more limited history of imitation and adaptation, it again paralleled Defoe's more famous work. Also examines the importance of *The Hermit* for children's literature, in relation to the influence of *Robinson Crusoe* on Rousseau and his theories of education propounded in *Emile*.   The latter saw mankind and childhood as corrupted by the artificialities of society, and would remove the child from the malign influences of urban life and bring him up in rural seclusion. Maintains that Quarll realizes this idea more fully than Crusoe. Also investigates the sharp decline in the popularity of Longueville's novel in the mid-19c, and its total neglect in the 20c. Detailed notes and bibliography (71-73).

———

LUSSAN, Marguerite de

The life of the Countess de Gondez (1729, pp. 279)

NCBEL II 992[10]; McBurney 245; Morgan 593; ECSTC 3466L2
Trans. Penelope AUBIN.
Adventure and morality.

———

LYLY, John

Euphues and Lucilla: or the false friend and inconstant mistress (1716; 5 edns by 1732; n.p.)

NCBEL II 988[2]; ECSTC 3539L2
Modernized version, rewritten and recast, of *Euphues* (1578).

STUDIES

1604 HARNER, James L. 1) *English Renaissance prose fiction, 1500-1600: an annotated bibliography.* (Reference Publications in Literature.) Boston, MA: G. K. Hall, 1978. pp. xxiv, 556; 2) *English Renaissance prose fiction: an annotated bibliography, 1500-1660 (1976-1983).* Boston: G. K. Hall, 1985, pp. xxi, 228; 3) *English Renaissance bibliography, 1500-1660 (1984-1990)* (New York: G. K. Hall and London: Maxwell Macmillan International, 1992), pp. ix, 185.

Comprehensive annotated bibliography of editions and studies with updates to 1990:
1) Nos. 1767-1980 (pp. 287-320);
2) Nos. 515-587 (pp.104-17);
3) Nos. 336-375 (pp. 78-86).

———

LYTTLETON, George, Baron

Letters from a Persian in England to his friend at Ispahan (1735 [4 edns]; spurious continuation in the same year, as *The Persian letters continued*; at least 11 edns by 1800; pp. 254)

NCBEL II 994[1]; McBurney 299; Morgan 632; ECSTC 3610L10
Influential, much imitated; foreign commentator on English institutions derived from Montesquieu, *Lettres persanes.*

STUDIES

1605 BLUNT, Reginald. *Thomas Lord Lyttleton: The portrait of a rake, with a brief memoir of his sister, Lucy Lady Valentine. With an introduction by Maud Wyndham.* London: Hutchinson, 1936; pp. 288.

Account of the life of Lyttleton based on his voluminous correspondence with Elizabeth Montague. Nine appendices are of special interest: pedigree, the Lyttleton letters, the epistle to the Clentiles, the Libertine Macaroni, Pitt Place, Epsom, Wraxall's account of Lyttleton's death, the gaming clubs, the Angelsey peerage, Lyttleton and Junius. Bibliography (276-78). Index. Illustrations.

1606 DAVIS, Rose Mary. *The good Lord Lyttleton: A study in eighteenth-century politics and culture.* Columbia Univ. diss. Bethlehem, PA: Times Publishing Co., 1939; pp. ix, 442.

Study covering Lyttleton's political and literary activities, and related to both, his activities as a man of letters (with regard to Fielding, *Tom Jones*; Thomson's *The Seasons*). Divided into four parts: 1) "Preparartions for Life (1709-30)"; 2) "In the Opposition (1735-44)"; 3) "In the Government (1744-56)"; 4) "In the House of Lords (1756-73)". Appendices (406-15). Bibliography (416-32).

1607 OLNEY, Clark. "Lucy revisited.' *NQ* 103 (1958): 538-40.

Wordsworth's Lucy perhaps inspired by Lyttleton's 'Monody' in memory of his wife Lucy Fortescue.

1608 RAO, Ananda Vittal. *A minor Augustan: Being the life and works of George, Lord Lyttleton, 1709-1773*. Calcutta: The Book Company, Ltd., 1934; pp. viii, 387. 5 illus.

Gives a complete account of Lyttleton's career, both political and literary, and of his friendships with, and patronage of, men of letters, as well as an examination of his works. Covers early life, Oxford (1726 to 1728), the Grand Tour (1728 to 1730), entry into politics (1730 to 1735) and *The Persian Letters*, opposition politics (1735 to 1742) and marriage, literary friendships, the 'Monody' and other poems (1743 to 1750), Shenstone and landscape gardening politics (1750 to 1760), the antipathy of Smollett and Johnson, more friendships, the blue stockings, the tour to Wales, 'The Dialogues of the Dead', 'The History of King Henry II', last days, personal features and character. Bibliography (335-62). Selections from unpublished works (363-68). Index (369-87). Of particular pertinence is the detailed discussion of *The Persian Letters* (70-82).

1609 ROBERTS, S. C. "An eighteenth-century gentleman." *London Mercury* 11 (1925): 290-97.

Brief and entertaining acount of Lyttleton's life and work. He emerges as "the idealised Whig" with a real enthusiasm for literature, a power of oratory, a genuin piety. He was awkward, angular, lacking a sense of humour, and fell short of greatness, "a blend of Horace Walpole and the Prince Consort" (297).

1610 TODD, William B. "Patterns in press figures: a study of Lyttleton's 'Dialogues of the Dead'." *SB* 8 (1956): 230-35.

Three distinct editions of Lyttleton's 'Dialogues' (1760) were all printed in less than a week. He and his printer, Samuel Richardson, accomplished this miracle, the book being a testimony to their remarkable achievement.

———

MADDEN, Samuel

Memoirs of the twentieth century: being original letters of state under George the Sixth (1733, 1763 [as *The reign of George VI*]; pp. 527)

NCBEL II 993[12]; McBurney 284; ECSTC 610M5
Satire against George II and his Court; 6 vols were projected, but it was suppressed after vol. 1.

STUDIES

1611 STRACHAN, L. R. M. "'Words are daughters of the earth'." *NQ* 183 (1942) 27.
About Dr Johnson and Sam Madden, whose verse Johnson may have revised. Perhaps it stuck in Johnson 's memory and so contributed to the new phrasing in the Preface to the *Dictionary* (1755).

———

MANLEY, Mary Delarivière

1. *Letters written by Mrs Manley, to which is added a letter from a suppos'd nun in Portugal* (1696, 1713, 1725 [as *A stage coach journey to Exeter*], 1735 [in *Mr Pope's literary correspondence*]; pp. 88)

   WING M434; NCBEL II 983[17]; ECSTC 923M9
   Lively account of a journey, imitating Mme D'AULNOY'S methods and based on actual correspondence; itself much imitated in the following decades.

2. *The secret history of Queen Zara and the Zarazians* (1705; 5 edns by 1749; pp. 119)

   NCBEL II 985[7]; McBurney 18; Morgan 436; ECSTC 923M14
   Sensational account of Sarah, Duchess of Marlborough. French trans. in 1708)

3. *A lady's pacquet of letters, taken from her by a French privateer in her passage to Holland* (1707, 1708; [pt 1, pbd with D'AULNOY, *Memoirs of the Court of England*; pt 2, pbd with D'AULNOY, *History of the Earl of Warwick*]; 1711 [complete, 41 letters, as *Court Intrigues*; pp. 220)

NCBEL II 985[16]; McBurney 26; ECSTC 923M8
Epistolary fiction of several varieties, excellent technique.

4. *Secret memoirs and manners of several persons of quality of both sexes from the new Atalantis* (1709; at least 7 edns by 1736; pp. 246)

NCBEL II 986[7]; McBurney 45; Morgan 459; ECSTC 923M15
Alleged secrets of numerous contemporary notables; the archetypal scandal novel; highly popular.

5. *Memoirs of Europe, towards the close of the eighth century. Written by Eginhardus, secretary and favourite to Charlemagne* (1710, 1711 etc, 1720 [with *The New Atalantis* as *Secret Memoir*]; 7th edn by 1736; pp. 380)

NCBEL II 986[10]; McBurney 51; Morgan 463; ECSTC 923M21
Continuation of a scandal-chronicle of contemporary personages.

6. *The adventures of Rivella; or the history of the Author of the Atalantis [...]. Delivered in a conversation to the young Chevalier D'Aumont [...] by Sir Charles Lovemore. Done into English from the Fr.* (1714, 1717, 1725; pp. 120)

NCBEL II 988[9]; McBurney 72; Morgan 474; ECSTC 923M4
Lively fictionalized autobiography; secret history, scandal.

7. *The power of love, in seven novels, viz., I, The Fair Hypocrite; II, the Physician's Strategem; III, The Wife's Resentment; IV-V, The Husband's Resentment in two examples; VI, The Happy Fugitive, VII, The Perjur'd Beauty* (1720, 1741; pp. 368)

NCBEL II 989[3]; McBurney 115; Morgan 503; ECSTC 923M12
Free adaptations from BANDELLO, perhaps from versions in William PAINTER'S collection of translations, *Palace of pleasure* (1566, 1567, 1575).

EDITIONS

1612 'Letter 33' ("From a lady to a lady") from *A lady's pacquet of letters*. Ed. WÜRZBACH in (pp. 37-52) *The novel in letters* etc., **149**.

Introd. (39-40). "The care with which Mrs Manley motivates her characters and interprets their actions goes far beyond anything we find in most of her fiction."

1613 *The secret history of Queen Zarah.* Preface ed. BOYCE in *Prefaces to fiction* etc. See ANTHOLOGIES, Ch.2, **121**.

1614   *The Secret History of Queen Zarah and the Zarazians.* Ed. BACKSCHEIDER and RICHETTI in (pp. 45-80) *Popular fiction by women, 1660-1730: an anthology* etc.See ANTHOLOGIES, Ch. 2, **119**.

BIBLIOGRAPHY

1615 SAAR, Doreen Alvarez. "Manley, Delarivière." In (pp. 360-90) SAAR and SCHOFIELD, *Eighteenth-century Anglo-American women novelists: a critical reference guide* etc., **93**..

Annotated criticism from 1900 to 1992 (168 items).

SELECTED PRE-1992 STUDIES

1616 ANDERSON, Paul Bunyan. "Delarivière Manley's prose fiction." *PQ* 13 (1934): 168-88.

Queen Anne's redoubtable defender, and the most representative professional figure among Englishwomen who first tried to make a living by literature, has been left in the obscurity of her scandalous reputation. The article provides extensive 5-part investigation of Manley's autobiogrpahical *Adventures of Rivella*. This is an open self-glorification, but it provides an exact picture of her mind in its naïve candour, its untrained ignorance, and its eagerness to gain masculine approval. Beneath the alluring surface of her narratives lies a structure of objective fact. Extensive examinations of life and work with full footnotes.

1617-----"Mistress Delarivière Manley's biography." *MP* 33 (1936): 261-78.

Examines life and works of the first English woman to achieve success in a general literary career as a courageous feminist pioneer. As a practitioner of prose fiction she also deserves honor as a pioneer. The restricted range of her subject matter and situations was as much a heritage from traditional fiction as her own fault. As a contriver of attractive prose fiction, certainly not as a moralist, she found it expedient to add to the salacious appeal of her material, the interest of intimate psychology, of subtler nature, of unusual detail. Although ill-trained, she had a technique and a personal vision which transformed the life she knew into the pattern she wanted for it. If she failed to write a real novel, she contributed to the means at her disposal of her successors and gave them an audience.

1618-----"The historical authorship of Mrs Crackenthorpe's *Female Tatler*." *MP* 28 (1931): 354-60.

"*The Female Tatler*, by Mrs Crackenthorpe, a Lady that knows every thing" was the most vigorous rival of the *Tatler* and appeared on 8 July 1709. With humour, impudence and dignity, she maintained her *Female Tatler*, not as an imitation, but as the counterpart to its masculine contemporary. The original Mrs Crackenthorpe was Mrs Manley. For further light on the spurious *Female Tatler* see R. T. MILFORD *MP* 29 (1932): 350-51. There were 26 numbers of Thomas Baker's rival paper. The Bodleian Library (Hope fol.91) has a complete set of both the original and rival *Female Tatlers*.

1619 ANON., "Sunderland v. Manley." *Factotum* 21 (1985): 22-23.

Politicians of the early 18c were much exercised as to the best means of dealing with the frequent attacks launched against them by party journalists. But most of them found that of all the methods available, direct legal prosecutions was the most futile. The actions taken by the Whigs against Mrs Manley after the publication of her notorious *roman à clef*, the *New Atalantis*, was a case in point. Lord Sutherland, the Whig Secretary of State, achieved little by his interrogation of Mrs Manley, who with her publisher had been taken into custody for her scandalous revelations concerning the private lives of the leading Whigs. He succeeded only in furnishing her with some excellent copy for her autobiographical novel, *The Adventures of Rivella*, which appeared some years later. She was bailed almost at once, and undaunted by her subsequent appearance before the Court of Queen's Bench, set to work at once on a sequel to the *New Atalantis*.

1620 BLOOM, Edward A. and BLOOM, Lilian D. "Steele and his answerers: May 1709-February 1714." In (pp. 167-97) WHITE, Robert B., Jr. (ed.). *The dress of words: essays in honour of Richmond P. Bond* etc., **1046**.

Mrs Manley sketched Steels's portrait in the first volume of *The New Atalantis* (1709), just a month after the *Tatler* came to London. Steele may have been selected for punishment because of his performance as gazeteer, or he may have been a last minute choice, Mrs Manley's answer to the threat of the *Tatler*, which burst upon the capital with its satires of easily indentifiable persons.

1621 CLARK, Constance. "The Female Wits: Catherine Trotter, Delarivière Manley, and Mary Pix -- three women playwrights who made their debuts in the London season of 1695-6." Unpub. doct. diss., City Univ.

of New York, 1984. [*DA* 45 (1984): 19A.]

The three women in question were prolific professional writers, Trotter had five plays produced and published, Manley four and Pix twelve. Each published in other genres as well. Their biographies are presented, their plays analyzed, and other works discussed. Sources and influences, including that of their predecessor Aphra Behn, are considered. An evaluation is made of each of these writers' place in the theater of their times, and their influence upon the English drama of the 18c.

1622-----*Three Augustan women playwrights.* (American Univ. Studies, 4; Anglo-Saxon Language and Literature, 40.) New York; Bern; Frankfurt: Lang, 1986; pp. 355.

Investigation of Catherine Trotter, Mary Pix, Delarivière Manley, Mary Rich, "The Female Wits". The women playwrights of the Restoration have been grouped together as 'minor' writers and perhaps doomed to be ignored because of their alleged mediocrity. They can be assessed only as more is brought to light about them as individuals, and about their differing degrees and areas of talent. Whatever their individual merits, they will always be grouped together because it was as a group that they were a phenomenon in the London season of 1695-96. Bibliography (335-48).

1623   DAY, Robert Adams. "Muses in the mud: the Female Wits anthropologically considered." *Women's Studies* 7:3 (1980) 61-74.

Although Pix, Manley, Trotter and Behn possessed very considerable talent, and each wrote in several genres enough to fill 2 stout volumes, none was able to attain the combination of a comfortable living, a respectable status in society, fame, or general recognition of merit in literary circles. For a woman to earn her living by a profession which was new and unclassified was therefore taboo.

1624   DUFF, Dolores Diane Clark. "Materials toward a biography of Mary Delarivière Manley." Unpub. doct. diss., Univ. of Indiana, 1966. [*DA* 26 (1966) 6695.]

Offers materials towards a biographical restoration of the image of Mrs Manley. Her literary career is examined after discussion of three major relationships (with Steele, John Barker, Swift). She used drama as a testing ground for her theories, her treatment of drama as a luxury. An examination of her fiction deals with her literary theory and practice, her psychological realism, her use of contemporary materials, views of the novel as forum for social comment, obsessions with recurring themes, treatment of selected situations, mature treatment of the theme of love, and sophisticated and satirical uses of autobiographical materials.

1625 FINKE, Laurie A. "The satire of women writers in *The Female Wits*." *Restoration* 8 (1984): 66-71.

The last decade of the 17c witnessed a renewed inquiry into the intellectual abilities and education of women. The same decade saw the emergence of the first group of professional women writers, playwrights conscious of themselves as an intellectual group, and of their precarious roles in the theatrical world of the late 17c and early 18c London (Manley, Pix and Trotter). As a masculine response to the relative success of these female playwrights, the anonymous 1697 rehearsal play *The Female Wits* occupies an important historical position in the 17c. This can be read as a masculine indictment of female presumption as well as a satire on Manley's excesses in *The Royal Mischief*. Both *The Female Tatler* and the commendatory verses Manley, Pix and Trotter wrote to each other suggest the extent to which playwriting during the 1690s became an area for sexual warfare. It may well have succeeded in driving Manley from the theater for ten years. During the decade 1696 to 1705 she published nothing but a poem on Dryden's death, and she did not write another play until she brought out the feminist tragedy *Almyna* in 1706.

1626 FOXTON, Rosemary. "Delarivière Manley and 'Astrea's vacant throne'." *NQ* 33:1 (1986) 41-42.

"Elegy upon the death of Mrs A. Behn, the incomparable Astrea". Manly at seventeen strongly admired Aphra Behn, and implicitly admitted to literary aspirations of her own. She subsequently reworked constituents of Behn's elegy into an enconium which acknowledged Trotter's achievements. The friendship between the two women was even at this early date in the careers of both not without an element of rivalry.

1627 GRAHAM, Walter. "Thomas Baker, Mrs Manley, and the *Female Tatler*." *MP* 34 (1937): 267-72.

Favors the traditional acceptance of Baker as the author of the Bragge-Baldwin *Female Tatler* until better explanations are found. Thomas Baker, a minor dramatist of the period, was regarded by his contemporaries as the author of the *Female Tatler*. Anderson's case for Mrs Manley's authorship can hardly be accepted until further explanations are made. The two periodicals with all their conflicting claims and contradictory statements, mean that the problems of authorship can never be solved in a satisfactory way. It appears as well to accept the tradition that Thomas Baker was the author.

1628 HOOK, Lucyle (ed.). *'The Female Wits' (Anonymous) (1704)*. with an introd. (Augustan Reprint Soc. 124.) Los Angeles: Clark Memorial Library, UCLA, 1967; pp. xviii, 68.

The Female Wits (Theatre Royal in Drury Lane, 1696, pub. 1704) is a devastating satire attacking all plays by women playwrights, particularly Manley's *The Royal Mischief* (1696). It is directed not only at the subject matter and style, but supplies searing portraits of recognizable persons, esp. Mary Manley, and to a lesser degree, Mary Pix and Catherine Trotter. Manley became one of the leading Tory pamphleteers, political editors and literary hacks in London, employed and respected by Steele and Swift. Her *New Atalantis* (1709) and semi-autobiography *The Adventures of Rivella* (1714) caused government enquiries, and she never ceased to be a controversial figure.

1629 KÖSTER, Patricia. "Delarivière Manley and the DNB: a cautionary tale about following black sheep, with a challenge to cataloguers." *ECL* 3 (1977): 106-11.

Detailed investigation of the correct form of her name."Mary" was used only in the 19c. Until further information is forthcoming, she should be known as "Delarivière" Manley.

1630-----"New light on Maria Williamina Manley." *PQ* 57 (1978): 133-36.

Establishes definitively that this woman is not to be confused with the novelist.

1631 LOCK, F. P. "Astraea's 'Vacant Throne': the successors of Aphra Behn." In (pp. 25-36) FRITZ, Paul; MORTON, Richard (eds). *Women in the eighteenth century, and other essays.* (Pbns of the McMaster Univ. Assn for Eighteenth-Century Studies, 4.) Toronto; Sarasota, FL: Samuel Stevens; Hakkert, 1976; pp. x, 343.

Women dramatists before Mrs Behn are few and unimportant: after her there are many, and with the exception of Mrs Centlivre (1669-1723), unimportant. Investigate the dramatic contributions of Trotter, Pix and Manley. Concludes that Pix and Trotter were very unconsiderable figures in the history of the English drama, and if Mrs Manley is better known than her fellow wits, it is chiefly because of her *chroniques scandaleuses*.

Mrs. Centlivre was the only active woman dramatist after 1706. Several of her plays remained stock pieces in the 18c and through the 19c.

1632   McKEE, Francis. "Early criticism of *The Grumbling Hive.*" *NQ* 35:2 (1988): 176-77.

Queen Zarah was part of the wave of Tory invective using the techniques of the *roman à clef* to attack particularly Sarah Churchill. The first volume was published in Aug. 1705 and focused on the rise to power of the Marlboroughs. The second volume appeared by Nov. and concentrated its attack on Sarah Churchill's ambition and greed in the reign of Queen Anne. The attention paid to Bernard Mandeville's poem "The Grumbling Hive" in *Queen Zarah* helps to situate it more definitively within the political context of the time. It does not limit the poem's attack to specific party themes, or eliminate the paradoxical qualities inherent in it.

1633 MAISON, Margaret. "Pope and the two learned nymphs." *RES* 29 (1978): 405-14.

Discusses the scurrilous reputation of Catherine Trotter and Mary Manley, Manley's satire of Trotter in *The New Atalantis*, and the relationship of both to Pope and his literary treatment of the Establishment.

1634 MORGAN, Fidelis (ed.). *A woman of no character: an autobiography of Mrs Manley*. London: Faber & Faber, 1986; pp. 176.

Compilation of selected writings of Mrs Manley, using all the episodes within her published work which are widely acknowledged to be autobiographical, arranged in their true chronology, as far as this is known. The gaps are bridged with short links explaining who is talking and where. Where events are important to understanding her life as a whole, chapters have been written which include as many Manley quotes as possible. Provides a family tree, a chronology, a key to pseudonyms, a complete list of works, and a select bibliography (169-72). Index.

1635 NEEDHAM, Gwendolyn B. "Mary de la Rivière Manley: Tory defender." *HLQ* 12 (1949): 255-88.

Long detailed assessment of Mrs Manley as a political writer. She has never been fully appreciated in this role because she has remained the victim of one book's amazing success, *The New Atalantis* (1709) which became a bestseller and established her reputation. But she deserves to be remembered equally as an ardent defender of Queen Anne and the Tory Party. The effects of her political writings (1705-14) were recognized both by her party and the political opposition. Although it brought her personal satisfaction, there was little reward and considerable suffering.

1636-----"Mrs Manley: an eighteenth-century wife of Bath." *HLQ* 14 (1951): 259-84.

Account of life and works. This amazing woman not only dared deviate from the fixed pattern for her sex, but boldly challenged the very premises of its structures. She earned the title to several female firsts: first gentlewoman to gain her living by her pen, first political journalist, first author of a bestseller, first to be jailed for her writings, and perhaps most daring of all, first to assail by deed and word the double standards of morality. In her own time she was scorned and vilified. Swift, Steele and Prior admired her, and she achieved much as a pioneer rebel against women's restricted position.

1637 PALOMA, Dolores. "A woman writer and the scholars: a review of Mary Manley's reputation." *Women and Literature* 6:1 (1978): 36-46.

Investigates the general attitude to Manley, finding it lacking in substance. There is unrelenting emphasis on her sexuality and the eroticism of her work which leaves no time to explore its innate qualities.

1638 PAYNE, Linda R. "Genre and gender: women as writers of prose fiction and drama in Restoration and early eighteenth-century England" etc., **750**.

1639 SUTTON, John L. "The source of Mrs Manley's preface to *Queen Zarah*." *MP* 82:2 (Nov. 1984): 167-72.

Viewed from the perspective of English critical tradition, Manley's Preface is a theoretical landmark, but perhaps it is not so unique, nor Mrs Manley its original author. It belongs to an older and more sophisticated tradition of prose criticism; in fact, is a literal translation of an essay on prose fiction contained in a French "courtesy book" published in 1702 -- the Abbé Morvan de Bellegarde's *Lettres curieuses de littérature et de morale* which enjoyed great popularity in France and England in the first half of the 18c. The thought expressed came directly from Du Plaisir's *Sentiments*, which embodied the recent change in literary fashion that led French novelists to give up writing long, multi-volume, heroic romance in favor of a shorter, more tightly constructed, more realistic kind of novel, variously described as "nouvelle" or "petite histoire" which reached its maturest form in Mme de Lafayette's *La Princesse de Clèves*.

Mrs Manley's preface is part of the great wave of French Neo-Classical ideas which entered England in the late 17c and early 18c.

1640 SYNDER, Henry L. "New light on Mrs Manley." *PQ* 52 (1973): 767-70.

Publishes a petition written on 24 December 1706 to Queen Anne from a widow imprisoned for debt, and suggests that the petitioner might be Mrs Manley. Koster investigates a petition sent 14 years earlier to King William III, and observes that because there is "a confusing tendency to overlap (duplication of spouses, petition writing), and that they all have the *Manley* surname, perhaps it will be possible to distinguish them a little more clearly in future" (135).

1641 TODD, Janet. "Life after sex: the fictional autobiography of Delarivière Manley." *Women's Studies* 15:1-3 (1988): 43-55.

Manley was a woman who tried to give the conventional tale a subverting comic turn and provide sexualized femininity with a cheerful rather than horrific aim. Her early years can be glimpsed through her own creations, esp. in her fictional autobiography *The Adventures of Rivella* (1714). Female desire need not result in distress, but instead yield delight and money through its representations. "The whore becomes the storyteller of man's lust and historian of the comical history of 'virtue in distress' made entertaining and popular" (55).

1642 WEBER, Donna-Lee. "Fair game: rape and sexual aggression on women in some early eighteenth-century prose fiction" etc., **1035**.

1643 WINTON, Calhoun. "Steele, Mrs Manley, and John Lacy." *PQ* 42 (1963): 272-75.

Most of Steele's early associates gravitated towards the Whigs after the Tory triumph in 1710 (Addison, Garth, Congreve). Two who did not leave and became Steele's bitter foes were Swift and Mrs Manley: their pens were certainly the most effective on the Tory side in the furious pamphlet war over the Succession. "The Ecclesiastical History" (1714) with its half-true scandalous anecdotes and close knowledge of Steele's life points to Mrs Manley as author, or co-author with Swift. John Lacy did not write it.

1644 WOODCOCK, George. "Mary Manley and Eliza Haywood." *Room of One's Own* 2:4 (1977): 49-65.

Manley in the 1690s took over Behn's position as the leading she-wit in

English letters. She was less talented, but not unlike Behn in character and career. Her writing is smoother in texture, and shows sharper awareness of the everyday scene, but lacks Behn's vigorous style and variety of imagination. It can seem flat and trivial because of her affected preoccupation with petty intrigue."Love is no longer, as with Aphra Behn, a heroically transfiguring passion; the Augustan society in which Manley moved had reduced it to a social game, a play of feeling poised between sentiment and prurience" (50). She was best known for her key novels in which political propaganda was mingled with amorous sensationalism, and is important as the pioneer of the novel of tendency, one of the earliest writers to use the novel to explore the world of politics.

STUDIES (1992-1999)

1645 ALLIKER, Melinda. "The Manl(e)y style: Delarivière Manley and Jonathan Swift." In (pp. 125-53) MELL, Donald (ed.). *Pope, Swift, and women writers*. Newark: Delaware UP; London and Toronto: Assoc. UPs, 1996; pp. 251.
Manley's *New Atalantis* (1709) was one of her most popular narratives, with a distinct ironic style. Concentrates on Manley as a political satirist. Manley's association with Swift is not her claim to fame, but a means of seeing her accomplishments more clearly, and of correcting some of old misconceptions in Swift studies. Proposes a way of reading Manley as a satirist, using as illustrative texts the *New Atalantis*, the *Examiner* (1711), and *A True Narrative of what pass'd at the Examination of the Marquis De Guiscard* (1711).

1646 BENEDICT, Barbara M. "The curious genre: female enquiry in amatory fiction." etc. See above under HAYWOOD, **1564**.

1647 CHEN, Jue. "Poetics of historical referentiality: *roman à clef* and beyond." Unpub. doct. diss., Princeton Univ., 1997. [*DA* 58 (1997): 856A.]

Focuses on the European *roman à clef* and the Chinese *yingshe* method of composition in fiction. Comparing the two, the *yingshe* or element of historical referentiality (historical people and events being explicitly portrayed in fiction) has played a central role in the overall development of traditional Chinese fiction. The European side focuses on Mlle. de Scudéry and Mrs Manley. The poetics of historical referentiality distiguishes the analogical imagination from the mimetic imagination.

1648 CONNOR, Margarette Regina. "Heirs to 'Astrea's vacant throne': Behn's influence on Trotter, Pix, Manley and Centrelivre." Unpub. doct. diss., Univ. of New York, 1995. [*DA* 56 (1995): 1788A:]

Examines how the influence of Behn is apparent in the writing of Trotter, Pix, Manley, and Centrelivre. These later writers consciously modelled themselves in a specifically female literary tradition. Although most are playwrights, they all published in other genres. The most important links with Behn is a shared sense of feminism. Like Behn, they reflected interest in current politics, with Manley and Centlivre the most political. There is an intricacy of relationship between politics, religion and literature during the Restoration and early 18c. Analyzes Behn's work and the major themes which later appeared in the work of her heirs: feminism, politics, philosophy and homosexuality. Each one of the writers is given a biographical sketch, with a tracing of Behn's themes and their work through a close reading of the texts.

1649 CONWAY, Alison Margaret. "Private interests: spectatorship, portraiture and the novel in eighteenth-century England."etc. See above under HAYWOOD, **1568**.

1650 DUCROCQ, Jean. "Du bon usage de la fiction: *The New Atalantis* de Delarivière Manley." *RANAM* 26 (1993): 63-74.

In French. "[...] nous voudrions évoquer quelques aspects de la fiction de Delarivière Manley qui nous paraissent faire de leur auteur à la fois le révélateur de la crise esthétique et morale de son temps et un écrivain que sa marginalité même a contraint à concilier traditions, soumission aux goûts du public et originalité [...]" (65). L'éthique qui est à l'oeuvre dans *The New Atalantis* sera l'objet d'une critique radicale dans les grands romans du dix-huitième siècle [...]" (74).

1651 FABRIKANT, Carole. "The shared world of Manley and Swift:" In (pp. 154-78) MELL, Donald (ed.). *Pope, Swift and women writers* etc., **665**.

Examines how Manley represents the possibility of blurred boundaries, intensifying fears of being unable to discriminate between great art and hack writing, between elite and popular culture. Manley was and continues to be transformed into the contemptible Other that serves by contrast to shore up a culturally sanctioned Augustan identity and to define the 'true' Augustan moral and literary values. One should ponder the many ways in which Manley's relationship to Swift, as a fellow satirist and political propandist, would invariably have been treated differently by her contemporaries and subsequently in literary history if she had been a man.

1652 HOLLIS-BERRY, Elizabeth Ann. "Sexual politics in Delarivière Manley's *Secret Histories*." Unpub. doct. diss., Univ. of Alberta, 1993. [*DA* 94

(1994): 3446A.]

In her prose fiction, Manley writes both for and against the established order. Her writing shows her cavalier roots while simultaneously demonstrating her passionate opposition to a system in which women were often violently exploited. Her skill as a political satirist places her within the canonical scope of developing novelistic forms, while her marginal position as a wronged woman writing against the social grain allows her to claim excitingly unfamiliar territory where she mediates herself. Throughout her amatory fiction she anatomizes an entire social system lived out in the boudoirs and bowers of the great and not so great. Her multiple narratives create a series of fictional worlds peopled by characters who enact in satiric miniature the shifting problematic nature of individual relationships between men and women. She explores epistemological questions and dramatizes sexual politics through layers of allusive text.

1653 KIM, Elizabeth Sungeun. "Exploiting rape: women's literary representations of rape in early eighteenth-century prose fiction," **566**.

1654 LOWENTHAL, Cynthia. "Portraits and spectators in the late Restoration playhouse in Delarivière Manley's *Royal Mischief*." *ECent* 35:2 (1994): 119-34.
Investigates the problem of power relations within the context of the historicity of gendered spectatorship by examining the construction of female identity as it emerges in the problem of representating 'new' female interiority in Behn's *The Rover* (1677) and as it is modified by Manley in *The Royal Mischief* (1696). Reveals the ways that two female playwrights participate and comment on the gendering of the spectatorial economy by bringing to sight the mediating force the theater exerts in allowing and prohibiting the representation of *female* desire.

1655 MERRENS, Rebecca Beth. "Troping tragedy: Women, nature, and theories of order in early modern England." Unpub. doct. diss., Univ. of Washington, 1994. [*DA* 56 (1995): 1370A.]

Argues that late 16c and 17c science and literature functioned as mutually authorizing discourses which were isotropically invested in identifying and conquering feminized corruption as a means to (re)constitute masculinity as authoritative and cohesive. Defining 'corruption' as feminine enabled masculine communities, and indeed masculinity, to author itself as masterful, coherent and controlling - particularly during a period marked by fears of political, theological, and socio-cultural chaos, and by a decided shift in representation and responses to the feminine. The second half examines responses to masculine tragedy by Margaret Cavendish, Delarivière Manley, and Catherine Trotter who interrogate the assumptions of tragic troping in science and literature to resist efforts to scapegoat women and feminized nature for crises endemic to homosocial communities.

1656-----"Unmanned with thy words: regendering tragedy in Manley and Trotter." In (pp. 31-53) QUINSEY, Katherine (ed.). *Broken boundaries: women and feminism in Restoration drama.* Lexington: Kentucky UP, 1996; pp. v, 244.

Manley's *The Royal Mischief* and Trotter's *The Fatal Friendship* reject a repressive tradition of blaming women for socio-political strife, and instead locate the source of tragedy explicitly within the contradictions and violence of the paterlineal order.

1657 ONEY, Jay Edward. "Women playwright during the struggle for control of the London theater, 1695-1710." Unpub. doct diss., Ohio State Univ., 1996. [*DA* 57 (1997): 2745-6A.]

Concerns the playwrights Pix, Manley, Trotter and Centlivre. The Actors' Rebellion (1695) and the return to only one-play-producing theater in London (1710) provide a convenient interval. Investigates how they became playwrights, and evaluates their plays according to number of performances in the initial run, number of revivals, acceptance of subsequent work for production, plays' merits, première dates, casting and playwrights' reaction to the reform movement, relations to theater company personnel, responses to competition between 1695 and 1710. Examines how politics, patronage, and public influenced the womens' literary careers. The difference between Pix, Trotter and Manley's inexperience in 1696 and Centlivre's maturity in 1709 provides the key to understanding why the Three Female Wits are associated with the 17c and Centlivre is considered an 18c writer. Important for placing Manley's career as an 18c novelist in precise perspective.

1658 RABB, Melinda Alliker. "Angry beauties: (wo)manley satire and the stage." *TSL* 37 (1995): 127-58.

Critical assessment of Manley must contend with the relationship between gender and genre that underlies the study of satire. Satire has conventionally been associated with men. By modifying the conventions of both comedy and heroic tragedy, Manley regendered satire to accommodate women's indignation. Promiscuous desire for sexual gratification, and uncontrollable desire for economic or political power became confused. This ironic device is central to her most famous work, *The New Atalantis*, in which political satire on the Whig government is framed in amorous episode. The transgressive woman as desired object/or desiring subject reappears. Extensive notes (154-56) and bibliography (156-58).

1659 RICHETTI, John, "Amatory fiction: Behn, Manley, Haywood." In (pp. 18-51) *The English novel in history, 1700-1780*, **806**.

1660 RUBIK, Margarete. "'My life, my soul, my all is fixed upon enjoyment': the unbalanced expressions of female desire in *The Royal Mischief*." *Gramma* 4 (1996): 165-79.

After the outrage occasioned by *The Royal Mischief* (1696), Manley turned to fiction, esp. her *romans à clef* about the love lives of the Whig upper crust. The play attests to the author's skill at portraying female sexual desire with fervor and unusual candor, and it deserves to be remembered as an unabashed expression of female desire and an almost unique document of its time.

―――

MARINI, Giovanni Ambrogio

The desparadoes: an heroick history. Tr. from the Italian [...] of Giovanni Ambrogio Marini (1733, pp. 284)

NCBEL II 993[13]; McBurney 286; Morgan 619; ECSTC 1113M1
Trans. of French version, *Les désespérés*, 1732.
Tale of mistaken identities and melodramatic adventure.

―――

MARIVAUX, Pierre Carlet de Chamblain

1. *Le paysan parvenu: or the fortunate peasant* (1735, pp. 286)

NCBEL II 994[2]; McBurney 307; Morgan 642
Contains only the first four parts of the French original, all that had appeared by then.

2. *The life of Marianne: or the adventures of the Countess of* *** (3 vols. 1736-42; Vol. I, 2 pts, pp. 3-254)
NCBEL II 994[10]; McBurney 318; Morgan 643
Extremely popular and influential; many edns.

EDITIONS

1661 *Ouevres complètes.* 12 vols. Paris: Duchesne, 1781.

1662 *Romans.* Paris: Bibliohthèque de la Pléiade, Gallimard, 1949.

SELECTED STUDIES

1663 ARLAND, Marcel. *Marivaux.* Paris: Gallimard, 1950; pp. 270.

In French. Study of the life and works. Part I looks at the novel (11-94). His youth is described (*Pharsamon, Les Effets de la Sympathie*) and then his growing maturity (*La Vie de Marianne, Le Paysan parvenu, Histoire de la Religieuse*). Part II is devoted to the theatrical works and Part III to the essays and "Le visage de Marivaux". No critical apparatus of any kind.

1664 BROOKS, Peter. *The novels of worldliness: Crébillon, Marivaux, Laclos, Stendhal* etc., **1211**.

1665 DELOFFRE, Frédéric. *Une Préciosité nouvelle: Marivaux et le Marivaudage. Étude de langue et du style.* (Annales de l'Université de Lyons, 3me serie, 27.) Paris: Société d'Éditions Les Belles Lettres, 1955; pp. 603.
Detailed account of life, works and style. "Marivaux et son temps, Les Problèmes généraux du style; Le Vocabulaire, Le Mot dans la phrase et dans la pensée; Le matériel grammatical: La Phrase." Chronology of the life and work (503-62). Grammatical and stylistic index, lexicographical index. Index of names (567-80). Bibliography (581-98).

1666 DÉDÉYAN, Charles. "Marivaux à l'école d'Addison et de Steele." *Annales de l'Université de Paris* 25 (1955): 5-17.
Abstract not available.

1667 GELOBTER, Hanna. "*Le Spectateur* von Pierre Marivaux und die englischen Wochenschriften." Doct. diss., Frankfurt-am-Main, 1936; pp. 94.
Abstract not available.

1668 HUGHES, Helen Sard. "Translations of the *Vie de Marianne* and their relations to contemporary English fiction." *MP* 15 (1917): 491-512.

Investigates inaccurate and incomplete statements about the translations of Marivaux. There is evidence that by 1746 three translations were in circulation. The number of the translations makes clear the ground of their appeal, and the relation of Marivaux and Richardson to fictional developments before and during the period in which *Pamela* appeared.

1669 JAMIESON, Ruth Kirkby. *Marivaux, a study in sensibility.* New York: King Crown Press, 1941; pp. 212.

Marivaux is known chiefly as the author of a group of delightful comedies, but his first considerable literary efforts were novels. *La Vie de Marianne* and *Le Paysan parvenu* were widely read in their day in France and England, where Mariavaux was favorably compared to Richadson and Fielding. Looks at the author in the context of the *salons*, "Les effets suprenants de la sympathie", the sensitive heart, "amour-propre", "amour-tendresse", the morality of sentiment, Marivaux's humanitarianism, sense and sensibility. Bibliography (162-69). Notes (170-200).

1670 MEISTER, Anna. *Zur Entwicklung Marivaux'.* (Studiorum Romanicorum Collectio Turicensis, 8.) Bern: Francke, 1955; pp. 93.

In German. Investigates the works, trying to make obvious the opposition between the *Paysan parvenu* and the early works. Looks at the move from aristocrat to parvenu, chance, relations, the person as actor, the presentation of people, characteristics of language. Bibliography (92-93).

1671 MERRETT, Robert James. "Marivaux translated and naturalized: systematic contraries in eighteenth-century British fiction." *CRCL* 17:3-4 (Sept.-Dec. 1990): 227-54.

Marivaux's texts were adapted and naturalized into English in a manner which exposed the polarities informing and defining British fiction when viewed as a complex, institutional system. Compares Sterne and Defoe: systematic relations between him and the British writers query those truisms of literary history which declare Sterne to be atypical and Defoe to be marginal. All three share a keen interest in narrative mediation, fostered at the cost of political and religious orthodoxy. This explains why all three receive no more than equivocal recognition from literary history. Their experimental, playful and even subvertive interest in narrative render them suspect.

1672 PARRISH, Jean. "Illusion et réalité dans les romans de Marivaux." *MLN* 80 (1965): 301-06.

In French. "Marivaux débutant par la parodie du roman d'aventures se moque de nos illusions chevaleresques. Mais la distinction formelle entre illusion romanesque et le réel fictif tend à disparaître dans les oeuvres maîtresses [...]. Dans l'ambiguïté foncière de notre rapport aux autres, Marivaux a compris qu'illusion et realité deviennent presque impossible à démêler et, qui en plus, sont à la merci du moment" (306).

1673 PETERSON, H. "Notes on the influence of Addison's *Spectator* and Marivaux's *Spectateur français* upon *El Pensador*." *Hispanic Review* 4 (1936): 256-63.

Spanish *costumbrismo* underwent both English and French influence as early as 1762 when the first numbers of *El Pensador* began to appear. The English influence upon this journal came from the *Spectator* through the medium of a French translation. It is not merely an imitation of the English paper in general form and content, but it contains among its numbers translations of seven whole *Spectators* and direct imitations of 6 others. The French influence is slight, but definite. It takes the form of two essays, *Pensamiento* 22 and the second part of 66, which owe their existence to the *Feuilles* of Marivaux's *Spectateur français* (1722-23).

1674 STADLER, Eva Maria. "Defining the female body within social space: the function of clothes in some early eighteenth-century novels." In (pp. 468-73) BAUER, Roger and FOKKEMA, Douwe (et al eds.). *Proceedings of the XIIth Congress of the International Comparative Literature Association, Munich III: space and boundaries in literature* (Proceedings of the Congress of the International Comparative Literature Association, 12:3.) Munich: Iudicium, 1990; pp.509.

Analyzes the function of clothing in three novels written during the first half of the 18c: Defoe's *Moll Flanders* (1722), Marivaux's *La Vie de Marianne* (1731-41) and Richardson's *Pamela* (1740). All three are novels of apprenticeship and, although written by men, all three focus on the female experience. In *Moll Flanders* cloths and clothes are strong indicators of wealth and wordly possessions, in *Marianne* clothes are weapons in the encoded seduction game between men and women, as well as signs of social position. In *Pamela* the danger of dress is used explicitly as a personal social act, and clothing is related to social position, wealth and seduction. In the 18c, English novelists are primarily concerned with the correspondence of words to things, while in France the continuing classical influence produced more stylized words, and greater emphasis on concision and elegance. The language of clothing and personal adornment bears this out. Clothing functions not only as a referential marker, but also as a link between the female body and the world. As an encroachment by society upon her space, clothing can also be a protective skill that a woman uses to assert and assure her position.

1675 THOMAS, Ruth P. "The art of the portrait in the novels of Marivaux." *French Review* 42 (1968): 23-31.

The modern reader of *Le Paysan parvenu* and *La Vie de Mariane* is immediately struck by the number, variety and length of the portraits in the novels. About every chapter, regardless of importance, receives a portrait of some sort, often very long, Since the middle of the 17c, the portrait of living persons came into vogue in the *salons* of the *précieux*. Marivaux continues this genre, and makes a significant contribution. He has taken a conventional, highly literate form, and made it an actual representation of fictional and real personages. He has understood that the literary portrait must have a clearly definable, not morally simplistic, point of view. The narrator sympathizes with, or is detached from, the characters, and so enables the reader to share the narrator's view of the personages, and see them from the same angle. Investigates the portraits in these two psychological novels.

1676 WEINSTEIN, Arnold. "The Self-Made Woman 2 (*La Vie de Marianne*". In (pp. 100-13) *Aspects of the Self* etc., **1039**.

"Marivaux's heroine Marianne - seemingly so different, yet ultimately so like Moll Flanders - pursues a dazzling course of self-assertion in her itinerary from orphanhood to aristocracy" (100).

1677 WILLIAMS, Ioan. "The Early Marivaux; Experiments in Modernism, 1712-15" and "*La Vie de Marianne*: The Novel as Portrait". In (pp. 137-39 and 162-200) *The idea of the novel* etc., **1056**.

Marivaux introduced a new idea of the novel and took a fundamental step forward, "the basis of a great achievement and of great historical significance" (163).

MISSON, François

A new voyage to the east-Indies by Francis Leguat and his companions (1708, pp. 248)

NCBEL II 986[3]; McBurney 39; ECSTC 2737M2
Partly Utopian.

EDITIONS

1678 *The Voyage of François Leguat of Bresse to Rodriguez, Mauritius, Java, and the Cape of Good Hope. Transcribed from the first English Edition. Edited and Annotated by Captain Pasfield OLIVER.* London: The Hakluyt Society, 1891. 2 vols. I, lxxxviii + 137; II, xviii + 139-433.

Vol. I has tables of contents, illustrations and maps, editor's preface, bibliography. Introd., chronology, addenda and corrigenda, dedicatory letter (Dutch ed.), table of contents (Dutch ed.). Facs. titlepage of orginal English ed., letter of dedication to the Duke of Kent. Vol. II has contents, lists of illus. and maps, bibliography (lx-xiv). Second part (from Rodriguez to Mauritius, Java, the Cape of Good Hope, return to Holland, thanksgiving hymn). Appendices A-E. Index (384-433).

STUDIES

1679 ATKINSON, Geoffrey. "A French desert island novel of 1708." *PMLA* 36:4 (1921): 509-28.

Gives a history of the desert isle and shipwrecked crew stories in French literature (1603-1707), and a full account of the first French edition of Leguat, and the English and Dutch translations. For over 200 years this work by "the philosophic Huguenot" has been considered by many to be a true story. Atkinson contends that the story is not the authentic account of a real voyage, but on the contrary a novel. The book is not an account of the real Leguat's travels and observations, but a mosaic of observations of many travellers in Africa and America. It is a voyage made in an armchair. As a novel, written in 1707, often reprinted and believed to be an essentially true story for 200 years, it is without parallel. Its carefully authenticated realism -- borrowed largely from the forgotten naturalists Du Tertre and Du Bois -- has deceived modern readers and critics.

1680 NORTH-COOMBES, Alfred. *The Vindication of François Leguat, first resident and historian of Rodriguez (1691-1693).* Mauritius: Organisation Normale des Enterprises Limitée, 1979; Rev. Rose Hill, Mauritius: Société de l'Histoire de l'Ile Maurice, 1991; pp. xxxix, 306.

Comprehensive appraisal of Leguat's natural history observations in the island of Rodriguez (1708) and a thorough refutation of his detractors from Buffon and Cuvier to Atkinson and his supporters. Chronology, appendices, bibliographic notes. Bibliography (267-89). Index (291-306).

———

MONCRIF, François-Augustin-Paradis de

Indian tales: or the adventures of Zeloide and Amanzarifdine(1718, pp. 7-179)

> NCBEL II 988[7]; McBurney 92
> Sentimental novel in French historical mode.

EDITIONS

1681   *The Adventures of Zeloide and Amanzarifdine. Translated with an Introduction by C. K. Scott MONCRIEFF.* (The Broadway Library of XVIII Century French Literature.) London: George Routledge & Sons, Ltd., 1929; pp. xlvii, 205.

Extended introd. by SCOTT MONCRIEFF (ix-xlvi). Explains the origins of the name and family of the author, before providing a detailed account of his life and works, and a bibliographic note on the text used in the trans. The text itself is divided into 7 tales.

STUDIES

1682   SHAW, Edward P. *François-Augustin-Paradis de Moncrif (1687-1770).* New York: Bookman Associates, 1958; pp. 179.

Discusses life and work in tandem. Covers early years, introduction to polite and literary society, first literary compositions, *L'Histoire des chats*, social relationships and financial emoluments, election to the French Academy, early relationships with Voltaire, ejection by the Comte de Clermont, the circle around Marie Leszcynska and poetry written for the Queen, Mme. de Pompadour and the Théâtre des Petits Cabinets, *Zélindor, Roi des sylphes* and other ballets, the *Parade*, Stanislas and the Society of Nancy, the exile of Comte d'Argenson, functions and intrigues as an academician, late relationships with Voltaire, activities as a Royal Censor, poetical work, last years and death. Of particular interest is ch. 20 "Moncrif the Poet" which discusses his poetic work in critical detail. Bibliographic notes (145-66). Bibliography (167-72). Index (173-79).

——

MONTESQUIEU, Charles Secondat, Baron de

Persian letters (1722, 1730; 6 edns by 1773; 2 pts, pp. 271 + 309)

> NCBEL II 989[16]; McBurney 136
> Trans. John OZELL.

Epistolary; pioneering psychological, sociological fiction; influential and much imitated.

BIBLIOGRAPHIES

1683 CABEEN, David C. "Montesquieu: a bibliography." *BNYPL* 51 (1947): 231-38, 359-83, 423-30, 513-19, 545-65, 593-616.

Extensive bibliography in 5 parts with a prefatory note in which it is described as "an annotated , critical bibliography of the editions of Montesquieu's works in the New York Public and Columbia Univ. Libraries, and of all studies on him in the United States which the compiler has been able to consult." Aims at completeness. Montesquieu is important in the fields of literature, politcal science, history, law, philosophical economy and political economy. Lists bibliographies, works by Montesquieu, material on Montesquieu's family, studies on Montesquieu. Index (609-16).

1684-----"Montesquieu studies: a brief survey." *French Stud* 22 (1948): 25-31. Continuation of the above.

SELECTED STUDIES

1685 CRISAFULLI, Alessandro S. "A neglected English imitation of Montesquieu's *Lettres persanes.*" *MLQ* 14 (1953): 208-16.

Contributes to the history of the pseudo-oriental letter novel after Montesquieu. The fiction *Letters from an Armenian in Ireland to his Friends at Trebizond* (Dublin, 1756) is one of the many works stemming from the vogue for Montesquieu's *Persian letters* (1721), and also *Letters from a Persian in England to his Friends at Ispahan* (1735).

1686-----"Parallels to ideas in the *Lettres persanes.*" *PMLA* 52 (1937): 773-77.

The *Lettres persanes* (1721) on which Montesquieu worked for 10 years, reflect to a large extent the voluminous reading he must have done. The great variety of subjects implies numerous possible sources. Considers the possible influence of Malbranche, Leibniz and Shaftesbury. There is also a relationship of ideas between Montesquieu and these three writers, which implies some influence since Montesquieu esteemed them all.

1687 DEDIEU, Joseph. *Montesquieu.* (Les Grands Philosophes.) Paris: Félix Alcan, 1913; pp. vii, 358.

Life and works covering the formation and the spirit, the origins of his sociological method, Montequieu's political and moral ideas, his social, economic, religious ideas. Chronological Table (339-46). Bibliography (347-55) covers: 1) general monographs; 2) biography; 3) *Les Lettres persanes*; 4) *Les Considérations sur la grandeur*; 5) *L'Esprit des lois*; 6) influence.

1688 DODDS, Muriel. *Les récits de voyages, sources de' l'Esprit des lois' de Montesquieu.* Paris: Champion, 1929; pp. 304.

Considers the knowledge of foreign countries in France in the late 17c and 18c. Part I investigates Montesquieu's sources in Germany, Italy, Turkey, Persia, Ethiopia, North Africa, Guinea, the East Indies, Siam, China, Japan, Tartary and Russia, the two Americas and the West Indies. Part II explores the sources of the idea of despotism in *L'Esprit des lois*, the role of China, Montesquieu's handling of sources, esp. those which influenced his account of voyages. There is tabulation of sources (175-200), an appendix (291-95) and a bibliography (296-303).

1689 FALVEY, John. "Aspects of fictional creation in the *Lettres persanes*, and of the aesthetic of the rationalist novel." *Romanic Review* 56 (1965): 248-61.

Examines the propositions that an important and hitherto largely unrecognized narrative process in the *Lettres persanes* is a realism of the manner akin to the "formal realism" discovered by Ian Watt in the English novel of the period, and that the success of the work can be more closely understood when Montesquieu's performance is viewed directly as rationalistic technique. Looks at individualization by means of psychological perspectives, by means of formal arrangements, by means of the intellectual dialogue. The unique charm of the *Lettres persanes* lies in the empathy which the writing engenders, in that it can give the reader's mind, at the moment of contact, an impetus which sets it working in the manner of an 18c rationalist. This empathy emanates from the strength of Montesquieu's personality, is conveyed by his masterly control of manner, and makes possible those pleasures analyzed in the *Essai sur le goût* which are experiences of the soul through elegant style, functional order, and the exercise of reason. See pp. 248-9 for further Montesquieu bibliography.

1690 GREEN, F. C. "Further evidence of realism in the French novel of the eighteenth century." *MLN* 40 (1925): 257-70.

The earliest novelist aims at the reproduction of *unidealized* nature. In selecting his subjects, he is naturally led to prefer the ugly to the beautiful so that the unity of his picture is not complicated by idealistic elements. In 1744, the Président Caulet launched an attack on novels in general, all of which he would suppress if he could. He did admit that the novel of his time had increased in probablility. Despite the existence of a considerable body of opinion opposed to realism in the novel, there is a steady growing current of realist fiction in the 18c. At the end of the 17c realism was an adjunct to satire, as in Antoine Furetière's *roman bourgeois*, and in Charles Sorel's *roman comique*. In the second half of the 18c, realism became the medium of sentiment. The object of writers like Rousseau was to move their readers, to harrow them with realities of passionate and unhappy love with all its complications.

1691-----"Montesquieu the novelist and some imitations of the *Lettres persanes*." *MLR* 20 (1925): 32-42.

Circumstances have conspired to direct attentions of critics from the importance played by Montesquieu in the evolution of the French novel. This reputation as a publicist has excluded a proper consideration of the *Lettres persanes*. The fictitious element has been dismissed, and the vogue for oriental exoticism has passed. Montesquieu furthermore held novelists in contempt. He felt the novel should be true to life, felt the *merveilleux* had been abused, and was anxious to show in the *Lettres persanes* what could be done by someone who understood the production of a good novel. The critic would be a novelist. His theories were excellent, but like those of Diderot on the theater, they failed when applied by the author. He was extremely deficient in psychological penetration; there is not sufficient central action, there are no adventures, either physical or psychological, leading up to the dénouement. The spirit of tragedy was to find a worthy successor to Racine in the novels of Prévost. The *Lettres persanes* was an attempt to write a novel of letters, but some of the imitators of this new form led to a retarding of the development of the epistolary novel, as love was subordinated to criticism of *moeurs*. Montesquieu moved beyond Lesage and paved the way for the divorce between the *conte* and the novel, which was, however, not to become effective until nearly 1750.

1692 KETTLER, David. "Montesquieu on love: notes on *The Persian Letters*." *American Political Science Review* 58 (1964): 658-61.

The Persian Letters is often considered as a collection of fragments, but it is here discussed as a meaningful whole, a book which has the theme of love and its relation to social institutions. Montesquieu treats love as a decisive manifestation of humanity. The lover is more truly human than other men, his potentialities as a man are more fully realized. His critique of the dehumanization of society eventuates in pessimism rather than radical reform. Having discovered true love to be an accidental phenomenon on the margin of analysis, he abandons it as a tool of analysis, or a goal to be sought. To evaluate society by the criteria of love reveals too much. More relative criteria are needed to discern the possible.

1693 LAUFER, Roger. "La réussite romanesque et la signification des *Lettres persanes* de Montesquieu." *Revue d'histoire littéraire de la France* 61 (1961): 188-203.

In French. Is the *Lettres persanes* a novel? Investigates the external unities of the work, biography, the romanesque genre, its rococo style, its voices, its movement, the natural law and the tyranny of the seraglio, the character of Usbek, a tragic hero. "Au moins avait-il écrit dans *Les Lettres persanes* le premier roman de l'adolescence futilement révoltée contre l'ordre social qui la soutient et qui presque toujours la récupère après quelques années" (203).

1694 MAHMOUD, Parvine. "Les Persanes de Montesquieu." *French Review* 34 (1960): 44-50.

In writing the *Lettres persanes*, Montesquieu wanted to satirize French *moeurs*. He wrote his book in the form of letters by 2 Persians who write to their family and friends in Persia. The Iranian elements bear little resemblance to reality, but it is to Montesquieu's credit that with so little material he created the illusion of an authentic Persia.

1695 RANUM, Orest. "Personality and politics in the *Persian Letters*." *Political Science Quarterly* 84 (1969): 606-27.

Montesquieu's perception of political crisis in France after 1715, and his own adolescent crisis, combined to fix him in his purpose for the rest of his life. The *Spirit of the Laws* was an outgrowth of the maturing young author of the *Persian Letters*. He abhorred despotism in all its forms, whether in Ispahan, the realm of the political ideology, the Palais Royal (a source of unlimited power which made him despair), or in his father's château of La Brède.

1696 SHACKLETON, Robert. *Montesquieu: a critical biography.* London: Oxford UP, 1961; pp. xv, 432. 3 plates.

Detailed account of life and works in critical tandem. Ch. 2 covers the *Lettes persanes* (27-46): the literary tradition, society and government, religion, philosophy and history. The bibliography (400-18) covers: 1) original works by Montesquieu; 2) extracts and analyses made by Montesquieu (collections, indiv. works). Index (419-32).

1697 VAN ROOSBROECK, Gustave L. "Persian letters before Montesquieu." *MLR* 20 (1925): 432-42. As book: New York: Institute of French Studies, 1933; pp. 147.

New facts on the early history of the 'foreign observer' genre. The foreign pseudo-letter had its humble beginnings in Marana's *Letters of a Turkish Spy* some thirty years before it culminated in Montesquieu's *Lettres persanes*. The evolution inside the genre sprang from a denunciatory spirit of the times which seized upon them as a new and safe vehicle for incisive criticism of society. The *Lettres persanes* are a complex result of several contemporary currents of thought, literary examples, personal observations and experience, sifted through and harmonized by a personality. The austere *Letters*, spurred on by philosophy, and transformed through successive mutations, becomes an image of a period in intellectual crisis in the *Lettres persanes*. During the next decades the picture changed to a more detailed image of contemporary life and customs, and sometimes to caricature rather than portrayal.

1698 VARTANIAN, Aram. "Eroticism and politics in the *Lettres persanes.*" *Romanic Review* 60 (1969): 23-33.

There is no reason why a literally erotic fiction in the artistic context should not on occasion symbolize a veiled *non-erotic* content to the point of prefiguring some abstract idea with which its author might be philosophically obsessed. A study of the *Lettres persanes* from such a perspective will show that the real motive behind Montesquieu's use of the *roman du sérail* in its pages was the clarification that it brought, by analogy, to certain political truths which, for him, were essential. Montesquieu regarded the novelistic material as the proper framework for the presentation of his philosophical criticisms. Unable to attack French absolutism directly, he turned to the expedient of invoking fictionally in the minds of the reader its affinities with the inefficiency and self-destructiveness of Oriental tyranny. The manner in which the *Lettres persanes* sought to bring out this dangerous convergence of absolutism and despotism proved to be the first notable instance of the eroticization of philosophical ideas which became thereafter a characteristic of French 18c thought.

———

MOTTLEY, John

Joe Miller's jests: or the wit's vademecum (1739 [3 edns]; many further edns and versions; pp. 70)

NCBEL II 995[1]; ECSTC 3642M11
The classic jestbook of the period; some anecdotes approach short fiction. 247 jests.

EDITIONS

1699 Facsimile of the 1739 edition. N.p., 1861; pp. 70.

1700 *Joe Miller's Jests. Being a Collection of The most Brilliant Jests and most pleasant short Stories in the English Language -- The greater Part of which are taken from the Mouth of that facetious Gentleman whose Name they bear.* In (pp. 288-94) ASHTON, John. *Chapbooks of the eighteenth century* etc., **118**.

Selection of jests, with brief introd. Facs. of the title page of an edition later than the original.

1701 Facsimile edition. Ed. Robert HUTCHINSON. New York: Dover, 1963. Preface pp. xix, facs; pp. 70.

Joe Miller died in 1735, but the Fleet Street publisher T. Reed conceived of publishing a book of jests, and commissioned an impecunious writer, John Mottley, to write it. He attached the still popular name of Joe Miller to it, and the book attained immediate and lasting popularity. Discusses Mottley's and a survey of the history of jest books from Greek and Roman times. The Augustan Age was a period of wit in England. The humor of the previous period with its medieval trappings and stories from Plutarch was simply incomprehensible. It was the world of the theater that enchanted the people of Mottley's time. "No matter now if Mottley had used diverse sources, or if many of the jokes fell flat, [...] to us the book is a piece, and it is the very air and breathing reality of the period that produced it, the eighteenth century" (xvi). [...] the whole century is here, and one need only open the book to see it come to life" (xvii). Its healthiness is attested to by nine generations taking it into their homes. Neglects to identify which edition was used for the copy.

STUDIES

1702 ANDERSON, Paul Bunyan. "Thomas Gordon and John Mottley, *A Trip* *through London, 1728." PQ* 19 (1940): 244-60.

A Trip through London is inherently very lively and had many reprintings. It is an odd collaboration between Thomas Gordon and a pamphleteer of 1725, probably John Mottley. It is made up of the early humorous and realistic journalism of Thomas Gordon, chiefly of 1718-9, selected from Gordon's volumes of collected essays, *The Humourist* (1720, 1724), and accompanied by a few contributions from the collaborative hands on Welsh servants, Irish fortune hunters, undertakers, Templars, and London citizens and apprentices -- the whole seasoned with a few ripe jests. Because of Gordon's personal associations with Mottley, and the interest he took in his particular psychology and tastes, Gordon asked him in *Pasquin* (1723-4), as Giles Bookit, to sketch a picture of the lower levels of Grub Street and the Jacobite camp followers who indulged in dreams of a Stuart restoration.

1703 WILLIAMS, Franklin B., Jr. "Joe Miller on Thomas More." *Moreana* 38 (1973): 59-61.

Evidence of the survival of Thomas More's reputation for wit and repartee into the age of the Enlightenment is found in the fact that no less than 4 anecdotes appear in the 1739 first edition of the most famous joke book of the time. The compilation was the work of the miscellaneous writer John Mottley, under the pseudonym of Elijah Jenkins. A modern reader is impressed by the literary quality of many of the stories. Copies of the first edition are more numerous than one might expect.

———

MOUTHY, Charles de Fieux, Chevalier de

The fortunate country maid: being the entertaining memoirs of the present celebrated Marchioness of L. V. (1740, 1741; at least 5 edns by 1792; 2 vols, n.p.)
NCBEL II 995[2]; Beasley 30
Trans. of *La Paysanne parvenue*, 1738; Eliza HAYWOOD'S trans. as *The virtuous villager*, 1742.
Distressed heroine; theme of *Pamela* and *Marianne*.

———

OLDMIXON, John

The secret history of Europe (1712; 4 edns by 1724; pp. 251)

NCBEL II 986[16]; McBurney 61; ECSTC 312O50

Secret history with Whig bias.

STUDIES

1704 FISHER, George T. "John Oldmixon, early Whig historian." Unpub. doct. diss., Ohio State Univ., 1972. [*DAI* 33 (1972): 693A.]

Claims that Oldmixon (1673-1742) was a forerunner of the Whig historians of the 19c. Begins with an account of his life, then turns to a discussion of the salient characteristics of later Whig historiography (based on the works of Hallam and Macaulay). Examines Oldmixon's view of England in Medieval, Tudor and Stuart times which shows how he anticipated the characteristics of later Whig historians.

1705 MADDEN, R. J. (ed.). *John Oldmixon. An Essay on Criticism (1728)*. With an introd. (Augustan Reprint Soc. 107-8.) Los Angeles: Clarke Memorial Library, UCLA, 1964; pp. v, 94.

Oldmixon's *Essay on Criticism* (1728), like his *Reflections on Dr Swift's Letter to the Earl of Oxford, about the English Tongue*, provides evidence to support Dr Johnson's description of its author as "a scribbler for a party", and indicates that Oldmixon must have been devoted to gathering examples of what appeared to be the good, and bad in literature. He was concerned with the English need for guidance in "right thinking". It is more than an example of the interrelation of literature and politics in the 18c, and it is more than a step on the way to its author's immortalizing. It presents, albeit not very imaginatively, a statement of many of the literary theories and attitudes of the Augustan Period. His remarks about the language of poetry and the effects of certain literary passages are of interest as imperfect examples of a type of practical criticism, and show him to have been a man of literary taste, sense and intelligence.

1706 ROGERS, J. P. W. "A lost poem by Oldmixon." *PBSA* 63 (1969): 291-94.

In Oct. 1714 Bernard Lintot recorded publication of a new poem by Oldmixon, "Britannia Liberata", written to celebrate the Hanoverian Accession, but no trace of it survives. One is diposed to believe that it did exist, and a copy will one day emerge for critical discussion.

1707-----"Congreve's first biographer: the identity of 'Charles Wilson'." *MLQ* 31 (1970): 330-44.

Discusses the authorial controversy surrounding the *Memoirs of the Life,*

Writing, and Amours of William Congreve, Esq (1739), considering the candidature of Edmund Curll and John Oldmixon. The evidence is not conclusive enough for a definite attribution.

1708 ROGERS, Pat. "John Oldmixon and a translation of Boileau." *RLC* 43 (1969): 509-13.
The first English translation of Boileau's work to be designated as a comprehensive whole appeared in 1711-13. John Ozell and Samuel Cobb appeared to have played the main part. However, Oldmixon also claimed to have contributed a share of the labour. Draws attention to the evidence on support of this claim, which includes a letter to Lord Halifax and the prior publication of a Boileau epistle.

1709-----"The conduct of the Earl of Nottingham: Curll, Oldmixon and the Finch family." *RES* 21 (1970): 175-81.

Examines a series of letters linking Oldmixon to the production of *The Conduct of the Earl of Nottingham* which appeared only in 1941 after its initial suppression in 1717.

1710-----"Two notes on the John Oldmixon and his family." *NQ* 215/17 (1970): 293-300.

Investigates details of Oldmixon's family with parish entries and family tree. Also considers possible additions to the Oldmixon canon, examining claims by the Earl of Oxford in a MS held by the British Museum.

1711-----"John Oldmixon and *An Impartial Enquiry* (1715)." *SB* 24 (1971): 163-65.
A series of letters preserved in the Finch MSS (Leicester Record Office) makes it possible to explain a hitherto obscure allusion in one of Pope's pamphlets, and furnishes valuable evidence concerning the mode and financing of publication in the early 18c. In June 1715 James Roberts brought out a work in reply to Mrs Manley's "Conduct of the Duke of Ormonde". The pamphlet is now in the Bodleian Library, shorn of its plan. It is virtually certain that Oldmixion wrote the *Enquiry*. Gives various reasons why. Oldmixon may have reaped more financial reward from a book which was suppressed than from among the 70-odd he wrote which did find their way into the bookshop.

1712-----"*The Catholick Poet* (1716): John Oldmixon's attack on Pope." *BLR* 8 (1971): 277-84.

This rare work found only in the Yale University Library is part of an anti-Pope move. Examines this rare copy of a broadsheet ballad, pointing out that it encapsulates a good deal of literary history, the Pope-Curll quarrel, the *ripostes* of the duncely party, the beleaguered conditions of the book-selling trade. The ballad has its moments of fun, but it is only when it is read in context, with its proper prose lamentation intact, that its full energies are released and full meaning disclosed. It looks, from both press advertisements and from the work itself, as if Oldmixon thought he was in some ways on Pope's side of things.

1713-----"The dunce answers back: John Oldmixon on Swift and Defoe." *TSLL* 14 (1972): 33-34.

For over a generation, the obstinate Whig pamphleteer enshrined in a variety of works a huge collection of abusive reference, much of it directed explicitly at Swift or Defoe. The Oldmixon bibliography "forms an index to a veritable thesaurus of invective". Singles out the entries covering these two authors, and attempts some differentiation in the tone and contents of Oldmixon's remarks.

1714 SHEPPERSON, Wilbur S. and FOLKES, John G. "Biographical notes on Sir John Oldmixon." *NQ* 207 (1962): 4-5.

Attempt to penetrate the mixture of myth and misinformation surrounding Oldmixon and his family. Investigates the descendants.

———

OLIVIER, J.

Memoirs of the life and adventures of Signor Rozelli (1709; 5 edns by 1725; continuation 1724; pp. 325)

NCBEL II 986[8]; McBurney 46; Morgan 458; ECSTC 347O1
Trans. has been doubtfully assigned to Defoe.
Picaresque adventures; anti-Catholic propaganda.

———

P., W. [William PITTIS?]

The Jamaica lady: or the life of Bavia (1720, pp. 100)

NCBEL II 989[4]; McBurney 108; ECSTC 98P6
Female rogue.

EDITIONS

1715 Ed. McBURNEY in *Four before Richardson* etc.See ANTHOLOGIES, Ch. 2, **133**.

STUDIES

1716 NEWTON, Theodore F. M. "William Pittis and Queen Anne journalism." *MP* 32 (1935): 169-86.

Account of Pittis's role in the journalistic bickering which erupted in the third year of the reign of Queen Anne. Embittered by the Queen's conversion to the temperate policies of her ministry, the Tory extremists launched a virulent paper warfare, not only against the Whiggish opponents, but against any apostle of moderation.

1717-----"William Pittis and Queen Anne journalism II." *MP* 33 (1936): 279-302.

The journalistic frenzy died of its own futility, but brought out one of the most provacative journals of the reign, *Whipping Post*, at a new session of Ayer and Terminer for the scribblers which offered valuable, if biased, comments on the affairs of day (1705). This, and *Heraclitus ridens* (1703-04), were written by a former fellow of Oxford named Wiliam Pittis. He became a close friend of Tom Brown, whose place as Pittis's closest companion was taken by Ned Ward, and was also associated with the publisher Curll. Only a dozen of his 50 works bear his name, and in his scurrility, he is most valuable in presenting a new light on peoples and problems of his day.

———

PERRAULT, Charles

Tales of Mother Goose (1729; several edns by 1800)

NCBEL II 992[11]; ECSTC 1534P1
Trans. G. M. GENT (11th ed. 1719); trans. Robert SAMBER (1729).
Many titles, versions, selections. Authorship now questioned.

EDITIONS

1718 BARCHILON, Jacques (introd. and crit. text). PERRAULT, Charles. *Tales of Mother Goose: The Dedication Manuscript of 1695. Reproduced in Collotype Facsimile.* New York: Pierpont Morgan Library, 1956; pp. 108.

The introd. gives an account of the authorship of the Tales, the sources, Parrault's textual improvements, his literary achievement, and a biographical sketch. Bibliography (105-8).

1719 BRERETON, Geoffrey. (introd. and trans.). *Fairy Tales*. Harmondsworth: Penguin Books, 1957; pp. xli, 114.

Introd. (ix-xli) looks at: 1) Folklore and the Fairy Tale (ix-xvi); 2) Perrault and Mother Goose (xvii-xxii); 3) The Individual Tales (xxli-xli). "It appears likely that he meant his tales to not so much moral in the ethical sense as 'exemplary' or instructive. They taught children what the world was like, bad and dangerous as well as good. To overcome the bad it was not always enough to be good oneself. One must also be wary and cleaver. What more beneficial lesson could there be? "(xxi). The illustrations used as headings to the tales are reproductions of the woodcuts appearing in the first English edition of Perrault, a copy of which is known to exist. This is the so-called 'eleventh' edition, *The Tales of Mother Goose*, "Englished by G. M. Gent (probably Guy Miege) and dated 1719. The designs were inspired by the 1677 (Paris) edition of the original French text.

1720 *Contes de Perrault*. (Collection "renard poche".) Paris: L'école des loisirs, 1978.; pp. 126.

Complete edition of the original text of 1697 with omission of the final moralizing verses, following the practice of Jules Hetzel in his edition of 1860. Particularly interesting for the reproduction of the illustrations by Gustave Doré, also done for the Hetzel edition (40 pl.).

1721 ZIPES, Jack (trans.). The ten tales of *Histoires ou contes du temps passé*. In (pp. 21-74) *Beauties, beasts and enchantment* etc., **150**.

These tales form part of a selection and translation of a series of French fairy tales, using John Robinson PLANCHÉ'S two collections *Four-and-twenty Fairy Tales selected from those of Perrault, etc* (1858) and *Countess D'Aulnoy's Fairy Tales* (1885) as a basis, with the aim of providing a modern version of the major tales, and reintroducing the public to the neglected archaeologist and writer.

STUDIES

1722 HALSBAND, Robert. "An imitation of Perrault in England: Lady Mary Wortley Montague's 'Carabosse'." *Comparative Lit* 3 (1951): 174-77.

Lady Mary's imitation of Perrault is a canvas she used to sketch her own spiritual portrait, and she displays in it the subtlety and cynicism with which she had been bestowed in her real life. She also imitated Perrault's courtly style and etiquette. If she borrowed from the French, she generously paid back, since her popularization of innoculation inspired the *philosophes.*

1723 MORGAN, Jeanne. *Perrault's morals for moderns.* (American Univ. Studies; Series II, Vol. 28.) New York: Peter Lang, 1985; pp. 179.

Reconsiders the multiple context within which Perrault's *Contes* were created in order to clarify controversies surrounding them and to attain an understanding of the text which is consistent with its distinctive stylistic qualities. Reconstructs what the *Contes* meant to Perrault and to his target audience of the late 17c. Analyzes style and moralities which close the Tales, suggesting that he intended his stories for adult readers rather than children. In those stories not of classical inspiration, he develops a 'modern' genre in which the final moral statement is suitable for the age of Louis XIV. Looks at the author, creation of a modern genre, sources, parallel versions and originality, the *contes du temps passé.* Selected Bibliography (171-79).

1724 PALMER, Nancy B. and PALMER, Melvin D. "The French *conte de fée* in England" etc., **733.**

1725 SORIANO, Marc. *Les contes de Perrault, culture savante et traditions populaires.* Paris: Gallemard, 1968; pp. 525.

In French. Detailed study of the Fairy Tales, and Perrault's life: "Une enquête difficile - La Piste du Folklore"; "Le Père et le Fils"; "Les Bessons"; "Les Questions les plus générale". Bibliography (497-509).

1726-----*Le Dossier Perrault.* Paris: Hachette, 1972; pp. 438.

In French. Full critical biography and survey of works.

1727 ZIPES, Jack. "The Rise of the French Fairy Tale and the Decline of France". In (pp. 1-12) *Beauties, beasts and enchantment* etc., **150.**

1728----"Charles Perrault". In (pp. 17-19) *Beauties, beasts and enchantment* etc.

Succinct critical introd. to the life and works, discussing Perrault's transformation of several folk tales, with all their superstitious beliefs and magic, into moralistic tales that would appeal to both adults and children, and demonstrating a modern approach to literature. He was the greatest stylist among the writers of fairy tales in the 1690s, offering an enduring contribution to the debate about values, norms, politics, and civility. Zipes asks whether the Age of Reason has in fact "led to the progress and happiness promised so charmingly in Perrault's tales" (19).

—

PÉTIS DE LA CROIX, François

1. *Turkish tales; consisting of several extraordinary adventures [...] now done into English* (1708, pp. 323)

   NCBEL II 986[4]; McBurney 41; Morgan 450; ECSTC 1677P2

2. *The Persian and the Turkish tales, compleat, tr. formerly from those languages into French by M. Pétis de la Croix (assisted by A. R. Le Sage) and now translated into English by Dr. King and several other hands* (1714, 1718 etc; 6 edns by 1750; 3 vols: *Persian Tales*, pp. 1-459; II *Persian Tales*, pp. 499-755; + *Turkish Tales*, 1-229, 230-39, 240-52)

   NCBEL II 988[10]; McBurney 75; Morgan 478
   Trans. William KING et al from *Les milles et un jour* and *Histoire de la sultane de Perse, contes turcs*; Ambrose PHILIPS'S version of the former, 1714, had 5 edns by 1738. Extremely popular and influential.

—

PLANTIN, Arabella

Two novels: The Ingrateful; Love led astray (1727, 1731 [as a filler in miscellanies relating to the Duke of Wharton]; 2 pts, pp. 33-37 + 38-58)

   NCBEL II 991[20]; McBurney 217; ECSTC 2592P1
   Romances with a moral tone.

—

PÖLLNITZ, Karl Ludwig

Les amusements de Spa: or the gallantries of the Spaw in Germany (1737, 1737, 1739, 1740, 1745; 2 vols: I, 232; II, 270)

   NCBEL II 994[14]; McBurney 325
   Travelogue, anecdotes, secret histories.

—

PRÉCHAC, Jean, Sieur de

The disguis'd Prince; or the beautiful Parisian (1728; 2 pts, pp. 58 + 54)

McBurney 238.

———

PRÉVOST D'EXILES, Antoine-François, Abbé

1. *The life of Mr Cleveland, natural son of Oliver Cromwell* (1731, 1734-5 etc,
   [Dublin] 1736; numerous edns through the century; 5 vols: I, 1-248; II,
   1-277; III, 3-422; IV, 3-298; V, 3-299)

   NCBEL II 993[1]; McBurney 265; ECSTC 1636L33/3537P7
   Several different trans., from *Le Philosophe anglais* (1731-39).
   Sensibility and deism; complex series of adventures; the hero an
   autodidact. Extremely popular and influential; much imitated.

2. *Memoirs of a man of quality* (1738, 1740; 7 edns by 1770 [with other titles]; pp.
   299)

   NCBEL II 994[16]; McBurney 327; ECSTC 3567P5
   Trans. J. WILFRED (1738); ANON. "A new edition" (1770). There is no
   material difference between the text of the 2 editions. Autobiographical
   adventures; pathos and sentiment.

EDITIONS

1729 *Adventures of a Man of Quality. Translated with an Introduction by Mysie
   E. I. ROBERTSON.* (The Broadway Library of XVIII Century French
   Literature.) London: George Routledge & Sons, Ltd., 1930; pp. 208. 4
   illus.
   Trans. of Vol. 5; Vol. 7 *Manon Lescaut* is omitted. Introd. (1-58).
   Translator's Note (59-60). Prologue [summary of Vol. 1-5] (61-74). Text
   of Vol. 5 *Adventures of a Man of Quality in England* (75-184). Epilogue
   [summary of Vol. 6] (185-94). Bibliography (195-208). Extended 4-part
   introd. provides details of life and work, esp. Prévost's experiences in
   London, as well as discussion of the novel, its genesis, sources, content,
   form and style, and history of its translation.

1730 *The History of Manon Lescaut and the Chevalier de Grieux. Translated
   with an Introduction by George Dunning GRIBBLE.* (Broadway
   Translations.) London: George Routledge & Sons, Ltd. and New York:
   E.P Dutton & Co., 1925; pp. 269.

Introd. "The Abbé Prévost and the Story of *Manon*" (1-48). Preface by the Author (49-52). *The History of Manon Lescaut* (53-266). The Principal Works of the Abbé Prévost (267-69).

1731 *The Story of Manon Lescaut and the Chevalier des Grieux*. Trans. H. WODDEL. New York: The Heritage Press, 1935.

1732 *Manon Lescaut*. Trans. L. W. TANCOCK. Harmondsworth: Penguin Books, 1949; pp. 190. Rpt. 1967.

Introd. (7-17) to the life of Prévost and nature of the work and the English translation. "*Manon Lescaut* [...] has the economy, the logic, the dignity and the morality of a classical tragedy, especially of the classical tragedy of Racine" (13).

1733 *Histoire du Chevalier des Grieux et de Manon Lescaut*. Ed. Frédéric DELOFFRE and Raymond PICARD. Paris: Éditions Garnier Frères, 1965; pp. clxxvii, 337. 34 illus.

Introduction (iii-clxxvii) gives genesis, meaning, contemporary opinions of the novel. Text has extended critical footnotes. Bibliography (254-63). Lists of contemporary editions (265-304). Notes on the iconography (305-19). Glossary (322-52). Index (333-7).

BIBLIOGRAPHY

GENERAL

1734 ROBERTSON, Mysie E. I. *Adventures of a Man of Quality*, etc.. London, 1930.
Provides extensive bibliography (195-208) pertinent to Prévost's life in England: I. Sources A. Prévost's two visits to England (195-6); B. Work published prior to 1731 (196-99); C. Other sources for the period (199-202); II. Secondary Works (202-8);III.Works of Reference (208).

1735 SGARD, Jean. *Prévost: Romancier*. Paris: Librairie Jesé Corti, 1968; pp. 692.
Extensive bibliography (641-70):1. work devoted to Prévost (644-50); 2. old sources (651-63); 3. modern works (19-20cc) (664-70).

PARTICULAR

1736 BIBLIOTHÉTHQUE NATIONALE. *Manon Lescaut à travers deux siècles*. Paris, 1963. pp. x, 50. 6 illus.

Introduces a list of 304 items connected with all aspects of Prévost's most famous work. 1) L'Abbé Prévost et ses oeuvres (1. vie, 2. oeuvres); 2) *Manon Lescaut* (1. L'epoque et le décor, 2. Les editions du vivant de l'auteur); 3) L'Illustration de *Manon Lescaut* (1. Les editions illustrées, 2. Les images et les imitations); 4) *Manon Lescaut* et la posterité (1. Les commentateurs, 2. Suites romanesques et les imitations, 3. traductions); 5) *Manon Lescaut* dans les spectacles (1. oeuvres dramatiques, 2. oeuvres lyriques, 3. oeuvres cinémato-graphiques).

1737 DELOFFRE and PICARD, *Histoire du Chevalier des Grieux et de Manon Lescaut* etc., **1733**.

Extensive bibliography (245-63) lists contemporary editions, modern editions, works relating to Prévost and *Manon Lescaut*.

SELECTED STUDIES

1738 ENGEL, Claire-Eliane. *Figures et aventures du XVIIIe siècle: Voyages et découvertes de l'Abbé Prévost.* (Études de littérature, d'art et d'histoire, 5.) Paris: Editions 'Je sers', 1939; pp. 277.

In French. Survey of the English scene as Prévost knew it. Investigates the Abbé's relations with England in detail. The Introduction provides a survey of English society and literature from 1727 to 1740. Part I looks at Prévost's English impressions, his journey, London and the English countryside, the English Revolution, the refuge for Frenchmen, adventure at sea (South Sea Company, Defoe), romanesque themes (esp. *Pamela*). Part II examines the aesthetic scene, the conception of history, the English novels of the time, the dramatic scene, truth and the psychology of the Abbé. Bibliography (249-61). Index.

1739 FACULTÉ DES LETTRES ET SCIENCES HUMAINES D'AIX. *Abbé Prévost.* (Actes du Colloque d'Aix-en-Provence 20 et 21 Décembre 1963. Nouvelle série, No. 50.) Aix-en-Provence: Publications des Annales de la Faculté des Lettres, 1965; pp. 270.

In French. Introd. J. FABRE. Series of 26 essays covering various aspects of the life, thought and fiction of Prévost. Includes:
- J. FABRE, "Prévost et le roman noir" (39-56);
- R. MEIER, "Le thème oriental dans les romans de Prévost" (85-92);
- A. LEBOIS, "Amitié, amour et inceste dans *Cleveland*" (125-38);
- F. PRUNER, "Pychologie de la *Grecque moderne*" (139-46);
- H. COULET, "Le comique dans les romans de Prévost" (173-84);
- R. MAUZI, "Le thème de la retraite dans les romans de Prévost" (185-

96);

- J. ROUSSET, "Prévost romancier: la forme autobiographique" (197-206);
- K. WAIS, "L'Abbé Prévost et le renouvellement du roman en Europe" (247-54).

1740 FOSTER, James R. "The Abbé Prévost and the English novel." *PMLA* 42 (1927): 443-64.

The novels of Mmes De Layette, D'Aulnoy, De Tancin, Riccoboni and De Genlis, and those of Marivaux and Prévost were animated by the spirit of that philosophy of the heart which Richardson made so savoury. Adaptations and copies of the French were often the most significant and important; in fact they determined to a great extent the form taken by the novel of the last two decades of the century. Prévost was known in England, France and Germany. He gave concrete expression and engaging form to the new philosophy of feeling. An anti-classicism was inherent to his conception of character, and the romantic craving for the exotic and the strange was evinced in his romanesque themes. Because his main business was to write an interesting narrative, he did not preach or go out of his way to develop ideas. Like Mmes D'Aulnoy and De Nerval, he was fond of English characters and a quasi-historical background. Marvellous and moving adventures, shipwrecks, piracy, abduction, incredible coincidence, robbery and the supernatural became episodes in the frame of a sentimental love story. His treatment of love is notable. The English critical press gave him generous notice, and the storehouse of his romanesque themes was extensively plagiarised.

1741 HARRISSE, Henry. *L'Abbé Prévost: Histoire de sa vie et ses oeuvres. (Documents nouveaux)*. Paris: Calmann Lévy, 1896; pp. 465.

In French. Introduction (1-82). La famille Prévost (1480 to 1895). Year by year examination of life and works (1697 to 1762) with documentation of many kinds, most esp. letters, and details of the various editions of his works. Index (455-65). Illus.

1742 HAVENS, George R. *L'Abbé Prévost and English literature*. (Elliott Monographs in the Romance Languages and Literatures.) Princeton: Princeton UP, 1921. Rpt. New York: Kraus Reprint Corporation, 1965; pp. 135.

The French refugees played a leading role in spreading on the Continent a knowledge of English institutions, science and literature. They prepared the way for the work of three great men, Béat de Muralt, Voltaire and the Abbé Prévost. Considers the life of Prévost in England, the general aims of the *Pour et Contre* its authorship, the general principles of Prévost's criticism, his preparation, his attitude to Voltaire's *Lettres philosophes*, to Shakespeare, Addison, Dryden, Milton, Pope, Shaftesbury, Steele, Swift, Lillo, other English authors. Investigates his sources and influence (117-31). Bibliography (132-35).

1743 JACCARD, Jean-Luc. *Manon Lescaut: Le personnage - romancier*. Paris: A.-G. Nizet, 1975; pp. 254.
In French. Devoted to *Manon Lescaut* looking in Part I at "Les particularités du discours" and in Part II at "Les étapes de l'idéalisation". Bibliography (249-50).

1744 JOSEPHSON, Miriam. *Die Romane des Abbé Prévost als Spiegel des 18. Jahrhunderts*. Winterthur: P. G. Keller, 1966; pp. 72.

In German. Looks at:1) Die Auflösung der Gemeinschaft; 2) Der Einbruch der Materie; 3) Die Frau als Zentrum; 4) Verlust der Einheit; 5) Die neue Religion; 6) *Manon Lescaut*: Kampf zweier Welten. Investigates "eine Welt, die trotz allem weitgehend ein Spiegel der geistigen Situations Frankreichs in der erste Hälfte des 18. Jahrhunderts ist, mag sie auch Züge enthalten, die auf Kommendes hinweisen. Zweck dieser Arbeit soll sein, diese Welt, wie sie in Werk des Abbé Prévost lebt, zur Darstellung zu bringen und in ihren Zusammenhängen zu untersuchen". Bibliography (72).

1745 KORY, Odile A. *Subjectivity and sensitivity in the novels of the Abbé Prévost*. Paris: Didier, 1972; pp. 135.

Prévost's writings reveal the 18c mind at work. Analyzes the themes recurrent through his novels in the light of 18c intellectual, literary and emotional atmosphere. The rise of the novel as a legitimate means to express new ideas and sensitivities resulted in Prévost giving fictional life to his ideas and his conception of man. He was at once encyclopedic and creative. His position was determined as both priest and scholar: he was constantly pulled between traditional unquestioning adherence to Christian dogma, and the new world of intellectual curiosity. Looks at the nature of sensibility, realism and subjectivity, the problems of morality, the search for an identity. It is the alienation of his heroes that provided a vivid model for the 19c romantic hero.

1746 LABRIOLLE-RUTHERFORD, M. R. de. "*Le Pour et Contre* et les romans de l'abbé Prévost." *Revue d'histoire littéraire de la France* 62 (1962): 28-40.
In French."*Le Pour et Contre* contient des commentaires et des

éclaircissements intéressants sur les romans que l'Abbé Prévost composa avant 1740. Dans le Tome III de ce périodique se trouve un éloge de *Manon Lescaut* qui dut paraître en février ou mars 1734".

1747 MONTY, Jeanne R. *Les romans de l'abbé Prévost.* (SVEC, 78.) Geneva: Institut et Musée Voltaire, Les Delices, 1970; pp. 272.

In French. Devotes a chapter to each principal work: *Mémoires d'un homme de qualité*; *Histoire de Cleveland*; *Le Doyen de Killerine*; *Histoire d'un Greque moderne*; *Mémoire d'un honnête homme*. Bibliography (1. works of Prévost, 2. works on Prévost, 3. general studies) (259-68). Index (269-72).

1748 MÜLLER, Walter. *Die Grundbegriffe der gesellschaftlichen Welt in den Werken des Abbé Prévost.* (Marburger Beiträge zur romanischen Philologie, 19.) Marburg/Lahn: Hans Michaelis Braun, 1938; pp. 100.

In German. Surveys the Prévost research to date, and investigates certain dominant themes, e.g. the central concern with money and wealth (1. "Geld als Medium des Widerspruchs der Liebe"; 2. "Geld als abstraktes Prinzip gesellschaftlicher Gliederung"; 3. "Die subjektiven und objektiven Bedingungen der Hypotrophe der Geldkategorie bei Prévost"). The second part looks at the "Weltbild Prévosts" (1. theory and practice, the role of *hazard*, a discussion of "Willensfreiheit und Subjektivierung der Moral" and "die utopische Planung der Wirklichheit". Bibliography (96-8).

1749 SGARD, Jean. *Prévost: Romancier.* Paris: Librairie Jesé Corti, 1968; pp. 692.
In French. Large study of life and works discussed chronologically and critically in tandem: Part I (1720-1728), II (1731), III (1734-1740), IV (1741-1763). Appendices provide a list of Prévost's works (607-22) and discuss his correspondence (622-40). Major bibliography (641-70).

1750 TURNELL, Martin. "The Abbé Prévost." In (pp. 31-60) *The art of French fiction: Prévost, Stendhal, Zola, Maupassant, Gide, Mauriac, Proust.* London: Hamish Hamilton, 1959; pp. 394.

Looks at the position of a priest-novelist in the 18c, examining *Manon Lescaut,* and the forgotten novels. "It is one of Prévost's shortcomings that, like Marivaux, his novels were too much the product of the age in which he lived, and that he did not possess either the toughness of the highly individual sensibility - a sensibility that creates new patterns of feeling - which stamp a man as a great writer" (60).

1751 WEINSTEIN, Arnold. "Old Worlds, New Worlds (*Manon Lescaut*)". In (pp. 131-45) *Aspects of the self* etc., **1039**.

Prévost suggests that our most authentic experiences emanate from "the lunar landscape of the heart", and he shows us with considerable power that we cannot live there. "Passion betokens an awakening of the self and a threat to society; gratification is brief; reconciliation with this world, impossible; transcendence to another, impossible" (145).

1752 WILCOX, Frank Howard. "Prévost's translations of Richardson's novels." *University of California Publications in Modern Philology* 12 (1927): 341-411.
Monograph which attempts to illustrate certain characteristics of French taste in the 18c by an examination of the change which Prévost introduced into his versions of Richardson's novels. Divided into 6 chapters: 1) the growth of English influence in France; 2) Prévost's translations; 3) Richardson and the laws of good taste; 4) and 5) Richardson's realism and preaching, 6) conclusion. Bibliography (409-11). During the latter half of the 17c, the literary fashion was from France to England. During the first half of the 18c, the current turned in the other direction. It is not so much that French letters ceased to exert an influence in England (the novels of Marivaux, Le Sage, and Prévost were read with enthusiasm in both countries), but at the time the French public first became aware of English literature and discerned its strange and attractive qualities. The real impulse towards the knowledge of English literature came from the exiled Huguenots. Then came the *Lettres anglaises* of Voltaire. An even more influential interpreter of the English to the French was the Abbé Prévost. In his career as priest, soldier and man of letters, he fled to England in 1728, and returned in 1733. Altogether he spent three-and-a-half years in England, acquired a thorough knowledge of English, became enthusiastic for the country of his exile, its institutions, manners and literature. The fruits of this are seen in his novels, *Mémoirs d'un homme de qualité* and *Cleveland*. After 1740 he abandoned *Le Pour et Contre* (1733-40), a literary journal in which he intorduced a great deal of English attitudes to the French and gave place to serious literary criticism and translations. His most notable labor was the translation of Richardson's novels.

1753 WILLIAMS, Ioan. "Enlightenment and Absurdity; Prévost's *Le Philosophe anglais*". In (pp. 156-61) *The idea of the novel* etc., **147**.

Even though his view of the novel was more advanced than that of his predecessors, *Le Philosophe anglais* is not a successful work of fiction. Rather than lie with the narrator and his experiences, attention in the novel is devoted to the author's didactic purposes in promoting a secular and humane view of the world. "His rationalism short-circuited experience and involved him necessarily in gross manipulation and consequent absurdity" (162).

1754 WINNACK, Paul. "Some English influences on the Abbé Prévost." In (pp. 285-312) MASON, Haydn (gen.ed.). *Studies on Voltaire and the eighteenth century.* Vol. 182. Oxford: Voltaire Foundation, 1979; pp. 357.
Many of the novelists of the early 18c seemed to have fluctuated between the writing of plays and the writing of novels. Fielding, Crébillon, Marivaux spring to mind as both novelists and dramatists. The Abbé Prévost was an exception to such a list, an absence which is all the more remarkable when one remembers his obvious enthusiasm for the theater. *Le Pour et Contre* bears witness to Prévost's knowledge and appreciation of the English stage with its reports and translations of the plays which he considered important enough to introduce to the French reading public. His outlook and approach to French literary traditions was influenced by his exposure to and appreciation of English literature (Farquhar, Lillo, Aphra Behn).

———

QUINTANA, Francisco de

The most entertaining history of Hippolito and Aminta: being a collection of delightful novels (1718, 1721 etc.; pp. 391)

NCBEL II 988[8]; McBurney 93; ECSTC 85Q1
Trans. John STEVENS from the Spanish novel of 1627.

———

RENNEVILLE, René-Auguste

The French inquisition: or the history of the Bastille in Paris (1715, pp. 322)

NCBEL II 987[15]; McBurney 81; ECSTC 745R1
Trans. from *L'Inquisition française*, 1715.
Sensational memoir in the manner of DEFOE; anti-clerical.

———

ROWE, Elizabeth Singer

1. *Friendship in death in twenty Letters from the Dead to the Living* (3 pts 1728-32; at least 18 edns by 1800; pp. 70, 138, 253)

NCBEL II 992[7]; McBurney 234; Morgan 581; ECSTC 1996R7
Letters from the dead to the living as a device for pious instruction.

2. *Letters, Moral and Entertaining in Prose and Verse* (3 pts 1729-33; numerous
   later edns)

NCBEL II 992[12]; Morgan 592; ECSTC 1996R18
Similar to the earlier work, but better as fiction.

EDITIONS

1755 *Friendship in Death*, selections. Ed. BACKSCHEIDER and RICHETTI in
(pp. 323-34) *Popular fiction by women, 1660-1730: an anthology* etc.
See ANTHOLOGIES, Ch. 2, **119**.

STUDIES

1756 HUGHES, Helen Sard. "Elizabeth Rowe and the Countess of Hertford."
PMLA 59 (1944): 726-46.

Mrs Rowe learned various lessons from Isaac Watts. Her piety and the
enthusiastic order of the Dissenters, were expressed with the
conventional elegance of her day. More noteworthy was her employment
on occasion of the ardent language of her own romantic heart. Both in
the elegance and in the quality of her romantic feeling and imagination
which marked her prose and verse, she was encouraged by another
friend, and a correspondent of more than 20 years, the Countess of
Hertford, a patroness of young poets. This friendship was woven into her
literary work, and casts light on the writings, as well as being interesting
from the human aspect. Extensive quotation from the correspondence.

1757 RICHETTI, John J. "Mrs Elizabeth Rowe: the novel as polemic." *PMLA* 82
(1967): 522-29.

Critical review of life and work. Dr Johnson recognized that Mrs Rowe's
works were the touchstone for those who aspired to combine devotion
with literary pleasure. Her books are a literary polemic against unbelief,
waged on the emotional and human level, for assurance of immortality
and salvation is provided ultimately through conjugal love (or the
capacity for it) which is elevated to the status of beatitude. Death, the
great problem that rationalism and infidelity cannot solve, is defeated by
true and pure love, the great human necessity which reason cannot
explain or eliminate. The novel develops in its main direction (that is, as
a powerful moral and social force) by learning to embody the theological

antithesis between the simple believer and faithless world in a persuasive narrative form. Mrs Rowe's *Letters* is nothing less than an important symptom of the gradual accommodation of fiction to the idelogical needs of the time.

———

RUSSEN, David

Inter-lunare: or a voyage to the moon (1703, 1707; pp. 147)

NCBEL II 985[2]; McBurney 11; ECSTC 2235R2
Whimsical Utopian romance.

———

SAINT EVREMOND, Charles

A novel [*The Irish prophet*] (1700, pp.21)

WING S301
Contained in *Works* (1700), vol.2, pp.78-99.
Novel set in the Restoration.

STUDIES

1758   COHEN, Gustave. "Le séjour de Saint-Evremond en Hollande (1665-1670)." *RLC* 5 (1925): 431-54; *RLC* 6 (1926): 28-78, 402-23.

Extensive biographical investigation into the life of Saint-Evremond in Holland. Describes his relations with Vossius, Huygens, Spinoza. Includes an appendix of several autograph letters in the Record Office mentioned neither in the *Calendar of State Papers*, nor included among those of 1666 published by Melville Daniels, but pointed out by the Dutch historian Jaspike.

1759   HOPE, Quentin M. *Saint-Evremond: the Honnête Homme as critic.* (Indiana Univ. Humanistic Series, 51.) Indiana UP, 1962; pp. 146.

Saint Evremond, who never wanted to be anything other than an *honnête homme*, is by reputation the best critic of his day. He presented no carefully elaborated doctrine, no systematic approach to literature. This lack of system may explain his appeal: his critical essays do mirror a distinctive personality, being short, stimulating and idiosycratic, written not for the general public, but for his friends. Molière, Racine and Boileau preached in their prefaces, and demonstrated in their works, the crucial importance of *l'art de plaire* - the art of engaging and holding the whole interest of the reader. Saint Evremond, by creating the new genre of the informal critical essay, the form of which he borrowed from Montaigne, and which he adapted to the manners of his own time, with a more exclusively literary subject matter, was the first to bring *l'art de plaire* into literary criticism. Looks at his reputation, the *honnête homme*, the psychological approach, the historical perspective, the intellectual response, key works. Bibliographical notes. Selected bibliography (135-39). Index.

1760   SPALATIN, K. *Saint-Evremond.* (Séminaire de Philologia Romane de l'Université de Zagreb.) Zagreb, 1934 and Paris: Société d'Éditions Les Belles Lettres, 1935; pp. 180.

In French. Account of life and works. I." La Vie et l'Oeuvre"; II. "L'Esprit de Saint-Evremond (amour et amitié, philosophie et réligion, histoire et critique)". Bibliography (165-74). Chronology of works (175-80). Of particular interest is the section I e) "L'Oeuvre" (97-118) which describes his work in England, and his influence on English literature (115-8). "Grâce à l'enorme prestige français de cette époque et à sa propre finesse, Saint-Evremond à contribué en grande partie au raffinement, pour ainsi dire, du public, des manières et du style anglais" (116). He exerted special influence on Hamilton, and was at one with Chesterfield and Addison in condemning the excesses of the French and English theater.

1761   TERNOIS, René. "En écoutant Saint-Evremond." *Revue d'histoire littérature de la France* 60 (1960): 165-76.

In French. "Le vrai Saint Evremond ce n'est pas dans les notes et la notice bavarde de ses editions [...] mais ailleurs -- dans la préface de *Silvestre* si discrète qu'elle soit, dans des lettres inédites, dans les documents qu'on peut encore découvrir, et en particulier dans ce cahier de notes, où on entend le vieil homme parler de lui-même, de sa jeunesse, et de ses écrits" (176).

———

SAINT HYACINTHE, Themiseul de

The adventures of Pomponious, a Roman knight (1726; 2 pts, pp. 144, 152)

NCBEL II 991[6]; McBurney 200
Trans. S. MACKY.
A scandal novel of the French Court.

STUDIES

1762 MISH, Charles Carol. "A voyage to the moon." *NQ* 200 (Dec. 1955): 527-29.

This comparatively little-known piece of early 18c prose fiction is a trans. by Spring MACKY from the French. A persistent tradition connects the book with the Abbé Prévost, who is credited with having revised, and sometimes with publishing, it. Basically the book is a topical satire: religious, literary, historical. Besides the treatment of historical characters, religious groups, such as the Jesuits, come in for satire, as do the various agitations in France caused by the papal bull *Unigenitus*. The specific persons jibed at are identified in a series of notes (39 pp.), offering a key to the work. The topic of the lunar voyage is unusual in that the satire starts as a romance, so that the hero's trip to the moon comes as a jolt. Here it becomes satire. The moon is a country like, and yet unlike, the earth, so that visitors get along, and yet have characteristic adventures. The last part of the book provides 84 pp. of miscellaneous material, dealing with the regency of Louis XV.

———

SEGRAIS, Jean-Regnauld de

Five novels (1725 [2 formats]; 4 edns by 1736; n.p.)

> NCBEL II 990[23]
> Trans. from *Nouvelles françaises*, reissued 1722.
> Condensed romances.

———

SMITH, Alexander

1. *The history of the lives and robberies of the most noted highway-men* (1713; 6 edns by 1720 [2-3 vols.]; 1734 [with Charles JOHNSON, *General history of the pirates*]; pp. 288 + 288 [2nd. ed.]; 326 + 364 [5th ed.])

> NCBEL II 987[3]; McBurney 68; Morgan 475; ECSTC 2824S3
> Collection of short rogue biographies, male and female; lively and often obscene; highly popular.

2. *The secret history of the lives of the most celebrated beauties, ladies of quality and jilts from fair Rosamund down to the present day* (1715, 1716 [as *The school of Venus* and *The court of Venus*], 1730 [as *Court intrigues*]; pp. 262)

NCBEL II 987[16]; McBurney 80; Morgan 484; ECSTC 2824S2
Large collection of brief lives of famous courtesans and royal favourites;
lively, anecdotal style; inserted letters.

3. *Memoirs of the life and times of the famous Jonathan Wilde.* 1726; pp. 287.

NCBEL II 991[7]; ECSTC 2824S5
One of several rogue biographies of Wild.

EDITIONS

1763   *A Complete History of the Lives and Robberies of the most notorious*
Highwaymen, Footpads, Shoplifts, and Cheats of Both Sexes, Wherein
the most Secret and Barbarous Murders, Unparalleled Robberies,
Notorious Thefts and Unheard-of Cheats are set in a true Light and
exposed to Public View, for the Common Benefit of Mankind. Ed. Arthur
L. HAYWARD. London: George Routledge & Sons Ltd., 1926; pp. xxii,
607. 17 illus.
Introd. places the work in historical context, describes the genre and
existing literature, criminality and the underworld of early 18c London.
Points out that nothing is known about Capt. Smith. "This edition [...] is
reprinted from the 5th edition, published in three 12mo volumes in 1719.
The spelling and punctuation have been modernized, but the phraseology
has been left untouched and to all intents and purposes this book is as the
author wrote it" (xix). Includes Preface to vol. I (1-3).

STUDIES

1764   KATANKA, Margaret C. "'Captain Smith's' plagiarism." *NQ* 24 (1977):
222-23.
Captain Alexander Smith was responsible for three works containing
honestly collected and dubiously accurate biographies. His subjects
ranged from celebrities of the underworld (1714), to the bailiffs of the
law (1723). Encouraged by the success of his criminal biographies, he
produced a history of cuckolds (1716) in the preface of which he
described the characteristics of a whore. In this he plagiarized the ideas
of Sir Thomas Overbury in his book *A Wife, now the Widow of Sir*
Thomas Overbury (1614).

1765   SECORD, A. W. "Captain Alexander Smith." *TLS* (19 April 1934): 288.

Although no copies of the first, third and fourth editions of Capt. Smith's
Lives of the Highwaymen are now known, it is clear from newspaper
advertisements that the first was issued by Morphew on 10 Nov. 1713,

the second on 24 Dec. 1713, or early 1714. Six works were attributed to Smith :

1) *Lives of the Highwaymen*;
2) *The secret history of the most celebrated beauties* (2 vols, 1716);
3) *The court of Venus* (2 vols, 1716);
4) *The comical and tragical history of the Bayliffs* (1723);
5) *Memoirs of the life and times of Jonathan Wild* (1726);
6) *Court Intrigues; or an account of the secret amours of the British nobility* (1730).

Nos. 2, 3 and 6 are identical.

——

'SYMSON, William'

A new voyage to the East Indies (1715, 1720, 1732; n.p.)

NCBEL II 978[17]; ECSTC 5320S1
A probable source of *Gulliver's travels*.

STUDIES

1766 FRANTZ, R.W. "Gulliver's cousin Symson." *HLQ* 1 (1938): 329-34.

In 1726 Swift released *Gulliver's Travels* for publication, and included a prefatory statement by a certain Symson who declared his relationship to Gulliver. 'William Symson' never existed. The book bearing his name is spurious. Those portions of it which describe the voyage to and from the East Indies were taken from John Ovington's trustworthy *Voyage to Suralt* (1696). Swift used Symson not Ovington: he took certain materials from *A Voyage to the East Indies* which masqueraded as the work of a real voyager named Capt. William Symson. The pilfering of one small passage from this work gives it a distinction it would otherwise not deserve: Swift honored this one of many accounts of actual voyages in the early 18c by his slight borrowing.

——

TENCIN, Claudine-Alexandrine-Guérin de

The siege of Calais by Edward of England (1740; 4 edns by 1751; pp. 288)

NCBEL II 995[3]; Beasley 32
Trans. Charles DENNIS?
Romantic treatment of history; unusual amount of historical detail, setting.

TERRASSON, Jean

The life of Sethos. Taken from private memoirs of the Ancient Egyptians. Translated from a Greek Manuscript into French and now faithfully done into English by Mr. Lediard (1732; 2 pts pp. 460 + 480)

NCBEL II 993[7]; McBurney 276; Morgan 617; ECSTC 602T3
Trans. Thomas LEDIARD from *Sethos*, 1731.
Historical novel with moral purpose in imitation of Fénelon, *Télémaque*.

THEOBALD, Lewis

The history of the loves of Antiochus and Stratonice (1717, 1721; pp. 290)

NCBEL II 988[3]; McBurney 88; ECSTC 695T26
Retelling of a legend, with a French novel as intermediary.

STUDIES

1767 FRAZIER, Harriet. C. *A babble of ancestral voices: Shakespeare, Cervantes, and Theobald.* (Studies in English Literature 73.) The Hague: Mouton, 1974; pp. 161.

Throughout the early 18c, the additional seven plays attributed to Shakespeare (*The London Prodigal, The History of Thomas Lord Cromwell, Sir John Oldcastle, Lord Cobham, The Puritan Widow, A Yorkshire Tragedy, The Tragedy of Locrine*) appeared in standard editions of Shakespeare. Theobald excluded the vagrant seven. In 1727 he claimed to have in possession three MSS copies of a lost play by Shakespeare, *The Double Falsehood.* Considers Theobald's early interest in Elizabethans, Theobald as Shakespeare editor, *Don Quixote* in the 18c (the adventures of Cardenio). There is considerable evidence that Theobald forged the *The Double Falsehood*, which dramatizes one of the two most popular narratives from *Don Quixote* and adapts the language of Shakespeare's most popular plays (esp. *Hamlet*) for the dramatization of *Cardenio*. This arises from his desire to profit from the enormous vogue which Shakespeare and Cervantes were enjoying in the 18c. Bibliography (154-59).

1768 HINES, Philip, Jr. "Antedatings, postdatings, and additions to O. E. D. in Theobald, 1714-19." *NQ* 23 (1976): 346-48.

Listing of Theobald's supplements to the O.E.D.

1769 INGRAM, William H. "Greek drama and the Augustan stage: Dennis,
      Theobald, Thomson." Unpub. doct. diss., Univ. of Pennsylvania, 1966.
      [*DAI* 27 (1966): 1338A.]

      Study of the fortunes of the Athenian drama in England in the late 17c
      and early 18c. Considers the theories of translation current in the period,
      discussion of pertinent examples, a survey of Classical scholarship and
      Augustan texts of the three tragedies. Then considers three special
      instances of the adaptation of Greek tragedy: *Iphegenia* (1700, John
      Dennis), *Orestes* (1731, Lewis Theobald), *Agamemnon* (1737, Jane
      Thomas).

1770 THOMAS, D. S. "Theobald and Fielding's *Don Tragdio*." *ELN* 2 (1965):
      266-71.
      Judging from the annotations in *The Tragedy of Tragedies*, Fielding drew
      suggestions from *The persian Princess* when he wrote *Tom Thumb*. The
      frenzied style of Theobald's first plays is remarkably like that of
      Fielding's burlesque.

1771 WIDMAN, R. L. "Morgann's copy of Theobald." *NQ* 17 (1970): 125.

      The Folger Shakespeare Library in Washington DC possesses Vol. I of
      Maurice Morgann's 1733 edition of Shakespeare.

1772 WOODS, Charles B. "Fielding's epilogue for Theobald." *PQ* 28 (1949):
      419-24.
      When Fielding was a young dramatist, he wrote a prologue and two
      epilogues for plays by other authors. A third epilogue which has escaped
      the notice of his biographers was published in April 1731 in *Orestes: A
      Dramatic Opera* by Lewis Theobald, the 'hero' of *The Dunciad*.

      ———

THIBAULT, Gouveneur de Talmont

*The life of Pedrillo del Campo intermixed with several entertaining and delightful
novels. Translated into English by Ralph Brookes* (1723, pp. 197)

      NCBEL II 990[1]; McBurney 149; Morgan 530; ECSTC 779T1
      Trans. Ralph BROOKES.
      Spanish picaresque modified for the French taste as a *roman comique*.

      ———

TYSSOT DE PATOT, Simon

The travels and adventures of James Massey (1733, 1743 [another version]; pp. 318)

NCBEL II 993[14]; McBurney 287; ECSTC 2337T1
Trans. Stephen WHATLEY.

STUDIES

1773 ANDREWS, S. G. "The Wandering Jew and *The travels and adventures of James Massey.*" *MLN* 72 (1957): 39-41.
The many details in *The travels and adventures* indicate that the portrait of the Wandering Jew was suggested by the mysterious wanderer in Giovanni Marana's *Letters of a Turkish Spy.* The picture of Tyssot's Wandering Jew is a traditional one, nor is it the first time that the legend had been used as a sort of framework for a rapid survey of famous historical characters and events. The account is unique in one respect, however: here for the first time the Wandering Jew is introduced in order to make an authoritative pronouncement upon a typical fine point of medieval theology -- the condition of the body in the afterlife.

1774 KNOWLSON, J. R. "The ideal languages of Veiras, Foigny, and Tyssot de Patot." *JHI* 24 (1963): 269-78.

In their knowledge of precise schemes of universal languages, the three authors were more than interested amateurs. Their curiosity was wide-ranging, although the areas into which it was channelled were quite unrecognized. Their ideal languages reflect some of the ways in which 17c and 18c scholars aimed at constructing a perfect *lingua mundi.*

1775 McKEE, David Ria. *Simon Tyssot de Patot and the seventeenth-century background of critical deism.* (Johns Hopkins Studies in Romance Literatures and Languages, 40.) Baltimore: Johns Hopkins Press; London: Humphrey Milford, Oxford UP; Paris: Société d'Editions 'Les Belles Lettres', 1941; pp. 105.

James Massey contained the germ not only of Voltaire's later thought, but also that of Diderot and Rousseau. It enjoyed considerable success in the 18c, and Voltaire drew upon it for some of his critical arguments against the doctrine of the resurrection. Voltaire indeed counted the anonymous author among the freethinkers. Looks at the life of Tyssot, the attack on revealed religion, the 17c background, science and metaphysics, political, social and ethical views. Extensive bibliographical notes. Bibliography (97-102). Index (103-5).

1776 STORER, Mary Elizabeth. "Bibliographical observations on Foigny, Lahontan, and Tyssot de Patot." *MLN* 60 (1945): 143-56.

Biographers have listed two 1710 editions of Tyssot's *Voyages des aventures de Jacques Massé*. One very rare, bears the imprint of Cologne (508 pp.). But there were three entirely different 1710 Bordeaux editions; furthermore, there was a fourth from Cologne. Tyssot, alias Jacques Massé, would gladly have thrown responsibility for his deistic ideas on Lord Bolingbroke and the English writers of his kind. But the more we become acquainted with the multiple fictitious imprints of his works, the more we realize that the French libertines of the late 17c needed no bridge to cross the Channel. Investigations in this field show increasingly the diffusion of these philosophic utopias in what seems superficially to have been a strictly censored situation in France.

———

VALDORY, Guillaume

The adventures of the celebrated Madam de Muci (1731, pp. 3-103)

> NCBEL II 993[2]; McBurney 266
> Trans. of *Histoire de Madame de Muci*.
> Epistolary; adventures, disguises, amorous intrigues.

———

VEGA CARPIO, Lope Felix de

The pilgrim: or the stranger in his own country (1738; 2 pts, pp. 1-127, 137-284)

> NCBEL II 994[17]; ECSTC 221V1
> Trans. from *Peregrino en su patria*, 1604.
> Collection of novels, with *Montemayor and Gil Polo, Diana*. Already pub. in *Applebee's Original Weekly Journal*.

———

WALKER, Capt Charles

Authentick memoirs of the life intrigues and adventures of the celebrated Sally Salisbury (1723, 1724; pp. 150)

> NCBEL II 990[3]; McBurney 146; ECSTC 246W1
> Lively memoir of the famous courtesan; inserted letters from her clients;

combines jestbook with rogue biography.

———

WALPOLE, Sir Robert

The present state of fairy-land in severall letters from Esquire Hush (1713, n.p.)
NCBEL II 987[4]; ECSTC 446W27

Anti-Tory propaganda in the form of a letter to Louis XIV from an English squire which replies to an attack on Walpole, *The testimonies of several citizens of Fickleborough.*

STUDIES

1777 PLUMB, J. H. *Sir Robert Walpole.* London: Allen Lane, The Penguin Press, 1956. 2 vols. I, xvii, 407; II, xii, 363. Illus.

Provides a definitive account of his distinguished political career: I, *The Making of a Statesman*; II, *The King's Minister.* Preface, introduction, sources, index. Supports Walpole's supposed authorship of *The Present State of Fairyland in severall letters from Esquire Hush*, which came as a reply to a particularly scurrilous and tasteless sally on Walpole: " [...] the pamphlet contains a brilliantly satirical attack on the ministry's policy towards France. The writing has all the marks of Walpole's own emphatic skill in argument, and it would seem that he himself turned the tables with real journalistic flair on the Grub Street hacks" (I: 183).

1778 WINTON, Calhoun. "Voltaire and Sir Robert Walpole: a new document." *PQ* 46 (1967): 421-24.

The legend persists that Voltaire, while in England during the years 1726-29, acted as a government informer for Sir Robert Walpole. Unless a more plausible explanation is offered, it appears probable that Walpole made Voltaire the gift of 200 pounds sterling with the expectation that he would provide information about Bolingbroke's opposition, or perhaps on the basis of information already provided. This would seem to be true.

———

WARD, Edward

1. *The London spy* (18 pts, 2 vols 1698-1700, 1 vol 1700; first published in book form in 1703 as *The London Spy compleat*; 7 or more edns by 1724)

NCBEL II 984[2]; Morgan 428; ECSTC 569W26/W27

Lively account of rambles through London streets.

2. [et al]. *A pacquet from Will's* (1701 [in *Works of Voiture*, vol. 2], 1724 [in *Familiar lettres of love*]

NCBEL II 984[16]; ECSTC 666V1
Miscellany of narrative letters, humorous and satirical.

EDITIONS

1779 *The London spy.* Ed. with notes and introd. by Kenneth FENWICK. London: Folio Soc.; New York: Duschnes, 1955; pp. xv, 327.
The text is that of 1703, but punctuation has been modernized, as has the use of capital letters and italics. The introd. (xi-xiv) locates the book in its social context and briefly discusses Ward's life and works.

BIBLIOGRAPHY

1780 TROYER, H. W. *Ned Ward of Grubstreet: A study of sub-literary London in the eighteenth century.* Cambridge, MA: Harvard UP, 1946; pp. xi, 290.
Discusses Ward's life and works in the context of the social, political and literary context of late 17c and early 18c London. Ward played a significant role in the development of periodical literature. Provides bibliographical references in the notes (211-18), a list of writings (231-77), and doubtful attributions (278-82).

1781 CAMERON, W. J. "Bibliography of Ned Ward (1667-1731)." *NQ* 198 (July 1953): 284-86.

Provides additions to N. W. Troyer's list of authentic works (1946).

1782 JONES, Claude E. "Short-title checklist of works attributed to Edward Ward (1667-1731)." *NQ* 190 (1946): 135-39.

Ward was one of the most prolific of Samuel Butler's successors, and provided much interesting and informative writing about the London of his day, as well as being a prolific writer of characters, imaginative voyages and realistic prose. Provides a short-title checklist of writings attributed to him.

1783 WARD, S. H. "The works of Edward Ward." *NQ* 198 (Oct. 1953): 436-38.
Provides a list of editions of Ward's works not noted by Troyer, Cameron, and Jones.

STUDIES

1784 ANON. "Defoe, Ward, Brown and Tutchin, 1700-1703." *NQ* 162 (1932):
418-23.
Collection of newspaper references.

1785 ALLEN, Robert Joseph. "Ned Ward and *The Weekly Comedy*." *Harvard
Studies and Notes in Philology and Literature* 17 (1935): 1-14.

Argues that a careful study of *The Weekly Comedy* of 1707 "shows that
Ward's authorship [...] is, in part at least, open to question [...]."
Discusses the two publications entitled *The Weekly Comedy*, positing that
Ward's authorship of the 1699 publication is certain, but presents textual
and historical evidence to suggest that he may have not authored the
1707 publications.

1786 DAY, W. G. "The language of Ned Ward." *NQ* 215 (1970): 421-23.

Words and usages earlier than, or absent from, the O.E.D.

1787 KAWAI, Michio. "The 'scurrilous' language of *The London Spy*." *Anglica*
5 (1962): 20-35.

Discusses the linguistic provocation of *The London Spy*.

1788 MATTHEWS, William. "The character-writings of Edward Ward."
Neophilologus 21 (1936): 116-34.

Personages described in *The London Spy*.

5

A Selected Chronological Shortlist
of Prose Fiction in English
Published between 1700 and 1740

Page references indicate the length of the respective volumes.

1700

1. ANON. *The amours of Edward the IV*; pp. 120.

2. ANON. *Bateman's tragedy: or the perjured bride justly rewarded* [1700?]; pp. 13.

3. ANON. *Johnny Armstrong*; pp. 24.

4. BEHN, Aphra. *The dumb virgin: The unhappy mistake*; pp. 34.

5. BOYER, Abel. *The wise and ingenious companion*; pp. 232.

6. BROWN, Thomas. *Amusements serious and comical, calculated for the meridian*; pp. 160.

7. COURTILZ DE SANDRAS, Gatien. *The French spy: or the memoirs of John Baptist de la Fontaine*; pp. 371.

8. CR[AWFORD], D[avid]. *Several letters containing: The unfortunate Dutchess, Love after enjoyment, The unhappy mistake*; n.p.

9. DELERAC, François-Paulin. *Polish Manuscripts*; pp. 290.

10. SAINT EVREMONT, Charles. *A novel* [*The Irish prophet*]; pp. 21.

1701

11.   WARD, Edward, et al. *A pacquet from Will's*; n.p.

1702

12.   ANON. *The adventures of Lindamira, a lady of quality*; pp. 228.

13.   ANON. *The perfidious P--: being letters from a nobleman to two ladies*; pp. 143.

1703

14.   RUSSEN, David. *Inter-lunare: or a voyage to the moon*; pp. 147.

1704

15.   BOCCALINI, Traiano. *Secretaria di Apollo: or letters from Apollo*; n.p.

16.   DAVYS, Mary. *The amours of Alcippus and Leucippe*; n.p.

1705

17.   AVELLANEDA, Alonso Fernandez de. *A continuation of the comical history of the most ingenious knight Don Quixote*; pp. 437.

18.   DAVYS, Mary. *The fugitive*; pp. 204.

19.   MANLEY, Mary Delarivière. *The secret history of Queen Zarah and the Zarazians*; pp. 119.

1706

20.   ANON. *The jilted bridegroom: or the London coquet*; pp. 55.

21.   GALLAND, Antoine. *The Arabian nights entertainments: consisting of one thousand and one stories*; pp. 592.

1707

22.   ANON. *The pleasant intrigues and surprising adventures of an English nobleman at the last carnival of Venice*; pp. 156.

23. ANON. *The Spanish libertines: or the lives of Justina, Celestina and Estervanillo Gonzales*; n.p.

24. D'AULNOY, Marie. *The diverting works of the Countess D'Anois*; pp. 648.

25. -----*The history of the Earl of Warwick, sirnam'd the Kingmaker*; pp. 199, 175, 78.

26. -----*Memoirs of the Court of England*; pp. 220, 353-518, 521-616.

27. LA CHAPELLE, Jean de. *The adventures of Catullus, and history of his amours with Lesbia*; pp.400.

28. MANLEY, Mary Delarivière. *The lady's pacquet of letters, taken from her by a French privateer in her passage to Holland*; pp. 220.

1708

29. ANON. *An account of some remarkable passages in the life of a private gentleman, with reflections thereon*; pp. 308.

30. ANON. *A voyage to the new island Fonseca, near Barbadoes*; pp. 44.

31. ALEMAN, Mateo. *Guzman de Alfarache*; pp. 116.

32. D'AULOY, Marie. *Hypolitus Earl of Douglas, with the secret history of Mack-Beth; the amours of Count Schlick*; pp. 256, 97, 63.

33. GILDON, Charles. *The new metamorphosis: being the golden ass of Lucius Apuleius*; pp. 380, 325.

34. LE SAGE, Alain-René. *Le diable boiteux: or the Devil upon two sticks*; pp. 278.

35. MISSON, Francois. *A new voyage to the east-Indies by Francis Leguat and his companions*; pp. 248.

36. PÉTIS DE LA CROIX, François. *Turkish tales*; pp. 323.

1709

37. ANON. *The life and adventures of Capt. John Avery, the famous English pirate*; pp. 64.

38.   GILDON, Charles. *The golden spy: or a political journal of the British nights entertainments*; pp. 304

39.   .MANLEY, Mary Delarivière. *Secret memoirs and manners of several persons of quality of both sexes from the new Atalantis*;pp.246.

40.   OLIVIER, J. *Memoirs of the life and adventures of Signor Rozelli*; pp. 325.

1710

41.   [CIBBER, Colley?]. *The secret history of Arlus and Odolphus, ministers of state to the Empress of Grandinsula*; pp. 40.

42.   MANLEY, Mary Delarivière. *Memoirs of Europe, towards the close of the eighth century*; pp. 380.

1711

43.   ANON. *The generous rivals: or love triumphant*; pp. 270.

44.   ANON. *The tell-tale: or the invisible witness*; pp. 67.

45.   BORDELON, Laurent. *A history of the ridiculous extravagances of Monsieur Oufle*; pp. 303.

1712

46.   ANON. *The history of Prince Mirabel's infancy, rise and disgrace; with the sudden promotion of Novicus.*; pp. 90 + 80 + 80.

47.   ANON. *The history of the proceedings of the mandarins and proatins of the Britomartian empire*; pp. 78.

48.   OLDMIXON, John. *The secret history of Europe*; pp. 251.

1713

49.   ANON. *The infernal congress; or news from below*; n.p.

50.   ANON. *Letters of Abelard and Heloise; to which is prefix'd a particular account of their lives, amours and misfortunes*; n.p.

51.   ANON.   *A new voyage to the islands of fools, representing the policy, government and present state of the Stultitians*; pp. 1-58 + 59-62.

52.   BARKER, Jane. *Love's intrigues: or the history of the amours of Bosvil and Galesia*; pp. 71.

53.   BLAND, Captain. *The northern Atalantis: or York spy*; pp. 70.

54.   SMITH, Alexander. *The history of the lives and robberies of the most noted highway-men*; pp. 288 + 288.

55.   [WALPOLE, Robert?] *The present state of fairy-land*; n.p.

1714

56.   ANON. *The Court of Atalantis*; pp. 153-78.

57.   ANON. *The ladies tale, exemplified in the virtues and vices of the quality*; pp. 264.

58.   ANON. *The rover*; n.p.

59.   HAMILTON, Anthony. *Memoirs of the life of the Count de Grammont*; pp. 356.

60.   MANLEY, Mary Delarivière. *The adventures of Rivella*; pp. 120.

61.   PÉTIS DE LA CROIX, François. *The Persian and the Turkish tales*. I, 495; II, 499-755; 1-252.

1715

62.   ANON. *The fatal effects of arbitrary power*; n.p.

63.   ANON. *The German Atalantis*; pp. 143.

64.   ANON. *The history of Menuthia; with an account of the chief transactions in that kingdom*; pp. 52.

65.   BARKER, Jane. *Exilius: or the banish'd Roman; written after the manner of Telemachus*; pp. 172 + 142.

66.   RENNEVILLE, René. *The French Inquisition: or the history of the Bastille*; pp. 322.

67. SMITH, Alexander. *The secret history of the lives of the most celebrated beauties*; pp. 262.

68. 'SYMSON, William'. *A new voyage to the East Indies*; n.p.

1716

69. DuNOYER, Anne Marguerite Petit. *Letters from a lady at Paris to a lady at Avignon*; pp. 239.

70. GUEULETTE, Thomas-Simon. *A thousand and one quarters of hours: being Tatarian Tales*; pp. 254.

71. LE SAGE, Alain-René. *The history and adventures of Gil Blas of Santillane*; 2 vols.

72. LYLY, John. *Eupheus and Lucilla: or the false friend and inconstant mistress*; n.p.

1717

73. THEOBALD, Lewis. *The history of the loves of Antiochus and Stratonice*; pp.290.

1718

74. ANON. *The double captive: or chains upon chains*; n.p.

75. HEARNE, Mary. *The lover's week: or the six days adventures of Philander and Amarylis*; pp. 56.

76. LE NOBLE DE TENNELIÈRE, Eustache. *Pure love, a novel: being the history of the Princess Zulima*; pp. 257.

77. MONCRIF, François-Augustin-Paradis de. *Indian tales: or the adventures of Zeloide and Amanzarifdine*; pp. 179.

78. QUINTANA, Francisco de. *The most entertaining history of Hyppolito and Aminta: being a collection of delightful novels*; pp. 391.

1719

79. ANON. *Passionate love letters between a Polish princess and a certain chevalier*: pp. 72.

80. ANON. *The secret history of the Prince of the Nazarenes and two Turks; The fatal amour between a beautiful lady and a young nobleman*; pp. 1-25, 27-66.

81. BARKER, Jane. *The entertaining novels of Mrs Jane Barker*; pp. 310.

82. BUTLER, Sarah. *Milesian tales: or instructive novels for the happy conduct of life*; pp. 130.

83. DEFOE, Daniel. *Robinson Crusoe*; pp. 364.

84. GILDON, Charles. *The post-man robb'd of his mail: or the packet broke open*; pp. 340.

85. HAYWOOD, Eliza. *Love in excess: or the fatal enquiry*; pp. 56.

86. HEARNE, Mary. *The female deserters*; pp. 109.

1720

87. ANON. *The German rogue*; pp. 111.

88. ANON. *A select collection of novels in six volumes*; n.p.

89. BLACKAMORE, Arthur. *The perfidious brethren: or the religious triumvirate, displayed in three ecclesiastical novels*; pp. 104.

90. CHETWOOD, William Rufus. *The voyages, dangerous adventures and imminent escapes of Capt. R. Falconer*; pp. 76, 136, 176.

91. DEFOE, Daniel. *Captain Singleton*; pp. 344.

92. -----*Memoirs of a cavalier*; pp. 338.

93. GILDON, Charles. *Miscellanea aurea: or the golden medley*; n.p.

94. MANLEY, Mary Delarivière. *The power of love, in seven novels*; pp. 368.

95. P.W. [William Pittis?] *The Jamaica lady or the life of Bavia*; pp. 100.

1721

96.   ANON. *The secret history of Pythagorus*; pp. 36.

97.   AUBIN, Penelope. *The life of Madam de Beaumont, a French lady*; pp. 143.

98.   -----*The strange adventures of the Count de Vinevil and his family*; pp. 138.

99.   BOURSAULT, Edmé. *Letters from a lady of quality to a chevalier*; pp. 86.

100.   CHAMBERLEN, Paul. *Love in its empire, illustrated in seven novels*; pp. 180.

101.   LE NOBLE DE TENNELIÈRE, Eustache. *Ildegerte, Queen of Norway*; pp. 56, 66.

1722

102.   ARMENO, Cristoforo. *The travels and adventures of three Princes of Sarendip*; pp. 276.

103.   AUBIN, Penelope. *The life and amorous adventures of Lucinda, an English lady*; pp. 1-260, 261-76.

104.   -----*The noble slaves: or the lives and adventures of two lords and two ladies*; pp. 202.

105.   COURTILZ DE SANDRAS, Gatien de. *The unfortunate marriage*; pp. 296.

106.   DEFOE, Daniel. *Colonel Jack;* pp. 399.

107.   -----*A journal of the plague year*; pp. 287.

108.   -----*Moll Flanders*; pp. 424.

109.   HAYWOOD, Eliza. *The British recluse: or the secret history of Cleomira, suppos'd dead*; pp. 138.

110.   MONTESQUIEU, Charles de Secondat. *Persian letters*; pp. 271, 309.

1723

111. ANON. *Love letters between a certain late nobleman and the famous Mr Wilson*; pp. 49.

112. AUBIN, Penelope. *The life of Charles Du Pont*; pp. 282.

113. BARKER, Jane. *A patch-work screen for the ladies*; pp. 38 + 143.

114. BLACKAMORE, Arthur. *Luck at last: or the happy unfortunate*; pp. 112.

115. HAYWOOD, Eliza. *Idalia: or the unfortunate mistress*; pp. 74 + 66 + 67-135.

116. -----*Lasselia: or the self-abandon'd*; pp. 80.

117. THIBAULT, Gouveneur de Talmont. *The life of Pedrillo del Campo*; pp. 197.

118. WALKER, Capt. Charles. *Authentick memoirs of the life intrigues and adventures of the celebrated Sally Salisbury*; pp. 150.

1724

119. ANON. *Love upon tick: or implicit gallantry*; pp. 143.

120. ANON. *A narrative of all the robberies, escapes etc of John Sheppard*; pp. 31.

121. A., Ma. *The prude*; pp. 87.

122. DAVYS, Mary. *The reform'd coquet*; pp. 171.

123. DEFOE, Daniel. *Roxana, or the fortunate mistress*; pp. 407.

124. E., G. *Authentic memoirs of the life and surprizing adventures of John Sheppard*; pp. 82.

125. GOMEZ, Madeleine. *La belle assemblée: or the adventures of six days*; pp. 138 + 105 + 119.

126. HAYWOOD, Eliza. *The fatal secret: or constancy in distress*; pp. 61.

127.   -----*The masqueraders: or fatal curiosity*; pp. 47.

128.   -----*A spy upon the conjurer*; pp. 259.

129.   -----*The works of Mrs Eliza Haywood.*; I, 323; II, 138; III, 74 + 135.

130.   'JOHNSON, Capt. Charles'. *A general history of the robberies and murders of the most notorious pyrates*; pp. 17-320.

131.   -----*The history of the life and intrigues of that celebrated courtezan and posture-mistress, Eliz. Mann*; pp. 49.

1725

132.   BUSSY-RABUTIN, Roger de. *The amorous history of the Gauls*; pp. 232.

133.   DAVYS, Mary. *The works of Mrs Davys*; I, 272; II, 308.

134.   GUEULETTE, Thomas-Simon. *Chinese tales: or the wonderful adventures of the mandarin Fum-Hoam*; I, 275; II, 264.

135.   HAYWOOD, Eliza. *Bath-intrigues*; pp. 51.

136.   -----*Fantomina: or love in a maze*; pp. 275-91.

137.   -----*Memoirs of a certain island adjacent to the kingdom of Utopia*; I, 77; II, 92.

138.   -----*Secret histories, novels and poems*; I, 259; II, 114; III, 162; IV, 45 + 93 + 50

139.   SEGRAIS, Jean Regnauld. *Five novels*; n.p.

1726

140.   AUBIN, Penelope. *The life and adventures of the lady Lucy*; pp. 131.

141.   BARKER, Jane. *The lining for the patch-work screen*; pp. 201.

142.   CHETWOOD, William Rufus. *The voyages and adventures of Capt. Robert Boyle*; pp. 374.

143. HAYWOOD, Eliza. *The city jilt: or the alderman turn'd beau*; pp. 60.

144. -----*The mercenary lover: or the unfortunate heiresses*; pp. 62.

145. SAINT HYACINTHE, Themiseul de. *The adventures of Pomponius, a Roman knight*; I, 144; II, 152.

146. SMITH, Alexander. *Memoirs of the life and times of the famous Jonathan Wilde*; pp. 287.

1727

147. 'BRUNT, Samuel'. *A voyage to Cacklogallinia*; pp. 167.

148. CHASLES, Robert. *The illustrious French lovers*; I, 267; II, 347.

149. DAVYS, Mary. *The accomplish'd rake: or modern fine gentleman*; pp. 196.

150. HAYWOOD, Eliza. *Cleomelia: or the generous mistress*; pp. 104.

151. -----*The fruitless enquiry*; pp. 274.

152. -----*Letters from the palace of fame*; pp. 24 (incomplete).

153. -----*The life of madam de Villesache, written by a lady, who was an eye-witness of the greatest part of her adventures*; pp. 63.

154. -----*Love in its variety*; pp. 250.

155. -----*The perplex'd Dutchess, or treachery rewarded: being some memoirs of the Court of Malfy*; pp. 60.

156. -----*Philidore and Placentia: or l'amour trop delicat*; pp. 46, 48.

157. -----*The secret history of the present intrigues of the Court of Caramania*; pp. 348.

158. LONGUEVILLE, Peter. *The hermit: or the unparalleled sufferings and surprising adventures of Mr Philip Quarll, an Englishman*; pp. 264.

159. PLANTIN, Arabella. *Two novels: the ingrateful; Love led astray*; pp. 33-58.

1728

160.   ANON. *The illegal lovers: a true secret history*; n.p.

161.   ANON. *Some memoirs of the amours and intrigues of a certain Irish dean*; pp. 68.

162.   ANON. *The velvet coffee-woman*; pp. 46.

163.   BEAUCHAMPS,Pierre-François-Godart de. *The history of King Apprius, translated from a Persian manuscript*; pp. 116.

164.   HAYWOOD, Eliza. *The agreeable Caledonian: or memoirs of signiora di Morella, a Roman lady*; pp. 93.

165.   -----*Irish artifice: or the history of Clarina*; pp. 41.

166.   PRÉCHAC, Jean de. *The disguis'd Prince: or the beautiful Parisian*; pp. 58, 54.

167.   ROWE, Elizabeth. *Friendship in death*; pp. 70, 138, 253.

1729

168.   BIGNON, Jean Paul. *Adventures of Abdella, son of Hanif*; pp. 169.

169.   HAYWOOD, Eliza. *The fair Hebrew*; pp. 53.

170.   LUSSAN, Marguerite de. *The life of the Countess de Gondez*; pp. 279.

171.   PERRAULT, Charles. *Tales of Mother Goose*; n.p.

172.   ROWE, Elizabeth. *Letters moral and entertaining*; n.p.

1730

173.   ANON. *The brothers: or treachery punish'd*; pp. 166.

174.   ANON. *The unnatural mother and ungrateful wife* [1700?]; pp. 107.

175.   [CAMPBELL, John?]. *The polite correspondence: or rational amusement* [1730?]. n.p.

176.   HAYWOOD, Eliza. *Love-letters on all occasions lately passed between*

persons of distinction; pp.224.

177.   L., S. *The amours of Philarus and Olinda: or the intrigues of Windsor*; pp. 70.

1731

178.   ANON. *A view of the beau monde: or memoirs of the celebrated Coquetilla*; pp. 60.

179.   ANON. *Winter evenings tales*; pp. 284.

180.   COSTEKER, John Littleton. *The constant lovers*; pp. 248.

181.   DESFONTAINES, Pierre-François-Guyot. *The travels of Mr John Gulliver, son to Capt. Lemuel Gulliver*; I, 212; II, 198.

182.   PRÉVOST D'EXILES, Antoine-François. *The life of Mr Cleveland, natural son of Oliver Cromwell*; I, 248; II, 277; III, 422; IV, 298; V, 299.

183.   VALDORY, Guillaume. *The adventures of the celebrated Madam de Muci*; pp. 103.

1732

184.   ANON. *The fair concubine: or the secret history of the beautiful Vanella*; pp. 17-49.

185.   ANON. *Memoirs of love and gallantry*; pp. 74.

186.   ANON. *The perjur'd citizen: or female revenge*; pp. 55.

187.   BOYD, Elizabeth. *The happy-unfortunate: or the female-page*; pp. 340.

188.   TERRASSON, Jean. *The life of Sethos*; I, 460; II, 480.

1733

189.   ANON. *The finished rake: or gallantry in perfection*; pp. 59.

190.   ANON. *Love without artifice: or the disappointed peer*; pp. 47.

191.   ANON. *The secret history of Mama Oella, Princess Royal of Peru*; pp. 51.

192.   FONTANIEU, Gaspard Moïse de. *Rosalinda: a novel*; pp. 347.

193.   MADDEN, Samuel. *Memoirs of the twentieth century: being original letters of state under George the Sixth*; pp. 527.

194.   MARINI, Giovanni Ambrogio. *The desparadoes: an heroic history*; pp. 284.

195.   TYSSOT DE PATOT, Simon. *The travels and adventures of James Massey*; pp. 318.

1734

196.   GOMEZ, Madeleine. *L'entretien des beaux esprits*; I, 272; II, 264.

197.   GUEULETTE, Thomas-Simon. *Peruvian tales, related in one thousand and one hours*; pp. 187.

1735

198.   ANON. *The English nobleman: or peasant of quality*; pp. 88.

199.   CRÉBILLON, Claude-Prosper-Jolyot de. *Letters from the Marchioness de M*** to the Count de R****; pp. 304.

200.   -----*The skinner: or the history of Tanzai and Néadarné.* I, 271; II, 144.

201.   LYTTLETON, George. *Letters from a Persian in England to his friend at Ispahan*; pp. 254.

202.   MARIVAUX, Pierre Carlet de Chamlain de. *Le paysan parvenu: or the fortunate peasant*; pp. 286.

1736

203.   ANON. *Celenia: or the history of Hyempsal king of Numidia*; I, 319; II, 321-642.

204.   ANON. *The history of Autonous*; pp. 117.

205. ANON. *Letters from a Moor at London to his friends at Tunis*; pp. 274.

206. CORDONNIER, Hyacinthe. *The history of prince Titi, a royal allegory*; pp. 204.

207. GUEULETTE, Thomas Simon. *Mogul tales: or the dreams of men awake*; I, 288; II, 238.

208. HAYWOOD, Eliza. *Adventures of Eovaai, Princess of Ijaveo*; pp. 244.

209. LOCATELLI, Francesco. *Lettres moscovites: or Muscovian letters*; pp. 190.

210. MARIVAUX, Pierre Carlet de Chamblain de. *The life of Marianne: or the adventures of the Countess of ****; pp. 254.

1737

211. ANON. *A letter from Mrs Jane Jones, alias Jenny Diver*. n.p.

212. BERINGTON, Simon. *The memoirs of Sigr Gaudentio di Lucca*; pp. 335.

213. LE SAGE, Alain René. *The bachelor of Salamanca: or memoirs of Don Cherubim de la Ronda*; pp. 259.

214. PÖLLNITZ, Karl Ludwig. *Les amusements de Spa: or the gallantries of the Spaw in Germany*; I, 232; II, 270.

1738

215. LEDIARD, Thomas. *The German spy, in familiar letters*; pp. 436.

216. PRÉVOST D'EXILES, Antoine-François. *Memoirs of a man of quality*; pp. 299.

217. VEGA, Lope Felix de. *The pilgrim: or the stranger in his own country*; pp. 127 + 137-284.

1739

218. ANON. *The life and adventures of Mrs Christian Davies, commonly call'd Mother Ross*; pp.104.

219. ANON. *The unfortunate Dutchess: or the lucky gamester*; pp. 78.

220.   D'ARGENS, Jean-Baptistede Boyer. *The Jewish spy: being a philosophical, historical and critical correspondence*; 5 vols.

221.   MOTTLEY, John. *Joe Miller's jests: or the wit's vademecum*; pp. 70.

1740

222.   MOUHY, Charles de Fieux. *The fortunate country maid: being the entertaining memoirs of the present celebrated Marchioness of L.V.*; 2 vols.

223.   RICHARDSON, Samuel. *Pamela: or virtue rewarded*; 2 vols.

224.   TENCIN, Claudine-Alexandrine-Guérin de. *The siege of Calais by Edward of England*; pp. 288.

Index of Scholars

All numbers in boldtype refer to entries, not pages.

ANONYMOUS, **114, 151, 152, 153, 154, 1095, 1164, 1619, 1784**
ADAMS, Percy G., **155, 156, 157**
ADAMS, Robert M., **158**
ADAMS, Stephen, **1311**
ADAMSON, David McLaren, **159**
ADBURGHAM, Allison **160**
ANDREWS, S. G., **1773**
AITKENS, G. A., **1231**
ALDINGTON, R., **115**
ALDISS, Brian W., **161**
ALLEN, C. Leonard, **525**
ALLEN, Don Cameron, **162**
ALLEN, Robert Joseph, **1785**
ALLEN, Robert R., **586**
ALLEN Walter, **163**
ALLIKER, Melinda, **1645**
ALLISTON, April, **164**
ALLOTT, Miriam, **116**
ALTER, Robert, **165**
ALTMAN, Janet Gurkin, **166**
AMELINCKX, Frans C., **167**
AMOS, Flora Ross, **168**
AMPRIMOZ, Alexandre
ANDERSON, G. L., **1506**
ANDERSON, Howard, **169**
ANDERSON, Paul Bunyan, **1616,**

1617, 1618, 1702
ANDERSON, Philip B., **2**
ANDREW, Donna T., **170**
ANDREWS, S. G., **1773**
ANDREWS, William L., **117**
ANDRIES, Lise, **1386**
ANNANDALE, E. T., **171**
*ANNUAL BIBLIOGRAPHY OF
ENGLISH LANGUAGE
AND LITERATURE,* **1**
ARAVMUDAN, Srinivas, **172**
ARLAND, Marcel, **1663**
ARMISTEAD, J. M., **29, 803**
ARMSTRONG, Katherine A., **1312, 1472**
ARMSTRONG, Nancy **174, 175, 176, 177**
ASHLEY, Leonard R. N., **178, 1189, 1190**
ASHTON, John, **118, 1700**
ATKINSON, Geoffroy, **179, 180, 181, 182, 183, 1679**
AUSTIN, Michael, **1313**
AUTY, Susan Garis, **184, 185**
AVERLEY, G., **91**

BABB, Moira Campbell Ferguson,

Subject and Thematic Index

All numbers in boldface refer to entries, not pages.

About the Author

ROBERT IGNATIUS LETELLIER is a member of the Salzburg Centre for Research in the Early English Novel at the University of Salzburg. He is also a member of Trinity College and the Board of Continuing Education at Madingley Hall, the University of Cambridge. His previous books include *The English Novel, 1660–1700: An Annotated Bibliography* (Greenwood, 1997).